Lecture Notes in Computer Science　13580

More information about this series at https://link.springer.com/bookseries/558

Chunhua Su · Kouichi Sakurai · Feng Liu (Eds.)

Science of Cyber Security

4th International Conference, SciSec 2022
Matsue, Japan, August 10–12, 2022
Revised Selected Papers

 Springer

Editors
Chunhua Su [iD]
University of Aizu
Aizuwakamatsu, Fukushima, Japan

Kouichi Sakurai
Kyushu University
Fukuoka, Japan

Feng Liu
Institute of Information Engineering
Chinese Academy of Sciences
Beijing, China

ISSN 0302-9743   ISSN 1611-3349 (electronic)
Lecture Notes in Computer Science
ISBN 978-3-031-17550-3   ISBN 978-3-031-17551-0 (eBook)
https://doi.org/10.1007/978-3-031-17551-0

This Springer imprint is published by the registered company Springer Nature Switzerland AG
The registered company address is: Gewerbestrasse 11, 6330 Cham, Switzerland

Preface

This volume contains the papers presented at the 4th International Conference on Science of Cyber Security (SciSec 2022), which was held as a hybrid conference during August 10–12, 2022, in Matsue, Japan. SciSec is an annual international forum for researchers and industry experts to present and discuss the latest research, trends, breakthroughs, and challenges in the domain of cybersecurity. SciSec 2022 featured three keynote speeches given by Moti Yung, Yi Deng, and Akira Otsuka, along with paper presentations. This year we received 88 submissions of excellent quality from around the world. Each paper was reviewed by at least three Program Committee members in a single-blind process, and on average 2.8 reviews were received for each paper.

Although there were many good papers submitted, in order to maintain the high quality of SciSec 2022 we could only select a very small portion of them to be included in the proceedings. After extensive discussion among the Program Committee, we decided to accept 32 full papers and four short papers. We would like to express our thanks to all Program Committee members. Without their hard effort in reviewing papers in such a short time, the conference would not have been successful. We would also like to thank our general co-chairs, Feng Liu and Akihito Nakamura, they both devoted a large amount of time for the preparation of this conference.

August 2022

Chunhua Su
Kouichi Sakurai

Organization

General Co-chairs

Feng Liu   Institute of Information Engineering, Chinese
Academy of Sciences, China
Akihito Nakamura   University of Aizu, Japan

Program Committee Co-chairs

Chunhua Su   University of Aizu, Japan
Kouichi Sakurai   Kyushu University, Japan

Program Committee

Habtamu Abie   Norwegian Computing Centre, Norway
Richard Brooks   Clemson University, USA
Jiageng Chen   Central China Normal University, China
Hung-Yu Chien   National Chi Nan University, Taiwan
Sherman S. M. Chow   The Chinese University of Hong Kong, China
Kapal Dev   Munster Technological University, Ireland
Chun-I Fan   National Sun Yat-sen University, Taiwan
Thippa Reddy Gadekallu   VIT Vellore, India
Dieter Gollmann   Hamburg University of Technology, Germany
Arash Habibi Lashkari   University of New Brunswick, Canada
Daojing He   East China Normal University, China
Huawei Huang   Sun Yat-sen University, China
Celestine Iwendi   University of Bolton, UK
Hiroaki Kikuchi   Meiji University, Japan
Lingguang Lei   Institute of Information Engineering, Chinese
Academy of Sciences, China
Yingjiu Li   University of Oregon, USA
Xiwei Liu   Tongji University, China
Pratyusa K. Manadhata   Hewlett-Packard Laboratories, UK
Weizhi Meng   Technical University of Denmark, Denmark
Thomas Moyer   UNC Charlotte, USA
Kazumasa Omote   University of Tsukuba, Japan
Noseong Park   Yonsei University, South Korea
Zhiri Tang   City University of Hong Kong, China

Ding Wang	Peking University, China
Lingyu Wang	Concordia University, Canada
Yu Wang	Guangzhou University, China
Chengyi Xia	Tianjin University of Technology, China
Jia Xu	Nanjing University of Posts and Telecommunications, China
Maochao Xu	Illinois State University, USA
Xin-Jian Xu	Shanghai University, China
Toshihiro Yamauchi	Okayama University, Japan
Ge Yan	Rensselaer Polytechnic Institute, USA
Kuo-Hui Yeh	National Dong Hwa University, Taiwan
Chuan Yue	Colorado School of Mines, USA

Additional Reviewers

Jin, Shuyuan
Li, Peng
Lian, Zhuotao
Qiu, Chen
Shorna, Sabira Khanam
Tian, Youliang
Wang, Weizheng
Wang, Ziyue
Ye, Guang

Contents

Blockchain and Applications

ChainSCAN: A Blockchain-Based Supply Chain Alerting Framework
for Food Safety 3
Jorge Castillo, Kevin Barba, and Qian Chen

BlockRAT: An Enhanced Remote Access Trojan Framework
via Blockchain 21
Yanze Kang, Xiaobo Yu, Weizhi Meng, and Yining Liu

Adapted PBFT Consensus Protocol for Sharded Blockchain 36
Ling Yang and Huawei Huang

A Practical Blockchain-Based Maintenance Record System for Better
Aircraft Security 51
Wictor Lang Jensen, Sille Jessing, Wei-Yang Chiu, and Weizhi Meng

Redactable Blockchain with Fine-Grained Autonomy and Transaction
Rollback 68
Chunying Peng and Haixia Xu

Cryptography and Applications

Pitch in: A Secure Extension Signature Based on SM9 87
Chuyi Yan, Haixia Xu, Yongheng Mu, and Jiong Ding

Verifiable DOPE from Somewhat Homomorphic Encryption,
and the Extension to DOT 105
Amirreza Hamidi and Hossein Ghodosi

Scalable M+1st-Price Auction with Infinite Bidding Price 121
Po-Chu Hsu and Atsuko Miyaji

The Shared Memory Based Cryptographic Card Virtualization 137
Chen Li, Bibo Tu, and Yanchang Feng

Network Security

Feature Transfer Based Network Anomaly Detection 155
Tao Chen and Kun Wen

Hybrid Routing for Efficient Fine-Grained Management of Specific
Services in SDN 170
    Kun Jia, Jiazhi Liu, Wen Wang, and Feng Liu

AtNet: A Novel Anti-tracking Network with Multi-Party Judgement
Capability Based on Cross-Domain Small-World Topology 186
    Wenjie Qin, Chengwei Peng, Tao Yin, Changbo Tian, and Guangze Zhao

A Two-Stage Method for Fine-Grained DNS Covert Tunnel Behavior
Detection 201
    *Bingxu Wang, Gang Xiong, Peipei Fu, Gaopeng Gou, Yingchao Qin,
    and Zhen Li*

Analysis and Detection Against Overlapping Phenomenon of Behavioral
Attribute in Network Attacks 217
    Jiang Xie, Shuhao Li, and Peishuai Sun

Integration of Cybersecurity Related Development Processes by Using
a Quantification Method 233
    *Hassan Noun, Florian Rehm, Guillaume Zeller, G. Rajesh,
    and Roland Lachmayer*

Cyber-Physical System

ZoomPass: A Zoom-Based Android Unlock Scheme on Smart Devices 245
    Thomas Gleerup, Wenjuan Li, Jiao Tan, and Yu Wang

Metasploit for Cyber-Physical Security Testing with Real-Time Constraints 260
    Sulav Lal Shrestha, Taylor Lee, and Sebastian Fischmeister

Passive User Authentication Utilizing Consecutive Touch Action Features
for IIoT Systems 276
    Guozhu Zhao, Pinchang Zhang, Yulong Shen, and Xiaohong Jiang

Malware

Malware Classification Based on Semi-Supervised Learning 287
    *Yu Ding, XiaoYu Zhang, BinBin Li, Jian Xing, Qian Qiang, ZiSen Qi,
    MengHan Guo, SiYu Jia, and HaiPing Wang*

Malware Detected and Tell Me Why: An Verifiable Malware Detection
Model with Graph Metric Learning 302
    *Xiao Chen, Zhengwei Jiang, Shuwei Wang, Rongqi Jing, Chen Ling,
    and Qiuyun Wang*

Malware Detection Using Automated Generation of Yara Rules
on Dynamic Features 315
  Qin Si, Hui Xu, Ying Tong, Yu Zhou, Jian Liang, Lei Cui, and Zhiyu Hao

Mobile System Security

Question Answering Models for Privacy Policies of Mobile Apps: Are We
There Yet? 333
  Khalid Alkhattabi, Davita Bird, Kai Miller, and Chuan Yue

Design of End-To-End Security for MQTT 5.0 353
  Hung-Yu Chien

DroidFP: A Zero-Permission Detection Framework for Android Devices
Based on Gated Recurrent Unit 364
  Xinyu Liu, Wu Zhao, Langping Chen, and Qixu Liu

System and Web Security

An Intrusion Detection System Based on Deep Belief Networks 377
  Othmane Belarbi, Aftab Khan, Pietro Carnelli,
  and Theodoros Spyridopoulos

HINCDG: Multi-Meta-Path Graph Auto-Encoders for Mining of Weak
Association Malicious Domains 393
  Jiawei Sun, Guangjun Wu, Junnan Yin, Qiang Qian, Junjiao Liu, Jun Li,
  and Yong Wang

AttVAE: A Novel Anomaly Detection Framework for Multivariate Time
Series 407
  Yi Liu, Yanni Han, and Wei An

BASNEA: Threat Hunting for Ethereum Smart Contract Based
on Backtrackless Aligned-Spatial Network Entity Alignment 421
  Xiangyu Du, Zhengwei Jiang, Jun Jiang, Kai Zhang, Zijing Fan,
  Fangming Dong, Ning Li, and Baoxu Liu

Multi-region SRAM-Based TCAM for Longest Prefix 437
  Qian Zou, Ning Zhang, Feng Guo, Qingshan Kong, and Zhiqiang Lv

Security in Financial Industry

A Solution for the Offline Double-Spending Issue of Digital Currencies 455
  Zhexuan Hong and Jiageng Chen

A Hierarchical Macroeconomic Copula Model for Cyber Damages Based
on Current Cyber Insurance Prices 472
    Daniel Kasper and Jens Grossklags

Social Engineering and Personalized Security

Cyber Social Engineering Kill Chain 487
    Rosana Montanẽz Rodriguez and Shouhuai Xu

Towards Practical Personalized Security Nudge Schemes: Investigating
the Moderation Effects of Behavioral Features on Nudge Effects 505
    Leilei Qu, Ruojin Xiao, and Wenchang Shi

Spear Phishing Email Detection with Multiple Reputation Features
and Sample Enhancement 522
    *Zhiting Ling, Huamin Feng, Xiong Ding, Xuren Wang, Chang Gao,
    and Peian Yang*

Privacy and Anonymity

TraceDroid: A Robust Network Traffic Analysis Framework for Privacy
Leakage in Android Apps 541
    *Huajun Cui, Guozhu Meng, Yan Zhang, Weiping Wang, Dali Zhu,
    Ting Su, Xiaodong Zhang, and Yuejun Li*

A k-Anonymity-Based Robust Watermarking Scheme for Relational
Database 557
    Jing Yu, Shuguang Yuan, Yulin Yuan, Yafan Li, and Chi Chen

Author Index 575

Blockchain and Applications

ChainSCAN: A Blockchain-Based Supply Chain Alerting Framework for Food Safety

Jorge Castillo$^{(\boxtimes)}$ (ID), Kevin Barba (ID), and Qian Chen (ID)

The University of Texas at San Antonio, San Antonio, TX 78249, USA
jorge.castillo@utsa.edu

Abstract. Supply Chain Management (SCM) systems provide a digital platform for the supply chain organizations to communicate and exchange information. In the food industry, SCMs provide the essential software components for monitoring food transportation and product handling. However, contemporary SCM systems suffer from non-traceability, non-interoperability and poor resiliency. Global food supply chains are at risks from cyber threats, which will lead to food shortages and poor quality control. In this paper, we present ChainSCAN, a three-layer design of a fully decentralized and blockchain-based SCM system that protects data security, privacy, and remove single point of failures of traditional SCMs. In addition, ChainSCAN provides a transparent environment to protect physical security of assets from stolen and record all activities of the food supply chain. ChainSCAN leverages four smart contracts to automate and regulate interactions of supply chain participants with the ledger, which can enforce the best practices among all supply chain organizations. Furthermore, ChainSCAN contains a notification system that automatically alerts consumers about food recalls and/or potential misbehaviors.

Keywords: Blockchain · Smart contracts · Decentralized applications · Supply chain

1 Introduction

Supply chain is a network of organizations focusing on transforming raw materials to finished products, and bring these goods and services to customers [14]. Supply chain organizations are composed by producers, suppliers, retailers and consumers. The food supply chain is one of the cornerstones to support our daily life, and this industry must be responsible to produce high quality materials (i.e., food). More importantly, the food industry should ensure food safety standards, and enforce the best practices in agricultural economics [10]. According to the World Health Organization (WHO), almost one out of 10 people in the world become ill after eating contaminated food (i.e., E. coli, Salmonella) and 420,000 people die every year [38]. Recently, the food supply chain started to scale down operations aiming at preventing contamination from epidemics and pandemics (i.e., COVID-19). This increases the risk of food supply chains to become a new target for cyber threats.

C. Su et al. (Eds.): SciSec 2022, LNCS 13580, pp. 3–20, 2022.
https://doi.org/10.1007/978-3-031-17551-0_1

Supply Chain Management (SCM) systems provide a platform for the supply chain network organizations to communicate and exchange information. Besides regulating information, SCM also manages capital, logistics and business flows to establish a collaborative partnership between producers, suppliers and retailers [24,29]. In the food industry, SCMs are the essential software components for monitoring food transportation and product handling. However, supply chain cyber attacks increased 51% in 2021 [36]. In particular, there has been instances where the food supply chain has been affected by cyber attacks [1,5,19]. For example, the world's largest meat processing company JBS has recently paid over $11M dollars in ransom after some computers were compromised by attackers, where they injected a ransomware infection into the IT infrastructure of the company [5].

Current contemporary SCM systems have many drawbacks due to their centralized and monopolistic design such as non-traceability, production deficiency, the lack of provenance and trust [41]. Today, food products must traverse among many intermediaries before reaching their consumers. Each intermediary has their own systems of quality assurance and product handling. These customized SCM systems are not synchronized among supply chain organizations which may increase food fraud incidents and threaten consumer's health [16]. To solve existing challenges of SCMs, we should design a new system that allows fine-grained data sharing and automatic notifications, providing a transparent environment with an enhanced trust model. We also observed that the current third party certifications (TPC) have flaws and data integrity can be easily compromised [25]. To increase product traceability (i.e., from farms to consumers), this new SCM system should also log and share ownership of food supply chain's physical assets such as meat from slaughterhouses, and fruits and vegetables from farms. A promising solution to realize such a SCM system is to leverage the decentralization and immutability properties of the blockchain technology.

While blockchain is known as the main ingredient of cryptocurrencies like Ethereum [11], its unique properties are a perfect fit to enhance current SCM systems. In particular, Non-Fungible Tokens (NFTs) allows systems to represent ownership of digital and/or physical assets by storing the food supply chain's transaction records in the blockchain ledger. The food organizations (e.g., food distributors) who own a NFT proves the existence and ownership of their physical assets (e.g., fruits/vegetables) without requiring a third party's certification/verification. Furthermore, the use of NFTs for food SCM systems can improve food traceability and enable liability attribution if food products are potentially mishandled (e.g., product recall).

This paper introduces our design of a fully decentralized SCM system for the food supply chain based on smart contracts named ChainSCAN. ChainSCAN protects the information stored in ledgers and enables auditability to each produced asset with the utilization of NFTs. ChainSCAN therefore provides a secure and trusted business environment for food supply chains. Smart contracts automate and regulate interactions with the ledger, which can enforce the best practices among all supply chain organizations. Furthermore, ChainSCAN contains a notification system to automatically alert consumers about food recalls and/or potential misbehaviors. Such a notification and alerting system can propagate and share important timely news among all supply chain participants.

The remainder of this paper is organized as follows. In Sect. 2, we present the state-of-the-art research studies of blockchain-based SCMs. Section 3 discusses the threat model. Section 4 introduces the ChainSCAN framework and its components. Section 5 provides ChainSCAN evaluation and results. We conclude this study in Sect. 6.

2 Related Work

Recent studies validate the applicability of blockchain to manage supply chain [4,13,15,17,23,27,35,39-41]. However, most of these studies are still in the initial phase without providing technical details of how to design and deploy blockchain-based SCMs in real world scenarios [7,8,22]. Many challenges of contemporary SCM systems have not been solved, which consequently lead to food fraud, threatening human health [16]. These challenges include non-traceability (lack of provenance and transparency), non-interoperability, and non-resiliency against natural disaster events (e.g. COVID-19 pandemic, earthquake, and hurricane) and cyber attacks [12]. For instance, the COVID-19 pandemic forced supply chains to restructure to include risk-management processes [2] to manage food assets. This is because current SCM systems are centralized, and the monopolistic design lacks of trust according to [41].

Traceability. According to the work of Lim *et al.* [24] and Sunny *et al.* [37], current SCMs suffer from lack of transparency and product traceability. To address this challenge, supply chain information and data should be classified and isolated to reduce their visibility to non-relevant members in the supply chain [21]. Moreover, transparency is a key metric to measure the overall performance of SCM [6]. In this study, we design ChainSCAN, leveraging the transparency property of the blockchain ledger, to provide asset traceability and liability attribution to every supply chain participant (i.e., producer, supplier, and consumers).

Interoperability. SCMs are composed of various participants from many countries around the world. Each of them has their own food handling standards, which result in interoperability hurdles [32]. Henninger and Mashatan agreed that the key to improve current SCM systems is to provide "Distributed Interoperable Records" [18] to supply chain participants. Additionally, there is a growing demand by consumers and governmental organizations for the interoperability between every SCM stakeholder (e.g. brands, manufacturers, producers, retailers, distributors, transportation carriers) [33]. To address the interoperability challenge, ChainSCAN uses multiple smart contracts regulated by an Access Control List (ACL) to provide the same level of data access and interoperability to each of supply chain participant.

Resiliency. The absence of SCM resiliency was observed during the start of the pandemic when there was a sudden shift in food demands from restaurants towards food consumed at home [20]. The distribution channels were exacerbated, with near-complete loss as reported by Chenarides *et al.* [9]. This incident reveals food supply chain lacks enough regulation and reporting, which has led to product recalls [28]. In order to improve food supply chain resiliency, we must design a adaptable and flexible SCM system [20]. Moreover, supply chain is also a cyber-physical system and we should protect its resiliency from both cyberspace (i.e., cyber attacks) and the physical world (i.e., natural disasters) [1,5,19,31].

Blockchain-Based SCM Systems. According to Duan *et al.* [13], blockchain technology can enable current SCMs' food traceability, support information transparency and enhance product recall efficiency. In addition, the value of blockchain in supply chain's sustainability has been studied by Niu *et al.* [30], who validates the performance of the overall system has been enhanced by using the blockchain technology. Rizou *et al.* [34] proposed safety measures and guidelines in the food sector for every stage of the SCM, and Malik *et al.* [26] focused on food provenance and security of SCM with the application of blockchain technology. However, neither of them provide a fully implemented blockchain-based SCMs. Instead, they validated ideas in a simulated environment. In contrast, ChainSCAN provides security and privacy to supply chain entities and enhance SCM resiliency by using Access Control Lists (ACL) and smart contracts. We also provide evaluation and security analysis of ChainSCAN in real world scenarios.

3   Threat Model

Current centralized SCM systems are vulnerable to cyber attacks. This section, we present two cyber threats. The first is insider attacks, which compromise SCMs' data integrity, and the second is external ransomware attacks that compromise data availability.

Threat 1 - Insider Attackers Maliciously Modify Original Asset Information to Avoid Liability. Food supply chain participants who are held liable for damage-causing events would seek scapegoats to take their responsibility. These insider attackers may attempt to change/overwrite information about the original assets to avoid their liability.

Threat 2 - External Attackers Compromise Supply Chain Data Availability. Similar to enterprise information systems, SCM systems are also extremely vulnerable to ransomware attacks. To disrupt supply chain's normal operations, an external attacker can exploit ransomware attacks to infect supply chain's computing network and maliciously encrypt essential files. This operational disruption may cause delays or even damage assets.

4   ChainSCAN Framework

ChainSCAN, presented in Fig. 1, is a blockchain-based supply chain management system consisting of three layers, namely the data layer, the blockchain

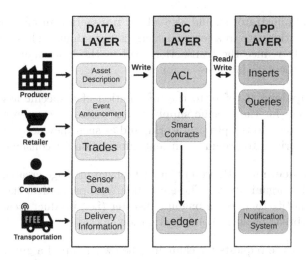

Fig. 1. Three layer structure of ChainSCAN.

(BC) layer, and the application (APP) layer.[1] The data layer collects information generated from different organizations of the food supply chain (i.e., producer, retailer, consumer, transportation), either from the Internet of Things (IoT) sensors or data retrieved from the traditional information systems (e.g., databases, email or text messages). For instance, data generated by a fruit or vegetable producer can include the food's maturity status, optimal harvest date, and its price. The BC layer aims at transforming supply chain data collected by the data layer from each organization to a correct blockchain transaction format. Blockchain transactions are regulated by the Access Control List (ACL) module, which also restricts data accessibility for certain organizations. The application layer allows legitimate supply chain participants to interact with the blockchain such as using their *off-chain* applications to connect with the blockchain to obtain product delivery status or generate a new transaction to the ledger such as an announcement for recalling products.

4.1 Data Layer

The data layer collects information from supply chain organizations such as asset descriptions, announcements, trades, IoT sensor collected (near) real-time data and delivery information. In this data layer, heterogeneous and big data is automatically compiled and formatted to blockchain transactions. The extremely large volume of supply chain data and limited computing resources can make ChainSCAN very difficult to scale-up. To enhance ChainSCAN scalability, not all supply chain raw data should be stored in the blockchain, instead processing raw data and store not relevant information off-chain is a better choice. Also, the

---

[1] Source code found in https://github.com/jacastillo8/ChainSCAN.

ChainSCAN administrator should also adjust transaction submission frequency such as limiting this rate to a few transactions per minute. These two methods would effectively reduce the transaction load in the blockchain network. The components of the data layer are as follows.

Asset Description. It refers to the information of a specific asset produced by the producers for the specific supply chain. These assets represent objects (e.g., food products) in the physical world, and as such they need to be properly labeled and described to provide sufficient information for consumers.

Event Announcement. Represents a customized message created by the producer or retailer organizations. These events are propagated to the appropriate consumers to notify them of an ongoing disaster (i.e., product recall), such as a salmonella outbreak or an E. coli investigation.

Trades. Constitute requests for changing the ownership of a given asset. After assets have been properly defined, producers would start to generate trade events among the supply chain participants. Both the current owner and potential buyers should be notified of the pending trades. However, generating a pending trade does not guarantee that the current owner is willing to pass ownership. ChainSCAN allows the current owners to decide whether or not they would accept the trades.

Sensor Data. With the development of 5G and IoT technology, supply chain organizations are utilizing sensors to obtain live information of the supply chain (i.e. the location of assets). The data collected by IoT devices/systems must be frequently submitted to the ledger of blockchain-based SCMs. The stream of information collected from the sensors is the record of assets' historical provenance. However, not all participants of the supply chain can access to sensor generated data due to privacy concerns. For example, only the organizations who are involved in a given trade can access assets delivery information generated by transportation sensors. Further details of transaction visibility are discussed in Sect. 4.2.

Delivery Information. This should be provided to participants who engage in a certain asset trade. Delivery services, as an important component of ChainSCAN, frequently submit information of the trading asset, from initial pick up from the producers until the moment the asset is delivered to consumers.

4.2   BC Layer

This BC layer maintains the distributed blockchain ledger of ChainSCAN. As presented in Fig. 1, transactions submitted to the ChainSCAN blockchain network are controlled by the rules specified in an Access Control List (ACL). The ACL is defined and implemented in smart contracts, which regulates supply chain organization's activities based on their roles. Through the ACL, private consumer's information is protected and only certain supply chain users who meet

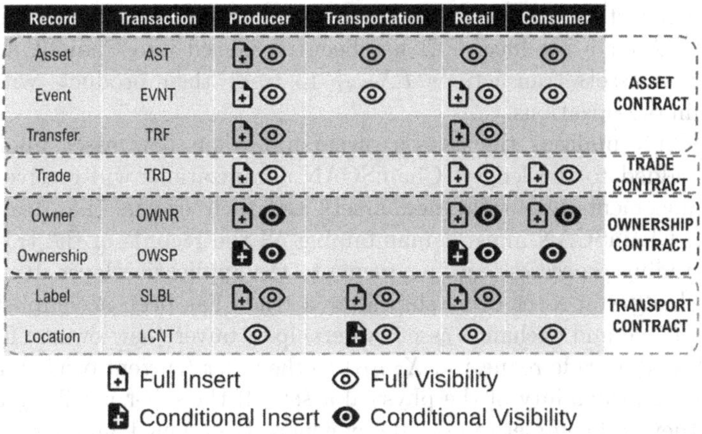

Record	Transaction	Producer	Transportation	Retail	Consumer	
Asset	AST	🗎◉	◉	◉	◉	ASSET CONTRACT
Event	EVNT	🗎◉	◉	🗎◉	◉	ASSET CONTRACT
Transfer	TRF	🗎◉	◉	🗎◉		ASSET CONTRACT
Trade	TRD	🗎◉		🗎◉	🗎◉	TRADE CONTRACT
Owner	OWNR	🗎◉		🗎◉	🗎◉	OWNERSHIP CONTRACT
Ownership	OWSP	🖿◉		🖿◉	◉	OWNERSHIP CONTRACT
Label	SLBL	🗎◉	🗎◉	🗎◉		TRANSPORT CONTRACT
Location	LCNT	◉	🖿◉	◉	◉	TRANSPORT CONTRACT

🗎 Full Insert   ◉ Full Visibility

🖿 Conditional Insert   ◉ Conditional Visibility

Fig. 2. Record keeping properties for transaction as per the ACL.

the specific conditions can access consumer's information. The implementation of ACL in ChainSCAN can effectively enhance data privacy. Figure 2 presents ChainSCAN supporting four different smart contracts (asset, trade, ownership and transport contracts), and each contract has specific transaction types. For example, the asset contract contains asset, event and transfer transactions. To protect supply chain data security, we define full vs. conditional access rights and grant the permissions to participants based on their roles. This access control method helps ChainSCAN to (1) limit organizations to arbitrarily insert or create new transactions of a given type of transactions to the blockchain. (2) It can also enhance data privacy by decreasing transaction visibility, and only the users who have the full rights can visualize private information (e.g., trades progress). We discuss the different transaction types and smart contracts as follows.

Transactions. As demonstrated in Fig. 2, ChainSCAN utilizes 7 different transaction types to maintain the distributed blockchain-based SCM functionality along with one special transaction type, the owner transaction (TX_{OWNR}), to support new entity registration. Five transaction types among the seven including (1) asset transaction (TX_{AST}), (2) event transaction (TX_{EVNT}), (3) trade transaction (TX_{TRD}), (4) transfer transaction (TX_{TRF}), (5) sensor location transaction (TX_{LCTN}) are synchronized with information collected from the data layer. The other two transaction types namely (6) shipping label (TX_{SLBL}) and (7) ownership (TX_{OWSP}) transactions are automatically generated and submitted to the blockchain every time when new transfer transactions TX_{TRF} have been inserted into the ledger.

To access ChainSCAN, a new user must first register as user of the system, and generate a new owner transaction TX_{OWNR} to the blockchain. Once ChainSCAN administrators receive the new user's registration request, they should first verify the identity of new users, and then return a unique owner identifier and granting the users correct access rights based on the organizations they belong to. For instance, $\mathbb{PID}$ and $\mathbb{RID}$ map to a producer and retailer identifiers, respectively. After a producer $\mathbb{PID}$ has been registered into ChainSCAN, they can start new assets transactions TX_{AST} to trade their products with other supply chain organizations.

ChainSCAN updates the asset's ownership when new asset information TX_{AST} is added to the ledger. ChainSCAN organizations will receive system wide announcements about the new assets and their owners (i.e., transaction TX_{OWSP}.) ChainSCAN aims at maintaining all the records of the trades and delegates trading processes (e.g., payment) to the application layer. It also supports the changes in asset ownership after a trade has been accomplished. To complete a trade and exchange asset ownership, a buyer (new owner) first generates and send a trade request (TX_{TRD}) to the seller (current owner) and asks for purchasing availability of the physical assets. If the seller is willing to trade the asset, they will complete the trade by generating a new transfer transaction (TX_{TRF}). Once the transfer transaction is added to the ledger, ChainSCAN automatically generates a new ownership transaction TX_{OWSP} to change the ownership property of the asset to the new owner (buyer). ChainSCAN also automatically creates a new shipping label transaction TX_{SLBL}, which returns a label identifier $\mathbb{LID}$. At this stage, ChainSCAN notifies transportation services about a pending shipment for the given asset.

Once the packages are accepted by the transportation organization, TX_{SLBL} transactions would be updated as the transportation services should continuously update the tracking information. This generates package location transactions TX_{LCTN} using captured data from IoT sensors until the assets are delivered to buyers. IoT sensors may generate a large volume of location transactions to unintentionally flood the blockchain network if no regulations have been set up. Therefore, system administrators should decide and set up a reasonable TX_{LCTN} transaction frequency (e.g., one transaction per minute) to protect system throughput. If producers and retailers found out the traded assets are defective or unsafe, they can use ChainSCAN to generate event transactions TX_{EVNT} to alert consumers and initiate a product recall process.

Smart Contracts. They eliminate the regulation of supply chain operations conducted by third parties and improve the performance of ChainSCAN in a secure, efficient and automated manner. As a decentralized application, ChainSCAN separates its functionalities into four aspects, namely, assets, trade, ownership and transportation. Every functionality is regulated by a smart contract as presented in Fig. 2. This design can avoid *cross-talk* between smart contracts, which can efficiently protect data privacy and security. The four smart contracts are elaborated as follows.

1. *Asset Contract.* The asset contract manages and supports all activities related to physical assets. These activities include creating new assets by producers, querying asset's information, transferring assets from sellers to buyers, and generating announcements about asset recall. The asset contract implements security checks (i.e., validate owners before changes in ownership) to protect

data integrity and prevent assets from being stolen by misbehaving users. For example, when a new asset transaction is requested to replace an asset's original information, the asset contract first checks the user's roles and organizations. If the user is not the owner of the assets, the transaction request will be declined. Similarly, the contract will first verify the ownership of an asset before approving any trade and transfer transactions.

2. *Trade Contract.* This contract supports and tracks all trade events created and completed by asset's owners. These trading activities include initiating new trades among different owners, and obtaining a given owner's historical trade records. Since the asset contract implements security checks that can protect asset data integrity and physical security, we do not implement security checks in the trade contract. This is also because the trade contract only initiates trade requests among supply chain participants, but it does not guarantee the fulfillment of the trade.

3. *Ownership Contract.* This ownership contract keeps the records of the existing asset's owners and allows new owners to register their assets in ChainSCAN. However, none of the supply chain organizations or participants can directly interact with the ownership contract. Instead, the assets' owners are added or modified through the transactions managed by asset and trade contracts. This ownership contract uses the same security check mechanisms as the asset contract (i.e., owner validation).

4. *Transportation Contract.* This contract aims at regulate and manage asset shipment and provide package tracking information in near real-time. The shipment label and package location transactions are controlled and managed automatically in ChainSCAN by the transportation contract. This contract heavily relies on ACLs to provide privacy to the location of assets.

4.3 APP Layer

The application layer provides a website interface for the supply chain organizations to access asset, trade, ownership and shipment information provided by ChainSCAN. The notification system (alerts and announcement) of ChainSCAN is designed and deployed in the App layer. Supply chain participants or consumers can receive updated notifications without requiring access the blockchain ledger. This section introduces the functionality of App layer in details.

Inserting New Transactions to Ledger. Legitimate supply chain participants can use the app layer to insert new transactions such as asset and trade transactions into the ledger. Smart contracts are used to approve or reject such requests, which reduces the system administrator's burden to manually verify request. However, human administrators still need to verify and manually approval new ownership transactions.

Obtaining Information from Ledger. Legitimate users, based on their roles, can send queries to obtain the transactions in the ledger through the app layer. The BC layer follows the predefined ACL rules to retrieve information from ledger and display it in app layer for users to review.

Notification System. The notification system is designed to provide announcements to consumers. The system continuously monitors for contract notifications to send queries to BC layer and retrieve product recall messages generated by the supply chain producers and retailers. Once a new message has been retrieved, the notification system collects all information of the assets and broadcast the notifications to consumers via emails.

5 ChainSCAN Prototype Evaluation

This section first design the prototype of ChainSCAN and then we conduct experiments to evaluate ChainSCAN's performance. We also provide the analysis of ChainSCAN's security.

5.1 Prototype Implementation

Our framework is implemented on the Hyperledger Fabric platform [3], which is a private and permissioned blockchain used to implement business models. Chain-SCAN's blockchain network requires a single or consortium of system administrators to manage operations. These system administrators fully control the blockchain network such as adding new users to ChainSCAN and deploying smart contracts. The end-to-end communications of ChainSCAN are as follows.

1. Asset owners (i.e., producers) register in ChainSCAN by submitting a single TX_{OWNR} transaction through the app layer. Once the system administrator has verified the new owners' identity and their assets information, the TX_{OWNR} transaction would be fully committed, ChainSCAN will generate a unique identifier $\mathbb{PID}$ associated with new asset transactions in our ChainSCAN supply chain network.
2. Similarly, interested and approved retailers register in ChainSCAN through the app layer. ChainSCAN blockchain network returns a unique identifier $\mathbb{RID}$, and this identifier will be used by retailers to requests asset's information and create trading events with asset owners (producers).
3. The asset producer generates a new asset transaction, which returns a unique asset identifier $\mathbb{AID}$. Immediately, ChainSCAN automatically assigns the asset's original ownership to asset ID $\mathbb{AID}$ with a new ownership transaction TX_{OWSP}.
4. After the asset with identifier of $\mathbb{AID}$ has been correctly added in the ledger, supply chain participants such as retailers can request information of the new assets, and initiate product trading by creating a new trading transaction TX_{TRD}.
5. TX_{TRD} is then sent to, reviewed and approved by the owner of the asset $\mathbb{AID}$. The owner later transfers the asset to the buyer by generating a TX_{TRF} transaction and ChainSCAN automatically updates the new ownership of the asset after a new shipping label of TX_{SLBL} is generated with an identifier of $\mathbb{LID}$.

6. The transportation services receives the physical asset $\mathbb{AID}$ (packages), and creates a transport identifier $\mathbb{TID}$ and submit the TX_{SLBL} transaction to the ledger associated with asset ID $\mathbb{AID}$. At this stage, neither the producer or the transportation services are allowed to modify the shipping label since all of the asset related activities (i.e., delivery information) is provided by our framework through the pre-defined smart contracts. This immutable and transparent property of ChainSCAN guarantee the trust of supply chain trading processes.

7. The asset (package) locations are continuously updated by IoT sensors until the assets are delivered to retailers or consumers. IoT sensors submit TX_{LCTN} frequently to the ledger. This near real-time updates allow participants to monitor delivery status of the assets through the app layer's query function.

8. When the physical asset received by their new owners, the IoT sensors and transportation services submit a new transaction to deactivate the shipping label transaction TX_{SLBL} of asset ID $\mathbb{AID}$.

9. Steps 4–8 can be repeated multiple times depending on the number of middlemen between the producers and consumers.

10. If malicious activities such as asset data integrity is compromised by cyber attacks or misbehaving users steal physical assets during the trading process of the asset ID $\mathbb{AID}$ are detected, system administrators, retailers and producers can create an event transaction TX_{EVNT} to notify trading parties and participants.

11. TX_{EVNT} is constantly being monitored by an automatic notification system running in the application layer (off-chain). Once a new event is registered, it notifies the end consumers of the event.

Off-Chain Notification System. As described in *Step 11*, a notification system is designed to send alerts and announcement to consumers by asset producers, retailers (and/or ChainSCAN system administrators). In our design, a NodeJS application receives automatic notifications from the asset contract. Once a new event has been successfully retrieved, the notification system immediately sends a query to obtain the asset's current owner contact information from the *ownership contract*. The notification system then creates an alert email and send it to the current owner and also the consumer of the assets. We use Google APIs (Gmail) to automatically send notification messages to consumers.

5.2   Performance Evaluation

Our blockchain framework's performance efficiency is determined by the number of new transactions, new transactions' frequency and underlying block's structure. To evaluate the performance, we investigate the parameters impacting the blocks' generation, and stability to maximize throughput. These parameters are defined as follows: the block generation timeout (*BlockTimeout*), the maximum number of transactions allowed per block (*TxPerBlock*), and the maximum amount of bytes permitted in a single block (*BlockSize*). The combination

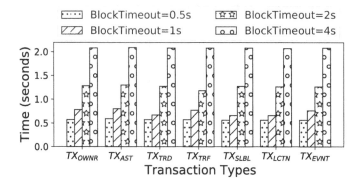

Fig. 3. Latency analysis for transaction types using BlockTimeout.

of all three parameters influence the generation of new blocks. For example, a new block is generated if BlockTimeout is triggered. In our study, we set up the block size as 2MB, to clearly define the influence of the BlockSize parameter.

Experiment Settings. We compare ChainSCAN performance using Hyperledger Caliper, a blockchain benchmark tool. Our ChainSCAN blockchain framework contains a solo orderer blockchain node with a single endorsing peer for each of the *four* participating organizations, namely, producers, retailers, transportation services and consumers. Our framework uses a single communication channel for ledgers to interact with smart contracts. Performance evaluation experiments are conducted on a CyberPowerPC with Intel Core i7 at 2.6 GHz and 16 GB of RAM.

ChainSCAN Transaction Types and Latency. The first experiment aims at finding out ChainSCAN network's bottleneck of latency, and determine which transaction types (i.e. seven transaction types such as TX_{AST}, TX_{TRD}, etc.) significantly influence network latency. To conduct evaluation experiments, we first assume smart contracts have been correctly initialized and tested and there is no delays in the network caused by smart contracts errors. To evaluate the network latency regarding to seven different transaction types, we generate 10 transactions at a rate of 1 transaction per second (TPS) for each transaction type while modifying the value of BlockTimeout.

Figure 3 compares the transaction latency with different BlockTimeout values from 0.5 s to 2 s. Each bar represents the average time (in seconds) a submitted transaction takes to be fully committed into the ledger. Large latency variations are observed when $BlockTimeout \geq 1s$. This is because a larger BlockTimeout value allows the blockchain network to add more transactions into a single block. Comparing with one transaction per block, it effectively reduces the latency of some transactions. Note that every transaction type shows similar latency effect on the network, which is due to the low computational complexity of every transaction type. Therefore, we have selected asset transactions TX_{AST} to be the bottleneck of the network, since asset transactions are the most common transaction types in ChainSCAN (new assets require new TX_{AST}).

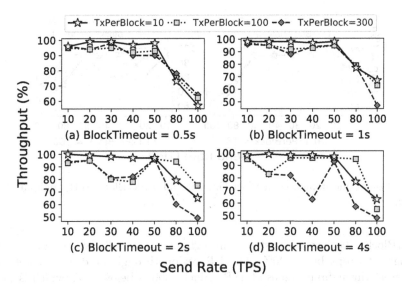

Fig. 4. Throughput analysis of 200 TX_{AST} using TxPerBlock and BlockTimeout as references.

ChainSCAN TX_{AST} Throughput Analysis of BlockTimeout, TxPer-Block and TPS. In this experiment, we use the asset transaction type TX_{AST} to evaluate the throughput of our framework (since we acknowledge that the asset transaction type is the bottleneck of ChainSCAN latency). Our goal is to maximize the transaction throughput performance by modifying the underlying block structure such as the maximum number of transactions allowed per block (TxPerBlock). In this experiment, we extend the evaluation method of the latency experiments to analyze the effect of three parameters, namely, TxPerBlock, BlockTimeout and the transaction sending rate (or transactions per second - TPS) to throughput. Figure 4 illustrates that ChainSCAN network throughput (y-axis) is influenced by all of these three parameters. We define three values of 10, 100, and 300 to limit the maximum number of transactions per block (i.e., TxPerBlock=10, 100, 300). These three numbers are represented by three lines (star, square and diamond lines) in each subfigure of different BlockTimeout (i.e., BlockTimeout=0.5, 1, 2, 4 s) in Fig. 4. X-axis values of each subfigure represent the sending rate of the 200 transactions, which varies from 10 TPS to 100 TPS.

The send rate can be divided into two regions, namely, *lower-rate when* $TPS < 50$ **(LR)** and *upper-rate when* $TPS >= 50$ **(UR)**. Figure 4a shows that our network throughput is higher than 90% in the LR region when BlockTimeout is 0.5 s. The throughput performance significantly reduces in the UR region to 60%, regardless of variations of TxPerBlock values. When the BlockTimeout is increased from 0.5s to 1s, throughput values of LR are still as stable as before when TxPerBlock values are 10 and 100. However, we observe in the LR region,

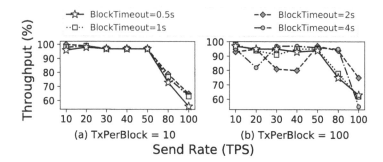

Fig. 5. Comparing influences of BlockTimeout and TxPerBlock to throughput of 200 TX_{AST}.

TxPerBlock=300 has a less stable throughput, specifically when TPS=30, the throughput drops below 90%. The UR region throughput drops as well, but the lowest throughput values of TxPerBlock=300 is below 50%, which is worse than its values when BlockTimeout is smaller. Similarly, when BlockTimeout increases to 2 and 4 s, in the LR region, a larger number of TxPerBlock preforms less stable of network throughput. The throughput of TxPerBlock=300 drops to 60% when BlockTimeout=4s and TPS=40. In the UR region, the smaller TxPer-Block values result in a better throughput but not higher than 80%. In Fig. 5, we compare the different BlockTimeout values to the network throughput when TxPerBlock values are 10 and 100. These two subfigures, again, validate that BlockTimeout has little influence to the stability of throughput in the LR region when TxPerBlock is small. However when TxPerBlock value increases, a smaller value of BlockTimeout results in a more stable network throughput in the LR region. No significant differences for the UR region regardless of the variations of BlockTimeout.

TX_{AST} **Latency Analysis of BlockTimeout and TxPerBlock.** We further combine the first two analysis of latency, transaction types and throughput to conduct the third experiment to evaluate blockchain network, specifically committed transactions' latency caused by different values of TxPerBlock and BlockTimeout. Similar to Fig. 3, where the bars represent the average latency of committed transactions, Fig. 6 shows the impact latency caused by different TxPerBlock values. More specifically, in Fig. 6a we observe that fast commits (low latency) in LR due to the smaller number of transactions per block. Therefore, we observe much lower latency about 0.5 even though BlockTimeout increases to 4s. Compared with evaluation results in Fig. 3, it is much faster. However, similar to throughput drops in the UR region, the latency also increases sharply because a larger number of blocks are required to commit all transactions. At this moment an increased value of BlockTimeout can relax the system's load. Therefore, we observe in Fig. 6a, latency values are smaller when BlockTime-out=2s, 4s and TPS=80, 100. In contrast, Fig. 6b encounters slower commits due to an increase in TxPerBlock which forces the framework to wait slightly longer to fulfill one of the defined conditions, i.e., BlockTimeout or TxPerBlock. These delays begin to drop when TPS increases, which is why we see a slight surge in throughput in Fig. 5b, as these events are related to each other.

Therefore, a proper block configuration is extremely important to reduce latency and maintain a stable throughput of the blockchain system. From experiment results, we propose two different configurations for the LR and UR regions. For a system to handle the LR region ($TPS < 80$) with great stability and low latency we propose the use of $TxPerBlock = 10$ in combination with $BlockTimeout = 2s$. On the other hand, if a system TPS setting is larger than 80, it is better to choose $TxPerBlock = 100$ with $BlockTimeout = 4s$.

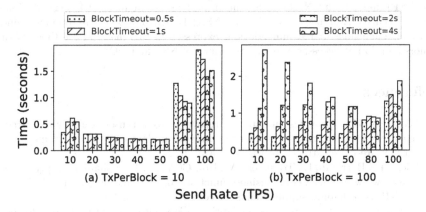

Fig. 6. Comparison BlockTimeout and TxPerBlock influences to latency with 200 TX_{AST}.

5.3 Security Analysis of ChainSCAN

To enhance ChainSCAN resiliency against byzantine participants (i.e., overwrite information to avoid liability), we leverage the immutability property provided by blockchain technology. For instance, a participant may attempt to modify the condition/quality of a generated/traded asset after ownership has been transferred to other supply chain institutions (i.e., supplier, retailer). Since Chain-SCAN follows the strict ACL rules to provide provenance of an asset and prevent participants from attempting to modify data. Furthermore, ChainSCAN uses multiple smart contracts (i.e., decentralized application) to remove potential single-point of failures from the system as contracts are deployed in a decentralized way. Hence, ChainSCAN, a blockchain-based SCM system increases data availability and reduce system bottleneck, and it is resilient to cyber attacks such as Denial-of-service (DoS) or ransomware attacks.

6 Conclusion

We present ChainSCAN, a fully decentralized blockchain-based supply chain management system, that manages, regulates and records activities in food supply chain. The three layers design of ChainSCAN solve many challenges of the current SCM systems such as enhancing supply chain data integrity, availability and privacy, as well as effectively removing the single-point failure by using blockchain technology. ChainSCAN operates automatically using four different smart contracts, and leverages the concept of NFTs to provide traceability of assets through ownership. ChainSCAN provides a transparent environment for liability attribution. Furthermore, we demonstrate the feasibility of deploying ChainSCAN in real world to replace current SCM systems by analyzing its performance under different scenarios.

Acknowledgments. This research is sponsored by the National Science Foundation (NSF) under Grant No.1812599, and in part by Department of Energy/National Nuclear Security Administration (DOE/NNSA) DE-NA0003985. Any opinions, findings, and conclusions or recommendations expressed in this material are those of the authors and do not necessarily reflect the views of NSF and DOE/NNSA.

References

1. AGCO: AGCO provides update on recovery from ransomware cyber attack. https://news.agcocorp.com/news/agco-provides-update-on-recovery-from-ransomware-cyber-attack. Accessed 12 Apr 2022
2. Alicke, K., Barriball, E., Trautwein, V.: How COVID-19 is reshaping supply chains. https://www.mckinsey.com/business-functions/operations/our-insights/how-covid-19-is-reshaping-supply-chains. Accessed 18 Apr 2022
3. Androulaki, E., et al.: Hyperledger fabric: a distributed operating system for permissioned blockchains. In: EuroSys Conference (2018)
4. Arena, A., Bianchini, A., Perazzo, P., Vallati, C., Dini, G.: Bruschetta: An IoT blockchain-based framework for certifying extra virgin olive oil supply chain. In: 2019 IEEE International Conference on Smart Computing (SMARTCOMP), pp. 173–179 (2019). https://doi.org/10.1109/SMARTCOMP.2019.00049
5. BBC: Meat giant JBS pays $11m in ransom to resolve cyber-attack. https://www.bbc.com/news/business-57423008. Accessed 12 Apr 2022
6. Beske-Janssen, P., Johnson, M.P., Schaltegger, S.: 20 years of performance measurement in sustainable supply chain management-what has been achieved? Supply Chain manag. **20**(6), 664–680 (2015)
7. Cahn, D.: When supply chains and blockchains become pervasive. https://talkinglogistics.com/2019/10/24/when-supply-chains-and-blockchains-become-pervasive/. Accessed 18 Apr 2022
8. Chen, T., Wang, D.: Combined application of blockchain technology in fractional calculus model of supply chain financial system. Chaos, Solitons Fractals **131**, 109461 (2020). https://doi.org/10.1016/j.chaos.2019.109461
9. Chenarides, L., Manfredo, M., Richards, T.J.: COVID-19 and food supply chains. Appl. Econ. Perspect. Policy **43**(1), 270–279 (2021). https://doi.org/10.1002/aepp.13085
10. Christiansen, L.: A guide to the food supply chain. https://altametrics.com/food-supply-chain.html. Accessed 21 Mar 2022
11. Dannen, C.: Introducing Ethereum and Solidity. Apress, Berkeley, CA (2017). https://doi.org/10.1007/978-1-4842-2535-6

12. DoE: Colonial pipeline cyber incident. https://www.energy.gov/ceser/colonial-pipeline-cyber-incident. Accessed 18 Apr 2022

13. Duan, J., Zhang, C., Gong, Y., Brown, S., Li, Z.: A content-analysis based literature review in blockchain adoption within food supply chain. Int. J. Environ. Res. Public Health **17**(5), 1784 (2020). https://doi.org/10.3390/ijerph17051784

14. Folkerts, H., Koehorst, H.: Challenges in international food supply chains: vertical co-ordination in the European agribusiness and food industries. Br.Food J. **100**(8), 385–388 (1998)

15. Fraser, I.J., Mueller, M., Schwarzkopf, J.: Transparency for multi-tier sustainable supply chain management: a case study of a multi-tier transparency approach for SSCM in the automotive industry. Sustainability **12**(5), 1814 (2020)

16. Galvez, J.F., Mejuto, J., Simal-Gandara, J.: Future challenges on the use of blockchain for food traceability analysis. TrAC, Trends Anal. Chem. **107**, 222–232 (2018). https://doi.org/10.1016/j.trac.2018.08.011

17. Grecuccio, J., Giusto, E., Fiori, F., Rebaudengo, M.: Combining blockchain and IoT: food-chain traceability and beyond. Energies **13**(15), 3820 (2020)

18. Henninger, A., Mashatan, A.: Distributed interoperable records: the key to better supply chain management. Computers **10**(7) (2021). https://doi.org/10.3390/computers10070089

19. Henriquez, M.: Blackmatter's ransomware attack on new cooperative may impact food supply chain. https://www.securitymagazine.com/articles/96135-blackmatters-ransomware-attack-on-new-cooperative-may-impact-food-supply-chain. Accessed 12 Apr 2022

20. Hobbs, J.E.: Food supply chain resilience and the COVID-19 pandemic: what have we learned? Can. J. Agr. Econ./Revue canadienne d'agroeconomie **69**(2), 189–196 (2021). https://doi.org/10.1111/cjag.12279

21. Jiang, Q., Ke, G.: Information sharing and bullwhip effect in smart destination network system. Ad Hoc Netw. **87**, 17–25 (2019)

22. Katsikouli, P., Wilde, A.S., Dragoni, N., Høgh-Jensen, H.: On the benefits and challenges of blockchains for managing food supply chains. J. Sci. Food Agric. **101**(6), 2175–2181 (2021). https://doi.org/10.1002/jsfa.10883

23. Kouhizadeh, M., Sarkis, J.: Blockchain practices, potentials, and perspectives in greening supply chains. Sustainability **10**(10), 3652 (2018)

24. Lim, M.K., Li, Y., Wang, C., Tseng, M.L.: A literature review of blockchain technology applications in supply chains: a comprehensive analysis of themes, methodologies and industries. Comput. Indus. Eng. **154**, 107133 (2021)

25. Liu, C.: Is USDA organic a seal of deceit: The pitfalls of USDA certified organics produced in the united states, China and beyond. Stan. J. Int'l L. **47**, 333 (2011)

26. Malik, S., Kanhere, S.S., Jurdak, R.: ProductChain: scalable blockchain framework to support provenance in supply chains. In: 2018 IEEE 17th International Symposium on Network Computing and Applications (NCA), pp. 1–10 (2018). https://doi.org/10.1109/NCA.2018.8548322

27. Mohan, T.: Improve food supply chain traceability using blockchain (2018)

28. Morris, A.: Baby formula shortage reveals gaps in regulation and reporting. The New York Times (2022)

29. Mou, W., Wong, W.K., McAleer, M.: Financial credit risk evaluation based on core enterprise supply chains. Sustainability **10**(10), 3699 (2018)

30. Niu, B., Shen, Z., Xie, F.: The value of blockchain and agricultural supply chain parties' participation confronting random bacteria pollution. J. Clean. Prod. **319**, 128579 (2021). https://doi.org/10.1016/j.jclepro.2021.128579

31. Oladimeji, S., Kerner, S.: SolarWinds hack explained: everything you need to know. https://www.techtarget.com/whatis/feature/SolarWinds-hack-explained-Everything-you-need-to-know. Accessed 20 Apr 2022

32. Pazos Corella, V., Chalmeta Rosalen, R., Martinez Simarro, D.: SCIF-IRIS framework: a framework to facilitate interoperability in supply chains. Int. J. Comput. Integr. Manuf. **26**(1–2), 67–86 (2013)

33. Provenance: Blockchain: the solution for supply chain transparency. https://www.provenance.org/whitepaper. Accessed 20 Apr 2022

34. Rizou, M., Galanakis, I.M., Aldawoud, T.M., Galanakis, C.M.: Safety of foods, food supply chain and environment within the COVID-19 pandemic. Trends Food Sci. Technol. **102**, 293–299 (2020). https://doi.org/10.1016/j.tifs.2020.06.008

35. dos Santos, R.B., Torrisi, N.M., Pantoni, R.P.: Third party certification of Agri-food supply chain using smart contracts and blockchain tokens. Sensors **21**(16), 5307 (2021). https://doi.org/10.3390/s21165307

36. Stone, B.: Supply chain cyberattacks jumped 51% in 2021. https://www.techrepublic.com/article/supply-chain-cyberattacks-jumped-51-in-2021/. Accessed 12 Apr 2022

37. Sunny, J., Undralla, N., Pillai, V.M.: Supply chain transparency through blockchain-based traceability: an overview with demonstration. Comput. Indus. Eng. **150**, 106895 (2020)

38. WHO: Food safety. https://www.who.int/news-room/fact-sheets/detail/food-safety. Accessed 21 Mar 2022

39. Yiannas, F.: A new era of food transparency powered by blockchain. Innov. Technol. Gov. Global. **12**(1–2), 46–56 (2018). https://doi.org/10.1162/inov_a_00266

40. Zhao, F., Guo, X., Chan, W.K.V.: Individual green certificates on blockchain: a simulation approach. Sustainability **12**(9), 3942 (2020). https://doi.org/10.3390/su12093942

41. Zhao, G., Liu, S., Lopez, C., Lu, H., Elgueta, S., Chen, H., Boshkoska, B.M.: Blockchain technology in Agri-food value chain management: a synthesis of applications, challenges and future research directions. Comput. Ind. **109**, 83–99 (2019). https://doi.org/10.1016/j.compind.2019.04.002

BlockRAT: An Enhanced Remote Access Trojan Framework via Blockchain

Yanze Kang[1], Xiaobo Yu[1], Weizhi Meng[2], and Yining Liu[1(✉)]

[1] School of Computer Science and Information Security, Guilin University
of Electronic Technology, Guilin 541004, China
ynliu@guet.edu.cn
[2] Department of Applied Mathematics and Computer Science, Technical University
of Denmark, 2800 Kongens Lyngby, Denmark

Abstract. Remote Access Trojan (RAT) is a type of malicious software, aiming to infect victims' computers through targeted attacks. Most existing RATs require a hacker to purchase a server, a domain name and many network resources to construct the infrastructure with a Command and Control (C2) channel. However, hackers' information may be leaked or become traceable during the purchase of C2 channels and network resources. In this work, we propose BlockRAT, a blockchain-based RAT framework that can hide the hacker's personal information with untraceability and low cost. We also introduce a method to help assess the suitability of blockchain types. In the evaluation, we take Network Infrastructure for Decentralized Internet (NKN) as a case study, and compare our BlockRAT with existing studies. The results indicate that BlockRAT can achieve upstream and downstream anonymity, low cost, and good extensibility.

Keywords: Blockchain technology · Remote access trojan · Command and control · Network attack · NKN

1 Introduction

Remote Access Trojan (RAT) is a type of malicious software that uses backdoors to gain a higher privilege control over infected victims' computers [11]. That is, it offers a high level permission and control over compromised computers to hackers. In practice, it is often used to scan cyber-space for flawed hosts in large numbers by various infection methods, and to create one-to-one or one-to-many network architecture [23].

RATs are mainly used to monitor the infected victims, such as documents, video, audio, and even exfiltrate personal files. Hackers often send modified programs to victims by implanting shellcode with malicious functions [18]. Currently, there are two major attacking methods: *targeted attacks* that use phishing emails, spoofed documents to exploit weak passwords, and vulnerability identification in operational systems and platforms to conduct automated attacks

C. Su et al. (Eds.): SciSec 2022, LNCS 13580, pp. 21–35, 2022.
https://doi.org/10.1007/978-3-031-17551-0_2

and capture vulnerable devices [20]. Due to this, RATs are widely used in bot-nets, i.e., Botmaster (botnets administrator) can communicate with the infected nodes via a Command and Control (C2) communication channel and modified RAT.

In practice, RATs are designed in various forms, but the communication infrastructure has not been changed a lot. For instance, a RAT often sets up a C2 channel with the hacker's servers, which can receive data and give commands to victims' computers. Hackers are commonly hiding or masking their malicious traffic via specific encryption and decryption. Figure 1 illustrates two main prob-lems: single point of failure and traceability, in the communication channel of the C2 infrastructure. In this case, hackers may leak their personal information when purchasing network resources for building a C2 channel.

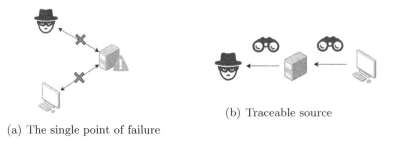

(a) The single point of failure

(b) Traceable source

Fig. 1. Possible faults encountered with the RAT

To address the main problems, blockchain-based botnet schemes have been studied, aiming to ensure anonymity and security during C2 communications. In terms of cost, performance and availability, we found there are still some prob-lems in these schemes, i.e., they can only be adapted to a specific blockchain with a limited role. In addition, some variants of botnets have also been explored to leverage blockchain technology to infect victims and hide malicious events in the cyber-space [1]. Hence, it is an interesting topic to investigate how a blockchain can be used as C2 medium for benefiting botnets, especially RAT.

Motivated by the above observations, we make the following contributions in this paper.

- We propose an enhanced blockchain-based RAT infrastructure, which can provide untraceability and low cost. It can avoid information leakage effec-tively when purchasing network resources, as compared to common RATs.
- We introduce a method to evaluate various blockchain platforms and identify suitable blockchains as a medium for RAT. This method provides a glimpse into the development tendency about the blockchain-based RATs or botnets in the future.

– The blockchain-based RAT can be adaptable according to particular remote control scenarios with traffic obfuscation, persistence enhancements.

The paper is structured as follows: Sect. 2 discusses background and related work. Section 3 describes the blockchain-based RAT, including system design and main workflow. The challenges and solutions are discussed in Sect. 4. Section 5 evaluates the effectiveness and performance of our proposed blockchain-based RAT. We conclude the paper in Sect. 6.

2   Background and Related Work

2.1   RAT, Botnets and C2 Channel

A RAT can offer a highly level permission and control over compromised computers to hackers; thus, it has been widely used in botnets, as one major cyber threat nowadays. Botnets often target home networks, routers, gateways, cameras and PC hosts, among other devices. Some trained hackers may target on government entities and corporations with political and highly technical backgrounds. As a result, there are some motivated botnet attackers in the cyber threat campaign, most of which are aimed at stealing confidential information.

The C2 channel is primarily used for messaging and interaction between hackers and botnets servers, i.e., hackers can manage their acquired infected hosts and also protect their personal privacy. The common C2 channel mechanisms, such as IRC (Internet Relay Chat) protocol-based and HTTP protocol-based communication, often adopt a centralized C2 architecture, which offers rapid deployment capability due to the simple design, while causing a single point of failure (SPOF) problem [17].

Though P2P protocol-based botnets can improve the concealment of botnet communication and avoid the SPOF problem, they still suffer from incomplete decentralization during initialization. In order to ensure the security of traffic in C2 communication, hackers often resort to P2P-derived protocols, traffic encryption, signatures and Tor communication methods, as shown in Fig. 2.

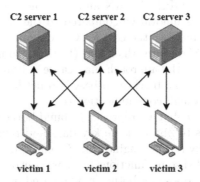

Fig. 2. Decentralized C2 structure

2.2   Blockchain Technology in RAT

Blockchain is a technical infrastructure in the form of decentralized P2P networks, which features smart contracts and distributed ledgers for applications [16]. It can be considered as a new application model that integrates distributed data storage, peer-to-peer transmission, consensus mechanisms, encryption algorithms and various network technologies [15]. The transactions are processed based on different nodes in the blockchain, which can protect from unauthorized mortification by any individual or organization. This makes blockchains a potential medium for C2 communication.

2.3   Related Work

Early botents such as Gtbot [7] often used IRC (Internet Relay Chat) protocol for C2 command communication, through a chat system with plaintext transmission. The C2 infrastructure of botnets implemented based on the IRC protocol is easy to use; however, the main issue is the poor concealment due to the plaintext transmission. Then Rustock [19] and SocioBot [14] used HTTP protocol as the main communication protocol, which can well hide the hacker's traffic and make it more difficult for traceability analysis. While it is easy to identify HTTP features via the hard-coded or static addressing of botnets, hackers start using dynamic addressing for channel transmission, including Domain-Flux [24] and Fast-Flux [12] botnets. They used a large number of domain names and mapped them to IP pools, which can dynamically generate domain names through DGA (Domain Generation Algorithm) and resolve them to C2 servers.

The advent of blockchain technology introduces a new way of designing a RAT, botnet and detection framework. Lekssays [13] proposed a dynamic botnet detection framework, which can ensure immutability and transparency by leveraging on blockchain. Spathoulas [21] used smart contracts for exchanging information and detected distributed denial of service (DDoS) by lightweight agents installed at IoT devices. Ali et al. [4,5] proposed a botnet model based on bitcoin network, inheriting the advantages of anonymity as well as decentralization, based on the P2P protocol. It could perform a C2 communications and update via bitcoin's OP_RETURN and Unspendable Transaction Output (UTXO). This method is innovative compared to the common RAT, but it is still traceable and may increase the cost for C2 communication. Frkat [11] used Edwards-curve Digital Signature Algorithm (EdDSA) to maintain stealthier in bitcoin blockchain. While the approach may cause a 10min delay as compared to [4,5]. Falco [10] proposed a blockchain-based botnet based on neuromesh, but this model still suffers a high communication cost.

Sweeny [22] then presented an approach to build botnets via a private chain, but it allows the others to obtain some key data and take over some nodes in the private blockchain by reverse engineering. Omar [6] used smart contracts for creating botnet and called some functions of smart contracts for C2 communications. Baden et al. [8] proposed a botnet model based on Ethereum whispering protocol. Compared to Zombiecoin, this method poses no cost for C2 communication, whereas the Whisper botnets may take down an Ethereum network in practical usage.

Leon [9] made an experimental analysis of some existing blockchain-based botnets in feasibility and detectability, and discussed potential countermeasures.

3 Our Approach

In this section, we propose an enhanced blockchain-based RAT framework, called BlockRAT, which can hide the hacker's personal information with untraceability and low cost.

3.1 System Design

C2 Programs. The C2 programs are build on blockchain application layer, which can be flexible and adaptive to various platforms and give full play to the benefits of the blockchain. It consists of the following components:

C2 Server. It is responsible for receiving information from victims and sending evil commands by nodes. In order to prevent the replaying of commands and messages, the C2 Server always use the encryption algorithms to protect communication security. There is also a need to create a private channel by designating to the specific seeds.

C2 Client. The program is initially executed on victim's PC, which can get pre-set seeds to connect to the nearest node server and send response to C2 server. Blockchain communication channel can automatically transfer the response traffic to C2 server, which is unpredictable.

Blockchain Communication Channel. This communication channel consists of node servers on the blockchain, which normally requires no additional configuration. Unless that blockchain does not support software development at the application layer, we can only write information to a storage space on the block that can be queried.

Work Process. As shown in Fig. 3, victims can calculate the C2 domain name or channel address according to the algorithm or information pre-set inside the program, and can send an online message to that address. During this process, the C2 Server listens to the channel and receives the uplink information. Once the victim host is obtained, it can send commands through the channel. Then the victim side sends back the result of its execution based on the commands.

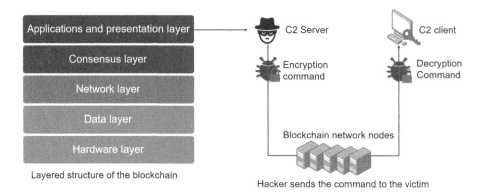

Fig. 3. C2 program's work process

3.2   Attack Characteristics

To understand the attack characteristics, we have to know how C2 traffic is transmitted across the blockchain network. Normally, C2 traffic needs to maintain the anonymity by transmitting over the blockchain channel, including both upstream and downstream, as shown in Fig. 4.

Upstream Transmission: Response result from victim will be given over the blockchain node servers to hacker in the upstream. Hackers can also send a C2 command to control victim in the upstream. Simply understood, the upstream transmission process can be considered as the control process of hackers. During this transmission, hackers may encode the C2 commands into a pubic block and control a victim, by listening to the pre-set channel in the upstream stage. If the hackers choose the former, then they may have a significant transaction cost, especially for Bitcoin.

Downstream Transmission: In the downstream transmission, victim needs to request the C2 server address or pre-set channel to connect with hackers' side for C2 communications, when they executed the C2 client program. The downstream transmission always includes the victims' received C2 commands and the execution results back to hackers after the C2 channel is established.

From this above processes, we can understand the attack characteristics of blockchain-based RAT and the urgent need for strengthening:

Blockchain Selection. Although hackers do not need to purchase server resources, they may still spend on block trading. Thus it is important to choose a suitable blockchain for C2 infrastructure's construction. For example, Bitcoin-based RAT may require a significants cost to maintain C2 communications. Therefore, keeping communication cost as low as possible is also an issue to be considered.

Obvious Traffic Characteristics. In the downstream, the victim can send an uptime message to the hacker in a number of ways when the C2 Client is

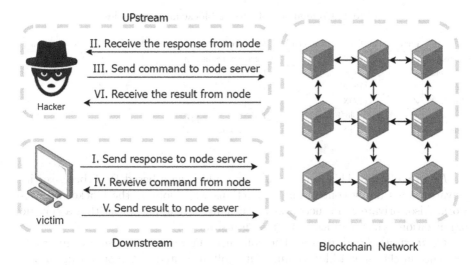

Fig. 4. Workflow

firstly executed. It can calculate the domain name of C2 server through DGA and then resolve it through decentralized DNS, or send a request directly to the nearest blockchain node server. In either way, the C2 Client always has to send a request to the blockchain network. Security administrators can filter these packets with blockchain names (e.g., Bitcoin, Ether) and block blockchain-based RAT responses.

Backdoor Persistence. The loss of a few hosts from a large botnet does not fatally affect the performance. On the other hand, the blockchain-based RAT needs to be guaranteed to be persistent and covertly online in order to better execute the hacker's commands. Fortunately, existing security software does not detect blockchain-based RATs well, because their action features are relatively novel and the signature code does not exist in previous virus repositories. Thus, we can focus more on the persistence of backdoor.

4   Implementation Detail

In this section, we introduce how to address three major challenges during the implementation.

4.1   Challenge and Solution 1: Blockchain Selection

How to select a suitable blockchain platform is a challenge. Table 1 describes several main platforms and in this work, the blockchain platform with the lowest transaction cost can be selected. Below are some factors should be considered for the selection.

Table 1. Comparison of several blockchain properties

	Public chain	Consensus mechanism	Main application	DApp development	Suitable for channel
Bitcoin	✓	POW	Currency trading	✗	✗
Ethereum	✓	POS	DApp	✓	✓
Namecoin	✓	POW	DNS	✓	✓
NKN	✓	POX	DApp	✓	✓
Fabric	✗	Solo/Kafka/raft	Ledger	✗	✗
Filecoin	✓	IPFS	Data storage	✓	✗

Public Chain. This is necessary for a blockchain-based RAT because the private chains imply control and restrictions when joining the blockchain network. Also, private chain networks are usually only applicable within a specific organization, which can lead to a rise in instability.

Consensus Mechanism. The consensus mechanism is also an important reference in choosing a blockchain, as it is often related to the operating principles of a blockchain network. For example, filecoin, which is based on the IPFS consensus mechanism, is dependent on the amount of storage to work.

Main Application. We can understand the main application aspects of the blockchain network and decide the role what they play in the blockchain-based RAT. If the main application of a blockchain is only in cryptocurrency and data storage, we must find a way to store our C2 information in the accessible part of the public block for C2 channel communication. In addition, the blockchain-based DNS allows us to get the convenience of anonymity in domain name resolution.

DApp Development. The availability of DApp development is an important factor in choosing a blockchain. The DApp facilitates RAT development and rapid deployment. It also hands over C2 traffic to the blockchain network for transmission with the help of blockchain's open SDK. In other words, the ideal blockchain-based RAT is a decentralized application.

With the above considerations, we can use blockchains such as Ethereum and NKN that support DApp development, in order to achieve peer to peer and real-time communication of C2 traffic, circumventing the usual transaction steps required for C2 command delivery.

4.2   Challenge and Solution 2: Obvious Traffic Characteristics

The blockchain-based RAT can send some requests to blockchain nodes, which carries a distinct traffic profile. We can obfuscate C2 traffic to avoid being filtered by firewalls and other security software. There is an encryption module in the C2 program for securing our communication and further reducing the possibility of intermediate nodes that steal information during the communication process.

In the common RAT, we can use traffic forwarding to protect our C2 traffic from security engineers, which can be disguised as communication with highly reputable domains at the same time, mostly used for covert communication between the Trojan's side and the control side. However, we cannot simply apply the domain fronting technology to blockchain-based RAT, because we do not know which blockchain node is hiding behind and whether the CDN is enabled or not. However, we can hide our behavior by forwarding traffic with characteristics through some features of CDN, such as cloudflare workers. With this method, the victim can only observe that the C2 client sends information to the CDN just like the shaded part as shown in Fig. 5, while not discovering the subsequent transmission phase.

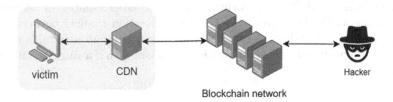

Fig. 5. Traffic Forwarding

If the victim sends plaintext packets when negotiating communication with the blockchain network, we can further obfuscate the traffic by manually adding an encryption module to the development library by encrypting the sent plaintext into unrecognizable ciphertext.

4.3   Challenge and Solution 3: Backdoor Persistence

Backdoor persistence is a relatively important work of RAT. Conventional backdoor persistence methods are relatively easy to implement such as Task Schedule, regedit, services and so on, which may lead to security software for these places of strict defense in Windows. We can consider the DLL hijacking approach to achieve hidden sensitive behavior. This method circumvents the whitelisting mechanism of security software by injecting code into the DLL files of common software, in order to achieve the effect of persistent hiding. Also, if the user launches the hijacked software, our malicious program will be launched automatically. While the disadvantage is also obvious, we need to know the applications on the victim's host and mine those software for DLL vulnerabilities.

5   Evaluation

5.1   Comparison with Common RATs

We evaluate our proposed blockchain-based RAT framework compared with the common RATs. Table 2 describes the comparison regarding five features. It is seen that blockchain-based RAT has the following advantages:

Anonymity. The blockchain-based RAT infrastructure has the inherent anonymity from blockchain, making it harder for security analysts to trace back to the source, whether it is critical control information hosted on a block or malicious traffic generated by a hacker. Compared to common RATs, our blockchain-based RATs can provide the anti-traceability and avoid the leakage of personal information in the process of purchasing network C2 resources.

Robustness. Better network scalability and performance can be provided by the blockchain-based RATs, benefiting from the large number of blockchain nodes acting as the medium of the C2 communication channel between hackers and victims. Blockchain network will automatically find a suitable channel based on the specific blockchain network mechanism even if a single-point failure exists.

Flexibility. The infrastructure can adapt to various consensus mechanisms. Any community blockchain project can become the medium for RAT C2 communications, as long as the blockchain platform supports extension and application development.

Simplicity. For better C2 communication and security, blockchain-based RAT does not need to purchase expensive network resources, as the C2 program can be created on the existing blockchain application layer.

5.2   Effectiveness Evaluation

To evaluate the effectiveness of our C2 programs, we selected three types of properties, including imperceptibility, availability and blockchain performance. The anti-virus detection for the C2 programs were conducted in VirusTotal [3]. We uploaded the program to Virustotal for online testing. From the detection results shown in Fig. 6, the C2 programs have only 4% malicious code detection rate, and prove that the blockchain-based RAT programs are able to circumvent most anti-virus software.

The availability evaluation was conducted in a virtual machine environment, where C2 server and client were running in laptop with Windows 10 and AMD Ryzen 7 5800H Radeon (3.2 GHz). Windows 10 Vmware environment was used to send C2 commands with 3.5GB RAM, dual processors and quad core. Windows 7 Vmware was used and controlled with 2.0GB RAM, dual processors and quad core. In this experiment, the hacker executed the C2 server-side program, and sent the command to execute the calculator to the channel, after which the victim successfully executed it locally, proving the availability of the program, as shown in Fig. 7.

Fig. 6. VirusTotal scan result

Fig. 7. Availability of the C2 programs

5.3   Comparison with Existing Blockchain-based RATs/botnets

In this section, we further compared the existing blockchain-based botnets according to Table 2. From this table, we can easily see that the Bitcoin-based botnets are disadvantageous, because it possesses a higher cost as well as uncertain anonymity. Since Bitcoin-based RATs can only read and execute C2 commands through blocks in the downstream stage of the transmission process, which does not provide good protection of anonymity and security for hackers. Although Monero's costs less than Bitcoin-based blockchain, it does not solve the upstream anonymity and zero transaction cost. Sweeny does not need any communication cost to build C2 channel by private chains, but it may lose security and non-traceable properties.

Table 2. Comparison of existing blockchain-based botnets or RATs

	Blockchain	Zero transcation cost	Upstream anonymity	Downstream anonymity	Public blockchain	Extensibility
Zombiecoin [5]	Bitcoin	✗	✗	✓	✓	?
ChainChannel	Bitcoin	✗	✗	✓	✓	✓
Redaman	Bitcoin	✗	✗	✓	✓	✗
NeuroMesh [10]	Bitcoin	✗	✗	✓	✓	?
Monero [17]	Monero	✗	✗	✓	✓	✗
Botract [6]	Ethereum	✗	✓	?	✓	✓
UnblockableChains [25]	Ethereum	✗	✓	✓	✓	✓
Whispering [8]	Ethereum	✓	✓	✓	✓	✗
Sweeny [22]	Ethereum	✓	✓	✗	✗	?
Fbot	EmerCoin	✗	✗	✗	✓	?
NKN	NKN	✓	✓	✓	✓	✓

✗ Does not possess features ✓ Possessing features ? Not specified.

NKN and ETH have good scaling performance among the current blockchains that support DApp development, but Whispering is practically unusable because the key whisper API has been removed in Ethereum python library web3 [2]. Even though the Whispering can be used, its extensibility and rapid deployment is poor than NKN.

In addition, the bitcoin-based blockchain botnets such as Zombiecoin rely mainly on OP_RETURN, UTXO, hiding C2 commands by specific transactions amount value, subliminal channels, key leakage [5], so these methods have some limitations on command transmission. Thus, we can only use 80 bytes to send command by OP_RETURN function, and 20 bytes of data by UTXO due to function and programming limitations. The Ethereum-based botnet can use smart contracts to build a botnet C2 channel, allowing more space to send commands, but it still does not solve the problem of transmitting files. For our approach, the C2 commands what we can send are not limited in length and we can also transfer files as shown in Fig. 8.

5.4   Limitation and Discussion

However, there are also some limitations in our approach. Firstly, only a small size of files can be transferred, whereas we can add a slice transfer feature into the C2 program, making it possible to transfer large files. Then code development of the blockchain-based RAT is limited by the interface provided by the blockchain network, which leads to possibility that the code may have to be updated with the blockchain upgrade. Although the blockchain interface upgrade is uncommon, it still has the potential to happen. Thus, we need to add the update module into our C2 Client program, in order to prevent from rendering the client program unusable.

Fig. 8. Transferring files

6   Conclusions

With the escalation of cyber-space confrontation, the common RAT commands and control mechanisms may no longer meet the needs of attackers, and there is a trend towards building a more robust, covert and flexible botnet and RAT. The popularity and application of blockchain networks offer new possibilities for this purpose. In this work, we proposed BlockRAT, an enhanced blockchain-based RAT framework that can hide the hacker's personal information with untraceability and low cost. We also introduced a method for selecting a suitable blockchain for BlockRAT. In our experiments, we selected NKN blockchain as the medium to implement BlockRAT and proved imperceptibility, availability. Then we showed that our approach can have certain advantages as compared with existing blockchain-based RATS / botnets. We further found that Whisper protocol can be a good alternative option in our future study.

Acknowledgments. This work was supported by Natural Science Foundation of China under grant No. 62072133, Key projects of Guangxi Natural Science Foundation under grant No. 2018GXNSFDA281040

References

1. Bitcoins, blockchains, and botnets. https://www.akamai.com/blog/security/bitcoins--blockchains--and-botnets
2. Remove whisper API. https://github.com/ethereum/web3.py/pull/1791
3. Virustotal. https://www.virustotal.com/

4. Ali, Syed Taha, McCorry, Patrick, Lee, Peter Hyun-Jeen., Hao, Feng: ZombieCoin: powering next-generation botnets with bitcoin. In: Brenner, Michael, Christin, Nicolas, Johnson, Benjamin, Rohloff, Kurt (eds.) FC 2015. LNCS, vol. 8976, pp. 34–48. Springer, Heidelberg (2015). https://doi.org/10.1007/978-3-662-48051-9_3

5. Ali, S.T., McCorry, P., Lee, P.H.J., Hao, F.: Zombiecoin 2.0: managing next-generation botnets using bitcoin. International J. Inf. Secur. **17**(4), 411–422 (2018)

6. Alibrahim, O., Malaika, M.: Botract: abusing smart contracts and blockchain for botnet command and control. Int. J. Inf. Comput. Secur. **17**(1–2), 147–163 (2022)

7. Atluri, Anoop Chowdary, Tran, Vinh: Botnets threat analysis and detection. In: Traoré, Issa, Awad, Ahmed, Woungang, Isaac (eds.) Information Security Practices, pp. 7–28. Springer, Cham (2017). https://doi.org/10.1007/978-3-319-48947-6_2

8. Baden, M., Torres, C.F., Pontiveros, B.B.F., State, R.: Whispering botnet command and control instructions. In: 2019 Crypto Valley Conference on Blockchain Technology (CVCBT), pp. 77–81. IEEE (2019)

9. Böck, L., Alexopoulos, N., Saracoglu, E., Mühlhäuser, M., Vasilomanolakis, E.: Assessing the threat of blockchain-based botnets. In: 2019 APWG Symposium on Electronic Crime Research (eCrime), pp. 1–11. IEEE (2019)

10. Falco, G., Li, C., Fedorov, P., Caldera, C., Arora, R., Jackson, K.: Neuromesh: IoT security enabled by a blockchain powered botnet vaccine. In: Proceedings of the International Conference on Omni-Layer Intelligent Systems, pp. 1–6 (2019)

11. Frkat, D., Annessi, R., Zseby, T.: Chainchannels: Private botnet communication over public blockchains. In: 2018 IEEE International Conference on Internet of Things (iThings) and IEEE Green Computing and Communications (GreenCom) and IEEE Cyber, Physical and Social Computing (CPSCom) and IEEE Smart Data (SmartData), pp. 1244–1252. IEEE (2018)

12. Holz, T., Gorecki, C., Rieck, K., Freiling, F.C.: Measuring and detecting fast-flux service networks. In: NDSS (2008)

13. Lekssays, A., Landa, L., Carminati, B., Ferrari, E.: Pautobotcatcher: a blockchain-based privacy-preserving botnet detector for internet of things. Comput. Netw. **200**, 108512 (2021)

14. Makkar, I.K., Troia, F.D., Visaggio, C.A., Austin, T.H., Stamp, M.: Sociobot: a twitter-based botnet. Int. J. Secure. Network. **12**(1), 1–12 (2017)

15. Meng, W., Li, W., Zhou, J.: Enhancing the security of blockchain-based software defined networking through trust-based traffic fusion and filtration. Inf. Fusion **70**, 60–71 (2021)

16. Meng, W., Li, W., Zhu, L.: Enhancing medical smartphone networks via blockchain-based trust management against insider attacks. IEEE Trans. Eng. Manag. **67**(4), 1377–1386 (2020)

17. Mengidis, A.: Blockchain-based command and control for next generation botnets (2019)

18. Or-Meir, O., Nissim, N., Elovici, Y., Rokach, L.: Dynamic malware analysis in the modern era-a state of the art survey. ACM Comput. Surv. (CSUR) **52**(5), 1–48 (2019)

19. Quarterman, J.S., Sayin, S., Whinston, A.B.: Rustock botnet and ASNs. TPRC (2011)

20. Silva, S.S., Silva, R.M., Pinto, R.C., Salles, R.M.: Botnets: a survey. Comput. Netw. **57**(2), 378–403 (2013)

21. Spathoulas, G., Giachoudis, N., Damiris, G.P., Theodoridis, G.: Collaborative blockchain-based detection of distributed denial of service attacks based on internet of things botnets. Future Internet **11**(11), 226 (2019)

22. Sweeny, J.: Botnet resiliency via private blockchains. SANS Institute Information Security Reading Group (2017)
23. Yin, M., Chen, X., Wang, Q., Wang, W., Wang, Y.: Dynamics on hybrid complex network: Botnet modeling and analysis of medical IoT. Secur. Commun. Netw. **2019**(5), 1–14 (2019)
24. Zhang, L., Yu, S., Wu, D., Watters, P.: A survey on latest botnet attack and defense. In: 2011IEEE 10th International Conference on Trust, Security and Privacy in Computing and Communications, pp. 53–60. IEEE (2011)
25. Zohar, O.: Unblockable chains. https://github.com/platdrag/UnblockableChains. Accessed 12 Dec 2018

Adapted PBFT Consensus Protocol for Sharded Blockchain

Ling Yang and Huawei Huang[(✉)]

School of SSE, Sun Yat-sen University, Guangzhou, China
`huanghw28@mail.sysu.edu.cn`

Abstract. As the foundation of a blockchain, consensus algorithm significantly affects the blockchain system's performance. To a consortium blockchain, Practical Byzantine Fault Tolerance (PBFT) has been widely believed as a good candidate consensus due to its many advantages. However, PBFT is not particularly designed for a consortium blockchain. Thus, there is still a large improvement space to implement the PBFT algorithm in a sharded blockchain. Based on network sharding, we aim to address the problems incurred by the traditional PBFT algorithm. Because when there are large number of nodes in a P2P network, PBFT can lead to a significant performance degradation. Even worse, Byzantine nodes cannot be found timely in a large-scale blockchain network where the PBFT algorithm is adopted. In this paper, we propose an adapted version of BFT consensus for the sharded blockchain. The proposed cross-shard BFT consensus mainly consists of a two-phase consensus mechanism after performing network sharding. In the first phase, Raft consensus is first adopted within each shard, in which a leader is elected. In the second phase, those leaders from all shards form a committee and perform a committee-wise PBFT consensus. Through introducing anchor nodes within each shard, the security of the proposed two-phase consensus is guaranteed. We analyze the security of the cross-shard BFT consensus based on a committee-wise monitoring framework. Through simulations, we find out that the proposed cross-shard BFT consensus yields a higher throughput, lower latency than the original PBFT. The fault-tolerance ability of the proposed consensus is around 1.5× to 2× of PBFT.

Keywords: Blockchain · Consensus algorithm · Practical byzantine fault tolerance · Network sharding

1 Introduction

Blockchain, a new distributed ledger technology, is decentralized, de-trusted, tamper-evident and anonymous. It can enable nodes to reach consensus without the existence of a trusted third party, and is hailed as a new technology that will revolutionize society [1].

The core of blockchain is the consensus algorithm, which determines the way in which the nodes in the consensus network finally agree on specific data.

C. Su et al. (Eds.): SciSec 2022, LNCS 13580, pp. 36–50, 2022.
https://doi.org/10.1007/978-3-031-17551-0_3

Consensus algorithm also determines the performance of the blockchain, such as throughput, latency, and security.

Blockchains have different ways of classification according to different criteria, and can be divided into the public, private and consortium blockchains according to the way they are deployed [2]. Depending on application scenarios and performance requirements, different consensus algorithms can be considered.

In the public blockchain, any node can join or leave the network at any time without any permission. The most commonly used consensus algorithms in public chains are Proof of Work (PoW) [3], Proof of Stake (PoS) [4] and Delegate Proof of Stake (DPoS) [5]. For example, the consensus algorithm used by Bitcoin and Ethereum [6] is PoW. Although security is greatly guaranteed, the efficiency is very low. Its reliance on computer arithmetic to reach consensus is very inefficient and leads to a huge waste of resources. Bitcoin's transaction throughput is only about 7 transactions per second [7], and Ethereum's transaction throughput is about 15 transactions per second. Therefore, in order to improve consensus efficiency, many new consensus algorithms have been proposed, such as PoS and DPoS. But all of these algorithms must rely on digital currency in order to reach consensus, so they are less practical.

Unlike the public blockchain, the private blockchain are generally limited to the internal use of enterprises or individual individuals, and there are no Byzantine nodes in the network [8], which deliberately send wrong information and cause the whole network to fail reaching consensus. Thus most of the private blockchains use the traditional distributed consistency algorithm, such as Raft [9], as their consensus.

The consortium blockchain is often implemented internally by an organization, with certain identity restrictions. In those organizations, their data on the chain cannot be accessed externally. Thus, the security and privacy of the internal data can be greatly guaranteed when using a consortium blockchain. Thereby, consortium blockchains have a wide application scenarios in the fields of banking and medical care. The most popular consensus algorithm of the consortium blockchain is Practical Byzantine Fault Tolerance (PBFT) [10], which exploits signature verification, hashing and other cryptography algorithms to ensure immutability in the message transmission process.

When implementing a consortium blockchain, people have been trying to adopt PBFT as its consensus. However, PBFT is not particularly designed for a consortium blockchain. Thus, there is still a large improvement space to implement the PBFT algorithm in a sharded blockchain. From the process of the PBFT algorithm, it can be seen that it relies on a large number of inter-node communications with a network complexity of $O(N^2)$. When there are large number of nodes in a P2P network, PBFT can lead to a significant performance degradation. In addition, when the network latency is large or there are too many nodes, the consensus may not be completed within a certain time. This can lead to frequent view-change and even eventually rendering the consensus ineffective. Therefore, it is necessary to reduce the communication complexity and network dependence of PBFT.

In this paper, we propose an adapted version of BFT consensus for the sharded blockchain by combining the advantages of high consensus efficiency of Raft protocol and Byzantine fault tolerance security of PBFT algorithm. In addition, an anchor node is introduced in each shard to monitor the leader, which solves the problem that the Raft protocol cannot address Byzantine behaviors. Anchor nodes ensure the security of the consensus of the proposed two-phase BFT. Meanwhile, a sorter is introduced to replace the primary node in the conventional PBFT protocol. A sorter is used to sort requests submitted from clients and notify those requests to all leaders. The meaning of such sorter is to prevent that the primary node may commit malicious behaviors once it too powerful.

Through simulations, we find out that the cross-shard BFT consensus algorithm proposed in this paper yields a higher throughput, lower latency than the original PBFT, and still maintains high performance as the number of nodes increases. The fault-tolerance ability of the proposed consensus is around $1.5\times$ to $2\times$ of PBFT.

Our study in this paper includes the following contributions.

- We proposed an adapted BFT protocol for sharded blockchains.
- The security guarantee of the proposed two-phase consensus is analyzed using a committee-wise monitoring framework.

The rest of the paper is organized as follows. Section 2 reviews the related work. In Sect. 3, the relevant background is presented. In Sect. 4, a new cross-shard BFT consensus algorithm is proposed. Then, the consistency, safety and liveness is analyzed. In Sect. 5, the cross-shard BFT consensus algorithm and the original PBFT algorithm are tested in terms of throughput, latency and fault tolerance, respectively, and the test results are analyzed. Finally, the paper is concluded in Sect. 6.

2 Related Work

2.1 Sharded Blockchain

Elastico [11] is viewed as the first sharding system designed for public blockchain. Zilliqa [12] is the first implementation of elastico protocol. Interestingly, Zilliqa blockchain exploits both PoW and PBFT algorithms for its consensus, in which the committee formation adopts PoW while block generation in each shard utilizes PBFT.

OmniLedger [13] uses RoundHound and VRF protocols to randomly assign Validators to different shards. The consensus of each shard uses the PBFT algorithm. Omniledger tolerates no more than $\frac{1}{3}$ of the Byzantine nodes.

RapidChain [14] uses state sharding technology to achieve near-linear scaling of blockchain performance, while also largely solving the problem of huge storage costs faced by blockchain scaling.

Monoxide [15] provides linear scaling by dividing the workload of all key components of the blockchain system without compromising decentralization and security.

2.2 PBFT Algorithms

In 1999, Castro and Liskov proposed the PBFT algorithm [10], which is the first widely available Byzantine fault-tolerant algorithm. However, the PBFT algorithm to solve the Byzantine general problem requires a network communication with time complexity of $O(N^2)$, which puts a great pressure on the network. In response to this problem, many researchers at home and abroad have optimized the PBFT consensus algorithm, which basically focuses on the three-stage consensus process, primary selection and view change.

The RBFT [16] improves the system performance under the worst conditions by reducing the system performance under the optimal conditions, so as to improve the robustness of the whole system. However, due to the addition of one more stage than the PBFT algorithm, RBFT is higher than the PBFT algorithm in terms of communication overhead and latency.

FastBFT [17] arranges the replica nodes in a tree structure, with the primary node as the root of the tree. Ideally, the message complexity of FastBFT can be reduced to $O(nlogn)$. However, in the case of failure the message complexity is still $O(N^2)$.

DBFT [18] combines the DPoS [5] and PBFT. DBFT selects some of the nodes to participate in consensus based on their share voting results, which greatly reduces the amount of communication between nodes. However, DBFT has the same problem as DPoS algorithm, it requires digital currency to complete the consensus.

Zyzzyva [19] simplifies the consistency protocol of the PBFT algorithm in the absence of Byzantine nodes in the network, which reduces the time complexity of the entire consensus process from $O(N^2)$ to $O(N)$. However, in the presence of Byzantine nodes, Zyzzyva's performance degrades to $O(N^2)$.

Hot-Stuff [20] is another protocol based on Byzantine fault tolerance. Once the network is in a synchronized state, the Hot-Stuff algorithm allows a leader to initiate consensus at a fixed interval. The network communication overhead of this algorithm is linearly related to the number of replica. However, its time complexity is still $O(N^2)$ if it is executed as normal.

Tendermint [21] optimizes the PBFT algorithm through a locking mechanism. It combines the PoS with BFT and requires only two rounds of voting to reach consensus. Tendermint elects the nodes that pack the blocks based on the weight of the assets. Therefore, Byzantine nodes can break the consensus by increasing their own equity.

3   Background and Preliminaries

3.1   Blockchain Sharding

Originated from database technology, sharding was initially proposed to reduce the pressure of data access on a single server and improve the overall performance of the database. Sharding is to divide the data in the database into multiple independent data shards in a certain way, and then put these data shards into different servers. Sharding can overcome the hardware performance bottleneck of a single server and improve the performance of the database system as a whole.

Blockchain sharding technology borrows the idea of database sharding and divides the consensus network into several mutually independent networks that can independently perform consensus. The introduction of the sharding technology greatly reduces the amount of computation and redundant storage for blockchain nodes to perform consensus. Each node only needs to perform verification and consensus on the transactions within its own shard thus saving a lot of time and network resources.

Based on the degree of sharding, blockchain sharding can be classified into three categories: network sharding, transaction sharding, and state sharding.

Network Sharding is the most basic type of sharding. It divides nodes at the network level into multiple sub-networks that can be independently consensual. Both transaction sharding and state sharding are based on network sharding.

Transaction sharding is between network sharding and state sharding. Transactions are assigned to different shards according to certain rules. Each shard is responsible for processing only the transactions assigned to that shard.

State sharding is the most challenging of all sharding approaches. It divides blockchain data into multiple disjoint data sets and then let different parts be stored by different shards. Each node does not need to store the complete blockchain state, but only needs to be responsible for processing the sharded data assigned to it.

3.2   BFT Consensus Algorithms

In 1982, Lamport, Pease and Shostak proposed the "Byzantine General Problem" [8]. It investigates the problem of reaching consistency in a scenario where a few nodes are allowed to be evil (messages can be forged). The Byzantine general problem has also become the basis of consensus algorithm research. Byzantine nodes are the nodes that will be evil in the consensus and deliberately create false messages to prevent consensus reaching.

Byzantine Fault Tolerance (BFT) consensus algorithms are fault-tolerant algorithms for Byzantine problems, which is how to reach consensus among normal nodes assuming the existence of normal, faulty and Byzantine nodes in the blockchain network.

BFT consensus algorithms can be classified as Practical Byzantine Fault Tolerance(PBFT), Federated Byzantine Agreement (FBA), and Delegated Byzantine Fault Tolerance(DBFT), among which PBFT is the most widely used BFT Consensus Algorithm.

4   Solution: A New Cross-shard BFT Consensus

We proposed a cross-shard BFT to solving the consensus in sharded blockchain (Fig. 1).

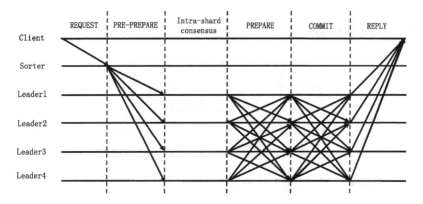

Fig. 1. The procedures of proposed cross-shard BFT consensus.

4.1 Committee-wise Monitoring

The presence of anchor node is a major improvement to Raft's security. The addition of anchor node gives Raft the ability to resist Byzantine nodes.

In the Raft consensus mechanism, if the leader is evil and sends malicious messages to the followers in the shard, it will break the consistency of the consensus. Anchor nodes are responsible for supervising the leaders within the shard. Thus anchor nodes do not participate in the leader election, but only participate in the intra-shard Raft consensus as followers. At the same time, anchor nodes need to ensure anonymity to prevent targeted fraud by leaders.

Let one anchor node be assigned for every r shards, then the number of anchor nodes s satisfies

As shown in Fig. 2, assuming the number of shards is 4 and one anchor node is assigned to every 3 shards, $s \geq 2$. Then anchor node 1 is assigned to shard 1, shard 2 and shard 3, and anchor node 2 is assigned to shard 2, shard 3 and shard 4 at the same time.

In this paper, a signature verification session is added in the intra-shard consensus phase. When the leader sends a message to the followers, it needs to sign the message. After receiving the message from the leader, the anchor node needs to verify the signature and compare the contents, so as to determine whether the leader is a Byzantine node.

The supervision process of the supervision node for the leader is divided into three main stages: evidence collection, evidence presentation and verification.

1. **Evidence Collection.** When performing Raft intra-shard consensus, anchor nodes can listen to messages sent from leaders to followers in multiple shards, screen messages sent by leaders after verifying node signatures, and determine a leader as a Byzantine node when it is found that the messages sent by a leader are different from other leaders. The identity of the node is locked according to the node signature and forensics is performed.

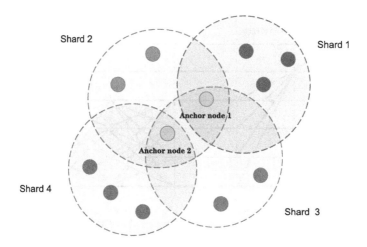

Fig. 2. Assignment of anchor nodes in shards ($k = 4$, $r = 3$).

2. **Evidence Presentation.** After the forensics on the Byzantine node is completed, the anchor node packages a proof message $< PROOF, t, m, i >$ and sends the message to the sorter, where $PROOF$ is the message identifier, t is the forensic timestamp, m is the forensic content, and i is the node number of the anchor node for forensics.

3. **Verification.** Based on the contents of the proof, the sorter determines the public key and other information of the malicious node being proved and verifies the legitimacy of the proof, and makes a decision on whether to remove the leader identity of the malicious node.

4.2   How Does It Work?

The consensus among the leaders follows the PBFT consensus algorithm. As shown in Fig. 3, the steps of the cross-shard BFT consensus algorithm are as follows.

1. **PROPOSE** The client sends a $REQUEST$ to the sorter.
2. **PRE-PREPARE** After the sorter verifies that the signature is correct, it assigns number n to the request and broadcasts a $PRE\text{-}PREPARE$ message to all leaders.
3. **Intra-shard Consensus** The leaders send the requests from the sorter to all the followers within the shard, and the followers respond to the requests. When the leaders receive more than half of the valid returned messages from the nodes within the shard, they enter the cross-shard consensus.
4. **PREPARE** The leader broadcasts $PREPARE$ messages to other leaders, while validating the received $PREPARE$ messages. If the verification does not pass, it is discarded. And move to the next stage when $2f + 1$ (including itself) validated $PREPARE$ messages are received.

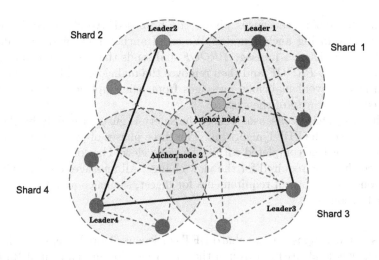

Fig. 3. Communication between nodes in the cross-shard consensus ($k = 4$, $r = 3$).

5. **COMMIT** The leader broadcasts *COMMIT* messages to other leaders and simultaneously verifies the received *COMMIT* messages. If the verification does not pass, it is discarded. And sends *REPLY* messages to the client if it receives $2f+1$ (including itself) *COMMIT* messages that pass the verification.
6. **REPLY** Consensus is reached when the client receives a *REPLY* message from $f + 1$ leaders.

4.3 Performance Guarantee Analysis

We analyze the performance guarantees of the proposed cross-shard BFT consensus algorithm from three perspectives: consistency, safety and liveness.

Consistency. The proposed cross-shard BFT consensus algorithm guarantees the final consistency of each node through PBFT consensus mechanism and the AppendEntry RPC mechanism in the Raft.

In the intra-shard consensus phase, it can proceed smoothly when the number of Byzantine nodes $f \leq \frac{m-1}{2}$ (m is the number of nodes in each shard, satisfy $m \geq 3$). If a leader fails, a new leader election is held for that leader's shard. The new leader will synchronize logs from other leaders to maintain consistency. Other nodes in the shard synchronize messages via the AppendEntry RPC mechanism.

In the cross-shard consensus phase, consensus can proceed smoothly when the number of Byzantine nodes $f \leq \frac{k-1}{3}$ (k is the number of shards, satisfy $k \geq 4$).

Safety. The proposed cross-shard BFT consensus algorithm ensures safety by the consensus feature of PBFT and the introduction of anchor node and sorter.

In the intra-shard consensus phase, the proposed two-phase BFT ensures safety by introducing anchor nodes. When an anchor node finds a malicious leader, it will packages a message $PROOF$ and sends the message to the sorter. The sorter verifies $PROOF$ and then removes the malicious leader in time. This mechanism can avoid malicious messages from being uploaded, which greatly guarantees the security of the system.

In the cross-shard consensus phase, the safety is ensured mainly by the consensus feature of the PBFT algorithm. The three phases of pre-prepare, prepare and commit must be completed within the same view. The completion time cannot exceed the time required for the view change. All messages comply with the PBFT consensus protocol requirements for digest, sequence number and signature verification.

Liveness. The proposed cross-shard BFT consensus algorithm ensures the liveness of the whole algorithm through the leader election mechanism of Raft and the viewchange mechanism of PBFT.

In the intra-shard consensus phase, the heartbeat detection mechanism can determine whether the leader is down or not. When the leader is down, a new leader can be elected in time through the leader election mechanism. This is an excellent way to ensure the liveness of intra-shard consensus.

In the cross-shard consensus phase, leaders from all shards form a committee and perform a committee-wise PBFT consensus. If a leader fails, a new leader is quickly re-elected for that leader's shard. The new leader will quickly synchronize the latest messages and continue the cross-shard consensus. This mechanism nicely improves the liveness of the whole algorithm and enhances the failure resilience of the committee members. Meanwhile, the viewchange mechanism of the PBFT algorithm also largely ensures the activity of the algorithm.

5   Performance Evaluation

5.1   Settings

The host system chosen for the experimental environment is Window 10, the processor is Intel i7-8550U, the host memory is 8g, and the development environment of the test platform software is Ubuntu 20.04/Golang 1.16.

5.2   Baseline Algorithms

In this paper, we use our own PBFT algorithm implemented in the same network environment configuration as baseline algorithms.

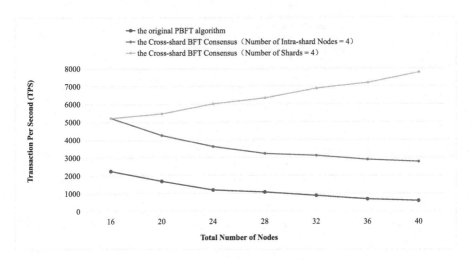

Fig. 4. Throughput of PBFT and the proposed cross-shard BFT consensus.

5.3   Performance Discussion

We tested the proposed cross-shard BFT consensus algorithm and the original
PBFT algorithm in terms of throughput, consensus latency, and fault tolerance.
After analyzing the simulation results, we find out that the proposed cross-shard
BFT consensus can yield a higher throughput, lower latency than the original
PBFT. The fault-tolerance ability of the proposed consensus is around 1.5× to
2× of PBFT.

Throughput. Throughput is the number of transactions processed by the system per unit of time. In general, a higher TPS indicates a better performance of
the blockchain system. In this paper, throughput is calculated using the ratio of
the total number of transactions processed, M, and the consensus time required,
t, which is

Throughput can be a good reflection of the performance of the consensus
algorithm. We conduct 20 simulations at different node numbers. The average
of the 20 simulations is taken as the throughput at that number of nodes. The
simulations results are shown in Fig. 4.

As seen in Fig. 4, the throughput of both the original PBFT algorithm and
the cross-shard BFT consensus algorithm with a fixed number of nodes of 4
decreases as the number of nodes increases. At the same time, the throughput
of the cross-shard BFT consensus algorithm with a fixed number of shards of 4
increases as the number of nodes increases. This is because the throughput and
consensus efficiency of the original PBFT algorithm decreases significantly as
the size of the consensus network nodes increases. For the proposed algorithm
with a fixed number of nodes within a slice, when the number of nodes increases,
it is equivalent to increasing the number of nodes in the PBFT consensus phase.

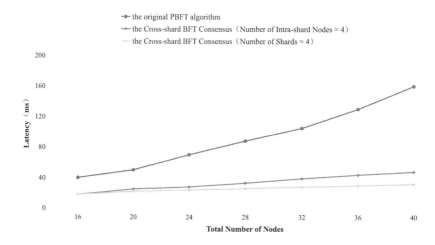

Fig. 5. Latency of PBFT and the proposed cross-shard BFT consensus.

At this point consensus efficiency becomes the main factor affecting throughput, and naturally throughput decreases. And when the number of shards is fixed, when the number of nodes increases, it is equivalent to increasing the number of nodes in the Raft consensus phase. At this time, the main factor affecting the system throughput changes from the consensus latency to the concurrency of nodes, and the natural throughput will gradually increase.

Latency. The latency refers to the time required for a request to be sent from the client to the final network-wide consensus. The smaller the latency, the shorter the time required for the message to be consensus by the network, and the better the performance.

We conduct 20 simulations at different node numbers. The average of the 20 simulations is taken as the latency at that number of nodes. The simulations results are shown in Fig. 5.

From Fig. 5, it can be seen that the consensus latency increases gradually as the number of nodes increases. Among them, the original PBFT algorithm grows the fastest, while the cross-shard BFT consensus algorithm with a fixed number of shards of 4 is the slowest. Therefore, the cross-shard BFT consensus algorithm can still ensure high consensus efficiency when the number of nodes increases. When the number of nodes is the same, the consensus latency of the cross-shard BFT consensus algorithm is still much smaller than that of the original PBFT algorithm.

As the number of nodes increases, the growth rate of latency of the proposed algorithm with a fixed number of nodes within a shard of 4 is greater than that of the proposed algorithm with a fixed number of shard of 4. This is because the proposed algorithm is a two-phase BFT algorithm, and the efficiency of intra-shard consensus is higher than the efficiency of cross-shard consensus. Increasing the number of shards essentially expands the committee size and increases the consensus elapsed time in the cross-shard consensus phase of PBFT, so increasing the number of shards will have a greater impact on the consensus latency.

Number of Nodes Tolerable. Let f_1, f_2 be integers greater than 0, the number of nodes in each shard m satisfies $m \geq 2f_1 + 1$, and the number of shards k satisfies $k \geq 3f_2 + 1$. Each r group is assigned one anchor node ($r \geq 2$), and assuming that the number of nodes in each shard is the same, then the total number of nodes N satisfies

$$N = k \cdot m - \frac{k}{r}(r - 1) - l(r - 1), \tag{1}$$

where l is defined by

$$l = \begin{cases} 0, & k \bmod r = 0; \\ 1, & k \bmod r \neq 0. \end{cases} \tag{2}$$

The maximum fault tolerance of the PBFT consensus phase is $\frac{k-1}{3}$ and the maximum fault tolerance of the Raft consensus phase is $\frac{m-1}{2}$. With the participation of anchor nodes, the maximum fault tolerance of the cross-shard BFT consensus algorithm in this paper is

$$F \leq \frac{k-1}{3}m + \left(r - \frac{k-1}{3}\right)\left(\frac{m-1}{2} - 1\right)$$
$$+ \left[\left(k - \frac{k-1}{3}\right) - \left(r - \frac{k-1}{3}\right)\right]\left(\frac{m-1}{2}\right) \tag{3}$$
$$= 4f_1 f_2 + 2f_2 + f_1 - r.$$

The simulation assume that the number of nodes contained in all the shards is the same, and one anchor node is set to be assigned to every three shards ($r = 3$).

The increase in the number of anchor nodes does not affect the throughput and latency of the proposed algorithm, but it does affect its maximum fault tolerance. It does not affect the throughput and latency of the proposed algorithm because the supervisory behavior of the anchor nodes is independent of the consensus process, and the increase in communication from them has no effect on the overall consensus communication. It affects the maximum fault tolerance because once an anchor node has a problem, it is equivalent to a problem in all the shards where it is located. The maximum fault tolerance of the proposed algorithm is given by Eq. (3).

From Fig. 6, it can be seen that the cross-shard BFT consensus algorithm has higher fault tolerance than the original PBFT algorithm. For the cross-shard BFT consensus algorithm, when the number of nodes in each shard is fixed to 4, increasing the number of shard, the fault tolerance of PBFT dominates. When the number of shard is fixed to 4 and the number of nodes within the shard increases, the fault tolerance of Raft dominates. Keeping the number of shards

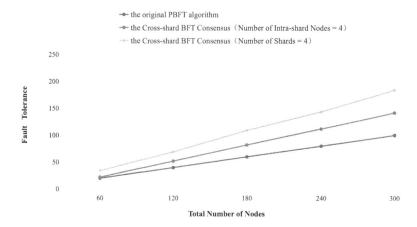

Fig. 6. Number of nodes tolerable by PBFT and the proposed cross-shard BFT consensus, respectively.

constant tolerates a higher maximum number of Byzantine nodes than keeping the number of nodes within a shard constant. As the size of the network nodes increases, the fault tolerance of the proposed algorithm also increases. It is clear that the cross-shard BFT consensus algorithm is highly secure.

6   Conclusion

In this paper, we aim to address the problems incurred when introducing the traditional PBFT to the sharded blockchain. In the context of network sharding, we propose an adapted version of BFT consensus for sharded blockchains. The proposed two-phase BFT includes an intra-shard consensus and a cross-shard consensus. In the intra-shard consensus phase, Raft is first adopted within each shard, in which a leader can be elected. Anchor nodes within each shard can monitor whether the leader within that shard is malicious or not. In the cross-shard consensus phase, leaders from all shards form a committee and perform a committee-wise PBFT consensus.

Through simulations, we find out that the proposed cross-shard BFT consensus can yield a higher throughput, lower latency than the original PBFT, and still maintains high consensus efficiency and liveness with the increasing number of nodes. The fault-tolerance ability of the proposed consensus is around 1.5× to 2× of PBFT. The introduction of anchor nodes within each shard ensures that Byzantine nodes can be found timely, which also largely improves the security of the whole consensus algorithm.

Acknowledgment. This Work is partially supported by National Natural Science Foundation of China (Grant No. 61902445), and CCF-Huawei Populus euphratica forest fund (Grant No. CCF-HuaweiBC2021004).

References

1. Swan, M.: Blockchain: Blueprint for a New Economy. O'Reilly Media Inc., Sebastopol (2015)
2. Zheng, Z., Xie, S., Dai, H., Chen, X., Wang, H.: An overview of blockchain technology: Architecture, consensus, and future trends. In: 2017 IEEE International Congress on Big Data (BigData congress), pp. 557–564. IEEE (2017)
3. Nakamoto, S.: Bitcoin: a peer-to-peer electronic cash system. Decentralized Business Review, p. 21260 (2008)
4. Vasin, P.: Blackcoin's proof-of-stake protocol v2 71 (2014). https://blackcoin.co/blackcoin-pos-protocol-v2-whitepaper.pdf
5. Larimer, D.: Delegated proof-of-stake consensus. R (2018)
6. Wood, G., et al.: Ethereum: A secure decentralised generalised transaction ledger. Ethereum Project Yellow Paper, vol. 151(2014), pp. 1–32 (2014)
7. Sompolinsky, Y., Zohar, A.: Secure high-rate transaction processing in bitcoin. In: Böhme, R., Okamoto, T. (eds.) FC 2015. LNCS, vol. 8975, pp. 507–527. Springer, Heidelberg (2015). https://doi.org/10.1007/978-3-662-47854-7_32
8. Lamport, L., Shostak, R., Pease, M.: The byzantine generals problem. In: Concurrency: The Works of Leslie Lamport, pp. 203–226 (2019)
9. Huang, D., Ma, X., Zhang, S.: Performance analysis of the raft consensus algorithm for private blockchains. IEEE Trans Syst. Man Cybern. Syst. **50**(1), 172–181 (2019)
10. Castro, M., Liskov, B., et al.: Practical byzantine fault tolerance. In: Proceedings of USENIX Symposium on Operating Systems Design and Implementation (OSDI), vol. 99, pp. 173–186 (1999)
11. Luu, L., Narayanan, V., Zheng, C., Baweja, K., et al.: A secure sharding protocol for open blockchains. In: Proceedings of ACM SIGSAC Conference on Computer and Communications Security (CCS 2016), pp. 17–30 (2016)
12. Team, T.Z.: The zilliqa technical whitepaper (2017). Accessed 16 Sept 2019
13. Kokoris-Kogias, E., Jovanovic, P., Gasser, L., Gailly, N., Syta, E., Ford, B.: Omniledger: a secure, scale-out, decentralized ledger via sharding. In: Proceedings of IEEE Symposium on Security and Privacy (SP 2018), pp. 583–598 (2018)
14. Zamani, M., Movahedi, M., Raykova, M.: Rapidchain: scaling blockchain via full sharding. In: Proceedings of ACM SIGSAC Conf. on Computer and Communications Security (CCS 2018), pp. 931–948 (2018)
15. Wang, J., Wang, H.: Monoxide: scale out blockchains with asynchronous consensus zones. In: Proceedings of 16th {USENIX} Symposium on Networked Systems Design and Implementation (NSDI 2019), pp. 95–112 (2019)
16. Aublin, P.L., Mokhtar, S.B., Quéma, V.: RBFT: redundant byzantine fault tolerance. In: 2013 IEEE 33rd International Conference on Distributed Computing Systems, pp. 297–306. IEEE (2013)
17. Liu, J., Li, W., Karame, G.O., Asokan, N.: Scalable byzantine consensus via hardware-assisted secret sharing. IEEE Trans. Comput. **68**(1), 139–151 (2018)
18. Crain, T., Gramoli, V., Larrea, M., Raynal, M.: DBFT: efficient leaderless byzantine consensus and its application to blockchains. In: 2018 IEEE 17th International Symposium on Network Computing and Applications (NCA), pp. 1–8. IEEE (2018)

19. Kotla, R., Alvisi, L., Dahlin, M., Clement, A., Wong, E.: Zyzzyva: speculative byzantine fault tolerance. In: Proceedings of Twenty-First ACM SIGOPS Symposium on Operating Systems Principles, pp. 45–58 (2007)
20. Yin, M., Malkhi, D., Reiter, M.K., Gueta, G.G., Abraham, I.: Hotstuff: BFT consensus with linearity and responsiveness. In: Proceedings of the ACM Symposium on Principles of Distributed Computing (PODC 2019), pp. 347–356 (2019)
21. Kwon, J.: Tendermint: consensus without mining (2014)

A Practical Blockchain-Based Maintenance Record System for Better Aircraft Security

Wictor Lang Jensen, Sille Jessing, Wei-Yang Chiu, and Weizhi Meng[✉]

SPTAGE Lab, Department of Applied Mathematics and Computer Science,
Technical University of Denmark, Kgs. Lyngby 2800, Denmark
`weme@dtu.dk`

Abstract. Public transportation not only has a high utilization rate but also has a high density of population on-board. Keeping these facilities safe-to-use and well-functioned is the highest priority since it is heavily relevant to public safety. A malfunctioning may cause an accident ranged from slight to severe, even fatal. In particular, civil aviation (aircraft) is one of the public transportation industries that requires the highest safety standards. However, several accidents on aircraft maintenance system have revealed that there is an emerging need to secure the record integrity and traceability. Motivated by this observation and supported by an airline company, in this work, we propose and implement AirChain, a blockchain-based aircraft maintenance record system, in which the data can be stored in a way that is resistant to tampering but is easy to access. In the evaluation, we examine the system performance in the aspects of storage growth and processing time. The results indicate the viability and practicability of our system.

Keywords: Blockchain technology · Decentralized application · Aircraft security · Smart contract · Record maintenance

1 Introduction

Keeping a good and well-maintained records, on occasion, can be considered as a nice addition to our daily utility, just like neat hand-writing. In many cases, these records do not relate or cause direct consequences to the damage of properties. However, it is not the case when being applied in public transportation [8]. Not only the utilization rate, but also the transportation density of these vehicles are very high. Keeping these vehicles well-operated and safe is the top priority, since they are heavily responsible for public safety. Some simple malfunctions of these vehicles may cause as small as inconvenience and the delay of time; however, some can be fatal, making a damage beyond estimation and affordability. Hence the detailed and careful maintenance is a must. To carry out a precise and careful maintenance, keeping track of records is a basic and fundamental requirement, where integrity is one of the most important properties [17].

© The Author(s), under exclusive license to Springer Nature Switzerland AG 2022
C. Su et al. (Eds.): SciSec 2022, LNCS 13580, pp. 51–67, 2022.
https://doi.org/10.1007/978-3-031-17551-0_4

Generally, unclear or falsified records can cause misinterpretation and miscommunication within repair crews, resulting in incorrect repair work, or unsatisfactory overhaul. Hence - garbage in, garbage out. In particular, civil aviation is one of the public transportation industries that requires the highest safety standards [32]. As previously mentioned that correct records will play a crucial role in maintenance, it is of great importance for a system that can keep tracks of records with integrity warranty and can be audited by all participating parties [35]. However, such requirement of record keeping is expected in all civil airliners, the human errors and cultural environment can still affect the outcome result in practice. Kind of unauthorized and intentional alteration of existing records may directly or indirectly cause serious incidents [7].

Motivation. Although civil aviation needs a high safety standard, there are many airline accidents and incidents reported almost every year. For instance, a small incident has been reported by an U.S news agency in 2015, stating that a man hacked into the aircraft maintenance system and altered several existed records [16]. Though no further report has been made, it raises a concern about the security practice in the system and the data integrity held by the system. As another example, China Airlines (Taiwan) reported that a series of workers disregarded the standard procedure and failed to keep the maintenance records' integrity, which caused an accident that perished hundreds in 2002 [5]. Recently in 2019, Ethiopean Airline, with an accident that perished hundreds, was busted by an insider, who stated that: "A history at the company of falsifying records and signing off on dodgy maintenance and repair jobs" [6].

Contributions. Providing a record system with integrity warranty from both the procedure and the design perspective is urgently needed. Using blockchain as the underlying datastore is one of the promising solutions. Such datastore uses the power of masses to perform collective-booking and consensus-reaching, in which it is able to remain its integrity in a decentralized zero-trust network. This can create a database that is append-only, record-traceable, and cannot be altered once written. Our contributions can be summarized as below.

- The maintenance records within the aviation industry require high integrity and traceability. Focused on this issue, we develop and implement AirChain, a blockchain-based aircraft maintenance record system. To make the system more practical and closer to a real-world scenario, we got support from China Airlines (Taiwan), which provided the format of Cabin Log Book (CLB), Technical Log Book (TLB) and their partial procedure.
- In the evaluation, with the help from airline's technical personnel, we simulate an experimental setup with both clients and servers, and examine the system performance in the aspects of storage growth and processing time. The results demonstrate the viability and effectiveness of our system.

Organization. Sect. 2 introduces the background on blockchain technology and related work on the blockchain applications in aircraft maintenance. Section 3 details the design of our proposed AirChain including platform selection, system overview, and front-end design & implementation. Section 4 presents our evaluation and results. Section 5 discusses some limitations and challenges, and Sect. 6 concludes our work.

2   Background and Related Work

Blockchain has been applied into many different disciplines (e.g., software defined networking [9,13], smart city [23,27], trust management [26,28], intrusion detection [11,14,29,31], insurance industry [25]), which usually focuses on providing a unified, auditable, and immutable data storage in a decentralized network [15]. Record keeping is one common usage in many blockchain applications, while it is one critical function in aircraft maintenance that requires an extremely high integrity standard.

In the literature, it is found that the combination of blockchain technology and aircraft's maintenance record keeping has not been widely studied. In this section, we briefly discuss the background of blockchain and the importance of its underlying consensus algorithms. Then we introduce the existing state-of-the-art in aircraft maintenance for ensuring data integrity and the motivation for our proposed system – AirChain.

2.1   Background on Blockchain

In order to provide a currency system that has the capability of self-governance and could not be controlled by any party in a decentralized and zero-trust network, cryptocurrency is derived from digital currency. To achieve this, protocols must be carefully designed and developed in a way of maintaining the state of the system (such as the amount of total currency, and the balance status of each account) within a decentralized network, where all participants must agree and recognize the latest state. Otherwise, the credibility of such system will be in vain. There are past attempts to create such system, though some of them remained in concept, there is one system provides a possible clue on solving the issue [2]. People learnt from the idea and implemented the scheme into Bitcoin, which was later tuned as Blockchain.

The name of Blockchain is coming from the data structure of this datastore. A basic storage unit, named *block*, is connected with its previous blocks and the next block cryptographically. Blocks will be generated periodically by miners, and consensus algorithms are involved to enable the miners to reach a consensus on which (next) block should be added to the current chain. In particular, consensus algorithms can provide a cryptographic proof of a block, securing it from being tampered. There are many types of consensus algorithms with different advantages and disadvantages. We can roughly categorize them as below.

- **The Proof-of... Family:** The main characteristic of Proof-of-X family is to require miners to pay effort or resources, or provide provable indexes that can be compared, e.g., storage capacity. One of the well-known algorithms in this category is Proof-of-Work (PoW). If a miner is willing to put more "work" into the competition, he or she can have a higher chance of winning the competition and leading the consensus. The miner who can successfully propose its block as the next one to be connected to the chain is called *sealer*. To reach this, a computationally hard problem with probabilistic outcome is involved. A *difficulty index* controls how hard the problem will be, e.g., hash competition game [2].

This type of consensus algorithms provides security through the challenge of reaching the resources putting on competition. Many public permissionless blockchain platforms utilize the Proof-of-X-based consensus algorithms. Some consensus algorithms belong to this family are straightforward and intuitive, but all of them have their own merits and limitations in different environments [3]. For example, the 51% attack plagued some algorithms in this family, e.g., the 51% attack on PoW-based blockchain indicated that if a party owns 51% or more computational power of the whole network, then it can have the utmost advantage in leading the chain. Others, based on their implementation, may suffer different kinds of 51% attack [4].

– The Byzantine Fault Tolerance (BFT) Family: To ensure that the chain's latest state is unified, the sealer should be counted as few as one on each term. This approach is effective and intuitive, while keeping all participants taking the same action can be another method of achieving this goal. The BFT-based method implements the solution of Byzantine General problem, which is designed to ensure all nodes running the correct command in an asynchronous system [20]. Compared with many Proof-of-X based consensus algorithms, BFT-family is relatively quicker and more responsive. These algorithms, rather than conducting several rounds of selection or competition, have rounds of confirmation between nodes. However, the broadcast-like way of reaching consensus makes it difficult to scale. On a large-scale network, it may generate too much traffic for the underlying infrastructure, resulting in an inefficient operation and high communication load. There are also some research studies focused on fixing the incapability of expanding BFT-based networks [19].

Due to the nature of its design, BFT-based algorithms might be difficult to apply in a large-scale network, especially a constantly expanding public blockchain. However, in a small-scale environment, e.g., a semi-fixed network, BFT-based algorithms can provide a fast and efficient way to operate with both malicious- and fault-tolerance.

– The Raft/Paxos-like Family: Different from competitive Proof-of-X family, and the gossiping BFT-family, the Raft/Paxos adopts another main idea [22]. That is, if you like to propose something to all participants, you have to convince all of them why should they accept it. The accepted proposer, in this case, is the consensus result of the network.

2.2   Blockchain in Aircraft Maintenance

As we previously discussed, maintenance record integrity is critical and essential with regard to aircraft maintenance. In the literature, there are several studies taking blockchain as a solution. They focused on different aspects of aircraft maintenance. For instance, Madhwal and Panfilov [32] introduced the aircrafts' supply-chain management with blockchain integrated, and discussed the difficulties in smart supply-chain management in aviation industry. They particularly pointed out two important blockchain characteristics that can mend the difficulties, as below:

- **Transparency**: Transaction Records are embedded within the network as a whole.
- **It cannot be corrupted**: Alternating any existing information (especially PoW-based algorithm) indicates that an attacker must use a huge amount of computational power to override the entire network.

They also pointed out that the expected developing amount of airline travels in the future could result in a growing trend of aircrafts and their parts' supplement. The soaring demands may add pressure on the supply chain, accounting for the increasing rate of errors. Blockchain's characteristics can provide a solution to address the issue, and help create more efficient and reliable supply chain management systems.

Then Rajkov [33] presented a survey on evaluating the effect of integrating blockchain into aircrafts' spare part management. It concludes the impact of blockchain on the business model as follows:

- Key Partnerships
- Key Activities
- Value Proposition
- Cost Structure
- Customer Relationships
- Customer Channels

However, the above research work only proposed a concept, until 2019, Schyga *et al.* [34] proposed a relevant prototype system based on Hyperledger, which can create a Permission Blockchain System for aircraft maintenance, repair, and overhaul. It fully utilizes the ability of channeling in Hyperledger, making such system capable of interconnecting different organizations with the control of information sharing instantly.

Then similar to [34], Ho *et al.* [35] proposed a similar blockchain-based system for aircraft maintenance. Their system focused on parts' traceability and trackability for the inventory management. It could detail the traceability information of parts and utilize the Hyperledger Fabric's advantage of channeling. Compared with Schyga *et al.*'s work [34], they presented a structure that is more close to realization.

Discussion. However, the existing systems, though somehow involved with the repair and overhaul departments, are coming from the perspective of a supply chain. It is understandable that both efficiency and integrity can be considered as a direct impact to the supply chain management, which would affect the revenue potentially. However, there is few work focusing on record integrity of the maintenance work in aircraft. It is noted that keeping the record integrity on maintenance work might not directly offer profitability, but it can enhance the airliner's safety and maintain its reputation.

Aleshi *et al.* [30] focused on the aircraft maintenance records and explored the feasibility of applying a blockchain. This is the most relevant work to ours, but their system was mainly relied on the information from a private plane, and they did not show any performance result. Motivated by this observation, our work designs and implements AirChain, a practical blockchain-based aircraft maintenance record system, which creates a database in which all traces will be left and all records are traceable to the original. We argue that the cooperation between the correct parts' information and the fluency in both supply chain management and repair work can maximize the power of blockchain in aircraft industry. We also demonstrate the system performance regarding storage and processing time. As our work is supported by an airline, our implemented system is believed to be more practical.

3   Our Proposed System - AirChain

As we previously discussed, data integrity in aircraft maintenance should not be compromised, but the traditional database techniques may require additional extensions and security practices in order to ensure data integrity. Thus, blockchain technology can provide a method of storing and distributing data in a decentralized zero-trust network. That is, the use of blockchain can prevent the potential malicious activities of manipulating the existing records [10,12,24]. In this section, we introduce the design of our proposed AirChain – a blockchain-based aircraft maintenance record system.[1]

Though blockchain sounds solid and suitable for building an aircraft maintenance record system, it does not mean that any type of blockchain is suitable. For this reason, in the section, we first discuss the selection of blockchain platforms, and then introduce the system overview and design workflow of AirChain. We also briefly discuss the difficulty of upgrading smart contracts.

3.1   Blockchain Platform Analysis and Selection

Blockchain is a method that utilizes consensus algorithms to create a decentralized datastore among nodes, with traceability and auditability. Though all blockchain platforms aim to reach this primary goal, the core idea of different consensus algorithms may provide distinct advantages and disadvantages. In this case, we need to select a suitable blockchain platform with consensus algorithm for our proposed system. Below are the required characteristics for a suitable blockchain platform in our application scenario.

---

[1] A previous version of AirChain can be referred to our poster at ICBC 2022 [1].

- **Semi-Fixed Access Devices**: Due to the importance, the access scope of such system is limited to the internal network of an airliner. The endpoint devices that can access this system have little variety from time to time. For most of the time, it seldom changes. Compared to a blockchain-based cryptocurrency platform, most joined nodes are already known or registered in the internal network. Hence, the join process should be controlled by system administrators.
- **Mandatory Access Control**: Intuitively, different system roles should have various permissions for the aircraft maintenance. For example, captain can fill in Cockpit Log Book (CLB), while the repair crew should not. By contrast, the repair report (Taken Action) can only be fulfilled by repair crew. The sign-off of a case only can be done by certified professionals. In practice, some roles can be granted with multiple actions by system administrators.
- **Hide and seek's hunt game**: Though most of the devices that access this blockchain system are internal and well-known, not all of them are trusted devices. Also, we cannot ensure that a trusted device is always honest and doing well, i.e., some may be infected by malware. Thus, the blockchain platform should not only be fault-tolerance, but also be malicious-tolerance.
- **Time-Sensitive**: When a record has been issued, it should be properly sealed and updated through all participants within the acceptable time. For instance, the duration of several minutes may be unfavorable, while the duration of several hours should be considered as unacceptable.

By observing these requirements, we argue that a private blockchain should be preferred. As a result, performance-eating and power-hungry consensus algorithms are not suitable. Hence, we exclude most of the algorithms from Proof-of-X family, even though some of them are considered as the most secure. This is because they may require too many environmental resources, with excessive cost and the time consumption in updating data. In addition, as the blockchain should be ideally malicious-tolerable in a non-fully-trusted environment, Raft may not be favorable.

Another consideration is the compatibility of our system, where users can switch platforms if a better option is found in the future. Though we cannot expect what might be in the future; however, the most widely supported smart contract platform is EVM/Solidity. Hence, if we choose to build our own system based on EVM, we can have a better chance to upgrade the platform in the future. Meanwhile, EVM has some advantages that can protect our endpoint in some perspectives. Since EVM is a dedicated environment that executes its own intermediate binary code, it is a challenge for malicious smart contracts to escape from the virtual machine and run code on bare metal. This is a possible security threat on some platforms that might be vulnerable to Remote Code Execution attack [36].

As depicted in Table 1, we also compare the transaction speed among blockchain platforms that support both BFT-like algorithms and Solidity. It is noticed that the FISCO BCOS can provide significantly better speed when deploying contracts. However, when looking into the speed of finishing a single transaction, they can all finish at instance without any significant delay.

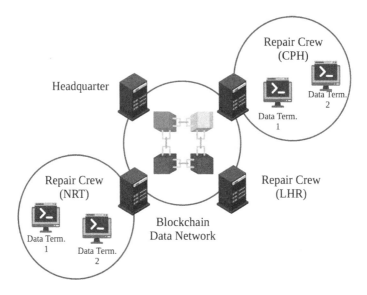

Fig. 1. The system overview of AirChain

Table 1. Transaction speed with deploying one contract

Platform	Algorithm	0.5K	10K	100K	1M
Ethereum	Clique	4,110 ms	3,835 ms	4,063 ms	4,360 ms
BCOS	PBFT	810 ms	747 ms	762 ms	781 ms
Besu	IBFT	2,985 ms	3,610 ms	3,471 ms	3,450 ms

However, though FISCO BCOS supports Solidity, it requires a further extension to support Web3j interface. This interface-set aims to provide communication between EVM and other applications, which is officially supported by other
platforms that utilize EVM as a smart contract platform. Though FISCO BCOS
has its own implementation of Web3 extension, it still requires to change some
codes accordingly. This is because most of other platforms can use the official
Web3 interface directly.

Due to these advantages and disadvantages, in order to keep the development
process simple and efficient, we decide to choose **Hyperledger Besu** as our
development platform, which supports both EVM and the official Web3 interface.

3.2 System Overview

Our proposed aircraft maintenance record system – AirChain involves one or
multiple servers located on different sites, so that multiple access clients can
connect to their local servers.[2] These local servers can maintain the blockchain

---

[2] The source code of our AirChain is available at: https://sptage.compute.dtu.dk/file/
AirChain.zip.

and work in a collaborative mode, as shown in Fig. 1. There are several major smart contracts in our system, as below.

- **The Log Book**: CLB and TLB are short for Cabin Log Book and Technical Log Book. These are the two main documents for recording aircraft faults. In particular, they can be roughly divided into two sections: one section is used for when an error is firstly recorded and the other one is used for when some actions have been taken to fix the error, which in turn should be recorded. Generally, it has a structure that can be divided between new added error and what has been fixed. Each new case with an instance of an error should be assigned with an ID, which can be used to update that specific document with the fix specifications later. Finally, the document needs to be approved by certified professional or manager before it can be eventually published as official. Our system designs the structure of CLB and TLB with the embedment of Permission Manager – a smart contract that manages roles and permissions. Such design can control each user's access to each function provided by the smart contract.
- **Permission Manager**: This smart contract records what can be accessed by each user. When a function in either CLB or TLB is triggered, such function will consult Permission Manager to obtain the access right of the called user. Then, it utilizes the provided information to decide whether accept or reject a user's request.
- **Main Contract**: Though keeping a "main" contract here may look confusing, such main contract is the most important smart contract that connects the system up with security in mind. When a smart contract is deployed, it is immutable. Although the state of the contract can be changed, the code cannot, even if the possibility of invalidating the contract is decided by a programmer. If no destructor has been described, such smart contract will continue running. This means that when a logic error or a flaw is discovered in the smart contract, we have to invalidate the contract, or forcefully update the front-end program to direct itself to the newly updated smart contract.

  To avoid the inconsistency during the updating process between clients, we add our front-end program to this main contract, which can keep track of all other contracts and provide an access point for programs. If there is an improved and more advanced smart contract that has been proposed, not only such proposal has to be accepted, but also the creator of such newly updated contract has to trust the main contract unconditionally. Though our "hub"-like method might be primitive, it provides system administrators with the right to declare the updated access method to different contracts directly. In addition, all programs have to consult the main contract to reach the latest (updated) version of each contract.

3.3 Front-End Design and Implementation

Solidity only runs upon EVM, an environment that cannot directly interact outside the border of EVM. The front-end program must inquire EVM to operate

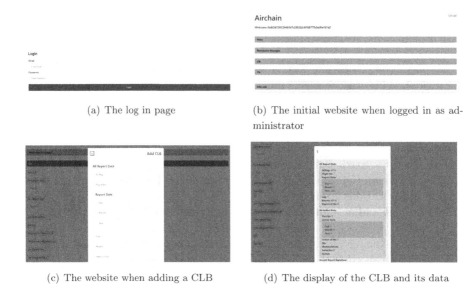

(a) The log in page

(b) The initial website when logged in as administrator

(c) The website when adding a CLB

(d) The display of the CLB and its data

Fig. 2. The WebUI of AirChain

the smart contract. Such task can be easy, or be challenging. Since we allow the system to have the flexibility within each contract, it is not possible to hard-code our front-end. This requires an infinite case loop to make sure that all contracts can be displayed correctly. More generally, for the data of every contract, the default way of generating displayed content should rely on web-page's program logic to parse the announced application binary interface (ABI) in the main contract, and then to determine what should be displayed.

As the ABI is essentially a list of public methods on the contract along with both inputs and outputs, the web server can generate a section for each contract, as well as *callers* and *output fields* for each method. Although this practice may reduce kind of user friendliness when the system expands, it ensures that as long as the function is deployed, users can interact with the function instantly.

The input forms are generated by firstly assigning the form with an ID based on the contract's name. By then, iterating via the methods and inputs therein, a series of forms can be created with each field having a name that uses the ID as a prefix, followed by the parameter name. In the case of a complex parameter – *structs* (a declaration of data structure in Solidity), a modal window can be instead generated to allow for compact and easily understandable inputs.

When the web server starts, it will firstly request a full list of contracts from the "main" contract, and then obtain the "Permission Manager" from the contract list. When a user logs into the platform, the web server can instantly access the permission information and arrange the web interface.[3]

---

[3] A demo is available at: https://sptage.compute.dtu.dk/doc/AirChain.mp4.

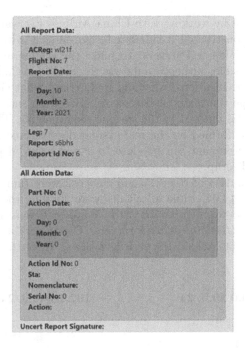

Fig. 3. An example of CLB record.

The website design is tailored to be intuitive and user-friendly. Figure 2 depicts four different scenarios. More specifically, in Fig. 2(a), the login page is designed to ask for credentials. Though in a blockchain-based system, it works differently from a simple username and password, we have to make the operation recognizable; otherwise, the users might find it hard to operate. After a successful login, the user will get into the AirChain system as shown in Fig. 2(b). Since all functions are mainly differentiated by contracts, our designed user interface aims for not only easy access but also for easy system maintenance. Based on different user permissions, the displayed content varies. For example, administrator can propose a new permission manager and add new users.

Figure 2(c) shows a typical data creation screen (i.e., adding a CLB). It is designed to display the different fields that are needed to be completed in a compact way. Then, a complete record is shown in Fig. 2(d), which uses different grey shades to highlight different fields. Figure 3 shows an example of CLB record, including registration number, flight number, report date, leg, report number and report ID number.

4   Evaluation

In this section, we introduce the experimental setup and the results in the aspects of storage growth and processing time.

We collected data by working with China Airlines (Taiwan), e.g., CLB and TLB format, and constructed a simulated environment with a set of virtual machines as both clients and servers. To make the system as applicable to an actual airport as possible, authentic data was received from China Airlines. From the airline's data specifications, we could understand what circumstances it is acceptable to change the maintenance record. Based on such information, the system was able to be tailored to the specific requirements. Though our experiments cannot be performed on the real system due to some privacy concerns, our established environment can be close to a real setup in practice. Figure 4 depicts the detailed setup.

The server computers of *Server*1 and *Server*2 were running the Vagrant's variance of Ubuntu 14.04, while all clients were running the latest version of Lubuntu. The Clients from *Computer A* to *Computer F* were split into two networks. Each was assigned to different servers. The servers were, however, connecting to the same blockchain (Hyperledger Besu) where they acted as miners and authorities.

10.0.10.0/24   **192.168.1.0/24**

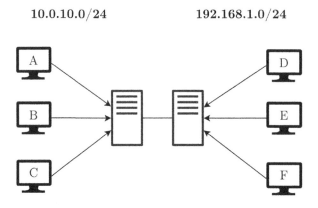

Fig. 4. The network configuration of clients and servers

To test the network performance and functionalities, we deliberately entered an invalid dataset and observed how the system could react. Though the generated test datasets have been all correctly accepted or rejected, it provides a possibility for us to observe the sustainability and availability of the system.

In addition to deliberately entering both correct and invalid data, we performed another type of testing – fuzz testing, an automated software testing technique that can provide invalid, unexpected, and random data as inputs to a computer program. The advantage of fuzzing test is that we can test the system and its ability of handling random data quickly and easily. For this purpose, we wrote a script – *testData.js*, which can check what type of data that the given field requires to randomly generate a value of that type. Hence it was possible to generate a log, such as TLB, with all the data needed. This made it possible to test the system easily throughout the process.

4.1   Storage Growth

This test aims to examine how much storage the full chain should take if such solution is implemented. As TLBs are, by far, the largest transactions aside from contract deployment, both in terms of data stored and gas required, it was selected as the contract to test. We performed by measuring the file size of the data directory during the first run in the blockchain according to two conditions, 1) after the initial setup had been completed, and 2) finally after storing several TLBs. The testing result on storage can be seen in Table 2.

Table 2. Storage required for the blockchain

Item	Size
After Genesis Init	6.31 KB
After First Deploy	118 KB
nTLB = 10000	104 MB

Depending on how often a TLB should be filled out, this might eventually grow to a size where it will become difficult to manage. Taking Taoyuan Airport (Taiwan) as an example, it had more than 129,000 regular flights coming in and out in the year of 2019 [37]. If we assume that each of these flights requires to fill and submit at least one TLB, it would cost 1,341 MB storage, or a little over a gigabyte (GB) storage in every node after a year. This does, of course, only account for the largest common transactions.

4.2   Processing Time

This test aims to examine whether our system works properly in an expected network structure, and investigate how fast a miner node was able to process the requests. As there was no way for computers to communicate with outside client, it is hard to ensure when all the data was received on the end server. This also largely depended on the connection speed, and thus these results are merely an estimation that can be used to check whether the system is usable. The tests were performed by:

- Generating 100, 1000 and 10,000 CLBs: We directly requested *Server*1 to generate these requests simultaneously.
- Manually submitting a CLB.
- Requesting a list of CLB.

After each increment, CLBs have to be signed and completed, based on the request. Table 3 describes the completion time measured with the following criteria.

– `Getting, Updating, Getting Updated`: By adding a single CLB, the computed time should consider the full request to be completed, measured using the Firefox browsers. That is, it measures from the moment when the client sends the request to when the response is fully received.
– `Adding`: The time is measured using the built-in *time*-command in the Linux command-line. This also includes the time consumption for unlocking accounts at the beginning of execution, as well as printing results out to the console.

Table 3. Time completion table

nCLB/Time	Adding	Getting	Updating	Getting Updated
0	N/A	0.78 s	N/A	N/A
1	0.85 s	0.80 s	0.76 s	0.80 s
100	7.32 s	1.53 s	0.77 s	2.05 s
1,000	50.29 s	20.03 s	0.81 s	2.25 s

There appears to have a large discrepancy between the time it required to receive the updated documents alone versus all documents submitted. This is most likely caused by the server compiling every CLB into an HTML document before sending the result to the client. This compilation time along with the transferred massive text is likely the main reason for the delay.

Discussion. Based on the experimental results, our proposed system of AirChain could work well as intended in practice. A user can log in and, depending on their clearance and permissions, they can both add logs and sign them. The system is built upon a private blockchain, which creates a unique possibility to have access to all previous data as well as ensuring a level of security to the data integrity on the chain itself. The system was developed using multiple different aspects of the blockchain technology, involving everything from the deployment of a smart contract to the usage of a user's address as a focal point for managing the user-specific data.

5   Limitations and Discussion

Though our evaluation presented promising results on the system feasibility and performance, some limitations are remained to update in our future work.

5.1   Scalability: Adding Smart Contracts

The expandability of our system is important. If our proposed system was about to be expanded, it can add more smart contracts and/or change the ones already implemented. As we previously discussed, the "main" contract has been developed to keep the program always using the latest version of the contract.

If this system were to be expanded and scaled, then it needs to add contracts. The main focus is on the TLB and the CLB and how to manage the corresponding data, i.e., inventory management and the data such as lost luggage. By adding more features gradually, the system is able to handle more and more airport's data. In this case, we can create a digitalized and secure system, which is also an easily accessible platform. A more detailed scalability evaluation will be one of our future plans.

5.2 Security

Our system currently handles access control in a way that an attacker is not able to tamper with data without accessing to an authorized account, but it cannot prevent from viewing the data if one can access the internal network and dump the blockchain itself. This is not the focus in our current work, but we are trying to apply data encryption methods, and utilize the blockchain platform's built-in private transaction function or channeling function to ensure the data privacy. This is an important topic in our future work.

6 Conclusion

Due to the importance of aircraft maintenance, in this work, we developed and implemented AirChain, a blockchain-based aircraft maintenance record system, which can ensure the record integrity and traceability. We further selected Hyperledger Besu as our development platform, introducing the system design and evaluating the system performance by cooperating with an airline, in the aspects of growth storage and processing time. Our results demonstrate the viability and practicability of our proposed AirChain. Our future work will focus on scalability evaluation and how to make the system more versatile. We also plan to investigate the potential merits of FISCO BCOS in the future.

Acknowledgments. The authors would like to thank the support from China Airlines. This project is partially supported by the EU H2020 DataVaults project with GA Number 871755.

References

1. Jensen, W.L., Jessing, S., Chiu, W.Y., Meng, W.: AirChain - towards blockchain-based aircraft maintenance record system. In: Proceedings of the 2022 IEEE International Conference on Blockchain and Cryptocurrency (ICBC), pp. 1–3 (2022)
2. S. Nakamoto, Bitcoin, A Peer-to-Peer Electronic Cash System (2008). https://bitcoin.org/bitcoin.pdf
3. Wang, W., et al.: A survey on consensus mechanisms and mining strategy management in blockchain networks. IEEE Access **7**, 22328–22370 (2019)

4. Sayeed, S., Marco-Gisbert, H.: Assessing blockchain consensus and security mechanisms against the 51% attack. Appl. Sci. **9**(9), 1788 (2019)
5. China Airlines Flight 611. https://planecrash.fandom.com/wiki/China_Airlines_Flight_611. Accessed 5 May 2022
6. Ethiopian Airlines denies it tampered with flight records after crash. https://www.straitstimes.com/world/africa/ethiopian-airlines-denies-it-tampered-with-flight-records-after-crash. Accessed 5 May 2022
7. The FAA Bulletin November 1993: Preventing Falsification of Maintenance Records. https://flightsafety.org/amb/amb_nov-dec93.pdf
8. Papadimitratos, P., Calandriello, G., Hubaux, J.-P., Lioy, A.: Impact of Vehicular Communications Security on Transportation Safety. CoRR abs/0808.2666 (2008)
9. Li, W., Wang, Y., Meng, W., Li, J., Su, C.: BlockCSDN: towards blockchain-based collaborative intrusion detection in software defined networking. IEICE Trans. Inf. Syst. **E105D**(2), 272–279 (2022)
10. Li, W., Wang, Y., Li, J.: Enhancing blockchain-based filtration mechanism via IPFS for collaborative intrusion detection in IoT networks. J. Syst. Architect. **127**, 102510 (2022)
11. Li, W., Wang, Y., Li, J., Au, M.H.: Towards a blockchain-based framework for challenge-based collaborative intrusion detection. Int. J. Inf. Secur. **20**(2), 127–139 (2021)
12. Li, W., Meng, W., Yang, L.: Enhancing trust-based medical smartphone networks via blockchain-based traffic sampling. In: Proceedings of The 20th IEEE International Conference on Trust, Security and Privacy in Computing and Communications (TrustCom), pp. 122–129 (2021)
13. Li, W., Tan, J., Wang, Y.: A framework of blockchain-based collaborative intrusion detection in software defined networking. In: The 14th International Conference on Network and System Security (NSS), pp. 261–276 (2020)
14. Li, W., Tug, S., Meng, W., Wang, Y.: Designing collaborative blockchained signature-based intrusion detection in IoT environments. Futur. Gener. Comput. Syst. **96**, 481–489 (2019)
15. Meng, W., et al.: Position paper on blockchain technology: smart contract and applications. In: Au, M.H., et al. (eds.) NSS 2018. LNCS, vol. 11058, pp. 474–483. Springer, Cham (2018). https://doi.org/10.1007/978-3-030-02744-5_35
16. Man claims to have hacked into airplane's computer system. https://wjla.com/news/political/man-claims-to-have-hacked-into-airplane-s-computer-system-114056. Accessed 5 May 2022
17. Mansor, H., Markantonakis, K., Akram, R.N., Mayes, K., Gurulian, I.: Log your car: reliable maintenance services record. In: Proceedings of Inscrypt, pp. 484–504 (2016)
18. Du, M., Ma, X., Zhang, Z., Wang, X., Chen, Q.: A review on consensus algorithm of blockchain. In: Proceedings of the IEEE SMC, pp. 2567–2572 (2017)
19. Gao, S., Yu, T., Zhu, J., Cai, W.: T-PBFT: an Eigentrust-based practical byzantine fault tolerance consensus algorithm. China Commun. **16**(12), 111–123 (2019)
20. Castro,M., Liskov, B.: Practical byzantine fault tolerance. In: Proceedings of the OSDI, vol. 99, no. 1999, pp. 173–186 (1999)
21. Lamport, L.: Paxos made simple. ACM SIGACT News **32**(4), 18–25 (2001)
22. Ongaro, D., Ousterhout, J.: In search of an understandable consensus algorithm. In: Proceedings of the 2014 USENIX Annual Technical Conference, pp. 305–319 (2014)
23. Chiu, W.Y., Meng, W.: EdgeTC - A PBFT blockchain-based ETC scheme for smart cities. Peer-to-Peer Networking Appl. **14**, 2874–2886 (2021)

24. Chiu, W.Y., Meng, W., Jensen, C.D.: My data, my control: a secure data sharing and access scheme over blockchain. J. Inf. Secur. Appl. **63**, 103020 (2021)
25. Chiu, W.Y., Meng, W.: Towards decentralized bicycle insurance system based on blockchain. In: Proceedings of the 36th ACM/SIGAPP Symposium on Applied Computing (ACM SAC), pp. 249–256 (2021)
26. Meng, W., Li, W., Zhou, J.: Enhancing the security of blockchain-based software defined networking through trust-based traffic fusion and filtration. Inf. Fusion **70**, 60–71 (2021)
27. Meng, W., Li, W., Tug, S., Tan, J.: Towards blockchain-enabled single character frequency-based exclusive signature matching in IoT-assisted smart cities. J. Parallel Distributed Comput. **144**, 268–277 (2020)
28. Meng, W., Li, W., Zhu, L.: Enhancing medical smartphone networks via blockchain-based trust management against insider attacks. IEEE Trans. Eng. Manage. **67**(4), 1377–1386 (2020)
29. Meng, W., Li, W., Yang, L.T., Li, P.: Enhancing challenge-based collaborative intrusion detection networks against insider attacks using blockchain. Int. J. Inf. Secur. **19**(3), 279–290 (2020)
30. Aleshi, A., Seker, R., Babiceanu, R.F.: Blockchain model for enhancing aircraft maintenance records security. In: Proceedings of the IEEE International Symposium on Technologies for Homeland Security (HST), pp. 1–7 (2019)
31. Tug, S., Meng, W., Wang, Y.: CBSigIDS: towards collaborative blockchained signature-based intrusion detection. In: Proceedings of the First IEEE International Conference on Blockchain (Blockchain), pp. 1228–1235 (2018)
32. Madhwal, Y., Panfilov, P.B.: Blockchain and supply chain management: aircrafts' parts' business case. In: Proceedings of the 28th DAAAM International Symposium on Intelligent Manufacturing and Automation, pp. 1051–1056 (2017)
33. Rajkov, D.: Blockchain for aircraft spare part management: evaluating the robustness of the Maintenance, Repair and Overhaul business model, Master thesis, Delft University of Technology (2018)
34. Schyga, J., Hinckeldeyn, J., Kreutzfeldt, J.: Prototype for a permissioned blockchain in aircraft MRO, In: Proceedings of the Hamburg International Conference of Logistics, pp. 469–505 (2019)
35. Ho, G.T.S., Tang, Y.M., Tsang, K.Y., Tang, V., Chau, K.Y.: A blockchain-based system to enhance aircrafts and traceability and trackability for inventory management. Expert Syst. Appl. **179**, 115101 (2021)
36. Li, Z., Wang, Y., Wen, S., Ding, Y.: Evil Chaincode: APT attacks based on smart contract, frontiers in cyber security, pp. 178–196 (2020)
37. History of Aircraft Volume. Taoyuan International Airport Corporation Ltd. (2020). https://www.taoyuanairport.com.tw/main_en/flight/FlightsQuery.aspx?uid=398&pid=357. Accessed 5 May 2022

Redactable Blockchain with Fine-Grained Autonomy and Transaction Rollback

Chunying Peng[1,2,3] and Haixia Xu[1,2,3(✉)]

[1] State Key Laboratory of Information Security, Institute of Information Engineering, CAS, Beijing 100093, China
{pengchunying,xuhaixia}@iie.ac.cn
[2] School of Cyber Security, University of Chinese Academy of Sciences, Beijing 100049, China
[3] Data Assurance and Communication Security Research Center, Chinese Academy of Sciences, Beijing 100093, China

Abstract. Redactable blockchain is an innovative but controversial research field emerging in recent years, aiming at revising the blockchain data in a safe and controlled manner without eroding the nature of the blockchain. In this paper, we weigh the conflict between the immutability and editing of blockchain, present a redactable consortium blockchain with fine-grained autonomy and transaction rollback, supporting user data self-management, mandatory deletion of harmful information and recovery of wrong transfers within a specific time. In order to achieve the first two requirements, we put forward a double trapdoor key-exposure free chameleon hash function (DTCH), ensuring the dual needs of data modification and chain governance. In addition, we leverage the concept of temporary accounts to realize transaction rollback.

Keywords: Redactable blockchain · Chameleon hash ·
Self-management · Transaction rollback · Key-exposure free

1 Introduction

Blockchain as the underlying core supporting technology of the digital cryptocurrency system, was pioneered by Satoshi Nakamoto in "Bitcoin: A peer-to-peer electronic cash system" [22]. It can be regarded as a distributed ledger, an innovative and revolutionary technology that has been developed rapidly in recent years. Blockchain is characterized by tamper-proof, traceable, transparent and immutable. The immutability ensures the integrity and invariance of historical transaction data, which is an important feature to be satisfied in many practical applications. However, in some scenarios or even legal requirements, we require it to break the invariance in a controllable way.

From the perspective of network information security, the current research and application of blockchain focuses more on the storage security of data on the chain, while ignoring the content security and legitimacy. At present, pornographic links, viruses and other illegal content have been found in blockchain

C. Su et al. (Eds.): SciSec 2022, LNCS 13580, pp. 68–84, 2022.
https://doi.org/10.1007/978-3-031-17551-0_5

applications such as Bitcoin and Ethereum, which has become an effective way to spread harmful information. Blockchain users joining and running blockchain nodes means storing and spreading these illegal contents, potentially exposing themselves to legal risks. This is not conducive to the healthy development of the blockchain.

For the sake of privacy protection, the nature of blockchain data's transparency and immutability infringes users' privacy rights, which also runs counter to the requirements of some laws and regulations. For example, the "General Data Protection Regulations (GDPR)" [27] promulgated by the European Union in 2018 stipulated that users have the "right to be forgotten", and users could request the responsible party to hide or delete sensitive information stored in the blockchain, such as contract documents, medical information and notarized records, etc. Therefore, only redactable blockchain can be compatible with relevant legal requirements.

At the meantime, blockchain is a constantly developing new technology, whose essence is a decentralized database, so there may be erroneous data and vulnerabilities caused by subjective or objective reasons, and to revise erroneous data or update content requires secure and controllable editing technology to support.

In summary, taking into account all the factors above, blockchain controllable editing has the dual needs of practical application and legal obligations, it can contribute to the sustainable development and healthy development of the blockchain.

Our Contributions. To the best of our knowledge, we present the first redactable blockchain system that simultaneously supports transaction rollback as well as *transaction-level rewriting*. We refine the modification authority, and both users and the regulatory committee (a pre-selected set of nodes responsible for reviewing user information revisions and information governance) have editing rights. To be specific, we have two technical contributions.

- *Redactable blockchain protocol with fine-grained autonomy and transaction revocable.* In this paper, we put forward the redactable blockchain system with illegal and harmful information forced deletion. There is a clear division of labor and mutual restriction among users, regulatory committee and miners. Leveraging the double trapdoor key-exposure free chameleon hash function (DTCH), it can not only enable users to legally revise their own information and protect the "right to be forgotten", but also realize the mandatory deletion of harmful information on the chain by the regulatory committee. The system also supports transaction rollback. If there is a transfer error within a certain period of time, the wrong transaction initiator can apply for withdrawal.
- *Double trapdoor key-exposure free chameleon hash function (DTCH).* In order to achieve the purpose that both users and the regulatory committee have editing authority, we propose the double trapdoor key-exposure free chameleon hash function (DTCH). The user and the regulatory committee

each have a trapdoor key. The user's trapdoor key is used to legally modify private information, etc. While the second trapdoor key is used by the regulatory committee to delete harmful information compulsorily. This function solves the key exposure problem by introducing customized identity. The trapdoors of this chameleon hash function cannot be calculated when different collision pairs with the same hash value are obtained. In addition, we introduce a random number jointly generated by the regulatory committee as the temporary private key to ensure that the deletion of harmful information is democratic, legal and fair.

Related Work. Although redactable blockchain is an emerging field of small scale exploration, some achievements have been made. A non-exhaustive overview of related work is presented. At present, it is mainly divided into three categories. First, by means of cryptography, the block is revised by the participants who have the authority (key or satisfy strategy). Second, based on consensus (voting), miners can vote for the proposed amendment. The third is the revision of the protocol layer.

In 2017, Ateniese et al. [2] first proposed the concept of redactable blockchain. They put forward to replace the conventional SHA256 with chameleon hash function. When the trapdoor key is given, the collision can be effectively calculated to modify the block content and keep the state of the chain unchanged. In 2019, Derler et al. [10] proposed a policy-based chameleon hash function, in which people with enough privileges satisfying the policy can calculate the collision of a particular hash, supporting fine-grained and controllable modification, which is an elegant solution. Since then, other researchers have conducted more detailed and comprehensive studies. For example, Ashritha et al. [1] proposed to build a modifiable blockchain with an enhanced chameleon hash function, Hou et al. [15] proposed a fine-grained controllable editable blockchain that can forcibly delete harmful information, Zhang et al. [30] proposed a consortium blockchain controlled by Multi-authority CP-ABE, Huang et al. [16] proposed an extensible editable blockchain that can be updated and anonymous, Jia et al. [17] proposed an editable blockchain that supports supervision and self-management, and so on.

Consensus-based mutable blockchain was first proposed by Peddu et al. [24] in 2017, who proposed μchain. In order to replace the data records, the concept of mutation was introduced. Mutation is controlled by policy, enforced by consensus, and can be verified as a regular transaction. However, a malicious user can set his transaction not to be changed, or only himself can change it. In addition, the use of MPC protocol has affected the scalability and effectiveness of μchain. In 2019, the first redactable blockchain in the permissionless setting was born, which was proposed by Deuber et al. [11], using consensus-based voting. It does not rely on heavy cryptographic primitives or additional trust assumptions. Participants propose amendments, if the block verification algorithm is satisfied, the voting stage can be entered, and the amendments can be made in the ledger if there are enough miners to vote within a certain period of time. In 2021, Li et al. [20] proposed an instantly redactable blockchain protocol in permissionless setting, achieving better security and faster revision speed than previous research results in the permissionless setting, and also providing public verifiability.

The third category is editing at the framework and protocol layer. Dousti et al. [12] proposed the moderated redactable blockchains, which is a definitional framework with an efficient construct. In 2021, Thyagarajan et al. [29] proposed Reparo, a general protocol that can publicly repair any blockchain, by introducing external data structures to store content without changing the block structure.

As far as we know, so far, research on redactable blockchain that simultaneously satisfies user data self-management, on-chain harmful information governance, and transaction revocation is still blank.

2 Preliminaries

In this section, we first describe the notation and definitions that will be used in the later work, then introduce the cryptographic building blocks and basic knowledge of blockchain.

2.1 Notation

We use n to denote the main cryptographic security parameter through the paper and $\mathbb{Z}_q$ to denote the set of integers modulo an integer $q \geq 1$. For a nonnegative integer k, $[k]$ denotes $\{1, \cdots, k\}$. Negligible function in n is written as $negl(n)$, which vanishes faster than the inverse of any polynomial in n.

2.2 Gap Diffie-Hellman (GDH) Group

Let G be a cyclic multiplicative group generated by g, whose order is prime q. We assume that the inversion and multiplication in G could be calculated efficiently. We draw into the following assumptions.

- **Discrete Logarithm Problem (DLP)**: Given two elements g and h, to find an integer $a \in \mathbb{Z}_q^*$, such that $h = g^a$ whenever such an integer exists.
- **Computational Diffie-Hellman Problem (CDHP)**: Given (g, g^a, g^b) for $a, b \in \mathbb{Z}_q^*$, to compute g^{ab}.
- **Decisional Diffie-Hellman Problem (DDHP)**: Given (g, g^a, g^b, g^c) for $a, b, c \in \mathbb{Z}_q^*$, to decide whether $c \equiv ab \bmod q$.
- **Square Computational Diffie-Hellman Problem (Squ-CDHP)**: Given (g, g^a) for $a \in \mathbb{Z}_q^*$, to compute g^{a^2}.
- **Inverse Computational Diffie-Hellman Problem (Inv-CDHP)**: Given (g, g^a) for $a \in \mathbb{Z}_q^*$, to compute $g^{a^{-1}}$.

The *Gap Diffie-Hellman group* is defined as in which DDHP can be solved in polynomial time, while CDHP can not be solved by a polynomial time algorithm with non-negligible probability. We can find such groups on supersingular elliptic curves or hyperelliptic curves over finite fields. For more details, see [5,9,14,23].

Two variations of CDHP: Squ-CDHP and Inv-CDHP are equivalent under the optimal reduction conditions. Namely Squ-CDHP, Inv-CDHP and CDHP are polynomial-time equivalent to each other in G. For more details, see [4,21,25].

The tuple $< g, g^a, g^b, g^c >$ is a valid Diffie-Hellman tuple only if $c \equiv ab \bmod q$.

2.3   Double Trapdoor Chameleon Hash Function

We briefly review the concept of double trapdoor chameleon hash function introduced by Catalano et al. [7].

Definition 1. *A double trapdoor chameleon hash function is a tuple of polynomial-time algorithms as follows:*

$KG(1^n)$: *a probabilistic algorithm that takes as input the security parameter* 1^n, *outputs a triplet of public/private keys* (pk, sk_0, sk_1);

$TKG(1^n, i)$: *a probabilistic algorithm which, on input the security parameter* 1^n *and a bit* i, *outputs a pair of public/private keys* (pk, sk);

$CH_{pk}(m, r)$: *the evaluation algorithm that, on input the public key* pk, *a message* m *and a random nonce* r, *outputs a hashed value;*

$Coll(sk_i, m, m', r)$: *the collision finding algorithm which, on input one of the two private keys* sk_i, *two messages* m, m' *and a nonce* r, *outputs a new nonce* r' *such that* $CH_{pk}(m, r) = CH_{pk}(m', r')$.

The security requirements of double trapdoor chameleon hash function are as follows:

Distribution of Keys: Let $\overline{KG}(1^n, i)$ the algorithm that executes $KG(1^n)$ and restricts its output to (pk, sk_i). It is required that the distribution of the output of $TKG(1^n, i)$ and $\overline{KG}(1^n, i)$ to be the same.

Collision Resistance: Let $KG(1^n) = (pk, sk_0, sk_1)$.

1) For $i = 0$ or $i = 1$, with knowledge of pk and sk_i, it is infeasible to find sk_{1-i}.
2) Furthermore, there exists an efficient algorithm A that takes as input the public key pk and a collision (m, r, m', r') finds at least one of the trapdoors sk_i.

Therefore, it is impossible to find collisions without at least one of the trapdoors sk_i.

Distribution of Collisions: For every m, m', random r, and every $i = 0, 1$, the distribution of $r' = Coll(sk_i, m, m', r)$ is uniform, even when given pk, $h = CH_{pk}(m, r)$, m and m'. In the case of a "normal" chameleon hashing, this means that the function is information-theoretically hiding commitment. Furthermore, it implies that the distributions of the openings are the same no matter what trapdoor one uses.

2.4   The Chameleon Hashing Without Key Exposure

In 2004, Chen and Zhang et al. [8] proposed their full chameleon hashing scheme without key exposure by leveraging the idea of "Customized Identities" [3]. The details of the scheme are as follows.

- **System parameter generation:** For a gap Diffie-Hellman group G, whose generator is g, the order is prime q. Let $H : \{0,1\}^* \rightarrow G^*(G^* = G\backslash\{1\})$ be a secure cryptographic hash function. Define $I = H(ID_S||ID_R||ID_T)$, where ID_S denotes the identity of the signer, ID_R denotes the recipient's identity, and ID_T is the identity of the transaction, respectively. Then the system parameters are denoted by $SP = \{G, q, g, H\}$.
- **Key generation:** The private key is generated by the user randomly selecting an integer $x \in \mathbb{Z}_q^*$, the public key is defined as $y = g^x$. The validity of the public key can be guaranteed by the certificate of a trusted third party.
- **Hashing computation:** Choose a random integer $a \in \mathbb{Z}_q^*$, the hash function is defined as

$$h = Hash(m, I, g^a, y^a) = (g * I)^m y^a$$

where y is the public key and I is a customized identity.

2.5   A Discrete Log-Based Double Trapdoor Commitment Scheme

The double trapdoor commitment scheme was first introduced by Bresson et al. in [6], then Catalano et al. [7] gave a detailed definition. Here we briefly review this definition as follows.

- **Key generation:** Let G be a cyclic group of prime order q, g is the generator of G. Pick two random values $x, y \in \mathbb{Z}_q$ and compute $h_1 = g^x$ and $h_2 = g^y$. Then the public key is (G, q, g, h_1, h_2), the private key is (x, y).
- **Commitment function:** For message $m \in \mathbb{Z}_q$, two random values $r, s \in_R \mathbb{Z}_q^*$, the commitment is defined as $C(m, r, s) = g^m h_1^r h_2^s$.

2.6   Blocks and Chain

Blocks: A block B is represented by a tuple, such as (P, C, V, W) [12], containing various components. In the most common case, P denotes the prefix of the block, C is the content of the block, V represents the version of the block, and W is the witness of the block. In this paper, the block we introduce is in the spirit of [13], and we define the block form as $B :=< s, x, w, r >$, where $s \in \{0,1\}^k, x \in \{0,1\}^*$. The s denotes the state of the previous block, x is the block data, w is the consensus witness and r is nonce.

Time and Slots: We consider that the whole system has a global clock. With reference to literature [18], we divide the time into discrete units, which are named slots. Everyone in the system is equipped with (roughly synchronized) clocks to indicate the current slot. For more details, see [18].

Chain: There are three types of blockchains that occur in real-world applications: *public blockchain, consortium blockchain* and *private blockchain* [2]. *The public blockchain* is completely decentralized, anyone in the world is allowed to read, send transactions to the network and include the valid transactions in the blockchain. *The consortium blockchain* is a blockchain where the consensus process is controlled by a predetermined set of parties, it can be considered as "partially decentralized". The right to read the blockchain can be public or limited to participants. *The private blockchain* is a blockchain where the write permissions are kept centralized to one authority, and the read permissions may be public or restricted. In this paper, we are working on the basis of consortium chain.

Account: In our system, the user's account contains two parts: an available balance portion and a temporary balance portion. The available balance can be directly consumed, but the temporary balance can't, and it can only be used as a transit account in the revocable period.

2.7 Publicly Verifiable Secret Sharing (PVSS)

The publicly verifiable secret sharing (PVSS) scheme, as recommended by Stadler [28], is a verifiable secret sharing scheme where anyone can verify the validity of the shares distributed by the dealer. In this work, we refer to the discrete logarithm based PVSS of [26], details are as follows.

- **Initialization:** The group G_q and two generators g and G are selected using the appropriate disclosure procedure. Participant P_i chooses a random value $x_i \in \mathbb{Z}_q^*$, and registers $y_i = G^{x_i}$. The public/private key pair is (x_i, y_i).
- **Distribution:**
  1) *Distribution of the shares.* The dealer picks a random polynomial $p(\cdot)$ of degree $d(\leq t-1)$ with coefficients $a_0, a_1, ..., a_d$, where $a_0 = s$. The dealer publishes the commitments $C_i = g^{a_i} (0 \leq i \leq d)$, as well as the encrypted shares $Y_j = y_j^{p(j)} (1 \leq j \leq n)$, and let $X_i = \prod_{j=0}^d C_j^{i^j} = g^{p(i)}$. The proof of the consistency of encrypted values $\log_g(X_i) = \log_{y_i}(Y_i)$ is attached.
  2) *Verification of the commitments.* The commitments can be verified by checking the proofs of discrete-log equality.
- **Reconstruction:**
  1) *Decryption of the shares.* The participant P_i gets the share $S(i)$ by computing $S_i = Y_i^{x_i^{-1}}$, and publishes the knowledge proof of equality of discrete-logarithms $\log_{S_i}(Y_i) = \log_{Y_i}(G)$.
  2) *Recover the shares.* On the premise that the participant P_i produces the correct S_i, the secret can obtained by Lagrange interpolation: $S = \prod_{j=1}^d S_{i_j}^{\lambda_j}$, where $\lambda_1, ..., \lambda_d$ are the Lagrange coefficients.

3   Double Trapdoor Key-exposure Free Chameleon Hash Function

The concept of chameleon hashing was first proposed by Krawczyk and Rabin [19]. As described in [19], a chameleon hash function is associated with user U, who has published the public hashing key PK, and holds the corresponding secret trapdoor T. The public-private key pair is generated by the user using the key generation algorithm. Then the chameleon hash function is denoted by the public key PK, it takes into a message m and a random string r, outputs the hash value. The chameleon hash function is also known as trapdoor commitment scheme [7]. In this paper, we learn from the achievement of Bresson and Catalano etc. [6] – trapdoor commitment scheme, and put forward a double trapdoor key-exposure free chameleon hash function. It generalizes the notion of chameleon hash by allowing the existence of two independent trapdoors. Knowing either of the two trapdoors, one can easily find collisions.

3.1   Our Double Trapdoor Key-Exposure Free Chameleon Hash Function

In our protocol, in order to avoid unilateral modification and key exposure, we have outlined the above concepts and definitions, and put forward a double trapdoor key-exposure free chameleon hash function (DTCH). The gap Diffie-Hellman group G generated by g and the prime order q are system parameters. We denote by G^* the set $G^* = G \backslash \{1\}$ where 1 is the identity of G.

The scheme comprises four algorithms, *KeyGen, Hash, Verify* and *Adapt*. It makes use of a full-domain hash function $H : \{0,1\}^* \to G^*$ and a cryptographic hash function $\mathcal{H} : \{0,1\}^* \to \mathbb{Z}_q$. Define the customized identity $I = H(transaction\_id \| sender\_id \| receiver\_id)$, and different identities correspond to different hash values. The security analysis views H as a random oracle. The specific algorithm is shown as follows.

- **Key generation:** Choose two random values $x_{user}, x_{regulator} \in \mathbb{Z}_q^*$, compute $h_1 = g^{x_{user}}$ and $h_2 = g^{x_{regulator}}$. The public key is (G, q, g, h_1, h_2), the private key is $(x_{user}, x_{regulator})$.
- **Hashing calculation:** For message m, pick two random values $a, b \in \mathbb{Z}_q^*$, the hash function is defined as

$$Hash(m, I, g^a, g^b) = (g * I)^{\mathcal{H}(m)} h_1^a h_2^b$$

  Set $h \leftarrow Hash(m, I, g^a, g^b)$, and $r \leftarrow ((g^a, h_1^a), (g^b, h_2^b))$.
  Return (h, r).
- **Verification:** On input public parameters $pk = (G, q, g, h_1, h_2)$, message m, hash value h, customized identity I, and randomness $r = ((g^a, h_1^a), (g^b, h_2^b))$, check if $g^a, g^b \in G$, and if $h = (g * I)^{\mathcal{H}(m)} h_1^a h_2^b$. If all checks hold, return 1. Otherwise, return 0.

- **Adaptation:** On input private key x_{user} or $x_{regulator}$, messages m and m', hash value h and randomness $((g^a, h_1^a), (g^b, h_2^b))$, the algorithm $\mathcal{F}$ computes the hash collision as follows:

  1) When the input private key is x_{user},

  $$\mathcal{F}(x_{user}, h, m, m', g^a, h_1^a, I) = (g^{a'}, h_1^{a'})$$

  where $g^{a'} = (g * I)^{x_{user}^{-1} * (\mathcal{H}(m) - \mathcal{H}(m'))} g^a$ and $h_1^{a'} = (g * I)^{(\mathcal{H}(m) - \mathcal{H}(m'))} h_1^a$.
  Note that

  $$
  \begin{aligned}
  Hash(m', I, g^{a'}, g^b) &= (g * I)^{\mathcal{H}(m')} h_1^{a'} h_2^b \\
  &= (g * I)^{\mathcal{H}(m')} (g * I)^{(\mathcal{H}(m) - \mathcal{H}(m'))} h_1^a h_2^b \\
  &= (g * I)^{\mathcal{H}(m)} h_1^a h_2^b \\
  &= Hash(m, I, g^a, g^b)
  \end{aligned}
  $$

  and $< g, h_1, g^{a'}, h_1^{a'} >$ is a valid Diffie-Hellman tuple. Therefore, the forgery is successful.
  Return $(m', r') \leftarrow (m', ((g^{a'}, h_1^{a'}), (g^b, h_2^b)))$.

  2) When the input private key is $x_{regulator}$, we need to add a temporary key t, t is a random number jointly generated by the regulatory committee (the details will be introduced in Section 4.1.2), the algorithm is as follows:

  $$\mathcal{F}(x_{regulator}, h, m, m', g^b, h_2^b, I, t) = (g^{tb'}, h_2^{tb'})$$

  where $g^{b'} = (g * I)^{x_{regulator}^{-1} * t^{-1} * (\mathcal{H}(m) - \mathcal{H}(m'))} (g^b)^{t^{-1}}$ and $h_2^{b'} = (g * I)^{t^{-1} * (\mathcal{H}(m) - \mathcal{H}(m'))} (h_2^b)^{t^{-1}}$.
  Note that

  $$
  \begin{aligned}
  Hash(m', I, g^a, g^{tb'}) &= (g * I)^{\mathcal{H}(m')} h_1^a h_2^{tb'} \\
  &= (g * I)^{\mathcal{H}(m')} \left[(g * I)^{t^{-1} * (\mathcal{H}(m) - \mathcal{H}(m'))} (h_2^b)^{t^{-1}} \right]^t h_1^a \\
  &= (g * I)^{\mathcal{H}(m)} h_1^a h_2^b \\
  &= Hash(m, I, g^a, g^b)
  \end{aligned}
  $$

  and $< g, h_2, g^{b'}, h_2^{b'} >$ is a valid Diffie-Hellman tuple. Therefore, the forgery is successful.
  Return $(m', r') \leftarrow (m', ((g^a, h_1^a), (g^{b'}, h_2^{b'})))$.

We notice that the two private keys are independent of each other. When calculating the collision, only the random number related to their own key is solved, while the other random number remains unchanged. Therefore, the reasonable collision changes only one random number compared with the original random pair.

Theorem 1. *Under the assumption of CDHP in G is intractable, the above scheme is a double trapdoor chameleon hash function in the random oracle model.*

Proof. We prove this theorem by proving that the scheme satisfies three main properties of the double trapdoor chameleon hash function.

Distribution of Keys: Here we show the TKG algorithm in detail. On input the security parameter 1^n and a bit i, it chooses two random generators $g, h_{i \oplus 1} \in G$, a random $sk_i \in \mathbb{Z}_q^*$ and sets $h_i = g^{sk_i}$. The public key is set as (G, q, g, h_1, h_2), the trapdoor is sk_i. It is simple to verify that all the required properties are met.

Collision Resistance: We prove this by contradiction. If an adversary $\mathcal{A}$ issuing at most q_H queries to the random oracle H_1 has the advantage ϵ to find a collision in the proposed scheme, then we can construct an algorithm $\mathcal{B}$ breaks the Inverse Computational Diffie-Hellman Problem (Inv-CDHP) in G with non-negligible probability $\epsilon \delta^{q_H}$ (suppose the probability that $\mathcal{A}$'s query is not terminated is δ^{q_H}).

$\mathcal{B}$ is given a challenge (g, g^{x_0}, g^{x_1}). $\mathcal{H} : \{0,1\}^* \to \mathbb{Z}_q$ is a public hash function. In setup, it constructs public key $h_1 \leftarrow (g^{x_0})$, $h_2 \leftarrow (g^{x_1})$. For each i, $1 \leq i \leq q_H$, $\mathcal{B}$ picks a random number $r_i \xleftarrow{R} \mathbb{Z}_p^*$, and sets $\sigma_i \leftarrow g^{r_i}$. When $\mathcal{A}$ requests a hash on a customized identity I_i, $\mathcal{B}$ responds with σ_i. After the query phase, $\mathcal{A}$ requests the hash of challenging customized identity I_{i^*} (on which $\mathcal{A}$ had not requested a hash), $\mathcal{B}$ picks a random number $r_{i^*} \xleftarrow{R} \mathbb{Z}_p^*$, sets $\sigma_{i^*} \leftarrow g^{r_{i^*}}$, and responds with σ_{i^*}. Finally, $\mathcal{A}$ halts, either conceding failure or returning a valid collision $(m, g^a, h_1^a, g^b, h_2^b)$ and $(m', g^{a'}, h_1^{a'}, g^{b'}, h_2^{b'})((g^a = g^{a'}, g^b \neq g^{b'})$ or $(g^a \neq g^{a'}, g^b = g^{b'}))$ where $Hash(m, I_{i^*}, g^a, g^b) = Hash(m', I_{i^*}, g^{a'}, g^{b'})$.

After receiving the collision, $\mathcal{B}$ first determines the type of collision. If $g^a \neq g^{a'}$, he can compute $g^{x_0^{-1}} = \left(\frac{g^a}{g^{a'}}\right)^{\frac{1}{(r_i^*+1)[\mathcal{H}(m')-\mathcal{H}(m)]}}$. If $g^b \neq g^{b'}$, he can compute $g^{x_1^{-1}} = \left(\frac{g^b}{g^{b'}}\right)^{\frac{1}{(r_i^*+1)[\mathcal{H}(m')-\mathcal{H}(m)]}}$. $\mathcal{B}$ outputs $g^{x_i^{-1}}$ ($i=0$ or 1), which is indeed the answer to the Inverse Computational Diffie-Hellman Problem challenge posed to it. From Sect. 2.2, we know it is equivalent to solve the CDHP in G.

Distribution of Collisions: We consider the two distributions:

$$\{a, b \leftarrow \mathbb{Z}_q^*, \mathcal{H}(m), \mathcal{H}(m') \leftarrow \mathbb{Z}q : \text{Coll}\left(sk_1, m, m', g^a, h_1^a, g^b, h_2^b\right)\}$$

$$\{a, b \leftarrow \mathbb{Z}_q^*, \mathcal{H}(m), \mathcal{H}(m') \leftarrow \mathbb{Z}q : \text{Coll}\left(sk_2, m, m', g^a, h_1^a, g^b, h_2^b\right)\}$$

In the first distribution Coll outputs a pair $(g^{a'}, h_1^{a'}, g^b, h_2^b)$ such that $g^{a'} = (g*I)^{sk_1^{-1}*(\mathcal{H}(m)-\mathcal{H}(m'))}g^a$ and $h_1^{a'} = (g*I)^{(\mathcal{H}(m)-\mathcal{H}(m'))}h_1^a$. We observe that if

g^a and h_1^a are uniformly distributed in G, then $g^{a'}$ and $h_1^{a'}$ are also uniformly distributed in G. In the second distribution Coll outputs a pair $(g^a, h_1^a, g^{b'}, h_2^{b'})$ such that $g^{b'} = (g * I)^{sk_2^{-1}*(\mathcal{H}(m)-\mathcal{H}(m'))}g^b$ and $h_2^{b'} = (g * I)^{(\mathcal{H}(m)-\mathcal{H}(m'))}h_2^b$. If g^b and h_2^b are uniform in G, then $g^{b'}$ and $h_2^{b'}$ are also uniform in G. Thus, both the two distributions are perfectly indistinguishable from uniform in G.

Theorem 2. *The above chameleon hashing scheme satisfies the property of key exposure freeness.*

Proof. Given two collisions $(m, g^a, h_1^a, g^b, h_2^b)$ and $(m', g^{a'}, h_1^{a'}, g^{b'}, h_2^{b'})((g^a = g^{a'}, g^b \neq g^{b'})$ or $(g^a \neq g^{a'}, g^b = g^{b'}))$, the information of $(g * I)^{x_i^{-1}}$ (i=0 or 1) can be recovered. However, it is impossible for anyone to compute x_i from $(g * I)^{x_i^{-1}}$ (i=0 or 1). Therefore, collision forgery cannot lead to leakage of the trapdoor information.

4   Blockchain Redacting Protocol

In this section, we will present our protocol, clarifying how to leverage and modify the existing cryptography technology to obtain a redactable blockchain system that supports fine-grained autonomy and transaction rollback.

4.1   Redactable Blockchain System

There are three roles in our system, namely users, regulatory committee and miners. Each of them performs its own duties and restricts each other. Users can publish transactions and legally revise transactions. The regulatory committee is responsible for reviewing and forcibly deleting harmful information. Miners take charge of uploading and rewriting the transaction. A simple system model is shown in Fig. 1.

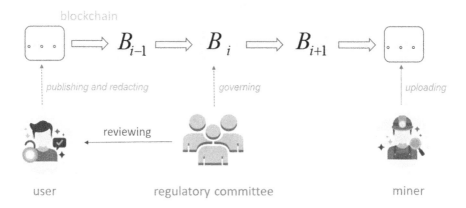

Fig. 1. System model of our redactable blockchain.

4.2   Technique Overview

We have recourse to the techniques in [10] and our proposed double trapdoor key-exposure free chameleon hash function (DTCH). The hash values of all transactions in a block constitute the leaf nodes of Merkle tree, and its root node is stored in the block header. We replace the hash function in the leaf nodes with our proposed DTCH, realizing the transaction-level rewriting. The nature of the chameleon hash function guarantees the invariance of Merkle tree's root hash (which is denoted by TX_ROOT), since changing the content of a transaction does not change the hash value of the transaction. Therefore, the state of the chain remains unchanged. Figure 2 presents the application of DTCH for transaction-level blockchain rewriting.

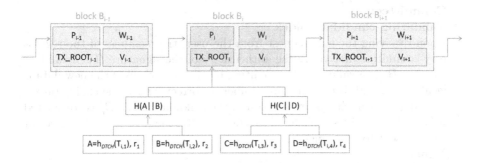

Fig. 2. DTCH for our redactable blockchain.

In Fig. 2, a block B_i contains a Merkle root, which accumulates four transactions: $T_{i,1}$, $T_{i,2}$, $T_{i,3}$ and $T_{i,4}$. They are all mutable transactions. Note that the randomness r_i is not included in the hash calculation of the aggregation, but is provided as the non-hashed part of the transaction, which is used for verification. When $T_{i,1}$ needs to be altered to $T'_{i,1}$, its owner or the regulatory committee could compute a valid hash collision r' without changing its hash value. Finally, the new transaction $T'_{i,1}$ along with the new randomness r' are updated.

4.3   Block Information Revision

In our system, there are two types of revisions. One is self-management of user data, and the other is the mandatory deletion of harmful information. The specific revision process is shown below.

User Data Self-management. For the legal modification of the transactions, users can calculate hash collisions themselves to make a redaction. Generally, a block B_i contained in $chain = (B_1, ..., B_n)$ can be edited by the following steps.
User:

1) **Calculating the hash collision**

   Any user in the system can propose an edit to block B_i for a particular data to be removed or replaced, he first calls the algorithm $\mathcal{F}$ to compute the hash collision $\mathcal{F}(x_{user}, h, m, m', g^a, h_1^a, I) = (g^{a'}, h_1^{a'})$, where m' is the new data and x_{user} is his own secret key.

2) **Proposing a redaction**

   After computing the collision, he constructs an edit request transaction $ET = (ID_{block}, PK_j, B_i^*)$ containing the block number ID_{block}, his public signing key PK_j and the new candidate block $B_i^* = (s, x', w, r')$, where $x' = m'$ and $r' = (g^{a'}, h_1^{a'}, g^b, h_2^b)$, s and w are the same as before. Moreover, his signature $Sig_{sk_j}(ET)$ is attached to the request transaction to ensure the authenticity. Then he submits the ET to the regulatory committee for review, which requires payment of a transaction fee.

   Committee:

3) **Validating candidate block**

   Upon receiving the edit request from the user, the members of the regulatory committee first verify the authenticity of the signature. Then validate whether B_i^* is a valid candidate editing block. They check if the new data is legal and logical, if the random number is correct, and if the chain state is unchanged. If all checks are successful, the candidate block B_i^* is considered valid, otherwise it is considered invalid. Finally, the review result (reject or pass) is sent to the miner.

   Miner:

4) **Redacting the block**

   If the candidate block passes the review of the regulatory committee, the miner redacts the content of corresponding block and broadcasts the revision of the block to the whole network. Then everyone in the system updates the chain.

Mandatory Deletion of Harmful Information When malicious information appears on the chain, the regulatory committee can jointly revise it. Each member of the regulatory committee knows the private key $x_{regulator}$, which acts as a long-term private key. While the temporary private key is a random number jointly calculated by them each time. We employ a coin tossing scheme to generate unbiased randomness, ensuring that all honest parties receive the output as long as there is an honest majority. By referring to [18], we put forward the following randomness generation protocol π_{GRN}.

Protocol π_{GRN}

The protocol π_{GRN} is implemented by the regulatory committee within a fixed period of time ($T = 10l$ slots), and each round (divided into three phases) generates an uniform randomness beacon. We will use the PVSS (as described in section 2.6) as a sub-protocol.

Input: Each party has the regulatory committee membership set S, a PKI of public keys $\{\text{pk}_i\}_{i \in S}$, and its private key sk_i. Let $H : \{0,1\}^* \rightarrow \mathbb{Z}_q^*$ be a cryptographic hash function. Without loss of generality, committee members involved in the random number generation are denoted by P_1, P_2, ..., P_n.

Phase 1 - Commitment ($4l$ slots): At the beginning of the round, committee member $P_i(i \in [n])$ samples an uniformly distributed random string s_i and a random number r_i for the commitment scheme. Then, distributes s_i using PVSS and generates shares $\theta_1^i, ..., \theta_n^i$. Each share $\theta_k^i(k \in [n])$ is encrypted with P_k's public key. Finally, P_i posts his commitment $Com(s_i, r_i)$ and encrypted shares to the blockchain.

Phase 2 - Reveal ($4l$ slots): During the reveal stage, which lasts for $4l$ slots, P_i opens his commitment $Com(s_i, r_i)$ by posting $Open(s_i, r_i)$ to the blockchain provided that the blockchain contains the effective shares of most committee member (P_1, P_2, ..., P_n); if not, each P_i terminates.

Phase 3 - Recovery ($2l$ slots): After slot $8l$, for any party P_b who did not participate in the reveal phase, $P_i(i \in [n])$ reveals the share θ_i^b it received to insert blockchain. When all shares $\theta_1^b, ..., \theta_n^b$ are available, each party P_i can compute $Rec(\theta_1^b, ..., \theta_n^b)$ to reconstruct s_b (regardless of whether P_b opens the commitment $Com(s_b, r_b)$ or not).

Output: The final random number is defined as $t = H(\bigoplus_{i=1}^n s_i)$.

After jointly calculating the random number t, the head of the regulatory committee calls the algorithm $\mathcal{F}$ to compute the hash collision

$$\mathcal{F}(x_{regulator}, h, m, m', g^b, h_2^b, I, t) = (g^{tb'}, h_2^{tb'}),$$

where $x_{regulator}$ is the long-term private key, m' is the new data after deleting the illegal data. Then, the new candidate block is denoted as $B_i^* = (s, x', w, r')$ where $r' = (g^a, h_1^a, g^{b'}, h_2^{b'})$ and x' is the new data after removing harmful information. Finally, after receiving the block ID and the candidate block B_i^*, the miner revises it and broadcasts to the whole network.

4.4 Transaction Rollback

Users can apply for transaction cancellation if they find a transaction error within a specific time. In our system, there is an intermediate account for temporarily storing the transfer amount, similar to Alipay. It means that the user's account consists of two parts, the available balance portion and the temporary balance portion. Upon receipt of a transfer, the change of the account balance will first occur in the temporary balance portion of the account. Only after the time (T) agreed by the system will the transaction amount be accumulated to the available balance, which also means that the transaction cannot be withdrawn. An example of transfer is presented in Fig. 3.

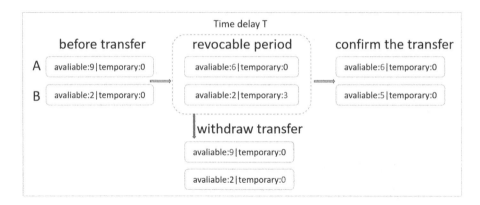

Fig. 3. A transfer 3 to B.

Design Rule. The specific rules are as follows.

1) Only the available balance can be spent.
2) The money received will be transferred to the temporary balance first.
3) The transaction cannot be withdrawn after the time delay T.

5   Conclusion

In this paper, we present a blockchain editing protocol that simultaneously supports fine-grained autonomy and transaction rollback. The feature of our scheme is that it meets the dual needs of chain governance and data modification. On the one hand, users can self-manage their own data; on the other hand, the regulatory committee can forcibly delete harmful information on the chain. To this end, we design a double trapdoor key-exposure free chameleon hash function. At the same time, the protocol also supports transaction cancellation within a specific time. Our work has taken a step forward in promoting the development of editable blockchain protocols.

References

1. Ashritha, K., Sindhu, M., Lakshmy, K.: Redactable blockchain using enhanced chameleon hash function. In: 2019 5th International Conference on Advanced Computing & Communication Systems (ICACCS), pp. 323–328. IEEE (2019)
2. Ateniese, G., Magri, B., Venturi, D., Andrade, E.: Redactable blockchain-or-rewriting history in bitcoin and friends. In: 2017 IEEE European Symposium on Security and Privacy (EuroS&P), pp. 111–126. IEEE (2017). https://doi.org/10.1109/EuroSP.2017.37
3. Ateniese, G., de Medeiros, B.: Identity-based chameleon hash and applications. In: Juels, A. (ed.) FC 2004. LNCS, vol. 3110, pp. 164–180. Springer, Heidelberg (2004). https://doi.org/10.1007/978-3-540-27809-2_19

4. Bao, F., Deng, R.H., Zhu, H.F.: Variations of Diffie-Hellman problem. In: Qing, S., Gollmann, D., Zhou, J. (eds.) ICICS 2003. LNCS, vol. 2836, pp. 301–312. Springer, Heidelberg (2003). https://doi.org/10.1007/978-3-540-39927-8_28

5. Boneh, D., Lynn, B., Shacham, H.: Short signatures from the Weil pairing. In: Boyd, C. (ed.) ASIACRYPT 2001. LNCS, vol. 2248, pp. 514–532. Springer, Heidelberg (2001). https://doi.org/10.1007/3-540-45682-1_30

6. Bresson, E., Catalano, D., Gennaro, R.: Improved on-line/off-line threshold signatures. In: Okamoto, T., Wang, X. (eds.) PKC 2007. LNCS, vol. 4450, pp. 217–232. Springer, Heidelberg (2007). https://doi.org/10.1007/978-3-540-71677-8_15

7. Catalano, D., Di Raimondo, M., Fiore, D., Gennaro, R.: Off-line/on-line signatures: theoretical aspects and experimental results. In: Cramer, R. (ed.) PKC 2008. LNCS, vol. 4939, pp. 101–120. Springer, Heidelberg (2008). https://doi.org/10.1007/978-3-540-78440-1_7

8. Chen, X., Zhang, F., Kim, K.: Chameleon hashing without key exposure. In: Zhang, K., Zheng, Y. (eds.) ISC 2004. LNCS, vol. 3225, pp. 87–98. Springer, Heidelberg (2004). https://doi.org/10.1007/978-3-540-30144-8_8

9. Choon, J.C., Hee Cheon, J.: An identity-based signature from gap Diffie-Hellman groups. In: Desmedt, Y.G. (ed.) PKC 2003. LNCS, vol. 2567, pp. 18–30. Springer, Heidelberg (2003). https://doi.org/10.1007/3-540-36288-6_2

10. Derler, D., Samelin, K., Slamanig, D., Striecks, C.: Fine-grained and controlled rewriting in blockchains: chameleon-hashing gone attribute-based. IACR Cryptol. ePrint Arch. p. 406 (2019). https://eprint.iacr.org/2019/406

11. Deuber, D., Magri, B., Thyagarajan, S.A.K.: Redactable blockchain in the permissionless setting. In: 2019 IEEE Symposium on Security and Privacy, SP 2019, San Francisco, CA, USA, pp. 124–138. IEEE (2019). https://doi.org/10.1109/SP.2019.00039

12. Dousti, M.S., Küpçü, A.: Moderated redactable blockchains: a definitional framework with an efficient construct. In: Garcia-Alfaro, J., Navarro-Arribas, G., Herrera-Joancomarti, J. (eds.) DPM/CBT -2020. LNCS, vol. 12484, pp. 355–373. Springer, Cham (2020). https://doi.org/10.1007/978-3-030-66172-4_23

13. Garay, J., Kiayias, A., Leonardos, N.: The bitcoin backbone protocol: analysis and applications. In: Oswald, E., Fischlin, M. (eds.) EUROCRYPT 2015. LNCS, vol. 9057, pp. 281–310. Springer, Heidelberg (2015). https://doi.org/10.1007/978-3-662-46803-6_10

14. Hess, F.: Efficient identity based signature schemes based on pairings. In: Nyberg, K., Heys, H. (eds.) SAC 2002. LNCS, vol. 2595, pp. 310–324. Springer, Heidelberg (2003). https://doi.org/10.1007/3-540-36492-7_20

15. Hou, H., Hao, S., Yuan, J., Xu, S., Zhao, Y.: Fine-grained and controllably redactable blockchain with harmful data forced removal. Security and Communication Networks 2021 (2021). https://doi.org/10.1155/2021/3680359

16. Huang, K., Zhang, X., Mu, Y., Rezaeibagha, F., Du, X.: Scalable and redactable blockchain with update and anonymity. Inf. Sci. **546**, 25–41 (2021). https://doi.org/10.1016/j.ins.2020.07.016

17. Jia, Y., Sun, S.F., Zhang, Y., Liu, Z., Gu, D.: Redactable blockchain supporting supervision and self-management. In: ASIA CCS 2021: ACM Asia Conference on Computer and Communications Security, Virtual Event, Hong Kong, pp. 844–858 (2021). https://doi.org/10.1145/3433210.3453091

18. Kiayias, A., Russell, A., David, B., Oliynykov, R.: Ouroboros: a provably secure proof-of-stake blockchain protocol. In: Katz, J., Shacham, H. (eds.) CRYPTO 2017. LNCS, vol. 10401, pp. 357–388. Springer, Cham (2017). https://doi.org/10.1007/978-3-319-63688-7_12

19. Krawczyk, H., Rabin, T.: Chameleon hashing and signatures. IACR Cryptol. ePrint Arch. p. 10 (1998). http://eprint.iacr.org/1998/010

20. Li, X., Xu, J., Yin, L., Lu, Y., Tang, Q., Zhang, Z.: Escaping from consensus: Instantly redactable blockchain protocols in permissionless setting. IACR Cryptology ePrint Archive p. 223 (2021). https://eprint.iacr.org/2021/223

21. Maurer, U.M.: Towards the equivalence of breaking the Diffie-Hellman protocol and computing discrete logarithms. In: Desmedt, Y.G. (ed.) CRYPTO 1994. LNCS, vol. 839, pp. 271–281. Springer, Heidelberg (1994). https://doi.org/10.1007/3-540-48658-5_26

22. Nakamoto, S.: Bitcoin: a peer-to-peer electronic cash system. Decentralized Business Review, p. 21260 (2008)

23. Okamoto, T., Pointcheval, D.: The gap-problems: a new class of problems for the security of cryptographic schemes. In: Kim, K. (ed.) PKC 2001. LNCS, vol. 1992, pp. 104–118. Springer, Heidelberg (2001). https://doi.org/10.1007/3-540-44586-2_8

24. Puddu, I., Dmitrienko, A., Capkun, S.: μchain: How to forget without hard forks. IACR Cryptology ePrint Archive, p. 106 (2017). http://eprint.iacr.org/2017/106

25. Sadeghi, A.-R., Steiner, M.: Assumptions related to discrete logarithms: why subtleties make a real difference. In: Pfitzmann, B. (ed.) EUROCRYPT 2001. LNCS, vol. 2045, pp. 244–261. Springer, Heidelberg (2001). https://doi.org/10.1007/3-540-44987-6_16

26. Schoenmakers, B.: A simple publicly verifiable secret sharing scheme and its application to electronic voting. In: Wiener, M. (ed.) CRYPTO 1999. LNCS, vol. 1666, pp. 148–164. Springer, Heidelberg (1999). https://doi.org/10.1007/3-540-48405-1_10

27. Shabani, M., Borry, P.: Rules for processing genetic data for research purposes in view of the new EU general data protection regulation. Eur. J. Hum. Genet. **26**(2), 149–156 (2018)

28. Stadler, M.: Publicly verifiable secret sharing. In: Maurer, U. (ed.) EUROCRYPT 1996. LNCS, vol. 1070, pp. 190–199. Springer, Heidelberg (1996). https://doi.org/10.1007/3-540-68339-9_17

29. Thyagarajan, S.A.K., Bhat, A., Magri, B., Tschudi, D., Kate, A.: Reparo: publicly verifiable layer to repair blockchains. In: Borisov, N., Diaz, C. (eds.) FC 2021. LNCS, vol. 12675, pp. 37–56. Springer, Heidelberg (2021). https://doi.org/10.1007/978-3-662-64331-0_2

30. Zhang, Z., Li, T., Wang, Z., Liu, J.: Redactable transactions in consortium blockchain: controlled by multi-authority CP-ABE. In: Baek, J., Ruj, S. (eds.) ACISP 2021. LNCS, vol. 13083, pp. 408–429. Springer, Cham (2021). https://doi.org/10.1007/978-3-030-90567-5_21

Cryptography and Applications

Pitch in: A Secure Extension Signature Based on SM9

Chuyi Yan[1,4], Haixia Xu[2,3,4(✉)], Yongheng Mu[2,3,4], and Jiong Ding[2,3,4]

[1] Institute of Information Engineering of Chinese Academy of Sciences,
Beijing, China
[2] State Key Laboratory of Information Security, Institute of Information Engineering
of Chinese Academy of Sciences, Beijing, China
{yanchuyi,xuhaixia,muyongheng,dingjiong}@iie.ac.cn
[3] Data Assurance and Communication Security Research Center of Chinese Academy
of Sciences, Beijing, China
[4] School of Cyber Security, University of Chinese Academy of Sciences,
Beijing, China

Abstract. SM9 is the identity-based cryptography (IBC) promulgated
by the State Cryptography Administration of China. SM9-IBS has
become an international standard in 2017 (the main part of ISO/IEC
14888-3/AMD1 standard). SM9-IBS reduces the certificate application
and verification phases, which has obvious advantages in identity authentication in mobile Internet, Internet of things (IoT), big data, and other
fields. Many researchers use SM9 as the underlying cryptography and
have successively proposed extended signatures such as group, ring, and
two-party cooperation. In order to further promote the application of
SM9, reduce the pressure of root KGC and improve the reliability of
the system, we present a secure and feasible hierarchical SM9 signature
scheme which is the first SM9-IBS (Identity-based Signature) extension.
Also, we prove its security is existentially unforgeable under adaptive chosen message and identity attacks (EUF-CMIA) in the standard model.
At the same time, the implementation of our scheme using Java does not
lead to an additional performance burden based on the SM9 algorithm.

Keywords: SM9-IBS · Identity-based signature · Hierarchical
signature · Bilinear paring · Information security

1 Introduction

The fundamental service of digital signature is identity authentication. Digital
signature aims at providing authentication and non-reputation. Nowadays, many
applications(APPs) linking in the network require the above goal, especially large

This work is supported by National Key R&D Program of China (2017YFB0802500),
Beijing Municipal Science and Technology Project (No. Z191100007119007) and Shandong province major science and technology innovation project (2019JZZY020129).

enterprises applications (like banks and governments). In terms of ensuring security, identity-based digital signature [1–3] can be considered for authentication, which is very suitable for the management mode of large enterprises.

In 2016, the State Cryptography Administration of China released identity-based cryptography SM9 using elliptic curve pairing. In 2018, SM9-IBS has become the ISO/IEC international standard. SM9-IBS has obvious advantages in authentication in the fields of Internet of Things [4], blockchain [5,6], and big data [7] because its consumption is low due to the reduction of certificate application and verification. And extended signatures such as SM9-based group and ring signatures [8] and two-party cooperation signatures [9] have been proposed successively. However, these works generally rely on a single KGC, which makes the pressure on a single KGC heavy. To further promote the application of SM9, reduce the burden of the root KGC, and improve the reliability of the system (When the lower-level KGCs are corrupted, it will not affect the higher-level KGCs), we present the first SM9-based hierarchical signature scheme, to our best knowledge. Compared with directly introducing several KGCs without hierarchical relationship, our scheme can better reflect the management relationship between KGCs and is more suitable for the current organizational structure.

In 2002, Gentry and Silverberg [10] introduced the idea of identity-based hierarchical cryptography for the first time. The system includes a hierarchical encryption system and hierarchical signature system that in the random oracle model, satisfy selected ciphertext security and 100% collusion resistance on an indefinite levels, but unfortunately, there is no relevant security proof in the article. Then Chow et al. [11] proposed the first provably secure identity-based hierarchical signature scheme, but it needs to prove its security by random oracle.

Since then, the research on identity-based hierarchical cryptography has been a hot spot in the academic field. It is especially useful for e-government structure.

1.1 Related Work

In 1984, the first identity-based cryptography was proposed by Shamir [2]. Since then, a large number of identity-based cryptography have emerged. Boneh et al., [12] proposed an identity-based encryption system using bilinear mapping on the elliptic curve in 2001, which is considered to be the first practical identity-based encryption system. In 2001, K. Ohgishi et al. [13] presented an elliptic curve pairing-based identity-based key sharing system. Boneh et al. proposed a sequential identity-based public-key encryption algorithm using the elliptic curve pairing [14–16]. These efforts have led to new developments in identity-based cryptography. In 2016, the State Cryptography Administration of China released identity-based cryptography SM9 using the elliptic curve pairing. In 2018, SM9-IBS became the ISO/IEC international standard, but so far, there is no hierarchical extension of SM9-IBS itself to the best of our knowledge.

Horwitz [17] proposed a two-level identity-based hierarchical signature algorithm that took the first step in the hierarchical signature. Later, Gentry and Silverberg [10] proposed a fully scalable hierarchical cryptography in the same year. In 2004, Chow et al. [11] constructed an identity-based hierarchical signature algorithm that is selective identity security under the random oracle model.

Then Yuen and Wei [18] proposed a scheme with a constant signature length but relied on the new OrcYW assumption. The solution proposed by Wu and Zhang [19] in 2011 solved the problem of excessive public parameter length but the verification phase requires four bilinear pairing operations.

1.2 Our Contribution

Symmetric bilinear pairings are used in many extension schemes, while SM9-IBS uses asymmetric bilinear pairing, so construction and proving are challenging. This paper proposes a secure SM9-IBS hierarchical identities extension and presents its implementation for the first time.

Our main contribution is as follows:

1. We propose the first hierarchical scheme compatible with SM9-IBS using an asymmetric bilinear pairing structural algorithm. The advantages of our scheme are as follows:
   a) It reduces the workload of a single KGC;
   b) When the lower-level KGCs are corrupted, it will not affect the higher-level KGCs, which enhances the reliability of the system;
   c) It get a step to promote the promotion of SM9-IBS;
2. We provide the security proof of our scheme and SM9-IBS as an integral element of our work since extension schemes require the security of the SM9-IBS.
3. We implement our scheme and analysis its performance, which shows the scheme is efficient and practical.

1.3 Organization

We organized our paper as follows: Sect. 2 introduces definitions and background information. Section 3 describes our scheme in detail. Section 4 analyzes the correctness and security of the scheme. Section 5 shows the implementation and performance of our scheme with java. Section 6 concludes the paper.

2 Preliminaries

Hierarchical identity usually consists of four efficiently algorithms: **Setup, Extraction, Signing** and **Verification**. The specific description is shown in Sect. 2.2. In the hierarchical structure, all the nodes (consists of the root KGC, lower-level KGCs, and users) form a $lev-$level tree structure where the root KGC is at the 0th level.

2.1 Definitions

We provide certain definitions in this part that are similar to those provided in [20, 21].

ID-Tuple: A vector indicates the user's position in the hierarchical structure, represented by $(ID_1, ID_2, ..., ID_m), 1 \leq m \leq lev$. The top level in the hierarchical structure is the root node, and the lower-level nodes are represented by ID-tuples$(ID_1, ID_2, ..., ID_i) : 1 \leq i \leq m$.

Setup: System initialization is divided into the root KGC's initialization and lower-level KGCs' initialization. The root KGC chooses a security parameter and returns the root KGC's secret as the master private key and the system public parameter *params*. *params* are public, and the root KGC only holds the master private key. The lower-level KGCs' initialization can only be started after obtaining the public parameters from the root KGC. In our scheme, the lower-level KGCs do not need to generate their own unique public parameters but still need to generate the current KGC's secret and the auxiliary information Q which is needed in the verification phase, so in essence, it is an IBS which is hierarchical only in structure, but it can lighten the single KGC's workload.

Extraction: A single KGC with $(ID_1, ID_2, ..., ID_m)$ uses its public parameters and master private key to generate signature private key for its child nodes with $(ID_1, ID_2, ..., ID_{m+1})$.

Signing: The signer uses the public parameter *params*, his private key ds, and the message $M \in \mathcal{M}$ to output the signature $S \in \mathcal{S}$ of the message M.

Verification: The verifier uses *params*, the signer's ID-tuple, $M \in \mathcal{M}$, $S \in \mathcal{S}$ and the auxiliary information Q can output "Success" or "Fail".

At the same time, **Signing** and **Verification** also have to satisfy consistency constraints.

Bilinear Pairing [22]: When $\hat{e} : \mathbb{G}_1 \times \mathbb{G}_2 \rightarrow \mathbb{G}_T$ (where $\mathbb{G}_1, \mathbb{G}_2$ is the additive cyclic group of order p (large prime number), $\mathbb{G}_T$ is the multiplicative cyclic group of order p) satisfies the following three properties, then it is said $\hat{e}$ is bilinear pairing:

1. Bilinearity: $\forall (P_1, P_2) \in \mathbb{G}_1 \times \mathbb{G}_2, \forall a, b \in \mathbb{Z}, \hat{e}(aP_1, bP_2) = \hat{e}(P_1, P_2)^{ab}$.
2. Non-degeneracy: $\forall P_1 \in \mathbb{G}_1, \hat{e}(P_1, P_2) = 1$ for all $P_2 \in \mathbb{G}_2$ if and only if $P_1 = \mathcal{O}$.
3. Computability: there exists efficient algorithms to calculate $\hat{e}(P_1, P_2)$, for $\forall (P_1, P_2) \in \mathbb{G}_1 \times \mathbb{G}_2$.

2.2   The SM9-IBS

Our scheme is based on the SM9-IBS, so we give some explanations on the SM9-IBS techniques.

In the **Key Generation** phase, the key generation center (KGC) will generate two types of keys: the master key pair and private key of each user.

Notation: P_1, P_2 are generators of respectively $\mathbb{G}_1$ and $\mathbb{G}_2$.

Key Generation

Participate: KGC

Input: ID_A (to generate its private key)

Output: P_{pub-s} and ds_{ID} (send user ID's private key through the secure channel)

Key Generation:

    1. Generate the master private key: a random number $s \in [1, p-1]$; compute master public key $P_{pub-s} = sP_2$ in $\mathbb{G}_2$. Keep s as secret and make P_{pub-s} public;

    ID_A is the identification of user A can be used to generate private key ds_A for signature.

    2. Compute $t_1 = H_1(ID_A, p) + s$, $t_2 = s \cdot t_1^{-1} \bmod q$ then computes $ds_A = t_2 P_1$;

    3. Send ds_A to user A through the secure channel.

In the **Signing** stage, M is the message waiting for signature, signer A uses his private key to obtain the digital signature (h, S).

Signing

Participate: Signer A

Input: Message M, A's private key ds_A and master public key P_{pub-s}

Output: Signature pair (h, S)

Signing:

    1. Compute $g = \hat{e}(P_1, P_{pub-s})$ of the group $\mathbb{G}_T$;

    2. Choose a random $r \in [1, p-1]$;

    3. Compute $\omega = g^r$ of the group $\mathbb{G}_T$;

    4. Compute $h = H_2(M \| \omega, p)$;

    5. Compute $l = (r - h) \bmod p$, if $l = 0$ then return to 2;

    6. Compute $S = l \cdot ds_A$ of the group $\mathbb{G}_1$;

    7. Output signature pair (h, S).

In the **Verification** phase, M' and (h', S') will be verified in this stage.

Verification

Participate: Verifier B

Input: Received message M', its digital signature (h', S'), ID of signer and master public key P_{pub-s}

Output: Success/Fail

Verification:

    1. Compute $g = \hat{e}(P_1, P_{pub-s})$ of the group $\mathbb{G}_T$;

    2. Compute $t = g^{h'}$ of the group $\mathbb{G}_T$;

    3. Compute $h_1 = H_1(ID_A, p)$;

    4. Compute $P = h_1 P_2 + P_{pub-s}$ of the group $\mathbb{G}_2$;

    5. Compute $u = \hat{e}(S', P)$ of the group $\mathbb{G}_T$;

    6. Compute $\omega' = u \cdot t$ of the group $\mathbb{G}_T$;

7. Compute $h_2 = H_2(M'||\omega', p)$;
8. Output Success iff $h_2 = h'$, otherwise output Fail.

2.3   q-Strong Diffie-Hellman Problem

Definition 1. *Giving bilinear map groups* $(\mathbb{G}_1, \mathbb{G}_2, \mathbb{G}_T)$ *and generators* $P_1 \in \mathbb{G}_1, P_2 \in \mathbb{G}_2$. *In groups* $(\mathbb{G}_1, \mathbb{G}_2)$, *the q-Strong Diffie-Hellman problem(q-SDHP) is finding a pair* $(c, \frac{1}{c+\alpha}P_2)$, *where* $c \in Z_p^*$ *(p is a large prime number), by given a* $(q + 2)$*-tuple* $(P_1, P_2, \alpha P_2, \alpha^2 P_2, ..., \alpha^q P_2)$ *as input.*

3   Our Scheme

After introducing preliminaries, based on the SM9-IBS, this section proposes a secure and feasible identity-based signature method.

3.1   Notation

In our scheme, all nodes (including the root KGC, low-level KGCs, users, etc.) form a $lev-$level tree structure, where the root KGC is at level 0. Considering time and space efficiency, the value of lev should not be too large (no more than 10), consistent with our actual management situation. The schematic diagram of the node structure is shown in Fig. 1. An ID vector represents the identity of the user. For example, the identity of the m-th level user is represented by the vector $(I_1, I_2, ..., I_m)$, and the identity of the user's ancestor nodes (except the root KGC) can be represented as $(I_1, I_2, ..., I_i), 1 \leq i \leq m$. The i-th level KGCs generate the signature private key and the auxiliary information using in the verification for the $i + 1$-th level KGCs or the users, where $0 \leq i \leq lev - 2$; users in the i-th level use the signature private key to sign message M where $1 \leq i \leq lev - 1$; any user can verify the signature of the i-th users with the auxiliary information, where $1 \leq i \leq lev - 1$.

Since our scheme is based on the SM9-IBS, it has the same public parameters as the SM9-IBS. Let the finite field $F_N(N>3$ and N is a prime) be the base field of the elliptic curve; a, b are the parameters of the elliptic curve equation; let p be the prime factor of the curve $E(F_N)$ and cf be the cofactor relative to p; let k be the curve $E(F_N)$ embedding times relative to p; let P_1 be the generator of the p-th order cyclic subgroup $\mathbb{G}_1$ of $E(F_{N^{d_1}})$ (d_1 divides k), and let P_2 be the generator of the p-th order cyclic subgroup $\mathbb{G}_2$ of $E(F_{N^{d_2}})$ (d_2 divides k); $\mathbb{G}_T$ is the p-th order cyclic group of the finite field $F_{N^k}^*$, the range of the bilinear pairing $\hat{e}$ is $\mathbb{G}_T$; $H_i(Z, n), i = 1, 2$ is a cryptographic function given in SM9 (GM/T 0044.2-2016), the input is a bit string Z and an integer n, and the output is an integer $h \in [1, q], q = p - 1$; uP refers to the u times of the element P in the additive groups $\mathbb{G}_1$ and $\mathbb{G}_2$. The security parameter is λ, where p is a large prime number and $p > 2^\lambda$.

Level 0

Level 1

Level 2

Level 3

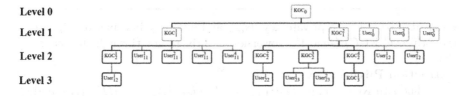

Note: The solid line represents KGC→KGC, the i-th level KGCs generate the signature private key for the i+1 level KGCs or the user; the dotted line represents KGC→User, the users in charge of the 0-th level KGCs are at first level, and the users in charge of the first level KGCs are at 2-th level. The user's participation is optional, which improves the scalability of the SM9-IBS.

Fig. 1. The schematic diagram of the node structure.

3.2 Construction

This section describes our scheme in detail. Our scheme is divided into four phases: **Setup**, **Extraction Pitch-in**, **Signing Pitch-in** and **Verification Pitch-in**, which are introduced below.

After selecting the security parameter λ, the root KGC selects the additive cyclic group $\mathbb{G}_1, \mathbb{G}_2$, the multiplicative cyclic group $\mathbb{G}_T$, and the bilinear pairing $\hat{e}(\cdot, \cdot)$. KGCs do the **Setup**.

Setup

Participate: Root KGC and lower-level KGCs

Input: Security parameter λ

Output: Master public key Q_0

Setup:

1. The root KGC chooses random $s_0 \in [1, p-1]$ and maintain as the master private key for the system;

2. The root KGC computes $Q_0 = s_0 P_2$ of $\mathbb{G}_2$ and then publics Q_0 as the master public key.

3. The i-th $(1 \leq i \leq lev - 2)$ KGC chooses random $s_i \in [1, N-1]$ and keep secret as the master private key of the i-th level.

In the **Extraction Pitch-in** phase, the i-th$(0 \leq i \leq lev - 2)$ level KGCs generate signature private key and auxiliary information required in verification for the $i+1$-th level KGCs or the users, including the following steps, the process is shown in Fig. 4.

Extraction Pitch-in

Participate: Root KGC and lower-level KGCs

Input: Master private key of the i-th level s_i, the i-th level's private key ds_i and ID-vector $(ID_1||ID_2|| \cdots ||ID_{i+1})$ (for the i-th level KGC)

Output: Lower-level's private key ds_{i+1} and auxiliary information Q_i (for the i-th level KGC) (send the lower-level's private key through the secure channel)

Extraction Pitch-in:

1. The i-th KGC computes $H_{1\_i+1} = H_1(ID_1||ID_2||\cdots||ID_{i+1}, p)$, and $t_{i+1} = H_{1\_i+1} + s_i$ and then:

   1) When $i = 0$, computes $ds_1 = \frac{s_0}{t_{i+1}}P_1$ as the signature private key of the first level KGCs or the users;

   2) When $i \geq 1$, computes $ds_{i+1} = \frac{1}{t_{i+1}}ds_i$ as the signature private key of the $i+1$-th level KGCs or the users;

2. The i-th ($i \geq 1$) KGC computes the auxiliary information required for **Verification**. The auxiliary information is a series of elements in $\mathbb{G}_2$. Expand $\prod_{j=0}^{i} t_{j+1}$ into 2^{i+1} terms and add them together. For each term, multiply the containing product of the master private keys. Denote the auxiliary information as

$$
\begin{aligned}
Q_i &= s_i \cdot Q_{i-1}||Q_{i-1}||s_i P_2 \\
&= ([ks_0]P_2, ..., [ks_i]P_2, [ks_0 ks_1]P_2, ..., [ks_0 ks_i]P_2, ..., \qquad (1) \\
&\quad [ks_0 ks_1 ks_2]P_2, ..., [ks_0 ks_1 ks_i]P_2, ..., [ks_0 ks_1 \cdot ... \cdot ks_i]P_2)
\end{aligned}
$$

3. Send ds_i to i-th level's KGCs or users through the secure channel and public Q_i.

Remark. Q_i is generated by the KGC of each layer, a trusted third party, so the verifier can trust Q_i. Q_i will be made public after it is generated at the current level, making it necessary for the verifier at the users' level can use Q_i for verification.

In the **Signing Pitch-in** phase, the i-th ($1 \leq i \leq lev - 1$) level user signs the message M, including the following steps, the process is shown in Fig. 3.

Signing Pitch-in

Participate: Signer A (The i-th level KGC or the user)

Input: Message M, A's private key ds_i and master public key Q_0

Output: Signature pair (h, S)

Signing Pitch-in:

1. Compute $g = \hat{e}(P_1, Q_0)$ of the group $\mathbb{G}_T$;
2. Choose a random $r \in [1, p-1]$;
3. Compute $\omega = g^r$ of the group $\mathbb{G}_T$;
4. Compute $h = H_2(M||\omega, p)$;
5. Compute $l = (r - h) \mod p$, if $l = 0$ then return to 2;
6. Compute $S = l \cdot ds_i$ of the group $\mathbb{G}_1$;
7. Output signature pair(h, S).

In the **Verification Pitch-in** phase, the i-th ($1 \leq i \leq lev - 1$) level user checks the received message M' and its signature (h', S'), including the following steps, the process is shown in Fig. 2.

Verification Pitch-in

Participate: Verifier B (the i-th level KGC or user)

Input: Received Message M', its digital signature (h', S'), auxiliary information Q_i of the signer, ID-vector $(ID_1||ID_2|| \cdots ||ID_i)$ of the signer and master public key Q_0

Output: Success/Fail

Verification Pitch-in:

1. Compute $g = \hat{e}(P_1, Q_0)$ of the group $\mathbb{G}_T$;
2. Compute $\nu = g^{h'}$ of the group $\mathbb{G}_T$;
3. Compute $P = \prod_{j=0}^{i} t_{j+1} \cdot P_2$ of the group $\mathbb{G}_2$ with the auxiliary information Q_i and the ID information $H_{1 \cdot j}(1 \leq j \leq i)$;
4. Compute $u = \hat{e}(S', P)$ of the group $\mathbb{G}_T$;
5. Compute $\omega' = u \cdot \nu$ of the group $\mathbb{G}_T$;
6. Compute $h_2 = H_2(M'||\omega', p)$;
7. Output Success iff $h_2 = h'$, otherwise output Fail.

---

4   Analysis

This section analyzes our scheme, which is divided into two parts: correctness analysis and security analysis.

4.1   Correctness

For any valid signature generated by our scheme, it satisfies:

$$S = l \cdot ds_i = \frac{l \cdot s_0}{\prod_{j=0}^{i} t_{j+1}} P_1 \tag{2}$$

in the verification phase, take S' in u if $S' = S$:

$$u = \hat{e}(S', P) = \hat{e}(\frac{l \cdot s_0}{\prod_{j=0}^{i} t_{j+1}} P_1, \prod_{j=0}^{i} t_{j+1} \cdot P_2) = \hat{e}(l \cdot P_1, Q_0) == g^l \tag{3}$$

and $\omega' = \nu \cdot u = g^{l+h} = g^r$; then put it into $h_2 = H_2(M'||\omega', p)$, finally $h_2 = h$.

4.2   Security Results

We analyzes our scheme's security. Firstly, define the security of the hierarchical signature, and then we prove its security theoretically. In the proof, we also prove the SM9-IBS, which is an essential part of our security proof.

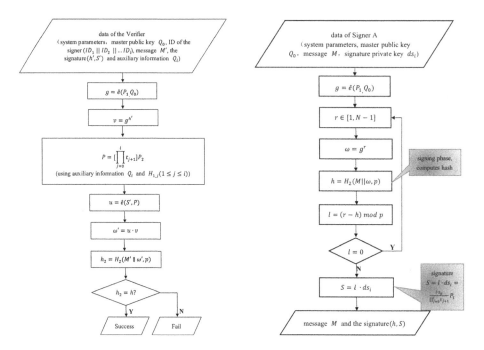

Fig. 2. Verification Pitch-in.   **Fig. 3.** Signing Pitch-in.

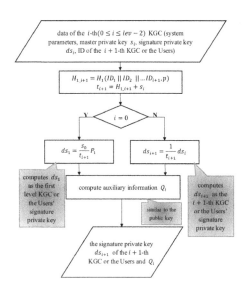

Fig. 4. Extraction Pitch-in.

Definition 2. *(Existentially Unforgeable of Hierarchical Signature.) If no adversary in this game has a non-negligible advantage in probabilistic polynomial time (PPT), under adaptive chosen message and identity attacks, an HIBS scheme is existentially unforgeable.*

1. *The challenger generates the system's parameters using the setup process and delivers them to the adversary.*
2. *The attacker sends a sequence of queries to the oracles listed below:*
   - *Hierarchical key extraction oracle: returns private keys for arbitrary identity tuples.*
   - *Hierarchical signature oracle: produces signature on arbitrary messages using the private key corresponding to arbitrary identity tuples.*
   - *Hierarchical key extraction oracle: private keys for arbitrary identity tuples are returned.*
   - *Hierarchical signature oracle: the private key belonging to arbitrary identity tuples is used to produce signatures on arbitrary messages.*
3. *A triple (ID^*, M^*, θ^*) consisting of an identity ID^*–ID^*'s private key was not extracted in the past time- and a message-signature pair (M^*, θ^*) that was never given to the signature oracle are forged by the adversary. If the triple (ID^*, M^*, θ^*) is accepted by the verification procedure, she wins.*

The scheme's security is established by the following lemmas. Lemma 1 only considers a weaker attack in which a forger is challenged with an attacker-chosen identity. The forking lemma is used to prove Lemma 2. [23,24]. Lemma 3 is based on the security of SM9-IBS, which is proved in Lemma 2 under the q-SDH problem.

Lemma 1. *If a forger $\mathcal{F}_0$ has advantage ϵ_0 to deploy an adaptively chosen message and identity attack on SM9-IBS scheme using time t_0 and querying the random oracle H_1 in q_{h_1} times, then an algorithm $\mathcal{F}_1$ will have advantage $\epsilon_1 \leq \epsilon_0(1 - \frac{1}{2^k})/q_{h_1}$ to deploy an adaptively chosen message and identity attack on our scheme using time $t_1 \leq t_0$. (The number of key extraction queries, signature queries and H_2-queries is same as in $\mathcal{F}_0$.)*

Lemma 2. *Assume that in order to attack SM9-IBS, an adaptively chosen message and given identity adversary $\mathcal{F}$ make a forgery message with probability $\epsilon \geq 10(q_s + 1)(q_s + q_{h_2})/2^\lambda$, querying random oracles $H_i(i = 1, 2)$ q_{h_i} times, querying the signing oracle q_s times, using less than time t. Then, algorithm $\mathcal{B}$ must be existed, which can solve q-SDHP using an probable time $t' \leq (120686q_{h_2}(t + \mathcal{O}(q_s \tau_{paring})))/\epsilon(1 - q/2^\lambda) + \mathcal{O}(q^2 \tau_{sca\_mult})$, using $q = q_{h_1}$, where τ_{paring} is the expense of one pairing evaluation and τ_{sca_mult} is the expense of one scalar multiplication in $\mathbb{G}_2$.*

Proof. Firstly, we simulate the attack environment to provide a consistent view with the adversary, and then use the oracle replay technology to solve the q-SDH problem. Algorithm $\mathcal{B}$ takes as input $(P_1, P_2, \alpha P_2, \alpha^2 P_2, ..., \alpha^q P_2)$ and is on the lookout for a pair $(c, \frac{1}{c+\alpha}P_2)$ with $c \in Z_p^*$.

Initialization: Firstly, $\mathcal{F}$ first outputs a selected identity ID^* and sends it to $\mathcal{B}$ as a given challenge ID^*, where $ID^* \stackrel{R}{\leftarrow} \{0,1\}^*$.

Setup: Construct $G \in \mathbb{G}_1$ and prepare $(\omega_i, \frac{\alpha}{\omega_i+\alpha}G)$ of $q-1$ pairs to answer the private key query, where $\omega_1, \omega_2, ..., \omega_{q-1} \in Z_p^*$.

1. choose random $\omega_1, \omega_2, ..., \omega_{q-1} \leftarrow Z_p^*$ and expand the polynomial $f(z) = \prod_{i=1}^{q-1}(z+\omega_i)$, satisfying $f(z) = \sum_{i=0}^{q-1} c_i z^i$ in order to get $c_0, c_2, ..., c_{q-1} \in Z_p^*$;
2. define a generator $H = \sum_{i=0}^{q-1} c_i(\alpha^i P_2) = f(\alpha)P_2 \in \mathbb{G}_2$ and a generator $G = \psi(H) = f(\alpha)P_1 \in \mathbb{G}_1$; define a element $H_{pub} \in \mathbb{G}_2$ as master public key, $H_{pub} = \sum_{i=1}^{q} c_{i-1}(\alpha^i P_2)$, which satisfied $H_{pub} = \alpha H$ ($\mathcal{B}$ does not know α);
3. for any i ($i \in [1, q-1]$), the polynomial $f_i(z) = \frac{f(z)}{z+\omega_i} = \sum_{i=0}^{q-2} d_i z^i$ was expanded by $\mathcal{B}$ to obtain $\sum_{i=0}^{q-2} d_i\psi(\alpha^i P_2) = f_i(\alpha)P_1 = \frac{f(\alpha)}{\alpha+\omega_i}P_1 = \frac{1}{\alpha+\omega_i}G$;
4. compute $\frac{\omega_i}{\alpha+\omega_i}G$, then find its inverse $-\frac{\omega_i}{\alpha+\omega_i}G$, and finally $\frac{\alpha}{\alpha+\omega_i}G = G - \frac{\omega_i}{\alpha+\omega_i}G$. $\mathcal{B}$ has already obtained $q-1$ pairs of $(\omega_i, \frac{\alpha}{\omega_i+\alpha}G)$ through 3 and 4 steps.

After the **Setup**, $\mathcal{B}$ can answer subsequent inquiries. Before inquiring, $\mathcal{B}$ initializes a counter $l = 1$.

Attack:

– For the queries about an identity $ID \in \{0,1\}^*$ to H_1:

$$\mathcal{B}(\lambda) = \begin{cases} \omega^* \stackrel{R}{\leftarrow} Z_p^*, & if\ ID = ID^* \\ \omega = \omega_l \in Z_p^*, & otherwise \end{cases}$$

$\mathcal{B}$ reserves (ID, ω) in the list, named L_1 in the above two cases.
– For the queries about key extraction when $ID \neq ID^*$: $\mathcal{B}$ finds the answer to (ID, ω) pair, which reserving in L_1 so she can send the corresponding answer $\frac{\alpha}{\omega+\alpha}G$.
– For the queries about signature corresponding to the message-identity pair (M, ID): to computes $r = \hat{e}(S, Q_{ID})\hat{e}(G, H_{pub})^h$, $\mathcal{B}$ needs to randomly choose $S \stackrel{R}{\leftarrow} \mathbb{G}_1$, $h \stackrel{R}{\leftarrow} Z_p^*$ and compute $Q_{ID} = H_1(ID)H + H_{pub}$. To maintain the consistence, $\mathcal{B}$ defines $H_2(M, r) = h$, where $h \in Z_p^*$. If $H_2(M, r)$ has already be defined, then $\mathcal{B}$ aborts.

Forgery: $\mathcal{F}$ outputs $< M^*, r^*, h^*, S^* >$ as the forge signature of ID^*.

After completing the simulation, use the oracle replay technology (on the basis of the forking lemma) to solve the q-SDH problem. We construct an F' of input (H_{pub}, ID^*) and recall $\mathcal{F}$ to obtain 2 sets of forgeries formed as $< M^*, r, h_a, S_a >, < M^*, r, h_b, S_b >$, satisfying $h_a \neq h_b$. After getting 2 sets of forgeries, $\mathcal{B}$ can be recovered (ID^*, ω^*) as it reserved in L_1, where $Pr[\omega^* \neq \omega_1, \omega_2, ..., \omega_{q-1}] \geq 1 - q/2^\lambda$. If both forgeries can get into signature verification, then we can get:

$$\hat{e}(S_a, Q_{ID^*})\hat{e}(G, H_{pub})^{h_a} = \hat{e}(S_b, Q_{ID^*})\hat{e}(G, H_{pub})^{h_b} \tag{4}$$

where Q_{ID^*} can be computed as $Q_{ID^*} = H_1(ID^*)H + H_{pub}$ and $Q_{ID^*} = (\omega^* + \alpha)H$. So there is that $\hat{e}((h_b - h_a)^{-1}(S_a - S_b), H) = \hat{e}(\frac{\alpha}{\omega^*+\alpha}G, H)$ and hence $(h_b - h_a)^{-1}(S_a - S_b) = \frac{\alpha}{\omega^*+\alpha}G$, invert both sides of the equation, add G and multiply $1/\omega^*$ to get the equation

$$T^* = \frac{1}{\omega^*}(G - (h_2 - h_1)^{-1}(S_1 - S_2)) = \frac{1}{\omega^* + \alpha}G \tag{5}$$

$\mathcal{B}$ extracts $\sigma^* = \frac{1}{\omega^*+\alpha}P_1$ [16]: then $\mathcal{B}$ gets $\gamma_{-1}, \gamma_0, ..., \gamma_{q-2} \in Z_p^*$ in $\frac{f(z)}{z+\omega^*} = \frac{\gamma_{-1}}{z+\omega^*} + \sum_{i=0}^{q-2} \gamma_i z^i$. Then it comes to $\sigma^* = \frac{1}{\gamma_{-1}}[T^* - \sum_{i=0}^{q-2} \gamma_i \psi(\alpha^i P_2)] = \frac{1}{\omega^*+\alpha}P_1$. $\mathcal{B}$ returns (ω^*, θ^*) as result. So far, Lemma 2 is proved.

Lemma 3. *Assume that in order to attack our hierarchical scheme, an adaptively chosen message and given identity adversary $\mathcal{A}$ make a forgery message with probability ϵ_A, querying random oracles $H_i(i = 1, 2)$ q_{h_i} times, querying the signing oracle q_s times, using less than time t_A. Then, adversary $\mathcal{F}$ must be existed, which is able to produce a produce a forgery of SM9-IBS with probability $\epsilon \geq \epsilon_A \cdot (1 - \frac{1}{h_{image}})^{u-1}(1 - \frac{1}{p})^{u-1}$ where h_{image} is the number of images in the hash function H_1, $h_{image} = p - 1$, p is the order of the group $\mathbb{G}_1, \mathbb{G}_2$, u is the maximum level of the adversary choosing, $u \in [1, lev]$, using an probable time $t = t_A + \mathcal{O}(\tau_{sca\_mult})$, where τ_{sca_mult} is the expense of one scalar multiplication in $\mathbb{G}_2$.*

Proof. Assuming that there exists an adversary $\mathcal{A}$ with the advantage of ϵ_A attacking our hierarchical scheme, at this time, an adversary $\mathcal{F}$ can be constructed to attack the SM9-IBS.

Initialization: Firstly, $\mathcal{A}$ outputs a selected identity $ID^* = (I_1^*, I_2^*, ..., I_u^*)$ of level $u \in [1, lev]$ and sends it to $\mathcal{F}$ as a given challenge ID^*, where $I_m^* \xleftarrow{R} \{0,1\}^*$, $m \in [1, u]$.

Setup: $\mathcal{F}$ sends I_1^* in the given ID^* to the above-mentioned adversary $\mathcal{B}$ to activate it, and then $\mathcal{B}$ performs the **Setup** phase in Lemma 2 and generate the group generator G,H and the master public key H_{pub}, sending to $\mathcal{F}$ as a public parameter, and then $\mathcal{F}$ sends it to $\mathcal{A}$.

Attack: In this stage, $\mathcal{A}$ can query for private key of q_E times, signature of q_S times, H_1 of q_{H_1} times, and H_2 of q_{H_2} times. The simulation of each phase is as follows:

-For the queries about key extraction when identity $ID \neq ID^*$ and ID is not the prefix of ID^*: when receiving $ID = (I_1, I_2, ..., I_u)$ where $u \in [1, lev]$, $\mathcal{F}$ records and stores the received ID in the list L_2 maintained by $\mathcal{F}$;

Case 1: Look up the first column ID of the list L_2. If I_1 does not appear in the first column of ID, $\mathcal{F}$ sends I_1 to adversary $\mathcal{B}$ then $\mathcal{B}$ computes the root signature private key ds_0 corresponding to I_1 and sends it to $\mathcal{F}$, then $\mathcal{F}$ chooses random $\omega_2, \omega_3, ..., \omega_u \xleftarrow{R} Z_p^*$ (as the answer to the query $H_1(I_1||I_2), H_1(I_1||I_2||I_3), ..., H_1(I_1||I_2||...||I_u))$ and random $\alpha_1, \alpha_2, ..., \alpha_{u-1} \xleftarrow{R} Z_p^*$ (as an answer to the query $s_1, s_2, ..., s_{u-1}$) and stores in the I_m, $m \in [1, u]$ of the list L_2. $\mathcal{F}$ computes $t_2 = \omega_2 + \alpha_1, t_3 = \omega_3 + \alpha_2, ..., t_u = \omega_u + \alpha_{u-1}$, then the private key is $ds_u = \frac{1}{\prod_{n=2}^u t_n} ds_0$ as $\mathcal{A}'$s reply.

Case 2: Look up the first column ID of the list L_2. If I_1 appears in the first column of ID, use I_2 to look up the second column ID of the list L_2 until I_k, $k \in [2, u]$ is in the k-th column of the list L_2 which does not appear so far. At this time, it means that the private key of $(I_1, I_2, .., I_{k-1})$ has already been computed as ds_{k-1}, so $\mathcal{F}$ chooses random $\omega_k, \omega_{k+1}, ..., \omega_u \xleftarrow{R} Z_p^*$ and random $\alpha_{k-1}, \alpha_k, ..., \alpha_{u-1} \xleftarrow{R} Z_p^*$ then stores in the corresponding position in the list L_2. $\mathcal{F}$ computes $t_k = \omega_k + \alpha_{k-1}, t_{k+1} = \omega_{k+1} + \alpha_k, ..., t_u = \omega_u + \alpha_{u-1}$, if $t_n = 0, n \in [k, u]$, then choose random α_{n-1} again, otherwise the private key is $ds_u = \frac{1}{\prod_{n=k}^{u} t_n} ds_{k-1}$ as $\mathcal{A}'$s reply.

- H_1 queries on an identity $ID = (I_1, I_2, ..., I_u)$: When receiving $ID = (I_1, I_2, ..., I_u)$, where $u \in [1, lev]$, finding the ω corresponding to ID from the list L_2 as the answer to maintain consistency.
- For the queries about signature corresponding to the message-identity pair (M, ID): when receiving (M, ID), sign it by the previously generated private key and get S, choose $h \xleftarrow{R} Z_p^*$ as the answer of H_2, and use the α array corresponding to ID in the list L_2 to generate the Q array, if the corresponding element is not found, it will be generated according to the steps of the private key query, and finally obtain (h, S) and Q as $\mathcal{A}'$s reply.

Forgery: $\mathcal{A}$ outputs a forgery (h^*, S^*) on ID^*. If (h^*, S^*) is a valid signature, then $\mathcal{A}$ sends it to $\mathcal{F}$.

If $\mathcal{A}$ has already asked $H_1(I_1^* \| I_2^*), H_1(I_1^* \| I_2^* \| I_3^*), ..., H_1(I_1^* \| I_2^* \| ... \| I_u^*)$ and the private key of $(I_1, I_2^*, ..., I_u^*)$, where $I_1 \neq I_1^*$, there would be records corresponding of ω and α in the list L_2, so that $T^* = (H_1(I_1^* \| I_2^*) + ks_1) \cdot (H_1(I_1^* \| I_2^* \| I_3^*) + ks_2) \cdot ... \cdot (H_1(I_1^* \| I_2^* \| ... \| I_u^*) + ks_{u-1})$, then $\mathcal{F}$ can forge SM9's signature $S_{SM9}^* = S^* \cdot T^*$, and $\mathcal{F}$ succeeds. Suppose $\mathcal{A}$ asked $H_1(I_1^* \| I_2^*), H_1(I_1^* \| I_2^* \| I_3^*), ..., H_1(I_1^* \| I_2^* \| ... \| I_u^*)$ and asked about the ID form of $(I_1, I_2^*, ..., I_u^*), (I_1' , I_2', I_3', ..., I_u'), ..., (I_1'', I_2'', ..., I_u^*)$'s private key where $I_1, I_1', ..., I_1'' \neq I_1^*$ is the event P_A, then $Pr[P_A] \geq (1 - \frac{1}{h_{image}})^{u-1}(1 - \frac{1}{p}^{u-1})$, and we can get $Pr[\mathcal{F}$ succeeds$] \geq \epsilon_A \cdot (1 - \frac{1}{h_{image}})^{u-1}(1 - \frac{1}{p})^{u-1}$, which is a non-negligible probability. So far, Lemma 3 is proved.

Combining the three lemmas, comes to Theorem 1.

Theorem 1. *Assume that in order to attack our hierarchical scheme, an adaptively chosen message and given identity adversary $\mathcal{A}$ make a forgery message with probability ϵ_A, querying random oracles $H_i(i = 1, 2)$ q_{h_i} times, querying the signing oracle q_s times, using less than time t_A. Then, algorithm $\mathcal{B}$ must be existed, which can solve q-SDHP using an probable time $t' \leq (120686q_{h_2}(t_A + \mathcal{O}(\tau_{sca\_mult}) + \mathcal{O}(q_s\tau_{paring})))/\epsilon(1 - q/2^\lambda) + \mathcal{O}(q^2\tau_{sca\_mult})$, using $q = q_{h_1}$, where τ_{paring} is the expense of one pairing evaluation and τ_{sca_mult} is the expense of one scalar multiplication in $\mathbb{G}_2$.*

According to Theorem 1, our scheme is security under the q-SDH problem.

5 Efficiency Discussions

This section briefly summarizes the implementation and efficiency of the system. The complete process of our scheme includes master public key and master private key generation function (genSignMasterKeyPair), user signature private key generation function (genSignPrivateKey), signature generation function (sign) and verification function (verify).

We implement the code of our scheme on a PC with Intel(R) Core(TM) i7-5600U CPU @ 2.60 GHz and 8G memory. The curve and groups used are the same as the sample in the SM9-IBS standard algorithm (See Appendix B for specific parameters). Efficiency is shown in Table 1.

The 0th-level KGC performance is the SM9-IBS time of the three algorithms. Each level thereafter showing the time after the upper level transmits the relevant information to the node, so the time is the incremental time relied on the SM9-IBS. Therefore, it is showed in the table that the root level requires the longest time of all types.

According to the results, it can be seen that our scheme does not lead to additional performance burden based on the SM9 algorithm less in 10 levels which can satisfy the above scenes like large enterprises or private groups.

Moreover, we compare our scheme performance with SM9-IBS, showed in Table 2. Using average times of each layers, our scheme is more efficient than a single KGC which uses SM9-IBS itself.

Table 1. Efficiency results.

Platform	The i-th KGC	Phase	Times (ms)
Windows + Eclipse2020	0 (SM9-IBS)	Next-level user private key generation	97
		Next-level user signing	2007
		Verification	1813
	1	Next-level user private key generation	16
		Next-level user signing	954
		Verification	1411
	2	Next-level user private key generation	10
		Next-level user signing	770
		Verification	1207
	3	Next-level user private key generation	8
		Next-level user signing	855
		Verification	1671

Note: The message length for signature and verification is 24 bytes, and the structure is 5 layers in total.

Table 2. Performance comparison With SM9.

	SM9-IBS times (ms)	Our scheme times (ms)
(Next-level) user private key generation	97	11.3
(Next-level) user signing	2007	859.7
Verification	1813	1429.7

6   Conclusion

We propose a secure SM9-IBS hierarchical identities extension, promoting the promotion of SM9 cryptography. At the same time, we proved our scheme's security together with SM9-IBS itself as an essential part of our work. Although the signature in our scheme does not increase with levels, the auxiliary information still grows with levels, so it is not suitable for the case where the levels are too high. Fortunately, in the real world, 10-levels are enough (e.g., the number of branches of the banking system (from the head office to the subordinate branches) generally does not exceed ten levels). Our scheme can be used in the authentication to the applications of large enterprises, and obviously, it can also be used for applications such as cloud storage, especially in the scenes where the key escrow is required.

Acknowledgements. This work is supported by National Key R&D Program of China (2017YFB0802500), Beijing Municipal Science and Technology Project (No. Z191100007119007) and Shandong province major science and technology innovation project (2019JZZY020129).

References

1. Aruna, J., Ashwani, D.: Improved identity based digital signature authentication using Feistel algorithm in cloud computing. In: Satapathy, S.C., Bhateja, V., Raju, K.S., Janakiramaiah, B. (eds.) Computer Communication, Networking and Internet Security. LNNS, vol. 5, pp. 347–354. Springer, Singapore (2017). https://doi.org/10.1007/978-981-10-3226-4_35
2. Shamir, A.: Identity-based cryptosystems and signature schemes. In: Blakley, G.R., Chaum, D. (eds.) CRYPTO 1984. LNCS, vol. 196, pp. 47–53. Springer, Heidelberg (1985). https://doi.org/10.1007/3-540-39568-7_5
3. Wang, J., Yu, J., Li, D., Bai, X., Jia, Z.: Combining user authentication with role-based authorazition based on identity-based signature. In: Wang, Y., Cheung, Y., Liu, H. (eds.) CIS 2006. LNCS (LNAI), vol. 4456, pp. 847–857. Springer, Heidelberg (2007). https://doi.org/10.1007/978-3-540-74377-4_89
4. H. Liao, D. Wang, J. Wang, L. Li, H. Wang, Research and application of sm9 in the ubiquitous electric iot, in: IEEE 5th Information Technology and Mechatronics Engineering Conference (ITOEC). IEEE **2020**, 1764–1768 (2020)
5. Park, S., Lee, K., Lee, D.H.: New constructions of revocable identity-based encryption from multilinear maps. IEEE Trans. Inf. Forensics Secur. **10**(8), 1564–1577 (2015)

6. Ma, X.-T., Ma, W.-P., Liu, X.-X.: A cross domain authentication scheme based on blockchain technology. ACTA ELECTONICA SINICA **46**(11), 2571 (2018)

7. Xuan, J., Wang, D., Li, Z., Zhang, S.: Design of secure and independent controllable email system based on identity-based cryptography. In: 2016 2nd IEEE International Conference on Computer and Communications (ICCC), pp. 217–222. IEEE (2016)

8. Ya-Tao, Y., Ju-Liang, C., Xiao-Wei, Z., et al.: Privacy preserving scheme in block chain with provably secure based on SM9 algorithm. J. Softw. **30**(6), 1692–1704 (2019)

9. Mu, Y., Xu, H., Li, P., Ma, T.: Secure two-party SM9 signing, Science China. Inf. Sci. **63**(8), 1–3 (2020)

10. Gentry, C.: Practical identity-based encryption without random oracles. In: Vaudenay, S. (ed.) EUROCRYPT 2006. LNCS, vol. 4004, pp. 445–464. Springer, Heidelberg (2006). https://doi.org/10.1007/11761679_27

11. Chow, S.S.M., Yiu, S.M., Hui, L.C.K., Chow, K.P.: Efficient forward and provably secure ID-based signcryption scheme with public verifiability and public ciphertext authenticity. In: Lim, J.-I., Lee, D.-H. (eds.) ICISC 2003. LNCS, vol. 2971, pp. 352–369. Springer, Heidelberg (2004). https://doi.org/10.1007/978-3-540-24691-6_26

12. Boneh, D., Franklin, M.: Identity-based encryption from the Weil pairing. In: Kilian, J. (ed.) CRYPTO 2001. LNCS, vol. 2139, pp. 213–229. Springer, Heidelberg (2001). https://doi.org/10.1007/3-540-44647-8_13

13. Sakai, R., Ohgishi, K., Kasahara, M.: Cryptosystems based on pairing, SCIS 2000–c20, Jan, Okinawa, Japan (2000)

14. Boneh, D., Boyen, X.: Short signatures without random oracles. In: Cachin, C., Camenisch, J.L. (eds.) EUROCRYPT 2004. LNCS, vol. 3027, pp. 56–73. Springer, Heidelberg (2004). https://doi.org/10.1007/978-3-540-24676-3_4

15. Boneh, D., Boyen, X.: Efficient selective-ID secure identity-based encryption without random oracles. In: Cachin, C., Camenisch, J.L. (eds.) EUROCRYPT 2004. LNCS, vol. 3027, pp. 223–238. Springer, Heidelberg (2004). https://doi.org/10.1007/978-3-540-24676-3_14

16. Boneh, D., Boyen, X.: Secure identity based encryption without random oracles. In: Franklin, M. (ed.) CRYPTO 2004. LNCS, vol. 3152, pp. 443–459. Springer, Heidelberg (2004). https://doi.org/10.1007/978-3-540-28628-8_27

17. Horwitz, J., Lynn, B.: Toward Hierarchical Identity-Based Encryption. In: Knudsen, L.R. (ed.) EUROCRYPT 2002. LNCS, vol. 2332, pp. 466–481. Springer, Heidelberg (2002). https://doi.org/10.1007/3-540-46035-7_31

18. Chow, S.S.M., Yuen, T.H., Hui, L.C.K., Yiu, S.M.: Signcryption in hierarchical identity based cryptosystem. In: Sasaki, R., Qing, S., Okamoto, E., Yoshiura, H. (eds.) SEC 2005. IAICT, vol. 181, pp. 443–457. Springer, Boston, MA (2005). https://doi.org/10.1007/0-387-25660-1_29

19. Wu, Q., Zhang, L.: Hierarchical identity-based signature with short public keys. In: Wang, G., Ray, I., Feng, D., Rajarajan, M. (eds.) CSS 2013. LNCS, vol. 8300, pp. 272–281. Springer, Cham (2013). https://doi.org/10.1007/978-3-319-03584-0_20

20. Gentry, C., Silverberg, A.: Hierarchical ID-based cryptography. In: Zheng, Y. (ed.) ASIACRYPT 2002. LNCS, vol. 2501, pp. 548–566. Springer, Heidelberg (2002). https://doi.org/10.1007/3-540-36178-2_34

21. Lim, H.W., Paterson, K.G.: Multi-key hierarchical identity-based signatures. In: Galbraith, S.D. (ed.) Cryptography and Coding 2007. LNCS, vol. 4887, pp. 384–402. Springer, Heidelberg (2007). https://doi.org/10.1007/978-3-540-77272-9_23

22. Barreto, P.S.L.M., Libert, B., McCullagh, N., Quisquater, J.-J.: Efficient and provably-secure identity-based signatures and signcryption from bilinear maps. In: Roy, B. (ed.) ASIACRYPT 2005. LNCS, vol. 3788, pp. 515–532. Springer, Heidelberg (2005). https://doi.org/10.1007/11593447_28
23. Pointcheval, D., Stern, J.: Security proofs for signature schemes. In: Maurer, U. (ed.) EUROCRYPT 1996. LNCS, vol. 1070, pp. 387–398. Springer, Heidelberg (1996). https://doi.org/10.1007/3-540-68339-9_33
24. Pointcheval, D., Stern, J.: Security arguments for digital signatures and blind signatures. J. Cryptol. **13**(3), 361–396 (2000)

Verifiable DOPE from Somewhat Homomorphic Encryption, and the Extension to DOT

Amirreza Hamidi$^{(\boxtimes)}$ and Hossein Ghodosi

James Cook University, Townsville, Australia
amirreza.hamidi@my.jcu.edu.au, hossein.ghodosi@jcu.edu.au

Abstract. Distributed oblivious polynomial evaluation (DOPE) is a special case of two-party computation where a sender party holds a polynomial $f(x)$ of degree t and a receiver party has an input x_2. They communicate with a set of distributed cloud servers to implement a secure computation such that the receiver party obtains $f(x_2)$, while the privacy of their inputs is preserved.

We present a verifiable and private DOPE protocol using additive homomorphic encryption in the presence of k distributed servers where k does not depend on the degree t. The sender is involved in the offline phase which can be implemented at any time well in advance of the actual online computation phase. Our protocol holds the unconditional security against a malicious sender in the offline phase and a static active adversary corrupting a coalition of at most $k-1$ dishonest servers in the online computation phase with negligible probability of error. In addition, it preserves strong privacy conditions for a DOPE system. The communication complexity is determined by the term kt which improves the DOPE approaches of [18] and [5]. Also, the proposed protocol can be extended to a protocol of secure $\binom{1}{2}$ distributed oblivious transfer with the linear communication complexity $O(k)$ where the same setting of security is achieved.

Keywords: Distributed oblivious polynomial evaluation · Homomorphic encryption · Distributed oblivious transfer · Message authentication codes

1 Introduction

Secure two-party computation is a setting of multi-party computation where two parties with their private inputs want to execute a function computation while the privacy of their inputs is preserved. In detail, parties P_1 and P_2, holding the inputs x and y, jointly compute some function such that the outputs for P_1 and P_2 are $f_1(x,y)$ and $f_2(x,y)$, respectively. This functionality is denoted by $(x,y) \rightarrow (f_1(x,y), f_2(x,y))$. Oblivious polynomial evaluation (OPE) is a special case of two-party computation where P_1 holds a polynomial $f(x)$ and P_2 has

© The Author(s), under exclusive license to Springer Nature Switzerland AG 2022
C. Su et al. (Eds.): SciSec 2022, LNCS 13580, pp. 105–120, 2022.
https://doi.org/10.1007/978-3-031-17551-0_7

a value x_2. They wish to perform a secure computation such that P_2 learns $f(x_2)$ and P_1 gains nothing which can be denoted by the functionality $(f(x), x_2) \rightarrow (\perp, f(x_2))$. In this system, an adversary either aims to learn information about the private inputs, called passive (semi-honest) adversary, or, in addition to that, he deviates from the protocol impacting the integrity of the computation in an arbitrary fashion, named active (malicious) adversary. Thus, a protocol must hold security properties dealing with these adversaries which are correctness and privacy. Correctness implies that the protocol computes the correct output at the end of the process. Privacy ensures private computation meaning that no information about the inputs of honest parties is leaked to the adversary. Moreover, an adversary may have limited computational power and time, known as the computationally-bounded adversary which is more practical in the real world, or it can be with unlimited time and power of computation, defined as the computationally unbounded adversary. Thus, we now can have a better definition of a OPE protocol:

Definition 1. *In a secure OPE protocol in the field $\mathbb{F}_q$ (where q is a prime number), a sender party P_1, holding the polynomial $f(x)$, wants to perform a secure computation algorithm with a receiver party P_2, who has the value x_2. The protocol ensures that P_2 learns $f(x_2)$ and P_1 gets nothing, while the privacy of the parties is achieved, i.e., P_1 gains no information relating to the value x_2 and P_2 does not obtain any information about $f(x)$ except the output $f(x_2)$.*

The recent development of cloud computing has enabled fast outsourced computation where a number of different servers can be employed to present more secure and efficient protocols [16]. An important application of this functionality is distributed oblivious polynomial evaluation (DOPE) where the two parties utilize a set of n distributed servers such that k servers suffice to implement the DOPE computation. Here the advantage is that P_1 and P_2 just communicate with the servers, i.e., they do not interact directly with each other [18]. This makes it possible that the two parties can be anonymous to each other resulting more flexible availability and better security for both parties. However, a challenge arises as the privacy of their inputs and the correctness of outcome need to be preserved.

1.1 Background

OPE was first introduced by Naor and Pinkas [21]. They employed oblivious transfer to present an OPE protocol where the polynomial f and the value x_2 are masked by random bivariate and univariate polynomials, respectively. OPE is the computation core of many cryptographic models and has been used in other fields such as oblivious neural networking [4], oblivious keyword search [10], oblivious transfer [23], privacy preserving data mining [20], set intersection [11], two-party RSA key generation [13] and private support vector machine [26].

In the literature, the privacy properties of the OPE protocols are either information-theoretic (unconditional) or computational (semantic). Some studies have utilized homomorphic feature of encryption systems to present their semantically secure OPE protocols. [12] employed additive (Paillier encryption) and multiplicative (ElGamal cryptosystem) homomorphic encryption methods (i.e., fully homomorphic encryption) to propose their OPE protocols for the multivariate case. A simulation-based secure protocol (in ideal/real paradigm) with this technique was studied by [15]. [10] proposed two OPE protocols for keyword search problem using homomorphic encryption and pseudorandom functions. Furthermore, some studies employed intermediate servers, as one or more trusted third parties. An information-theoretic secure OPE protocol with a trusted third party was studied by [14]. [17] conducted a study to minimize the communication of a computationally-private information retrieval protocol using a single database for the datasets with large length. Recently, [12] presented a verifiable and private OPE protocol, by employing homomorphic feature of Paillier encryption and a trusted server, to record medical datasets. A serious downside of the OPE protocols with just a single trusted third party is that corrupting only one server (the third party) causes a central point of failure that breaks the whole security of the protocols.

The protocols with a set of distributed servers (i.e., $k \geq 2$) offer higher security since an adversary must corrupt more than one server to break the privacy or forge the output. However, the security is achieved with a higher cost of communication overhead. [18] proposed an unconditionally secure DOPE protocol using a set of k distributed servers such that P_1 and P_2 distribute the shares of their inputs, $f(x)$ and x_2, among the servers with the polynomials of degrees $t - 1$ and $l - 1$, respectively. However, the privacy of the inputs is not preserved against the maximum required number of $k - 1$ servers, i.e., $k \geq t + l$, and increasing the security threshold of P_1 would decrease the security threshold of P_2 and vice versa. To deal with this problem, they introduced some publicly known information that increases the communication overhead. As a result, their protocol does not seem to be suitable and efficient for a system with large datasets. Recently, another unconditionally secure DOPE protocol was given by [5] which holds privacy for the inputs of $P_1(P_2)$ against a passive adversary corrupting a coalition of $k - 1$ servers and $P_2(P_1)$. However, their protocol requires P_1 to communicate directly with P_2. Besides, their protocol does not maintain the privacy of the receiver's input in the actual computation phase. The communication complexity of their protocol is determined by the factor $2kt$ for private interactions, where k is the number of servers and t is the degree of the sender's polynomial, which can be improved.

1.2   Our Contribution

We aim to present a secure DOPE protocol using additive homomorphic feature of Paillier encryption and secret sharing in the presence of n distributed servers where k number out of them can be chosen to perform the computation. An advantage of our protocol is that, unlike the protocol of [5], the sender and the receiver parties do not communicate directly, i.e. they can be anonymous to each other. This interesting feature would enable the protocol to have an offline phase well in advance of the actual online computation while the privacy of the sender's input is preserved. Thus, the receiver essentially must not be available in the offline phase giving a more flexible system. Our protocol holds unconditional security against a static active adversary corrupting P_1 in the offline phase and at most $k-1$ dishonest servers in the online computation phase using message authentication codes (MAC). The adversary tries to deviate from the protocol and forge the output of P_2. However, we assume P_2 is not corrupted by the active adversary since he aims to obtain the correct output while he can still remain semi-honest. To the best of the authors' knowledge, this is the first verifiable secure DOPE protocol against a malicious sender and at most $k-1$ servers. Furthermore, it preserves information-theoretic security for the sender's inputs against a passive adversary controlling a coalition of the receiver P_2 and $k-1$ servers before and after executing the protocol. This gives a security improvement on the DOPE protocol of [18] as their protocol is not privately secure against the maximum $k-1$ servers. The secure outsourced computation of the homomorphic encryption scheme is performed by the servers in parallel. Our protocol has the communication complexity with the factor kt where t is the degree of the sender's polynomial. This improves the communication overhead of [5] where it is determined by the term $2kt$.

In addition, the proposed protocol can be extended to a system of secure $\binom{1}{2}$ distributed oblivious transfer with the same security setting and the linear communication complexity $O(k)$ which is discussed after presenting the main DOPE protocol.

2 Preliminaries

2.1 Model

We propose a secure DOPE protocol where the sender party P_1, with the polynomial $f(x)$ of degree t, and the receiver party P_2, holding a value x_2, aim to perform a secure computation in the presence of a threshold number of k cloud servers (security parameter) such that P_2 computes $f(x_2)$ while the correctness and the strong privacy of the inputs are preserved. The idea is that the sender's polynomial along with its corresponding MACs are distributed among the servers using secret sharing over the integers. The MAC keys α_i are generated by the servers and used to verify the distributed shares in the offline phase, and a global MAC key (which is the additive secret of the keys α_i) authenticates the output to P_2. Any malicious behaviour can be detected by having P_2 verify the output using the corresponding MAC value received from the servers. Moreover, the outsourced computation technique enables fast computation of the large values over the field. Please note that in order to preserve the privacy of the sender's polynomial, the protocol with a fixed polynomial can only be implemented up to $k-1$ times.

This system can also be extended to secure DOT_1^2 as well, where P_1 holds two inputs, m_0 and m_1, and P_2 has $\sigma \in \{0,1\}$. Using the extended protocol, P_2 learns m_σ while the same security condition is met. We utilize Paillier public key system to encrypt the P_2's input as this cryptosystem is the most suitable additive homomorphic encryption scheme for large datasets [15].

2.2   Shamir's Secret Sharing

In this scheme, a secret value s is distributed among n participants using a random polynomial $p(x) = \sum_{j=0}^{t} a_j x^j \bmod q$, where $a_0 = s$, such that each party is given a share $p_i \leftarrow p(i)$ [25]. We employ this scheme over the integers where the computation is performed over a prime number q $(q > n)$, i.e., in the field Z_q. A set of at least $t+1$ parties, where $t+1 \leq n$, pools their shares and reconstructs the secret with no interaction using Lagrange interpolation.

Clearly, this scheme is information-theoretically private against a passive adversary corrupting up to t participants which implies it is a $(t+1, n)$ $(t+1$-out-of $n)$ private secret sharing scheme. We denote the t-sharings $[s]_t$ as a set of $t+1$ shares of a random polynomial with the threshold/degree t and the secret s. This method is linear and the participants can reconstruct any linear function with no interaction.

2.3   The Paillier Cryptosystem

This scheme is a trapdoor discrete logarithmic encryption system introduced by [24] as a quadratic residousity cryptosystem, and we discuss it in this section.

Key Generation: A probabilistic key generation algorithm $\mathsf{Gen}(1^k)$, with the security parameter k, is invoked to generate a pair of the keys $(pk, sk) \leftarrow \mathsf{Gen}(1^k)$. Let the public key be an RSA modulus $pk \leftarrow N$ with k bits where $N = pq$. The easiest way is to choose p and q two $k/2$-bit large prime numbers. The private key sk is the Euler's totient $sk \leftarrow \phi(N)$ where $\phi(N) = (p-1)(q-1)$ and $\gcd(N, \phi(N)) = 1$.

Encryption: To encrypt a plaintext $m \in Z_N$, the ciphertext $c \leftarrow \mathsf{Enc}_{pk}(m, r)$ is computed as follows:

$$\mathsf{Enc}_{pk}(m, r) = g^m r^N \bmod N^2$$

where g is an element in $Z_{N^2}^*$ and a non-zero multiple of N that is usually considered as $g = N + 1$, and r is a random number chosen in Z_N^*. Hence, the encryption algorithm has a probabilistic functionality.

Decryption: To invoke a deterministic decryption algorithm, one raises the ciphertext c to the private key $\phi(N)$. Based on Euler's theorem of the totient function, the random number $r^{N\phi(N)} \bmod N^2$ disappears because $\phi(N^2) = N\phi(N)$. Thus, we will have:

$$((N+1)^m r^N)^{\phi(N)} \bmod N^2 = N \cdot \phi(N) \cdot m + 1$$

since the property $(N+1)^x \bmod N^2 = Nx + 1$ can be proven by means of binomial coefficients for any positive integer x. Let the function $L(x)$ be defined as $L(x) = \frac{x-1}{N}$, the plaintext $m \leftarrow \mathsf{Dec}_{sk}(c)$ can be computed as:

$$\mathsf{Dec}_{sk}(c) = L(c^{\phi(N)} \bmod N^2) \cdot \phi(N)^{-1} \bmod N$$

This system is semantically secure, based on the decisional composite residuosity assumption (DCRA) [24]. It states that for any probabilistic polynomial time algorithm, an encrypted value is computationally indistinguishable from random values over the domain.

Definition 2. *Let two values x_0 and x_1 be encrypted under a public key with k bits. Assume that an adversary $\mathcal{A}$ is given an encryption of x_β for a random $\beta \in \{0, 1\}$. Let $p_0(\mathcal{A}, k)$ and $p_1(\mathcal{A}, k)$ be the probabilities that $\mathcal{A}$ can guess x_0 and x_1, respectively. The public key encryption scheme is semantically secure, if for any probabilistic polynomial time $\mathcal{A}$, $|p_0(\mathcal{A}, k) - p_1(\mathcal{A}, k)| \leq \varepsilon$ where ε is negligible in k.*

According to this definition, given two ciphertexts $\mathsf{Enc}_{\mathsf{pk}}(x_0, r_0)$ and $\mathsf{Enc}_{\mathsf{pk}}(x_1, r_1)$ using the Paillier's public key system, a probabilistic polynomial time algorithm can guess either of the plaintexts with any negligible advantage [7].

Homomorphic Property. This cryptosystem has the additively homomorphic feature where $\mathsf{Enc}(m_1) \times \mathsf{Enc}(m_2) = \mathsf{Enc}(m_1 + m_2)$ and $\mathsf{Enc}(m_1)^d = \mathsf{Enc}(dm_1)$ for any value d in Z_N. In detail, let m_1 and m_2 be two plaintexts, the homomorphic property of Paillier encryption is as follows:

$$\mathsf{Enc}_{\mathsf{pk}}(m_1, r_1) \times \mathsf{Enc}_{\mathsf{pk}}(m_2, r_2) \bmod N^2 = \mathsf{Enc}_{\mathsf{pk}}(m_1 + m_2 \bmod N, r_1 r_2 \bmod N)$$

$$\mathsf{Enc}_{\mathsf{pk}}(m_1, r)^{m_2} \bmod N^2 = \mathsf{Enc}_{\mathsf{pk}}(m_1 m_2 \bmod N, r^{m_2} \bmod N)$$

This feature ensures that given ciphertexts c_i of the plaintexts m_i (for $i = 1, \ldots, n$), the summation of the plaintexts $m = \sum_{i=1}^{n} m_i$ can be obtained without revealing any information about the values of m_i.

2.4　Message Authentication Code

The message authentication code (MAC) is an efficient method to protect secret shares from being manipulated by an active adversary and to verify the output. Due to the efficiency, this technique has been employed in MPC systems to detect any cheating in case of malicious behaviour, see e.g. [1,8,9].

The system has a random key α_i and the authentication code for any value m with the key α_i is represented as $\mathrm{MAC}(m) = \alpha_i \cdot m \bmod p$ in Z_p. We denote $\mathrm{MAC}(m)$ by $\gamma(m)$. Assume a party P_i, holding an input m, wants to send the input to the party P_j. In order to prove the authentication of m, P_i computes $\gamma(m)$ with the key α_i and sends the values m and $\gamma(m)$ to P_j who accepts m iff $\gamma(m) = \alpha_i \cdot m$, otherwise he outputs *fail* and aborts the protocol. We use a global key α which is the additive secret of the random keys α_i, and the MAC values $\alpha \cdot a_m$ of the polynomial $f(x) = \sum_{m=0}^{t} a_m x^m$ is secret-shared among the servers. The servers perform the computation and the output $f(x_2)$ is authenticated iff $\alpha \cdot f(x_2) = \gamma(f(x_2))$. This scheme is linear and the probability of cheating without being detected is equivalent to obtaining the global key α, i.e., $\varepsilon = 1/q$.

2.5   Security

In this section, we discuss ideal/real security models and the strong security requirements for DOPE protocols. It is assumed that there exists a simulator S in the ideal model who takes inputs from the participants and implements the functionality $\mathcal{F}$, denoted by $IDEAL_{\mathcal{F},S}$ such that the parties do not communicate with each other. Hence, this model doesn't have any type of adversary and it achieves the highest level of security. The view of this model is denoted by $VIEW_S$. On the other hand, a protocol Π is executed in the presence of a probabilistic polynomial-time adversary $\mathcal{A}$ in the real model $REAL_{\Pi,\mathcal{A}}$. The view of the coalition controlled by the adversary is denoted by $VIEW_{\mathcal{A}}$. Based on the simulation-based security model, the protocol Π is implemented securely iff $IDEAL_{\mathcal{F},S}$ and $REAL_{\Pi,\mathcal{A}}$ are computationally indistinguishable [19].

Suppose that P_1, with the polynomial $f(x)$, and P_2, holding a value x_2, aim to communicate with at least k distributed cloud servers to run a secure DOPE protocol. According to [2] and [18], the protocol must satisfy the following conditions to hold the strong security:

- **Correctness:** After implementation of the protocol, P_2 receives $f(x_2)$, while P_1 and a maximum number of the distributed servers obtain nothing. Here, an active adversary might attack the system to manipulate the outcome computed by P_2. Thus, the system must be secure against a malicious adversary corrupting a coalition of at most $k-1$ dishonest servers in the computation phase. Note that P_2 normally does not deviate from the protocol since he intends to obtain the correct output; however, he still remains semi-honest.
- **Receiver's Privacy:** Here, the adversary $\mathcal{A}$ corrupts a coalition of up to $k-1$ servers and P_1. The protocol must not leak any information about the P_2's input x_2 to $VIEW_{\mathcal{A}}$.
- **Sender's Privacy:** $\mathcal{A}$ controls a coalition of the maximum $k-1$ servers and P_2. **Before** and **after** running the online computation phase, $VIEW_{\mathcal{A}}$ must learn nothing about the polynomial $f(x)$ except what it can get from the outcome $f(x_2)$. Note that the protocol with the same sender must only be executed up to $k-1$ times since $\mathcal{A}$ can interpolate the sender's polynomial using k different shares.

3   Our Protocol

The proposed DOPE protocol is discussed in this section. The protocol consists of two different phases: *setup* and *computation*. The sender party P_1 interacts with the servers in the offline setup phase, whereas the receiver party P_2 communicates with the servers in the actual online computation phase. Each phase has the verifiable stage that authenticates the inputs and the output using the MACs, and the protocol *fails* in the case of detecting any malicious behaviour. It is assumed that the private communication channels are secure and synchronous.

3.1   Setup Phase

This phase is offline which can be executed at anytime before running the actual online computation phase. This property enhances the security and the flexibility (since P_2 is not available) of the system. In addition, each server checks the authentication of the given shares using the MAC scheme.

Assume P_1 wishes to distribute the polynomial $f(x)$ of degree t in the field Z_q among a set S of k distributed servers. Figure 1 shows the offline setup phase of the protocol Π_{DOPE}.

Inputs: P_1 has the polynomial $f(x) = a_0 + a_1 x + \ldots + a_t x^t$, where $a_m \in Z_q$ for $m = 0, 1, \ldots, t$.

- Each server $S_i \in S$ (for $i = 1, \ldots, k$) generates a MAC key $\alpha_i \in Z_q$ uniformly random. It sends the global key share α_i to P_1.

- P_1 generates $t + 1$ random polynomials of the degree $k - 1$ with the constant terms $a_0, a_1, \ldots, a_t$ and computes the shares $[a_m]_{k-1}$ over the integers. He performs the same process with the MAC values $\gamma_m \leftarrow \alpha \cdot a_m$, where $\alpha = \sum_{i=1}^{k} \alpha_i$, and computes the shares $[\gamma_m]_{k-1}$ over the integers. He gives the tuples $\langle a_{mi} \rangle$ to each server $S_i \in S$, which is defined as:

$$\{\forall S_i \in S, \ 0 \leq m \leq t : \quad \langle a_{mi} \rangle \leftarrow ([a_m]_{k-1}, \gamma_i([a_m]_{k-1}), [\gamma_m]_{k-1})\}$$

- P_1 leaves the protocol and takes no step further.

Verification

- Each S_i checks for the share $[a_m]_{k-1}$ that $\gamma_i([a_m]_{k-1}) = \alpha_i \cdot [a_m]_{k-1}$. It accepts the share iff OK, otherwise broadcasts $fail$ and aborts the protocol.

Fig. 1. The setup phase of the protocol Π_{DOPE}

The communication complexity of this phase is $O(kt)$ where the number of servers k can be selected as the security parameter. Note that the number of servers k does not depend on the degree t of the sender's polynomial.

3.2   Computation Phase

In this online phase, P_2 firstly encrypts his inputs and broadcasts the ciphertexts. Each server computes an encrypted share of the output using homomorphic encryption. It repeats the same process with the shares of the MACs to obtain the corresponding encrypted share of the MAC value. P_2 calculates the output and checks whether the final outcome satisfies the verification stage using the MACs he receives from the servers. Here, a static adversary, corrupting at most $k - 1$ servers, can forge the output without being detected with the small probability of error $\varepsilon = 1/q$. Based on [2], the strong security conditions of DOT and DOPE protocols can be acquired with at least two communication rounds between the servers and P_2. Figure 2 illustrates the online computation phase of the protocol Π_{DOPE}. In order to maintain the sender's privacy, the receivers are allowed to implement this phase only up to $k - 1$ times.

Note that since the inputs, $f(x)$ and x_2, and the output $f(x_2)$ are over the field of a prime number Z_q while the public key encryption and the homomorphic feature are computed in the field Z_N, we must determine the relation between these two fields. Therefore, in order to have the protocol work properly, it is required that $N = p_c q_c > q$; otherwise, P_2 would calculate $f(x_2) \ mod \ N$ not $f(x_2) \ mod \ q$. More precisely, because each term $x_2^m \cdot a_m$ is in modulo q^2, N must hold the condition $N > (t + 1)q^2$. It is recommended to choose two large values for the size of the prime numbers p_c and q_c, e.g., each at least 1024 bits.

It should be stated that the computation of the new encrypted shares and their corresponding MACs can be implemented by the servers in parallel which reduces the computation time of the protocol. The communication complexity is determined by the factor kt which gives an improvement of the DOPE protocols of [18] and [5].

4   Security Evaluation

In this section, we evaluate the protocol Π_{DOPE}, based on the security conditions described in Sect. 2.4.

Theorem 1. *The protocol Π_{DOPE} is unconditionally secure against a static active adversary $\mathcal{A}$ corrupting P_1 in the offline phase and a coalition of at most $k - 1$ dishonest servers in the online computation phase.*

Proof. Let C and H represent corrupted and honest parties/servers, respectively. In the ideal model, the simulator sends a list of $P_1, S_i \in C$ to the functionality. The simulator picks random values for the shares $[a'_m]_{k-1}$ in the offline phase simulating the errors $[a'_m]_{k-1} = [a_m]_{k-1} + \delta_{mi}$ by $\mathcal{A}$ in the real model. The errors can be detected using the corresponding MACs with the negligible probability of error $1/q$. In the online computation phase, the simulator sends random values c''_i and $c''(\gamma_{f_i})$ which is equivalent to introducing the errors $c''_i = c'_i + \delta_i$ and $c''(\gamma_{f_i}) = c'(\gamma_{f_i}) + \delta_{\gamma_{f_i}}$ by $\mathcal{A}$ to the real model. The simulator runs the functionality and sends the output $f'(x_2)$ to P_2 where $f'(x_2) = f(x_2) + \delta$. Similarly, the simulator calculates the global MAC key $\alpha' = \alpha + \delta_\alpha$ which can be considered as the MAC key cheated by $\mathcal{A}$ in the real model. Any inconsistency between the output and the MAC value $\gamma'(f(x_2))$ is detected with the probability $1 - 1/q$ in the verification stage, i.e., there is just one value for α' which results $\gamma'(f(x_2)) - \alpha' \cdot f'(x_2) = 0$.

If $P_1, S_i \in H$, the simulator receives their inputs and runs the protocol. It computes the encrypted shares c'_i which can be written as:

$$c'_i = \mathsf{Enc}_{\mathsf{pk}}((\sum_{m=0}^{t} x_2^m \cdot [a_m]_{k-1}) \times l_{0,i} \ mod \ N)$$

Input: P_2 has the value $x_2 \in Z_q$.
Output: P_2 learns $f(x_2)$.

- P_2 invokes the key generation algorithm $\mathsf{Gen}(1^k)$, described in section 2.3, to generate a pair of encryption keys (pk, sk) where $pk \leftarrow N$, $sk \leftarrow \phi(N)$ and $N = p_c q_c$. He encrypts the values x_2^m, for $m = 0, 1, \ldots, t$, to obtain the ciphertexts:

$$c_m \leftarrow \mathsf{Enc}_{\mathsf{pk}}(x_2^m)$$

  and broadcasts the respective ciphertexts c_m.

- Each $S_i \in S$ computes a new encrypted share:

$$c_i' = \left(\prod_{m=0}^{t} c_m^{[a_m]_{k-1}}\right)^{l_{0,i}} \ mod \ N^2$$

  where $l_{0,i}$ is the Lagrange coefficient of S_i as:

$$l_{0,i} = \prod_{\substack{j \in S \\ j \neq i}} \frac{-j}{i-j}$$

- Similarly, each S_i computes the encrypted share of the MAC value using another round of homomorphic encryption as follows:

$$c_i'(\gamma_{f_i}) = \left(\prod_{m=0}^{t} c_m^{[\gamma_m]_{k-1}}\right)^{l_{0,i}} \ mod \ N^2$$

  and it assigns them to the tuple $\langle C_i' \rangle \leftarrow (c_i', c_i'(\gamma_{f_i}), \alpha_i)$. It privately sends $\langle C_i' \rangle$ to P_2.

- P_2 obtains the output using the encrypted shares c_i' of the servers as:

$$c' = \prod_{i=1}^{k} c_i' \ mod \ N^2$$

$$f(x_2) \leftarrow \mathsf{Dec}_{\mathsf{sk}}(c')$$

Verification

- P_2 calculates the global MAC key $\alpha = \sum_{i=1}^{k} \alpha_i$.

- P_2 computes the MAC value of the output as follows:

$$c'(\gamma_f) = \prod_{i=1}^{k} c_i'(\gamma_{f_i}) \ mod \ N^2$$

$$\gamma(f(x_2)) \leftarrow \mathsf{Dec}_{\mathsf{sk}}(c'(\gamma_f))$$

- P_2 checks that

$$\gamma(f(x_2)) - \alpha \cdot f(x_2) = 0$$

  and he accepts $f(x_2)$ iff *OK*. Otherwise, he broadcasts *fail* and outputs $\perp$.

Fig. 2. The computation phase of the protocol Π_{DOPE}

The simulator employs another round of homomorphic encryption to compute the new encrypted value c' as:

$$c' = \mathsf{Enc_{pk}}(\sum_{i=1}^{k}([a_0]_{k-1} + x_2[a_1]_{k-1} + x_2^2[a_2]_{k-1} + \ldots + x_2^t[a_t]_{k-1}) \times l_{0,i} \bmod N)$$

$$= \mathsf{Enc_{pk}}(\sum_{i=1}^{k}(\sum_{m=0}^{t} x_2^m \cdot [a_m]_{k-1}) \times l_{0,i} \bmod N)$$

Finally, the simulator invokes the algorithm $\mathsf{Dec_{sk}}(c')$ to decrypt c' and obtains the output $\sum_{m=0}^{t} x_2^m \cdot a_m = f(x_2)$. It then sends the output to P_2 and the verification stage is performed.

We now aim to prove that the privacy of the receiver's input is held against the adversary $\mathcal{A}$. P_2 encrypts the values x_2^m and broadcasts the respective ciphertexts c_m. Furthermore, the security of the homomorphic encryption is determined by the semantic security of the initial Paillier cryptosystem. Thus, $VIEW_{\mathcal{A}}$ cannot distinguish between the input x_2 and random values in the field, and the receiver's privacy is held against the adversary in the real model. Therefore, the ideal and the real models are computationally indistinguishable.

Theorem 2. *A passive adversary $\mathcal{A}$, corrupting a coalition of $k-1$ servers and the receiver P_2, cannot gain any information about the polynomial $f(x)$ before and after executing the online computation phase of the protocol Π_{DOPE}.*

Proof. P_1 distributes the coefficients $a_0, a_1, \ldots, a_t$ among the k servers in the offline phase with random polynomials of degree $k-1$ such that each S_i receives $t+1$ shares. Without loss of generality, assume that the adversary $\mathcal{A}$ corrupts a coalition of $k-1$ servers $S_1, \ldots, S_{k-1}$ and the receiver P_2. Each S_i computes the encrypted share c_i' in the online computation phase as:

$$c_i' \leftarrow \mathsf{Enc_{pk}}((\sum_{m=0}^{t} x_2^m \cdot [a_m]_{k-1}) \times l_{0,i} \bmod N)$$

Since $VIEW_{\mathcal{A}}$ holds the private encryption key, it can decrypt c_i' to obtain the plaintext. Without loss of generality, let f_i be the respective plaintext which can be shown as:

$$f_i \leftarrow (\sum_{m=0}^{t} x_2^m \cdot [a_m]_{k-1}) \times l_{0,i} \tag{1}$$

where, based on information-theoretic security of the secret sharing method and since f_k (the decrypted share of S_k) has more than one unknown share, the polynomial $f(x)$ is uniformly random over the field and, thus, $VIEW_{\mathcal{A}}$ can learn no information relating to it.

After implementing the computation phase, $VIEW_{\mathcal{A}}$ calculates the output $f(x_2)$ which can be written as:

$$f(x_2) = f_1 + \ldots + f_k$$
$$= \sum_{i=1}^{k} f_i$$

$VIEW_{\mathcal{A}}$ has the plaintexts $f_1, f_2, \ldots, f_{k-1}$ and the output $f(x_2)$. It also learns the number of $k-1$ shares of each coefficient a_m. Hence, it can calculate f_k by the formula $f_k = f(x_2) - \sum_{i=1}^{k-1} f_i$. However, because the equation of f_k (Eq. 1) has more than one unknown share (i.e., at least for $m = 0, 1$) and due to the linear feature of the secret sharing, $VIEW_{\mathcal{A}}$ can gain no information relating to the shares $[a_m]_{k-1}$ of S_k. Therefore, $VIEW_{\mathcal{A}}$ can learn nothing about the coefficients $a_0, a_1, \ldots, a_t$ of the polynomial, and the sender's privacy is preserved.

5   Extension to DOT

Distributed oblivious transfer has been a subject of numerous studies, see e.g., [2,3,6,22]. Our protocol can also be extended to a system of secure $\binom{1}{2}$ distributed oblivious transfer, denoted by DOT_1^2. Basically, this system has a similar functionality to DOPE where P_1 holds two inputs, m_0 and m_1, and P_2 has the choice bit $\sigma \in \{0, 1\}$. They communicate with a set S of k distributed servers. A DOT_1^2 protocol is securely implemented such that P_2 receives m_σ and P_1 gains nothing while the security conditions (i.e., privacy and correctness) are preserved against the adversary [22]. Similar to the DOPE system, our extended DOT_1^2 protocol has two different offline and online phases and it holds the security setting described in Sect. 2.5. This improves the security of the protocol of [22] where the privacy of the parties' inputs is not preserved against coalition of $k - 1$ servers. The homomorphic encryption is employed to perform the private outsourced computation. Figure 3 shows the extension to the protocol $\Pi_{\text{DOT}_1^2}$.

Theorem 3. *The protocol $\Pi_{\text{DOT}_1^2}$ is unconditionally secure against a static active adversary corrupting P_1 in the offline phase and a coalition of $k - 1$ dishonest servers in the online computation phase with the small probability of error. The protocol is also secure against a passive adversary controlling a coalition of $P_2(P_1)$ and $k-1$ servers before and after the implementation of the online computation phase.*

Proof. It is straightforward to verify the correctness of the protocol $\Pi_{\text{DOT}_1^2}$. Let C and H represent the corrupted and honest parties/servers in the ideal model, respectively. If $P_1 \in C$ in the offline phase, the simulator sends the random shares $[m'_\tau]_{k-1}$ to the functionality which simulates the introduced errors δ_τ by the adversary $\mathcal{A}$ in the real model, i.e. $[m'_\tau]_{k-1} = [m_\tau]_{k-1} + \delta_\tau$. The simulator executes the functionality and the inconsistency is detected with the error probability of $1/q$. If $S_i \in C$ in the online computation phase, the simulator

Input: P_1 has the values m_0 and m_1 in Z_q. P_2 holds σ where $\sigma \in \{0,1\}$.
Output: P_2 learns m_σ.

Verifiable offline setup phase:

- Each server $S_i \in S$ (for $i = 1, \ldots, k$) generates a random MAC key $\alpha_i \in Z_q$ and sends it to P_1.

- P_1 generates $k-1$-sharings $[m_0]_{k-1}$, $[m_1]_{k-1}$ over the integers integers. He also calculates $\gamma_0 = \alpha \cdot m_0$ and $\gamma_1 = \alpha \cdot m_1$ where $\alpha = \sum_{i=1}^{k} \alpha_i$, and generates the $k-1$-sharings $[\gamma_0]_{k-1}$ and $[\gamma_1]_{k-1}$ over the integers. He sends the tuples $\langle m_0 \rangle$ and $\langle m_1 \rangle$ to each server S_i where:

$$\{\forall S_i \in S, \ \tau = 0,1 : \quad \langle m_{\tau i} \rangle \leftarrow ([m_\tau]_{k-1}, \gamma_i([m_\tau]_{k-1}), [\gamma_\tau]_{k-1})\}$$

- Each S_i accepts the share $[m_\tau]_{k-1}$ iff $\gamma_i([m_\tau]_{k-1}) = \alpha_i \cdot [m_\tau]_{k-1}$, otherwise broadcasts *fail* and aborts the protocol.

- P_1 leaves the protocol and takes no step further.

Online computation phase:

- P_2 generates two $k/2$-bit large prime numbers p_c and q_c to calculate a pair of the keys (pk, sk) where $N = p_c q_c$. He computes the ciphertext $c_0 \leftarrow \mathsf{Enc}_{pk}(1 - \sigma)$ and $c_1 \leftarrow \mathsf{Enc}_{pk}(\sigma)$ and broadcasts them.

- Each server $S_i \in S$ computes in parallel:

$$c_i' = (c_0^{[m_0]_{k-1}} \cdot c_1^{[m_1]_{k-1}})^{l_{0,i}} \bmod N^2$$

where $l_{0,i}$ is the Larange coefficient of S_i.

- Each S_i employs another round of homomorphic encryption to compute the encrypted share of the corresponding MAC value as:

$$c_i'(\gamma_{m_\sigma}) = (c_0^{[\gamma_0]_{k-1}} \cdot c_1^{[\gamma_1]_{k-1}})^{l_{0,i}} \bmod N^2$$

and it privately sends the tuple $\langle C_i' \rangle$ to P_2 where $\langle C_i' \rangle \leftarrow (c_i', c_i'(\gamma_{m_\sigma}), \alpha_i)$.

- P_2 obtains the output as follows:

$$c' = \prod_{i=1}^{k} c_i' \bmod N^2$$

$$m_\sigma \leftarrow \mathsf{Dec}_{sk}(c')$$

Verification

- P_2 calculates the global MAC key $\alpha = \sum_{i=1}^{k} \alpha_i$.

- P_2 computes the MAC value of the output as:

$$c'(\gamma_{m_\sigma}) = \prod_{i=1}^{k} c_i'(\gamma_{m_\sigma}) \bmod N^2$$

$$\gamma(m_\sigma) \leftarrow \mathsf{Dec}_{sk}(c'(\gamma_{m_\sigma}))$$

- P_2 checks

$$\gamma(m_\sigma) - \alpha \cdot m_\sigma = 0$$

and he accepts m_σ iff it is *Ok*. Otherwise, he broadcasts *fail* and outputs $\bot$.

Fig. 3. The extension of the protocol Π_{DOPE} to the protocol $\Pi_{\mathrm{DOT}_1^2}$

sends a list of corrupted parties to the functionality. The simulator picks random values c_i'', $c_i''(\gamma_{m_\sigma})$ and α' for their inputs. This is analogous to the condition where $\mathcal{A}$ deviates from the protocol by adding the errors δ_i, $\delta_{\gamma_{m_\sigma}}$ and δ_α in the real model which can be denoted as $c_i'' = c_i' + \delta_i$, $c_i''(\gamma_{m_\sigma}) = c_i'(\gamma_{m_\sigma}) + \delta_{\gamma_{m_\sigma}}$ and $\alpha' = \alpha + \delta_\alpha$. The simulator runs the functionality and sends the output $m_\sigma' = m_\sigma + \delta_\sigma$ to P_2 who is able to detect the any inconsistency between the output and the corresponding MAC value with the probability $1-1/q$ and aborts the protocol. If $P_1, S_i \in H$, the simulator runs the protocol and P_2 receives the new encrypted value $c' \leftarrow \mathsf{Enc_{pk}}((1-\sigma).m_0 + \sigma.m_1 \bmod N)$. Clearly, if $\sigma = 0$ or $\sigma = 1$, P_2 decrypts and receives either m_0 or m_1, respectively.

The privacy condition follows the security evaluation of the main protocol Π_{DOPE}. The protocol preserves the strong security in both the sender's and the receiver's sides and the communication overhead is linear $O(k)$. This gives an improvement on the protocol of [22] where the communication overhead is $O(kd_y)$ in which d_y is the variable degree of a bivariate polynomial with the free term m_σ.

6   Conclusion

DOPE has been the building block of many cryptographic models. In this study, we propose a verifiable and private DOPE protocol, using additive homomorphic encryption feature and secret sharing in the presence of k distributed cloud servers where k does not depend on the degree of sender's polynomial t. Our protocol has two offline and online phases, and the communication complexity is determined by the factor kt which gives an improvement on the previous DOPE protocols of [18] and [5]. The sender party is just involved in the offline phase which means that the receiver must not necessarily be available in the offline phase that is, also, an improvement on the protocol of [5]. Furthermore, the outsourced computations of the homomorphic encryption can be implemented by the servers in parallel which reduces the computation time.

The security is unconditionally preserved against a corrupted sender in the offline phase and a static active adversary corrupting a coalition of at most $k - 1$ dishonest servers in the online computation phase using MAC scheme. To the best of the authors' knowledge, this is the first verifiable secure DOPE protocol which authenticates the correctness of the receiver's output with the small probability of error. Moreover, the privacy is held in environment of the strong security where the privacy of the sender's/receiver's input(s) is preserved against a coalition of $k-1$ servers and the receiver/sender corrupted by a passive adversary. The security of the sender's inputs is information-theoretic before and after running the protocol, while the receiver's input holds semantic security of the encryption system.

Our DOPE protocol can be extended to a secure DOT_1^2 protocol with the linear communication complexity $O(k)$ which is an improvement on the protocol of [22] where the communication overhead is not linear.

References

1. Bendlin, R., Damgård, I., Orlandi, C., Zakarias, S.: Semi-homomorphic encryption and multiparty computation. In: Paterson, K.G. (ed.) EUROCRYPT 2011. LNCS, vol. 6632, pp. 169–188. Springer, Heidelberg (2011). https://doi.org/10.1007/978-3-642-20465-4_11
2. Blundo, C., D'Arco, P., De Santis, A., Stinson, D.: On unconditionally secure distributed oblivious transfer. J. Cryptol. **20**(3), 323–373 (2007)
3. Blundo, C., D'Arco, P., De Santis, A., Stinson, D.R.: New results on unconditionally secure distributed oblivious transfer. In: Nyberg, K., Heys, H. (eds.) SAC 2002. LNCS, vol. 2595, pp. 291–309. Springer, Heidelberg (2003). https://doi.org/10.1007/3-540-36492-7_19
4. Chang, Y.-C., Lu, C.-J.: Oblivious polynomial evaluation and oblivious neural learning. In: Boyd, C. (ed.) ASIACRYPT 2001. LNCS, vol. 2248, pp. 369–384. Springer, Heidelberg (2001). https://doi.org/10.1007/3-540-45682-1_22
5. Cianciullo, L., Ghodosi, H.: Unconditionally secure distributed oblivious polynomial evaluation. In: Lee, K. (ed.) ICISC 2018. LNCS, vol. 11396, pp. 132–142. Springer, Cham (2019). https://doi.org/10.1007/978-3-030-12146-4_9
6. Corniaux, C.L., Ghodosi, H.: A verifiable 1-out-of-n distributed oblivious transfer protocol. IACR Cryptol. ePrint Arch. **2013**, 63 (2013)
7. Damgård, I., Jurik, M.: A generalisation, a simplification and some applications of paillier's probabilistic public-key system. In: Kim, K. (ed.) PKC 2001. LNCS, vol. 1992, pp. 119–136. Springer, Heidelberg (2001). https://doi.org/10.1007/3-540-44586-2_9
8. Damgård, I., Keller, M., Larraia, E., Pastro, V., Scholl, P., Smart, N.P.: Practical covertly secure MPC for dishonest majority – or: breaking the SPDZ limits. In: Crampton, J., Jajodia, S., Mayes, K. (eds.) ESORICS 2013. LNCS, vol. 8134, pp. 1–18. Springer, Heidelberg (2013). https://doi.org/10.1007/978-3-642-40203-6_1
9. Damgård, I., Pastro, V., Smart, N., Zakarias, S.: Multiparty computation from somewhat homomorphic encryption. In: Safavi-Naini, R., Canetti, R. (eds.) CRYPTO 2012. LNCS, vol. 7417, pp. 643–662. Springer, Heidelberg (2012). https://doi.org/10.1007/978-3-642-32009-5_38
10. Freedman, M.J., Ishai, Y., Pinkas, B., Reingold, O.: Keyword Search and Oblivious Pseudorandom Functions. In: Kilian, J. (ed.) TCC 2005. LNCS, vol. 3378, pp. 303–324. Springer, Heidelberg (2005). https://doi.org/10.1007/978-3-540-30576-7_17
11. Freedman, M.J., Nissim, K., Pinkas, B.: Efficient private matching and set intersection. In: Cachin, C., Camenisch, J.L. (eds.) EUROCRYPT 2004. LNCS, vol. 3027, pp. 1–19. Springer, Heidelberg (2004). https://doi.org/10.1007/978-3-540-24676-3_1
12. Gajera, H., Giraud, M., Gérault, D., Das, M.L., Lafourcade, P.: Verifiable and private oblivious polynomial evaluation. In: Laurent, M., Giannetsos, T. (eds.) WISTP 2019. LNCS, vol. 12024, pp. 49–65. Springer, Cham (2020). https://doi.org/10.1007/978-3-030-41702-4_4
13. Gilboa, N.: Two party RSA key generation. In: Wiener, M. (ed.) CRYPTO 1999. LNCS, vol. 1666, pp. 116–129. Springer, Heidelberg (1999). https://doi.org/10.1007/3-540-48405-1_8
14. Hanaoka, G., Imai, H., Mueller-Quade, J., Nascimento, A.C.A., Otsuka, A., Winter, A.: Information theoretically secure oblivious polynomial evaluation: model, bounds, and constructions. In: Wang, H., Pieprzyk, J., Varadharajan, V. (eds.) ACISP 2004. LNCS, vol. 3108, pp. 62–73. Springer, Heidelberg (2004). https://doi.org/10.1007/978-3-540-27800-9_6

15. Hazay, C., Lindell, Y.: Efficient oblivious polynomial evaluation with simulation-based security. IACR Cryptol. ePrint Arch. **2009**, 459 (2009)
16. Kamara, S., Raykova, M.: Parallel homomorphic encryption. In: Adams, A.A., Brenner, M., Smith, M. (eds.) FC 2013. LNCS, vol. 7862, pp. 213–225. Springer, Heidelberg (2013). https://doi.org/10.1007/978-3-642-41320-9_15
17. Kiayias, A., Leonardos, N., Lipmaa, H., Pavlyk, K., Tang, Q.: Optimal rate private information retrieval from homomorphic encryption. Proc. Priv. Enhancing Technol. **2015**(2), 222–243 (2015)
18. Li, H.-D., Yang, X., Feng, D.-G., Li, B.: Distributed oblivious function evaluation and its applications. J. Comput. Sci. Technol. **19**(6), 942–947 (2004). https://doi.org/10.1007/BF02973458
19. Lindell, Y.: How to simulate it-a tutorial on the simulation proof technique. Tutorials on the Foundations of Cryptography pp. 277–346 (2017)
20. Lindell, Y., Pinkas, B.: Privacy preserving data mining. Journal of cryptology 15(3) (2002)
21. Naor, M., Pinkas, B.: Oblivious transfer and polynomial evaluation. In: Proceedings of the thirty-first annual ACM symposium on Theory of computing, pp. 245–254 (1999)
22. Naor, M., Pinkas, B.: Distributed oblivious transfer. In: Okamoto, T. (ed.) ASIACRYPT 2000. LNCS, vol. 1976, pp. 205–219. Springer, Heidelberg (2000). https://doi.org/10.1007/3-540-44448-3_16
23. Naor, M., Pinkas, B.: Efficient oblivious transfer protocols. In: SODA. **1**, 448–457 (2001)
24. Paillier, P.: Public-key cryptosystems based on composite degree residuosity classes. In: Stern, J. (ed.) EUROCRYPT 1999. LNCS, vol. 1592, pp. 223–238. Springer, Heidelberg (1999). https://doi.org/10.1007/3-540-48910-X_16
25. Shamir, A.: How to share a secret. Commun. ACM **22**(11), 612–613 (1979)
26. Tassa, T., Jarrous, A., Ben-Ya'akov, Y.: Oblivious evaluation of multivariate polynomials. J. Math. Cryptology **7**(1), 1–29 (2013)

Scalable M+1st-Price Auction with Infinite Bidding Price

Po-Chu Hsu[1] and Atsuko Miyaji[1,2] (✉)

[1] Osaka University, Suita, Japan
hsu@cy2sec.comm.eng.osaka-u.ac.jp, miyaji@comm.eng.osaka-u.ac.jp
[2] Japan Advanced Institute of Science and Technology, Nomi, Japan

Abstract. $M + 1$st-price auction, also called Vickrey auction, is a type of sealed-bid auction to sell M identical goods. B bidders secretly choose a bid. The top M bidders can buy the goods at the $M+1$st bidding price. In previous research, a trusted manager is commonly used to decide the $M + 1$st bidding price from these sealed ones and the top M bidders. In addition, there's an upper bound to the bidding price. We construct a scheme that removes all trusted parties such as managers and Mix servers in such a way that winning bidders themselves just prove that they are winners. By adopting a compact bit-slice design, the upper bound is removed, and the compact bit-slice design can also reduce the complexity of the number of bidders to sublinear. Our implementation shows that the gas usage reduces by 95% after we use zero-knowledge proof to replace Mix and Match. The overall gas usage is also reduced by 83%. This protocol reached the ultimate goal of decentralized apps (DApps): Decentralized: no TTP or manager is used. Scalable: unlimited bidding price and sublinear complexity to the number of bidders. Robustness, the auction does not necessarily need to restart if there are some malicious bidders at the first time.

Keywords: M+1st-price auction · Sealed-bid auction · Blockchain · Smart contract · Privacy

1 Introduction

$M + 1$st-price auction, also called Vickrey auction, is a type of sealed-bid auction. Bidders submit written bids without knowing other bidders' bids. A simplified version of the Vickery auction is a second-price auction. In a second-price auction, the bidder with the highest bidding price can buy the good at the second-highest bidding price. The $M + 1$st-price auction is used when there are M identical goods or the good can be divided into M equivalent parts. The top M bidders can buy goods by the $M + 1$st-price. All information except the identity of the top M bidders and the $M + 1$st-price should be secret. Table 1 is an example of $M = 2$. The top two bidders B_3 and B_5 can buy the goods by the B_1's bidding price \$400. Except for the boxed information, all other information is secret. These are called bids' secrecy and bidders' anonymity (Fig. 1).

C. Su et al. (Eds.): SciSec 2022, LNCS 13580, pp. 121–136, 2022.
https://doi.org/10.1007/978-3-031-17551-0_8

Table 1. Example of M + 1st-price auction. $M = 2$, $B = 5$

Bidding price	$100	$300	$400	$700	$900
Bidder	B_2	B_4	B_1	B_5	B_3

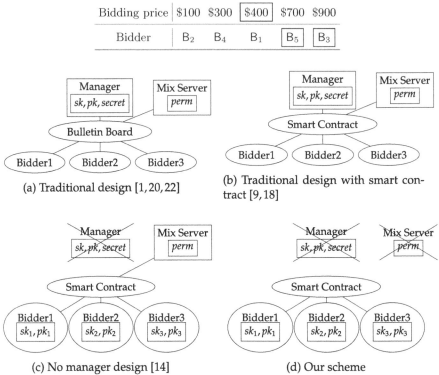

(a) Traditional design [1,20,22]

(b) Traditional design with smart contract [9,18]

(c) No manager design [14]

(d) Our scheme

Fig. 1. Auction schemes evolvement (boxed information are secret)

We focus on three important features: 1. no trusted manager, 2. scalability, 3. public verifiability. A trusted manager is commonly used [1,9,20,22]. However, these managers know all secrets, and it is impossible to prove that a side channel between the manager and a bidder does not exist. i.e., a manager may collude with a bidder. An approach to reduce the power of a trusted manager is to separate a trusted manager into two managers [17,25]. To construct a scheme without a manager, Smart Contract is a very plausible choice. A smart contract is a program running on top of a blockchain. It can be considered as a combination of a bulletin board, a trusted execution environment, and a monetary system. After the smart contract appeared, Hawk [18], as a universal smart contract framework that provides secure computations, gave an auction example. Even though all computations are public verifiable, the trusted manager in Hawk can still know all secrets. In 2018, Verifiable Sealed-Bid Auction [9] was proposed to fit the nature of smart contract protocol better. It aggregates the monetary system to provide financial fairness. However, their scheme also relies on a trusted manager to hide secrets. Furthermore, their scheme does not achieve a feature of public verifiability since it requires interactive proofs. The posterior bid secrecy and bidder anonymity also does not hold since a commitment scheme is opened at the end of the auction. Recently, schemes without trusted managers are proposed [12–14]. They removed the trusted manager from Abe, et al. [1]'s construction. We use the same concept that instead of asking managers to determine who is the winner, bidders need to interact with the smart contract independently to prove herself/himself as a winner.

As for the scalability, since we don't have a manager, we will only focus on the computation cost for each bidder. Compared with the online (smart contract) cost, the offline (local) cost is negligible. In a smart contract protocol, to make a function call to a smart contract, a participant has to create a transaction that includes the variables and transaction fee (gas fee). A transaction can be accepted only if the miner who creates the latest block verifies it at the cost of the transaction fee. Therefore, smart contract protocol is asynchronous by nature and the gas fee reflects all costs of the function call. In this research, we evaluate the time complexity and storage usage of a smart contract function call as it is the main portion of the gas fee.

We focus on the scalability of the number of bidders B and the number of possible bidding prices P. In previous researches [1, 9, 22, 25], the time complexity is $O(BPM)$ per manager and $O(P)$ per bidder. The time complexity of the manager is linear to B since there are B bidders, and the time complexity of both manager and bidder is linear to $P = |V|$, where V is the bidding vector. The bidding vector is the core concept of a bit-slice auction. It stores encrypted bits as an array that is used to hide the real bidding price.

Our main contributions are to improve the scalability of the number of bidders B, remove the upper bound of bidding price P, and remove the trusted manager and Mix server at the same time. The time complexity of our bidder is $O(M \log(|V|B))$. Our time complexity is sublinear to the number of bidders B since we use binary search to improve the efficiency to find the $M + 1$st price. Our time complexity is not related to the possible bidding price P since we use a compact bit-slice design. Auction prices can range from hundreds to billions. In previous research, a bidder can pick one bidding price and $|V| - 1$ dummy prices from $1, ..., |V|$ prices. By using a compact bit-slice design, bidders are allowed to pick one bidding price and $|V| - 1$ dummy prices from $1, ..., 2^{256}$ prices. Even though in compact bit-slice design, all $|V|$ prices are public, the probability for a malicious party to guess the real bidding price is the same as $\frac{1}{|V|}$. In a real-world auction, a bidder can have their own strategy to set the dummy bidding prices.

As for public verifiability, all messages sent by bidders need to attach a non-interactive zero-knowledge proof. The smart contract will verify this proof before accepting the request.

Features of our protocol are listed below:

– **Scalable on the bidding price:** The possible bidding prices are not bounded.
– **Scalable on the number of bidders:** The time complexity is sublinear in terms of the number of bidders.

- **No TTP:** No trusted third parties such as manager or Mix server.
- **Bid secrecy:** All bidding prices are secrets except the $M + 1$st-price.
- **Bidder anonymity:** Except for the top M winning bidders, all other bidders' identities are secret.
- **Posterior secrecy and anonymity:** Bid secrecy and bid anonymity hold after the auction ends.
- **Asynchronous:** In the same phase, the bidder does not need to wait for other bidders. For example, commutative decryption is asynchronous since one bidder does not need to wait for other bidders to decrypt.
- **Robustness:** The protocol can continue even if there are malicious bidders.
- **Public verifiability:** Every message is attached with non-interactive zero-knowledge proof to prove its correctness.
- **Financial fairness:** The smart contract can send malicious bidders' stakes to honest parties as compensation.

By utilizing smart contracts, this protocol not only improved traditional auction protocols but also reached the ultimate goal of decentralized apps (DApps):

- Decentralized: no TTP or manager is used.
- Scalable: unlimited bidding price and sublinear complexity to the number of bidders
- Robustness, the auction does not necessarily need to restart if there are some malicious bidders at the first time.

In this paper, we introduce the related studies in Sect. 2, and explain cryptographic preliminaries in Sect. 3, and propose an efficient and secure $M + 1$st-price auction protocol in Sect. 4, describe the implementation and optimization in Sect. 5, and compare our scheme with the previous researches in Sect. 6. Finally, we conclude our scheme in Sect. 7.

2   Related Works

There are many known $M + 1$st-price auction protocols. Franklin and Reiter [7] proposed a first-price auction, but the bids are revealed at the end of the auction. Naor, Pinkas, and Sumner [23] proposed a scheme that used Yao's secure computation and oblivious transfer (OT). However, the cost of communication is too high since they use OT bit by bit. Juels and Szydlo [17] improved [23] by using two independent auctioneers. Omote and Miyaji (OM) [25] also use two auctioneer designs, and use the p-th root problem to find the second-highest price. Abe and Suzuki [1] proposed a scheme based on semi-homomorphic encryption. Kurosawa and Ogata (KO) [19] used the bit-slice approach to construct a first-price and second-price auction. Using a binary format, they improved the computational cost of bidding price to $O(\log P)$. Mitsunaga, Manabe, and Okamoto (MMO) [20–22] used BGN encryption to improve the computation cost of KO. BGN is a Somewhat Homomorphic Encryption (SHE) that allows one homomorphic multiplication and many homomorphic additions. However, their algorithm used both addition and multiplication multiple times such that MMO's scheme needs full homomorphic encryption (FHE) to work.

After the invention of the Smart contract by Ethereum [26], Kosba, et al. [18] first build a general-purpose smart contract framework that can ensure public verifiability and financial fairness. Auction is one of their applications. CReam [27] is a smart contract enabled collusion-resistant e-auction. It is well organized and provides many experimental data. However, its design is based on a commitment scheme. The posterior bid secrecy and bidder anonymity can break when the commitments have been opened. CCL [4] is similar to CReam, but they used their blockchain called MinerGate. It also uses a commitment scheme and reveals the secrets at the end of the auction. Trustee [10] is a full privacy-preserving Vickrey auction on top of Ethereum. The design is similar to Hawk. All bidders encrypt their bids by managers' public key. The manager uses Intel SGX to decrypt the bid and determine the winner. The results are sent back to the smart contract with proof. Galal and Youssef (GY) [9] also proposed an efficient smart contract auction protocol that uses a commitment scheme and interactive zero-knowledge proof. However, at the end of the auction, the bid secrecy and bidder anonymity will be revealed. HM [14] is a smart contract auction protocol. It adopts AS's scheme to guarantee bid secrecy and bidder anonymity. By letting bidders act as managers, the trusted manager is removed from their scheme. It also adopts KMSWP [18] 's zero-knowledge proof idea to keep publicly verifiability and financial fairness.

3   Preliminaries

Definition 1 (DDH assumption). *Let t be a security parameter. A decisional Diffie-Hellman (DDH) parameter generator $I\mathcal{G}$ is a probabilistic polynomial time (PPT) algorithm that takes an input 1^k and outputs the description of a finite field $\mathbb{F}_p$ and a basepoint $g \in \mathbb{F}_p$ with the prime order q. We say that $I\mathcal{G}$ satisfies the DDH assumption if $\epsilon = |p_1 - p_2|$ is negligible (in K) for all PPT algorithms A, where $p_1 = PR[(\mathbb{F}_p, g) \leftarrow I\mathcal{G}(1^K); y_1 = g^{x_1}, y_2 = g^{x_2} \leftarrow \mathbb{F}_p : A(\mathbb{F}_p, g, y_1, y_2, g^{x_1 x_2}) = 0]$ and $p_2 = Pr[(\mathbb{F}_p, g) \leftarrow I\mathcal{G}(1^K); y_1 = g^{x_1}, y_2 = g^{x_2}, z \leftarrow \mathbb{F}_p : A(\mathbb{F}_p, g, y_1, y_2, z) = 0]$.*

Definition 2 (ElGamal encryption [5]). *Let p and q be large primes. Let $\langle g \rangle$ denotes a prime subgroup of $\mathbb{Z}_p^*$ generated by g whose order is q. Given a message $m \in \mathbb{Z}_p^*$, we define ElGamal [5] encryption as $\mathsf{Enc}_y(m) = (g^r, m \cdot y^r)$, where y is the public key and $r \in \mathbb{Z}_q^*$. Given a ciphertext $c = (g^r, m \cdot y^r)$, decryption is defined as $\mathsf{Dec}_x(c) = m$, where x is the private key.*

Definition 3 (ElGamal based multi-party encryption [14,15]). *Assume there are n encryptors with private key public key pairs $(x_i, y_i), i \in \{1, ..., n\}$ accordingly. Given a message m. The ElGamal ciphertext of m is defined as $\mathsf{Enc}_Y(m) = \mathsf{Enc}_{y_1}(...\mathsf{Enc}_{y_n}(m)) = c$, where $R = \sum_{i=1}^n r_i$ and $Y = \prod_{i=1}^n y_i$. The decryption is defined as $\mathsf{Dec}_X(c) = \mathsf{Dec}_{x_n}(...\mathsf{Dec}_{x_1}(m)) = m$, where $X = \{x_1, ..., x_n\}$.*

Theorem 1 (ElGamal based multi-entity decryption is commutative [14,15]**).** *Given two ciphertext* $Enc_{y_2}(Enc_{y_1}(m)) = c_1$ *and* $Enc_{y_1}(Enc_{y_2}(m)) = c_2$. *The decryption can be performed in any order.* $Dec_{x_1}(Dec_{x_2}(c_1)) = Dec_{x_2}(Dec_{x_1}(c_1)) = Dec_{x_1}(Dec_{x_2}(c_2)) = Dec_{x_2}(Dec_{x_1}(c_2)) = m$.

Theorem 2 (Plaintext equivalence proof of ElGamal ciphertext [3]**).** *Given an ElGamal ciphertext* (g^r, my^r) *and a plaintext* m', *the encryptor can prove the value of* $m = m'$ *without revealing* r. *This type of proof is based on the proof of the equality of two discrete logarithms. i.e.* g^r *and* my^r/m' *share the same discrete logarithm* r.

Theorem 3 (OR of the Two plaintext equivalence proof of ElGamal ciphertext [3]**).** *Given an ElGamal ciphertext* (g^r, my^r) *and plaintexts* m' *and* m'', *the value of* $m = m'$ *or* $m = m''$ *can be proved without revealing* m *and* r. *It is a variation of the plaintext equivalence proof. Helios [3] gave an example of how to construct this proof.*

Theorem 4 (Proof of knowledge of a discrete logarithm). *Given* $g \in \mathbb{Z}_p$ *and* $x \in \mathbb{Z}_q^*$, *the knowledge of* g^x *'s discrete logarithm* x *can be proved without revealing* x.

Theorem 5 (Proof of equality of two discrete logarithms). *Given* $g_1, g_2 \in \mathbb{Z}_p$ *and* $x_1, x_2 \in \mathbb{Z}_q^*$, *the knowledge of* g^x *'s discrete logarithm* x *can be proved without revealing* x. *This type of proof is a variation of the proof of knowledge of a discrete logarithm.*

Note that all proofs mentioned above can be non-interactive by using Fiat-Shamir heuristic [6].

Protocol 1 (Bit-slice). *Bit-slice is a common technique used in many auction protocols. It encodes real bidding prices into bits and encrypts each bit into an array such as* $[E_Y(z^0), E_Y(z^1), E_Y(z^0), E_Y(z^0)]$.

Algorithm 1 (Binary search)
Binary search [2] is an algorithm used to search on an ordered list. It can reduce the time complexity to $O(log(N))$, *where* N *is the number of elements.* $BiSearch[A, cmp] = i$:

- *Input: Given an ordered list* A *of* N *elements and a compare function cmp.*
- *Output: The index* j *of the target element* $A[j]$. *If there are no element satisfies the condition, output the largest* i *where* $cmp(i) = 1$.

Algorithm 2 (Mix and match [16]**)**
Mix and match is a technique used to examine whether the decryption of a ciphertext $Dec(c)$ *belongs to a set of plaintexts. It is based on Mix net, which can perform verifiable secret shuffle. The Mix server only knows their own permutation, they do not know the plaintext.* $MixMatch[c, S]$:

- *Input: Ciphertext* c *and a set of plaintexts* $S = \{m_1, m_2, ..., m_n\}$.
- *Output: True if* $Dec(c) \in S$. *Otherwise, output False.*

4   Our Protocol

Our protocol consists of a seller, who sells M goods; and bidders, who bid a price to the good. The M highest bidders can buy the goods by the $M + $ 1st-price. Remark that no other entity except seller and bidders is required in our protocol. In this section, we present our main ideas and then show our protocol.

In our protocol, two brilliant methods are newly introduced. One is a Compact Bit-Slice Design and the other is an Amortized $M + $ 1st-Price Decision. We present these two methods as follows.

In a real-world auction, a bidding price can be up to billions and does not have a predefined upper bound. However, in most auction schemes that use bit-slice design, the bidding price has an upper bound of P. This upper bound P is caused by the length of the bit-slice bidding vector $|V|$. In most research, $|V| = P$. We propose a compact bit-slice design that stores L key-value pairs. Key is an index, and value is a ciphertext. Similar to traditional bit-slice design, there are one real bidding price and $L - 1$ dummy prices. By using this design, $|V| = L$. $|V|$ has no relation with P. Therefore, the upper bound P of the bidding price is removed. The seller can choose preferred L as a security parameter.

price =	1	2	3	4	5	6	
$b_1 = 2, V_1 = [$	-	$(2, E_Y(z^1))$	-	$(4, E_Y(z^0))$	-	-	]
$b_2 = 6, V_2 = [$	$(1, E_Y(z^0))$	-	-	-	-	$(6, E_Y(z^1))$	]
$b_3 = 4, V_3 = [$	$(1, E_Y(z^0))$	-	-	$(4, E_Y(z^1))$	-	-	]
$a_1 = [$	-	$(2, E_Y(z^1))$	-	$(4, E_Y(z^0))$	-	-	]
$a_2 = [$	$(1, E_Y(z^1))$	-	-	-	-	$\boxed{(6, E_Y(z^1))}$	] win
$a_3 = [$	$(1, E_Y(z^1))$	-	-	$\boxed{(4, E_Y(z^1))}$	-	-	] win
$c = [$	$(1, E_Y(z^3))$	$(2, E_Y(z^3))$	-	$(4, E_Y(z^2))$	-	$(6, E_Y(z^0))$	]
Mix and Match $= [$	False	False	-	True	-	True	]
		j_{M+1st}					

Fig. 2. Example of $M = 2$ goods, $B = 3$ bidders and bidding vector length $L = 2$.

4.1   Auction Protocol

Smart Contract Deployment
The following parameters are deployed in the smart contract (SC) to start the auction.

– Cryptographic parameters: Large prime p, a basepoint g with prime order q, and a auction base $z \leftarrow \mathbb{Z}_p \backslash \{0, 1\}$.

– Seller initialization:
- Security parameter L, the length of the bidding vector V.
- Timeouts for each phase $T_1, ..., T_6$: Failed to submit things to the smart contract within a given period will be treated as a violation of the protocol and be financially penalized.
- Seller's stake S_S: Seller submits S_S amount of ether as a stake to start the auction.
- Bidders' stake requirement S_B: Bidders are required to submit S_B amount of ether as a stake to join the auction.

Phase 1. Bidder initialization
Bidders join the auction within time T_1 as follows. We assume that there are more than $M + 1$ bidders.

– Each bidder $B_i, i \in \{1, ..., B\}$ submit following messages to the SC:
- Public key $y_i = g^{x_i}$ for the ElGamal encryption, where $x_i \leftarrow \mathbb{Z}_q$ is a randomly chosen secret key.
- The proof of $y_i = g^{x_i}$: This proof can be constructed by using proof of knowledge of y_i's discrete logarithm x_i in Sect. 3.
- S_B amount of ether as stake.
– After this phase ends, an aggregated public key $Y = \prod_{i=1}^{B} y_i$ can be calculated by SC.

Phase 2. Bidder Submit Their Bids
All bidders must submit their bids to SC within time T_2 as follows:

– Each bidder $B_i, i \in \{1, ..., B\}$ submit following messages to the SC:
- Encrypted bidding vector $V_i = (V_{i1}, ..., V_{iL})$:

$$V_{ij} = \begin{cases} (p_j, \mathsf{E}_Y(z^1)) & \text{if } p_j = b_i \\ (p_j, \mathsf{E}_Y(z^0)) & \text{if } p_j \neq b_i \end{cases}$$

The bidder B_i first chooses a bidding point $b_i \in \mathbb{N}$, and generates the bidding vector V_i. V_{ij} is a price-value pair, $V_{ij}.p$ is the price, and $V_{ij}.v$ is the ciphertext. V_i should contain exactly one $(b_i, \mathsf{E}_Y(z^1))$ and $L - 1$ amount of $(r_j, \mathsf{E}_Y(z^0))$, where $r_j \leftarrow \mathbb{N}$ is a random value. An equivilant statement is

$$\left(V_{ij}.v \in \{\mathsf{E}_Y(z^0), \mathsf{E}_Y(z^1)\} \forall j\right) \wedge \left(\prod_{j=1}^{L} V_{ij}.v = \mathsf{E}_Y(z^1)\right)$$

- The proof of $V_{ij}.v \in \{\mathsf{E}_Y(z^0), \mathsf{E}_Y(z^1)\} \forall j$: This proof can be constructed by using an OR proof of $\mathsf{Dec}(V_{ij}.v) \in \{z^0, z^1\}$ in Sect. 3.
- The proof of $\prod_{j=1}^{L} V_{ij}.v = \mathsf{E}_Y(z^1)$: This proof can be constructed by using a plaintext equality proof of plaintext z^1 in Sect. 3.

Phase 3. $M + 1$st-Price Decision Preparation

In this phase, SC first calculates auxiliary arrays $a_1, ..., a_B$ for each bidder. Then calculates cumulative array $c = (c_1, ..., c_L)$ used for finding the $M + 1$st-price within time T_3. The protocol is as follows:

1. SC calculates array $a_i = (a_{i1}, ..., a_{iL})$ for all bidder B_i:

$$a_{ij} = (V_{ij}.p, \prod_{k=j}^{L} V_{ik}.v) = (V_{ij}.p, E_Y(z^{\sum_{k=j}^{L} t_{ik}}))$$

For all j, the value of $a_{ij}.v$ equals to $E_Y(z^1)$ if the bid b_i is larger than or equals to $a_{ij}.p$. Otherwise, $a_{ij}.v = E_Y(z^0)$. A simple way to reduce the time complexity from $O(L^2)$ to $O(L)$ is to compute

$$a_{ij} = (V_{ij}.p, a_{i(j+1)}.v \cdot V_{ij}.v)$$

2. SC calculates array $c = (c_1, ..., c_{L'})$:

$$c_j.v = \prod_{\forall V_{ij}.p \geq c_j.p} V_{ij}.v$$

Array c aggregates array $V_1, ..., V_B$ by price. Assume there are L' different prices. $L \leq L' \leq LB$. Assign these prices to $c_1.p, ..., c_{L'}.p$, and calculates $c_1.v, ..., c_{L'}.v$. The value of $c_j.v$ is the number of bidders whose bid b_i is larger than or equals to $c_j.p$. A simple way to reduce the time complexity from $O((LB)^2)$ to $O(LB \log(LB))$ is to sort all elements in all bidding vectors by price, then merge the elements that have the same price. Figure 2 provides an example of array a and array c.

Phase 4. $M + 1$st-Bid Decision

In this phase, Mix and Match is performed on array $c = (c_1, ..., c_{L'})$ to find the $M + 1$st-price within time T_4. In array $c = (c_1, ..., c_P)$, the value of $c_j.v$ is the number of bidders B_i whose bid b_i is larger than or equals to the price $c_j.p$. Thus, we can use Mix and Match to find out the bidding price $c_j.p$ where $Dec(c_j.v) \notin \{z^0, z^1, ..., z^M\}$, but $Dec(c_{j+1}.v) \in \{z^0, z^1, ..., z^M\}$. Since the c array is a decrementing array, binary search can speed up the search. We use j_{M+1st} as a symbol for this j. The protocol is as follows:

- By all bidders' help, SC finds the $M + 1$st-price $c_j.p$ that $\mathsf{MixMatch}[c_j.v, \{z^0, z^1, ..., z^M\}] = False$ but $\mathsf{MixMatch}[c_{j+1}.v, \{z^0, z^1, ..., z^M\}] = True$. Assume cmp is the compare function of binary search. $\mathsf{BiSearch}$ will return the j where $cmp(c_j) = -1$ but $cmp(c_{j+1}) = 1$. This $c_j.p$ is the $M + 1$st-price.

$$j_{M+1st} = \mathsf{BiSearch}[c, cmp]$$

$$cmp(c_j) = \begin{cases} 1 & \text{if } MixMatch\left[c_j.v, \{z^0, z^1, ..., z^M\}\right] = True \\ & \text{otherwise.} \end{cases}$$

Phase 5. Winner decision

Let the $M + 1$st price be P_{M+1}. In this phase, All bidders B_i whose bid b_i is larger than P_{M+1} can submit a proof that $\mathsf{Dec}(a_{i,j'}) = z^1$ to win the auction where $a_{i,j'}.p > P_{M+1}$. Here we pick the smallest j' that satisfies the condition. This behavior will not leak the bid b_i since $a_{i,j'} = \prod_{j=j'}^{P} V_{ij}$. All elements in $V_{i,j'}, ..., V_{iL}$ can be $\mathsf{E}_Y(z^1)$. The protocol is as follows:

- Bidders B_i whose bid $b_i > P_{M+1}$ can submit following messages to the SC:
  1. The proof of $a_{i,j'} = \mathsf{E}_Y(z^1)$: This proof can be constructed by using a plaintext equality proof of plaintext z^1 in Sect. 3. The j' should be the smallest j that satisfies the condition.

Phase 6. Payment

The bidders who win the auction send P_{M+1} amount of ether to the seller through SC. The protocol is as follows:

- All winning bidders pay P_{M+1} amount of ether to SC.
- The seller use winning bidders' public keys to encrypt the goods individually with proof and sends them to SC.
- SC sends bidders' payment to the seller.

4.2   Features and Security

The design of this protocol provides the following properties:

- **Scalable on the bidding price:** The bidding vector contains the L amount of price-value pairs. The price can be any value. It is not bounded by the length of the bidding vector.
- **Scalable on the number of bidders:** The time complexity and storage usages are sublinear to the number of bidders B.
- **Bid binding:** According to our implementation, the functions in SC will not allow bidders to change their bidding point after closing the bid submission phase.
- **Bid secrecy:** The bidding vectors $V_1, ..., V_B$ are encrypted by all bidders' public keys $Y = y_1 \cdots y_B$. Without all bidders' collaboration, the bids are kept as secrets. In phase 4, the Mix and Match algorithm itself ensures no information will be leaked except a plaintext of the ciphertext is in the given set $\{z^0, ..., z^M\}$ or not. In phase 5, winning bidders prove a ciphertext $a_{ij'}.v$ is $\mathsf{E}_Y(z^1)$ or not. This will not leak bid secrecy since all $V_{ij'}, ..., V_{iL}$ can cause $a_{ij'}.v = \mathsf{E}_Y(z^1)$.
- **Bidder anonymity:** Since $c_1, ..., c_{L'}$ are products of ciphertexts generated by all bidders, the identity of the $M + 1$st bidder is still a secret.
- **Posterior secrecy and anonymity:** The bidding points $b_1, ..., b_B$ and bidding vectors $V_1, ..., V_B$ are still secrets even after the auction ends. Thus, posterior secrecy and anonymity still hold.

- **Public verifiability:** All messages sent to SC are attached with a public verifiable non-interactive proof, which can be verified by smart contract immediately. Therefore, the correctness of the protocol is publicly verifiable.
  - Phase 1. Bidder initialization: A public key $y_i = g^{x_i}$ is submitted by each bidder B_i to SC, $i = 1, ..., B$. The proof of knowledge of x_i is publicly verifiable. Thus, the correctness of the public key is publicly verifiable.
  - Phase 2. Bidder submits their bids: A valid bidding vector $V_i = (V_{i1}, ..., V_{iL})$ consists of $L - 1$ amount of $E_Y(z^0)$ and one $E_Y(z^1)$.
    * For all $j = 1, ..., L$, an OR proof of $Dec(V_{ij}) \in \{z^0, z^1\}$ is submitted to SC to prevent malicious bidders from submitting V_{ij} other than $E_Y(z^0)$ and $E_Y(z^1)$.
    * A equality proof of $Dec(\prod_{j=1}^{L} V_{ij}) = z^1$ is used to prevent malicious bidders from chosing multiple bidding points.
    Thus, by using $L + 1$ non-interactive zero-knowledge proofs, the bidding vectors are public verifiable.
  - Phase 3. $M + 1$st-price decision preparation: This step is performed by the smart contract. Therefore, it is publicly verifiable.
  - Phase 4. $M + 1$st-bid decision: The Mix and Match protocol is publicly verifiable, and the binary search is performed by the smart contract. Thus, this phase is publicly verifiable.
  - Phase 5. Winner decision: A public verifiable equality proof of $a_{i,j'} = E_Y(z^1)$ is used to prove a bidder wins the auction. Thus, the winner's decision is publicly verifiable.
- **Financial fairness:** When they join the auction, the seller and all bidders are asked to deposit some ether in the smart contract. If they perform any malicious behavior, the smart contract can send their stake to others as compensation.

5 Implementation and Optimization

There are two main parts to this protocol, smart contract[1] and web3 client[2]. The gas usages are estimated by ganache-cli, a successor of ethereumjs-testrpc. Figure 3 shows the gas usage by the number of bidders. As we can see, the gas usage is sublinear to the number of bidders. Also, the gas usage is sublinear to the security parameter L. Compared with AS, a scheme that needs a manager, and HM, a scheme without a manager, Table 2 shows the gas usage of different phases. In the bid verification phase (phases 2 and 3), the most costly part of an auction protocol, the gas usage is reduced by 95% after we use zero-knowledge proof to replace Mix and Match. The overall gas usage is also reduced by 83%. We built a scheme that is sublinear to the number of bidders, and the security parameter L, with unlimited bidding price (Table 4).

---

[1] https://github.com/tonypottera24/m-1st_auction_ec_sol.
[2] https://github.com/tonypottera24/m-1st_auction_ec_py.

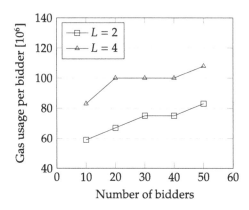

Fig. 3. Gas usage by number of bidders and security parameter L

Table 2. The gas usage of AS, HM, and our scheme (ECC 256, 3 bidders, 6 bidding prices, L = 6).

	AS	HM	Our scheme
Role	Manager	Bidder	Bidder
1	1	1	1
2	5	3	53
3	520	350	25
4	79	52	24
5	9	8	3
6	4	2	0.1
Overall	618	416	105

6   Comparison

The detailed comparisons of each phases are as follows:

1. **Phase 1. Bidder initialization:** In previous research such as AS, MMO and KO, the bids are encrypted only by the manager's public key. The bid secrecy, bidder anonymity, and many features rely on the trusted manager. On the other hand, in our scheme, the ciphertexts are encrypted by all bidders' public keys. Without all bidders' collaboration, no one can break the bid secrecy, bidder anonymity, and many other features.
2. **Phase 2. Bidder submit their bids:** A valid bidding vector $V_i = (V_{i1}, ..., V_{iL})$ should contain exactly $L-1$ amounts of $\mathsf{E}_Y(z^0)$ and one $\mathsf{E}_Y(z^1)$. In previous research such as AS, MMO and KO, bidding vector verification contains two parts. 1. $V_{ij} \in \{\mathsf{E}_Y(z^0), \mathsf{E}_Y(z^1)\}$; 2. $\sum_{j=1}^{L} V_{ij} = \mathsf{E}_Y(z^1)$. The first part is accomplished by Mix and Match. This requires T (trusted) Mix servers to perform Mix (secure shuffle [8,11,24]) and Match (ZK equality proof). The

Table 3. Comparison of previous researches and our scheme (TM: Trusted Manager, B: Bidder)

	Scalability (bidder)	Scalability (price)	Trusted Manager	Trusted Mix server	(Posterior) Bid Secrecy & Bidder Anonymity	Public Verifiability	Financial Fairness
AS	linear	linear	Yes	Yes	Based on TM	No	No
OM	linear	linear	Yes	Yes	Based on TM	No	No
MMO	linear	sublinear	Yes	Yes	Based on TM	No	No
GY	linear	linear	Yes	Yes	Based on TM	Interactive	Yes
HM	linear	linear	No	No	Yes	Yes	Yes
Our scheme	sublinear	unlimited	No	No	Yes	Yes	Yes

Table 4. Comparison of the complexities. (T: the number of trusted managers and Mix servers)

	Manager		Bidder	
	Total time complexity	Rounds	Total time complexity	Rounds
AS	$O(BPM)$	$O(\log P)$	$O(P)$	$O(1)$
OM	$O(BPM)$	$O(\log P)$	$O(P)$	$O(1)$
MMO	$O(B \log PM)$	$O(\log P)$	$O(\log P)$	$O(1)$
GY	$O(BPM)$	$O(B)$	$O(P)$	$O(1)$
HM	–	–	$O(BPM)$	$O(\log P)$
Our scheme	–	–	$O(M \log(LB))$	$O(\log(LB))$

second part is accomplished by asking trusted manager to decrypt $\sum_{j=1}^{L} V_{ij}$. In our scheme, instead of asking trusted managers to verify the bidding vector V_i, bidder B_i submit non-interactive zero-knowledge proofs to prove their bidding vector V_i is valid. SC can verify these proofs immediately without any other bidders' help. Compared with previous works, this reduces the local computation and communication costs from $O(BP)$ to $O(L)$.

3. **Phase 3 and 4.** M + **1st-bid decision:** In this phase, our approach is similar to previous research such as AS, MMO and KO. However, previous research used a trusted Mix server, and we use bidder to act as a Mix server. Also, the binary search used in previous research such as AS cannot improve performance. In AS, the length of bidding vector is $|V| = P$. The length of the array c is also P. Therefore, even though binary search reduce the complexity from $O(|c|) = O(P)$ to $O(\log |c|) = O(\log P)$ in this phase, the complexity in other phase still needs $O(|V|) = O(P)$. In our scheme, the length of the array c is BL'. The length of bidding vector is $|V| = L < BL'$. Therefore, the binary search can effectively reduce the total complexity from $O(BL')$ to $O(\log BL')$.

4. **Phase 5. Winner decision:** In previous research such as AS, trusted manager(s) decrypts all $a_{i,j'}$, $i = 1, ..., B$ to find out the winning bidders. In our scheme, each winning bidder B_i can provide proof that $\mathsf{Dec}(a_{i,j'}.v) = z^1$ to prove that he is a winner. Therefore, the time complexity is only $O(1)$ for each

bidder. Compared with previous works, this reduces the local computation and communication costs from $O(B)$ to $O(1)$.

5. **Phase 6. Payment:** Unlike previous research, the goods in our design are encrypted by the winners' public key and sent to SC. Seller also gets the ether from SC for the goods.

Compared with previous research, our design provides sublinear scalability on the number of bidders and an unlimited number of bidding prices. Table 3 shows that we do not use trusted manager and trusted Mix server. The (posterior) *bid secrecy* and *bidder anonymity* are also not based on TTPs. Also, the usage of smart contract and zero-knowledge proof ensures the *public verifiability* and *financial fairness*. MMO did great work to represent bids in binary format to reduce P to $\log P$. However, their construction is based on a trusted manager and full-homomorphic BGN encryption. In terms of computation and communication costs, we are better than them in terms of scalability on the number of bidders and the limitation on bidding price. Since our scheme does not use trusted Mix servers, our scheme is T times better than previous research. Also, since the bidding vector length is shorter than the length of the c array, binary search efficiently improved our scheme from $O(BLM)$ to $O(M \log LB)$. As a scheme without a trusted manager, this is a significant improvement compared with HM.

7   Conclusion

In our research, by utilizing smart contracts, this protocol reached the ultimate goal of decentralized apps (DApps): Decentralized: no TTP or manager is used. Scalable: unlimited bidding price and sublinear complexity to the number of bidders. Robustness, the auction does not necessarily need to restart if there are some malicious bidders at the first time.

Acknowledgement. This work is partially supported by JSPS KAKENHI Grant Number JP21H03443, Innovation Platform for Society 5.0 at MEXT, and JST Next Generation Researchers Challenging Research Program JPMJSP2138.

References

1. Abe, M., Suzuki, K.: M + 1-st price auction using homomorphic encryption. In: Naccache, D., Paillier, P. (eds.) PKC 2002. LNCS, vol. 2274, pp. 115–124. Springer, Heidelberg (2002). https://doi.org/10.1007/3-540-45664-3_8
2. Bentley, J.L.: Multidimensional binary search trees used for associative searching. Commun. ACM **18**(9), 509–517 (1975)
3. Bernhard, D., Warinschi, B.: Cryptographic voting — a gentle introduction. In: Aldini, A., Lopez, J., Martinelli, F. (eds.) FOSAD 2012-2013. LNCS, vol. 8604, pp. 167–211. Springer, Cham (2014). https://doi.org/10.1007/978-3-319-10082-1_7
4. Chen, Y.H., Chen, S.H., Lin, I.C.: Blockchain based smart contract for bidding system. In: 2018 IEEE International Conference on Applied System Invention (ICASI), pp. 208–211. IEEE (2018)

5. ElGamal, T.: A public key cryptosystem and a signature scheme based on discrete logarithms. IEEE Trans. Inf. Theory **31**(4), 469–472 (1985)
6. Fiat, A., Shamir, A.: How to prove yourself: practical solutions to identification and signature problems. In: Odlyzko, A.M. (ed.) CRYPTO 1986. LNCS, vol. 263, pp. 186–194. Springer, Heidelberg (1987). https://doi.org/10.1007/3-540-47721-7_12
7. Franklin, M.K., Reiter, M.K.: The design and implementation of a secure auction service. IEEE Trans. Software Eng. **22**(5), 302–312 (1996)
8. Furukawa, J., Sako, K.: An efficient scheme for proving a shuffle. In: Kilian, J. (ed.) CRYPTO 2001. LNCS, vol. 2139, pp. 368–387. Springer, Heidelberg (2001). https://doi.org/10.1007/3-540-44647-8_22
9. Galal, H.S., Youssef, A.M.: Verifiable sealed-bid auction on the ethereum blockchain. In: Zohar, A., et al. (eds.) FC 2018. LNCS, vol. 10958, pp. 265–278. Springer, Heidelberg (2019). https://doi.org/10.1007/978-3-662-58820-8_18
10. Galal, H.S., Youssef, A.M.: Trustee: Full privacy preserving vickrey auction on top of ethereum. arXiv preprint arXiv:1905.06280 (2019)
11. Groth, J., Lu, S.: A non-interactive shuffle with pairing based verifiability. In: Kurosawa, K. (ed.) ASIACRYPT 2007. LNCS, vol. 4833, pp. 51–67. Springer, Heidelberg (2007). https://doi.org/10.1007/978-3-540-76900-2_4
12. Hsu, P.C., Miyaji, A.: Bidder scalable m+1st-price auction with public verifiability. In: 2021 IEEE 20th International Conference on Trust, Security and Privacy in Computing and Communications (TrustCom), pp. 34–42. IEEE (2021)
13. Hsu, P.C., Miyaji, A.: Publicly verifiable m+1st-price auction fit for IoT with minimum storage. Secur. Commun. Networks **2021** (2021)
14. Hsu, P.C., Miyaji, A.: Verifiable m+1st-price auction without manager. In: 2021 IEEE Conference on Dependable and Secure Computing (DSC), pp. 1–8. IEEE (2021)
15. Huang, K., Tso, R.: A commutative encryption scheme based on Elgamal encryption. In: 2012 International Conference on Information Security and Intelligent Control, pp. 156–159. IEEE (2012)
16. Jakobsson, M., Juels, A.: Mix and match: secure function evaluation via ciphertexts. In: Okamoto, T. (ed.) ASIACRYPT 2000. LNCS, vol. 1976, pp. 162–177. Springer, Heidelberg (2000). https://doi.org/10.1007/3-540-44448-3_13
17. Juels, A., Szydlo, M.: A two-server, sealed-bid auction protocol. In: Blaze, M. (ed.) FC 2002. LNCS, vol. 2357, pp. 72–86. Springer, Heidelberg (2003). https://doi.org/10.1007/3-540-36504-4_6
18. Kosba, A., Miller, A., Shi, E., Wen, Z., Papamanthou, C.: Hawk: the blockchain model of cryptography and privacy-preserving smart contracts. In: 2016 IEEE Symposium on Security and Privacy (SP), pp. 839–858. IEEE (2016)
19. Kurosawa, K., Ogata, W.: Bit-slice auction circuit. In: Gollmann, D., Karjoth, G., Waidner, M. (eds.) ESORICS 2002. LNCS, vol. 2502, pp. 24–38. Springer, Heidelberg (2002). https://doi.org/10.1007/3-540-45853-0_2
20. Mistunaga, T., Manabe, Y., Okamoto, T.: A Secure M + 1st price auction protocol based on bit slice circuits. In: Iwata, T., Nishigaki, M. (eds.) IWSEC 2011. LNCS, vol. 7038, pp. 51–64. Springer, Heidelberg (2011). https://doi.org/10.1007/978-3-642-25141-2_4
21. Mitsunaga, T., Manabe, Y., Okamoto, T.: Efficient secure auction protocols based on the boneh-goh-nissim encryption. IEICE Trans. Fundam. Electron. Commun. Comput. Sci. **96**(1), 68–75 (2013)
22. Mitsunaga, T., Manabe, Y., Okamoto, T.: A secure m+ 1st price auction protocol based on bit slice circuits. IEICE Trans. Fundam. Electron. Commun. Comput. Sci. **99**(8), 1591–1599 (2016)

23. Naor, M., Pinkas, B., Sumner, R.: Privacy preserving auctions and mechanism design. In: Proceedings of the 1st ACM Conference on Electronic Commerce, pp. 129–139 (1999)
24. Neff, C.A.: A verifiable secret shuffle and its application to e-voting. In: Proceedings of the 8th ACM conference on Computer and Communications Security, pp. 116–125 (2001)
25. Omote, K., Miyaji, A.: A second-price sealed-bid auction with verifiable discriminant of p 0-th root. In: Blaze, M. (ed.) FC 2002. LNCS, vol. 2357, pp. 57–71. Springer, Heidelberg (2003). https://doi.org/10.1007/3-540-36504-4_5
26. Wood, G., et al.: Ethereum: a secure decentralised generalised transaction ledger. Ethereum Project Yellow Paper **151**(2014), 1–32 (2014)
27. Wu, S., Chen, Y., Wang, Q., Li, M., Wang, C., Luo, X.: Cream: A smart contract enabled collusion-resistant e-auction. IEEE Trans. Inf. Forensics Secur. **14**(7), 1687–1701 (2018)

The Shared Memory Based Cryptographic Card Virtualization

Chen Li[1,2], Bibo Tu[1,2(✉)], and Yanchang Feng[1,2]

[1] Institute of Information Engineering, Chinese Academy of Sciences, Beijing, China
{lichen,tubibo,fengyanchang}@iie.ac.cn
[2] School of Cyber Security, University of Chinese Academy of Science, Beijing, China

Abstract. Driven by cloud computing technology, traditional cryptography is transforming into cloud cryptographic service. Cryptographic cards must be virtualized if they are to be used in cloud. Hardware virtualization is the most commonly used cryptographic card virtualization solution, however, all existing hardware solutions rely on high-performance cryptographic cards that support Single Root I/O Virtualization (SR-IOV). Such cryptographic cards are expensive, providing a limited number of virtual cryptographic cards, making it challenging to support large-scale computing in cloud. Furthermore, existing software-based virtualization solutions perform poorly and do not support operations such as virtual machine(VM) migration and replication. This paper proposes a shared memory based cryptographic card software virtualization solution, which virtualizes a single PCIe cryptographic card into multiple virtual cryptographic cards, and encapsulates it as a virtual cipher machine (VCM) for users. This solution enables multiple VCMs to share hardware cryptographic resources effectively and reduce the hardware requirements for cloud servers to use cryptographic resources dramatically, realizing elastic expansion and an on-demand supply of cryptographic resources. Experimental results demonstrate that the performance of the solution proposed in this paper is better than the existing software virtualization solutions and can meet the requirements of high availability and high concurrency of cryptographic applications.

Keywords: Cloud computing · Shared memory · Cryptographic card virtualization

1 Introduction

Cloud computing is a rapidly evolving technology that has large-scale computing, on-demand resource provision, and flexible deployment capabilities. With a large amount of data transferring to the cloud, the emerging security issues have brought considerable challenges to the deployment of cloud computing. Data security issues consistently rank first as the top threats to cloud computing released by the Cloud Security Alliance (CSA) in February 2016 and September 2020 [1].

C. Su et al. (Eds.): SciSec 2022, LNCS 13580, pp. 137–151, 2022.
https://doi.org/10.1007/978-3-031-17551-0_9

Cryptography is the most effective technology to ensure the data security of information systems. However, the cryptographic technology is limited due to the poor scalability of corresponding cryptographic hardware, which cannot meet the requirements of large-scale cryptography in the cloud computing environment [2]. Cloud resources must have characteristics of dynamic expansion and on-demand services. These characteristics bring new challenges to cryptography. Accordingly, cryptography should be adjusted in both the deployment method and the service mode when applied to the cloud. Generally, the cloud platform deploys a cloud cryptographic resource pool separately and uses the cryptographic function through network. The cryptographic resource pool is a cluster of cryptographic hardware. The most widely used cryptographic hardware module is the cryptographic card or chip with a PCIe interface. Virtualizing the cryptographic card into independent virtual cryptographic cards is necessary.

The research on the virtualization of cryptographic card is still in its infancy, and has many problems. Most research focuses on hardware virtualization based on SR-IOV. For example, the cloud cryptographic platform solution proposed by Sansec [3], the cloud cryptographic resource pool proposed by Zhang et al. [4], and the cryptographic service cloud proposed by Wang et al. [5], all rely on high-performance cryptographic cards that support SR-IOV. SR-IOV based cryptographic cards are expensive and have strict compatibility for the software and hardware. They provide a limited number of virtual logical cryptographic cards with poor scalability, making it challenging to support VM migration and replication operations, and hard to meet large-scale computing needs in the cloud. There are fewer studies on software-based virtualization. The cryptographic card virtualization framework proposed by Sun et al. [6] does not support VM migration. The schemes proposed by Tang [7] and Zhang [8] have performance bottlenecks in terms of data transmission.

To solve the above problems, this paper proposes a cryptographic card software virtualization solution based on shared memory. Shared memory is the most efficient way to share data between processes. This solution enables multiple VCMs to share hardware cryptographic resources effectively and reduces the hardware requirements dramatically for cloud servers to use cryptographic resources, realising elastic expansion and on-demand supply of cryptographic resources.

Our contributions are as follows:

- We implement the shared memory mechanism by simulating a PCI device for VCMs in Virtual Machine Monitor (VMM), which realizes the communication between VCM and host by mapping the host's memory into the VCM's PCI device. Then we implement a cryptographic card software virtualization solution based on the shared memory mechanism. Our solution has no limit on the number of virtual cryptographic cards.
- We implement the prototype system of cryptographic card virtualization based on QEMU. The experiment shows the performance of this solution is better than the existing best-performing software based cryptographic card

virtualization scheme, and the data encryption speed is three times higher when data size exceeds 1 Mb.

- We optimize this method using Userspace I/O(UIO) technology, which improves the communication efficiency between the VM and the host. The experiments show that the performance improved by 2%–6.5%.

The rest of this paper is organized as follows: Sect. 2 introduces the latest work on cryptographic card virtualization and analyzes the existing problems. Section 3 shows the framework. Section 4 elaborates on the implementation. Section 5 verifies the effectiveness of the proposed solution through experiments. Section 6 summarizes the research of this paper.

2   Related Work

This section introduces the related work on the virtualization of the cryptographic card. As an I/O device, the cryptographic card can be virtualized by means of software virtualization and hardware-assisted virtualization.

2.1   Software Virtualization

Software virtualization solutions include full virtualization and paravirtualization. Full virtualization technique virtualizes the physical server at the operating system level [10,11]. It has been rarely used due to the high overhead, high-performance loss, and poor isolation.

Paravirtualization uses split drivers to handle I/O requests, which implements the efficient I/O operation of the VM through separate device drivers, including backend driver and frontend driver [12,13]. A backend driver is installed in privileged VM to access physical device. A frontend driver is installed in Guest OS, which handles Guest I/O requests and passes them to the backend driver. Tang et al. [7] and Li [9] proposed a software virtualization method for cryptographic cards based on the frontend and backend models of I/O. In these studies, efficient communication between multiple VMs and the host is completed by designing the frontend and backend drivers of the cryptographic card. The cryptographic card virtualization framework proposed by Sun et al. [6] adds a virtual cryptographic card domain based on the Xen virtualization platform. It implements an authentication module, a key management module, and a communication module in the domain, but the threshold value in the communication module of the framework is limited. The threshold setting has a performance impact, and VM migration is not supported. Zhang [8] proposed a privacy protection method based on cryptographic card virtualization, using KVM virtio technology to implement frontend and backend communication, improving the performance of the virtual cryptographic card by expanding the buffer capacity and encapsulating data packets. However, the cryptographic card only uses software simulation.

2.2 Hardware-Assisted Virtualization

Hardware-assisted virtualization can share physical devices at the hardware level directly, including device direct passthrough and SR-IOV. Ma et al. [14] designed a high-speed cryptographic card based on SR-IOV virtualization technology but only supported 160-bit hash operation, and resource scheduling cannot be achieved when the number of VMs is greater than the number of virtual cryptographic cards. Based on SR-IOV, Ren et al. [15] implemented a data interaction model for virtualized devices based on FPGA, which is used to solve the requirement of high-speed data interaction between cloud computing platforms and virtual devices. Yang et al. [16] proposed a security isolation framework on the Xen platform, combining the ideal of virtualization technology VT-d with trusted computing independent domain. Su [17] proposed three cryptographic card virtualization design schemes based on software virtualization and SR-IOV virtualization technology, but its software virtualization scheme uses full virtualization technology. Yang et al. [18] implemented a virtual trusted platform by using a cryptographic card supporting SR-IOV to replace the traditional TPM, providing trusted storage and measurement services for the application of the virtual platform, but it cannot be applied to the cloud server with multiple VMs running concurrently. In addition, traditional cryptographic infrastructure providers have also launched products and services suitable for cloud deployment to meet the needs of cloud service, such as the cloud encryption machine launched by Sansec and Tass [19]. Its core component is a high-performance cryptographic card that supports SR-IOV.

In summary, at present, there are few research on cryptographic card virtualization and the development is relatively lagging, lacking practical applications. Most of them focus on hardware virtualization based on SR-IOV, and only a few studies based on software virtualization. SR-IOV based cryptographic cards are expensive, and support a limited number of virtual logical cryptographic cards with poor scalability. Furthermore, existing software-based virtualization solutions perform poorly and do not support operations such as VM migration and replication.

This paper proposes a shared memory-based cryptographic card virtualization solution, which belongs to Paravirtualization. This solution does not need to modify the cryptographic card hardware and drivers, and has good compatibility while meeting the performance requirements.

3   Framework

This section introduces the framework of cryptographic card virtualization based on shared memory.

The cryptographic card is connected to the server through the PCIe interface. In this paper, multiple virtual cryptographic cards are virtualized through the virtualization technology based on shared memory and packaged as a VCM for users. Shared memory is the most efficient way to share data between processes

[20]. Multiple processes can share the same part of physical memory, and read or write memory directly without copying any data.

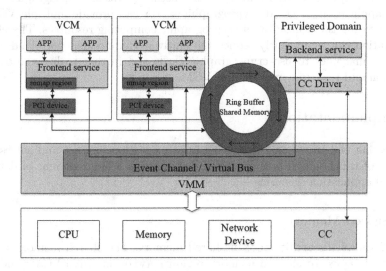

Fig. 1. Framework of Cryptographic Card Virtualization based on Shared Memory. (CC represents the cryptographic card.)

Figure 1 shows the framework of cryptographic card virtualization based on shared memory. We simulate a PCI device in VMM, which realizes the data transmission between VCM and the host by mapping the host's memory into the VCM's PCI device. Then we use event mechanism to achieve communication. VMM between the cryptographic card and the VCM runs in privileged mode, virtualizing a virtual hardware environment independent of the physical cryptographic card for each VCM, isolating and managing the VCM running at the upper layer. The VCM will copy the shared memory on migration to the destination host.

The architecture mainly include the frontend service and the backend service. The frontend service runs in VCM, and the backend service runs in host.

- The frontend service includes the cryptographic service interface of the cryptographic card and the shared memory frontend handler. The service receives the cryptographic service call of the application and writes the request to the PCI device through the *mmap* system call. The PCI device driver transfers the request to the shared memory, and then sends a notification to the backend service through the event mechanism.
- The backend service creates a shared memory object during initialization and monitors the VCM's request to the cryptographic card by listening on a UNIX domain socket. After receiving a request, the backend service calls the cryptographic card driver to complete the request, and then returns the response to the VCM through the shared memory.

In this architecture, we virtualize a virtual hardware environment independent of the physical cryptographic card for each VCM. The program running on the VCM is the same as running on the actual physical cryptographic card for the application. A cloud cryptographic server can provide multiple VCMs, thus improving the utilization of cryptographic computing resources. Therefore, this solution can significantly reduce the hardware requirement for cloud cryptographic machines to use cryptographic cards and further realize the elastic expansion and real-time migration of VCM.

4   Implementation

This section elaborates on the specific implementation method and solves the problem of using shared memory when dealing with a large amount of data in practical application scenarios.

4.1   Shared Memory

Figure 2 shows the architecture of shared memory. The shared memory mechanism is designed to share a memory region between multiple VCMs and the host. In order for all VCMs to pick up the shared memory area, it is modeled as a PCI device exposing shared memory to the VCM as a PCI BAR. The device can use a shared memory object on the host directly, or it can obtain one by the backend service.

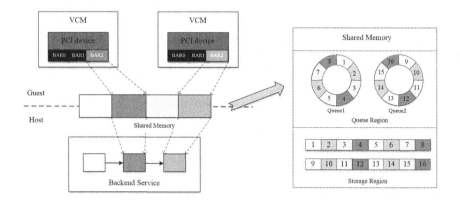

Fig. 2. Architecture of shared memory

The PCI device supports three base address registers BAR0, BAR1, and BAR2. BAR0 is a 1 KB Memory mapping I/O(MMIO) that supports registers and traditional interrupts. It includes four registers: Interrupt Mask, Interrupt Status, read-only IVPosition, and write-only Doorbell. IVPosition stores the VCM ID and can send interrupts to host by writing the Doorbell register. The device can additionally interrupt the backend service, and get interrupted by the backend service. BAR1 is used for MSI-X. BAR2 is used to access shared memory objects.

The right side of Fig. 2 shows the structure of shared memory area. The shared memory area is divided into queue region and storage region. The VCM ID and the index offset address of VCM are stored in the queue, the real data can be found in the storage area through the offset value. The storage area is a fixed-size memory area, and the size of each block is 2048 bytes.

4.2   Frontend Service

The frontend service runs in VCM, which includes the cryptographic service interface of the cryptographic card, the shared memory frontend handler.

The shared memory mechanism creates a PCI device for VCM when it starts up. We implement a kernel driver in the shared memory frontend handler, which is used to drive the PCI device, including registering and initializing the device. Algorithm 1 shows the PCI Device registration and initialization process.

Algorithm 1. PCI Device registration and initialization process

---

Input: *kvm_pci_dev, pdev*
Output: *result*
1: register_chardev(*kvm_pci_dev*)
2: result=pci_enable_dev()
3: **if** *result* **then**
4:     pci_name(*pdev, result*)
5:     **return**   *result*
6: **end if**
7: *result*=pci_request_regions(*pdev*)
8: **if** *result* < 0 **then**
9:     pci_disable
10: **else**
11:     ioaddr = pci_resource_start(*pdev*, 0, 2)
12:     ioaddr_size = pci_resource_len(*pdev*, 0, 2)
13:     ioaddr_size = pci_resource_len(*pdev*, 0, 2)
14: **end if**
15: **if** ! base_addr **then**
16:     pci_release()
17: **else**
18:     init_waitque_head()
19:     request_irq(kvm_pci_interrupt)
20: **end if**

---

1) By registering the character device, the kernel module obtains central device number, and realizes file operations such as reading and writing of the character device;

2) Then it initialize the device and wake up the device;
3) The module applies for memory space and configure memory resources according to the registered address space;
4) It sets the starting address and memory size of the mapped memory of BAR0 and BAR2, respectively, and maps BAR0 and BAR2 to the linear address space;
5) It registers interrupt callback.

The frontend handler receives the call from the cryptographic service API, writes the request into the shared memory mapped by the BAR2 register through the *mmap* system call, sends a request to the backend service on the host, and triggers an interrupt.

4.3   Backend Service

VCMs and the host share eventfd objects in addtion to shared memory. The shared resources are managed by the backend service. The backend service runs in privileged domain, it must be started before QEMU.

When the backend service is initializing, it creates a shared memory object through *shm_open* and *ftruncate*, initializes the shared memory size, queue number, queue information, etc., and creates a Unix socket, waiting for the QEMU process to connect. It establishes a socket connection with the service every time QEMU starts a VCM. The service assigns an ID to VCM and sends the ID and eventfd file descriptor to QEMU through the socket. QEMU stores the ID into the IVPosition register of ivshmem PCI device BAR0 in the VCM. Each VCM ID is unique and is used to identify the VCM when sending and receiving data, and the service identifies the address of the VCM in the shared memory through the VCM ID. Each VCM is listening on the eventfd bound to its ID. After receiving the interrupt request from the VCM, the service program reads the content of the shared memory, calls the cryptographic card driver to complete the request, and writes the response information back to the shared memory. The virtual interrupt controller of the kernel calls back the interrupt handler and notifies the VCM through its ID. The VCM receives the interrupt, reads the shared memory, and returns the response to the application.

Algorithm 2 shows the procedure of interrupt processing.

1) The VCM calls *ivshmem_send*, operates the ivshmem device to initiate an interrupt, and falls into the kernel through the privileged instruction *vmalunch*;
2) The kernel device driver calls *write()* to write the doorbell register of the device's BAR0, the kernel finds that it is a KVM virtual device, and the VCM exits to QEMU for processing;
3) QEMU calls *ivshmem_io_write*, and writes character 1 to the target eventfd file according to the incoming address;
4) The service program receives the eventfd signal, and implements interrupt injection;

5) The interrupt controller of the kernel calls back the interrupt function and performs interrupt processing according to the value of BAR0.

Algorithm 2. Interrupt process

Input: *fd, sema_irq, addr*
Output: *result*
1: result=ivshmem_send(*fd*, 0)
2: **if** *result* **then**
3:     ioctl(KVM_RUN)
4:     vmlaunch()
5: **end if**
6: kvm_ivshmem_ioctl(*sema_irq*)
7: write(bar0)
8: vmexit to QEMU
9: ivshmem_io_write(*addr*)
10: event_notifier_set(eventfds[vector],1)
11: *result* = ivshmem_IntrStatus_write(1)
12: **if** *result* **then**
13:     kvm_vm_ioctl(*result*)
14: **end if**
15: *result* = kvm_ivshmem_interrupt(dev_instance)
16: **if** *result* **then**
17:     kvm_ivshmem_ioctl()
18: **end if**

In the actual cloud cryptographic service scenario, considering a large amount of data block transmission, the size of the shared memory set may not be enough for one-time transmission during the initialization of the service program. This paper divides shared memory into multiple areas to solve this problem. We use the first memory area as flow control and introduce two variables, *usable* and *unusable*, to identify the read and write conditions of other memory blocks. *usable* represents the number of available memory areas, and *unusable* represents the number of unavailable memory areas. The two variables are protected with a lock each to achieve flow control.

5   Performance Evaluation

This section compares the data transmission performance and algorithm performance of the cryptographic card virtualization solution proposed in this paper and the current best-performing cryptographic card software virtualization solution. Then we optimize our solution and compare its performance with the original method.

5.1   Experiment Environment

The experimental environment includes 5 ThinkServer RQ940 servers, the processor model is Intel E7-4820, the number of CPU cores is 8, the memory is 32G, and each has 10 PCIe expansion slots. The operating system version is CentOS8.5-x86_64-2111, the kernel version is 4.18.0-348.2.1.el8_5.x86_64, and the QEMU version is 6.0.1. The cryptographic card adopts SJK1823 (#2) from Sansec. The VCM image is Ubuntu-18.04-desktop.qcow2.

5.2   Data Transfer Performance Test

For the software-based cryptographic card virtualization solutions, the vhost-based virtualization method proposed in [7,8,21] is widely used in existing research and is best-performing. This section compares the data transmission performance between this solution and the solution proposed in this paper.

This experiment tests the transmission time of data of different sizes. The data block size ranges from 0.1 Mb to 5 Mb. As shown in Fig. 3, with the increasing of data block size, the performance of shared memory is better than vhost. The transmission speed of shared memory is three times higher than vhost when the data block increases to 1 Mb.

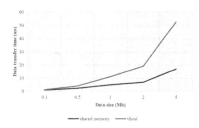

Fig. 3. Data transfer Time (ms)

5.3   Encryption Algorithm Performance Test

This experiment tests the performance of three commonly used international cryptographic algorithms in a single VM scenario and multiple VMs scenario and takes the performance of the cryptographic card on the host as a reference. The three commonly used algorithms include SHA256, RSA, and AES. The experiment method is to send cryptographic request cyclically on the VCM. We use a randomly generated string containing numbers and uppercase and lowercase letters as the input of the cryptographic algorithm, and the length gradually increases. This experiment obtains the number of operations in a fixed time to improve the accuracy. In addition, to exclude the chance of a single test, the test result is the average value of 10 tests after removing a maximum value and a minimum value. Each point in the figure represents the rate of cryptographic operations, which is calculated by multiplying the data length under the input by the number of operations divided by the running time.

First, we test the performance of the SHA algorithm. SHA is the most widely used hash algorithm at present, and the data bloack size increases from 16 bits to 16384 bits. Figure 4(a) shows the performance test results of the SHA256 algorithm of each solution in a single VM scenario. The performance of shared memory and vhost are 92% and 89% of the host when the data block size is 16 bits. As the data block size increases, the performance of shared memory increases slowly, and the performance of vhost gradually decreases. The performance of vhost is only 62% of shared memory when the data block size reaches 1024 bits. When it reaches 16384 bits, the performance of vhost is only 34% of shared memory. Figure 4(b) illustrates the results in the scenario of multiple VMs. The tested data block size is 256 bits. When the number of VMs exceeds 5, the overall performance of the two schemes exceed the host and tends to be stable. When the number of VMs is 10, the performance of shared memory and vhost is 107% and 105% of the host. Therefore, The performance of shared memory is better than vhost in SHA.

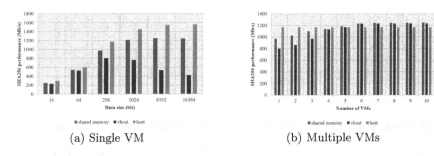

(a) Single VM   (b) Multiple VMs

Fig. 4. SHA256 performance (Mb/s)

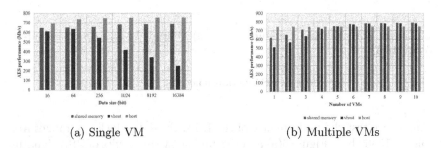

(a) Single VM   (b) Multiple VMs

Fig. 5. AES performance (Mb/s)

Then we test the performance of the AES algorithm. The AES is an symmetric encryption algorithm which the encryption and decryption keys are the same and is mainly used for the secure transmission of extensive data. The data block size ranges from 16 bits to 16384 bits. Figure 5(a) shows the performance test results of AES in a single VM scenario. The performance of shared memory and vhost are 93% and 88% of the host when data block size is 16 bits. As the data size increases, the performance of shared memory increases, and the performance of vhost gradually decreases. When the data block size reaches 1024 bits, the performance of vhost is only 61% of that of shared memory. After the data block size exceeds 1024 bits, the performance of shared memory gradually stabilize, while the performance of vhost decrease significantly. When it reaches 16384 bits, the performance of vhost is only 36% of shared memory. Figure 5(b) shows the results in the scenario of multiple VMs, and the data block size is 256 bits. When the number of VMs increases to 5, the overall performance of the two schemes begins to exceed the host and tends to be stable. When the number of VMs is 10, the performance of shared memory and vhost is 106% and 104% of the host. Therefore, the performance of shared memory is better than that of vhost in AES.

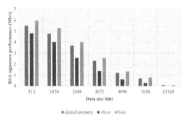

(a) Single VM of RSA Signature

(b) Multiple VMs of RSA Signature

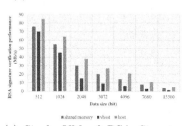

(c) Single VM of RSA Signature Verification

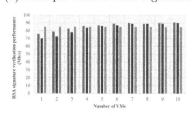

(d) Multiple VMs of RSA Signature Verification

Fig. 6. RSA performance (Mb/s)

Finally, we test the performance of the RSA, the data block size ranges from 512 bits to 15360 bits. Figure 6(a) and Fig. 6(c) show the results of RSA signature and signature verification algorithms in a single VM scenario. The performance degrades significantly when the data block size exceeds 1024 bits. The reason is that the message is hashed to generate a digest which the signature algorithm is used to sign. As the data block size increases, the hash will have a more significant impact on the overall performance of the signature algorithm. When the data block size is 512 bits, the performance of shared memory and vhost are 92% and 80% of the host in the signature algorithm and are 90% and 82% in the signature verification algorithm. When the data block size increases to 15360 bits, the performance of the signature and verification algorithms of vhost are 33% and 37% of shared memory. Figure 6(b) and Fig. 6(d) show the performance results in the scenario of multiple VMs. The data block size is 512 bits. When the number of VMs increases to 5, the performance of the two schemes begins to exceed the host and tends to stabilize. When the number of VMs is 10, shared memory and vhost performances are 108% and 106% of the host in the signature algorithm, and 107% and 106% in the signature verification algorithm. Therefore, the performance of shared memory is better than vhost in RSA.

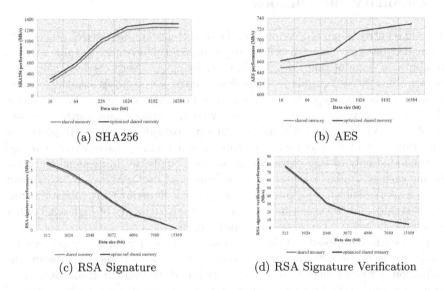

(a) SHA256

(b) AES

(c) RSA Signature

(d) RSA Signature Verification

Fig. 7. Performance comparison after optimization (Mb/s)

5.4   Performance Test After Optimization

In order to optimize the data transmission performance in the shared memory-based cryptographic card virtualization scheme, this paper introduces the UIO technology in the front-end driver. The general device drivers in Linux run in the kernel space, while most of the functions of the UIO driver run in the userspace, and only a tiny part runs in the kernel space. The client can directly operate the shared memory in the userspace with this technology. The user-mode driver is used to replace the kernel-mode driver, which reduces the data transmission time between the VM and the host. Next, we compare the performance of each encryption algorithm between the optimized solution and the original.

As shown in Fig. 7(a) and Fig. 7(b), the performance of SHA256 and AES is improved by 2% compared with the original scheme when the data block size is 16 bits. The performance of the optimized scheme is gradually improved as the data size increases. When data block size increased to 16384 bits, the optimized performance is 6% and 6.5% higher than the original solution. As shown in Fig. 7(c) and Fig. 7(d), the signature and verification performance of the RSA algorithm is improved by 2.2% and 2.3% when the data size is 512 bits. The performance of the optimized scheme is gradually improved as the data size increases. The performance of RSA signature and verification improved by 6% and 6.2% when data size increases to 15360 bits.

6   Summary and Outlook

As cloud security issues receive more and more attention, the research on cloudification of cryptographic services is in full swing, and cloud cryptographic services are also in a stage of rapid development. Existing password card virtualization solutions have various problems. Therefore, this paper proposes a software virtualization method of cryptographic cards based on shared memory. We virtualize a PCIe cryptographic card into multiple virtual cryptographic cards, encapsulate it as a VCM to provide users with cryptographic services, improve the utilization rate of cryptographic resources, and realize elastic expansion and on-demand supply of cryptographic resources. Finally, we implement a cryptographic card virtualization prototype system based on QEMU. The experiment proves that the solution proposed in this paper is superior to the existing software virtualization schemes and can meet the requirements of high-availability and high-concurrency cryptographic applications.

The solution proposed in this paper also have room for further improvement. Firstly, the isolation between virtual cryptographic cards based on software virtualization is weaker than that of hardware-based virtualization solutions. Secondly, user authentication mechanism and access control need to be enhanced at the software level. Then the problem of performance loss caused by the transformation needs to be further solved.

References

1. Top Threats to Cloud Computing. https://cloudsecurityalliance.org/press-releases. Accessed 28 Sept 2020
2. Cloud Cryptography Service Technical White Paper. http://www.bccia.org.cn/upload/files/2019/12/19f490f47a6d26bd.pdf. Accessed 4 Apr 2022
3. Sansec. https://www.sansec.com.cn/product/62.html. Accessed 1 Apr 2022
4. Yan, Z., Rongwei, C., Yuchao, S.: Application of cryptographic resource pool system in cloud computing environment. In: Research on Information Security, pp. 558–561 (2016)

5. Lei, S., Zewu, W., Kun, Z., Ruichen, S., Shuai, L.: Research and design of cryptography cloud framework. In: IEEE 3rd International Conference on Cloud Computing and Big Data Analysis 2018, pp. 147–154, (2018)
6. Sun, L., Wang, Z.W., Sun, R.C.: Research and design of cryptocard virtualization framework. In: Proceedings of 2016 International Conference on Wireless Communication and Network Engineering, pp. 311–319. Lancaster (2016)
7. Tang, L., Dou, T., Sang, H., Zhang, Y.: Software virtualization of password card based on I/O front-end and back-end model. In: Computer System Application, pp. 286–294 (2022)
8. Jiafu, Z.: Research on virtual desktop privacy protection based on password card virtualization. In: Huazhong University of Science and Technology. Wuhan (2017)
9. Li, Y.: The Research and Implementation of Cryptographic Algorithim Model in Cloud Computing Environment. In: Shandong University. Jinan (2016)
10. Rodríguez-Haro, F., Freitag, F., Navarro, L.: A summary of virtualization techniques. In: Procedia Technology, pp. 267–272 (2012)
11. Zhang, B., et al.: A Survey on I/O virtualization and optimization. In: 2010 Fifth Annual ChinaGrid Conference, pp. 117–123 (2010)
12. Barham, P., Dragovic, B., Fraser, K.: Xen and the art of virtualization. In: Proceedings of the 19th ACM Symposium on Operating System Principles, pp. 581–596 (2013)
13. Keir, F., et al.: Safe hardware access with the Xen virtual machine monitor. In: Proceedings of the 1st Workshop on Operating System and Architectural Support for the on demand IT InfraStructure, pp. 109–120 (2014)
14. Ma, L.: Design and implementation of high-speed password card based on SR-IOV virtualization technology. In: Shanghai Jiaotong University. Shanghai (2016)
15. Ren, J., Lin, S., Ye, Y.: Research and implementation of SR-IOV technology based on FPGA. In: Communication Technology, pp. 2321–2324. Shenzhen(2019)
16. Yang, Y., Yan, F., Yu, Z., et al.: Research on a virtual machine security isolation framework based on VT-d technology. In: Information Network Security, pp. 21–14 (2006)
17. Su, Z.: Research and implementation of password card virtualization technology. In: Integrated Technology, pp. 31–41 (2019)
18. Yang, W., Liu, J., Tu, Z., et al.: Design of virtualized trusted platform based on password card. In: Information Technology, pp. 171–176 (2016)
19. Tass. https://www.tass.com.cn/portal/article/index/cid/6/id/1.html. Accessed 2 May 2022
20. https://blog.csdn.net/LU_ZHAO/article/details/105237107 . Accessed 20 May 2022
21. Russell, R.: Virtio: towards a de-facto standard for virtual I/O devices. In: ACM SIGOPS Operating Systems Review, pp. 95–103 (2008)
22. Liu, Y., Niu, B.: Network request performance optimization of paravirtualization framework virtio. In: Small Microcomputer System, pp. 105–110 (2018)
23. El Amri, A., Meddeb, A.: Optimal server selection for competitive service providers in network virtualization context. In: Telecommunication Systems, pp. 451–467 (2021)

Network Security

Feature Transfer Based Network Anomaly Detection

Tao Chen and Kun Wen[✉]

Zhongyuan University of Technology, Zhengzhou 450000, China
wen@zut.edu.cn

Abstract. Network anomaly detection techniques can identify potential attacks from network traffic. However, they have been less than ideal in terms of detection accuracy. One important reason is that, for real network traffic data, different kinds of data have highly similar characteristics, thus leading to the situation that models misclassify the data with very similar characteristics. This situation accounts for the majority of misclassified samples. Accordingly, this paper proposes a feature transfer based neural network anomaly detection algorithm, which achieves complete detection of anomalous data, both known and unknown attacks (theoretically), by transferring the range of features common to highly similar normal and abnormal data to the range of anomalous data features. Since the algorithm's effectiveness depends on the feature variability of the normal data samples, and it isn't easy to obtain a pair of normal data samples with completely different features, this paper uses only one kind of normal data sample with good consistency. This paper uses the Transformer model to build the experimental framework and conduct 50 iterations of the experiment. The Corrected validation set from the KDD99 dataset is used to validate the model training effect. The experiments show that, relative to the original model, the error rate decreases by 1.38% on average after using this algorithm, the specificity of unknown attacks increases by 27.9% on average, and the number of attack categories with more than 90% specificity of unknown attacks increases from one to six.

Keywords: Transformer · Anomaly detection · Feature transfer · KDD99

1 Introduction

1.1 Motivation

Neural network models may not be able to correctly classify specific data because of problems such as insufficient data needed for training or defects in their structure. In general, we cannot predict what type of data the model will judge these incapable of classifying. For intrusion detection tasks, complete detection of anomalous data can be achieved if data that these models cannot correctly classify can be judged as anomalous. This is important for constructing a high-security system and enhancing the defense against unknown attacks.

C. Su et al. (Eds.): SciSec 2022, LNCS 13580, pp. 155–169, 2022.
https://doi.org/10.1007/978-3-031-17551-0_10

In this paper, we find that the main reason for the misclassification of data by neural networks is that the different kinds of data processed by neural networks have highly similar features to each other, and these data have a high degree of matching on such features. The problem can be expressed as follows: for a chunk containing both class A and class B data, the data in the chunk are highly similar, but their common highly similar features are not necessarily related to whether a particular data is class A or B. Because of the high significance of the common features, these features are decisive for the model to determine whether a data is a particular class compared to other features. However, this type of feature must have a great difference of significance in the range of features of different kinds of data so that the model can only judge the whole group as A or B class. If the model judges the chunk as A, the B data in the chunk is misclassified, and vice versa.

The primary way to deal with this classification error is to try to reduce the salience of common features and increase the salience of non-common features so that the model judges things according to the non-common features of each type of thing. Often, this isn't easy to achieve by adjusting the model structure itself, which is more related to the characteristics of the data itself and less connected to the model and the specific task. While we cannot directly reduce the salience of shared features and increase the salience of non-shared features, we can try to find out where these shared salient features correspond in the model. We can do this by controlling the data's consistency to narrow the data's range of features. By limiting the feature range of a specific type of data, the excluded features belonging to that type of data are subsumed into the features of other types of data that also have that type of feature, thus achieving the exposure of the features of that type. If the exposed features cover all the common features, the complete detection of other kinds of data can be achieved.

1.2   Related Work

Zhang et al. achieved high accuracy using unlabeled data to generate pseudo-labels to optimize the base LightGBM classifier [1]. Yuan et al. used three different Adaboost algorithms as weak classifiers to constitute a semi-supervised Triadaboost algorithm and achieved better results [2]. Jiang et al. used self-training and a standard boosting algorithm for semi-supervised learning and performed 97.64% accuracy on the KDD99 dataset [3]. Huang et al. proposed the IGAN-IDS model to generate a few class samples, significantly improving class imbalance detection [4]. Guo Pu proposed an unsupervised anomaly detection method by combining SVM and subspace clustering [5]. AlEroud A et al. proposed a content similarity-based detection model in the literature [6]. Song et al. offered a way to separately model known traffic classes using a single classification support vector machine to identify unknown attacks by determining whether the traffic belongs to a known type [7]. Li et al. proposed an attribute learning method, which identifies unknown attacks through an inter-class migration learning mechanism of attributes [8]. Zhang et al. proposed using a semantic self-encoder approach to detect unknown attacks by constructing feature-to-semantic mappings [9]. Chen P et al. offer a preprocessing data approach for unknown attacks in the literature [10], which uses statistical features of the training set as intrinsic features of the network environment to process the data and achieves better results. The importance of data preprocessing in network intrusion detection is described in great detail by DAJ Clark et al. in the literature [11]. Taeshik et al. proposed an SVM model based on unsupervised learning that effectively reduces the false alarm rate [12]. Lin et al. proposed the clustering center and nearest neighbor method CANN, effectively improving the detection rate and speed [13]. Ying-Yi Feng et al. proposed a category reorganization technique with FocalLoss loss function, significantly improving the detection accuracy for rare samples [14]. Xueli Xu et al. combined CNN and SVM to improve the model's generalization performance and learning speed [15]. One of the main reasons for the errors of neural network models in classification tasks is that they deal with different classes of data with highly similar characteristics, making it difficult for the model to distinguish them. Accordingly, this paper proposes a feature transfer-based anomaly detection algorithm, which detects anomalous data, both known and unknown attacks, by transferring the range of features common to highly similar normal and abnormal data to the range of anomalous data features.

2 Preliminaries

2.1 Transformer

The transformer is a neural network model proposed by Ashish Vaswani et al. in 2017 [16]. The overall structure of the Transformer model is as shown in Fig. 1.

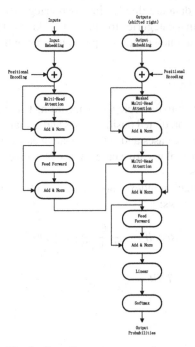

Fig. 1. Transformer structure diagram

Compared with traditional CNN, RNN, and other models, Transformer can simultaneously extract spatial and temporal features of data. Compared with the traditional time series model, it has better parallelism and stronger long-distance relational connection ability.

The Query, Key, and Value vectors are calculated as follows:

$$Q = W^Q * X \tag{1}$$

$$K = W^K * X \tag{2}$$

$$V = W^V * X \tag{3}$$

The formula for calculating the self-concentration layer is as follows:

$$Attention(Q, K, V) = softmax\left(\frac{QK^T}{\sqrt{d_k}}\right)V \tag{4}$$

2.2 Experimental Data Set

The dataset used in this experiment is the KDD-Cup-99 dataset [17]. The training set kddcup.data_10_percent contains 494021 data, and the validation set Corrected contains 311029 data. The sample data are divided into two categories: normal and abnormal. There are 39 attack types in 4 categories for anomalous kinds. There are 22 attack types in the training set, and 17 unknown attack types exist only in the test set.

2.3 Evaluation Indicators

The samples were classified into four categories according to the actual and predicted categories: True Positive (TP): predicted positive cases and actual positive cases; True Negative (TN): predicted negative cases and actual negative cases; False Positive (FP): predicted positive cases and actual negative cases; False Negative (FN): predicted negative cases, actual positive cases.

The experimental evaluation indexes are recall (Recall) and specificity (TNR). The detailed formulas are as follows:

$$Recall = \frac{TP}{TP + FN} \times 100\% \tag{5}$$

$$TNR = \frac{TN}{TN + FP} \times 100\% \tag{6}$$

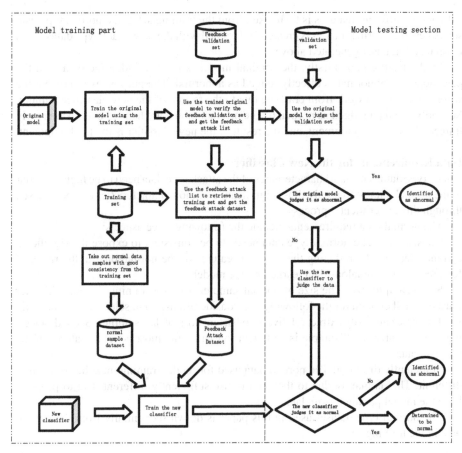

Fig. 2. Detection model framework

3 Feature Transfer Based Anomaly Detection Model

3.1 Framework

The detection model is divided into two major parts: the model training part and the model testing part, as shown in Fig. 2. Among them, the model training part completes training two transformer models. The model testing part uses the two trained models to make judgments on the validation set and calculate the evaluation metrics of the models.

Model training part: Use the training set to train the original transformer model, and then use the feedback validation set to test the trained model, collect the attack categories with poor recognition effect (FP>=TN) in the feedback validation set, and finally get a list of attack categories. This list only contains the attack categories poorly identified in the feedback validation set and does not contain specific sample data and labels. By retrieving this list, the attack types that exist in both this list and the training set are removed from the training set used to train the original model and combined into a new attack category dataset. A smaller sample of normal type data with more consistent but sufficiently different features is then taken from the training set as the normal type data set. A new transformer model is created and trained with the new attack type dataset and normal type dataset generated above.

Model testing part: Firstly, the original model is used to judge the data, and the part judged as abnormal is directly judged as abnormal. The purpose is to prevent the whole model framework from crashing due to the failure of the new classifier training. Secondly, the data judged as normal by the original model are handed over to the newly trained classifier for judgment, and the result of the new classifier is the final judgment.

Data Requirements for the New Classifier

Attack type data: The data characteristics of the attack type data need to be highly similar to the normal data so that only those significant common characteristics can be exposed through this experimental process.

The normal data requirements include the following three aspects:

Consistency: The normal type data needs to be consistent to expose the significant common features by reducing the range of features of the normal data to the range of features of the anomalous data learned by the model.

Small sample size: The size of normal samples used for training the new classifier must be small enough for the following two considerations: First, selecting a sufficiently small sample can easily extract relatively consistent normal data samples. Second, selecting a sufficiently small sample is sufficient to extract the most general features of the normal data.

Sufficiently different: The normal data used for model training must be sufficiently different. This is mainly due to the need to use sufficiently different data to properly keep the model parameters updated.

The normal type dataset used in this paper is drawn sequentially from the normal data in the training set.

Feature Transfer

Feature transfer is the process of transferring the features shared by highly similar normal data and abnormal data to the range of abnormal data features to achieve complete detection of abnormal data.

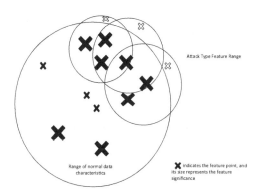

Fig. 3. The range of features learned by the original model

The feature range diagram can graphically represent the category features learned by the model. The circles in the graph indicate the range of features contained in a specific category of data; the fork symbols indicate the feature points, and their sizes indicate the significance of the feature; the solid fork symbols indicate the features of normal data, and the hollow fork symbols indicate the features of abnormal data only.

Let the significance of a feature point F_i be R_i; x be the input sample; $f_i(x)$ indicates the matching degree of x on the feature point F_i; n represents the number of feature points contained in a particular data category C; $S_C(x)$ denotes the relative magnitude of the model's confidence in whether the sample data x is a specific category C. Then the following equation is given:

$$S_C(x) = \sum_{i=0}^{n} R_i f_i(x) \tag{7}$$

Suppose that the significance of a feature point F_{i-} contained in the overlapping part of the feature range of a data category C and other data categories is R_{i-}, and the number of such feature points is n; the significance of the feature points contained in the non-overlapping part be R_{i+}, and the number of such feature points is m; the proportion of non-common features of a category C among all features learned by the model be G_C, then we have the following equation:

$$G_C = \frac{\sum_{i=0}^{m} R_{i+}}{\sum_{i=0}^{m} R_{i+} + \sum_{i=0}^{n} R_{i-}} \tag{8}$$

In general, the range of features learned by the original model is shown in Fig. 3. The features of the attack type data learned by the model that only belong to the attack type are usually not as significant as the part of the features they share with the normal data, and the significance of the normal type is greater than the significance of the abnormal type on the shared features. Therefore, the model will tend to identify these attacks as normal (Fig. 4).

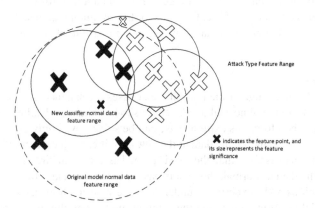

Fig. 4. The range of features learned by the model after reducing the range of features of normal data

In this paper, by narrowing the feature range of normal data, we try to judge all highly matched data on overlapping features as abnormal so that almost all data that is difficult to judge because of similar features can be judged as abnormal. This approach only reduces the range of overlapping normal data features and attack type features so that the part of features beyond that range is exposed. However, it is still difficult to fully classify the features of the overlapping region into the field of abnormal data features (Fig. 5).

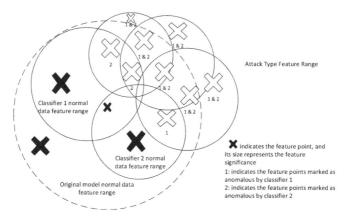

Fig. 5. The range of features learned by the model after supplemental training with normal data samples of different features

The problem can be well solved by using two normal data samples with completely different common features and good internal consistency to train two separate classifiers. (It is better to use normal data samples with completely different characteristics to prevent the influence of the widening range of abnormal data characteristics.) As long as one of the two classifiers judges the data as abnormal, it is directly judged as abnormal, and the rest is judged as normal. Since the range of normal data features learned by the two classifiers covers completely different regions for the common features, this enables the complete detection of abnormal data. However, it isn't easy to obtain such normal data samples.

Effect Stabilizer

Narrowing the feature range of the normal data causes the salience of those remaining features within the range of normal data's features to be enhanced, leading to a one-way model collapse. Therefore, this extreme case can be solved by simply using the trained original model before handing the data to the new classifier for judgment. If the original model judges the data as abnormal, the data is judged as abnormal directly. If the original model judges the data as normal, the data is passed to the new classifier for judgment.

In 50 repetitions of the experiment under the same state conditions, only once did the combined model perform worse than the original model, and the two were very close to each other. Accordingly, it can be concluded that the post-collapse model still has a significant advantage over the original model in judging the part of data judged as normal by the original model.

3.2 Data Pre-processing

The training set used in this experiment is kddcup.data_10_percent, the validation set is corrected, and the feedback validation set uses the validation set. The specific methods of data preprocessing are One-Hot coding, data normalization, and integer value mapping.

One-Hot Coding

One-Hot encoding [18] is a commonly used method for processing non-numeric attributes. One-Hot encoding converts a non-numeric attribute into an attribute class equal to the value type of the attribute. For example, there are three types of TCP, UDP, ICMP attribute protocol_type converted into TCP, UDP, ICMP. These sub-attributes obtained by decomposing the original attributes are Boolean values of 0 or 1, indicating whether they are the sub-attributes.

Data Normalization

Data normalization is the mapping of the original values to a specific range. The normalization used in this paper is maximum-minimum normalization [19], by which the data is mapped to between (0, 1). The formula is as follows:

$$x = \frac{x - \min(x)}{\max(x) - \min(x)} \tag{9}$$

Normalization allows the values of attributes with different data ranges to be compared simply by mapping the data of all attributes to the same range. This approach can somewhat mitigate the adverse effects on the model caused by the different value ranges of different attributes.

Integer Value Mapping

After normalizing the One-Hot encoded data, an integer value is selected (101 is usually chosen for the KDD99 dataset). Next, the normalized data is allowed to multiply by this integer value minus one and finally rounded down. The above steps will transform the intrusion detection data into a dictionary marker for NLP tasks. The processed data can then be used as a padded statement vector for training or judgments to transform the intrusion detection task into a text classification task.

3.3 Model Training

Model Training Process

First, the original model is trained directly using the training set.

Second, create a new classifier. The training consists of 3 large rounds, each with 28 small rounds. Any value can replace the 28 here. The smaller the value, the smaller the range of features of the normal data. One thing to note here is the number of training sessions. Most of the instability of the model is caused by the lack of a sufficient number of training sessions. Each small round is first trained with a small sample of normal data and then with the full set of attack-type data. Each small round in the same large round uses different normal type data, and the corresponding small rounds of different large rounds use the same normal type data.

Algorithm 1. New classifier training.
Input: *Normal_data, Normal_label, Attack_data, Attack_label, Model*
Output: *Model*
Training sample size ←28
FOR *i1*←0 TO 2 DO
    FOR *i2*←0 TO 27 DO
        Use Normal_data[i2 * training sample size:(i2 + 1) * training sample size],Normal_label to train the Model
        Train Model with Attack_data,Attack_label
    END FOR
END FOR

Loss Value Changes During the Training of the New Classifier
In the early stages of the training process, the model is trained with a small sample of normal data, where the loss rate is high, indicating that the model is learning the data features of these data and has not yet fully learned them; the model is trained with a selected sample of abnormal data, where the loss rate is low because the sample size of the abnormal data is much larger than the normal data sample. Both eventually converge to the lower of the smooth values.

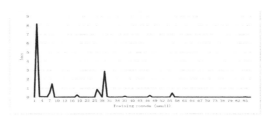

Fig. 6. The normal data loss rate of one training session with the number of training rounds (small)

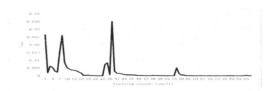

Fig. 7. Variation of data loss rate of attack types with training rounds (small) for one training

As seen in Fig. 6 and Fig. 7, the loss rate of normal data is usually much higher than the loss rate of these selected attack-type data. The attack types' loss rate fluctuates with the normal data's loss rate. The more significant sudden fluctuations in loss rate in the figure are related to the large training round turnover, and the more minor fluctuations may be related to the consistency changes in the normal data sample.

4 Experimental Results and Analysis

The Transformer model is continuously trained 50 times under the same conditions. Next, use the 50 trained original models to combine 50 trained new classifiers to obtain 50 combined models. Finally, the combined model is compared to the original model without combining the new classifier.

Each indicator (TP, TN, FP, FN) used in this paper is the average of 50 experiments. These averages do not imply the usual judging effect for a category but rather the probability value of judging the situation for such a category. For example, if the TN of a specific type of attack is 5 and the FP is 5, it does not necessarily mean that the model judged the number of 10 samples of that type correctly at each time is about 5. It may also mean that the model repeated the experiment 10 times and judged all of them correctly five times, all of them incorrectly five times.

4.1 Identification of Various Types of Known Attacks

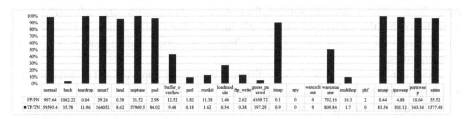

	normal	back	teardrop	smurf	land	neptune	pod	buffer_o verflow	perl	rootkit	loadmod ule	ftp_write	guess_pa sswd	imap	spy	warezcli ent	warezma ster	multihop	phf	nmap	ipsweep	portswee p	satan
FP/FN	997.64	1062.22	0.04	39.26	0.38	31.52	2.98	12.52	1.82	11.38	1.46	2.62	4169.72	0.1	0	0	792.16	16.3	2	0.44	4.88	10.64	55.52
TP/TN	59595.4	35.78	11.96	164052	8.62	57969.5	84.02	9.48	0.18	1.62	0.54	0.38	197.28	0.9	0	0	809.84	1.7	0	83.56	301.12	343.36	1577.48

Fig. 8. Identification of normal data and various types of known attacks by the original model

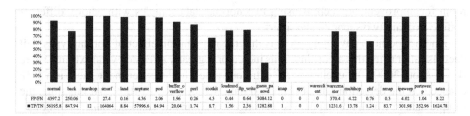

	normal	back	teardrop	smurf	land	neptune	pod	buffer_o verflow	perl	rootkit	loadmod ule	ftp_write	guess_pa sswd	imap	spy	warezcli ent	warezma ster	multihop	phf	nmap	ipsweep	portswee p	satan
FP/FN	4397.2	250.06	0	27.4	0.16	4.36	2.06	1.96	0.26	4.3	0.44	0.64	3084.12	0	0	0	370.4	4.22	0.76	0.3	4.02	1.04	8.22
TP/TN	56195.8	847.94	12	164064	8.84	57996.6	84.94	20.04	1.74	8.7	1.56	2.36	1282.88	1	0	0	1231.6	13.78	1.24	83.7	301.98	352.96	1624.78

Fig. 9. Identification of normal data and various types of known attacks by the combined model

The horizontal coordinates of Fig. 8 and Fig. 9 indicate each data category; the vertical coordinates indicate the recall or specificity, which represents the rate at which a specific type of data is correctly identified; the table below lists the values of the metrics for each category.

From Fig. 8, it can be seen that the original model can get good recognition on most types and performs very well on all of these types. However, the recognition effect is poor on some other attack types (specificity below 90%), and the specificity is less than 10% on half of these attack types, less than 20% on 70% of them, and less than 30% on 80% of them.

From the above experimental data, it is easy to draw the following analysis: It is not that the Transformer model does not learn the data features of these poorly identified attack types. This is because if the model does not learn these attack types well, it should not know how to classify them. In the end, it would have a 50% chance of being either normal or aggressive, rather than the experimental data suggests: most poorly identified attack types' specificity is very low. We have to assume that the model is not badly learning the characteristics of these attack-type data. Instead, it is because the model knows the features of these attack types so well that it cannot detect them well. The results of validation experiments on the Transformer model by reducing the sample size show that the model can fully detect SNMPGETATTACK when the sample size of the training set is 100,000, which indicates that the model has already learned data characteristics of this attack type. However, after expanding the sample size to 200,000, the model is almost entirely unable to identify this attack type and instead judges this attack type data almost wholly as normal. More importantly, when the CNN-LSTM model was used to do the same experiment on these 100,000 data, the CNN-LSTM was also almost entirely unable to correctly identify SNMPGETATTACK. But the sum of FN and FP of SNMPGETATTACK of CNN-LSTM and Transformer models is practically equal. Both models determine whether these data are attacks with very high confidence. This shows that these two models can only identify this type of attack and the normal data related to it as normal or abnormal. These two types of data have very similar characteristics.

As seen in Fig. 9, the models have different degrees of improvement in detecting all attack types of data after using this algorithm.

Although this algorithm has significantly improved the recognition of attack types that are otherwise poorly identified, the recognition of these attack types is still poor compared to other attack types. This is mainly because the more consistent sample of normal data selected still contains some disturbing features. This also means there is still room for improvement, such as using two normal data samples with wholly different features to train two separate classifiers.

Another point to pay attention to is that the recognition effect of normal types will decrease after using this algorithm. This indicator is greatly affected by the extreme value (FN is about 3000 after excluding the extreme value). In the experiment, there is a 10% chance that the detection rate of abnormal data will be close to 100%. At this time, the sample data in which normal data is misjudged as anomalous data account for 1/4 of all normal data. As mentioned earlier, this is the result of deliberately narrowing the range of features of normal data so that common features are exposed and classified as abnormal. This approach makes all data that are difficult to judge be judged as abnormal, which leads to some normal data that were judged to be normal by the original model being mistakenly judged as abnormal. This may mean that only further adjustments to this experimental framework are needed to achieve near-complete detection of anomalous data. However, further processing of data misjudged as abnormal is still required. The most suitable method to solve this problem is to directly adjust the weight parameters, which is also the main direction of the following work. This phenomenon also proves that some data of different categories have highly similar features, and some data have a high degree of matching on such features, which is the cause of model classification errors.

4.2 Identification of Various Types of Unknown Attacks

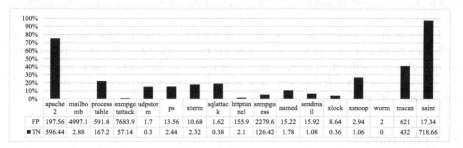

	apache2	mailbomb	process table	snmpgettattack	udpstorm	ps	xterm	sqlattack	httptunnel	snmpguess	named	sendmail	xlock	xsnoop	worm	mscan	saint
FP	197.56	4997.1	591.8	7683.9	1.7	13.56	10.68	1.62	155.9	2279.6	15.22	15.92	8.64	2.94	2	621	17.34
■ TN	596.44	2.88	167.2	57.14	0.3	2.44	2.32	0.38	2.1	126.42	1.78	1.08	0.36	1.06	0	432	718.66

Fig. 10. Identification of various types of unknown attacks by the original model

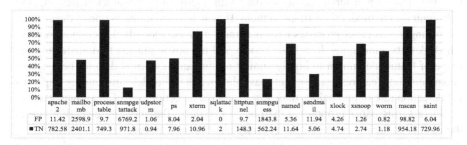

	apache2	mailbomb	process table	snmpgettattack	udpstorm	ps	xterm	sqlattack	httptunnel	snmpguess	named	sendmail	xlock	xsnoop	worm	mscan	saint
FP	11.42	2598.9	9.7	6769.2	1.06	8.04	2.04	0	9.7	1843.8	5.36	11.94	4.26	1.26	0.82	98.82	6.04
■ TN	782.58	2401.1	749.3	971.8	0.94	7.96	10.96	2	148.3	562.24	11.64	5.06	4.74	2.74	1.18	954.18	729.96

Fig. 11. Identification of various types of unknown attacks by the combined model

As can be seen from Fig. 10, the overall recognition of unknown attacks by the original model is poor. Only the specificity of attacks such as saint is over 90%, the specificity of apache2 is 75%, the specificity of mscan is 41%, and the rest are all below 30%. Among them, there are eight types of attacks with specificity equal to or lower than 10%, four types between 10% and 20%, and two types between 20% and 30%.

As in the above analysis, attack types such as Saint and apache2 are better identified because these attack types have very similar characteristics to some known attacks. These characteristics must be significant enough and not included in the feature range of normal data. The other attack types that are less well-identified, such as worm, mailbomb, etc., are because the model correctly learns the more salient features of these data. Still, these features are included in the range of features of the normal data and are therefore judged to be almost completely normal by the model.

As can be seen from Fig. 11, after using this algorithm, the combined model improved the recognition effect of all unknown attacks. In addition, except for saint, the recognition effect of other types of unknown attacks has been significantly improved. Among them, the number of attack types with specificity over 90% increased from 1 to 6, and the number of attack types between 80% and 90% increased from 0 to 1.

For those attack types for which the specificity increased to a very high level using this method, we can infer that the new classifier learned some relevant features of the attack type data from the known attacks. These features may not be significant in the original model. Or it is judged as abnormal because these attack-type data match too high on the overlapping features learned by the original model. These features are not included in the range of features for the well-consistent normal data used for training the new classifier.

For those attack types whose specificity remained low but improved after using this method, we can assume that this is because the normal data samples used for training the new classifier still retain some overlapping features. This part of the characteristics is dominant in the characteristics of these attack types, so the model still tends to judge these attack data as normal.

5   Conclusion

One of the main reasons for the errors of neural network models in classification tasks is that they deal with different classes of data with highly similar characteristics, making it difficult for the model to distinguish them. Hence, it has to judge as one of the classes. Accordingly, this paper proposes a feature transfer-based anomaly detection algorithm, which detects anomalous data, both known and unknown attacks, by transferring the range of features common to highly similar normal and abnormal data to the range of anomalous data features. Experiments have shown that the model substantially improves the detection rate of anomalous data, especially the detection rate of unknown attacks.

In fact, this paper proposes a method to maximize the anomaly detection rate at the cost of reducing the recall rate. It may also be used in reverse, i.e., to maximize the model's recall at the anomaly detection rate cost. The former can be used if higher security is needed and some usability can be sacrificed. The latter can be used if a higher availability is needed and some possible attacks can be spared. The two states can be switched arbitrarily in different conditions, such as using the former in a crisis and the latter in a normal situation, and the effect size can be adjusted by controlling the range of features, just like human wariness.

During the experiments, it was also found that different models, such as CNN, RNN, and LSTM, apply to the algorithm. In theory, the algorithm is independent of the specific neural network model, but the performance and the number of training sessions required vary slightly from model to model. The use of different models and ranges of normal data features may significantly differ in recognition of different types of attacks, and perhaps a filtering mechanism could be designed based on this.

References

1. Zhang, H., Li, J.: A new network intrusion detection based on semi-supervised dimensionality reduction and tri-LightGBM. In: 2020 International Conference on Pervasive Artificial Intelligence (ICPAI), pp. 35–40 IEEE (2020)
2. Yuan, Y., Huo, L., Yuan, Y., et al.: Semi-supervised tri-Adaboost algorithm for network intrusion detection. Int. J. Distrib. Sens. Netw. **15**(6), 1550147719846052 (2019)
3. Jiang, E.P.: A semi-supervised learning model for intrusion detection. Intell. Decis. Technol. **13**(3), 343–353 (2019)
4. Huang, S., Lei, K.: IGAN-IDS: an imbalanced generative adversarial network towards intrusion detection system in ad-hoc networks. Ad Hoc Netw. **105**(8), 350–368 (2020)
5. Guo, P., Wang, L., et al.: A hybrid unsupervised clustering-based anomaly detection method. Tsinghua Sci. Technol. **26**(02), 14–21 (2021)
6. AlEroud, A., Karabatis, G.: Detecting unknown attacks using context similarity. In: Alsmadi, I., Karabatis, G., Aleroud, A. (eds.) Information Fusion for Cyber-Security Analytics. SCI, vol. 691, pp. 53–75. Springer, Cham (2017). https://doi.org/10.1007/978-3-319-44257-0_3
7. Song, J., Takakura, H., Okabe, Y., et al.: Unsupervised anomaly detection based on clustering and multiple one-class SVM. IEICE Trans. Commun. **92**(6), 1981–1990 (2009)
8. Li, Z., Qin, Z., Shen, P., Jiang, L.: Zero-shot learning for intrusion detection via attribute representation. In: Gedeon, T., Wong, K., Lee, M. (eds.) ICONIP 2019. LNCS, vol. 11953, pp. 352–364. Springer, Cham (2019). https://doi.org/10.1007/978-3-030-36708-4_29
9. Zhang, Z., Liu, Q., Qiu, S., et al.: Unknown attack detection based on zero-shot learning. IEEE Access **8**, 193981–193991 (2020)
10. Chen, P., Guo, Y.F., Zhang, J.P., et al.: A deep neural network preprocessing method for unknown attack detection. J. Inf. Eng. Univ. **22**(2), 200–207 (2021)
11. Davis, J.J., Clark, A.J.: Data preprocessing for anomaly-based network intrusion detection: a review. Comput. Secur. **30**(6), 353–375 (2011)
12. Taeshik, S., Jongsub, M.: A hybrid machine learning approach to network anomaly detection. Inf. Sci. **177**(18), 3799–3821 (2007)
13. Lin, W., Ke, S.W., Tsai, C.F.: CANN: an intrusion detection system based on combining cluster centers and nearest neighbors. Knowl. Based Syst. **78**(1), 13–21 (2015)
14. Feng, Y.Y., Shi, Z.B.: CNN-based network intrusion detection under imbalanced data. J. North Cent. Univ. (Nat. Sci. Ed.) **42**(4), 318–324 (2021)
15. Xueli, X., Juan, D., Chuangbai, X., et al.: Message intrusion detection method based on CNN and SVM. Comput. Syst. Appl. **29**(6), 39–46 (2020)
16. Vaswani, A., Shazeer, N., Parmar, N., et al.: Attention is all you need, pp. 2999–3007. arXiv 2017. arXiv preprint arXiv:1706.03762 (2017)
17. Ambwani, T.: Multi-class support vector machine implementation to intrusion detection. In: International Joint Conference on Neural Networks. IEEE (2003)
18. Hu, Z., Wang, L., Qi, L., et al.: A novel wireless network intrusion detection method based on adaptive synthetic sampling and an improved convolutional neural network. IEEE Access **8**, 195741–195751 (2020)
19. Yan, Y., Qi, L., Wang, J., et al.: A network intrusion detection method based on stacked autoencoder and LSTM. In: ICC2020–2020 IEEE International Conference on Communications (ICC), pp. 1–6. IEEE (2020)

Hybrid Routing for Efficient Fine-Grained Management of Specific Services in SDN

Kun Jia[1,2] , Jiazhi Liu[1,2], Wen Wang[3], and Feng Liu[3(✉)]

[1] State Key Laboratory of Information Security, Institute of Information Engineering, CAS, Beijing 100093, China
`jiakun@iie.ac.cn`
[2] School of Cyber Security, University of Chinese Academy of Sciences, Beijing 100049, China
[3] Institute of information Engineering, CAS, Beijing 100093, China
`liufeng@iie.ac.cn`

Abstract. Software Defined Networking (SDN), a novel network architecture providing a global field of vision through separating data planes and control planes, has recently attracted a lot of attention because of its programmability and centralized control. However, to support some customized services such as resource allocation, anomaly detection, and traffic engineering, most advanced SDN designs require fine-grained management of specific flows, which may quickly exhaust the flow table of an SDN switch and lead to undesired processing overhead. Therefore, this paper proposes to balance the trade-off between customized services and resource consumption through hybrid routing. We formulate the installment of hybrid rules as integer linear programming problems. Rounding-based algorithms are proposed to acquire reasonable solutions which instruct the controller to install forwarding rules. Further experiments show the high efficiency of our algorithm. Compared with the benchmark work, our work reduces the maximum number of flow rules in SDN switches by at least 20.1% and shows better network performance in packet loss ratio and flow setup delay.

Keywords: Software defined network · MiniNet · Fine-grained management · RYU controller · Flow rules · Hybrid routing

1 Introduction

With the popularity of the Internet of things and social media, the era of big data has officially arrived. The increasing number of online terminals has led to a significant burden on network management. Meanwhile, resource constraints are a common problem, whether in the Internet of things [25], campus network,

Supported by the National Key R&D Program of China with No. 2018YFC0806900, Beijing Municipal Science & Technology Commission with Project No. Z191100007119009 and NSFC No. 61902397.

or data center [27]. Therefore, achieving effective management and, at the same time, meeting the requirement of customized services has become an essential issue in industry and academia. The traditional network is becoming increasingly outdated in some scenarios, such as data centers and clouds, due to its vendor-dependent devices, inability to scale the network architecture and adapt to the varying network environment, etc. [13]. Therefore, Software Defined Networking (SDN) emerges as the times require.

SDN is a new paradigm [16,28] that decouples the control and data planes into separated devices (e.g., controller and switches) to support flexible and agile flow control and resource management. The controller in SDN can adopt multiple open standard protocols such as OpenFlow [2,27], to control the underlying infrastructure. Due to its advantages, SDN can provide multiple customized services; for instance, resource allocation [23], anomaly detection [14,19], traffic engineering [12], and application identification [22]. However, to achieve heterogeneous management, most of them require per-application or per-flow fine-grained control of specific flows [13,18]. Technological developments and our increased interconnection to the Internet lead to the increase in cybercrimes [15] thus, per-application or per-flow management may lead to undesired overhead and depletion of resources. Attackers may even deliberately launching a DDoS [6,9,32] to paralyze the switches. Thus, balancing the trade-off between customized services and resource consumption is necessary.

Commonly, the simplest way to achieve per-flow management for specific flows is to install exact-match rules along the forwarding paths [7]. However, it consumes many flow rules, thus unacceptable in real life. Therefore, some advanced work proposed hybrid rule placement approaches. As a result, resources have been significantly saved by dispersing traffic, applying wildcard rules, and grouping similar flows. For instance, Liu et al. [13] proposed to dynamically group similar flows into a cluster and achieve macro-flow management. Alternatively, Wang et al. [23] proposed to disperse traffic into multiple paths using pre-installed wildcard rules to decrease the maximum load of links. However, all these schemes focus on balancing global services and resource consumption, thus may not always ensure fine-grained management for some customized services. The main contributions of this paper are summarized as follows:

1) We proposed a promising scheme, which realized fine-grained management of specific services and users for the first time;
2) Since our method achieves fine-grained management through installing heterogeneous rules effectively and proactively without completely getting the permission of traffic management; it is scalable and fit for other wildcard rule installment schemes;
3) Compared with the benchmark work, our work reduces the maximum number of flow rules in SDN switches by at least 20.1% and shows better network performance in packet loss ratio and flow setup delay.

The rest of this paper is organized as follows. Section 2 introduces related work. Section 3 describes the motivation and our intuition. In Sect. 4, we introduce the network model, formally propose the hybrid routing for efficient fine-grained management in three cases. We validate the availability and performance in Sect. 5 through a small-scale testbed and a large-scale simulated topology. Finally, we conclude this paper in Sect. 6.

2   Related Work

The capacity of SDN switch and the visibility of SDN have attracted the most attention. Among them, the visibility of SDN is actually decided by the fine-grained management of flows. Furthermore, with the wide use of SDN, reliable schemes to reduce the overhead of SDN components and maintain efficient network management have become emerging topics in SDN research. In general, typical work can be divided into hybrid routing and extension approaches.

Hybrid Routing Approaches. The simplest way to save flow table is to replace the exact-match rules with the wildcard rule. However, it might be too aggressive as all the flows matching one wildcard rule have to be routed along one path, which decreases the network visibility [5] and degrades the performance [13]. Hence, hybrid routing approaches are provided. The main idea of hybrid routing is installing multiple granularity rules to manage traffic hierarchically.

Several work [13,23,24] attempted to realize the optimal arrangement of flow table resources through hybrid routing, but they do not take into account the fine-grained control requirements of services.

As far as I know, He et al. [11] were the first to apply hybrid routing for fine-grained management, and they proposed Presto to install exact-match rules and wildcard rules on the edge and internal switches, respectively. Similarly, Yang et al. [29] proposed to deploy a joint virtual switch to alleviate this problem, which is based on the idea that the virtual switch has a more powerful processing ability and flow table compared to a physical switch. However, the above research still suffers from the insufficiency of flow table, especially for the edge switches.

Later, some researchers proposed to realize fine-grained management by reasonably deploying flow rules without changing the network environment. For instance, Bera et al. [5] proposed an adaptive flow-rule placement system, Flow-Stat, applying greedy algorithms to install wildcard rules and exact-match rules for each forwarding path. They came up with the idea that fine-grained management requires only one exact-match rule along the forwarding path.

Further, Zhao et al. [31] developed this idea to design an algorithm to install flow rules with a different granularity, therefore, showing better scalability. Moreover, they formulate linear programming to instruct the installation optimally. Their work tries to reduce the size of flow rule and, at the same time, maintain fine-grained management. However, the fine-grained control for some services mentioned in the article only considers the traffic towards critical servers, thus not applicable to real life.

All the above work either does not propose fine-grained management for specific services, or the management requirements are not feasible in real life. Therefore, it is necessary to establish a new practical model.

Extension Approaches. Instead of reducing the consumption of resources like hybrid rule placement approaches, extension approaches mainly aim to add extension functions or tools to the SDN framework to improve their capability.

The works of [17,30] installed forwarding rules at software flow tables (RAM) and hardware flow tables (TCAM) based on dynamic requirements. However, their techniques require additional intelligence of switches and violate the principle of centralized management of SDN, which affects its scalability and availability. DevoFlow [8] augment the "action" part of a wildcard rule with a boolean CLONE flag to install exact-match rules without informing the controller, But they did not mention how to deploy this "action" optimally. Moreover, HS [26] realized the low occupancy of the flow table by redirecting individual flows. In contrast, those flow statistics cannot be acquired through pre-installed wildcard rules, so additional hardware/software is necessary. Rifai et al. [20] proposed to deploy MINNIE and compress the exact rules on each switch. Their method does not affect the forwarding path of flows but does not consider the fine-grained management of specific flows globally.

3 Motivation and Our Intuition

In this section, we illustrate how Zhao's work [31] deals with the fine-grained requirements of some specific services and introduce our work on this basis.

Initially, it is necessary to recognize two ways to install flow rules: proactively and reactively. Proactively installment means that the SDN controller proactively installs matching flow rules. Reactively installment means that a switch initiates the installation request through a Packet-In message, and the controller response flow rules according to the message information.

Generally, SDN customizes a forwarding path for every flow, which produce at least one matching rule on every switch, as shown in Fig. 1. Zhao's work assumes that u_0 is a server depositing key data; thus flows **towards** the critical server should be fine-grained controlled.

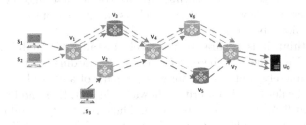

Fig. 1. Flows toward u_0 require fine-grained management.

Intuitively, we only need to reactively install exact-match rules for each flow on all switches (to be referred to as ER hereafter) along the forwarding path. Furthermore, the number of required rules for each switch is summarized in

Table 1. In contrast, Zhao proposes that HiFi reactively install exact-match rules only on switches v_3 and v_5; the rest of the switches along the forwarding paths are proactively installed with wildcard rules.

Table 1. Number of Required rules on Switches by ER and HiFi

Schemes	v1	v2	v3	v4	v5	v6	v7
ER	2	2	2	3	2	2	2
HiFi	1	1	2	2	1	1	1

It is evident that both schemes can realize that the flows toward the server are under fine-grained monitoring, but HiFi installs far fewer flow rules than ER. So far, HiFi has done a great job, but it assumes that only the flows **towards** critical servers require fine-grained management, while in real life, there may be more complex situations, such as the flow **towards and originating from** critical servers need to be fine-grained monitored, as shown in Fig. 2.

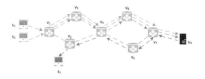 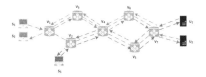

Fig. 2. Flows toward and originating from u_0 require fine-grained management.

Fig. 3. Flows toward and originating from u_0 require fine-grained management.

Another complicated case is that the security vendors specify fine-grained monitoring of **specific interactions** (all the traffic that may be included is referred to as critical flows here after), such as the flows from u_2 to s_2, from s_1 to u_1, and the flows between s_3 and u_1, as shown in Fig. 3.

One may think it is natural to reactively install exact-match rules for all critical flows. Nevertheless, there may be one forwarding path of non-critical flows that completely contains the forwarding path of a critical flow. If vendors install wildcard rules for all non-critical flows by default, then, no Packet-In message for critical flows will be encapsulated. Thus, reactively installment cannot work. Another possible idea is to install exact-match rules for all critical flows proactively. However, due to traffic dynamics, it may not be feasible. Therefore, a practical and feasible solution is to proactively install heterogeneous rules to filter out critical flows.

4 Network Mode and Hybrid Routing for Efficient Fine-grained Management

In this section, we first introduce the topology of our network model. Moreover, we discuss three cases of fine-grained requirements and design our hybrid routing algorithms.

4.1 Network Model

Table 2. Key notations.

Symbol	Semantics
Π	A set of flows
$\Pi_{(u)}$	A set of flows originating from u
Π_u	A set of flows toward destination u
$p(f)$	The forwarding path of flow f
$d(f)$	The destination of flow f
$s(f)$	The source of flow f
$c(v)$	The flow table size of switch v
$c_0(v)$	The space already occupied in the switch v

SDN network can be typically modeled by a graph $G(U \cup V, E)$ from the perspective of data plane, where $U = \{u_1, u_2, ..., u_k\}$, $V = \{v_1, v_2, ..., v_n\}$ and $E = \{e_1, e_2, ..., e_m\}$. Among them, U represents the set of terminals, V is the set of switches and E represents the set of directional links connetcting switches. Since this paper focuses on fine-grained management in the data plane, we assume that there is only one controller for ease of description (Table 2).

The flow set in the SDN is denoted by $\Pi = \{f_1, ..., f_i\}$. And the Π_u^v indicates the flows passing by switch v and toward destination u. Prior works [4,10,21] show that we can get the information including the flow set, the traffic throughput and the flow duration with low prediction error.

4.2 Heterogeneous Rule Installment for Case A

In this section, we first assume that there are a specific set of servers (or services) depositing crucial information, and all flow toward these servers is required to be controlled with fine-grained management. Zhao's work [31] has analyzed this scenario. Therefore, we will only briefly introduce how it works in this section.

Definition of HEI-A Problem. Since we install wildcard rules according to destination-based OSPF, all flows except those toward critical servers can be installed with wildcard rules. Thus, we only need to consider the flows that need fine-grained management. For simplicity, critical flows mentioned in this section refer to those that require fine-grained management. Zhao [31] first builds a tree T_u rooted at u that branches according to the flow set Π_u and proposes that there are two cases for each switch v on T_u.

1) $q_u^v = 0$. Proactively installing a wildcard rule on switch v for destination u.
2) $q_u^v = 1$. Reactively installing exact-match rules on switch v for flows in Π_u^v.

That is, for each flow passing by switch v, there is only one matching exact-match rule or one matching wildcard rule. Zhao expects to minimize the maximum number of flow rule utilization ratio η among all switches, thus formulating the rule installment as a linear programming problem as follows:

$$min \quad \eta$$

$$S.t. \begin{cases} \sum_{v \in p(f)} q_{d(f)}^v \geq 1, & \forall f \in \Pi \\ b(v) = \sum_{u \in U, v \in T_u} (q_u^v \cdot |\pi_u^v| + 1 - q_u^v) + c_0(v) & \forall v \in V \\ b(v) \leq \eta \cdot c(v), & \forall v \in V \\ q_u^v \in \{0, 1\}. & \forall v \in V, u \in U \end{cases} \quad (1)$$

4.3   Heterogeneous Rule Installment for Case B

Although Zhao's work perfectly solves the heterogeneous rule installment problem for the case A, security vendors usually need to monitor both the upstream and downstream traffic. In other words, traffic towards and originating from the critical servers should be fine-grained managed. In this section, we assume that there are a specific set of servers (or services) $\mathbb{S}$ depositing crucial information, and all flows toward and from these servers are required to be monitored.

Definition of HEI-B Problem. To achieve fine-grained management of critical servers, each flow toward or from these servers $\mathbb{S}$ will match at least one exact-match rule along its forwarding path. In the Case A, we have solved the problem of routing the traffic towards critical servers, so now we should focus on the traffic from $\mathbb{S}$.

A feasible solution is to install flow rules with different priorities, i.e., hierarchical routing, to separate the traffic requiring fine-grained management. Specifically, first, we install wildcard rules for all non-critical traffic according to the OSPF path and set the priority to 0. Then, we install heterogeneous rules for traffic that requires fine-grained management, such as $\{ip\_src = u_0, out\_port = controller, priority = 1\}$ on one switch along the forwarding path. Finally, the controller reactively instructs to install corresponding exact-match rules for all flows in $\Pi_{(s)}$. In order to prevent other packets of the same flow from triggering the controller repeatedly, we should install the exact-match rule on the same switch where the heterogeneous rules are located and configure them to a higher priority.

Deploying these heterogeneous rules optimally is a challenge. For ease of understanding, we need to model the infrastructure layout as a mathematical graph. Similar to the flows toward the critical server, it is easy to build a tree $T_{(s)}$ rooted at the critical server s that branches according to the flow set $\Pi_{(s)}$ originating from it. Further, we still use the variable $q^v_{(s)}$ to denote whether we install the heterogeneous rule on switch v for flows $\Pi^v_{(s)}$.

- $q^v_{(s)} = 1$: We install the heterogeneous rule on switch v for flows $\Pi^v_{(s)}$. That is to say, the traffic originating from the source s and passing through the switch v match the heterogeneous rule and be encapsulated to the controller;
- $q^v_{(s)} = 0$: We will not install the heterogeneous rule on switch v for flows $\Pi^v_{(s)}$. It is worth noting that $q^v_{(s)} = 0$ does not mean that flow in $\Pi^v_{(s)}$ cannot find a matching flow rule. Instead, it will directly match the pre-installed wildcard rules.

Logically, for simplicity, it is necessary to ignore those wildcard flow rules that have nothing to do with critical servers $\mathbb{S}$. Therefore, we only need to count the number of these wildcard rules $c_0(v)$ on each switch v. Nevertheless, we still aim to minimize the maximum number of flow rule utilization ratio ω among all switches. Therefore, the HEI (Heterogeneous rule Installment) problem is formulated as follows:

$$min \quad \omega$$

$$S.t. \begin{cases} \sum_{v \in p(f)} q^v_{d(f)} \geq 1, & \forall f \in \Pi_{d(f) \in \mathbb{S}} \\ \sum_{v \in p(f)} q^v_{(s(f))} \geq 1, & \forall f \in \Pi_{s(f) \in \mathbb{S}} \\ b(v) = \sum_{u \in \mathbb{S}, v \in T_u} (q^v_u \cdot |\pi^v_u| + 1 - q^v_u) \\ \quad + \sum_{s \in \mathbb{S}, v \in T_{(s)}} (q^v_{(s)} \cdot (|\pi^v_{(s)}| + 1)) + c_0(v) & \forall v \in V \\ b(v) \leq \omega \cdot c(v), & \forall v \in V \\ q^v_u, q^v_{(s)} \in \{0, 1\}. & \forall v \in V; s, u \in \mathbb{S} \end{cases} \tag{2}$$

The first set of inequalities is built to ensure fine-grained management of flows toward critical servers $\mathbb{S}$, which denotes that there will be at least one exact-match rule along the forwarding path. The second set of inequalities is built to ensure fine-grained management of flows originating from critical servers $\mathbb{S}$, which denotes that there will be at least one exact-match rule along the forwarding path. Finally, the third set of inequalities denotes that the total number of required rules on each switch v consists of three parts: rules for flows towards critical servers $\mathbb{S}$, rules for flows originating from critical servers $\mathbb{S}$ and rules for non-critical flows. The rules here include wildcard rules, exact-match rules, and heterogeneous rules. The objective is to minimize the maximum flow rule utilization ratio among all switches, i.e., minimizing ω.

Algorithm Design for HEI-B Problem. This section introduces a rounding-based algorithm to solve the HEI-B problem. The proposed algorithm consists of two main steps.

In the first step, we relax the integer linear programming problem 2 so as to acquire the fractional solutions $\tilde{q}_u^v, \tilde{q}_{(s)}^v$ in polynomial time.

In the second step, the fractional solutions need to be rounded to $\{0, 1\}$ considering that only $\{0, 1\}$ solutions make sense in real life. Therefore, it is necessary to design the rounding process to fit the optimal solution reasonably. That is, minimize the value of ω. To realize it, we design a rounding-based algorithm.

For traffic towards key servers Π_d, we randomly select an unvisited flow f in it. Then, we chooses a switch v_0 with maximum $\tilde{q}_{d(f)}^v$ among all switches along the forwarding path, and set $q_{d(f)}^{v_0} = 1$. Subsequently, all traffic towards $d(f)$ and passing by v_0 will be removed from Π_d. This step will end when Π_d is null. Similar strategy for traffic originating from key servers $\Pi_{(s)}$ is adopted. Subsequently, we proactively install heterogeneous rules according to the integer solutions, thus achieve fine-grained monitoring of specific flows. The algorithm is programmatically described in Algorithm 1.

Algorithm 1: Heterogeneous rule Installment for HEI-B

Input: The SDN graph $G(U \cup V, E)$;
The flow set Π_d, $\Pi_{(s)}$;

1 **Step 1: Solving the relaxed HEI-B problem**
2 Construct the relaxed linear program in 2;
3 Acquire the fractional results $\tilde{q}_u^v, \tilde{q}_{(s)}^v$.
4 **Step 2: Deriving the 0-1 Solution**
5 **while** $\Pi_d \neq \emptyset$ **do**
6   Randomly select f in Π_d;
7   Choose the switch v_0 with maximum $\tilde{q}_{d(f)}^v$;
8   Modify $q_{d(f)}^{v_0} = 1$;
9      $\Pi_d = \Pi_d - \Pi_{d(f)}^{v_0}$;
10 **end**
11 **while** $\Pi_{(s)} \neq \emptyset$ **do**
12   Randomly select f in $\Pi_{(s)}$;
13   Choose the switch v_0 with maximum $\tilde{q}_{(s(f))}^v$;
14   Modify $q_{(s(f))}^{v_0} = 1$;
15      $\Pi_{(s)} = \Pi_{(s)} - \Pi_{(s(f))}^{v_0}$;
16 **end**

4.4   Heterogeneous Rule Installment for Case C

More complicated than case A and case B is that the security vendors specify fine-grained monitoring of certain specific interactions, such as $\{s_1 \leftrightarrow s_2, s_2 \rightarrow s_1, s_1 \rightarrow s_3\}$. The above methods cannot be directly applied to this scenario. Therefore, we need to establish a new model to meet this requirement.

Definition of HEI-C Problem. First, we assume there are suspicious communications $\Pi_0 = \{s_i \rightarrow s_j | (i, j)\}$. Here we only discuss the flows $s_i \rightarrow s_j$ because the reverse flows can also be expressed by $s_j \rightarrow s_i$. Out of caution, we are required to monitor all flows from s_i to s_j in a fine-grained manner, and the existing routing scheme is wildcard-based.

Similarly to case B, it is necessary to filter out the critical traffic first. Thus, we install the heterogeneous rules, set their match elements, and designate its output port as the controller, i.e. $\{ip\_src = s_0, ip\_dst = u_0, out\_port = controller, priority = 1\}$. Then, the controller will reactively install exact-match rules for flows requiring fine-grained management. We aim to optimally deploy these rules next. For simplicity, we use the variable $q^v_{s,u}$ to denote whether we install the heterogeneous rule on switch v for flows from s to u.

- $q^v_{s,u} = 1$: We install the heterogeneous rule on switch v for flows from s to u. That is to say, the traffic from the source s to u, which will pass through switch v, can match the heterogeneous rule and be encapsulated to the controller;
- $q^v_{s,u} = 0$: We will not install the heterogeneous rule on switch v for flows from s to u. It is worth noting that $q^v_{s,u} = 0$ does not mean that flows from s to u cannot find matching flow rules. Instead, they will directly match the pre-installed wildcard rules.

Since OpenFlow supports real-time monitoring of the capacity of the switch table [2], it is easy to count the number of flow rules $c_0(v)$ on each switch v. We still aim to minimize the maximum number of flow rule utilization ratio λ among all switches. Therefore, the HEI-C (Heterogeneous rule Installment for Case C) problem is formulated as follows:

$$min \quad \lambda$$

$$S.t. \begin{cases} \sum_{v \in p(f)} q^v_{s(f),d(f)} \geq 1, & \forall f \in \Pi_0 \\ b(v) = \sum_{f \in \Pi, v \in p(f)} (q^v_{s(f),d(f)} \cdot (|\pi^v_{s(f),d(f)}| + 1)) + c_0(v), & \forall v \in V \\ b(v) \leq \lambda \cdot c(v), & \forall v \in V \\ q^v_{s(f),d(f)} \in \{0, 1\}. & \forall v \in V, f \in \Pi_0 \end{cases}$$

$$(3)$$

The first set of inequalities is built to ensure fine-grained management of flows in Π_0, which denotes that there will be at least one exact-match rule along the forwarding path. The second set of inequalities denotes that the total number of required rules on each switch v consists of rules for flows in Π_0 and rules for non-critical flows. The rules here include wildcard rules, exact-match rules, and heterogeneous rules. The objective is to minimize the maximum flow rule utilization ratio among all switches, i.e., minimizing λ.

Algorithm Design for HEI-C Problem. This section introduces a rounding-based algorithm to solve the HEI-C problem. The proposed algorithm consists of three main steps. In the first step, we relax the integer linear programming problem 3 to acquire the fractional solutions $\tilde{q}^v_{s,d}$ in polynomial time. Afterward, the fractional solutions need to be rounded to $\{0,1\}$ considering that only $\{0,1\}$ solutions make sense in real life. It is necessary to design the rounding process to fit the optimal solution reasonably. That is, minimize the value of λ. To realize it, we initialize a flow set equal to Π_0. For each flow f in Π_0, we chooses a switch with maximum $\tilde{q}^v_{s(f),d(f)}$ among all switches along the forwarding path, and set $q^v_{s(f),d(f)} = 1$. Subsequently, we proactively install heterogeneous rules according to the integer solutions, thus achieve fine-grained monitoring of specific flows. The algorithm is programmatically described in Algorithm 1. The algorithm is programmatically described in Algorithm 2.

Algorithm 2: Heterogeneous rule Installment

Input: The SDN graph $G(U \cup V, E)$;
The flow set Π_0, $\Pi'_0 = \Pi_0$;

1 **Step 1: Solving the relaxed HEI-C problem**
2 Construct the relaxed linear program in 3;
3 Acquire the fractional results $\tilde{q}^v_{s,d}$.
4 **Step 2: Deriving the 0-1 Solution**
5 **for** $f \in \Pi'_0$ **do**
6   Choose the switch v_0 with maximum $\tilde{q}^v_{s(f),d(f)}$;
7   Modify $q^{v_0}_{s(f),d(f)} = 1$
8 **end**
9 **Step 3: Installing the Heterogeneous Rules**
10 **for** $f \in \Pi'_0$ **do**
11   **for** $v \in p(f)$ **do**
12   **if** $q^v_{s(f),d(f)} == 1$ **then**
13   Install the heterogeneous rule on switch v for f
14   **end**
15   **end**
16 **end**

---

5   Performance Evaluation

To validate the feasibility and efficiency of our work, we conducted a testbed evaluation using MiniNet, and a simulation evaluation using networkx regarding similar work [13,29,31]. We compare our work with Presto [11] which installs fine-grained rules at the edge switches. Since Presto aims to support fine-grained management for all flows, we need to extend this design to specific flows for a fair comparison. That is, we install the heterogenous rules at the edge switches.

We apply four metrics in evaluation to compare the performance of our method (Hybrid Routing) and Presto, including (1) The number of required flow rules; (2) The number of Packet-In messages; (3) The flow setup delay; (4) packet loss ratio. Encapsulating Packet-In messages and installing flow rules will consume the CPU, bandwidth, and memory in both the switch and the controller [31]. Thus, too many Packet-In messages may lead to high flow setup latency and a high loss ratio. We set the maximum Packet-In message rate that each switch can handle as 150 per second according to [24]; thus, a Packet-In loss will occur if the uplink load exceeds the threshold.

5.1   Testbed Evaluation

For testbed evaluation, we use Mininet to implement an Epoch topology [1] with 6 nodes and 7 links. Each link has a capacity of 1 Gbps. The controller is deployed at another remote virtual machine with a Core i7 processor and 6 GB of RAM. We run RYU version 4.32 as the controller software. To simulate the regular communications, we generate TCP and UDP flows, originating from some randomly-selected hosts and towards other randomly-selected servers, through Iperf3. The traffic arrival rate of TCP, UDP is set to 1, 0.5 Mbps, respectively. Each flow traverses through the OSPF path for legacy management as [31] by default.

Evaluation Results. In the first experiment, we observe the number of required flow rules and the number of Packet-In messages on all switches. For simplicity, we only carried out the experiment for cases C since case B is a special example of case C. The results are shown in Fig. 4 and Fig. 5. Figure 4 indicates that our work and Presto need 55, 98 flow rules at most, respectively. Figure 5 indicates that our work and Presto consume 102, 176 Packet-In messages at most, respectively. Experiment results indicate that our method can significantly decrease the switch overhead. That is because our method deploys fine-grained flow rules in a balanced and decentralized manner based on the load of the switches. Note that the performance gap between our work and Presto will be more evident if the source of the flows requiring fine-grained management is more concentrated and the scale of network topology is larger, considering a larger topology usually implies that the decentralization can be more evenly.

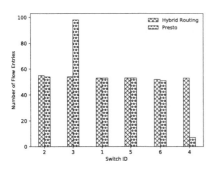

Fig. 4. No. of flow rules on each switch.

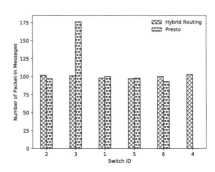

Fig. 5. No. of Packet-In on each switch.

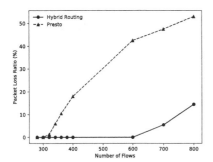

Fig. 6. Packet loss ratio versus No. of flows.

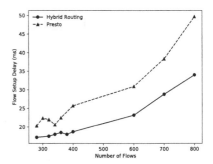

Fig. 7. Flow setup delay versus No. of flows.

In the second experiment, we obtain the flow setup delay and packet loss ratio by changing the number of flows in the network. Specifically, we generate more new critical flows (280–800) and observe their impact on network communication. As shown in Figs. 6 and 7, when we generate 320 new flows, packet loss occurs in Presto, while in our method, it starts to happen when more than 600 flows are generated. Meanwhile, our method always requires less time to setup a new flow compared with Presto. That is because our hybrid routing optimally installs flow rules so that congestion caused by Packet-In messages can be alleviated.

5.2   Simulation Evaluation

For simulation evaluation, we build a large-scale topology fat-tree [3] using the networkx and evaluate the efficiency of our work with different percentages of critical flows. Ultimately, we still compare our work with the benchmark method Presto. The pod of this fat tree is set as 6, and each pod is connected with 9 servers which means that there are 45 switches and 54 servers. For convincing, we try to randomly vary the traffic load and interaction pattern as much as possible.

Therefore, we choose to randomize the number of flows between terminals, suspicious flow sets, and suspicious server sets. Finally we acquire the average values. In addition, we also vary the percentage of suspicious terminal-terminal and the percentage of suspicious servers to further observe our method's availability.

Evaluation Results. We run two sets of experiments on fat-tree topology for HEI-B and HEI-C in simulation evaluation. Each set of experiments is executed 100 times with different random seeds.

We observe the average number of maximum flow rules by changing the percentage of suspicious terminal-terminal in Fig. 8 and servers in Fig. 9. As can be seen from these figures, the maximum number of flow rules increases with the increase of the percentage of suspicious terminal-terminal, which is reasonable as expected. Moreover, both figures clearly outline that our scheme can reduce the required flow rules by at least 20.1%, proving that our method can steadily reduce the maximum number of flow rules due to hybrid and decentralized routing.

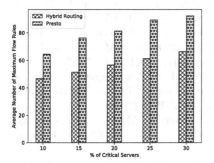

Fig. 8. Average number of maximum flow rules in case HEI-B.

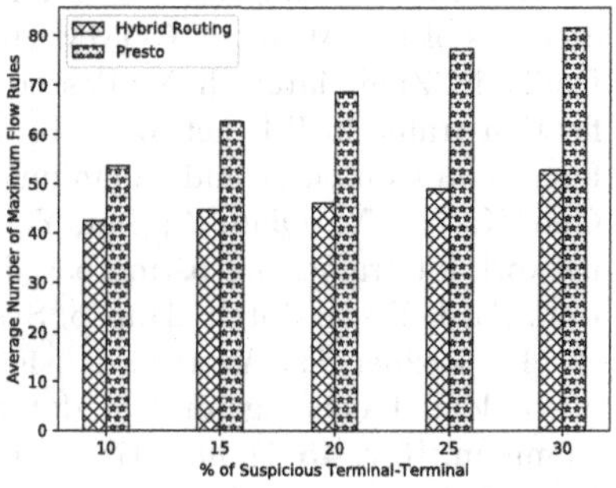

Fig. 9. Average number of maximum flow rules in case HEI-C.

6 Conclusion

In this paper, we propose a hybrid routing approach to achieve efficient fine-grained management of specific services in SDN. We assume two potential scenarios in real life, and linear programming functions are designed to give quantitative descriptions. We have implemented our algorithm on a small-scale testbed and a large-scale simulated topology. Compared with Presto, our method can save at least 20.1% of the maximum flow rules, thus fully proves its efficiency.

Acknowledgements. This work was supported by the National Key R&D Program of China with No. 2018YFC0806900, Beijing Municipal Science & Technology Commission with Project No. Z191100007119009, NSFC No. 61671448 and NSFC No.61902397.

References

1. The epoch topology. http://www.topology-zoo.org/maps/Epoch.jpg (2021)
2. Openflow specification v1.3. http://opennetworking.wpengine.com/wp-content/uploads/2014/10/openflow-spec-v1.3.2.pdf (2021)
3. Al-Fares, M., Loukissas, A., Vahdat, A.: A scalable, commodity data center network architecture. ACM SIGCOMM Comput. Commun. Rev. **38**(4), 63–74 (2008)
4. Azzouni, A., Pujolle, G.: NeuTm: a neural network-based framework for traffic matrix prediction in SDN. In: NOMS 2018–2018 IEEE/IFIP Network Operations and Management Symposium, pp. 1–5. IEEE (2018)
5. Bera, S., Misra, S., Jamalipour, A.: Flowstat: adaptive flow-rule placement for per-flow statistics in SDN. IEEE J. Sel. Areas Commun. **37**(3), 530–539 (2019)
6. Chen, K.Y., et al.: SDNshield: NFV-based defense framework against DDoS attacks on SDN control plane. IEEE/ACM Trans. Netw. **30**(1), 1–17 (2022)
7. Cohen, R., Lewin-Eytan, L., Naor, J.S., Raz, D.: On the effect of forwarding table size on SDN network utilization. In: IEEE INFOCOM 2014-IEEE Conference on Computer Communications, pp. 1734–1742. IEEE (2014)
8. Curtis, A.R., Mogul, J.C., Tourrilhes, J., Yalagandula, P., Sharma, P., Banerjee, S.: DevoFlow: scaling flow management for high-performance networks. In: Proceedings of the ACM SIGCOMM 2011 Conference, pp. 254–265 (2011)
9. Dodia, P., Zhauniarovich, Y.: Poster: SDN-based system to filter out DRDoS amplification traffic in ISP networks. In: Proceedings of the 2019 ACM SIGSAC Conference on Computer and Communications Security, pp. 2645–2647 (2019)
10. Guo, K., Hu, Y., Qian, Z., Sun, Y., Gao, J., Yin, B.: Dynamic graph convolution network for traffic forecasting based on latent network of Laplace matrix estimation. IEEE Trans. Intell. Transp. Syst. **23**(2), 1009–1018 (2022)
11. He, K., Rozner, E., Agarwal, K., Felter, W., Carter, J., Akella, A.: Presto: edge-based load balancing for fast datacenter networks. ACM SIGCOMM Comput. Commun. Rev. **45**(4), 465–478 (2015)
12. Hong, C.Y., et al.: Achieving high utilization with software-driven WAN. In: Proceedings of the ACM SIGCOMM 2013 Conference on SIGCOMM, pp. 15–26 (2013)
13. Liu, Y.F., Lin, C.J., Tseng, C.C.: Dynamic cluster-based flow management for software defined networks. IEEE Trans. Serv. Comput. **PP**(99) (2019)
14. Long, Z., Jinsong, W.: A hybrid method of entropy and SSAE-SVM based DDoS detection and mitigation mechanism in SDN. Comput. Secur. **115**, 102604 (2022)
15. MacDermott, Á., Baker, T., Buck, P., Iqbal, F., Shi, Q.: The internet of things: Challenges and considerations for cybercrime investigations and digital forensics. Int. J. Dig. Crime Forensics (IJDCF) **12**(1), 1–13 (2020)
16. McKeown, N., et al.: Openflow: enabling innovation in campus networks. ACM SIGCOMM Comput. Commun. Rev. **38**(2), 69–74 (2008)
17. Mimidis-Kentis, A., Pilimon, A., Soler, J., Berger, M., Ruepp, S.: A novel algorithm for flow-rule placement in SDN switches. In: 2018 4th IEEE Conference on Network Softwarization and Workshops (NetSoft), pp. 1–9. IEEE (2018)
18. Phan, T.V., Nguyen, T.G., Bauschert, T.: Deepmatch: fine-grained traffic flow measurement in SDN with deep dueling neural networks. IEEE J. Sel. Areas Commun. **39**(7), 2056–2075 (2021)
19. Phan, T.V., Nguyen, T.G., Dao, N.N., Huong, T.T., Thanh, N.H., Bauschert, T.: Deepguard: efficient anomaly detection in SDN with fine-grained traffic flow monitoring. IEEE Trans. Netw. Serv. Manage. **17**(3), 1349–1362 (2020)

20. Rifai, M., Huin, N., Caillouet, C., Giroire, F., Lopez-Pacheco†, D.: Too many SDN rules? compress them with MINNIE. In: IEEE Global Communications Conference (2015)
21. Saha, A., Ganguly, N., Chakraborty, S., De, A.: Learning network traffic dynamics using temporal point process. In: IEEE INFOCOM 2019-IEEE Conference on Computer Communications, pp. 1927–1935. IEEE (2019)
22. Suárez-Varela, J., Barlet-Ros, P.: Flow monitoring in software-defined networks: finding the accuracy/performance tradeoffs. Comput. Netw. 135, 289–301 (2018)
23. Wang, H., Xu, H., Qian, C., Ge, J., Liu, J., Huang, H.: PrePass: load balancing with data plane resource constraints using commodity sdn switches. Comput. Netw. 178, 107339 (2020)
24. Wang, P., Xu, H., Huang, L., He, J., Meng, Z.: Control link load balancing and low delay route deployment for software defined networks. IEEE J. Sel. Areas Commun. 35(11), 2446–2456 (2017)
25. Wu, C., et al.: A hybrid intrusion detection system for IoT applications with constrained resources. Int. J. Dig. Crime Forensics (IJDCF) 12(1), 109–130 (2020)
26. Xu, H., Huang, H., Chen, S., Zhao, G.: Scalable software-defined networking through hybrid switching. In: IEEE INFOCOM 2017-IEEE Conference on Computer Communications, pp. 1–9. IEEE (2017)
27. Jianfeng, W.L.X., Zhen, X.: Survey on resource consumption attacks and defenses in software-defined networking. J. Cyber Secur. 5(4), 72–95 (2020)
28. Yan, Q., Yu, R., Gong, Q., Li, J.: Software-defined networking (SDN) and distributed denial of service (DDoS) attacks in cloud computing environments: a survey, some research issues, and challenges. IEEE Commun. Surv. Tutorials 18(1), 602–622 (2016)
29. Yang, X., Xu, H., Huang, L., Zhao, G., Xi, P., Qiao, C.: Joint virtual switch deployment and routing for load balancing in SDNs. IEEE J. Sel. Areas Commun. 36(3), 397–410 (2018)
30. Zhang, J., Xi, K., Luo, M., Chao, H.J.: Load balancing for multiple traffic matrices using SDN hybrid routing. In: 2014 IEEE 15th International Conference on High Performance Switching and Routing (HPSR), pp. 44–49. IEEE (2014)
31. Zhao, G., Xu, H., Fan, J., Huang, L., Qiao, C.: Achieving fine-grained flow management through hybrid rule placement in SDNs. IEEE Trans. Parallel Distrib. Syst. 32(3), 728–742 (2020)
32. Zhou, Y., Cheng, G., Yu, S.: An SDN-enabled proactive defense framework for DDoS mitigation in IoT networks. IEEE Trans. Inf. Forensics Secur. 16, 5366–5380 (2021)

AtNet: A Novel Anti-tracking Network with Multi-Party Judgement Capability Based on Cross-Domain Small-World Topology

Wenjie Qin[1,2], Chengwei Peng[3(✉)], Tao Yin[1], Changbo Tian[1], and Guangze Zhao[1]

[1] Institute of Information Engineering, Chinese Academy of Sciences, Beijing, China
{qinwenjie,yintao,tianchangbo,zhaoguangze}@iie.ac.cn
[2] School of Cyber Security, University of Chinese Academy of Sciences, Beijing, China
[3] National Computer Network Emergency Response Technical Team/Coordination Center of China, Beijing, China
pengchengwei@cert.org.cn

Abstract. Anti-tracking network plays an important role to protect the participants from being associated in a conversation. Centralized networks are probably blocked or leak users' communication privacy. So anti-tracking network is usually a decentralized P2P overlay network. It needs good network robustness. The existing anti-tracking networks are lack of defense capability. A malicious node can easily find the key points or even all participants in the network systems. To address these problems, we propose AtNet, a novel **anti-tracking net**work based on cross-domain small-world topology. First, we generate a small-world topology with more uniform domain distribution based on greedy thought. Then we show a recursive requesting method to maintain the network's properties. Last, we explain the multi-party judgement mechanism. With the collaboration of near nodes, a node's abnormal requests can be found. Compared with three state-of-the-art anti-tracking network topologies, AtNet obviously has better robustness. Moreover, we implement the prototype system and evaluate the maintenance effect and defense effect. The experiment results show that AtNet can keep good robustness, anti-tracking capability, small-world property and high clustering when nodes randomly join in or exit the network, and a node can only averagely detect 7.71 nodes in the network with 1000 nodes when allowing nodes to lie twice.

Keywords: Anti-tracking network · Overlay network · Topology · Multi-party collaboration · Distributed system security

---

Supported by the National Key Research and Development Program of China under Grant No. 2019YFB1005205.

1   Introduction

The Internet has involved the most aspects of our lives, such as finance, health care, communication, social network and so on, which potentially threats the online privacy of network users [10,13]. The network monitors can find the position, action track, circle of friends etc. through traffic analysis. While hiding the contents of a conversation has a lot of solutions, hiding the associated metadata(participants, duration, frequency) remains a challenge [1]. In order to protect users' communication privacy, some anonymous networks [19] are proposed. These networks are usually based on Mix-net [8], PIR [4] or DC-nets [6]. They often need secure multi-party protocols, verifiable process, noise generation based on Poisson process or broadcast, so the communication overhead and network delay are high. And the nodes of system services are a few, so the service is easily to be blocked by ISPs or countries. The anti-tracking network based decentralized P2P network can migrate end-to-end traffics to the overlay networks. Motivated by this, we propose a novel P2P anti-tracking network base on cross-domain small-world network. AtNet can defense network detection and has high anti-tracking performance and robustness.

Small-world topology has small characteristic path and good connectivity, so this topology can provide good robustness. Adjacent nodes have different domains in AtNet's topology. We use greedy thought to make the domain distribution as uniform as possible, so a link can go through more domains. Communications in different domains are more difficult to be tracked. Our self-maintenance mechanism includes the process of recursive requesting. This process can not only keep AtNet cross-domain and small-world property, but also enhances clustering. Nodes can only communicate with neighbors. When a node request for adding neighbors, it must say why. Nodes near it have some probability to judge whether it's honest or not by the reason. The high clustering and recursive requesting of AtNet increase the probability. So AtNet can defense network detection. A node can only find a few other nodes, so AtNet is hard to be blocked.

We make three key contributions in this paper as follows.

- We propose a cross-domain small-world network topology construction method based on greedy thought for anti-tracking network. The topology has two features: cross-domain and small-world property. These two properties separately ensure AtNet has better anti-tracking performance and robustness. While CPTs [14] with 5000 nodes don't split until 40% of nodes randomly exit, AtNet with the same count of nodes don't split until 80% of nodes randomly exit.
- We propose a self-maintenance mechanism to maintain network features when nodes join in or exit AtNet. While other state-of-art anti-tracking networks don't run in real environment, we implement the prototype system of AtNet. And experiment results based on our prototype system show that the maintenance mechanism can not only maintain features, but also enhance clustering. High clustering can also improve the identification probability of multi-party judgement.

– We propose multi-party judgement mechanism to prevent adversaries from detecting the count and IPs of existing nodes in AtNet. A node's abnormal request behavior can be found and prevented by nodes near it. Experiment results show that a node can only detect 7.71 new nodes on average in AtNet with 1000 nodes. However, the state-of-art anti-tracking networks haven't considered to protecting the identities of relay nodes.

2   Related Work

Anti-tracking network is used for preventing adversaries from associating senders and receivers. There are many related researches. AppBot [21] is a P2P cross-domain network for high anti-tracking performance (the domains can be countries, network number, organizations, etc.), but it's used for one-way communication and the topology it generates possibly has cut points. CPT [13] is a model of anti-tracking network based on convex-polytope topology, and each surface of convex-polytope is a triangle. It maintains this feature and aims for the network robustness. CPTs [14] introduces a method of topology self-optimization for CPT, and gets the optimum CPT network. STon (alias NN) [17] proposed a smart topology maintenance method. Each node collects the local network state. The information is passed to the neural network and the program decides to add or remove neighbors. TresMep [15] achieves dynamic communication path for anti-tracking network. It combines Chord protocol [11] and DC-Nets [3]. Every position of Chord ring is a DC-Nets group. The links randomly change in different communication rounds to resist tracking. It eliminates the risk of fixed communication links by randomly choosing relay nodes. FMC [16] is a mechanism of message segmentation, multiplex transmission and reconstruction. It is inspired by Sudoku game. It reconstructs messages from partially lost packets by solving equations. These methods can solve partial problems in anti-tracking networks. But there are still some challenges:

– **Cut Point and Key Point Problem.** The exit of cut points will probably split the anti-tracking network based on P2P network. Cut points decrease the robustness of the network. They are weaknesses of network system and make the system likely suffer from network attack. Key points are points that must be passed during communication. The key points are easily to be blocked. If key points are blocked, the service of anti-tracking network will be unavailable.

– **The Cost of Network Maintenance.** Relay nodes in some existing network systems are hard to extend, such as Dissent [12] and Karaoke [9], or need multicast or broadcast, such as Riposte [5]. When maintaining topology, the communication cost is high, and it influences the whole network. Network maintenance with high communication overhead is not conducive to horizontal scalability.

– **Lack of Defense Capability.** Anti-tracking networks usually provide services, but not protect the identifies of relay nodes who provide services.

The relay nodes are exposed in air. A malicious node can passively collect relay nodes who participate in the construction of network topology through traffic analysis [20].

3   Designing AtNet

To make an overall perception of our proposal, we firstly introduce the overview of AtNet. Then we begin constructing the cross-domain small-world topology of AtNet based on greedy thought. Next we give the maintenance mechanism to keep AtNet's cross-domain and small-world property. Last, we show the multi-party judgement mechanism.

3.1   The Overview of AtNet

AtNet is a fully distributed and unstructured P2P overlay network where nodes are equivalent, as illustrated in Fig. 1. The illustrative topology has 24 nodes and 6 domains. Each domain is represented by one identify number or one color.

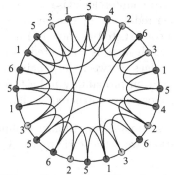

*Different digits represent different domains.
Colored dot represents nodes.

Fig. 1. An example of AtNet topology (Color figure online)

Each node has several neighbors and runs two types of threads to maintain the topology and defense network detection with the help of surrounding nodes. When the count of neighbors is less than the defined lower threshold, the node will request for a new neighbor. When the count of neighbors is up to the defined upper threshold, the node won't agree to add new neighbor. Neighbors keep connected through periodic heartbeat packets. When a node requests for new neighbors, nodes surrounding it will monitor it and suppress malicious requests.

3.2   The Construction of AtNet

AtNet's topology is based on small-world network, and any adjacent nodes' domains are different. The classic approaches of generating small-world network topology are WS model and NW model [7]. To construct a topology without cut point, we refer to NW model.

For the given N nodes and each node's domain, we use greedy thought to make nodes of the same domain as dispersed as possible. Therefore, a link will go through more domains and communication behavior is more difficult to be tracked. The constructing process takes two main steps shown as follows:

i) **Constructing a K-Distance Heterochromatic Ring**, where the adjacent K nodes have different colors. **First**, we use a priority queue to store three tuples: each domain, the count of available nodes and the count of used nodes in the domain. The bigger the count of available nodes, the bigger the count of used nodes, the higher priority the corresponding domain. **Second**, we place a window of size K (initialized by N) on the ring, as shown in Fig. 2(a). We get one node from the head of the priority queue, and try to put it in the middle of the window. If there is already one node of the same domain, then we must try the next domain from the queue. If there is no domain conflict, then move the window one gird counterclockwise as shown in Fig. 2(b). If there is no suitable domain, then reduce K by one and rearrange. **Last**, K-distance heterochromatic ring is constructed as show in Fig. 2(c).

ii) **Adding Edges**. First, each node is connected to its adjacent k ($k \leq \frac{K-1}{2}$) neighbors. Then, add edges between any pair of cross-domain and no-associated nodes with a given probability p. Last, an AtNet based on cross-domain small-world topology is constructed as shown in Fig. 2(d).

This construction process runs in an ordinary computer instead of nodes in AtNet. After the construction, we get a static topology of AtNet. This topology has two features:

- **Cross-Domain.** The concept of domain can be higher bits of IP address, country that the IP address belongs to, etc. Nodes between different domains usually don't cooperate. For example, there is interest competition, unfriendly relationship between them, or just for the reason of no permission. So, a communication link (can include more than three nodes) across multiple domains is more difficult to be tracked.
- **Small-World Property.** The topology based on NW model has small characteristic path length [2] and doesn't have cut point. The small-world property makes the AtNet have good network robustness and makes any two node can in a communication link.

3.3   The Maintenance of AtNet

After deploying the topology of AtNet, there are maybe some nodes joining in or exiting. We propose a self-maintenance mechanism as shown in Fig. 3 to keep

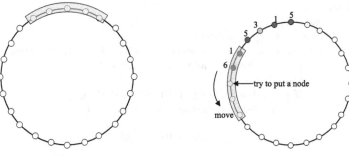

(a) place a window on the ring

(b) put a suitable node in the middle of the window and move one grid

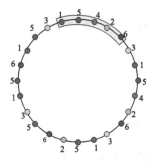

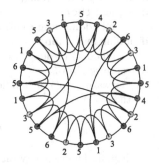

(c) K-distance heterochromatic ring

(d) cross-domain small-world topology

Fig. 2. Constructing process of an example of AtNet topology including 6 domains with 5, 3, 4, 2, 6, 4 nodes respectively

AtNet's two features and increase clustering coefficient [18]. Each node runs two types of threads: active thread and passive thread.

In Fig. 3a, lines 1∼3 show that the node periodically detects whether neighbors survive. Lines 4∼5 show that if any neighbor is disconnected or the count of neighbors is less than the defined lower threshold (named LOW_THRESHOLD) of neighbor set, the node will wait for a moment and prepare to request for new nodes. Line 6 is waiting other nodes to perceive the offline nodes and update their neighbor set. Lines 7∼8 show that after the waiting time expires, the node checks whether it needs new neighbors or not. If yes, the node will send a request message indicating which neighbor is offline and its ExceptionCount (used in Sect. 3.4) to a random neighbor.

In Fig. 3b, lines 1 and 10 are used for resisting detection next section. Line 2 shows the node is monitoring messages from its neighbors. Lines 3∼9 show there are four types of messages. The **ping_msg** is from one of the node's neighbors to make sure whether the node is online. Receiving **req_msg** represents certain node is seeking for new neighbor. The node that receives req_msg will randomly select one of its neighbors as a candidate and ask whether the candidate agrees

```
1: loop
2:     wait(Δ₁)
3:     error ← ping(neighbors)
4:     if error ≠ NULL or |neighbors| <LOW_THRESHOLD then:
5:         // the follows are added to threadPool
6:         wait(Δ₂)
7:         if |neighbors| <LOW_THRESHOLD then:
8:             request_node(error, ExceptionCount)
```

(a) active thread

```
 1: prehandle()
 2: receive msg from neighbors
 3: if ping_msg then: pong()
 4: if req_msg then:
 5:     send adding_msg to a random neighbor except the requester
 6: if adding_msg then:
 7:     addnode() or deny(), response()
 8: if resp_msg then:
 9:     forward_resp() or handle_resp()
10: posthandle()
```

(b) passive thread

Fig. 3. The topology maintenance mechanism of AtNet

to connect to the initiator. When the candidate receives **adding_msg**, it carries out a series of inspections and gives response message. If its domain is different from the initiator's, the size of its neighbors hasn't been up to the defined upper threshold of neighbor set, and the initiator isn't in its neighbor set, the candidate will agree to add the initiator as its neighbor. When a node receives **resp_msg**, if it's the initiator, it handles the response, or it helps to forward the response message. If the initiator doesn't successfully add a neighbor and still needs new neighbors, it will randomly choose a neighbor and send a req_msg again.

Node Exiting. Active exiting or abnormal disconnection of nodes are the same for AtNet. The processing action is to wait for neighbors to perceive and update their neighbor set. After updating, if the size of neighbor set is less than LOW_THRESHOLD, the node sends req_msg.

Node Joining. New node gets an existing node as its introducer. The information of existing nodes can be gotten from the original network deployers or social network. The introducer is the preset neighbor of the new node. Under its introducer's help, the new node gets some other nodes as its neighbors by sending req_msg. In Fig. 4, we present two examples of successful requesting process. Example 1 shows that a new node of black domain sends a req_msg to its introducer of white domain, and successfully adds a new neighbor of gray domain. Note that the new node, its introducer and its new neighbor form a complete triangle. This triangle increases the clustering coefficient [18] of AtNet. Example 2 shows a new node of black domain sends req_msg to its introducer. However, its introducer chooses a candidate1 of black domain. Its introducer forwards req_msg instead of adding_msg to candidate1. Then the candidate1 chooses another node (called candidate2) and sends adding_msg. The process of Example 2 can help two nodes far away from each other connect and help AtNet keep small characteristic path length. Note that the recursive request path will not exceed 3 hops, because the new node and candidate1 have the same domain and the domain of candidate2 must be different from the new node's.

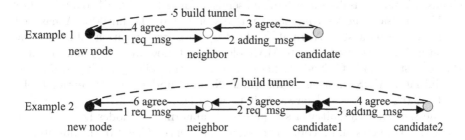

Fig. 4. The process of requesting a new neighbor

3.4   Multi-party Judgement Mechanism on AtNet

Based on the high clustering and recursive requesting of AtNet, we propose multi-party judgement mechanism to protect nodes' identifies from adversaries detecting. AtNet is a fully distributed and unstructured P2P overlay network. There isn't a central node as administrator to monitor the whole network. So, the defense work has to rely on multi-party collaboration. Note that, we don't talk about how to ensure the integrity and confidentiality when communicating. We think it's a code implementation problem. We assume that adversaries can block traffic, replay traffic and randomly modify traffic, but they can't validly modify traffic. Because the session can be encrypted and authenticated.

Analyzing Detection Behavior. In the AtNet, a node only responses to nodes who are in its neighbor set. When the size of node's neighbor set is within the upper and lower limits of the defined threshold, the node will not request for new neighbors. If adversaries control a node and want to detect more nodes in the AtNet, they need to block the connections between the node controlled with its neighbors. The blocking event triggers the node to send req_msg.

How to Defense Detection. We design the req_msg that contains a variable *ExceptionCount* and the information indicating which node is disconnected. Req_msg is like saying that *node x is disconnected, the initiator has*

lied ExceptionCount times and it needs you to help it add a new neighbor.
Combined with the recursive requesting process, this message will pass through
two or three nodes except the initiator. When these nodes find that node x is
still in their neighbor set, they can say the request is abnormal. This check is
done in the function prehandle() of the passive thread in Fig. 3b. In the function posthandle(), nodes will record the maximum *ExceptionCount* of initiators
in a table called ExceptionTable. When a node's *ExceptionCount* is up to the
defined upper limit, it can't send req_msg and others will not help it. These
two functions can be implemented by aspect oriented programming. If they are
removed, the maintenance mechanism can normally maintain the network.

In Fig. 5, we show an example of multi-party judgement process. Node A
claims that node x is disconnected, and sends req_msg $\{x, A, 2, N\}$ to its neighbor
B. This message means that node x is disconnected, the initiator A has lied
2 times. The request is *N*ormal. Node B updates its ExceptionTable (set the
initiator A's ExceptionCount to MAX(old value: 1, new value: 2)) and forwards
the request to node C. Node C finds node x is still online, so it's certain that
the initiator A's requesting is abnormal. Node C updates its ExceptionTable,
modifies the req_msg and forwards it to node D. Node D gives response with
the message that the initiator's requesting is abnormal, so nodes D, C, B, A all
know the bad news and record the maximum ExceptionCount of the initiator A.

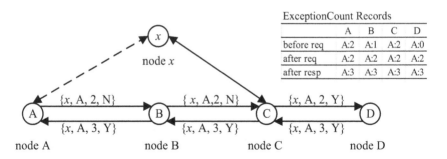

	ExceptionCount Records			
	A	B	C	D
before req	A:2	A:1	A:2	A:0
after req	A:2	A:2	A:2	A:2
after resp	A:3	A:3	A:3	A:3

* $\{x, A, 2, N\}$: Node x is disconnected, the initiator A has lied 2 times.
N: the requesting is Normal; Y: the requesting is Abnormal.

Fig. 5. An example of multi-party judgement process

Issues in Multi-party Collaboration. Note that, when a node x exits AtNet,
its neighbors can't perceive this event at the same time. If one of its neighbors
sends req_msg to another neighbor who hasn't known node x is offline. The
initiator will be wrongly considered as a liar. To solve this problem, the initiator
needs to wait some time (longer than heartbeat period, waiting other neighbors
of the exiting node perceive the exiting event), then sends req_msg, as shown in
line 6~8 in Fig. 3a.

Because of the recursive requesting, high clustering and persistent records
of nodes' *ExceptionCount*, AtNet can respond quickly and prevent network

detection events. Note that, the multi-party judgement process don't cause extra communication behavior, and just needs to attach a few bits message when nodes send req_msg. In short, multi-party judgement mechanism is effective, modular and low cost.

4   Experiment and Evaluation

In this section, we compare AtNet with three prior anti-tracking network topologies on network robustness. One is based on the convex-polytope topology (CPT) [13], one is the optimum structure of CPT (CPTs) [14] and another is based the neurual network (NN) [17]. We implement the prototype system and evaluate the network maintenance effect of AtNet when nodes join in or exit the network. Last, we use some nodes as malicious nodes to detect AtNet and evaluate the multi-party judgement capability.

4.1   Evaluation of Network Robustness

Firstly, we use (1) to calculate the network robustness (β): the ratio of the node count of maximum connected graph (MCG) to the total node count of the network (G).

$$\beta = \frac{|MCG(G)|}{|G|} \tag{1}$$

Then, we respectively generate the topologies of AtNet, CPTs, CPT and NN with 5000 nodes. Next, we remove nodes from networks by two strategies:

- **Random-p Removal.** Randomly select p proportion of nodes and remove them and their associated edges.
- **Top-p Removal.** Sort nodes by descending order of degrees. If nodes have the same degree value, shuffle them to avoid the influence of node order. Then we remove the top p proportion of nodes.

For every removal operation, we evaluate the robustness of the remain network. The experiment results are shown in Fig. 6.

From the results in Fig. 6, AtNet obviously has better robustness than CPTs, CPT and NN in both situations of Random-p Removal and Top-p Removal. What's more, AtNet doesn't split until more than 80% of nodes exit the network in Random-p Removal situation, and it doesn't split until more than 70% of the top-degree nodes exit the network in Top-p Removal situation. This is due to the small-world property of AtNet. Nodes have the similar degrees and the network has small characteristic path. However, CPT still has the potential threat from key points [13].

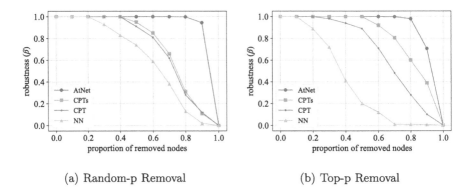

(a) Random-p Removal   (b) Top-p Removal

Fig. 6. The evaluation of network robustness

4.2   Evaluation of Maintenance Effect

To evaluate the maintenance effect of AtNet, we develop the prototype system of AtNet[1] according to the construction method and topology maintenance mechanism. We deploy it with 1000 nodes and 20 domains (set the parameters in Sect. 3.2: $k = 6, p = 0.005$) in three Linux Servers with 128 cores and 256 GB memory. Each node runs a process and occupies one port. We add a monitor to the network. The monitor passively records the neighbor information posted by all nodes, so we can know the network topology information. The monitor only exists in experiment stage and doesn't affect the evaluation result. In experiments, 1% proportion of the nodes gradually join in or exit the network every time, until half nodes join in or exit, and we observe the changes of network properties including robustness, anti-tracking performance, small-world property and clustering coefficient. The evaluation methods of the latter three properties are as follows:

– **Anti-Tracking Performance:** Convert overlay networks to weighted colored graphs (G). According to the domains of normal nodes and nodes controlled by adversaries, we add weights to edges with corresponding float values. The values represent the tracking probabilities. Each node (v) searches the network with a probability threshold $\bar{p}$. If the multiplicative value of a path is less than $\bar{p}$, nodes give up deeper search. The evaluation result of anti-tracking performance (α) is one minus the maximum ratio of the count of nodes tracked to the total count $(|G|)$ of the network. The calculation formula is (2).

$$\alpha = 1 - \frac{\text{MAX}_{v \in G}(\text{Search}(G, v, \bar{p}))}{|G|} \qquad (2)$$

– **Small-world property:** It's a feature that the network size is large and there is a relatively short path between any two nodes. And it is mathematically characterized by an average shortest path length (also known as characteristic

---
[1] https://gitee.com/wjsay/AtNet.

path length) [2]. The calculation formula is (3). The symbol $d_{u,v}$ is the shortest path length of nodes u and v in the network G.

$$L = \frac{1}{|G|\,(|G| - 1)} \sum_{u,v \in G, u \neq v} d_{u,v} \tag{3}$$

– **Clustering Coefficient:** The fraction of connected triples of nodes which also from triangles [2]. The calculation formula of clustering coefficient (C) is (4).

$$C = \frac{3 * |\text{trangles in } G|}{|\text{connected triples of nodes in } G|} \tag{4}$$

The evaluation results of network maintenance are shown in Fig. 7.

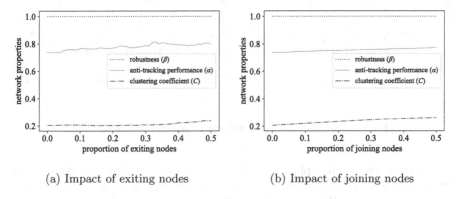

(a) Impact of exiting nodes   (b) Impact of joining nodes

Fig. 7. The evaluation of network maintenance effect

From the results in Fig. 7, the network robustness doesn't change. This shows that slow network turbulence can't split AtNet. The anti-tracking performance of the network enlarges a little. This is related to the edges reduce or the network scale enlarges. The clustering coefficient also increases a little along with the nodes exiting and nodes joining. This is because the process of requesting new neighbors will form more triangles between nodes. High clustering is an important property for multi-party judgement mechanism. In addition, the average shortest path length (L) is in scale 3.35~3.73 when no more than 50% nodes exit or join in the network. So, our self-maintenance mechanism can keep the anti-tracking performance, cross-domain, small-world property and high clustering of the topology of AtNet.

4.3 Evaluation of Multi-party Judgement Capability

To evaluate the multi-party judgement capability of AtNet, we deploy AtNet with 1000 nodes and let 10% of the nodes as malicious nodes block the connections to their neighbors. The blocking event triggers the process of requesting new neighbors. We want to see how many new nodes the malicious nodes can detect. The count of nodes detected is also used to reflect the defense effect.

Because there may be deliberate attacks, network exception etc., we probably allow nodes to send abnormal req_msg more than once. So we set the limit of ExceptionCount to 1∼6 and take six rounds of experiments. The evaluation results of multi-party judgement are shown in Fig. 8.

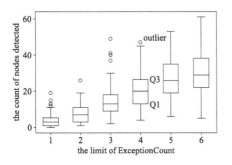
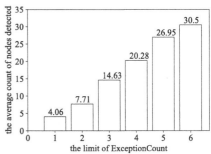

(a) full view of detection results

(b) how many nodes a node can detect on average

Fig. 8. The evaluation of multi-party judgement capability

In Fig. 8a, we use box plot to display the data (counts of nodes detected by 100 malicious nodes) distribution in a standardized way using five-number summary - minimum, Q1 (first quartile), median, Q3 (third quartile) and maximum. The three horizontal lines of the grid respectively represent Q1, median and Q3. Using box plot, we can see the detection results closely. The counts of nodes detected by most malicious nodes are similar. There are several outliers in single round experiment. This means very few nodes can detect more information than the most nodes, because multi-party judgement is based on uncertain probability. Overall, the greater the limit of ExceptionCount, the more the count of nodes detected. In the topology of this experiment, the average degree of nodes is 10.69. When the limit is 2, most nodes can only detect less than 10 existing nodes in the AtNet. In Fig. 8b, we show the average count of nodes detected under different limits of ExceptionCount. When the limit is 2, a node can averagely detect 0.771% of new nodes in the network. The multi-party judgement mechanism is quite effective. This mainly benefits from the high clustering and recursive requesting of AtNet. However, all anti-tracking networks mentioned in related work section can't protect the identifies of relay nodes.

5   Conclusion and Future Work

In this paper, we propose AtNet. It has good network robustness and can prevent malicious nodes from collecting more network information. We firstly construct a fully distributed and unstructured P2P network topology based on NW small-world model. We use greedy thought to make the network cross-domain and domain distribution more uniform. Then we maintain the cross-domain characteristic and small-world property through recursive requesting. With the collaboration of near nodes, an abnormal request of a node can be quickly identified and recorded by others. This multi-party judgement capability relays on high clustering and recursive requesting of AtNet, and it hardly needs extra communication cost. To evaluate the network robustness, we compare AtNet with three other topologies: CPT, CPTs and NN. The experiment results show that AtNet has the best network robustness. We also evaluate the maintenance effect and defense effect. The experiment results show that the maintenance mechanism can keep AtNet connected, good anti-tracking performance, small-world property and high clustering, and a node can only averagely collect 7.71 new nodes in the experimental network with 1000 nodes.

We want to construct a P2P overlay network to protect users' communication privacy. This paper mainly focuses on construction, maintenance and defense about topology. In the future, we will research on building communication tunnels and provide APIs for developing anti-tracking applications.

References

1. Angel, S., Setty, S.: Unobservable communication over fully untrusted infrastructure. In: 12th USENIX Symposium on Operating Systems Design and Implementation (OSDI 16), pp. 551–569 (2016)
2. Boccaletti, S., Latora, V., Moreno, Y., Chavez, M., Hwang, D.U.: Complex networks: structure and dynamics. Phys. Rep. **424**(4–5), 175–308 (2006)
3. Chaum, D.: The dining cryptographers problem: unconditional sender and recipient untraceability. J. Cryptol. **1**(1), 65–75 (1988). https://doi.org/10.1007/BF00206326
4. Cheng, R., Scott, W., Parno, B., Zhang, I., Krishnamurthy, A., Anderson, T.: Talek: a private publish-subscribe protocol. Tech. rep., Technical Report UW-CSE-16-11-01, University of Washington Computer Science ... (2016)
5. Corrigan-Gibbs, H., Boneh, D., Mazières, D.: Riposte: An anonymous messaging system handling millions of users. In: 2015 IEEE Symposium on Security and Privacy, pp. 321–338. IEEE (2015)
6. Golle, P., Juels, A.: Dining cryptographers revisited. In: Cachin, C., Camenisch, J.L. (eds.) EUROCRYPT 2004. LNCS, vol. 3027, pp. 456–473. Springer, Heidelberg (2004). https://doi.org/10.1007/978-3-540-24676-3_27
7. Guan, J., Tang, M., Huang, G., Zhu, W., Zhou, S., Ji, G.: A new small-world network model for instant messaging chat network. In: 2016 11th System of Systems Engineering Conference (SoSE), pp. 1–5. IEEE (2016)
8. Kwon, A., Lazar, D., Devadas, S., Ford, B.: Riffle. Proc. Priv. Enhancing Technol. **2016**(2), 115–134 (2016)
9. Lazar, D., Gilad, Y., Zeldovich, N.: Karaoke: distributed private messaging immune to passive traffic analysis. In: 13th USENIX Symposium on Operating Systems Design and Implementation (OSDI 18), pp. 711–725 (2018)

10. Shirazi, F., Simeonovski, M., Asghar, M.R., Backes, M., Diaz, C.: A survey on routing in anonymous communication protocols. ACM Comput. Surv. (CSUR) **51**(3), 1–39 (2018)

11. Stoica, I., et al.: Chord: a scalable peer-to-peer lookup protocol for internet applications. IEEE/ACM Trans. Netw. **11**(1), 17–32 (2003)

12. Syta, E., Corrigan-Gibbs, H., Weng, S.C., Wolinsky, D., Ford, B., Johnson, A.: Security analysis of accountable anonymity in dissent. ACM Trans. Inf. Syst. Secur. (TISSEC) **17**(1), 1–35 (2014)

13. Tian, C., Zhang, Y., Yin, T.: Modeling of anti-tracking network based on convex-polytope topology. In: Krzhizhanovskaya, V.V., et al. (eds.) ICCS 2020. LNCS, vol. 12138, pp. 425–438. Springer, Cham (2020). https://doi.org/10.1007/978-3-030-50417-5_32

14. Tian, C., Zhang, Y., Yin, T.: Topology self-optimization for anti-tracking network via nodes distributed computing. In: Gao, H., Wang, X. (eds.) CollaborateCom 2021. LNICST, vol. 406, pp. 405–419. Springer, Cham (2021). https://doi.org/10.1007/978-3-030-92635-9_24

15. Tian, C., Zhang, Y., Yin, T., Tuo, Y., Ge, R.: Achieving dynamic communication path for anti-tracking network. In: 2019 IEEE Global Communications Conference (GLOBECOM), pp. 1–6. IEEE (2019)

16. Tian, C., Zhang, Y.Z., Yin, T., Tuo, Y., Ge, R.: A loss-tolerant mechanism of message segmentation and reconstruction in multi-path communication of anti-tracking network. In: Chen, S., Choo, K.-K.R., Fu, X., Lou, W., Mohaisen, A. (eds.) SecureComm 2019. LNICST, vol. 304, pp. 490–508. Springer, Cham (2019). https://doi.org/10.1007/978-3-030-37228-6_24

17. Tian, C., Zhang, Y.Z., Yin, T., Tuo, Y., Ge, R.: A smart topology construction method for anti-tracking network based on the neural network. In: Wang, X., Gao, H., Iqbal, M., Min, G. (eds.) CollaborateCom 2019. LNICST, vol. 292, pp. 439–454. Springer, Cham (2019). https://doi.org/10.1007/978-3-030-30146-0_31

18. Touli, E.F., Lindberg, O.: Relative clustering coefficient. arXiv preprint arXiv:2106.05145 (2021)

19. Tyagi, N., Gilad, Y., Leung, D., Zaharia, M., Zeldovich, N.: Stadium: a distributed metadata-private messaging system. In: Proceedings of the 26th Symposium on Operating Systems Principles, pp. 423–440 (2017)

20. Winter, P., Ensafi, R., Loesing, K., Feamster, N.: Identifying and characterizing sybils in the ToR network. In: 25th USENIX Security Symposium (USENIX Security 16), pp. 1169–1185 (2016)

21. Yin, T., Zhang, Y., Li, J.: AppBot: a novel p2p botnet architecture resistant to graph-based tracking. In: 2016 IEEE Trustcom/BigDataSE/ISPA, pp. 615–622. IEEE (2016)

A Two-Stage Method for Fine-Grained DNS Covert Tunnel Behavior Detection

Bingxu Wang[1,2], Gang Xiong[1,2], Peipei Fu[1,2], Gaopeng Gou[1,2],
Yingchao Qin[1,2], and Zhen Li[1,2(⊠)]

[1] Institute of Information Engineering, Chinese Academy of Sciences, Beijing, China
lizhen@iie.ac.cn
[2] School of Cyber Security, University of Chinese Academy of Sciences,
Beijing, China

Abstract. DNS protocol is one of the most important protocols on the Internet. Network firewall and intrusion detection system generally do not block the DNS protocol, and a large number of malwares use DNS protocol as the covert tunnel for remote control. Therefore, it is very important to enhance the detection of DNS covert tunnel. At present, the researches always select closed data set to detect different tunnel tools and can not distinguish the specific attack behaviors such as download in the tunnel. This paper proposes a two-stage method for DNS covert tunnel behavior identification, which mainly identifies the DNS covert tunnel traffic and the different behaviors in the tunnel in a real-world network environment. In the first stage, by measuring and analyzing a large number of DNS traffic, the core feature threshold method is proposed to distinguish normal and tunnel traffic. The second stage mainly analyzes five kinds of DNS tunnel behaviors and classifies them with machine learning methods. Finally, more than 50 millions normal DNS sessions traffic is collected from the real network environment, and tunnel traffic is produced by DNS covert tunnel tools. Through experiments, using threshold method, the precision and recall rate of DNS covert tunnel detection reach 99%, and time processing efficiency is much higher than machine learning methods. In terms of behavior recognition, the precision and recall of five behaviors reach to 93% and 94%.

Keywords: DNS covert tunnel · Traffic behavior · Machine learning

1 Introduction

At present, Internet technology is developing rapidly, but there are a large number of harmful applications that endanger the security of the network, such as APT attack, botnet, ransomware and so on. After the attackers invade the user's computer, they will establish C&C channel (command and control channel) with the control server for command sending, data stealing and so on. In order to evade the detection of network firewall, attackers usually transmit data through covert tunnel.

© The Author(s), under exclusive license to Springer Nature Switzerland AG 2022
C. Su et al. (Eds.): SciSec 2022, LNCS 13580, pp. 201–216, 2022.
https://doi.org/10.1007/978-3-031-17551-0_13

Covert tunnel is a packet encapsulation technology, which encapsulates the original packet in another different protocol for transmission [11]. Many tunnel technologies are implemented using application layer protocols, such as HTTP protocol [12], DNS protocol [13], etc. DNS protocol is the most commonly used protocol on the Internet and its main function is to convert domain names into IP addresses. Because it has the function of public network service, most network firewalls allow DNS protocol traffic to pass smoothly. Therefore, more and more malicious tools choose DNS protocol as the transmission tunnel of harmful information. At the RSA conference held in 2012, malicious software based on DNS covert tunnel was listed as one of the six most dangerous network attacks [14]. Many malwares based on DNS covert tunnel have also been found in the industry. Palo Alto found that APT tool webky [15] used DNS request and response as the command and control channel. Cisco [16] found the DNS messanger attack, which put command and control instructions into the txt field of DNS. In recent years, the use of DNS covert tunnel has attracted the attention of academia. The researchers analyzed the core characteristics of DNS covert tunnel from multiple dimensions such as domain and traffic features, and identified tunnel traffic combined with machine learning and deep learning technologies.

Although there are many researches about DNS covert tunnel, they have two main problems. Firstly, most of the researches extract features from closed data sets, and use machine learning methods to establish models to classify different DNS tunnel tools. These models generally achieve good recognition effect on closed data sets, but the detection effect significantly reduces in real-world traffic environment. In addition, the time detection performance of the machine learning model is low. When the DNS traffic is large, it can not be processed quickly in real time. Secondly, the current researches mainly focus on the detection of different tunnel tools, and there is less research on the identification of specific behaviors such as download, shell in the tunnel.

This paper mainly studies the identification of DNS covert tunnel traffic and its behaviors in the tunnel. The main contributions of this article are as follows:

Firstly, a Two-Step Detection Method is Proposed. We use a hierarchical method to detect DNS tunnel behaviors. We first use the core feature threshold method to detect the tunnel traffic, and then use the machine learning method to fine-grained identify different tunnel behaviors.

Secondly, We Extract Core Features and Thresholds. In order to accurately detect the tunnel traffic, the distinguishing features and thresholds are extracted. In the stage of behavior recognition, we extract spatiotemporal features and detect different hehaviors combined with machine learning methods.

Thirdly, We Evaluate the Method Through Experiments. We extract more than 50 million normal DNS sessions and produce more than 11000 DNS covert tunnel session data. Through experiments, the precision and recall rate of threshold method reach to 99% and the execution time efficiency is more than

100 times faster than other machine learning methods. For behavior recognition, the precision and recall of different behaviors reach to 93% and 94%.

The rest of the article can be summarized as follows: the second section mainly introduces the background and related work of DNS covert tunnel. The third section mainly introduces the proposed method for detecting DNS covert tunnel and behaviors in the tunnel. The fourth section mainly carries out experiments to evaluate the detection effect. Finally, we summarize this article.

2   Background and Related Work

2.1   DNS Covert Tunnel

DNS covert tunnel refers to the channel that uses the fields in DNS packets to transmit secret information. As shown in Fig. 1, DNS covert tunnel can be used for data leakage, malicious transmission, C&C and other behaviors. Remote control trojan, botnet, ransomeware and APT often use DNS covert tunnel as control and data transmission channel.

In terms of protocol, DNS covert tunnel can be divided into two types: tunnel based on IP protocol and tunnel based on TCP protocol. The tunnel based on IP protocol encapsulates IP packets into DNS messages for transmission. It redirects IP layer packets to virtual network such as tun through DNS protocol, and uses this method to solve the problem of data fragmentation. Common DNS tunnels based on IP include IODINE [1] and DNSCAT [2]. The tunnel based on TCP protocol redirects TCP traffic to DNS channel, and then uses socks proxy and other technologies to communicate without relying on virtual network. Typical DNS tunnels based on TCP include DNS2TCP [3].

In terms of transmission mode, DNS covert tunnel is divided into IP direct connection tunnel and domain relay connection tunnel. For the IP direct connection tunnel, the controlled computer communicates directly with the DNS tunnel server, and the traffic is explicit in the DNS protocol format. In this mode traffic does not been transited through the DNS recursive server, so it is easy to expose its own IP address. For domain relay connection tunnel, DNS tunnel service is used as an authoritative server, DNS tunnel traffic go through recursive server firstly. Network firewalls can only see the IP address of recursive server, but cannot find the IP address of DNS tunnel server.

DNS tunnel mainly carries transmission data through A, AAAA, NS, CNAME, TXT and other fields in the protocol. Different tunnel tools usually choose different types.

2.2   Related Work

There are three main methods for DNS covert tunnel identification. Identification method based on abnormal DNS payload, identification method based on machine learning and identification method based on deep learning.

The identification method based on abnormal DNS payload is commonly used. When malware use DNS protocol as the data transmission channel, its behaviors

Fig. 1. DNS Tunnel

are obviously different from that of normal DNS traffic. For example, the length of domain in DNS covert tunnel is longer than normal DNS service, there are more capital letters and numbers in domain, and the frequency of request packets is higher. At present, there are many studies in this field. Born K [4] and others use information entropy to detect the confusion degree of domain. Normal domains are generally composed of regular words with low entropy, while DNS tunnel domains are generally composed of codes with high entropy. Bilge [5] found that the number of dictionary words in normal domains are much larger than that in DNS tunnels by collecting common words and sentences as dictionaries. Ellens [6] identified the DNS tunnel by detecting the traffic speed. For the DNS tunnel, multiple data packets need to be sent to transmit information. In a short time window, the messages generated by the DNS tunnel are much larger than the normal DNS traffic. The identification method based on abnormal DNS payload is generally based on rule threshold. This method is not flexible in detection and is easy to be bypassed in the process of traffic identification.

DNS covert tunnel identification method based on machine learning is also widely used. Almusawi [7] proposed a multi label support vector machine method to detect DNS covert tunnels, and also classified HTTP, FTP, HTTPS, POP3 and other protocols in DNS tunnels. Nadler [8] detected low-speed DNS covert tunnel traffic by extracting multi-dimensional features combining iforest model. Jawad [9] adjusted and trained a machine learning algorithm to use the benign data set of the top-level primary domain to detect exceptions in DNS query traffic. Engelstad [10] used unsupervised machine learning algorithm k-means to detect DNS tunnel, mainly by using stateful attributes to identify infected mobile devices, including the size of DNS query/response of the device and the time between DNS query and corresponding response.

DNS covert tunnel detection based on machine learning also has shortcomings, such as the extracted features are not comprehensive and strongly depends on expert experience. The current deep learning method is applied to the detection of DNS covert tunnel. Liu [21] proposed for the first time to use neural network to build a classifier to identify the DNS covert tunnel that convert each byte into a 257 dimensional vector through coding, and detect the traffic through

CNN model. Wu [22] used neural network to automatically obtain the characteristics for detection and learned the features of normal DNS traffic, and detected the DNS covert tunnel by calculating the variance between normal samples and malicious samples.

3 Method

This paper identify the tunnel traffic and specific behaviors in the tunnel in two-steps based on the core features. Firstly, we analyze the behaviors of DNS covert tunnel and design the framework of tunnel detection. On this basis, we introduce the feature threshold method of tunnel traffic detection and behavior detection method in tunnel respectively.

In order to analyze DNS covert tunnel behavior, we define several related definitions:

CC_DNS_S: It represents the DNS covert tunnel server, which is the control server of malicious remote software.

CC_DNS_C: It represents the DNS covert tunnel client, which is the controlled computers of malicious remote control.

CC_HEART: It represents the heartbeat keep alive traffic in the DNS covert tunnel.

CC_DATA: It represents the control command traffic and response data traffic in DNS covert tunnel.

DNS Session: Because the normal DNS protocol is a "one request one response" mode, it is limited to request and response packets in a DNS session. In addition, the suffix of the request domain name is added to distinguish DNS requests of different services. Therefore, the DNS protocol session can be described by six tuples.

When a host sends a message to destination IP 8.8.8.8 , destination port 53 through source IP address 1.2.3.4, source port 55445 to request domain www.golang888.xyz which can be described as:

   < 1.2.3.4, 55445, 8.8.8.8, 53, DNS, golang888.xyz >

Time Window: DNS tunnel established by malware are generally used for data theft, program remote control execution and other behaviors. It is difficult for a single DNS session to complete data transmission. Generally, the task can be completed through multiple DNS sessions. Therefore, this paper proposes the concept of time window to identify DNS covert tunnel through the traffic behavior of multiple DNS sessions in a certain time window. In this paper, we establish a time window to 600s.

3.1   DNS Covert Tunnel Behavior Detection Framework

According to the traffic characteristics of DNS covert tunnel, a layered tunnel behavior recognition method is proposed and is shown in Fig. 2. This method is mainly composed of two stages. The first stage is feature threshold method that mainly extracts the distinguishing features to detect the normal DNS traffic and DNS covert tunnel traffic. In the second stage, from the tunnel traffic, we further analyze behavior characteristics such as sleep, download, upload and exec, and classify them by machine learning methods.

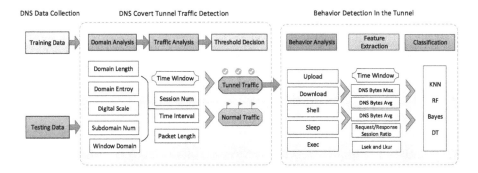

Fig. 2. DNS covert tunnel behavior detection framework

3.2   DNS Covert Tunnel Traffic Detection

In this paper the core idea of DNS covert tunnel identification is to measure and analyze a large number of normal DNS traffic and DNS covert tunnel traffic, and we extract their distinguishing features and thresholds to achieve identification.

3.2.1   Tunnel Feature Extraction
The feature extraction of DNS covert tunnel is mainly carried out from two aspects: domain features and traffic features. For the traffic feature, we extract the characteristics in the 600s time window. We extracted seven core features.

F1. Domain Length: The length of normal domain is usually short, such as www.google.com www.facebook.com. When DNS protocol is used as a covert tunnel, the CC_DNS_C encapsulate the data to domain to sent the CC_DNS_S, which leads to the length of the domain in the DNS covert tunnel is significantly larger than the domain of normal DNS services.

F2. Domain Entropy: Entropy is mainly used to measure the degree of information confusion. For normal domains, they are generally composed of some meaningful words, while the domains in DNS covert tunnels are usually encrypted or encoded. Generally speaking, the data entropy after encryption or coding is significantly larger than that of normal domain. This difference can be used as an indicator to distinguish between normal domain and DNS covert tunnel domain. The formula for calculating entropy is shown in the figure below.

$$Ent(D) = -\sum_{k=1}^{|y|} p_k \log_2 p_k \tag{1}$$

F3. Proportion of Numbers in Domain: We analyze a large number of domain and find that the characters in the domains are mostly letters, while the domain of DNS covert tunnel contains large numbers. The proportion of numbers in the domain can also be used as an important indicator to judge whether it is a DNS covert tunnel domain.

F4. Number of Subdomains: For normal network services, there is usually one or only a few subdomains. For the DNS covert tunnel, the data transmitted from CC_DNS_S to the CC_DNS_C is generally large, and multiple request packets are required to deliver the data. Therefore, in a time window, multiple subdomains generally appear.

F5. Number of Subdomain Sessions: According to the above analysis, for the same subdomain, the number of sessions in DNS tunnel is significantly more than that in normal DNS service in a specific time window.

F6. Request Packet Length: DNS request packet length refers to the payload length of UDP. We count the packet length distribution of the same subdomain in the time window. Statistics show that for normal DNS requests, the packet length is generally less than 80 bytes. For the DNS covert tunnel, because the transmitted content should be encapsulated in the domain name, that causes the request packet length to be much largeer than the length of normal DNS request packet.

F7. Request Time Interval: Time interval refers to the time between two DNS subdomains requests generated by the same client. When the malware transmits data through the DNS covert tunnel, it will automatically send multiple packets, and the time interval between DNS request packets is short. While normal DNS requests are generated by people operating electronic devices (such as browsing web pages, using app, etc.), and there will be a longer time interval.

3.2.2   Feature Threshold Analysis

Based on the features extracted above, we quantify the threshold of the core features. We conduct extensive measurement and statistics on the two types of traffic. For normal DNS services, we deploy passive traffic probes at the network gateway of our organization to obtain more than 30 million DNS sessions, a total of 3783909 domain names. For the DNS covert tunnel, we built the mainstream DNS tunnel tools DNScat2, Iodione, and used the malicious software Cobalt Strike [18] to build the DNS covert C&C tunnel to extract more than 6000 DNS sessions.

Table 1 shows the length distribution of domains. For DNS covert tunnels, the length of domains greater than 79 bytes account for 97.2%, while the proportion of normal domains is only 1.4%. In this article, the domain length threshold is set to 80 byte.

Table 1. DNS domain length threshold analysis.

Domain Len	2–19 bytes	20–39 bytes	40–59 bytes	60–79 bytes	Longer 70 bytes
Normal domain	52.7%	35.9%	4%	4%	1.4%
Tunnel domain	0	0.2%	0.8%	1.8%	97.2%

We calculate the entropy threshold of the collected black-and-white domains respectively. As shown in the Fig. 3, for normal DNS domains, the entropy of more than 97.4% domains lower than 2.6. However, for tunnel domains, the entropy of more than 88% domains larger than 2.5. In this paper, we set the threshold of domain entropy to 2.6.

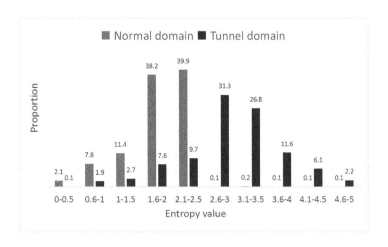

Fig. 3. DNS domains entropy analysis

Through analysis, we find that the proportion of numbers in the normal domains is only 2.4%. In the DNS covert tunnel, the number in domains accounts reach to 53.7%. In this article, the proportion threshold of numbers in domains is set to 40%. In the time window, we also analyze the time interval between the normal DNS service and the DNS covert tunnel request packets. The average time interval of the normal DNS service is 2.8s, while the DNS covert time interval is about 0.08 s. We set the DNS request interval threshold to 0.2 s (Table 2).

Table 2. Number proprotion and time interval analysis.

Feature	Num proprotion	Time interval	DNS sessions
Normal DNS	2.4%	2.8 s	15
Tunnel Traffic	53.7%	0.08 s	30

We also count the number of subdomains and DNS sessions in the time window. The specific threshold is shown in Table 3. For normal DNS services, the session number of subdomains is generally less than 15, while subdomains in DNS covert tunnels appear frequently, generally larger than 30. This article sets the threshold for the number of DNS sessions to 20. The number of subdomain is set to 8.

Table 3. DNS covert feature threshold.

Feature	Threshold
Domain Length	80
Domain Entropy	2.6
Proportion of Numbers in Domain	40%
Number of Subdomains	8
Number of Subdomain Sessions	20
Request Packet Length	100
Request Time Interval	0.2 s

3.3 DNS Covert Tunnel Behavior Detection

At present, many studies in industry and academia focus on the identification of DNS covert tunnel, but lack the identification of specific behaviors in the covert tunnel. In this paper, based on the detection of DNS covert tunnel, we carry out fine-grained analysis of the behaviors.

We use the DNS tunneling tool DNSCAT2 and malware software Cobalt Strike as experimental objects to extract five common behaviors: sleep, upload, download, shell and exec. Next, we analyze the features of each behavior and extract the distinguishing features. The behaviors are shown in Fig. 4.

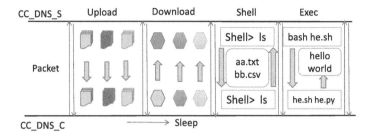

Fig. 4. DNS covert tunnel behavior

B1. Sleep Behavior: Sleep behavior is the keep-alive data packet in the covert tunnel. The controlled computers send data packet to the control service every certain time to inform that is still connected. For sleep behavior, its traffic characteristics are obvious, data packets are generated in a specific time interval, and the length of its request and response packets is shorter than that of other behaviors.

B2. Upload Behavior: Upload behavior is used to send data from the CC_DNS_S to the CC_DNS_C. At the traffic level, the DNS response packet length is large, and the data types are generally TXT and MX.

B3. Download Behavior: Download behavior is that CC_DNS_S downloads the required data from the CC_DNS_C. In terms of traffic, it is mainly reflected in the long length of the requested domains, and the traffic is sudden with a large number of packets and bytes. Its behavior is quite different from upload behavior.

B4. Shell Behavior: Shell behavior is to pop up the command control at CC_DNS_S and execute various commands. Different commands lead to different traffic behaviors. Because the result will be returned to CC_DNS_S after executing the command, so the domain length is long. There are similarities between shell behavior and download behavior, which makes it difficult to distinguish.

B5. Exec Behavior: Exec behavior mainly runs the program of CC_DNS_C through CC_DNS_S. Generally, malicious programs make the program execute in the background. In terms of traffic, CC_DNS_C and CC_DNS_S has several interaction processes, but the traffic is less than upload, download, shell and other behaviors.

Combined with the above behavior analysis, we extract features in a specific time window. The specific features are as follows table. We mainly extract the traffic features, including the maximum, average, proportion and total bytes of request and response direction, as well as the time interval information. Skewness is a feature that describes the symmetry of packet length distribution and kurtosis is a descriptor of the shape of a probability distribution. The detailed formulas are as follows (Table 4).

$$Lsek = \frac{\frac{1}{n}\sum_{i=1}^{n}(len - \bar{t})^3}{(\frac{1}{n-1}\sum_{i=1}^{n}(len - \bar{t})^2)^{\frac{3}{2}}} \tag{2}$$

$$Lkur = \frac{\frac{1}{n}\sum_{i=1}^{n}(len - \overline{len})^4}{(\frac{1}{n}\sum_{i=1}^{n}(len - \overline{len})^2)^2} - 3 \tag{3}$$

Table 4. DNS covert tunnel behavior feature.

Feature	Description
Time_interval	The time interval of DNS request
Num_session	The number of DNS sessions
Request/Response_byte	All bytes of DNS requests and responses
Response_byte	All bytes of DNS responses
Ratio_byte	The ratio of response bytes and request bytes
Max_request/response	Max packet length of requests and responses
Lsek	The symmetry of packet length distribution
Lkur	The shape of a probability distribution

After extracting features in a specific time window, machine learning algorithms are used to classify various behaviors of DNS tunnel. We use four commonly used machine learning algorithms: random forest, KNN, naive Bayes and gradient lifting decision tree.

4   Evaluation

In this part, we evaluate the detection effect of the above method on DNS tunnel traffic and behavior detection. First, we introduce the composition of the data set and how to evaluate the performance of our model. Secondly, we evaluate the recognition effect of DNS tunnel traffic using core threshold method. Finally, the detection effect of various tunnel behaviors using machine learning algorithms on is evaluated.

4.1   Dataset

In order to analyze the normal DNS traffic and DNS covert tunnel traffic, we use Cisco's JOY tool [24] to collect traffic for 30 days at the gateway of our research institution and filter core features, collecting more than 50 million DNS sessions, a total of 4173391 domains. Among them, 60% sessions and 3783909 domains are extracted as training and analysis samples. Others are used as testing samples.

At the same time, we build DNS tunnel tool DNScat2 and malware Cobalt Strike on the virtual server from Alibaba cloud company, and collect more than 11000 DNS covert tunnel sessions. Among them, 60% are used as training samples, and the rest are used as testing samples. The generated DNS covert tunnel traffic includes sleep, shell, exec, upload and download (Table 5).

Table 5. Dataset for Evaluation.

Data type	Normal DNS	All tunnel	Sleep	Shell	Exec	Upload	Download
Train Num	31036209	6702	3685	745	669	812	791
Test Num	20697472	4469	2457	497	446	541	529

4.2   Performance Metrics

In order to evaluate the effect of our method, we define TP, FP, FN and TN, which represent true positive, false positive, false negative, and true negative. We use precision (P), recall (R) and F1 score (F1) as the dns covert tunnel detection evaluation indicators. The formula is as follows:

$$P = \frac{TP}{TP + FP} \tag{4}$$

$$R = \frac{TP}{TP + FN} \tag{5}$$

$$F1 = \frac{2 * P * R}{P + R} \tag{6}$$

4.3   DNS Covert Tunnel Traffic Detection Evaluation

Domain White List: This paper mainly identifies DNS covert tunnel traffic by extracting effective features and analyzing reasonable thresholds. Through the analysis of a large number of domains, it is find that some normal domains are similar to those in DNS covert tunnels, such as the length of domains is long and the entropy of domains is high. These domains are easily mistaken for DNS covert tunnel domains. After analyzing these, we find that they mainly focus on several specific subdomains. For example, subdomains of Mcafee company account for more than half of the misdetected domains. After excluding such domains, the detection effect is greatly improved.Here are some common subdomains that are easy to be misidentified:

<mcafee.com> <in-addr.arp> <ipv6.arpa> <online-metrix.com>

Feature Number Usage Evaluation: In the above, we extract seven features and analyze the corresponding thresholds. Is it true that the traffic with all seven features meeting the corresponding threshold can be determined as DNS covert tunnel? Through our evaluation, we find that if all seven features meet the threshold, it shows an precision rate of 99.91%, but it results in a recall rate of only 90.74%. Because the traffic of DNS covert tunnel is relatively diverse, which may not meet the seven features at the same time in a certain time interval. We conduct experiments to decide the number of features to observe the precision and recall rates. The results are shown in Fig. 5: we find that when the five features are met at the same time, the precision remains at 99.67% and the recall rate is significantly increased to 99.31%, that shows the best effect.

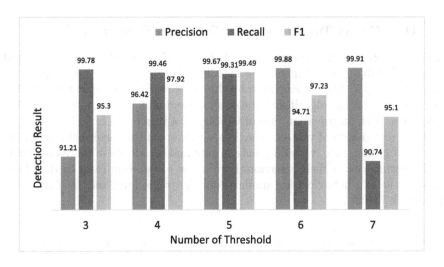

Fig. 5. Feature number usage evaluation

Threshold Method Compared With Other Methods: In this paper, our threshold method is compared with the machine learning methods. The machine learning method also achieves good detection effect. It is only slightly lower than the threshold method in precision and recall, but far lower than the threshold method in recognition time performance. The recognition time of every 10000 DNS sessions is counted, our threshold method takes about 0.6s, while the machine learning methods exceeds 80s.

This paper also compares with similar studies in the academic field. Almusawi [24] proposed a multi labels support vector machine method to detect and classify DNS covert tunnel. This paper extracts the relevant features and tests them on the sample data set, and also achieves more than 99% accuracy and recall. But it takes a long time than our threshold method. Through comparison, it is find that various methods have achieved high recognition rate for DNS covert tunnel. The advantage of our threshold method is that it has fast execution time and can be used in real online network environment (Table 6).

Table 6. Comparison with different threshold method.

Method	P	R	Time
Almusawi et al. [24]	99.53%	99.21%	117 s
Nadler et al. [25]	**99.71%**	99.1%	129 s
Threshold method(5 Features)	99.67%	**99.31%**	**0.6 s**
RF method	99.36%	99.29%	118 s
SVM method	99.12%	98.89%	107 s
DT method	99.09%	99.15%	129 s
Bayes method	99.32%	99.54%	112 s

4.4   DNS Covert Tunnel Behavior Detection Evaluation

This paper extracts the features of five behaviors sleep, shell, upload, download and exec in DNS covert tunnel, and classifies them by using common machine learning methods. The classification results are shown in the below table. In the comparison of various algorithms, the effect of random forest is better than other algorithms, with an precision rate of 93.4% and a recall rate of 94.3%.

In the recognition of various behaviors, sleep, upload and exec behaviors have a high recognition rate, with an precision rate and recall rate of more than 98%. While download and shell behaviors have a low recognition rate. In the above analysis, the two behaviors are similar from the traffic level and are difficult to distinguish (Table 7).

Table 7. Tunnel behaviors detection with different machine learning method.

Behavior	RF			BAYES			KNN			DT		
	P	R	F1	P	R	F1	P	R	F1	P	R	F1
Upload	**98.7**	**99.1**	98.90	97.9	98.2	98.05	97.2	98.5	97.85	97.2	98.4	97.8
Sleep	**98.5**	**98.9**	98.70	98.1	97.4	97.75	97.3	98.2	97.75	96.7	97.9	97.3
Exec	**97.9**	**98.8**	98.35	97.1	98.3	97.7	97.6	98.5	98.05	97.1	98.8	97.94
Download	**89.8**	**92.1**	90.94	90.1	87.4	88.73	90.3	90.1	90.2	90.6	90.4	90.5
Shell	**91.4**	**90.6**	91.00	88.5	90.2	89.3	87.8	91.3	89.52	88.1	90.1	89.09
All	**93.4**	**94.3**	93.85	91.7	92.1	91.9	91.1	92.3	91.7	90.1	92.9	91.48

5   Conclusion

This paper uses a two-step method to identify the DNS covert tunnel traffic and the behaviors in the tunnel. In the first step, we extract the core features from the domain and traffic level, and determine the threshold of each feature through the analysis of a large number of black-and-white sample data. In the second step, the key features of sleep, shell, upload, download and exec behaviors in the tunnel are extracted, and the machine learning methods are used for classification. Finally, we evaluate the recognition effect in real-world environment. The results show that the precision and recall rate of DNS covert tunnel traffic reach 99% and it has faster time detection performance, which is much greater than other methods. In terms of behavior recognition, the precision reached 93%, and the recall reached 94%.

Acknowledgements. This work is supported by The National Key Research and Development Program of China (No. 2020YFE0200500).

References

1. Andeersson, B., Ekman, E.: Iodine [EB/OL] (2014). http://code.kryo.se/iodine/
2. Pietraszek, B.: T.DNScat (2005). http://tadek.pietraszek.org/projects/DNScat/
3. Dembour, C.: DNS2TCP (2010). http://www.hsc.fr/ressources/outils/dns2tcp/
4. Born, K., Gustafson, D.: NgViz: detecting DNS tunnels through n-gram visualization and quantitative analysis. In: Proceedings of the Sixth Annual Workshop on Cyber Security and Information Intelligence Research, pp. 1–4 (2010)
5. Bilge, L., et al.: Exposure: finding malicious domains using passive DNS analysis. In: NDSS, pp. 1–17 (2011)
6. Ellens, W., Żuraniewski, P., Sperotto, A., Schotanus, H., Mandjes, M., Meeuwissen, E.: Flow-based detection of DNS tunnels. In: Doyen, G., Waldburger, M., Čeleda, P., Sperotto, A., Stiller, B. (eds.) AIMS 2013. LNCS, vol. 7943, pp. 124–135. Springer, Heidelberg (2013). https://doi.org/10.1007/978-3-642-38998-6_16
7. Almusawi, A., Amintoosi, H.: DNS tunneling detection method based on multilabel support vector machine. Secur. Commun. Netw. **2018**(6), 1–9 2018
8. Nadler, A., Aminov, A., Shabtai, A.: Detection of malicious and low throughput data exfiltration over the DNS protocol. Comput. Secur. **80**, 36–53 (2019)
9. Ahmed, J., Gharakheili, H.H., Raza, Q., et al.: Monitoring enterprise DNS queries for detecting data exfiltration from internal hosts. IEEE Trans. Netw. Serv. Manage. **17**(1), 265–279 (2019)
10. Do, V.T., Engelstad, P., Feng, B., van Do, T.: Detection of DNS tunneling in mobile networks using machine learning. In: Kim, K., Joukov, N. (eds.) ICISA 2017. LNEE, vol. 424, pp. 221–230. Springer, Singapore (2017). https://doi.org/10.1007/978-981-10-4154-9_26
11. Zander, S., Armitage, G., Branch, P.: A survey of covert channels and countermeasures in computer network protocols. IEEE Commun. Surv. Tut. **9**(3), 44–57 (2007)
12. Dusi, M., Crotti, M., Gringoli, F., et al.: Tunnel Hunter: detecting application-layer tunnels with statistical fingerprinting. Comput. Netw. **53**(1), 81–97 (2009)
13. Van Horenbeeck, M.: Deception on the network: thinking differently about covert channels (2006)
14. Skoudis, E.: The six most dangerous new attack techniques and what's coming next. In: RSA Conference (RSA2012) (2012)
15. Grunzweig, J., Scott, M., Lee, B.: New wekby attacks use DNS requests as command and control mechanism. Palo Alto Networks (2016)
16. Brumaghin, E., Grady, C.: Covert channels and poor decisions: the tale of DNS-Messenger. Accessed 10 Jun 2017 (2019)

17. https://www.alexa.com/ (2022)
18. https://www.cobaltstrike.com/
19. Friedman, J.H.: Greedy function approximation: a gradient boosting machine. Ann. Stat. **29**(5), 1189–1232 (2001)
20. Collins, M., Schapire, R.E., Singer, Y.: Logistic regression, adaboost and bregman distances. Mach. Learn. **48**(1), 253–285 (2002). https://doi.org/10.1023/A:1013912006537
21. Liu, C., et al.: A byte-level CNN method to detect DNS tunnels. In: 2019 IEEE 38th International Performance Computing and Communications Conference, pp. 1–8. IEEE Press, Piscataway (2019)
22. Wu, K.M., Zhang, Y.Z., Yin, T.: TDAE: autoencoder-based automatic feature learning method for the detection of DNS tunnel. In: 2020 IEEE International Conference on Communications, pp. 1–7. IEEE Press, Piscataway (2020)
23. Zhang, M., Sun, H.L., Yang, P.: Identification of DNS covert channel based on improved convolutional neural network. J. Commun. **41**(1), 169–179 (2020)
24. Almusawi, A., Amintoosi, H.: DNS tunneling detection method based on multilabel support vector machine. Secur. Commun. Netw. **2018**(6), 1–9 2018

Analysis and Detection Against Overlapping Phenomenon of Behavioral Attribute in Network Attacks

Jiang Xie[1,3], Shuhao Li[1,2(✉)], and Peishuai Sun[1,3]

[1] Institute of Information Engineering, Chinese Academy of Sciences, Beijing, China
{xiejiang,lishuhao,sunpeishuai}@iie.ac.cn
[2] Key Laboratory of Network Assessment Technology, University of Chinese Academy of Sciences, Beijing, China
[3] School of Cyber Security, University of Chinese Academy of Sciences, Beijing, China

Abstract. Various network attacks have brought great threats to cyber security. It is beneficial to build various datasets for detecting these network attacks. In these datasets, a sample has only one label. Traditional detection methods based on these data also belong to single-label learning, giving only one label to each sample. However, there is a noteworthy overlapping phenomenon of the behavioral attribute between attacks in the real world, i.e., network behavior could be multi-labeled. Reflected in the attack dataset is that multiple samples have the same features but different labels. This paper verifies and analyzes the overlapping phenomenon in well-known datasets UNSW-NB15 and CIC-AndMal-2020. For instance, in UNSW-NB15, a sample has an average of 1.689 labels. Then, we re-label these data as multi-label attack datasets based on the phenomenon. In addition, using multi-label methods to detect overlapping network attacks can support tracing attack sources and building better IDSs. Therefore, several multi-label detection methods are also adopted to detect these network attacks. Experiments in UNSW-NB15 show that multi-label methods are better than related single-label methods.

Keywords: Network attack analysis and detection · Overlapping phenomenon · Multi-label learning

1 Introduction

With the development of the Internet, various network attacks pose a significant threat to cyber security. To effectively detect network attacks, many researchers and organizations publish differently labeled attack datasets [3,13,16,17]. These datasets are collected from the real network environment and collated to support detection research in related fields. A network behavior record usually has only one label in these datasets. The detection methods based on these datasets also belong to single-label learning and just give one label for each sample.

Such methods are intuitive and effective, but we cannot get deeper correlation information about network attacks from the detection process. Furthermore, it is beneficial to obtain as much information as possible from a network behavior for the source tracing of network attacks and the construction of an Intrusion Detection System (IDS) [14].

In this paper, we discover that various network attacks exist the overlapping phenomenon of the behavioral attribute in the real world. Network behaviors belonging to different attacks show the same behavior features. That is, in an attack dataset, multiple network behavior records have the same features but different labels. We further describe and analyze the overlapping phenomenon in Sect. 2.

Analyzing the overlapping phenomenon can help the researcher obtain more information from a network behavior to support the tracing of attack source and build IDS. For instance, DoS is a malicious attempt to make a server unavailable to users; Fuzzers is an attack in which an attacker an attack in which the attacker attempts to discover security loopholes in a program, operating system, or network by feeding it to the massive input of random data to make it crash [16]. If a network behavior is considered as belonging to both DoS and Fuzzers, in this case, we can infer that the attacker attempts to make a server unavailable to users by continuously feeding it the randomly generated data.

The overlapping phenomenon causes a network behavior to have multiple labels. In this paper, we call network attack data existing overlapping phenomenon as multi-label network attack data. However, traditional detection methods belong to single-label learning and are difficult to detect these multi-label data. Therefore, detecting these attacks in a multi-label manner is a better choice. Corresponding detection methods belong to multi-label learning (MLL). Although this paper mainly focuses on analyzing the overlapping phenomenon, several multi-label baseline detection methods are also used to detect network attacks.

The main contributions of this paper are as follows.

- We discover the overlapping phenomenon of the behavioral attribute between network attacks in the real world. A network behavior could be multi-labeled and belongs to multiple attacks. That is, in a network attack dataset, there are multiple samples with the same features, but they have different labels. This phenomenon reflects the complex connections between attacks.
- We perform statistical analysis in well-known network attack datasets (UNSW-NB15 [16], CIC-AndMal-2020 [13,17]). The experimental results validate our findings on the overlapping phenomenon. In UNSW-NB15 and CIC-AndMal-2020, a sample has an average 1.689 and 1.413 labels, respectively. In addition, we re-label these data and make them publicly available to support related research[1].
- Based on the analysis of the overlapping phenomenon, we also use several multi-label methods for network attack detection. Experiments in

---

[1] The re-labeled dataset and related code can be found at https://anonymous.4open. science/r/processed-multi-label-dataset-D4C3/.

UNSW-NB15 (normal and nine types of attacks) show that RF-CC (Random forest with classifier chains [18]) can achieve better results than related single-label methods (3.61%~5.59% higher in $F1$).

The remainder of this paper is organized as follows. Section 1 introduces the background and related work. In Sect. 2, we analyze the overlapping phenomenon. Section 3 is multi-label attack detection and evaluation. Finally, Sect. 4 is the discussion, and Sect. 5 is the conclusion.

2 Background and Related Work

2.1 UNSW-NB15

UNSW-NB15[2] [16], is a dataset that hybrids the real modern normal and the contemporary synthesized attack activities of the network traffic. The tcpdump tool was utilized to capture 100 GB of the raw traffic (*e.g.*, Pcap files). This dataset has nine types of attacks, namely, Fuzzers, Analysis, Backdoors, DoS, Exploits, Generic, Reconnaissance, Shellcode, and Worms. A partition from this dataset was configured as a training set and testing set, namely, UNSW_NB15_training-set.csv and UNSW_NB15_testing-set.csv respectively. The number of records in the training set is 175,341 records, and the testing set is 82,332 records from the different types of attack and normal. The samples are in units of TCP traffic flows and are characterized by various statistical features about the flows. Each record has 42-dimensional features and a label.

Jing *et al.* [12] propose Support Vector Machine (SVM) with a new scaling method for binary-classification and multi-classification experiments. In UNSW-NB15, the proposed SVM method can achieve the testing accuracy of 85.99% for binary-classification and the testing accuracy of 75.77% for multi-classification. Yang *et al.* [22] propose a novel intrusion detection model, ICVAE-DNN. Experiments show that it outperforms six well-known models in the NSL-KDD [19] and UNSW-NB15 datasets. Yang *et al.* [21] also propose a network intrusion detection model called SAVAER-DNN, in which WGAN-GP is used to learn the latent data distribution. Experiments show that the SAVAER-DNN outperforms eight well-known classification models.

2.2 CIC-AndMal-2020

CIC-AndMal-2020[3] [13,17], is a new comprehensive and huge android malware dataset from the real world. The dataset is constructed based on the Canadian Institute for Cybersecurity (CIC) project in collaboration with Canadian Centre for Cyber Security (CCCS). It includes 200K benign and 200K malware samples totaling 400K android apps with 14 major malware categories and 191 eminent

---

[2] https://research.unsw.edu.au/projects/unsw-nb15-dataset.
[3] https://www.unb.ca/cic/datasets/andmal2020.html.

malware families. The samples are in units of software. Its features are composed of the static features of the software and the dynamic features displayed when running in a simulated environment. Each software has 9,503-dimensional features and a label.

Fiky *et al.* [7] propose two machine learning methods for dynamic analysis of android malware: one is used to detect and identify the category, and the other is used to detect and identify the family. Durmucs *et al.* [5] apply statistical calculation methods to the analysis output model. Then, an understandable scenario is created, and a model for cyber security intervention is provided. Liu *et al.* [15] apply an unsupervised malware detection method to detect Zero-day attack. They propose an unsupervised feature learning algorithm, SRBM, to reduce the data dimension. Experiments show that the features learned by SRBM perform better than those learned by other reduction methods.

The above detection methods based on UNSW-NB15 and CIC-AndMal-2020 have excellent performance in single-label detection. However, the overlapping phenomenon between network attacks is not considered.

3   Analysis of Overlapping Phenomenon

In this section, we analyze the overlapping phenomenon. Then, we re-label the data in UNSW-NB15 and CIC-AndMal-2020 based on the analysis results.

3.1   Overview

We discover the overlapping phenomenon of the behavioral attribute between network attacks. The phenomenon causes a sample to be multi-labeled. Figure 1 shows the overlapping phenomenon in the network attack dataset sampled from the Internet, i.e., there are multiple samples with the same features but with different labels (for instance, x_1 has two labels y_1 and y_2).

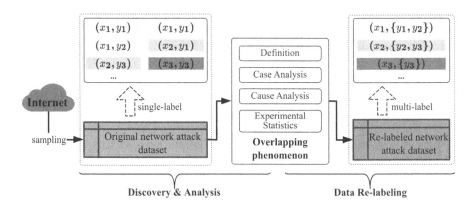

Fig. 1. The analysis process of the network attack dataset with the overlapping phenomenon of the behavioral attribute (x_*: the sample in the dataset. y_*: the label).

3.2 Definition of Overlapping Phenomenon

The formal description of the phenomenon is as follows. In a network attack dataset D, in which a sample is $x = [x^{(1)}, x^{(2)}, ..., x^{(d)}]$ and d is the feature size of the sample x. D consists of M attack sub-datasets $(D_1, D_2, ..., D_M)$, where the attack i has $|D_i|$ samples. We define two samples x and x' with overlapping the behavioral attribute as $x = x'$, as shown in Eq. (1), which are strictly the same in all features.

$$x = x' \Leftrightarrow \left\{ x^{(i)} = x'^{(i)}; i = 1, 2, ..., d \right\} \tag{1}$$

We define that if there is the overlapping phenomenon in the network attack dataset D, then: $\exists (x_1 \in D_1, x_2 \in D_2, ..., x_k \in D_k; k \leqslant M)$, has $x_1 = x_2 = ... = x_k$.

3.3 Case Analysis of Overlapping Phenomenon

Analysis, Backdoor, DoS, Exploits, and Fuzzers in UNSW-NB15. There is the overlapping phenomenon of the behavioral attribute in the Analysis, Backdoor, DoS, Exploits, and Fuzzers, i.e., they have the same samples. For instance, DoS is a malicious attempt to make a server unavailable to users, and Fuzzers is a technique that attempts to crash a program or network by feeding it the randomly generated data [16]. Therefore, if an attacker uses the technology of Fuzzers during the DoS attack, then the corresponding network behavior data can be considered to belong to both DoS and Fuzzers, and is multi-labeled. Table 1 shows an actual multi-label sample sampled from UNSW-NB15.

Table 1. An actual network behavior record in UNSW-NB15.

Feature Name	Dur, proto, service, state, spkts, dpkts, sbytes, dbytes, rate, sttl, dttl, sload, dload, sloss, dloss, sinpkt, dinpkt, sjit, djit, swin, stcpb, dtcpb, dwin, tcprtt, synack, ackdat, smean, dmean, trans_depth, response_body_len, ct_srv_src, ct_state_ttl, ct_dst_ltm, ct_src_dport_ltm, ct_dst_sport_ltm, ct_dst_src_ltm, is_ftp_login, ct_ftp_cmd, ct_flw_http_mthd, ct_src_ltm, ct_srv_dst, is_sm_ips_ports
Feature Value	$9 \times 10^{-6}, 120, 0, 5, 2, 0, 200, 0, 111111.11, 254, 0, 8.888889 \times 10^7, 0, 0, 0, 0.009, 0, 0, 0, 0, 0, 0, 0, 0, 0, 0, 100, 0, 0, 0, 6, 2, 2, 2, 2, 6, 0, 0, 0, 3, 6, 0$
Label	Analysis, Backdoor, DoS, Exploits, Fuzzers

Trojan and Zeroday in CIC-AndMal-2020. In CIC-AndMal-2020, a Trojan is defined as a software or script that accepts instructions to perform malicious actions in the host of victim [17]. The attacker usually communicates with the

Trojan by C&C channels; the Zeroday is relatively broader. Generally, any network attack that uses unknown vulnerabilities or backdoors can be considered Zeroday [13, 17]. Therefore, if an attacker uses unknown vulnerabilities to transmit Trojan or directly uses it as a C&C channel, it can belong to both Trojan and Zeroday. Since one sample in CIC-AndMal-2020 has 9,503 features, we show the actual sample in our Github repository.

There is also other overlapping phenomenon (Reconnaissance and Exploits in UNSW-NB15, Adware and Riskware in CIC-AndMal-2020, *etc.*). The overlapping phenomenon between network attacks is a universal problem that cannot be ignored.

3.4   Cause Analysis of Overlapping Phenomenon

The overlapping phenomenon reflects the complex relationship between the network attacks. We believe that there are the following reasons.

Overlapping of Different Attack Definitions. The definitions of different attacks are not mutually exclusive. Their boundaries are unclear, resulting in network behavior that may be inherently multi-labeled. For instance, a Fuzzer can crash a system, which can be considered a type of DoS, and the same is also true for an Exploit. While not all Fuzzers and Exploits can be considered DoS, attacks under two different definitions take the same actions in some cases, making these attacks a natural similarity.

Different Levels of Attacks. The different definitions of network attack are not at the same level. Generally, a network attack consists of other lower-level techniques in the implementation process. For instance, a DoS attack may use Exploit technology in a specific scenario. In this case, the DoS is at a higher-level, while the Exploit is at a lower-level.

Different Stages of Same Behavior. In the real world, the various actions that an attacker takes to achieve malicious behavior are complex. The corresponding representation of the network data is also complex and can be divided into different phases. The malicious features exposed at different phases classify this network behavior into different attacks. For instance, a Trojan-based attack can consist of two phases: in the intrusion phase, the Trojan uses the Zeroday vulnerability to attack the host, and after the intrusion is completed, it uses the Exploit technology to obtain and transmit private information. In this case, this attack behavior has different attack labels at different phases.

Weak Feature Extraction. Existing feature engineering is not comprehensive enough in extraction methods, and extracting unique and mutually exclusive features of different network behaviors is challenging. For instance, in encrypted traffic, the external features of data (packet length sequence, timestamp sequence, *etc.*) corresponding to two different attacks based on the same C&C encrypted channel are very similar. Therefore, if a feature engineer only computes external statistical features, these features cannot effectively distinguish different attacks.

3.5   Experimental Statistics of Overlapping Phenomenon

Data Sampling. We sample data from UNSW-NB15 and CIC-AndMal-2020, respectively. The data sampling results are shown in Table 2 and Table 3. For UNSW-NB15, we select the official training set and test set, as shown in Table 2. A detailed description of these attacks can be found here [16]. For CIC-AndMal-2020, the data is randomly sampled. We select part of the benign data (Ben0.csv) and all the malicious data, as shown in Table 3. A detailed description of these attacks can be found here [13,17].

Table 2. The data sampling results in UNSW-NB15.

Category	Size (Training set + Test set)	Category	Size (Training set + Test set)
Analysis	2,677 (2,000+677)	Generic	58,871 (40,000+18,871)
Backdoor	2,329 (1,746+583)	**Normal**	93,000 (56,000+37,000)
DoS	16,353 (12,264+4,089)	Reconnaissance	13,987 (10,491+3,496)
Exploits	44,525 (33,393+11,132)	Shellcode	1,511 (1,133+378)
Fuzzers	24,246 (18,184+6,062)	Worms	174 (130+44)
Total	257,673 (175,341+82,332)		

Table 3. The data sampling results in CIC-AndMal-2020.

Category	Size	Category	Size	Category	Size
Adware	47,198	FileInfector	669	Scareware	1,556
Backdoor	1,538	NoCategory	2,296	SMS	3,125
Banker	887	PUA	2,051	Spy	3,540
Benign	32,084	Ransomware	6,202	Trojan	13,542
Dropper	2,302	Riskware	97,349	Zeroday	13,327
Total	227,666				

Statistical Results. We statistically analyze the overlapping phenomenon in UNSW-NB15 and CIC-AndMal-2020 from two perspectives. Both the sample statistics in the dataset and multi-label metrics are calculated.

Sample Statistics. The results of sample statistics in UNSW-NB15 are shown in Table 4. It can be found that there is the overlapping phenomenon in UNSW-NB15. For instance, the number Total = 188 in the *sample* 1 column means that there are 188 samples that are the same as *sample* 1, 66 of which are labeled as DoS and 76 are labeled as Exploits.

Table 4. The top 5 multi-label network attack samples in the overlapping phenomenon of the behavioral attribute in UNSW-NB15 (The number represents the number of times this sample is repeated in the dataset).

Category	Network attack records					
	sample 1	sample 2	sample 3	sample 4	sample 5	...
Analysis	10	7	6	6	5	
Backdoor	10	7	4	6	4	
DoS	66	47	38	42	31	
Exploits	76	62	60	54	50	
Fuzzers	10	7	6	6	5	
Generic	6	1	0	0	0	...
Normal	0	0	0	0	0	
Reconnaissance	10	7	6	6	5	
Shellcode	0	0	0	0	0	
Worms	0	0	0	0	0	
Total	188	138	120	120	100	

The results of sample statistics in CIC-AndMal-2020 are shown in Table 5. It can be found that there is also the overlapping phenomenon in CIC-AndMal-2020. For instance, the number Total = 5,975 in the *sample* 1 column means that there are 5,975 samples that are the same as *sample* 1, 3,612 of which are labeled as Trojan and 2,363 are labeled as Zeroday.

Multi-label Metrics Calculation. In addition, we also employ two multi-label metrics to analyze the overlapping phenomenon, which quantitatively measures the overlapping distribution.

The label diversity, *LDiv*, is the number of different label sets in the dataset, as shown in the Eq. (2). The larger this value, the greater the multi-label diversity in the dataset.

$$\text{LDiv} = |\{Y \mid \exists \boldsymbol{x} : (\boldsymbol{x}, Y) \in \mathbf{D}\}| \tag{2}$$

The label cardinality, *LCard*, is the average label number of one sample, as shown in the Eq. (3). The larger the value, the more multi-label samples in the dataset.

$$\text{LCard} = \frac{1}{N} \sum_{i=1}^{N} \mid Y_i \mid \tag{3}$$

Table 5. The top 5 multi-label network attack samples in the overlapping phenomenon of the behavioral attribute in CIC-AndMal-2020 (The number represents the number of times this sample is repeated in the dataset).

Category	Network attack records					
	sample 1	sample 2	sample 3	sample 4	sample 5	...
Adware	0	206	3	134	1,547	
Backdoor	0	0	0	58	0	
Banker	0	0	0	28	0	
Benign	0	0	0	12	0	
Dropper	0	0	0	94	0	
FileInfector	0	0	0	5	0	
NoCategory	0	0	0	59	0	
PUA	0	0	0	7	0	
Ransomware	0	0	0	1,057	0	
Riskware	0	2,602	2,544	288	186	
SMS	0	0	0	14	0	
Scareware	0	0	0	8	0	
Spy	0	0	0	199	0	
Trojan	3,612	0	0	93	0	
Zeroday	2,363	0	0	301	0	
Total	5,975	2,808	2,547	2,357	1,733	

The two metrics are calculated to measure the multi-label distribution of network attacks. The multi-label analysis results are shown in Table 6. In UNSW-NB15, there are 10 basic categories and 57 label sets. On average, each sample has 1.689 categories. In CIC-AndMal-2020, there are 15 basic categories and 145 label sets. On average, each sample has 1.413 categories.

Table 6. The data analysis results of network attacks overlap.

	Basic category	LDiv	LCard
UNSW-NB15	10	57	1.689
CIC-AndMal-2020	15	145	1.413

3.6 Data Re-labeling

Based on the analysis of the overlapping phenomenon in the datasets, we re-label and de-duplicate the data sampled from UNSW-NB15 and CIC-AndMal-2020, respectively. For multiple samples with the same features but different labels, we only save one sample and all the corresponding labels. As shown in Fig. 1, these multi-label data compose the new re-labeled network attack datasets.

4   Multi-label Attack Detection and Evaluation

This paper refers to the network attack data with the overlapping phenomenon as multi-label attack data. Taking the re-labeled dataset from UNSW-NB15 for example, we detect these attacks in a multi-label manner.

4.1   Definition of Multi-label Attack Detection Problem

There is $\mathbf{X} \in \mathbb{R}^d$, d is the size of feature space, $\mathbf{Y} = \{y_1, y_2, ..., y_M\}$ is the label space. There is a network attack dataset $\mathbf{D} = \{(x_i, Y_i) | i = 1, 2, ..., N; x_i \in \mathbf{X}; Y_i \subseteq \mathbf{Y}\}$. We need to find a multi-label classification function h that maps x from the feature space $\mathbf{X}$ to the label space $\mathbf{Y}$, i.e., $x \in \mathbf{X} \rightarrow h(x) \subseteq \mathbf{Y}$.

4.2   Multi-label Detection Methods

This paper shows the training and detection process of a multi-label detection method, namely the multi-label model, as shown in Fig. 2. The training set is sampled from the re-labeled dataset to train the model. After the model converges, it enters the detection phase and provides detection results for unknown samples x' sampled from the Internet.

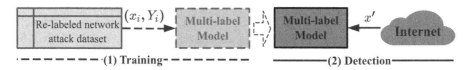

Fig. 2. The training and detection process of a multi-label model for network attacks with the overlapping phenomenon (x_i, x': the sample. Y_i: label set of x_i).

Multi-Label Learning Strategies. According to the strength of label correlation mining, methods for multi-label detection mainly have three strategies: first-order, second-order, and high-order [24].

First-order, ignores the correlation with labels and only builds binary-classifiers between single-label and samples [1,4,23]. For instance, it decomposes the multi-label classification of M base categories into M independent binary classification problems. The first-order structure is simple and can be constructed quickly using basic classifiers. However, this method cannot effectively utilize the correlation between labels, and the detection effect is often not high.

Second-order, explores the correlation features between pairs of labels [9], or dividing the labels into related and unrelated sets [6]. For instance, it constructs

$\frac{M(M-1)}{2}$ binary-classifiers of label pairs in a multi-label problem of M basic categories. The second-order locally considers the correlation between labels compared to the first-order.

High-order, considers the association between multiple labels [2,10,11,20]. For instance, it directly converts the label set of each sample in the dataset to specific natural numbers and then transforms the multi-label problem into a single-label multi-classification problem. In general, higher-orders can achieve better detection results in multi-label learning problems. However, the corresponding method of construction is also relatively more complex.

In multi-label learning, problem transformation and algorithm adaptation are two mainstream methods based on the above three strategies. Problem transformation converts multi-label problems into single-label problem combinations and then uses existing single-label algorithms. Algorithm adaptation improves the existing algorithm to detect multi-label problems directly. For instance, ML-KNN [23] refers to the clustering algorithm and directly determines the label set of the sample according to the neighbor characteristics.

Selection Methods. There is no related research on multi-label detection methods for network attacks with the overlapping phenomenon. Therefore, we select several classical multi-label methods for experimental evaluation.

The methods selected are shown in Table 7. These algorithms can be divided into problem transformation and algorithm adaptation based on the three strategies (first-order, second-order, and high-order). In the problem transformation, we select three transformations: Binary Relevance (BR) [1], Calibrated Label Ranking (CLR) [8], and Classifier Chains (CC) [18]. In the algorithm adaptation, we select the ML-KNN algorithm [23].

4.3   Experiment and Evaluation

Experimental Hyper-parameters Selection

Evaluation Metrics. This paper selects the example-based evaluation metrics to evaluate a model. Then, h is the model, N is the sample size, x_i is the sample, Y_i is the corresponding multi-label set, ΔY_i is the complement of Y_i, and $h(x_i)$ is the label set of x_i given by the model h.

As shown in the Eq. eqrefeqacc, the $Precision(P)$, $Recall(R)$, $Accuracy(Acc)$, and $F1$, imitate evaluation metrics in single-label classification and are also used to evaluate the detection performance of the model.

Table 7. Multi-label learning methods selected for experimental evaluation.

Method	Type	Strategy	Re-name
Bayes	BR	first-order	Bayes-BR
Decision Tree	BR	first-order	DT-BR
Random Forest	BR	first-order	RF-BR
SVM	BR	first-order	SVM-BR
Bayes	CLR	second-order	Bayes-CLR
Decision Tree	CLR	second-order	DT-CLR
Random Forest	CLR	second-order	RF-CLR
SVM	CLR	second-order	SVM-CLR
Bayes	CC	high-order	Bayes-CC
Decision Tree	CC	high-order	DT-CC
Random Forest	CC	high-order	RF-CC
SVM	CC	high-order	SVM-CC
ML-KNN [23]	Lazy Learning	first-order	ML-KNN

$$\text{Acc} = \frac{1}{N} \sum_{i=1}^{N} \frac{|Y_i \cap h(x_i)|}{|Y_i \cup h(x_i)|}$$

$$P = \frac{1}{N} \sum_{i=1}^{N} \frac{|Y_i \cap h(x_i)|}{|h(x_i)|} \qquad (4)$$

$$R = \frac{1}{N} \sum_{i=1}^{N} \frac{|Y_i \cap h(x_i)|}{|Y_i|}$$

$$\text{F1} = \frac{2 \times P \times R}{P + R}$$

Environmental Configuration. The system is Ubuntu16.04 LTS. Scikit-Learn is used to implement the above-mentioned multi-label methods. There are 16-core CPU and 128G RAM in the server.

Training Set and Test Set. In the re-labeled dataset sampled from UNSW-NB15, the official training set(101,040 samples after re-labeling and de-duplication) and test set(53,946 samples after re-labeling and de-duplication) are selected. The 5-fold crossover experiment is adopted in subsequent experiments.

Detection Results. The detection results are shown in Fig. 3, and RF-CC is superior to other methods in 3 of the 4 metrics. The Bayes-BR can get the best results on recall $R = 99.74\%$, but it fails in other metrics, such as the P of 27.52%. It means that Bayes-BR considers that the sample belongs to almost all categories when it detects a sample, which is unreasonable. In general, RF-CC can get better overall performance.

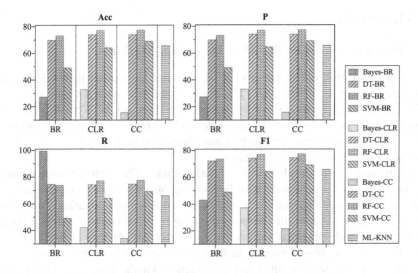

Fig. 3. Detection results of multi-label methods in UNSW-NB15.

Comparison with Related Single-label Methods. For a more comprehensive comparison, we implement the ICVAE-DNN [22] and SAVAER-DNN [21]. ICVAE-DNN consists of an improved conditional variational auto-encoder and a deep neural network. SAVAER-DNN consists of a supervised variational auto-encoder with regularization and a deep neural network. They can achieve 90+% accuracy in their respective single-label data.

The results are shown in Fig. 4. The performance of these two methods is lower than the multi-label methods (RF-CC, RF-CLR) because the single-label network attack detection methods can only give a single category for a sample. However, a sample could belong to multiple attacks in the overlapping phenomenon and is multi-label. Therefore, multi-label methods are more suitable for network attack detection in the overlapping phenomenon than single-label detection methods.

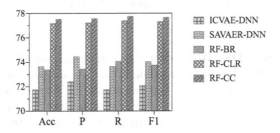

Fig. 4. Detection results of multi-label methods and related single-label methods in UNSW-NB15.

5   Discussion

5.1   Performance of Multi-label Detection Methods

Although the overall performance of RF-CC better than other methods, its various metrics are only 77+% (*Acc*, *F*1, *etc.*). There are two main reasons.

The first is the increased output space. For instance, in UNSW-NB15, the output space is increased from 10 categories to 57 categories after data processing and re-labeling based on the overlapping phenomenon. The increase in output space makes detection more difficult.

The second is the complexity of network attacks. There are not only overlapping behaviors but also similarities between network attacks. The similar phenomenon means that the network attack samples are not identical but rather similar. The feature space difference or distance between two samples is less than a threshold ϵ. This phenomenon makes it difficult for the model to distinguish different attack samples, resulting in false positives and false negatives.

In general, the basic multi-label detection methods have outperformed the single-label methods in the preliminary experiments. Therefore, we believe it is an excellent choice to detect network attacks with the overlapping phenomenon in a multi-label manner. However, limited by the length of the paper, we mainly focus on the analysis and statistics of the overlapping phenomenon in this paper. Our next work is based on this analysis, finding a better multi-label detection method.

5.2   Application Scenarios for Overlapping Phenomenon Analysis

Analyzing and detecting the overlapping phenomenon can help the researcher in two aspects.

Tracing the Source of Network Attack. The overlapping phenomenon causes a network behavior could be multi-labeled. Detecting samples in a multi-label manner can gain more information about the attackers behind them, such as more detailed attack techniques. We can infer that the actions taken by the attackers come from the intersecting regions defined by these attacks so that we can find the attackers more easily.

Building a Better IDS. We can get the distribution and similarity between attacks based on the multi-label method to detect network attacks with the overlapping phenomenon. We can find the similarity between attacks through multi-label and divide the clusters to get the distance between network attacks. Then, the detection process can be further divided into a series of steps, such as first separating attacks with larger feature distances for coarse-grained classification and then gradually subdividing the remaining attacks for fine-grained classification. Overall, multi-label information can help researchers build a more comprehensive defense scheme.

6 Conclusion

In this paper, we discover the overlapping phenomenon of the behavioral attribute between network attacks in the real world. Samples have the same features but different labels in the network attack dataset. We analyze the overlapping phenomenon and perform statistical experiments. For instance, in UNSW-NB15 and CIC-AndMal-2020, a sample has an average 1.689 and 1.413 labels, respectively. Based on the overlapping phenomenon, multi-label methods can help researchers better track the source of cyber attacks and build better IDS. Therefore, we select several multi-label methods for detection. Moreover, the experimental results in UNSW-NB15 show that RF-CC (Random forest with classifier chains) is better than related single-label methods (3.61% $\sim$ 5.59% higher in $F1$).

In the future, we will further explore the correlation between network attacks and build more suitable detection methods.

Acknowledgements. We thank the reviewers for their valuable suggestions. The corresponding author of this paper is Shuhao Li. This work is supported by the National Key Research and Development Program of China (Grant No. 2018YFB0804704) and the National Key Research and Development Program of China (Grant No. 2019YFB1005201).

References

1. Boutell, M.R., Luo, J., Shen, X., Brown, C.M.: Learning multi-label scene classification. Pattern Recogn. **37**(9), 1757–1771 (2004)
2. Cheng, W., Hüllermeier, E.: Combining instance-based learning and logistic regression for multilabel classification. Mach. Learn. **76**(2–3), 211–225 (2009)
3. Chou, D., Jiang, M.: Data-driven network intrusion detection: a taxonomy of challenges and methods. arXiv preprint arXiv:2009.07352 (2020)
4. Clare, A., King, R.D.: Knowledge discovery in multi-label phenotype data. In: De Raedt, L., Siebes, A. (eds.) PKDD 2001. LNCS (LNAI), vol. 2168, pp. 42–53. Springer, Heidelberg (2001). https://doi.org/10.1007/3-540-44794-6_4
5. Durmuş, Ö., Varol, A.: Analysis and modeling of cyber security precautions. In: 2021 9th International Symposium on Digital Forensics and Security (ISDFS), pp. 1–8. IEEE (2021)
6. Elisseeff, A., Weston, J.: A kernel method for multi-labelled classification. Adv. Neural. Inf. Process. Syst. **14**, 681–687 (2001)
7. Fiky, A.H.E., Shenawy, A.E., Madkour, M.A.: Android malware category and family detection and identification using machine learning. arXiv preprint arXiv:2107.01927 (2021)
8. Fürnkranz, J., Hüllermeier, E., Mencía, E.L., Brinker, K.: Multilabel classification via calibrated label ranking. Mach. Learn. **73**(2), 133–153 (2008)
9. Ghamrawi, N., McCallum, A.: Collective multi-label classification. In: Proceedings of the 14th ACM international conference on Information and knowledge management, pp. 195–200 (2005)

10. Godbole, S., Sarawagi, S.: Discriminative methods for multi-labeled classification. In: Dai, H., Srikant, R., Zhang, C. (eds.) PAKDD 2004. LNCS (LNAI), vol. 3056, pp. 22–30. Springer, Heidelberg (2004). https://doi.org/10.1007/978-3-540-24775-3_5
11. Ji, S., Tang, L., Yu, S., Ye, J.: Extracting shared subspace for multi-label classification. In: Proceedings of the 14th ACM SIGKDD international conference on Knowledge discovery and data mining, pp. 381–389 (2008)
12. Jing, D., Chen, H.B.: SVM based network intrusion detection for the UNSW-NB15 dataset. In: 2019 IEEE 13th International Conference on ASIC (ASICON), pp. 1–4. IEEE (2019)
13. Keyes, D.S., Li, B., Kaur, G., Lashkari, A.H., Gagnon, F., Massicotte, F.: Entroplyzer: android malware classification and characterization using entropy analysis of dynamic characteristics. In: 2021 Reconciling Data Analytics, Automation, Privacy, and Security: A Big Data Challenge (RDAAPS), pp. 1–12. IEEE (2021)
14. Liao, H.J., Lin, C.H.R., Lin, Y.C., Tung, K.Y.: Intrusion detection system: a comprehensive review. J. Netw. Comput. Appl. 36(1), 16–24 (2013)
15. Liu, Z., Wang, R., Japkowicz, N., Tang, D., Zhang, W., Zhao, J.: Research on unsupervised feature learning for android malware detection based on restricted Boltzmann machines. Futur. Gener. Comput. Syst. 120, 91–108 (2021)
16. Moustafa, N., Slay, J.: UNSW-NB15: a comprehensive data set for network intrusion detection systems (UNSW-NB15 network data set). In: 2015 military communications and information systems conference (MilCIS), pp. 1–6. IEEE (2015)
17. Rahali, A., Lashkari, A.H., Kaur, G., Taheri, L., Gagnon, F., Massicotte, F.: DiDroid: android malware classification and characterization using deep image learning. In: 2020 the 10th International Conference on Communication and Network Security, pp. 70–82 (2020)
18. Read, J., Pfahringer, B., Holmes, G., Frank, E.: Classifier chains for multi-label classification. Mach. Learn. 85(3), 333–359 (2011)
19. Tavallaee, M., Bagheri, E., Lu, W., Ghorbani, A.A.: A detailed analysis of the KDD cup 99 data set. In: 2009 IEEE Symposium on Computational Intelligence for Security and Defense Applications, pp. 1–6. IEEE (2009)
20. Yan, R., Tesic, J., Smith, J.R.: Model-shared subspace boosting for multi-label classification. In: Proceedings of the 13th ACM SIGKDD international conference on Knowledge discovery and data mining, pp. 834–843 (2007)
21. Yang, Y., Zheng, K., Wu, B., Yang, Y., Wang, X.: Network intrusion detection based on supervised adversarial variational auto-encoder with regularization. IEEE Access 8, 42169–42184 (2020)
22. Yang, Y., Zheng, K., Wu, C., Yang, Y.: Improving the classification effectiveness of intrusion detection by using improved conditional variational autoencoder and deep neural network. Sensors 19(11), 2528 (2019)
23. Zhang, M.L., Zhou, Z.H.: ML-KNN: a lazy learning approach to multi-label learning. Pattern Recogn. 40(7), 2038–2048 (2007)
24. Zhang, M.L., Zhou, Z.H.: A review on multi-label learning algorithms. IEEE Trans. Knowl. Data Eng. 26(8), 1819–1837 (2013)

Integration of Cybersecurity Related Development Processes by Using a Quantification Method

Hassan Noun[1(✉)], Florian Rehm[1], Guillaume Zeller[2], G. Rajesh[1], and Roland Lachmayer[3]

[1] ZF CVS, Hannover, Germany
hassan.noun@zf.com
[2] ZF CVS, Brussels, Belgium
[3] Leibniz University, Hannover, Germany

Abstract. The international standard ISO 21434 is used to derive new development processes, work products and roles during product development in the automotive industry. For a suitable development of security relevant vehicle systems, the new work steps must be integrated into the existing development process. The challenge is to apply a proper method for an integration of these additional activities. For the integration a quantification of the process maturity of the security relevant development processes supports thereby, in order to make a statement about the precondition for the treatment of security relevant vehicle systems. Furthermore, this identifies development fields in the process integration. This paper shows how a coefficient for measuring process maturity is established. Therefore, the functional security related activities are identified and isolated. In the next step supporting processes are defined. Further, weighted means are determined. The aim is to have an indicator for the security relevant development processes already at the beginning of the development and thus to be able to take appropriate measures in advance. As an application example, an automotive project for ADAS system is considered. This is followed by differentiated derivations of measures based on the established coefficients for the individual domains.

Keywords: Cybersecurity · Integration method · System security · Process integration

1 Introduction

In 2021 an additional binding international standard for road vehicles has been released. This is the first edition of the ISO 21434. It specifies the guideline for cybersecurity for electrical and electronic systems in the automotive industry. The purpose is to specify requirements for cybersecurity risk management, their components and interfaces, throughout engineering, production, operation, maintenance and decommissioning [1]. This standard is used to derive new security requirements for all road vehicles. This results in further processes, work products and roles in the development. The appropriate integration of the new processes is very different in the projects. In practice, the costs often exceed the effort estimations. In addition, important milestones in the projects are shifting. Furthermore, the start of series production can be delayed as a result. The reasons for inefficient use and application of the security related activities are often unclear and have different causes. One approach for the solution is to make the security related processes measurable in the projects. For this purpose, meaningful variables should be identified that are suitable for reflection in the development process. After determining several attributes, these can be brought into relations. The quantified processes can thus provide information about the extent to which the goals have been achieved. Furthermore, an iteration for a proper effort estimation for the entire security cycle can be realized [2].

1.1 Measurement of Cybersecurity Relevant Development Processes According to ISO 21434

Key Performance Indicators (KPI) can be used to represent the performance of activities. They help to measure success or failure. They also confirming the success of certain activities within a process [3]. Furthermore, in this way processes of an entire product development can be evaluated based of these performance indicators. Due to permanent monitoring, activities and measures can be adjusted and optimized accordingly. During implementing KPIs, the following steps should be generally considered [4–6]:

- Determination of the business processes which shall be evaluated.
- Breaking down of the process chain into modules.
- Consideration of the modules as isolated work steps within process chain.
- Establishing evaluation criteria.
- Implementation of a monitoring tool.

In order to measure the security relevant development processes, it is necessary to break them down into detailed blocks. Accordingly, these have to be considered as isolated steps within the process chain. It is therefore important to define all security relevant development processes of the entire product development.

In cybersecurity, key figures and metrics are also used. These describe, for example, the structural coverage at the software unit level and reflect the completeness and verification of the cybersecurity related mechanisms. Metrics are also used in software that incorporate diagnostic methodologies to describe the level of detection. However, these metrics summarize the technical security of an electronic system. For the application and realization of the security requirements, metrics have been used only to a limited extent. Quantified are the quality relevant development processes, in which only partially security relevant processes are considered [7, 8]. The publication of new security standards in the automotive industry results in an adaptation of existing processes. These must be suitably integrated. By considering the chain of security processes, it is necessary to develop a method for the integration of security related processes that is also consistent and applicable to new international industry standards.

1.2 Classification of the Security Relevant Processes in the V-Model

The decomposition of the process chain is based on the V-model of the VDI guideline 2206, in which an overview of all steps of the product creation is given [9, 10] (Fig. 1).

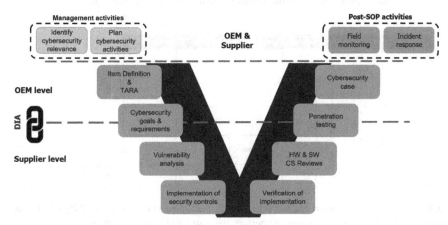

Fig. 1. Representation of the cybersecurity relevant development processes and work products in the V-Model. The left side of the V-Model reflects the development part and the right side the verification and validation part.

The security related activities always starting with an item definition and a threat analysis and risk assessment (TARA) of the vehicle system under consideration. This applies to all electrical and electronic vehicle (sub)systems even if they are apparently not dangerous for road traffic. Based on their functional characteristics, the TARA evaluates the possible attack feasibility. This results into the cybersecurity goals and determines the extent of the measures that must be implemented in the development [11, 12]. Once a function or a system has been identified as security critical, further steps are necessary to accompany the entire V-Model. First, a cyber security concept must be developed, which essentially includes a safe error response in the worst case. Further technical counter measures and control needs to be derived, which specifically considers the system architecture. Then the system and device requirements needs to be decomposed. At this point, the cybersecurity concept is technically implemented and impacts all other system components such as control units and software. In the next step a vulnerability analysis is performed on System, HW and SW level [13, 14]. The aim is to identify vulnerabilities resulting from weakness in cyber security requirements, architecture and design. The scope of the analysis depends on the engineering domain. All activities are resulting in security requirements that are incorporated into the product development. These have to be realized, implemented and finally tested. If there are delays in creating these requirements for the product or if they are missing, the system cannot be approved for the series production. It is therefore a high priority to integrate such processes correctly, as delays are associated with high costs and harms the reputation.

2   Quantification of the Cybersecurity Relevant Processes

In order to quantify a process, it is also necessary to record all steps and work products in detail. Furthermore, it is necessary to assign them to the phases of the product creation. The cybersecurity plan serves as the central document for this (Fig. 2).

Chapter	Work Product ID	Work Product	Responsible Role	Status	Development Phase
Management	2_1 2_2 2_n	2_1 .... 2_2.... 2_n....	CSM TPjM System Engineer		
Concept Phase	3_1 3_2 3_n	3_1 .... 3_2 .... 3_n	CSM		
System Development	4_1 4_2 4_n	4_1 .... 4_2 .... 4_n	CSM System Engineer		
Hardware Development	5_1 5_2 5_n	5_1 .... 5_2 .... 5_n	CSM eHW Architect eHW Developer		
Software Development	6_1 6_2 6_n	6_1 .... 6_2 .... 6_n	CSM SW Developer		

eHW: electronic Hardware
CSM: Cybersecurity Manager
SW: Software
TPjM: Technical Project Manager

Fig. 2. Tabular representation of the cybersecurity plan. The work products of ISO 21434 are shown in dependency of the responsible person, the status and the development phase [2].

The cybersecurity plan is used for the management of all security related activities, evidences and work products. This means that the isolated work steps can be derived from there. The artefacts based on the international standard ISO21434, are recorded. These are listed in the cybersecurity plan. Furthermore, the responsible persons are linked to the planned completion of the artifact as well as the associated project phase. This makes the document particularly suitable for recording the process chain, as all information is intertwined at this point.

2.1   Determination of the Supporting Processes for the Evaluation of the Preconditions

Maintaining a cybersecurity plan is, on the one hand, mandatory according to ISO21434 and, on the other hand, also necessary for planning. However, the mere listing of all activities does not significantly support the execution and completion. However, supporting processes and documents can be consulted in order to promote actual processing. This support should significantly improve the precondition of successful completion. Therefore, it is important to identify possible supporting processes which are reflecting the integration maturity. For the beginning, a clear definition of each artifact is indispensable to clarify the radius of action of all work products. Furthermore, there should be a reference of the definition to ISO21434, in order to be able to look up in the unfavorable case. A further support for the treatment in the development process are guidelines. These are guidelines for implementation in detailed form. Contained in it are descriptions to presupposed inputs, treatment as well as expected form of the results. Guidelines can contribute significantly to the self explanation of an artifact and serve to derive work instructions, which play an essential role in a project. Furthermore, guidelines define the actors and in which form they cooperate. An additional support is the use of templates. Templates are a set of documents with a predefined structure, which are very close to the final result of the work. The effectiveness of templates is very high, because they contain and store knowledge and experience. Furthermore, the provision of a professional tool can essentially support the creation of the artifacts. Furthermore, an associated training improves the understanding of the relevant work product for the responsible stakeholder. Subsequently, there is the possibility to use an automated support. These are tailored software solutions that can create and manage artifacts autonomously through a few parameterized settings. This type of tool combines the stored knowledge to create work products as well as editing. In order to use an automated and tailored solution, all the previously mentioned supporting processes are required, which have continued to experience a proven application. Finally, each work product can be supported by a global process supervisor. Such supervisors are process and technical experts who support the project to ensure the correct application and execution of the individual process steps. They are considered the point of contact within the company or organization. Thus, in the following are the listed supporting processes for the security related items:

- Process Definition
- Guidelines
- Templates
- Professional Software
- Tailored automated tools
- Process Expert/Supervisor

2.2 Preconditional Coefficient (PCC) for the Quantification of the Maturity

The approach to evaluating the preconditions for working on security relevant vehicle systems is due to the fact that certain preparations as well as knowledge should already exist at the beginning of a project. Since these are security critical systems in road traffic, the aim is to contribute some form of experience and knowledge. On the one hand, this can increase the security of the systems by avoiding potential sources of errors. On the other hand, the security relevant development processes can be reliably handled and completed in time for project milestones. To make the requirements for successful editing measurable, the identified supporting processes are weighted and related to the work products. To determine the extent to which the prerequisites for successful processing are met, a key performance indicator can be used:

$$PCC = \frac{\sum_{j=1}^{n_{AP}} \sum_{i=1}^{n_{UM}} U x U M_{Gi}}{n_{AP}} \tag{1}$$

Due to this formula the preconditional coefficient (PCC) can be calculated. This is obtained by multiplying the summed work products by the quantifier of the supporting processes (U). This is divided by the total number of work products n_{AP}. The key figure describes the degree to which a prerequisite support is available for all work products. Further, it can be also distinguished if the process has been used previously in at least one project. For this already practiced process an additional factor can be considered. This is shown as best practice in the evaluation table on the Fig. 3. This makes it possible to see how good the prerequisites are for successfully processing all work products or to what extent there is still a need for action. The status of the supporting processes (U) for the respective work products (AP) can be displayed in this way. The supporting processes receiving a quantifier (UM_G). On the one hand, a value can be assigned in this way and on the other hand, a suitable weighting can be assigned to the different processes in this way. A variable weighting is necessary because the influence and the importance are different. The values of the weightings come from expert surveys within the ZF Group company, Commercial Vehicles Control Systems. During the quality assurance of the project milestones, experts have evaluated it this way. For an initial practical application, the following weightings are assigned to the listed supporting processes from section II A.

Chapter	Workproduct ID	Workproduct	Definition Avail. 0,8	Definition Best Pract. 0,2	Guideline Avail. 0,8	Guideline Best Pract. 0,2	Template Avail. 0,8	Template Best Pract. 0,2	Tool Avail. 0,8	Tool Best Pract. 0,2	Autom. Support Avail. 0,8	Autom. Support Best Pract. 0,2	Expert/ Coach Avail. 0,8	Expert/ Coach Best Pract. 0,2
Chapter 2	2_1	2_1...	1	0	0	0	1	1	1	0	1	0	1	1
	2_2	2_2...	1	1	1	1	1	1	1	0	0	0	1	0
	2_3	2_3...	1	1	1	1	1	1	1	1	0	0	1	0
	2_n	2_n...	1	1	1	1	0	0	1	1	1	0	1	1
Chapter 3	3_1	3_1...	1	1	1	0	1	1	1	0	1	0	1	1
	3_2	3_2...	1	1	1	0	1	0	1	0	1	0	1	1
	3_3	3_3...	1	1	1	0	0	1	1	1	1	1	1	0
	3_n	3_n...	1	1	1	0	0	0	0	0	0	0	1	0
Chapter 4	4_1	4_1...	1	1	1	1	0	0	1	0	0	0	1	0
	4_2	4_2...	1	1	1	0	1	1	0	0	0	0	1	0
	4_3	4_3...	1	1	1	0	1	0	1	1	1	0	1	1
	4_n	4_n...	1	1	0	0	1	0	1	0	1	0	1	0
Chapter n	n_1	n_1...	1	1	0	0	1	0	0	0	1	0	1	1
	n_2	n_2...	1	1	1	1	0	0	0	0	1	1	1	1
	n_3	n_3...	1	0	1	0	0	0	1	1	1	0	1	0
	n_n	n_n...	1	1	1	1	1	0	1	0	0	0	1	1

Fig. 3. Tabular representation of the security relevant work products in connection with the weighted supporting processes[2].

Table 1. Table represents the quantifier for each supporting process.

Supporting Processes (UP)	Quantifier (UPG)
Definition	0,2
Guideline	0,25
Template	0,2
Software	0,1
Tailored automated Tool	0,1
Process Expert/Supervisor	0,15

With a completed definition of all work products, this results in a coefficient of 0,2. In a link with a complete definition of all work products, this can be the point at which the minimum process requirement for processing a security relevant project is reached. Before processing a security relevant project, it should be ensured that the security critical work products are known to the processing organization (Fig. 4).

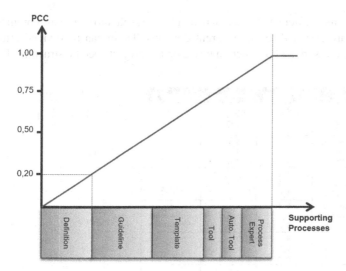

Fig. 4. Graphical representation of the preconditional coefficient as a function of the fulfilled supporting processes [2].

Another milestone for process development is the complete implementation of the guidelines for each security relevant work product. This is achieved from a PCC of 0,45. At this point, all work steps with the associated roles and their cooperation are defined. The PCC can then be systematically increased by integrating templates. In this way, the state of the security relevant process structure can be quantified. In this way, the PCC reflects the general preconditions for developing a security relevant system according to international standards.

3 Application Example on an Automotive Project for an ADAS System

In a pilot project of the Tier-1 supplier of the ZF Group, the preconditional coefficient is determined on the basis of the specified criteria. For this purpose, the security relevant process data from an automotive project for an ADAS system are collected. The table in Fig. 3 is used to record the existing processes. For this purpose, the entire security relevant work products of the ISO21434 have been listed with their reference from the cybersecurity plan. Based on an analysis of the existing process, all existing supporting processes have then been identified. Using Formula 1 and the weightings from section II, the following preconditional coefficient is thus obtained:

$$PCC = 26, 1/45.$$

The total PCC results in a value of 0,58.

3.1 Derivation of a Measure Based on the Result of the Preconditional Coefficient

Through this recording, the maturity of the security relevant processes can already be represented before the start of the project. However, in order to be able to take a suitable measure by this coefficient, it is useful to divide the result into sub areas. For this purpose, the values are assigned to the different domains. These can be divided into system, electronics, software and production based on the project specific structure (Fig. 5).

Chapter	Work Product ID	Work Product	Ressponsible Role
Chapter 2: Management	2_1 2_2 2_n	2_1 .... 2_2.... 2_n....	CSM TPjM System Engineer
Chapter 3: Concept Phase	3_1 3_2 3_n	3_1 .... 3_2 .... 3_n	CSM System Engineer
Chapter 4: System Development	4_1 4_2 4_n	4_1 .... 4_2.... 4_n	CSM System Engineer
Chapter 5: Hardware Development	5_1 5_2 5_n	5_1 .... 5_2 .... 5_n	CSM eHW Architect eHW Developer
Chapter 6: Software Development	6_1 6_2 6_n	6_1 .... 6_2 .... 6_n	CSM SW Developer
Chapter 7: Production	7_1 7_2 7_n	7_1 .... 7_2 .... 7_n	CSM TPjM

eHW: electronic Hardware
CSM: Cybersecurity Manager
SW: Software
TPjM: Technical Project Manager

System

Electronic Hardware

Software

Production

Fig. 5. Classification of the security related work products into the domains system, electronics, software and production.

By this assignment the PCC can be split up to make a need or a gap clear. For this purpose, the preconditional condition is determined with the same method for the individual domains (Fig. 6).

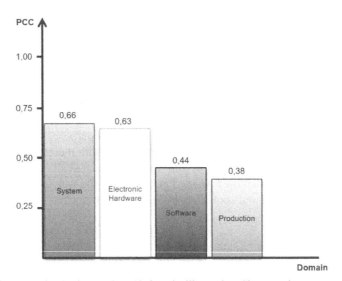

Fig. 6. A figure caption is always placed below the illustration. Short captions are centered, while long ones are justified. The macro button chooses the correct format automatically.

This breakdown shows that there is a need in the area of software and production. Here a PCC value of 0.44 and 0.38 has been achieved. This is due to incomplete guidelines and templates. Although the definitions are complete for the most part, no clear or partly clear process flow and no role responsibilities are defined. This means that measures must be taken in the run up to the project in order to make the effort required by security relevant processes plannable. For this reason, the decision is made early in this project to increase the planned working hours in the area of software and production. Furthermore, a further evaluation is planned after the concept phase. In this phase the progress will be checked separately. If necessary, it can be decided whether an additional expert in the area of software is called in. This qualified staff is connected with higher costs. However, this can compensate for the weaknesses in the process by its expertise. It is assumed at this point that the processes and the working method are known to this person and thus a low process maturity is not disadvantageous in the projects.

4 Summary and Discussion

For the development of a cybersecurity critical vehicle systems, additional development steps and work products are necessary due to international standards. The integration into the already existing development processes is complex. By establishing a preconditional coefficient, the security relevant process structure of a company can be represented by a key figure. It offers a close linkage of relevant supporting processes in the product development of security critical vehicle systems. The linked supporting processes also providing a guideline for process development from the identification of work steps and work products to their creation and application. Furthermore, it can be seen to what extent there is still a need for action in process integration. Thus, the achievement of certain values of the coefficient can be used for milestones in the process integration. According to international cybersecurity standards, the security relevant processes must be established in the company. Based on this, vehicle systems with cybersecurity goals are to be processed. However, there are no metrics or evidence in how far advanced these should be. This can now be represented by a preconditional coefficient. In further research, it can be considered whether a possible link between the criticality of a vehicle system and the PCC is useful. For example, an OEM (Original Equipment Manufacturer) may require proof of a chosen PCC value before having certain vehicle systems developed by a supplier. In addition, it can be investigated whether it makes sense to standardize these internationally. In this way, a minimum process structure can be demanded in order to increase the security of the vehicles already during product development. Furthermore, weightings of various supporting processes as shown in Table 1 can be examined in more detail. In this way, suitable values can be determined in order to be able to make a more precise statement with the coefficients.

References

1. ISO21434:2021: International Standard Organization (2021)
2. Noun, H.: Quantification of preconditions for processing safety relevant vehicle systems (2021). https://doi.org/10.1109/ICSRS53853.2021.9660689

3. Brudan, A.: The Production and Quality Management KPI Dictionary. CreatSpace: Independent Publishing Platform (2015)
4. Parmenter, D.: Key Performance Indicators: Developing, Implementing and Using Winning KPIs, 4th edn. Wiley, New York (2019)
5. Sihler, P.: Key Performance Indicators aus Controlling-Sicht. 1.Aufl. GRIN Verlag, München (2008)
6. Maute, C.: Zur Rolle und Nutzen von Key Performance Indicators (KPI). 1. Aufl München. GRIN Verlag (2009)
7. Wurm, M.: Automotive Cybersecurity: Security-Bausteine für Automotive Embedded Systeme. Springer, Heidelberg (2022). https://doi.org/10.1007/978-3-662-64228-3
8. Kshetri, N.: Cybersecurity Management: An Organizational and Strategic Approach. University of Toronto Press, Toronto (2021)
9. VDI2206: VDI-Richtlinie: Entwicklungsmethodik für mechatronische Systeme (2004)
10. Knöchelmann, M., Ley, P.-P., Kloppenburg, G., Mozgova, I., Lachmayer, R.: Methodische Entwicklung eines opto-mechatronischen Systems am Beispiel eines hochadaptiven Fahrzeugscheinwerfers, Tagungsband der VDI Fachtagung Mechatronik. Universität Paderborn, Paderborn (2019). https://doi.org/10.15488/4683
11. Möller, D.P.F., Haas, R.E.: Guide to Automotive Connectivity and Cybersecurity: Trends, Technologies, Innovations and Applications. Springer, Heidelberg (2019). https://doi.org/10.1007/978-3-319-73512-2
12. Kim, S., Shrestha, R.: Automotive Cyber Security Introduction, Challenges, and Standardization. Springer, Singapore (2020). https://doi.org/10.1007/978-981-15-8053-6
13. Schnieder, L., Hosse, R.S.: Leitfaden Automotive Cybersecurity Engineering: Absicherung vernetzter Fahrzeuge auf dem Weg zum autonomen Fahren. Springer, Wiesbaden (2018). https://doi.org/10.1007/978-3-658-23769-1
14. Zachäus, C., Meyer, G.: Intelligent System Solutions for Auto Mobility and Beyond: Advanced Microsystems for Automotive Applications. Springer, Cham (2021). https://doi.org/10.1007/978-3-030-65871-7

Cyber-Physical System

ZoomPass: A Zoom-Based Android Unlock Scheme on Smart Devices

Thomas Gleerup[1], Wenjuan Li[2,3]([✉]), Jiao Tan[4], and Yu Wang[3]

[1] Department of Electronic Systems, Aalborg University, Aalborg, Denmark
[2] Department of Electronic and Information Engineering, The Hong Kong
Polytechnic University, Hung Hom, China
wenjuan.li@polyu.edu.hk
[3] Institute of Artificial Intelligence and Blockchain, Guangzhou University,
Guangzhou, China
[4] KOTO Research Center, Macao, China

Abstract. Modern smart devices such as smartphones are able to provide various services, including checking online banking, watching video and listening to music. Due to the intelligence and popularity, such devices are also used as storage space for recording users' private information such as personal photos, credit card number, videos and more. This creates a need for protecting the devices from unauthorized access. Currently, many unlock schemes have been developed, in which Android unlock pattern is the most widely used scheme. However, traditional Android unlock pattern is vulnerable to different threats due to the limited pattern space. To enhance the security, one major direction is to combine biometric features with Android unlock pattern. In this work, motivated by this trend, we propose an enhanced Android unlock scheme based on zoom actions. More specifically, users can select two dots and perform a zoom action (either zoom-in or zoom-out) over each dot for authentication. In the study with 30 participants, our scheme demonstrates good performance in terms of usability and security.

Keywords: User authentication · Behavioral authentication · Zoom behavior · Smartphone security · Android unlock pattern · Touch dynamic

1 Introduction

With more and more personal/private information and data stored on smart devices (e.g., smartphones, iPad), such devices have become a major target by cyber-attackers [12]. Hence it is important to prevent the devices from unauthorized access by verifying the identity of user(s) [35]. Currently, textual password-based authentication is still the most widely adopted methodology, but there is a big challenge under many adversarial scenarios, e.g., recording attacks [4], and usability issues, e.g., the multiple password inference [36] and the limitation of long term memory [31,58].

© The Author(s), under exclusive license to Springer Nature Switzerland AG 2022
C. Su et al. (Eds.): SciSec 2022, LNCS 13580, pp. 245–259, 2022.
https://doi.org/10.1007/978-3-031-17551-0_16

As an alternative, graphical passwords, such as unlock patterns, are proposed as a popular means of authentication, which can authenticate users based on their input pattern(s) [22]. Graphical passwords are believed to be easier to memorize than textual passwords for phone users [41]. For instance, Jermyn *et al.* [14] introduced DAS (draw-a-secret) that requires users to draw their passwords on a 2D grid. Wiedenbeck *et al.* [57] developed *PassPoints* that allows creating users' credentials by clicking on some locations on an image. On smartphones, a typical example is Android unlock pattern that requires users to input a pattern in a 3×3 grid, with 4 dots at least and 9 dots at most. However, it still suffers traditional threats like brute-force attack [1] and many modern attacks such as recording attacks [42] and charging attacks [33,34,38,40].

Motivation. To enhance the security of Android unlock pattern, one way is to create more patterns. Forman and Aviv [11] proposed an enhanced scheme called *Double Patterns*, where a user has to select two sequential Android unlock patterns as their credentials. They believed that this scheme could help increase the visual complexity and password space. On the other hand, another way is to be integrated with biometric features, especially touch dynamics. For instance, De Luca *et al.* [5] introduced a hybrid scheme integrating behavioral biometric with Android unlock pattern based on dynamic time warping (DTW). Meng *et al.* [32] developed *TMGuard*, a touch movement-based unlock scheme to enhance the authentication security of Android unlock patterns, which could monitor and analyze users' touch movements by means of supervised learning classifiers. Afterwards, there are several studies focusing on leveraging particular touch actions to enhance the security of Android unlock pattern, such as swipe action [17,18], handwritten [55] and double-click action [20].

Contributions. Motivated by these studies, in this work, we advocate the advantage of combining behavioral features with unlock mechanism. We particularly focus on zoom actions, and propose ZoomPass – a Zoom-based unlock mechanism on smart devices. Under this scheme, users can choose two dots from the 3×3 grid and perform either Zoom-in or Zoom-out actions. The contributions of this work can be summarized as follows.

- We propose ZoomPass, an enhanced Android unlock scheme through verifying both the unlock pattern and the zoom actions. For registration, users can select two dots and perform either zoom-in or zoom-out actions over each dot. This unlock scheme is transparent and adopts traditional supervised learning classifiers, e.g., KNN, SVM.
- For performance evaluation, we conduct a user study with 30 common phone users. Based on the collected data and users' feedback, it is found that participants can perform well under our scheme with an authentication accuracy of around 98% in the best case. We consider ZoomPass can be an alternative to complement existing solutions.

Road Map. The reminder of this paper is structured as follows. Section 2 introduces related work on graphical passwords and touch behavioral authentication. Section 3 describes our scheme of ZoomPass in detail. Section 4 provides a user study with 30 participants and analyzes the collected data. We discuss some open challenges in Sect. 5 and conclude our work in Sect. 6.

2   Related Work

This section aims to introduce the state-of-the-art regarding graphical password schemes and touch behavioral authentication.

2.1   Authentication Based on Graphical Password

To complement the existing text-based user authentication, graphical passwords have been developed. Generally, there are three categories as follows [2,37,50]:

- *Recognition-based scheme.* This type of scheme requires a user to memorize and select one or several images out of a pool. For instance, *PassFaces* [43] scheme requires a user to recognize one human face out of nine faces for user authentication.
- *Pure recall-based scheme.* This type of scheme requires users to create a pattern on one image. As an example, Jermyn *et al.* [14] introduces a ('draw-a-secret') scheme – *DAS*, where a user has to draw something on a grid as the credential. Android unlock pattern, a revised version of Pass-Go [53] scheme, requires a user to draw a pattern on a screen and unlock the device. A valid pattern with 4 dots at least and 9 dots at most, within a grid of 3×3 points on smartphones.
- *Cued recall-based scheme.* This type of scheme requires a user to select an object on an image or more images. For instance, *PassPoints* [57] scheme needs a user to memorize five points on one image in a sequence. Followed this idea, Chiasson *et al.* [3] introduced Persuasive Cued Click-Points (PCCP), which requires a user to click one point on each of three images rather than on three click points on one image.

In the current literature, many graphical password schemes are hybrid, by combining the features from the above recognition-based and recall-based schemes. A typical example is *CD-GPS* – a click-draw based graphical password scheme, which can enhance the graphical password performance in both security and usability. This hybrid scheme includes two operational steps: image selection and secret drawing. In particular, users first choose an ordered sequence of images and then select some of them to click-draw their secrets [23,24,27,35].

Recently, map-based graphical passwords have received much attention, which can take world map as the background image [9,47]. For instance, Sun *et al.* [51] designed *PassMap* that requires users to select two locations (in an order) on a world map. Thorpe *et al.* [54] developed *GeoPass* that only requires users to select one map location as the credential. Meng *et al.* [37] indicated that there is no significant difference between the selection of one or two locations in practical usage. Meng [29] then designed *RouteMap*, a map-based scheme that demands users to create a route on a world map.

However, graphical passwords are also vulnerable to various issues, such as the multiple password interference. Meng *et al.* [36] performed a study with 60 participants to investigate the interference between textual passwords and map-based passwords under six account scenarios. It is found that participants in the map-based graphical password scheme could perform better than the textual password scheme in both short-term (one-hour session) and long term (after two weeks) password memorability tests. In addition, graphical passwords may suffer the same recording attacks [42] and charging attacks [33, 34, 38].

In practice, a balance should be made between security and usability in order to improve the performance of graphical passwords. Some more relevant studies on graphical passwords could be referred but not limited to [6, 7, 13, 16, 25, 30, 39, 59].

2.2   Touch Behavioral Authentication

Most of the current smart devices will feature a touchscreen, hence touch dynamics has become popular and important when designing a suitable behaviorial authentication scheme [28]. With a physically designed glove, Fen *et al.* [8] introduced a finger gesture-based authentication system on mobile devices, which could achieve an FAR of 4.66% and an FRR of 0.13% by meas of a random forest classifier. Meanwhile, Meng *et al.* [26] introduced a touch behavioral authentication scheme with 21 touch-related features on Android phones, which could achieve an average error rate of 3% by solely analyzing the touch behavior of users with a hybrid classifier of PSO-RBFN. Then *Touchalytics* was proposed by Frank *et al.* [10], which is a touch dynamics-based authentication scheme, which considered 30 features and provided a median equal error rate of around 4% (one week after the enrollment phase).

Zheng *et al.* [60] focused on users' tapping actions on a passcode-enabled smartphone, and introduced an authentication scheme by using a one-class algorithm. They could reach an averaged equal error rate of nearly 3.65%. Sharma and Enbody [49] explored how users can interact with the application interface, and introduced an authentication scheme using the SVM-based ensemble algorithm. They could reach a mean equal error rate of 7% in the evaluation. Shahzad *et al.* [48] focused on users' specific actions under some conditions and introduced an authentication scheme based on how users create a gesture or a signature, including features such as velocity, device acceleration, and stroke time. Meng *et al.* [32] introduced a touch movement-based security mechanism – TMGuard, which aimed to enhance the security of Android unlock pattern by examining a user's touch movements during pattern input. The evaluation with 75 participants demonstrated that users would perform a touch movement differently when interacting with the touchscreen and that users would perform somewhat stably for the same pattern after several trials.

Li *et al.* [17, 18] developed a machine learning-based unlock scheme called SwipeVLock, which could verify a user's entity based on their way of swiping the phone screen over a background image. There are two main steps: the first step is to select a background image from a pool, and the second step is to choose an image location and perform a swiping action. DCUS [20] is a similar scheme – a double-click-based unlock scheme on smart devices, which requires a user to unlock the device by double clicking on the right location on an image. For user authentication, the scheme should check the selected images, image location and double-click patterns. Li *et al.* [19] studied the inconsistency of phone users' touch behavior on Email applications and introduced an authentication scheme on smart devices. The evaluation with 60 participants demonstrated that users' touch behavioral deviation could be greatly decreased when users interact with Email applications (e.g., an average error rate of around 2.9%). Double-X [21] is a double-cross-based unlock scheme that requires a user to unlock the phone by inputting two cross shapes on the selected dots. For user authentication, it needs to check the selected dots and the behavioral features when drawing the cross shapes. More behavioral user authentication schemes can be referred to a survey [52].

3   ZoomPass Design

Our proposed ZoomPass can provide a promising alternative to existing unlock mechanisms such as Android unlock pattern on smartphones, by checking the behavioral features of zoom actions. It can provide many benefits: 1) it is transparent, 2) it does not need additional hardware, and 3) it is easy to implement. Figure 1 depicts the basic steps and the workflow of ZoomPass.

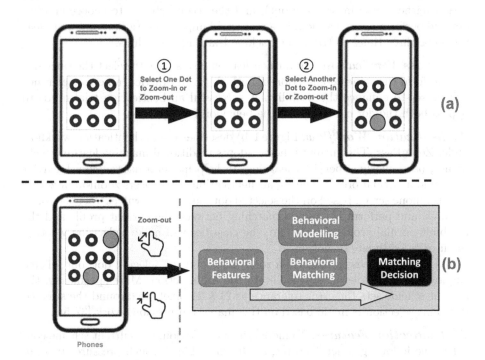

Fig. 1. a) ZoomPass steps: selecting one dot to perform either zoom-in or zoom-out action, and selecting another dot to perform either zoom-in or zoom-out action; and b) the authentication workflow for ZoomPass.

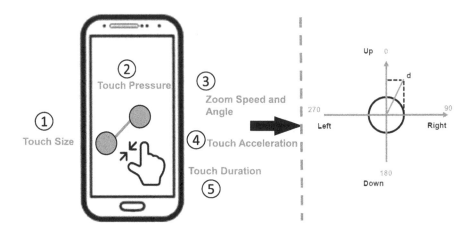

Fig. 2. Biometric features used in our scheme of ZoomPass.

ZoomPass Registration. As shown in Fig. 1(a), there are two basic steps in ZoomPass: the first step is to choose one dot out of 9 dots and perform a zoom action (either zoom-in or zoom-out); and the second step is to choose another dot and perform a zoom action. In a real-world implementation, users can repeat the steps three times to train the machine learning algorithms.

ZoomPass Verification. For authentication, users have to select the same dot and perform the same zoom action in both steps. In practice, an error tolerance will be set to enhance the usability. A successful authentication trial needs to bypass both the dot checking and the behavioral comparison.

Authentication Workflow. Figure 1(b) describes the authentication workflow under ZoomPass. The current scheme adopts traditional machine learning techniques, particularly supervised learning, to help model a user's zoom behavior and build a normal profile. During authentication, when users zoom-in or zoom-out the phone screen based on the selected dot, our scheme will extract the touch features, and perform behavioral matching between the current profile and the pre-built normal profile. In the end, the classifier will make a decision whether the user is legitimate or not.

As the user needs to perform a zoom action on the selected dot, our scheme employs an error tolerance to facilitate the zoom action. More specifically, the current scheme sets the error tolerance as 21×21 pixel box around the selected dot. This selection is made based on the analysis in previous work [37,54].

Authentication Features. To model the zoom action, our current scheme considers the following touch features, as shown in Fig. 2: touch pressure (two fingers), touch size (two fingers), touch duration, zoom speed and angle (two fingers), and touch acceleration (two fingers).

- *Touch pressure.* With the increasing capability of smartphones, current screen sensors are able to identify the values of touch pressure, which can be used to differentiate users' touch behavior.
- *Touch duration.* This feature can be computed by measuring the time difference between touch press-down and touch press-up. It is a common feature that is used to distinguish different users, i.e., some users may press longer while some may press shorter.
- *Touch size.* This feature can be used to measure the average human finger pad when touching the screen. It can help distinguish different users.
- *Touch speed and angle.* This feature can be used to describe the direction and speed of a zoom action. Based on previous work [32], suppose a swipe action starts from (x1, y1) and ends at (x2, y2), if we know relevant time of occurrence *T1* and *T2*, then we can calculate the touch speed and angle according to Eq. (1) and Eq. (2).
- *Touch acceleration.* Our work also considers touch acceleration with three vectors, such as the magnitude of acceleration when the touch is pressed down; the magnitude of acceleration when the touch is released; and the average value of magnitude of acceleration during touch-press to touch-release.

$$Touch\ Speed = \frac{\sqrt{(x2 - x1)^2 + (y2 - y1)^2}}{T2 - T1} \tag{1}$$

$$Touch\ Angle\ (d) = \arctan\frac{y2 - y1}{x2 - x1}, \theta \in [0, 360^\circ] \tag{2}$$

4   User Study

To explore the scheme performance of ZoomPass, we conduct a user study with 30 participants, who are common Android-phone users. Table 1 summarizes the participants' information in terms of age and occupation. More specifically, our study involved 15 males and 15 females aged in the range from 20 to 50. Regarding the occupation, up to 70% of them are students and the rest participants are business people and university staff. A $30 gift voucher was given to appreciate their attendance.

Table 1. Basic information of participants in the user study.

Information	Male	Female	Occupation	Male	Female
Age 20–30	12	11	Students	11	11
Age 30–40	1	2	University Staff	2	2
Age 40–50	2	2	Business People	2	2

Supervised Learning. The current ZoomPass adopts supervised learning to model and verify a user's entity. As a case study, we consider the following widely used machine learning algorithms: Decision tree (J48), Naive Bayes, SVM and Back Propagation Neural Network (BPNN).

- J48 is a decision tree classifier [44], which can label data based on the pre-trained tree-like structure.
- Naive Bayes is kind of supervised learning algorithms based on Bayes theorem by assuming conditional independence between every pair of features given the value of the class variable [45].
- BPNN is a kind of neural network classifier [46], using both a differentiable transfer function at each network node and an error back-propagation process to update the internal network weights after each round of training.
- Support Vector Machine (SVM) [15] is a linear model for both classification and regression tasks, through generating a line or a hyperplane that separates the data into classes.

To avoid any bias during classifier implementation, we adopted WEKA platform, which is an open-source machine learning collection in Java [56]. We used the default settings for all classifiers in the study. Below are two metrics used to evaluate the performance of ZoomPass.

- False Acceptance Rate (FAR): indicates the rate of how many intruders are classified as normal users.
- False Rejection Rate (FRR): indicates the rate of how many legitimate users are classified as intruders.

Study Procedure. In the lab study, all participants would be informed about our objectives and how we collect and store the data. During the study, each of them could get one Android phone (Samsung Galaxy Note) and they could have five trials to get familiar with the phone and the scheme of ZoomPass. The detailed study steps are summarized as below.

- Step 1. *Creation phase:* participants have to create their credentials according to ZoomPass' steps.
- Step 2. *Confirmation phase:* participants should confirm the password by verifying both the dot location and zoom behavior for 10 trials. They could change their credentials if they fail or want to do that.
- Step 3. *Distributed memory:* participants were provided with one paper-based finding task to distract them for 15 min.
- Step 4. *Login phase:* participants should try to unlock the phone for 10 times. The system recorded all the data for analysis.
- Step 5. *Feedback form:* participants could get a *feedback form* and provide scores to several questions in the aspect of scheme usage.
- Step 6. *Retention:* after three days, participants were asked to return and unlock the phone for 10 trials in our lab.
- Step 7. *Feedback form:* participants have to complete another *feedback from* regarding the scheme usage.

Table 2. The authentication performance under confirmation phase among different classifiers.

Metric	J48	NBayes	SVM	BPNN
FAR (%)	10.7	10.4	4.2	7.6
FRR (%)	11.3	12.7	3.9	7.5
AER (%)	11.0	11.55	4.05	7.55

Table 3. The authentication performance under login phase among different classifiers.

Metric	J48	NBayes	SVM	BPNN
FAR (%)	10.6	11.3	4.1	7.1
FRR (%)	11.7	10.2	3.8	7.2
AER (%)	11.15	10.75	3.95	7.15

Result Analysis. During the study, we could gather a total of 300 trials in the confirmation phase and the login phase, respectively. We used 60% of them as training data and the rest as testing data (with a cross-validation mode). We have the following observations.

- Table 2 depicts the authentication performance under confirmation phase. Among these classifiers, it is found that SVM reached better performance with an average error rate (AER) of 4.05% than the other classifiers, i.e., BPNN, J48 and NBayes could reach a rate of 7.55%, 11% and 11.55%, respectively. The errors in the confirmation phase were mainly caused by zoom behavior, i.e., some participants performed a zoom action too fast or too slow.
- Table 3 presents the authentication performance under login phase. The results verify that SVM could perform the best among these classifiers, with an AER of 3.95%. For the other algorithms, BPNN and NBayes also obtained a slightly increased rate. These may imply that the authentication rate can be enhanced by having more trials.
- After three days, we invited participants to return our lab, and 28 of them were successfully back. Table 4 summarizes the authentication performance, in which SVM could still provide a better error rate than the other classifiers, i.e., SVM 4.45%, J48 12.2%, BPNN 8.4%, NBayes 12.55%. There was a visible increase of errors in the retention phase, this is because participants may become uncertain about the zoom behavior after three days. However, the error rate of SVM was still acceptable.

In addition, we noticed that there are fewer errors caused by dot selection, validating that the selected error tolerance is suitable in practice. The majority of errors made in the study were mainly caused by behavioral matching process, hence how to control users' zoom behavior could directly influence the authentication performance.

Table 4. The authentication performance under retention phase among different classifiers.

Metric	J48	NBayes	SVM	BPNN
FAR (%)	12.3	12.5	4.2	8.6
FRR (%)	12.1	12.6	4.7	8.2
AER (%)	12.2	12.55	4.45	8.4

Table 5. Major questions and average scores from the user study.

Questions (Participant)	Average Scores
1. I could easily create a credential under ZoomPass	8.9
2. The login time is acceptable for ZoomPass	8.7
3. I could easily login to the system	8.8
4. I could easily remember the ZoomPass credentials	9.5
5. The security of ZoomPass may be lower than 4-digit PIN code	3.5
6. The security of ZoomPass may be lower than 8-digit PIN code	5.5
7. I would like to try this system in practice	8.5

User Feedback. In the study, we gave two feedback forms to each participant regarding the scheme usage. Ten-point Likert scales were used in each feedback question, where 1-score indicates strong disagreement and 10-score indicates strong agreement. Table 5 presents the questions and the average scores.

- *Usability.* For biometric schemes, usability is an important influencing factor. According to Table 5, most participants confirmed the easy-use characteristic of ZoomPass, i.e., giving an average score of 8.9 and 8.8 for credential creation and login process, respectively. They also considered that the login time is acceptable with a score of 8.7. In addition, most participants have an interest to use this scheme in their own phones, with a score of 8.5. These scores indicate the usability of ZoomPass.
- *Security.* We particularly asked the participants to compare ZoomPass with PIN code. For 4-digit PIN code, most participants believed that ZoomPass can provide a higher security level with a score of 3.5. While for 8-digit PIN code, many participants were not sure which one could be more secure, with a score of 5.5. We informally interviewed 12 participants, some of them voted for ZoomPass due to the use of biometric features, but some of them preferred 8-digit PIN code due to the password length.

Based on the feedback collected in the study, we believe that our scheme of ZoomPass has a great potential to be practical and adopted by many phone users. It can become a promising alternative to complement the existing textual passwords as well as phone unlock schemes.

5   Discussion

Our current ZoomPass scheme is still under development. Though we received many positive comments in the user study, there are many open challenges and limitations that need to be investigated in our future work.

- *Dot selection.* ZoomPass requires users to select two dots and perform either zoom-in or zoom-out. It is an interesting topic to explore any dot preference during the step of credential creation. This is because for a typical Android unlock pattern, users may have a bias on selecting the starting point of a pattern, i.e., starting from the top-left dot.
- *Zoom-action selection.* After each dot selection, users can choose either zoom-in or zoom-out. That is, attackers have to guess which zoom action the user may use. Similar to dot selection, it is an interesting topic to explore whether there is a preference on zoom-action selection among different users. This can be used by attackers to increase the hacking probability.
- *More participants.* In this work, we mainly involved 30 participants in the study. In our future work, we plan to recruit more participants with diverse background. In addition, it is also an interesting topic to investigate the difference between right handed and left handed participants.
- *Advanced attacks.* Our focus of this work is to investigate the performance of ZoomPass, so that we did not consider some adversarial scenarios, where an attacker may get the phone and try to unlock it, e.g., shoulder surfing [61]. This is an important topic in our future work, i.e., exploring the effect of recording attacks and mimic attacks.
- *Phone type.* In this work, we mainly used one type of Android phone in the user study, while it could be an interesting topic to explore whether phone models may affect the scheme performance. This is also an open challenge for most existing authentication schemes.
- *Machine leaning.* Supervised learning algorithms are widely adopted when designing a user authentication scheme [28,52]. In this work, we considered some common and popular machine learning schemes to verify users' behavior. Our future work plans to involve more diverse learning algorithms, e.g., deep learning, reinforcement learning.
- *Comparison with other schemes.* Our current work mainly focuses on evaluating the usability of ZoomPass. In the following work, we plan to provide a comparison with similar unlock schemes, e.g., DCUS, SwipeVLock. Also, we plan to investigate the time consumption among different schemes. This is an open challenge in this area, as there lacking a unified platform for scheme comparison.

6   Conclusion

Android unlock pattern is one widely used unlock scheme on smartphones, but it may suffer from various cyber-attacks such as screen recording attacks and USB charging attacks. To enhance its security, one promising approach is to integrate biometric features with Android unlock pattern. In this work, we develop ZoomPass, an enhanced Android unlock scheme based on zoom actions. Under our scheme, users can select two dots and then perform a zoom action (using either zoom-in or zoom-out), respectively. To model a user's action, we selected the features such as touch pressure (two fingers), touch size (two fingers), touch duration, zoom speed and angle (two fingers), and touch acceleration (two fingers). In the user study, we involved 30 participants and explored the error rates in the aspects of confirmation, login and retention phase. Based on the results, it is found that SVM classifier could be adopted when deploying ZoomPass in practice. The users' feedback also indicated that ZoomPass is a viable solution in terms of usability and security as compared with PIN code.

Acknowledgments. We would like to thank all the participants for their hard work in the user study. This work was partially supported by National Natural Science Foundation of China (No. 62102106).

References

1. Aviv, A.J., Gibson, K., Mossop, E., Blaze, M., Smith, J.M.: Smudge attacks on smartphone touch screens. In: Proceedings of the 4th USENIX Conference on Offensive Technologies, pp. 1–7. USENIX Association, (2010)
2. Chiasson, S., Biddle, R., van Oorschot, P.C.: A second look at the usability of click-based graphical passwords. In: Proceedings of the 3rd Symposium on Usable Privacy and Security (SOUPS), pp. 1–12. ACM, New York (2007)
3. Chiasson, S., Stobert, E., Forget, A., Biddle, R.: Persuasive cued click-points: design, implementation, and evaluation of a knowledge-based authentication mechanism. IEEE Trans. Dependable Secure Comput. **9**(2), 222–235 (2012)
4. Chakraborty, N., Anand, S.V., Mondal, S.: Towards identifying and preventing behavioral side channel attack on recording attack resilient unaided authentication services. Comput. Secur. **84**, 193–205 (2019)
5. De Luca, A., Hang, A., Brudy, F., Lindner, C., Hussmann, H.: Touch Me Once and I Know It's You!: implicit authentication based on touch screen patterns. In: Proceedings of CHI, pp. 987–996. ACM (2012)
6. Dirik, A.E., Memon, N., Birget, J.C.: Modeling user choice in the passpoints graphical password scheme. In: Proceedings of the 3rd Symposium on Usable privacy and security (SOUPS), pp. 20–28. ACM, New York (2007)
7. Dunphy, P., Yan, J.: Do background images improve "a secret" graphical passwords? In: Proceedings of the 14th ACM Conference on Computer and Communications Security (CCS), pp. 36–47 (2007)
8. Feng, T., Liu, Z., Kwon, K.-A., Shi, W., Carbunary, B., Jiang, Y., Nguyen, N.: Continuous mobile authentication using touchscreen gestures. In: Proceedings of the 2012 IEEE Conference on Technologies for Homeland Security (HST), pp. 451–456. IEEE, USA (2012)
9. Fox, S.: Future Online Password Could be a Map (2010). http://www.livescience.com/8622-future-online-password-map.html
10. Frank, M., Biedert, R., Ma, E., Martinovic, I., Song, D.: Touchalytics: on the applicability of touchscreen input as a behavioral biometric for continuous authentication. IEEE Trans. Inf. Forensics Secur. **8**(1), 136–148 (2013)

11. Forman, T.J., Aviv, A.J.: Double patterns: a usable solution to increase the security of android unlock patterns. In: ACSAC 2020, pp. 219–233 (2020)

12. Frik, A., Kim, J., Sanchez, J.R., Ma, J.: Users' expectations about and use of smartphone privacy and security settings. In: CHI 2022, 407, pp. 1–407:24 (2022)

13. Gołofit, K.: Click passwords under investigation. In: Biskup, J., López, J. (eds.) ESORICS 2007. LNCS, vol. 4734, pp. 343–358. Springer, Heidelberg (2007). https://doi.org/10.1007/978-3-540-74835-9_23

14. Jermyn, I., Mayer, A., Monrose, F., Reiter, M.K., Rubin, A.D.: The Design and Analysis of Graphical Passwords. In: Proceedings of the 8th Conference on USENIX Security Symposium, pp. 1–14. USENIX Association, Berkeley (1999)

15. LIBSVM - A Library for Support Vector Machines. https://www.csie.ntu.edu.tw/cjlin/libsvm/

16. Lin, D., Dunphy, P., Olivier, P., Yan, J.: Graphical passwords & qualitative spatial relations. In: Proceedings of the 3rd Symposium on Usable Privacy and Security (SOUPS), pp. 161–162 (2007)

17. Li, W., Tan, J., Meng, W., Wang, Y., Li, J.: SwipeVLock: a supervised unlocking mechanism based on swipe behavior on smartphones. In: The 2nd International Conference on Machine Learning for Cyber Security (ML4CS), pp. 140-153 (2019)

18. Li, W., Tan, J., Meng, W., Wang, Y.: A swipe-based unlocking mechanism with supervised learning on smartphones: design and evaluation. J. Netw. Comput. Appl. **165**, 102687 (2020)

19. Li, W., Meng, W., Furnell, S.: Exploring touch-based behavioral authentication on smartphone email applications in IoT-enabled Smart Cities. Pattern Recogn. Lett. **144**, 35–41 (2021)

20. Li, W., Wang, Y., Tan, J., Zhu, N.: DCUS: evaluating double-click-based unlocking scheme on smartphones. Mob. Networks Appl. **27**(1), 382–391 (2022)

21. W. Li, J. Tan, N. Zhu.: Double-X: towards double-cross-based unlock mechanism on smartphones. In: Proceedings of the 37th International Conference on ICT Systems Security and Privacy Protection (IFIP SEC), pp. 412–428 (2022)

22. Meng, W.: Graphical authentication. In: Jajodia, S., Samarati, P., Yung, M. (eds.) Encyclopedia of Cryptography, Security and Privacy. Springer (2021)

23. Meng, Y.: Designing Click-Draw Based Graphical Password Scheme for Better Authentication. In: Proceedings of the 7th IEEE International Conference on Networking, Architecture, and Storage (NAS), pp. 39–48 (2012)

24. Meng, Y., Li, W.: Evaluating the effect of tolerance on click-draw based graphical password scheme. In: Chim, T.W., Yuen, T.H. (eds.) ICICS 2012. LNCS, vol. 7618, pp. 349–356. Springer, Heidelberg (2012). https://doi.org/10.1007/978-3-642-34129-8_32

25. Meng, Y., Li, W.: Evaluating the effect of user guidelines on creating click-draw based graphical passwords. In: Proceedings of the 2012 ACM Research in Applied Computation Symposium (RACS), pp. 322–327 (2012)

26. Meng, Y., Wong, D.S., Schlegel, R., Kwok, L.: Touch gestures based biometric authentication scheme for touchscreen mobile phones. In: Kutyłowski, M., Yung, M. (eds.) Inscrypt 2012. LNCS, vol. 7763, pp. 331–350. Springer, Heidelberg (2013). https://doi.org/10.1007/978-3-642-38519-3_21

27. Meng, Y., Li, W., Kwok, L.-F.: Enhancing click-draw based graphical passwords using multi-touch on mobile phones. In: Proceedings of the 28th IFIP TC 11 International Information Security and Privacy Conference (IFIP SEC), IFIP Advances in Information and Communication Technology 405, pp. 55–68 (2013)

28. Meng, W., Wong, D.S., Furnell, S., Zhou, J.: Surveying the development of biometric user authentication on mobile phones. IEEE Commun. Surv. Tutorials **17**(3), 1268–1293 (2015)

29. Meng, W.: RouteMap: a route and map based graphical password scheme for better multiple password memory. In: Proceedings of the 9th International Conference on Network and System Security (NSS), pp. 147–161 (2015)

30. Meng, W.: Evaluating the effect of multi-touch behaviours on android unlock patterns. Inf. Comput. Secur. **24**(3), 277–287, Emerald (2016)

31. Meng, W., Li, W., Jiang, L., Meng, L.: On multiple password interference of touch screen patterns and text passwords. In: ACM Conference on Human Factors in Computing Systems (CHI 2016), pp. 4818–4822 (2016)

32. Meng, W., Li, W., Wong, D.S., Zhou, J.: TMGuard: a touch movement-based security mechanism for screen unlock patterns on smartphones. In: Proceedings of the 14th International Conference on Applied Cryptography and Network Security (ACNS), pp. 629–647 (2016)

33. Meng, W., Lee, W.H., Liu, Z., Su, C., Li, Y.: Evaluating the impact of juice filming charging attack in practical environments. In: Proceedings of ICISC, pp. 327-338 (2017)

34. Meng, W., Fei, F., Li, W., Au, M.H.: Harvesting smartphone privacy through enhanced juice filming charging attacks. In: Proceedings of ISC, pp. 291–308 (2017)

35. Meng, W., Li, W., Kwok, L.-F., Choo, K.-K.R.: Towards enhancing click-draw based graphical passwords using multi-touch behaviours on smartphones. Comput. Secur. **65**, 213–229 (2017)

36. Meng, W., Li, W., Lee, W., Jiang, L., Zhou, J.: A pilot study of multiple password interference between text and map-based passwords. In: Proceedings of the 15th International Conference on Applied Cryptography and Network Security (ACNS), pp. 145–162 (2017)

37. Meng, W., Lee, W., Au, M.H., Liu, Z.: Exploring effect of location number on map-based graphical password authentication. In: Proceedings of the 22nd Australasian Conference on Information Security and Privacy (ACISP), pp. 301-313 (2017)

38. Meng, W., Jiang, L., Wang, Y., Li, J., Zhang, J., Xiang, Y.: JFCGuard: detecting juice filming charging attack via processor usage analysis on smartphones. Comput. Secur. **76**, 252–264 (2018)

39. Meng, W., Zhu, L., Li, W., Han, J., Li, Y.: Enhancing the security of FinTech applications with map-based graphical password authentication. Futur. Gener. Comput. Syst. **101**, 1018–1027 (2019)

40. Meng, W., Jiang, L., Choo, K.K.R., Wang, Y., Jiang, C.: Towards detection of juice filming charging attacks via supervised CPU usage analysis on smartphones. Comput. Electr. Eng. **78**, 230–241 (2019)

41. Nelson, D.L., Reed, V.S., Walling, J.R.: Pictorial superiority effect. J. Exp. Psychol. Hum. Learn. Memory **2**(5), 523–528 (1976)

42. Nyang, D., Kim, H., Lee, W., Kang, S., Cho, G., Lee, M.K., Mohaisen, A.: Two-thumbs-up: physical protection for PIN entry secure against recording attacks. Comput. Secur. **78**, 1–15 (2018)

43. Passfaces. http://www.realuser.com/

44. Quinlan, J.R.: Improved use of continuous attributes in C4.5. J. Artif. Intell. Res. **4**(1), 77–90 (1996)

45. Rennie, J.D.M., Shih, L., Teevan, J., Karger, D.R.: Tackling the poor assumptions of naive bayes text classifiers. In: Proceedings of the 20th International Conference on Machine Learning, pp. 616–623 (2003)

46. Rumelhart, D., Hinton, G., Williams, R.: Learning representations by back-propagating errors. Nature **323**, 533–536 (1986)
47. Spitzer, J., Singh, C., Schweitzer, D.: A security class project in graphical passwords. J. Comput. Sci. Coll. **26**(2), 7–13 (2010)
48. Shahzad, M., Liu, A.X., Samuel, A.: Behavior based human authentication on touch screen devices using gestures and signatures. IEEE Trans. Mob. Comput. **16**(10), 2726–2741 (2017)
49. Sharma, V., Enbody, R.: User authentication and identification from user interface interactions on touch-enabled devices. In: Proceedings of the 10th ACM Conference on Security and Privacy in Wireless and Mobile Networks (WiSec), pp. 1–11 (2017)
50. Suo, X., Zhu, Y., Owen, G.S.: Graphical passwords: a survey. In: Proceedings of the 21st Annual Computer Security Applications Conference (ACSAC), pp. 463–472. IEEE Computer Society, USA (2005)
51. Sun, H., Chen, Y., Fang, C., Chang, S.: PassMap: a map based graphical-password authentication system. In: Proceedings of AsiaCCS, pp. 99–100 (2012)
52. Stylios, I., Kokolakis, S., Thanou, O., Chatzis, S.: Behavioral biometrics & continuous user authentication on mobile devices: A survey. Inf. Fusion **66**, 76–99 (2021)
53. Tao, H., Adams, C.: Pass-Go: a proposal to improve the usability of graphical passwords. Int. J. Network Secur. **2**(7), 273–292 (2008)
54. Thorpe, J., MacRae, B., Salehi-Abari, A.: Usability and security evaluation of GeoPass: a geographic location-password scheme. In: Proceedings of the 9th Symposium on Usable Privacy and Security (SOUPS), pp. 1–14 (2013)
55. Wang, L., Meng, W., Li, W.: Towards DTW-based unlock scheme using handwritten graphics on smartphones. In: The 17th International Conference on Mobility, Sensing and Networking (IEEE MSN), pp. 486–493 (2021)
56. Weka: Machine Learning Software in Java. https://www.cs.waikato.ac.nz/ml/weka/
57. Wiedenbeck, S., Waters, J., Birget, J.-C., Brodskiy, A., Memon, N.: Passpoints: design and longitudinal evaluation of a graphical password system. Int. J. Hum Comput Stud. **63**(1–2), 102–127 (2005)
58. Yan, J., Blackwell, A., Anderson, R., Grant, A.: Password memorability and security: empirical results. IEEE Secur. Priv. **2**, 25–31 (2004)
59. Yu, X., Wang, Z., Li, Y., Li, L., Zhu, W.T., Song, L.: EvoPass: evolvable graphical password against shoulder-surfing attacks. Comput. Secur. **70**, 179–198 (2017)
60. Zheng, N., Bai, K., Huang, H., Wang, H.: You are how you touch: user verification on smartphones via tapping behaviors. In: Proceedings of the 2014 International Conference on Network Protocols (ICNP), pp. 221–232 (2014)
61. Zhou, T., Liu, L., Wang, H., Li, W., Jiang, C.: PassGrid: towards graph-supplemented textual shoulder surfing resistant authentication. In: Proceedings of the 5th International Symposium on Security and Privacy in Social Networks and Big Data (SocialSec), pp. 251–263 (2019)

Metasploit for Cyber-Physical Security Testing with Real-Time Constraints

Sulav Lal Shrestha$^{(\boxtimes)}$, Taylor Lee , and Sebastian Fischmeister

University of Waterloo, Waterloo, Canada
{slshrest,taylor.lee,sfischme}@uwaterloo.ca

Abstract. Metasploit is a framework for cybersecurity testing. The Metasploit Framework provides the Hardware Bridge API to enable security testing of cyber-physical systems. Cyber-physical systems and tests/attacks on the systems are subject to real-time constraints. Hence, this research aims to study the timing characteristics of tests implemented using the framework. Several factors, such as the programming language used to write tests, overhead added by the framework, scheduling policies etc., affect the latency and jitter. This paper considers the Controller Area Network used in automotive systems to study the effect of those factors on the timing characteristics. The study evaluates (i) latency and jitter for transmission and reception of the messages in the network and (ii) the jitter in the periodicity in periodic transmission of messages. Based on the results, the study determines the best combination of the factors to minimize the latency and jitter in the tasks considered. The paper performs a case study on actual tests/attacks subject to real-time constraints and analyses the suitability of executing the tests using Metasploit. The study analyses the performance of tasks implemented as Metasploit modules and shows how choices of some factors can significantly improve the temporal characteristics without modifying the Metasploit Framework. The experimental results show some interesting findings related to Ruby and the Metasploit Framework.

Keywords: Cyber-physical systems · Security · Controller area network

1 Introduction

With advancements in computer-controlled physical systems and networked systems, physical systems are progressively going cyber-physical. The automotive industry is one such industry in which traditionally physical components like the powertrain are getting integrated with computing, and more essentially, networked computing [14]. Such integration allows attackers to access the systems inside the vehicle and compromise the subsystems [12].

Attacks on cyber-physical systems (CPS) can have real-time constraints. The Bus-Off attack [8] on the Controller Area Network (CAN) [4] of automotive

C. Su et al. (Eds.): SciSec 2022, LNCS 13580, pp. 260–275, 2022.
https://doi.org/10.1007/978-3-031-17551-0_17

systems is one such attack with timing constraints. The correctness of real-time processes depends upon the completion of the process within the given timing constraints. In the context of real-time attacks, the effectiveness or correctness of the attack depends on the timely execution of the attack.

For any given task, the use of a framework standardizes the process of executing the task. Such standardization makes the task execution uniform and makes knowledge transfer easier. This study focuses on a framework for cybersecurity: Metasploit [2]. The Metasploit Framework consists of a suite of tools used to test security vulnerabilities and execute attacks. Any task, such as scanning a target or exploiting the target, is implemented as a module in Metasploit. A framework, such as Metasploit, also promotes the reuse of code and components, in this case, the modules. For cyber-physical systems, it is important to test the security of both the cyber components and cyber-controlled physical components. The Hardware Bridge API in the Metasploit Framework extends the framework's support to hardware-related tests for cyber-physical systems like Internet-of-Things and Industrial Control Systems [26].

Several factors can affect the temporal characteristics of a process running in an operating system (OS). Such factors include the priority of the process, the scheduling policy used by the OS, and the language used to implement the software. Hence, to make the use of Metasploit suitable for executing real-time tasks, this research studies the temporal characteristics of a Metasploit module.

This work contributes to the understanding of performing security tests and assessment of networked embedded systems in the following ways:

- The work systematically analyzes and evaluates the effect of the implementation method and implementation language on the performance of temporal control in Metasploit.
- The work quantitatively analyzes the temporal jitter of the attacks through the Metasploit Framework.
- Based on the results, the work provides the best practices and recommendations for using Metasploit to test networked embedded systems.

2   Related Work

Researchers have studied the effects of different task compositions, schedules, and priorities [7,18] on the jitter in real-time tasks. Pozzobon et al. evaluated several CAN interface access modules for use in automotive security test frameworks, using round-trip latency and transmission-reception rates as the evaluation metrics [23]. In the case of a General Purpose Operating System, the user of the OS does not have much control over the scheduling policies. Linux does provide the ability to change the priority and scheduling algorithm for a process to some extent. Dubey et al. [10] implemented a control algorithm to control jitter in the sampling interval for a program running on a General Purpose Operating System. The authors treated jitter in the sampling interval as an error signal that the control system aimed to control. The suggested control algorithm ran in user-space instead of kernel-space, which made the use of the algorithm easier.

When the control task includes nodes in a network, the network latency also acts as a source of jitter. Roque et al. [25] evaluated the performance of an in-vehicle communication system by characterizing the jitter present in the timing of critical CAN messages. Imai et al. [16] used a time-delay compensation method to compensate for jitter in a networked control system. The method uses "Jitter Buffers" to suppress jitter due to time-varying network latency.

Researchers have dedicated efforts to integrate systems with special requirements into general-purpose systems. Bollella and Jeffay [3] designed a system in which a real-time kernel could co-exist with a general-purpose kernel to support real-time solutions in commercial systems. Ramamritham et al. [24] acknowledged that even though Windows NT is not a real-time OS, the timing requirements for the OS warranted a study due to the acceptance of the OS in industrial applications.

The use of Metasploit as a cyber-physical security testing tool for time-sensitive applications is yet to be explored. This study focuses on examining the timing characteristics of a task implemented as a Metasploit module.

3   Background: Cyber-Attack as a Real-Time Process

This section discusses how an attack on an automotive network can have real-time constraints. Researchers have identified and documented several attacks on the CAN Network [5,6,8,11,13,17,21]. This paper demonstrates the role timing characteristics play in cybersecurity-related tests/attacks using two attacks on the CAN Network (i) CAN-Flood Attack [6] and (ii) Bus-Off Attack [8].

Controller Area Network (CAN). CAN connects two or more nodes in a network. The messages transmitted by the nodes are broadcast messages. Only one node can transmit a message in the network at a particular instant of time. A CAN message does not consist of a transmitter or receiver identifier. Instead, each CAN frame consists of a message ID. The message ID provides the CAN frame its meaning and its priority. The lower the message ID, the higher the priority. A logic-0 in the CAN Network is called a dominant bit, and a logic-1 is called a recessive bit. When two nodes try to write to the bus and the bit being written are different, the bus is driven to a dominant bit state. To understand more about the CAN protocol, we encourage the readers to refer to Natalie et al. [9] and CAN Specification version 2.0 [4].

CAN-Flood Attack. In a CAN Network, if two nodes try to transmit messages with different CAN IDs simultaneously, the node that sends a message with a smaller CAN ID wins the arbitration. So, if a malicious node frequently sends a CAN message with a low CAN ID, non-malicious nodes do not get the chance to send messages with a higher CAN ID. Such contention for access to the bus leads to the non-malicious nodes experiencing Denial-of-Service.

In a CAN-Flood Attack, the adversary has the capability to transmit and receive messages in the targeted CAN network. The objective of the CAN-Flood attack is to transmit CAN messages with a low CAN ID as frequently as possible. The timing requirement is to minimize the temporal distance between two CAN messages sent by the malicious node.

Bus-Off Attack. The Bus-Off attack [8] focuses on causing a bit-error during the transmission of a message by the target node. When a node writes a bit onto the bus, the node monitors the state of the bus. If the bit monitored by the node is not the same as the one written by the node, the node concludes that something has gone wrong and aborts writing the message. If the detected discrepancy is during bus arbitration, the CAN node stops transmitting the message. If the detected discrepancy is not during bus arbitration, then the node increments the Transmission Error Counter (TEC) by 8. For a successful message transmission, the node decrements the TEC by 1.

Attack Setup. There are three nodes in a CAN network: $\mathcal{X}$, $\mathcal{V}$ and $\mathcal{A}$, where $\mathcal{X}$ is the trigger node, $\mathcal{V}$ is the target node, and $\mathcal{A}$ is the adversary node. The Bus-Off attack is executed with the help of preceded messages. The attack events progress as follows:

- $\mathcal{X}$ transmits Message $\mathcal{K}$ periodically with a period T.
- Immediately after transmitting Message $\mathcal{K}$, $\mathcal{X}$ transmits k preceded messages $P_1, P_2, ..., P_k$.
- When $\mathcal{V}$ and $\mathcal{A}$ receive Message $\mathcal{K}$, $\mathcal{V}$ transmits Message $\mathcal{M}$ (targeted message) and $\mathcal{A}$ transmits Message $\mathcal{C}$ (attack message). The attack message and target message must have the same CAN ID. The attack message must differ from the target message such that a bit in the attack message is dominant, whereas the corresponding bit in the target message is recessive.

Timing Requirements. If the instant at which $\mathcal{V}$ and $\mathcal{A}$ start writing the messages $\mathcal{C}$ and $\mathcal{M}$ onto the bus differs by even a single bit, the attack will fail. Considering a bitrate of 500 kbps, the bit-length is $2\,\mu s$. By making use of the preceded message, the timing requirement of the attack message injection becomes relaxed. Instead of 1 bit-length, the timing requirement is now the message length of the preceded message.

In this study, we take into account the difference in CAN message transmission latencies of the target and the adversary nodes. Let the delay between trigger message $\mathcal{K}$ and target message $\mathcal{M}$ be D_{target}, in the absence of preceded messages. Let the delay between $\mathcal{K}$ and attack message $\mathcal{C}$ be D_{attack}, in the absence of preceded messages. Jitter is known to follow a Gaussian distribution [8,15]. Hence, let D_{target} be characterised by a Gaussian distribution $\mathcal{N}(d_{target}, \sigma^2_{target})$, where, d_{target} is the mean delay in the target message and σ_{target} is the standard deviation in the delay. Similarly, let D_{attack} be characterised by a Gaussian distribution $\mathcal{N}(d_{attack}, \sigma^2_{attack})$, where d_{attack} is the mean delay in the attack message and σ_{attack} is the standard deviation in the delay. Let $D_{target,max}$ be the upper bound on D_{target} and $D_{attack,max}$ be the upper bound on D_{target}.

Let the temporal lengths of trigger, precede, target and attack messages be $t_{trigger}$, $t_{precede}$, t_{target} and t_{attack}, respectively. If t_k is the instant in time of the start of trigger message, then, the preceded messages should keep the bus busy until at least $t_k + max(D_{target,max}, D_{attack,max})$. Then,

$$k * t_{precede} \geq (max(D_{target,max}, D_{attack,max}) - t_{trigger}) \tag{1}$$

where, k is the number of preceded messages required to keep the bus busy such that the Messages $\mathcal{M}$ and $\mathcal{C}$ synchronize.

4 Methodology

The study aims to evaluate and improve the temporal control for modules in Metasploit. There are a number of choices available, from the creation of software to the execution of the software. The study considers such choices as *factors* that affect the timing of a task. The study considers the following factors: 1) Programming Language, 2) Process Scheduling Policy and Process Priority 3) Periodicity of a Periodic Task 4) Just-in-Time (JIT) Compilation 5) Effect of using the Metasploit Framework 6) Hardware Setup. To determine which combination of factors provides better temporal control, we perform experiments to estimate 1) jitter in the periodicity (Δt_p) of CAN message transmissions 2) transmission latency and jitter (Δt_{tx}) for a CAN message 3) round-trip latency and jitter (Δt_{rt}) for a CAN message under different combinations of factors. Additionally, jitter in the periodicity of periodic CAN message transmissions is estimated for different periods along with the program configurations.

4.1 Program Configuration

This paper uses the term *configuration* to denote a particular choice of *factor*. Instead of defining a separate configuration for each factor, we group some of the factors. Table 1 shows the different configurations and the values each configuration can have.

Framework Configuration. Framework configuration means if the program is a standalone program or implemented as a Metasploit module. A framework configuration can be *Standalone* or *Metasploit*. For interacting with a CAN interface, Metasploit provides an API which is a wrapper around *can-utils* (userspace utilities for SocketCAN) [1].

Language Configuration. Language Configuration shows which language is used to implement the program. Metasploit is implemented using Ruby. Metasploit modules are written in Ruby as well. Ruby is not a systems programming language and is not efficient or fast compared to a systems programming language like C [20]. Ruby is an interpreted language and provides the option to run Ruby programs with JIT enabled. The values for this configuration can be *C*, *Ruby* and

Ruby:JIT. Here, *Ruby* means the program written in Ruby is executed without enabling the JIT feature of the Ruby interpreter. *Ruby:JIT* means the program written in Ruby is executed with JIT enabled. Additionally, the study introduces another language configuration *Ruby:C*. *Ruby:C* means that the functionality is implemented as a function in a C shared library, which is then called from a Ruby program using Foreign Function Interface (FFI) [19]. This particular configuration is important because Metasploit modules can be implemented only in Ruby. So, to utilize the advantages offered by C, the actual intended functionality of the module is implemented in C as a shared library function which can then be called from a Metasploit module written in Ruby.

Scheduling Configuration. Scheduling Configuration combines the scheduling policy and process priority factors. The study considers three scheduling configurations: (i) *Default*, (ii) *FIFO*, and (iii) *RR*. *Default* scheduling configuration means that the program, when executed, uses the default scheduling policy, i.e. SCHED_OTHER and the default nice value of 0. *FIFO* scheduling configuration means that the scheduling policy used for the process is SCHED_FIFO and the process priority used is 99. *RR* scheduling configuration means that the scheduling policy used for the process is SCHED_RR and the process priority used is 99.

Table 1. Individual configuration and their possible values

Configuration	Values
Framework	Metasploit, Standalone
Language	C, Ruby, Ruby:JIT, Ruby:C
Scheduling	Default, FIFO, RR

For the evaluation of jitter in periodic CAN messages, the experiment uses the sleep method. One of the questions this paper considers is: does jitter in periodicity depend upon the duration of sleep? The period of a periodic task is not treated as a configuration. Rather, periodicity is treated as a parameter of the experiment.

Program Configuration and Naming Convention. This paper refers to a combination of individual configurations as a *program configuration*. To name the different program configurations used in the experiments, this paper uses the naming convention of *[Program Type]* - *[Language Configuration]* - *[Scheduling Configuration]*. For example, a program configuration mentioned as *Standalone-C-FIFO* means (i) the program is a standalone program (i.e., not a Metasploit module), (ii) the program is implemented in C, and (iii) the program is executed with *SCHED_FIFO* scheduling policy and a process priority of 99. To imply that a particular discussion is applicable to all the values of a specific configuration, the paper uses the wildcard character - asterisk (∗). For example,

Metasploit-Ruby-∗ means that the discussion is applicable for the program type configuration of Metasploit, language configuration of Ruby and all scheduling configurations.

4.2   Experimental Setup

The experimental setup is shown in Fig. 1. The figure shows a CAN bus connection between three nodes. Node 1 is the system-under-test (SUT). The SUT node is a 4-core i5 computer with 16 GB of RAM, and each core has a frequency of 1.60 GHz. SUT node uses the Metasploit framework - version *6.0.55-dev* running on Ubuntu 20.04 OS. The USB-to-CAN module used in Node 1 is *Peak CAN* [22]. Node 1 and Node 2 use USB-to-CAN modules to communicate with the CAN bus. Node 3 is a Raspberry Pi 3 computer with a CAN shield. The nodes are configured to use a bitrate of 500 kbps.

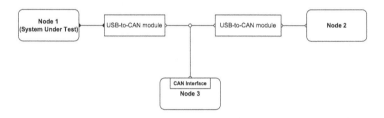

Fig. 1. Experimental setup showing a CAN bus network with three nodes. Nodes 1 and 2 are used for the experiments. Node 3, along with 1 and 2, is used in the case study with Bus-Off attack

4.3   Experiments

The study performs the following three experiments to evaluate temporal characteristics in a Metasploit module.

Experiment 1: Periodicity. Experiment 1 is designed to estimate the jitter in periodicity. Node 1 executes the task of sending a CAN message periodically with a period $T_{desired}$. If t_i is the instant at which i_{th} message is received by Node 2, then the jitter for i_{th} transmission $(\Delta t_{p,i})$ is calculated as,

$$\Delta t_{p,i} = t_i - t_{i-1} \tag{2}$$

The timing variable of interest - Δt_p is modelled as a Gaussian variable with mean μ_p and standard deviation σ_p, i.e., $\Delta t_p \sim \mathcal{N}(\mu_p, \sigma_p^2)$.

The periodic task is realized by Pseudocode 1. Implementations based on Ruby use the function *sleep* and implementations based on C use the function *usleep*. The experiment is repeated for 1000 sleep cycles. The mean (μ_p) and standard deviation (σ_p) of the jitter are then calculated for the 1000 sleep cycles.

The experiment is performed for each program configuration for Node 1. For each configuration, the sender program is run with different sleep durations of { 0.1s, 0.5s, 1.0s, 2.0s, 5.0s, 10.s, 20.0s }.

Pseudocode 1: Periodic CAN Message Sender

Input: Sleep Duration T, No. of iterations N

```
1 for i=0; i<=N; i++ do
2 |   send_can_msg();
3 |_  call_sleep_function(T);
```

Experiment 2: Transmission Latency. Experiment 2 is designed to estimate latency and jitter in the transmission of a CAN message. Pseudocode 2 realizes the task to be performed for Experiment 2. Node 1 sends two CAN messages without any explicit delay between the two transmissions. Let the transmission latency (Δt_{tx}) be defined as the temporal spacing between the two messages. Δt_{tx} is modelled as a Gaussian variable with a mean of μ_{tx} (called mean transmission latency) and standard deviation of σ_{tx} (called jitter in transmission latency), i.e., $\Delta t_{tx} \sim \mathcal{N}(\mu_{tx}, \sigma_{tx}^2)$.

Pseudocode 2: Program under test for the estimation of Δt_{tx}

Input: Sleep Duration T, No. of iterations N

```
1 for i=0; i<N; i++ do
2 |   send_CAN_message_1();
3 |   send_CAN_message_2();
4 |_  sleep_for_some_specific_time();
```

Let $t_{0,i}$ be the instance of time at the start of i_{th} CAN-Message-1. Let $t_{1,i}$ be the instance of time at the start of i_{th} CAN-Message-2. Let $t_{0,length}$ be the temporal length of CAN-Message-1. Then, the temporal spacing between i_{th} pair of CAN-Message-1 and CAN-Message-2 is given as,

$$\Delta t_{tx,i} = t_{1,i} - t_{0,i} - t_{0,length} \tag{3}$$

The temporal spacing between the two messages is calculated using Saleae Logic Analyzer 16. The process is repeated 1000 times under each configuration. The mean (μ_{tx}) and standard deviation (σ_{tx}) of the transmission latency is then computed for each run.

Experiment 3: Round-Trip Latency. Experiment 3 is designed to estimate the round-trip latency of the system-under-test in a CAN network. Pseudocode 3 realizes the task to be performed for this experiment. Node 2 sends a CAN message (say $P_{e,0}$) on the network. On receiving Message $P_{e,0}$, Node 1 sends another message (say $P_{e,1}$) on the network. Let the round-trip latency (Δt_{rt}) be defined as the temporal spacing between the two messages $P_{e,0}$ and $P_{e,1}$. Δt_{rt}

is modelled as a Gaussian variable with a mean of μ_{rt} (called mean round-trip latency) and standard deviation of σ_{rt} (called jitter in round-trip latency), i.e., $\Delta t_{rt} \sim \mathcal{N}(\mu_{rt}, \sigma_{rt}^2)$.

Let $t_{0,i}$ be the instance of time at the start of the trigger message i. Let $t_{1,i}$ be the instance of time at the start of the triggered message. Let $t_{0,length}$ be the temporal length of trigger message. Then, the temporal spacing between i_{th} pair of trigger message and triggered message is given as,

$$\Delta t_{rt,i} = t_{1,i} - t_{0,i} - t_{0,length} \tag{4}$$

The temporal spacing between the two messages is calculated using Saleae Logic Analyzer 16. The process is repeated 1000 times. The mean (μ_{rt}) and standard deviation (σ_{rt}) is then computed for the experimental runs under different configurations.

Pseudocode 3: Program under test for the estimation of Δt_{rt}

Input: No. of iterations N

```
1  for i=0; i<N; i++ do
2      wait_for_CAN_message();
3      send_CAN_message();
```

---

5   Results and Discussion

Figures 2 and 3 show the latency and jitter observed during the experiments. Based on the temporal characteristics observed for different program configurations, the program configurations with distinct temporal characteristics are 1. *Metasploit-Ruby-**, 2. *Standalone-Ruby-** and *Standalone-Ruby:JIT-**, and 3. *Standalone-C-** and **-Ruby:C-** Various observations from the experiments are discussed below.

Observation 1: Effect of Language Configurations. Language configuration had the most pronounced effect on the temporal characteristics in the experiments. For all the experiments performed, implementations using C or *Ruby:C* language configurations had the least latency and jitter. JIT compilation did not have any noticeable effect on the temporal characteristics. Considering the fact that for interacting with the CAN network, Ruby uses the bash utility *can-utils*, it is justified for the JIT compilation to not have any effect on the temporal characteristics.

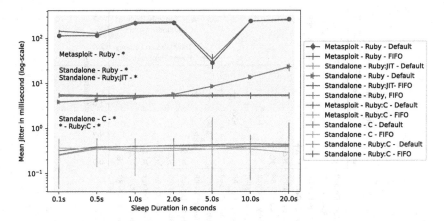

Fig. 2. Plot of mean jitter versus sleep duration for different program configurations. The plot shows three regions grouping the configurations based on their mean jitter. *-*-*RR* configuration follows a distribution similar to corresponding *-*-*FIFO* configuration. Hence, *-*-*RR* configuration plots are not included for clarity of the diagram.

Observation 2: Jitter in Periodicity in Ruby. For Experiment 1, the *Standalone-Ruby-Default* configuration demonstrated a peculiar behaviour, with the jitter showing an increasing trend with respect to the sleep duration. On closer inspection, it was found that the *sleep* function in Ruby uses a different system call compared to *usleep* function in C. While the *usleep* function in C uses the *clock_nanosleep* system call, the *sleep* function in Ruby uses *ppoll*. To confirm that the jitter increasing with sleep duration was due to the *ppoll* system call, the time spent in *ppoll* system call was captured using the *strace* utility, and the jitter was computed for different sleep durations. The jitter in the *ppoll* system call was found to be following a similar curve to the *Standalone-Ruby-Default* configuration.

Observation 3: Effect of using Metasploit Framework on CAN Message Transmission. The APIs provided by the Metasploit Framework seems to be adding overhead in accessing the hardware interface. The results show nearly two orders of magnitude increase in latency and jitter for *Metasploit-Ruby-** configurations compared to *Metasploit-Ruby:C-**. Using *strace* to monitor the system calls *Metasploit-Ruby-** is making in order to transmit a CAN message, we found that *Metasploit-Ruby-** is making more system calls compared to *Metasploit-Ruby:C-**, as shown in Table 2. Also, for *Metasploit-Ruby:C-**, the program needs to bind and connect to the socket once and close the socket once in the life cycle of the process to transmit or receive multiple CAN messages. However, in the case of *Metasploit-Ruby-**, the program establishes the connection and closes the connection for every call to the *can-utils* tool to transmit or receive CAN messages.

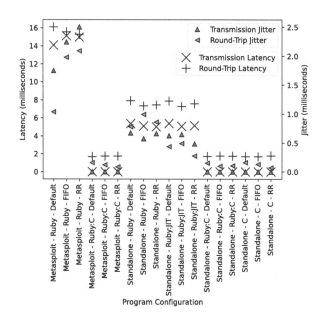

Fig. 3. Plot of transmission and round-trip latency and jitter for different program configurations. The left y-axis shows latency in milliseconds whereas the right y-axis shows jitter in milliseconds.

Observation 4: Behavior of Sleep Function in Metasploit-Ruby-.* From Fig. 2, μ_p for tasks implemented using *Metasploit-Ruby-** configurations is an order of magnitude higher compared to μ_p in *Standalone-Ruby-** configurations. In *Metasploit-Ruby-** configurations, μ_p is in the range of hundreds of milliseconds except for a period of 5.0 s, for which the jitter is in the range of tens of milliseconds. For *Metasploit-Ruby:C-** configurations, the jitter is not so different compared to *Standalone-C-** or *Standalone-Ruby:C-** configurations. Using the *strace* utility, it was found that in *Metasploit-Ruby-** configurations, sleep is implemented in 0.2 s quanta. Meaning that a specified sleep period of 0.1 s would result in an actual sleep period of at least 0.2 s. A sleep period of 0.21 s would instead result in a sleep period of at least 0.4 s. Another interesting behaviour is that the number of 0.2 s sleep blocks is sometimes more than the required number. These two observations explain the high jitter for *Metasploit-Ruby-** configurations. For 0.1 s and 0.5 s, the number of 0.2 s blocks of sleep was correct. For both of them, the sleep duration exceeded by 0.1 s as sleep was implemented in multiples of 0.2 s blocks of sleep. For 5.0 s sleep, the number of 0.2 s blocks of sleep was exact, i.e. 25, so the jitter observed was low compared to other sleep durations. For the 1.0 s, 2.0 s, 10.0 s and 20.0 s sleep durations, the number of 0.2 s blocks of sleep was one more than required, which explains the higher jitter compared to 0.1 s, 0.5 s and 5.0 s sleep durations.

Table 2. List of system calls made along with the number of times the system call was made to transmit a CAN message for *Metasploit-Ruby-** and *Metasploit-Ruby:C-**

System Call	Metasploit-Ruby-*	Metasploit-Ruby:C-*
socket	1	1
ioctl	1	1
bind	1	1
write	1	1
close	1	1
fcntl	1	0
fstat	1	0
getsockname	1	0
setsockopt	1	0
futex	25	0
connect	1	0
getpid	11	0
getsockopt	2	0
ppoll	3	0
select	2	0
sendto	1	0
recvfrom	1	0
read	2	0
getpeername	1	0
shutdown	1	0

Observation 5: Effect of Scheduling Configuration. Even though SCHED_FIFO and SCHED_RR are real-time scheduling policies for a Linux kernel, the *FIFO* and *RR* scheduling configurations showed no improvement in measured temporal characteristics compared to *Default* scheduling configuration. To understand why no discernible effect was seen on the temporal characteristics due to the scheduling configurations, we monitored the number of involuntary context switches (available in the \proc\PID\status file in Linux) and the amount of time the processes spent in the ready queue waiting for CPU time (available in the \proc\PID\schedstat file in Linux). The data in Table 3 shows that there was indeed a reduction in involuntary context switches and the time waited by the process in the ready queue. For a single iteration, the reduction in wait time is nearly 4 microseconds. Considering that the CAN message transmission latency for *Metasploit-Ruby-** is in the range of tens of milliseconds, the improvement due to scheduling configuration was not evident.

The *Standalone-Ruby-Default* configuration shows an increasing jitter with sleep duration in Experiment 1. The increasing jitter is not seen in *FIFO* and

RR scheduling configurations for *Standalone-Ruby-** program configurations. For the implementation in *Ruby:C*, *FIFO* and *RR* scheduling configurations had no significant effect on jitter when compared to the *Default* scheduling configuration.

Table 3. Number of involuntary context switches and wait time of a process in the ready queue for *Metasploit-Ruby-** program configurations for the program shown in Pseudocode 2 for 1000 iterations

Scheduling configuration	No. of involuntary context switches	Wait time in ready queue (microseconds)
Default	84	7184
FIFO	1	2976
RR	4	3091

6   Case Study

This section explores the configurations discussed above in effect. The case studies done below demonstrate the effect of the configurations on the timing characteristics studied in the experiments in Sect. 4.3 and consequently on the success of the attacks. We analyse how the *Metasploit-Ruby-Default* configuration compares to the *Metasploit-Ruby:C-Default* configuration in actual testing/attack scenarios.

CAN-Flood Attack. To effectively cause Denial-of-Service to non-malicious nodes, the malicious node needs to increase the bus load by sending messages with a low CAN ID. To monitor the bus load due to a malicious node, a node was designated as a malicious node in a CAN Network, with only the malicious node sending CAN messages. On using the *Metasploit-Ruby-Default* configuration to execute the CAN-Flood attack, the bus load increased from 0% to 3%. On using the *Metasploit-Ruby:C-Default* configuration, the bus load increased from 0% to 79%. The improvement offered by using C to implement the task compared to Ruby (3% to 79%) is significant.

Bus-Off Attack. To evaluate the Bus-Off attack, the setup shown in Fig. 1 was used. Node 1 used Metasploit to transmit the preceded messages periodically. Node 2 used Metasploit to transmit the attack messages, with the first preceded message sent by Node 1 acting as the trigger message. Node 3 (Raspberry Pi 3) was the target of the attack. Node 3 transmitted the target message on the reception of the first preceded message from Node 1.

For Node 3, the round-trip latency was estimated to be 541 µs with a jitter of 24 µs. For Node 2, we chose the *Metasploit-Ruby:C-Default* configuration. The round-trip latency for Node 2 is then 1682 µs with a jitter of 156 µs (from the data shown in Fig. 3). Since there is a difference in the round-trip latency of the target node and the adversary node, Node 2 must keep the bus busy such that the target message and the attack message synchronize. Let t_0 µs be the release time of the trigger message from Node 1. Considering a 95% confidence (i.e., $2\sigma_{rt}$), the greatest release time of target message is then $t_0 + 589$ µs. Similarly, the greatest release time of the attack message is $t_0 + 1994$ µs. Node 1 needs to keep the bus busy for at least 1774 µs (calculated using Eq. 1 and considering $t_{trigger} = 220$ µs and $t_{precede} = 248$ µs [8]), which is equivalent to 7 preceded messages. However, as Experiment 2 for the transmission latency showed, Node 1 cannot keep the bus busy completely. Hence, not all the attack messages succeed.

In the Bus-Off attack experiment discussed above, in 100 attempts, on average, 611 attack messages were needed before the target node entered the *Bus-Off* state. If we consider, Node 2 to be transmitting attack messages with the *Metasploit-Ruby-Default* configuration, the number of preceded messages needed is 73. And again, since the bus cannot be kept busy perfectly due to transmission latency, the target message would be transmitted before the attack message is transmitted, with a probability of 99.99% (equivalent to $4\sigma_{rt}$). When the Bus-Off attack experiment was performed with Node 2 using Raspberry Pi, in 100 attempts, on average, 56 attack messages were needed to force the target node into the bus-off state. This Bus-Off attack experiment highlights the drawback of the high latency in a Metasploit-based adversary compared to the target node.

7   Conclusion

It is necessary to ensure the security of both cyber and physical components in a CPS. The Metasploit Framework extended the support for testing cyber-physical systems by introducing the Hardware Bridge API. The authors argue that the framework needs to be evaluated with the real-time constraints of the tests under consideration. This study determined the latency and jitter in periodic transmission of CAN messages, the transmission of a CAN message and the round-trip time of a CAN message for different combinations of factors. The study showed that the APIs provided by Metasploit perform significantly more operations under the hood compared to a C implementation of the same functionality. Hence, using Metasploit-provided APIs can add significant latency and jitter to the task under consideration (in this case, CAN message transmission and reception).

For the periodic transmission of CAN messages, the study found a couple of interesting observations. First, the results showed increasing jitter in the period with respect to actual sleep duration in the *ppoll* system call used in the sleep function in Ruby when executed with the *SCHED_OTHER* scheduling policy. Second, the study showed that the sleep duration took effect in quanta of 200ms in Metasploit.

The results show that the improvement due to the real-time scheduling policies was too small. However, the number of involuntary context switches and wait time in the ready queue were reduced by using real-time scheduling policies with high process priorities. Enabling JIT in Ruby during the execution of a Ruby script did not bring any discernible improvement in the temporal characteristics for the task of interacting with the CAN network.

Each cyber-physical system is different, and each test can have different timing constraints. The timing characteristics need to be analyzed for each system-under-test, test and platform used for the test. Regardless, this paper has shown the extent of the effect of different factors on the temporal characteristics of Metasploit modules. This study has shown that the latency and jitter in transmission and reception of CAN messages using the Metasploit Framework are improved significantly by implementing the functionality in C as a shared library. This study also shows the extent of the impact of using real-time scheduling policies and JIT on the temporal characteristics of the Metasploit modules. The improvement in the temporal characteristics of Metasploit modules was also evidenced by the case studies on the CAN-Flood Attack and Bus-Off Attack. Therefore, the authors suggest implementing the tasks with real-time constraints as a C shared library instead of using the Metasploit-provided APIs for hardware access.

References

1. Socketcan userspace utilities and tools (2021). https://github.com/linux-can/can-utils
2. Metasploit - penetration testing software (2022). https://www.metasploit.com/
3. Bollella, G., Jeffay, K.: Support for real-time computing within general purpose operating systems-supporting co-resident operating systems. In: Proceedings Real-Time Technology and Applications Symposium, pp. 4–14 (1995). https://doi.org/10.1109/RTTAS.1995.516189
4. Bosch, R., et al.: Can specification version 2.0. Robert Bosch GmbH, Postfach 50 (1991)
5. Bozdal, M., Samie, M., Jennions, I.: A survey on can bus protocol: attacks, challenges, and potential solutions. In: 2018 International Conference on Computing, Electronics & Communications Engineering (iCCECE), pp. 201–205 (2018). https://doi.org/10.1109/iCCECOME.2018.8658720
6. Carsten, P., Andel, T.R., Yampolskiy, M., McDonald, J.T.: In-vehicle networks: attacks, vulnerabilities, and proposed solutions. In: Proceedings of the 10th Annual Cyber and Information Security Research Conference. CISR 2015. Association for Computing Machinery, New York, NY, USA (2015). https://doi.org/10.1145/2746266.2746267, https://doi.org/10.1145/2746266.2746267
7. Cervin, A.: Improved scheduling of control tasks. In: Proceedings of 11th Euromicro Conference on Real-Time Systems. Euromicro RTS 1999, pp. 4–10 (1999). https://doi.org/10.1109/EMRTS.1999.777444
8. Cho, K.T., Shin, K.G.: Error handling of in-vehicle networks makes them vulnerable. In: Proceedings of the 2016 ACM SIGSAC Conference on Computer and Communications Security, pp. 1044–1055 (2016)
9. Di Natale, M., Zeng, H., Giusto, P., Ghosal, A.: Understanding and using the controller area network communication protocol: theory and practice. Springer Science & Business Media (2012)

10. Dubey, A., Karsai, G., Abdelwahed, S.: Compensating for timing jitter in computing systems with general-purpose operating systems. In: 2009 IEEE International Symposium on Object/Component/Service-Oriented Real-Time Distributed Computing, pp. 55–62 (2009). https://doi.org/10.1109/ISORC.2009.28

11. Enev, M., Takakuwa, A., Koscher, K., Kohno, T.: Automobile driver fingerprinting. Proc. Privacy Enhancing Technol. **2016**, 34–50 (2016)

12. Goswami, D., et al.: Challenges in automotive cyber-physical systems design. In: 2012 International Conference on Embedded Computer Systems (SAMOS), pp. 346–354 (2012). https://doi.org/10.1109/SAMOS.2012.6404199

13. Groza, B., Murvay, P.S.: Security solutions for the controller area network: bringing authentication to in-vehicle networks. IEEE Veh. Technol. Mag. **13**(1), 40–47 (2018). https://doi.org/10.1109/MVT.2017.2736344

14. Haas, R.E., Möller, D.P.F.: Automotive connectivity, cyber attack scenarios and automotive cyber security. In: 2017 IEEE International Conference on Electro Information Technology (EIT), pp. 635–639 (2017). https://doi.org/10.1109/EIT.2017.8053441

15. Hu, T.: Deterministic and flexible communication for real-time embedded systems (2015)

16. Imai, R., Kubo, R.: Introducing jitter buffers in networked control systems with communication disturbance observer under time-varying communication delays. In: IECON 2015–41st Annual Conference of the IEEE Industrial Electronics Society, pp. 002956–002961 (2015). https://doi.org/10.1109/IECON.2015.7392552

17. Koscher, K., et al.: Experimental security analysis of a modern automobile. In: 2010 IEEE Symposium on Security and Privacy, pp. 447–462. IEEE (2010)

18. Lluesma, M., Cervin, A., Balbastre, P., Ripoll, I., Crespo, A.: Jitter evaluation of real-time control systems. In: 12th IEEE International Conference on Embedded and Real-Time Computing Systems and Applications (RTCSA 2006), pp. 257–260 (2006). https://doi.org/10.1109/RTCSA.2006.41

19. Meissner, W.: ffi—RubyGems.org (2021). https://rubygems.org/gems/ffi/

20. Nanz, S., Furia, C.A.: A comparative study of programming languages in Rosetta code. In: 2015 IEEE/ACM 37th IEEE International Conference on Software Engineering, vol. 1, pp. 778–788 (2015). https://doi.org/10.1109/ICSE.2015.90

21. Palanca, A., Evenchick, E., Maggi, F., Zanero, S.: A stealth, selective, link-layer denial-of-service attack against automotive networks. In: DIMVA (2017)

22. PEAK-System: PCAN-USB: can interface for USB (2022). https://www.peak-system.com/PCAN-USB.199.0.html?&L=1

23. Pozzobon, E., de, Weiss, N.: A survey on media access solutions for can penetration testing (2018)

24. Ramamritham, K., Shen, C., Gonzalez, O., Sen, S., Shirgurkar, S.: Using windows NT for real-time applications: experimental observations and recommendations. In: Proceedings. Fourth IEEE Real-Time Technology and Applications Symposium (Cat. No.98TB100245), pp. 102–111 (1998). https://doi.org/10.1109/RTTAS.1998.683193

25. Roque, A.S., Jazdi, N., Freitas, E.P., Pereira, C.E.: Performance analysis of in-vehicle distributed control systems applying a real-time jitter monitor. In: 2020 IEEE 18th International Conference on Industrial Informatics (INDIN), vol. 1, pp. 663–668 (2020). https://doi.org/10.1109/INDIN45582.2020.9442081

26. Smith, C.: Exiting the matrix: introducing Metasploit's hardware bridge (2017). https://www.rapid7.com/blog/post/2017/02/02/exiting-the-matrix/

Passive User Authentication Utilizing Consecutive Touch Action Features for IIoT Systems

Guozhu Zhao[1,2], Pinchang Zhang[3(✉)], Yulong Shen[4(✉)], and Xiaohong Jiang[1]

[1] Future University Hakodate, Hakodate, Hokkaido 041-8655, Japan
[2] Chuzhou University, Chuzhou 239000, Anhui, China
[3] Nanjing University of Posts and Telecommunications,
Nanjing 210023, Jiangsu, China
zpcap0505238@163.com
[4] Xidian University, Xi'an 710071, Shaanxi, China
ylshen@mail.xidian.edu.cn

Abstract. We propose a continuous and non-intrusive passive authentication method for the Industrial Internet of Things (IIoT) systems, based on user consecutive touch screen actions during routine work processes. In particular, utilizing both the temporal-variation characteristics of the user sequential touch screen actions and the constructed features from cumulative touch screen action trajectory images (CTTIs), we propose a novel touch-interaction based passive authentication method for IIoT systems. We use the Hidden Markov Model to characterize temporal-variation characteristics of user sequential touch screen actions, and also employ the PatternNet to depict the features of cumulative touch screen action trajectory images. Extensive experiments are conducted to illustrate the authentication performance in terms of equal-error rate and accuracy for resisting against impersonation attacks.

Keywords: Passive authentication · Hidden Markov Model · PatternNet · Continuous authentication

1 Introduction

Industrial Internet of Things (IIoT) is the extension and use of the internet of things (IoT) in industrial areas. By integrating cloud computing, big data and intelligent algorithms, IIoT has revolutionized world manufacturing patterns and becomes highly promising to promote the global collaboration, smart manufacturing and software defined manufacturing in the global manufacturing industry [1–3]. In the practical application of the IIoT, a large number of users access the cloud services or data centres through mobile smart devices to send/receive the data necessary to complete industrial production. Notice that the IIoT system stores and generates massive amounts of sensitive data in real time and users

C. Su et al. (Eds.): SciSec 2022, LNCS 13580, pp. 276–284, 2022.
https://doi.org/10.1007/978-3-031-17551-0_18

in the system generally have highly diverse authority right, making the efficient user authentication a challenging issue in such systems.

By now, some research efforts have been devoted to the development of passive authentication solutions for IIoT systems [4–6]. The authors in [7] conduct sufficient experiments to illustrate the discriminability and robustness for the intrinsic features from consecutive operation actions (e.g., walking, scanning, touch screen, and photographing-uploading), the Hidden Markov Model is constructed to determine user identities utilizing one-class classification technique. In [8], the authors proposed a passive user authentication method by using motion-sensor behaviors from user daily interaction with mobile phones, and provide both qualitative and quantitative analysis to verify the effectiveness of the proposed approach. The literature [9] exhibits 30 behavioral touch features extracted from raw touchscreen logs. Utilizing the 30 touchcreen features, a SVM-based classification technology is applied to verify user identities continuously.

The existing literatures show that touch-based features can effectively characterize user identities and realize user identity authentication in the corresponding specific scenarios. However, notice that the existing touch-based authentication solutions ignore touch screen features of cumulative consecutive touch screen action trajectories from user interaction with the smart mobile device, causing the existing methods to lack an important dimension in characterizing user identities using touchalytics for practical applications of IIoT systems. The main contributions of this paper are summarized as follows:

– We provide extensive experiment results to demonstrate that in IIoT systems the cumulative consecutive touch screen action trajectories from routine work processes exhibit a good discriminability and stability in discriminating user identities.
– To enhance the reliability and stability of the proposed authentication method, we construct a novel touch-based feature to characterize user identities for IIoT scenarios. We reproduce superposition effect of cumulative touch screen action trajectories as an image, namely the cumulative touch screen action trajectory image (CTTI), and extract user identity features using the SURF (Speeded Up Robust Features) algorithm from the CTTI.
– Utilizing Hidden Markov Model and PatternNet model respectively, both the time-varying features and CTTI features are employed to determine user identities in IIoT scenarios.

2 Consecutive Touch Actions Based Passive Authentication

2.1 User Identity Characterization Based on Time-Varying Touch Action Sequence

Time-Varying Touch Screen Action Events. Unlike daily interaction with personal mobile smart phone, a user generally interacts with the industrial smart mobile terminal according to the requirements of the work instruction manual(WIM) in IIoT scenarios. A WIM records in detail how the user uses the industrial APP embedded in the smart mobile terminal, and specifies the operation flow and general operation sequences to complete industrial production tasks. For example, a WIM for controlling the opening of the motor is: open the motor control page, click the motor self-test button, view the self-test message, self-test abnormal processing, abnormal diagnosis, confirm the motor intact, and turning on the motor switch. To finish specific industrial production business according to the WIM, a user usually performs some touch screen actions on the touchscreen of smart mobile terminal such as app page turning, browsing messages, viewing/confirming commands and switching contents.

It is noticed that a specific WIM is usually accompanied with the mutual switching of user touch screen actions. The resulting touch screen action sequences from different users can reflect different levels of temporal variations due to the individual difference of understanding ability (of the same WIM), operation habits, reaction speed and posture of holding the mobile terminal. In this paper, the HMM is used to model the temporal-variation patterns of user sequential touch screen actions, and thereby characterize the user's identity during the IIoT work processes.

Sequential Touch Action Events. During user routine work processes, the touch screen actions generally consist of sliding up, sliding down, sliding left, sliding right. To obtain fine-gained touch action sequence features, we employ the k-means clustering algorithm [10] to divide the sliding up action into three styles, i.e. sliding up slowly denoted by T_{sus}, sliding up normally T_{sun}, sliding up fast T_{suf}. Similar to the sliding up action, we can obtain three sliding down actions, three sliding left actions and three sliding right actions, i.e. $T_{sds}, T_{sdn}, T_{sdf}, T_{sls}, T_{sln}, T_{slf}, T_{srs}, T_{srn}$ and T_{srf}, respectively.

To construct sequential touch screen event sequences when a user works according to a specific WIM in IIoT scenarios, we employ $\Phi = \{T_{sus}, T_{sun}, T_{suf}, T_{sds}, T_{sdn}, T_{sdf}, T_{sls}, T_{sln}, T_{slf}, T_{srs}, T_{srn}, T_{srf}\}$ to denote the set of touch actions and use $\Psi = \{\mathbb{S}_1, \mathbb{S}_2, \ldots, \mathbb{S}_N\}$ to denote the set of steps (e.g. open the motor control page, click the motor self-test button, view the self-test message) in the WIM, where N is the number of steps in the WIM.

Training of HMM. We use $O^d = (o_1, \cdots, o_T)$ to denote the d-th observation sequence (i.e. touch screen action sequence) from user routine work processes, where $o_i \in \Phi$ denotes the i-th touch screen action in O^d; T is the length of O_d, $d = 1, 2, \ldots, D$ and D is the number of observation sequences. During user routine work processes, the steps user conducted according to the WIM active the corresponding observation touch screen actions in Φ. Hence, Ψ is regarded as hidden state set, and $Z = \{z_1, z_2, \ldots, z_T\}$ is employed to denote the state transition sequence with $z_i \in \Psi$ and $i = 1, \ldots, T$. Let us consider the HMM $\lambda = (\pi, A, B)$ parameterized by the initial state matrix π, the state transition matrix A, and the obfuscation matrix B, where $\pi = P(z_i = i)$, $A_{ij} = P(z_{t+1} = j | z_t = i)$, $B_i(j) = P(o_{t=j} | z_t = i)$.

Let $\chi = (O^{(1)}, O^{(2)}, \ldots, O^{(D)})$, where $O^{(i)} = (o_1^{(i)}, \cdots, o_T^{(i)})$, $o_j^{(i)} \in \Phi$, $i = 1, \ldots, D$, and D representing the number of touch action sequences. Because we can not give the hidden variables $z_j^{(i)}$ ($z_j^{(i)} \in Z$) for each $o_j^{(i)}$, Baum-Welch algorithm [11] is used to estimate λ^* from only χ, where $\lambda^* = \mathrm{argmax}_\lambda P(\chi; Z; \lambda)$ and λ is the learned parameterization of HMM from dataset χ with D touch screen sequences. Applying Baum-Welch algorithm, we can obtain the parameters π, A and B in λ by repeating the following steps until convergence:

$$\text{Step1}: \text{Compute} \quad Q(\lambda, \lambda^s) = \sum_{z \in Z} \log[P(\chi; Z; \lambda)] P(z | \chi; \lambda^s), \tag{1a}$$

$$\text{Step2}: \text{Set} \quad \lambda^{s+1} = \underset{\lambda}{\mathrm{argmax}}\, Q(\lambda, \lambda^s). \tag{1b}$$

User Identity Classification Based on HMM. To determine user identities during user routine work processes, we first collect user touch screen action dataset $\mathbb{D} = (\chi^{(1)}, \chi^{(2)}, \ldots, \chi^{(N)})$, where $\chi^{(i)}$ represents the touch action dataset from the i-th user, $i = 1, \ldots, N$, and N is the number of users in the IIoT scenario. We then construct a HMM for each user to obtain a set of HMMs $\boldsymbol{\lambda} = (\lambda^{(1)}, \lambda^{(2)}, \ldots, \lambda^{(N)})$ with $\lambda^{(i)}$ representing the HMM of the i-th user. Finally, according to (1) we can obtain the parameters of each HMM in $\boldsymbol{\lambda}$ by iterations.

For the i-th user to be authenticated, we collect his touch screen action sequence $O_i = (o_1, o_2, \cdots, o_\nu)$ with $o_j \in \Phi$, $j = 1, \ldots, \nu$, under the length of the operation sequence ν. Using the forward algorithm [12], the probability $P(O_i | \lambda^{(i)})$ is then calculated to authenticate the identity of the user under a given threshold.

2.2 User Identity Characterization Based on Cumulative Touch Screen Action Trajectories

Construction of CTTI. The HMM can only capture the time-varying features of sequential touch action sequences to determine the identities of users. However, some sophisticated imposers may record the speed, length and angle of the touch screen actions from legitimate users, and launch attacks by machine learning methods to impersonate the time-varying touch action sequences. To enhance the reliability and stability of the proposed authentication method, we use the touch trajectories generated by the accumulated touch screen actions to further confirm user identities.

In the observation touch screen sequence $O_i = (o_1, o_2, \cdots, o_\nu)$, each touch action generates a trajectory in the touchscreen of the mobile terminal. We record the coordinates of the touch trajectory on the mobile terminal screen and reconstruct the touch trajectory on the authentication server. Along with the touch actions happen, we construct all the touch trajectories in O_i. Then, we can obtain a CTTI denoted by F_i consists of the trajectories of touch actions in O_i. Corresponding to D touch action sequences from the i-th user $\chi_i = (O_i^{(1)}, O_i^{(2)}, \ldots, O_i^{(D)})$, we can obtain his CTTI set $\mathbb{F}_i = (F_i^{(1)}, F_i^{(2)}, \ldots, F_i^{(D)})$. Supposing there are N users in the IIoT scenario, we can obtain CTTI set of all users denoted by $\S = \{\mathbb{F}_1, \mathbb{F}_2, \ldots, \mathbb{F}_N\}$.

Feature Extraction and Dimensionality Reduction. The SURF (Speeded Up Robust Features) algorithm is a fast and robust algorithm for similarity invariant representation and comparison of images, which has been widely used in 3D reconstruction, image registration, and object recognition [13]. Applying the SURF algorithm, we first mine the 'interest points' of CTTIs for each element in $\S$, which are distinctive locations of CTTIs generated by the spatial distribution of the user's inherent touch habits on the mobile terminal screen. As shown in Fig. 1, we list the 'interest points' of CTTIs from three users. We can see from Fig. 1 that different users exhibit distinctive corners, blobs, and T-junctions in their CTTIs.

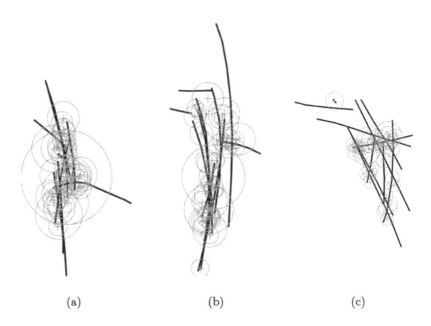

(a)   (b)   (c)

Fig. 1. The CTTI and corresponding distinctive locations of 'interest points' from user interaction with the mobile terminal screen for the same WIM. (a) CTTI and interest points from user1. (b) CTTI and interest points from user2. (c) CTTI and interest points from user3.

Then, the neighbourhood of every interest point corresponding to the CTTI is represented by a feature vector denoted by $V = (v_1, v_2, \ldots, v_n)$ with n representing the number of interest points. Finally, we apply Principal Component Analysis (PCA) [14] algorithm to reduce the dimensionality of the extracted feature vector V and obtain the lower dimensional features of CTTI denoted by s. Let us use $\mathbb{S}_i = (s_i^{(1)}, s_i^{(2)}, \ldots, s_i^{(D)})$ to denote the lower dimensional features of the i-th user corresponding to his CTTI set $\mathbb{F}_i = (F_i^{(1)}, F_i^{(2)}, \ldots, F_i^{(D)})$.

Classification Based on Patternnet. PatternNet (Pattern recognition network) [15] is a feedforward pattern recognition neural network consisting of a hidden layer, a training function and a performance function. We adopt PatternNet to realize the classification of CTTI features by setting hidden layer size 20, training function 'trainscg' (Scaled conjugate gradient backpropagation) and performance functio 'crossentropy'. In the training phase of the PatternNet model, we fist construct training sample set $F_{(i)} = \{(\mathbb{F}_i^{(1)}, L^{(i)}), \ldots, (\mathbb{F}_i^{(j)}, L^{(i)}), \ldots, (\mathbb{F}_i^{(D)}, L^{(i)})\}$, where $(\mathbb{F}_i^{(j)}, L^{(i)})$ and $L^{(i)}$ represent the CTTI features for the j-th touch screen action sequences of the i-th user and the label of the i-th user, respectively. We then use $F = \{F_{(1)}, \ldots, F_{(N)}\}$ to denote the set of all the training samples with N representing the number of users. In the training phase, F is used to train the PatternNet and the trained PatternNet model is stored in the IIoT system. Finally, in the classification phase the trained PatternNet model is employed to user identity classification and authentication for unknown users.

2.3 User Authentication Based on both HMM and PatternNet

Let us consider the observation touch screen action sequence $O_I = (o_1, o_2, \cdots, o_\nu)$ and its corresponding CTTI feature F_I for a claimed identity I. Our authentication method determines if $(I, [O_I, F_I])$ belongs to class ϖ_1 or ϖ_2 by

$$(I, [O_I, F_I]) \in \begin{cases} \varpi_1, & \text{HMM}(O_I) = I, \text{PatternNet}(F_I) = I, \\ \varpi_2, & \text{otherwise}, \end{cases} \tag{2}$$

where $\text{HMM}(O_I)$ represents $P(O_I|\lambda^I) > \varphi$ and φ is predefined threshold in the IIoT system; $\text{PatternNet}(F_I)$ is the classification result of F_I under the PatternNet model; ϖ_1 indicates that the claim is true (a legitimate user) and ϖ_2 indicates that the claim is false (an impostor).

3 Experiment and Analysis

We conduct extensive experiments to investigate the feasibility and resisting impersonation attack performance of the proposed continuous touch-based authentication method.

3.1 Influence of the Number of Touch Screen Actions

To explore how the number of touch actions (in a touch action sequence) l would affect the performance of the proposed touch-based passive authentication approach, we adopt 200 touch action sequences from 10 users in IIoT scenarios and present in Fig. 2(a) the impact of l on EERs by varying l from 6 to 18 in the IIoT scenarios. As shown in Fig. 2(a), the EERs when authenticating users utilize both the time-varying and CTTI feautes are always smaller than that of using single feature (i.e. only using time-varying or CTTI feature). At a level of 6 to 14 strokes, the EER values of the HMM&&PatternNet method converges to a range between 6.7% and 7.6% and stays there up to using 18 touch screen actions (e.g. $l = 18$).

3.2   Performance of Resisting Impersonation Attacks

To investigate the performance of resisting impersonation attacks of the proposed methods, we present in Fig. 2(b) the impacts of l on authentication accuracy based on 10 users. The 10 users are divided into two groups equally and the members in the two group impersonate each other in pairs. We can see from Fig. 2(b) that the performance of resisting impersonation attacks for HMM&&PatternNet significantly outperforms that of others (HMM and PatternNet), and the authentication accuracy of all the 3 cases (HMM, PatternNet and HMM&&PatternNet) monotonously increases as the number of touch screen actions increases from 6 to 18. It indicates that increasing the number of touch actions can effectively improve the accuracy of proposed user authentication approach, so as to better resist impersonation attacks in the IIoT scenario.

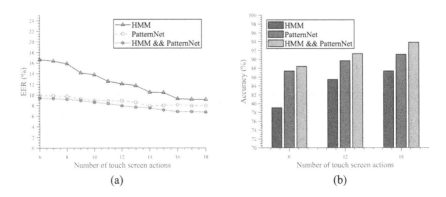

Fig. 2. Authentication performance analysis of the proposed method. (a) Authentication performance in terms of EERs. (b) Authentication performance of resisting impersonation attacks.

4   Conclusion

By exploiting the consecutive touch action features from user routine work processes in IIoT scenarios, we proposed a novel passive authentication method for such systems. We demonstrated that the new authentication method enables a flexible authentication performance control to be achieved by adjusting the system parameters like the length of the touch actions in a touch action sequence. Thus, the proposed authentication method is expected to serve as a good enhancement and complement to the traditional authentication solutions for IIoT systems.

Acknowledgements. This work was supported in part by the Academic Funding Project for Top Talents of Disciplines (Majors) in Universities of Anhui Province of China (No. gxbjZD2021080), the Key Project of Science Research in Universities of Anhui Province of China (No. KJ2021A1066, KJ2021A1067), the National Key R&D Program of China (No. 2018YFE0207600, 2018YFB2100403), the National Natural Science Foundation of China (No. U1736216, 61972308) and the Natural Science Basic Research Program of Shaanxi (No. 2019JC-17).

References

1. Gilchrist, A.: Industry 4.0: the Industrial Internet of Things. Apress, Berkeley, CA (2016). https://doi.org/10.1007/978-1-4842-2047-4
2. Qiu, T., Chi, J., Zhou, X., Ning, Z., Atiquzzaman, M., Wu, D.O.: Edge computing in Industrial Internet of Things: architecture, advances and challenges. IEEE Commun. Surveys Tutorials **22**(4), 2462–2488 (2020)
3. Mumtaz, S., Bo, A., Al-Dulaimi, A., Tsang, K.: Guest editorial 5G and beyond mobile technologies and applications for Industrial IoT (IIoT). IEEE Trans. Industr. Inf. **14**(6), 2588–2591 (2018)
4. Shahzad, M., Singh, M.P.: Continuous authentication and authorization for the Internet of Things. IEEE Internet Comput. **21**(2), 86–90 (2017)
5. Abuhamad, M., Abuhmed, T., Mohaisen, D., Nyang, D.: AUToSen: deep-learning-based implicit continuous authentication using smartphone sensors. IEEE Internet Things J. **7**(6), 5008–5020 (2020)
6. Qin, Z., et al.: Learning-aided user identification using smartphone sensors for smart homes. IEEE Internet Things J. **6**(5), 7760–7772 (2019)
7. Zhao, G., Zhang, P., Shen, Y., Jiang, X.: Passive user authentication utilizing behavioral biometrics for IIoT systems. IEEE Internet Things J. **9**(14), 12783–12798 (2022). https://ieeexplore.ieee.org/document/9663152
8. Shen, C., Li, Y., Chen, Y., Guan, X., Maxion, R.A.: Performance analysis of multi-motion sensor behavior for active smartphone authentication. IEEE Trans. Inf. Forensics Secur. **13**(1), 48–62 (2018)
9. Frank, M., Biedert, R., Ma, E., Martinovic, I., Song, D.: Touchalytics: on the applicability of touchscreen input as a behavioral biometric for continuous authentication. IEEE Trans. Inf. Forensics Secur. **8**(1), 136–148 (2013)
10. Hartigan, J.A., Wong, M.A.: A k-means clustering algorithm. J. Royal Stat. Soc. Ser. c (Appl. Stat.) **28**(1), 100–108 (1979)
11. Baggenstoss, P.: A modified Baum-Welch algorithm for hidden Markov models with multiple observation spaces. IEEE Trans. Speech Audio Process. **9**(4), 411–416 (2001)
12. Rabiner, L., Juang, B.: An introduction to hidden Markov models. IEEE ASSP Mag. **3**(1), 4–16 (1986)

13. Bay, H., Tuytelaars, T., Van Gool, L.: SURF: speeded up robust features. In: Leonardis, A., Bischof, H., Pinz, A. (eds.) ECCV 2006. LNCS, vol. 3951, pp. 404–417. Springer, Heidelberg (2006). https://doi.org/10.1007/11744023_32

14. He, R., Hu, B.-G., Zheng, W.-S., Kong, X.-W.: Robust principal component analysis based on maximum correntropy criterion. IEEE Trans. Image Process. **20**(6), 1485–1494 (2011)

15. Li, H., Ellis, J.G., Zhang, L., Chang, S.-F.: PatternNet: visual pattern mining with deep neural network. In: Proceedings of the 2018 ACM on International Conference on Multimedia Retrieval, pp. 291–299 (2018)

Malware

Malware Classification Based on Semi-Supervised Learning

Yu Ding[1,2], XiaoYu Zhang[1(✉)], BinBin Li[1], Jian Xing[1,2,3], Qian Qiang[1,2,4], ZiSen Qi[1,2], MengHan Guo[1], SiYu Jia[1,2], and HaiPing Wang[1,2]

[1] Institute of Information Engineering, Chinese Academy of Sciences, Beijing, China
{dingyu,zhangxiaoyu}@iie.ac.cn
[2] School of Cyber Security, University of Chinese Academy of Sciences, Beijing, China
[3] National Computer Network Emergency Response Technical Team/Coordination Center of China Xinjiang Branch, Urumqi, China
[4] National Computer Network Emergency Response Technical Team/Coordination Center of China, Beijing, China

Abstract. With the rapid evolution of malware in the past few years, it caused serious threats and damage to network security. To handle this, researchers began to propose effective classification approaches for various malware variants. However, these widely-used methods based on deep learning are in fully supervised manner, which suffers from two inevitable problems: 1) time-consuming: manually labeling data before training fully-supervised models require huge manual efforts. 2) resource-redundancy: a large amount of unlabeled data is not fully used, resulting in a resource waste. To solve the above problems, in this paper we propose a Malware Classification Method based on Semi-Supervised Learning namely MCM-SSL, which divides the model training into a pre-train stage using unlabeled data and a finetune stage using labeled data. The method proposed in this paper effectively uses a large amount of unlabeled data, and only needs a small amount of labeled data to achieve excellent performance. As a result, our method achieves an accuracy of 90.51% on the open-source Virus-MNIST dataset, which is superior to recent state-of-the-art methods. We also verify the generality and robustness of our method using a variety of common neural network algorithms. For the same algorithm, the accuracy of the pre-trained model is on average 2.4% higher than the model without pre-training.

Keywords: Malware classification · Semi-supervised learning · Contrastive learning

1 Introduction

Malware (malicious software) is a software program that enters into a user's computer with the intent to cause damage or steal sensitive information [8]. According to Kaspersky Lab's 2021 annual report "Kaspersky Security Bulletin

C. Su et al. (Eds.): SciSec 2022, LNCS 13580, pp. 287–301, 2022.
https://doi.org/10.1007/978-3-031-17551-0_19

2021. Statistics" [1], 15.45% of internet user computers worldwide experienced at least one Malware-class attack. Ransomware Trojans alone attacked 366,256 unique users, including 92,863 corporate users (excluding SMBs) and 12,699 users associated with small and medium-sized businesses. And Kaspersky identified more than 13,905 ransomware modifications and detected 33 new families.

In order to resist the harm of malware, machine learning and deep learning are often used to mine the identified features of malware and classify them based on the identified features of the malware. Due to the rapid evolution of malware, new malware variants are constantly developing. Despite the promising results of these methods aforementioned, the evolving malware over time has resulted in degrading performance of those classification models [24].

To solve this problem, the most common approach is to retrain the model periodically, which requires a large amount of labeled data for training and validation. However, acquiring so much labeled data is quite difficult, and time-consuming manual analysis and annotation must be performed. The large amount of unlabeled data obtained is not used effectively. Since labeled data is expensive and difficult to obtain, while unlabeled data is abundant and cheap, many researchers [5,7,11,16,17,21–23] have used semi-supervised methods such as pseudo-labeling to solve this problem.

In light of this background, We propose a novel malware classification method based on semi-supervised learning. The model first converts the malware binary to grayscale, then pre-train the neural network with unlabeled data, and finally finetune the model with labeled data. The main contributions are as follows:

- We propose a novel malware classification method named MCM-SSL based on semi-supervised learning, which solves the dependence of model training on a large amount of labeled data, and reduces the workload of manual data labeling. The effectiveness and robustness of the proposed method are verified by our experiments.
- The MCM-SSL method proposed in this paper is divided into two stages: pre-train and finetune. The pre-train stage could use unlabeled data to learn generic representations of malware samples, and the finetune stage only needs a small amount of labeled data to learn malware classification capabilities.
- Multiple neural network algorithms are used to train the malware classification model on the open source Virus-MNIST dataset. The accuracy of all algorithms is about 90%, and the best performance reaches 90.51%, which verifies the robustness of the proposed method.
- The pre-training process proposed in this method can improve the performance of the model. For the same algorithm, the accuracy of the pre-trained model is on average 2.4% higher than the model without pre-training.

2   Related Work

Malware classification has been a research hotspot in academia for a long time. Classic techniques for it can be categorized into three main types: Static, Dynamic, and Hybrid analysis [18]. Static analysis refers to analyzing the

Portable Executable files (PE files) without running them. Dynamic analysis executes infected files in a simulated environment using virtual machines or emulators to analyze their malicious functionality [12]. Hybrid analysis combines both static and dynamic methods for analysis improvement.

The advantage of static analysis is that it is fast and secure in malware analysis, but the disadvantage is that it cannot deal with the code obfuscation of malware. Static analysis is usually performed using binary grayscale images of malware samples, disassembly files, code, etc. Sriram S et al. [19] proposed a Spatial Pyramid Pooling Network (SPPNet) based on malware variant detection model. Malware binaries are converted to 8-bit vectors, which are then converted to grayscale images by treating each vector as a pixel value, and finally the grayscale images are classified using SPPNET. Tan Gao et al. [7] proposed a malware classification model based on malware visualization, and co-training of classifiers. The malware is transformed into grayscale images by visual methods, then a fusion method based on canonical correlation analysis(CCA) is utilized to fuse the local and global features extracted from the gray image to reduce time cost and improve feature relevance;

Dynamic analysis discloses the malwares' natural behavior, which is more resilient to static analysis. However, it is time intensive and resource consuming, thus elevating the scalability issues [6]. It has been proved to be effective against various code obfuscation techniques and newly released (zero-day) malware. Zhaoqi Zhang et al. [25] proposed a novel feature engineering method and a new deep learning architecture for malware detection over the API call sequence. They used Cuckoo (an open source binary behavior analysis tool) to run PE files and collect execution logs such as API calls. Samaneh Mahdavifar et al. [11] proposed an Android malware category classification system based on semi-supervised deep neural networks. And They trained deep neural networks in a semi-supervised manner with pseudo-labels.

Hybrid analysis gathers information about malware from static analysis and dynamic analysis, which combines the advantages of static and dynamic analysis [18]. Chao Ding et al. [4] proposed a hybrid analysis-based approach to Android malware detection and classification. They first analyzed malware using static features such as permissions and intent, and then further analyzed low-trust samples using dynamic features such as images of network traffic. The combination of static and dynamic analysis methods can effectively solve the problem that low-trust samples cannot be correctly detected.

3   Methodology

The overview of the proposed malware family classification method is shown in Fig. 1. This method first converts malicious sample data into grayscale images, and then completes the training of the model through two stages: pre-training and finetune. In the pre-train stage, the neural network model is pre-trained using unlabeled data, so that the model learns a generic representation of malware samples. During the finetune stage, the model is fine-tuned in a supervised manner using labeled data.

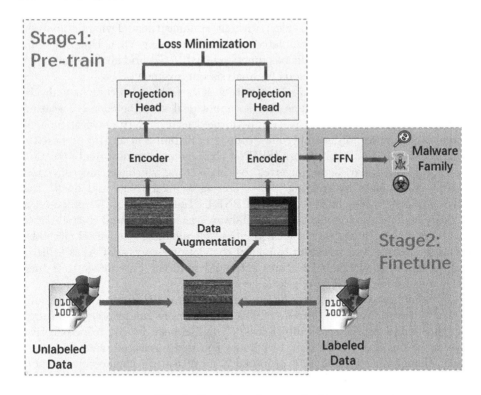

Fig. 1. Overview of our method.

3.1 Data Source

Portable Executable is a file format that is used by windows executables, object code, and DLLs. The PE file format contains a header followed by a series of sections. The PE file header contains metadata about the executable itself. It contains at least DOS stubs, signatures, the architecture of the file's code, timestamps, pointers, and various flags. The method proposed in this paper is a malware classification method based on Portable Executable (PE) file header. Different families of malware are designed for different purposes, which leads to their different structures. The PE file format is the most common file format for malware [15]. Therefore, malware could be classified using the information stored in the PE file header and the structural characteristics of the file.

3.2 Data Pre-processing

Inspired by the work of Nataraj et al. [13], the problem of malware classification problem could be transformed into an image classification problem. We visualize malware binary files as grayscale images. Figure 2 demonstrates the process of converting malware binary files to grayscale image. The malware binary is first divided into groups of 8 bit binary vectors, then the 8 bit binary vectors are converted to decimal values (for example, 8 binary digits [00000000] are converted to decimal values of [0], [11111111] to the decimal value [255]) [9]. Since the size of each PE file header is different, the length of the decimal vector is also different. In order to ensure that the length of each sample decimal vector is consistent, we take the first N values of the decimal vector as the final vector. Vectors of length less than N, padded with zeros. At last, the resulting decimal vector is reshaped to a 2D matrix and visualized as a grayscale image.

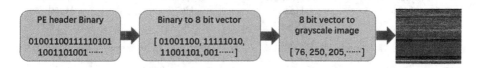

Fig. 2. PE file header as a graysacale image.

3.3 Pre-train

In order to make full use of unlabeled data resources, reduce the dependence of model training on labeled data. Inspired by contrastive learning [2], we present pre-train stage to learn generic representations of grayscale images by maximizing the consistency between different transformed views of the same image and minimizing the consistency between different transformed views of the image. It can be understood as: by making the transformed views of the same image "attract" each other, and let the transformed views of different images "repel" each other, so that the neural network learns the general representation of the image.

The pre-train stage is divided into three key steps: Data Augmentation, Encoding, and Loss Minimization of Representations. The overview of the pre-train stage is shown in Fig. 3.

- **Data Augmentation**: As shown in Fig. 3, the purpose of data augmentation is to construct self-supervised samples. Data augmentation draws samples from the training set and transforms each sample image twice using a combination of data augmentation (such as cropping, panning, zooming). Two augmented images of the same image are a positive pair, and augmented images of different images are a negative pair. The augmented positive and negative image pairs are used for subsequent Encoding.
  Different from the general Contrastive Learning method, we did not use flip, Gaussian Noise, Rotation, Color Jittering, etc. in the data augmentation stage. If the above data augmentation methods are used, the value of the image pixel will be greatly changed, which is equivalent to modifying the content of the PE header file. These augmentation method are not applicable in the malware classification scenario.

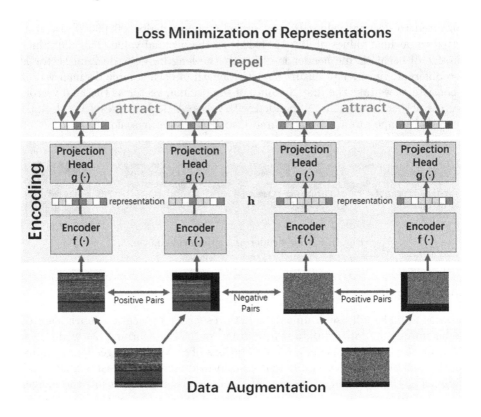

Fig. 3. Overview of pre-train stage.

- **Encoding**: Encoding could convert images into feature space vector representation and learn high-order features of images. The Encoding process is to use a neural network-based encoder to extract the representation vector of the augmented data, and then input the representation vector into a set of Feed Forward Network(FFN) called projection heads to convert the data to another space. Research by Ting Chen et al. [3] shows that using a projection head can improve performance.

In this paper, we use ResNet, DenseNet, MobileNet, VGG and other neural network models as encoders, use 2 FFN layers as projection head, and the activation function is Relu.

The encoder is represented by the function $h = f(x)$, and the projection head is represented by $z = g(h)$, then the Encoding process can be represented by the following formula:

$$z_i = g(f(x_i)) = W^{(2)} Relu(W^{(1)} f(x_i) + B^{(1)}) + B^{(2)} \tag{1}$$

where z_i represents the output of Encoding, $W^{(1)} + B^{(1)}$ and $W^{(2)} + B^{(2)}$ represent the two FFN layers of the projection head.

– **Loss Minimization of Representations**: Loss Minimization of Representations completes the learning of the $g(f(x))$ parameters in Encoding. The loss function is constructed based on the similarity of the representation vectors of the two images output from Encoding to train the parameters of Encoding model. In this method, we use the cosine similarity to measure the similarity of the two representation vectors, which is represented by $similarity(z_i, z_j)$. Cosine similarity measures the similarity of two vectors based on the angle between the two vectors in the feature space. The smaller the angle between the two vectors in the feature space, the more similar they are. The operation can be expressed as the following equation:

$$similarity(z_i, z_j) = \frac{z_i \cdot z_j}{|z_i| \times |z_j|} \tag{2}$$

We use NT-Xent (Normalized Temperature-Scaled Cross-Entropy Loss) to construct the loss function. With a mini-batch of augmented examples, the contrastive loss between a pair of positive example i, j (augmented from the same image) is given as follows:

$$\ell_{i,j}^{NT-Xent} = -log \frac{\exp(similarity(z_i, z_j)/\tau)}{\sum_{k=1}^{2N} \mathbb{1}_{[k \neq i]} \exp(imilarity(z_i, z_j/\tau))} \tag{3}$$

where $\mathbb{1}_{[k \neq i]} \in \{0, 1\}$ is an indicator function that takes value 1 when the event $(k \neq i)$ happens and value 0 when the event does not happen. $\mathbb{1}_{[k \neq i]}$ excludes the similarity of the sample to itself. The τ is a scalar temperature parameter. The temperature parameter is used to determine how "spiky" a probability distribution is. If the temperature is low, we get a spiky distribution, one with a single or a few prominent peaks. If the temperature is high, we get a flat distribution with no prominent peaks. According to the research of Ting Chen et al. [2], $\tau = 0.1$ in this method.

3.4   Finetune

In the pre-train stage, the model has learned the general representation of PE file header grayscale images. In order for the model to learn malware classification capabilities, we present finetune stage. Finetune is a common approach to adapt task-independent pretrained networks to specific tasks. In this paper, the model trained in the pre-train stage is fine-tuned using a small number of labeled samples in a supervised manner. In the fine-tuning process, the projection head composed of two layers of FFN is removed, only the encoder is retained, and an FFN layer is added after the encoder, and the activation function is Softmax. It can be understood that only $f(\cdot)$ is used in the fine-tuning stage, and $g(\cdot)$ is not used. At the same time, the weight W of the FFN layer for malware family classification is added, and the fine-tuning process can be expressed by the following formula:

$$f(x_i) = Softmax(W f(x_i) + B) \tag{4}$$

We employ the standard cross entroy loss as the objective function. After finetune, we use the finetuned model (encoder+FFN) as the final malware sample classifier.

4   Experiments and Result

In this section, we systematically evaluated the effectiveness of our method using different baseline models and different parameters, and compared it with what we know of other researchers' methods. We performed two sets of experiments, the first set of experiments to evaluate the overall performance of our method, and the second set of experiments to evaluates the advantages of our method under a small number of labeled training samples.

4.1   Dataset

We performed this work using an open source dataset called Virus-MNIST, published by Noever and Noever [14]. This dataset presents an image classification dataset consisting of 10 executable code varieties and 51,880 examples (48,422 training and 3,454 test). Each image in the dataset is the first 1024 bytes of the PE header, and the image shape is (32,32,1). The grayscale image of this dataset sample is shown in Fig. 4. The dataset can be downloaded from the Kaggle[1] and Github[2].

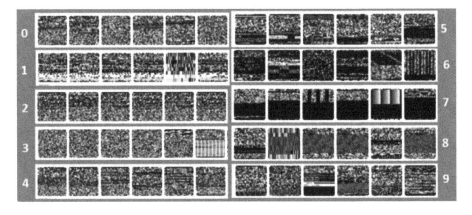

Fig. 4. Virus-MNIST contains 10 classes of samples, each sample is a grayscale image of size (32, 32, 1).

---

[1] https://www.kaggle.com/datamunge/virusmnist.
[2] https://github.com/reveondivad/virus-mnist.

4.2   Experiment Parameters

In the data augmentation process, we use RandomTranslation and Random-Zoom in keras.layers as data augmentation methods. We use ResNet, DenseNet, MobileNet, VGG and other neural network models as encoders. The size of the 2-layer FFN of the projection head is 1024. The epoch for pre-train is set to 200, the epoch for finetune and baseline models is set to 50, and the learning rate we use is 0.0001. We use accuracy, precision, recall, and F1-Score as performance evaluation metrics.

4.3   Result

In the two sets of experiments, we use the algorithm used by the encoder (without pre-train and finetune, and directly trained with labeled data) as the baseline model. These two sets of experiments were designed to answer two questions:

- **Experiment 1**: Verify that our proposed method has better performance on the problem of malware classification.
- **Experiment 2**: Verify that our proposed method has excellent performance using only a small amount of labeled data.

Table 1 and Table 2 present the performance of our method on two sets of experiments. The following subsections will illustrate the detailed experimental settings, and the comparison results of our method with the other scholars' methods.

Experiment 1. In this experiment, we use all the training datasets of the Virus-MNIST dataset to train our model, and use different neural network algorithms such as RestNet, DenseNet, MobileNet as the encoder. This experiment verifies the performance and robustness of our algorithm on different neural network algorithms.

As shown in Table 1, the encoder uses different neural network algorithms, all of the algorithms have excellent performance. The classification performance is best when encoder is ResNet50V2, with the accuracy rate of 90.51%, the precision rate of 90.08%, the recall rate of 90.51%, and the F1-Score of 90.19%.

As shown in Fig. 5 shows the normalized confusion matrix when encoder is ResNet50V2. Except for class 0 (which is a benign sample), the accuracy of all other classes has reached more than 85%.

Figure 6 shows the curve of accuracy and loss when the encoder is ResNet50V2. Due to the pre-training of the model in the pre-train stage, the model in the finetune stage can quickly achieve excellent performance. In addition, with the increase of epoch during finetune, the loss of the model increases slowly, and the accuracy also decreases slightly. This shows that the epoch of finetune should not be too many. Since there are fewer finetune samples used, too many epochs will make the encoder parameters of the pre-train deviate from the optimal value.

Table 1. The performance metrics of the first experiments.

Encoder algorithm	Baseline model				Our method			
	Accuracy	Prediction	Recall	F1-Score	Accuracy	Prediction	Recall	F1-Score
ResNet152V2	89.27%	87.86%	89.27%	88.18%	89.82%	89.54%	89.82%	89.63%
DenseNet201	88.06%	88.61%	88.06%	87.94%	90.28%	90.00%	90.28%	90.13%
ResNet152	84.27%	83.02%	84.27%	83.01%	90.37%	90.03%	90.37%	90.16%
DenseNet169	88.78%	88.38%	88.78%	88.19%	90.34%	89.78%	90.34%	89.70%
DenseNet121	90.34%	89.70%	90.34%	89.89%	90.43%	89.93%	90.43%	90.08%
ResNet101V2	87.07%	86.65%	87.07%	86.67%	90.05%	89.55%	90.05%	89.72%
ResNet101	85.25%	84.26%	85.25%	84.20%	90.23%	89.96%	90.23%	90.03%
ResNet50	89.01%	88.06%	89.01%	88.31%	90.23%	89.59%	90.23%	89.79%
ResNet50V2	89.36%	89.11%	89.36%	89.20%	**90.51%**	**90.08%**	**90.51%**	**90.19%**
VGG16	88.81%	88.59%	88.81%	88.60%	89.82%	89.59%	89.82%	89.59%
VGG19	89.73%	89.45%	89.73%	89.42%	90.37%	90.13%	90.37%	90.15%
MobileNet	85.54%	84.45%	85.54%	84.18%	90.02%	89.98%	90.02%	89.99%
MobileNetV2	84.99%	83.93%	84.99%	83.70%	89.53%	89.05%	89.53%	89.08%

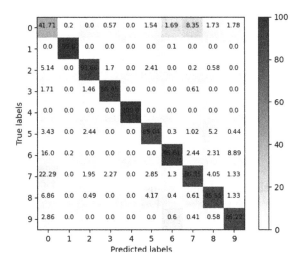

Fig. 5. The normalized confusion matrix when encoder is ResNet50V2.

This experimental result proves that the malware classification method proposed in this paper can effectively solve the problem of malware classification. It verifies the feasibility and effectiveness of treating the PE header-based malware classification as an image classification problem. And it proves the universality and robustness of this method when using different neural networks as encoders.

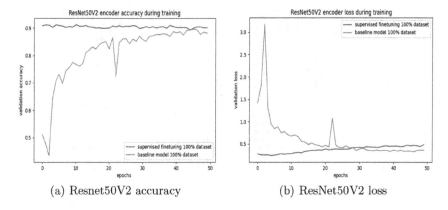

(a) Resnet50V2 accuracy   (b) ResNet50V2 loss

Fig. 6. The curve of accuracy and loss when encoder is ResNet50V2.

Experiment 2. In this experiment, we use 1%, 5%, 10%, 20%, 50% of the labeled training dataset for the training of the baseline model and the finetune of our method, respectively. In the pre-training phase, we used all unlabeled training dataset.

As shown in Table 2, our method requires only 50% of the labeled training dataset to achieve the performance of the baseline model using all labeled training datasets. Our method achieves excellent performance when using only 10% or less of the labeled training set. This proves that our method can greatly reduce the workload of manually labeling samples. In addition, our method can also use unlabeled data, which can make full use of data resources.

Table 2. The performance metrics of the second experiments.

Dataset fraction	Baseline model				Our method			
	Accuracy	Prediction	Recall	F1-Score	Accuracy	Prediction	Recall	F1-Score
1%	36.70%	43.91%	36.70%	31.05%	83.17%	82.05%	83.17%	82.35%
5%	59.22%	60.05%	59.22%	55.81%	86.03%	86.19%	80.44%	83.22%
10%	68.02%	66.45%	68.02%	66.27%	87.45%	85.02%	85.78%	85.40%
20%	77.85%	75.70%	77.85%	76.66%	86.84%	87.10%	86.84%	86.81%
30%	84.85%	83.79%	84.85%	83.56%	88.37%	87.89%	88.37%	88.08%
40%	86.23%	85.75%	86.23%	85.93%	89.39%	88.79%	89.39%	88.92%
50%	87.94%	87.03%	87.94%	87.25%	89.53%	88.96%	89.53%	89.17%

Figure 7 is the loss and accuracy curve using different fractions of the training data set. Our proposed method, the curve can converge faster and more stably. Even using only 1% of the labeled dataset, our proposed method achieves high performance around 10 epochs and remains stable in subsequent epochs. However, the curve of the base line model oscillates heavily and the performance is much lower than our method.

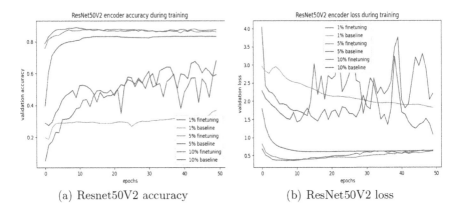

(a) Resnet50V2 accuracy   (b) ResNet50V2 loss

Fig. 7. Accuracy and loss curves when using different fractions datasets and the encoder is ResNet50V2.

Compared with Other Researhers. As far as we know, there have been several researches on the malware classification using the same dataset. As shown in Table 3, the best accuracy of other researchers' methods is 88% and F1-Score is 87.58%. The performance of our method is better than those of these scholars.

Table 3. Comparison with the methods of other scholars.

Researchers	Method	Accuracy	F1-Score
David A. Noever [14]	MobileNetV2	80.00%	\
W. K. WONG [20]	OVA	83.70%	78.94%
	OVO	81.80%	85.79%
	DR	83.70%	77.50%
	SR	84.10%	79.20%
Erik Larsen [10]	Light Gradient Boosting Machine	88.00%	87.58%
	Gradient Boosting	86.24%	86.05%
	Random Forest	85.74%	85.14%
	Extra Trees	85.18%	84.28%
	Logistic Regression	83.41%	83.99%
	Naïve Bayes	81.79%	80.77%
	SVM-Linear Kernel	81.30%	82.60%
Our Method		**90.51%**	**90.19%**

5 Conclusion

Due to the rapid evolution of malware, traditional machine learning and deep learning-based malware classification methods have to be regularly retrained to adapt to the latest features of malware. In order to reduce the dependence on a large amount of labeled data for regular training of the model and reduce the workload of manual labeling, we propose a semi-supervised learning based malware classification method named MCM-SSL. The method is divided into pre-train stage and finetune stage. The pre-train stage could use unlabeled data to learn generic representations of malware samples, and the finetune stage could use labeled data to learn malware classification capabilities.

The method proposed in this paper effectively uses a large amount of unlabeled data, and only needs a small amount of labeled data to achieve excellent performance. It achieves an accuracy of 90.51% on the open-source Virus-MNIST dataset. We also compare various neural network algorithms and other scholars' methods to verify the effectiveness and robustness of our method.

For the problem that the performance of traditional malware classification methods continues to degrade with the evolution of malware, our proposed method can only reduce the manual annotation workload required to periodically retrain the model, and does not solve the fundamental problem of model performance degradation. In future work we will investigate anti-aging methods for malware classification to slow down the aging of classification models.

Acknowledgment. We would like to thank Jie Yuan from Iowa State University for the valuable discussions and insightful comments. This work was supported by the National Natural Science Foundation of China (Grant 61871378 and U2003111), and Defense Industrial Technology Development Program (Grant JCKY2021906A001).

References

1. AMR: Kaspersky security bulletin 2021. statistics. https://securelist.com/kaspersky-security-bulletin-2021-statistics/105205/. Accessed 15 Dec 2021
2. Chen, T., Kornblith, S., Norouzi, M., Hinton, G.: A simple framework for contrastive learning of visual representations. In: International Conference on Machine Learning, pp. 1597–1607. PMLR (2020)
3. Chen, T., Kornblith, S., Swersky, K., Norouzi, M., Hinton, G.E.: Big self-supervised models are strong semi-supervised learners. In: Advances in Neural Information Processing Systems, vol. 33, pp. 22243–22255 (2020)
4. Ding, C., Luktarhan, N., Lu, B., Zhang, W.: A hybrid analysis-based approach to android malware family classification. Entropy **23**(8), 1009 (2021)
5. Duarte-Garcia, H.L., et al.: A semi-supervised learning methodology for malware categorization using weighted word embeddings. In: 2019 IEEE European Symposium on Security and Privacy Workshops (EuroS&PW), pp. 238–246. IEEE (2019)
6. Gandotra, E., Bansal, D., Sofat, S.: Malware analysis and classification: a survey. J. Inf. Secur. 2014 (2014)
7. Gao, T., Zhao, L., Li, X., Chen, W.: Malware detection based on semi-supervised learning with malware visualization. Math. Biosci. Eng. **18**(5), 5995–6011 (2021)
8. Goyal, M., Kumar, R.: A survey on malware classification using machine learning and deep learning. In. J. Comput. Networks Appl. **8**(6), 758–775 (2021)

9. Kalash, M., Rochan, M., Mohammed, N., Bruce, N.D., Wang, Y., Iqbal, F.: Malware classification with deep convolutional neural networks. In: 2018 9th IFIP International Conference on New Technologies, Mobility and Security (NTMS), pp. 1–5. IEEE (2018)

10. Larsen, E., MacVittie, K., Lilly, J.: Virus-mnist: machine learning baseline calculations for image classification. arXiv preprint arXiv:2111.02375 (2021)

11. Mahdavifar, S., Kadir, A.F.A., Fatemi, R., Alhadidi, D., Ghorbani, A.A.: Dynamic android malware category classification using semi-supervised deep learning. In: 2020 IEEE International Conference on Dependable, Autonomic and Secure Computing, International Conference on Pervasive Intelligence and Computing, International Conference on Cloud and Big Data Computing, International Conference on Cyber Science and Technology Congress (DASC/PiCom/CBDCom/CyberSciTech), pp. 515–522. IEEE (2020)

12. Mohamed, G.A.N., Ithnin, N.B.: Survey on representation techniques for malware detection system. Am. J. Appl. Sci. **14**(11), 1049–1069 (2017). https://doi.org/10.3844/ajassp.2017.1049.1069, https://thescipub.com/abstract/ajassp.2017.1049.1069

13. Nataraj, L., Karthikeyan, S., Jacob, G., Manjunath, B.S.: Malware images: visualization and automatic classification. In: Proceedings of the 8th International Symposium on Visualization for Cyber Security, pp. 1–7 (2011)

14. Noever, D., Noever, S.E.M.: Virus-mnist: a benchmark malware dataset. arXiv preprint arXiv:2103.00602 (2021)

15. Rezaei, T., Hamze, A.: An efficient approach for malware detection using PE header specifications. In: 2020 6th International Conference on Web Research (ICWR), pp. 234–239. IEEE (2020)

16. Santos, I., Nieves, J., Bringas, P.G.: Semi-supervised learning for unknown malware detection. In: Abraham, A., Corchado, J.M., Gonzilez, S.R., De Paz Santana, J.F. (eds.) International Symposium on Distributed Computing and Artificial Intelligence. pp. 415–422. Springer, Heidelberg (2011). https://doi.org/10.1007/978-3-642-19934-9_53

17. Santos, I., Sanz, B., Laorden, C., Brezo, F., Bringas, P.G.: Opcode-sequence-based semi-supervised unknown malware detection. In: Herrero, Á., Corchado, E. (eds.) CISIS 2011. LNCS, vol. 6694, pp. 50–57. Springer, Heidelberg (2011). https://doi.org/10.1007/978-3-642-21323-6_7

18. Sihwail, R., Omar, K., Ariffin, K.Z.: A survey on malware analysis techniques: static, dynamic, hybrid and memory analysis. Int. J. Adv. Sci. Eng. Inf. Technol. **8**(42), 1662–1671 (2018)

19. Sriram, S., Vinayakumar, R., Sowmya, V., Alazab, M., Soman, K.: Multi-scale learning based malware variant detection using spatial pyramid pooling network. In: IEEE INFOCOM 2020-IEEE Conference on Computer Communications Workshops (INFOCOM WKSHPS), pp. 740–745. IEEE (2020)

20. Wong, W., Juwono, F.H., Apriono, C.: Vision-based malware detection: a transfer learning approach using optimal ECOC-SVM configuration. IEEE Access **9**, 159262–159270 (2021)

21. Zhang, X.Y., Shi, H., Zhu, X., Li, P.: Active semi-supervised learning based on self-expressive correlation with generative adversarial networks. Neurocomputing **345**, 103–113 (2019)

22. Zhang, X.-Y., Wang, S., Jin, X., Zhu, X., Li, B.: Effective semi-supervised learning based on local correlation. In: Shi, Y., et al. (eds.) ICCS 2018. LNCS, vol. 10862, pp. 775–781. Springer, Cham (2018). https://doi.org/10.1007/978-3-319-93713-7_75

23. Zhang, X.Y., Wang, S., Yun, X.: Bidirectional active learning: a two-way exploration into unlabeled and labeled data set. IEEE Trans. Neural Networks Learn. Syst. **26**(12), 3034–3044 (2015)
24. Zhang, X., et al.: Enhancing state-of-the-art classifiers with API semantics to detect evolved android malware. In: Proceedings of the 2020 ACM SIGSAC Conference on Computer and Communications security, pp. 757–770 (2020)
25. Zhang, Z., Qi, P., Wang, W.: Dynamic malware analysis with feature engineering and feature learning. In: AAAI (2020)

Malware Detected and Tell Me Why: An Verifiable Malware Detection Model with Graph Metric Learning

Xiao Chen[1,2], Zhengwei Jiang[1,2], Shuwei Wang[1,2], Rongqi Jing[1,2], Chen Ling[1,2], and Qiuyun Wang[1(✉)]

[1] Institute of Information Engineering, Chinese Academy of Sciences, Beijing 100093, China
{chenxiao1998,jiangzhengwei,wangshuwei,jingrongqi,lingchen,
wangqiuyun}@iie.ac.cn
[2] School of Cyber Security, University of Chinese Academy of Sciences, Beijing 100029, China

Abstract. The amount of malware has proliferated in recent years because malware developers can easily exploit existing malware to develop new ones. To identify the interrelationships between old and new malware and unify the defense, researchers have continuously tried to automatically classify malware families, and deep neural networks have proven to be a reliable solution to this problem, but as the number of families increases, the robustness of the model is susceptible to data drift and deteriorates, and the validation work of deep neural networks remains insufficient. In this paper, we classify malware families based on semantic learning of disassembled code and graph neural networks, and also provide a judgment basis for family classification so that analysts can quickly verify the classification results. Experiments show that our model can effectively classify families and is robust to data drift.

Keywords: Malware · GNN · Metric learning

1 Introduce

In recent years, the number of malwares has exploded, and this phenomenon largely stems from the improvement of automatic malicious sample generation techniques, which allow attackers to easily transform existing malware into new malware using splicing, assembly, obfuscation, encryption, etc. Since this malware generation technique cannot be separated from the use of old code, the new malware generated is inevitably similar to the old malware in terms of code fragments, behavior patterns, etc. Those malware with similar code and functionality can be named as Family Malware. Struggling to cope with the sheer volume of malware samples, security and antivirus researcher are looking for an automated model that can identify malware or malware families, allowing them to focus on typical and new technology malware.

Machine learning and neural network is one of hot research direction, the researchers extracted static characteristics like binary string, ASCII string, import table, export

C. Su et al. (Eds.): SciSec 2022, LNCS 13580, pp. 302–314, 2022.
https://doi.org/10.1007/978-3-031-17551-0_20

table, function call graph, control flow graph and dynamic characteristics like API calls , training specific models to complete malware identification or family classification. However, most of the existing deep neural network research work is faced with following problems.

The first problem lies in the acquisition of training samples. High-precision supervised learning neural networks often need a large number of labeled samples for training, and these samples are required to be evenly distributed so that the model does not bias the samples to a specific category. In reality, however, researchers are able to obtain rare samples of tagged malware, especially new ones. On the other hand, the problem of data imbalance is particularly acute in the malware domain. Influenced by evasion techniques, researchers have easier access to malicious samples that are simple or exposed, and have difficulty obtaining those that are well hidden. This makes the distribution of malicious samples in the hands of researchers potentially different from that in real cyberspace.

The second problem occurs in model training. Malware update rapidly in real network, which is called data drift in the field of machine learning. Data drift also brings the problem of large number of families. In practice, we find that model tends to perform well in the classification of a small number of families, but its effect decreases significantly in the face of multi-family classification problem.

The third problem is the verifiability of the models. A large body of existing work, particularly deep learning models, only tells researchers what the family classification of a sample might be, but not what the basis of their predictions is. That is, when testing the model output researchers can only test the model output by analysing the sample from scratch, without being able to derive supporting information from the model to speed up the study. We define the model verifiability as the time saved by the model in helping the researcher to analyse the sample. The greater the validability of the model, the more time the researcher saves in validating the model results.

To deal with three questions, we propose a new malware family classification detection framework, which uses the disassembly code and function call graph as feature, vectorizes the functions in the program and carried out semantic learning. The framework include migration learning and semi-supervised technology to reduce the need for labeled samples, and uses the robustness of KNN to data drift to enhance the model's ability to recognize new family samples. Experiments show that our model can not only infer the family information of malicious software, but also provide the analyst with the information of suspicious functions inside it, which can effectively shorten the time for the analyst to verify and analyze the results of malware detection.

Contribution. In summary, our contributions are as follows:

- We propose a novel method to malware family classification, consisting of a pretrained model based on semantic learning, graph nerual network and metric learning. Experiment demonstrated that the model outperforms previous work and is robust to data drift.
- Our model is verifiable and, unlike the interpretability of traditional machine learning, the intermediate output of the model not only provides researchers with perceptual interpretation, but also helps them to analyse samples manually more quickly.

The rest of the paper is distributed as follow: In the second part, we introduce the related work in the fields covered by this paper, and in the third part, we introduce our model. In the fourth part, we verify the effectiveness of the model. In the fifth part, we discuss the conclusions and finally introduce our future work.

2 Related Work

2.1 Malware Detection

With the explosive growth of the number of malware, automatic analysis of malware has become a research focus, which can be divided into static and dynamic analysis of malware.

Dynamic malware analysis will run malicious software in sandbox or virtual machine and monitor it, studying the behaviors of malware such as API calls in the process of running. B. Ndibanje [1] use API call histogram classify malware, P.V. Shijo [2] model API calls as Bag-of-word, H. Kim [3] and Y. Ki [4] calculate the similarity of API sequences for research, J. Kang [5] use LSTM to learn API sequence features and Peng Wang [6] tried n-Gram of API sequence for cluster analysis. Dynamic analysis is prone to misjudgment caused by anti-virtualization, anti-sandbox and trigger means avoidance. In addition, dynamic analysis has high environment requirements for users.

Static malware analysis focus on the features extracted without really executing malware. These static features will be further processed into N-Gram distribution, Term Frequency or Inversed Document Frequency (TF-IDF) [7–10], control flow graph(CFG) [9], function length frequency(FLF) [12] and printable string information (PSI) [11–13] are also used to characterize file information. The advantages of static analysis are comprehensive software function analysis and less resource consumption, the disadvantage is that it is easily disturbed by obfuscation techniques.

2.2 Graph Neural Networks in Malware Detection

Unlike images, text messages, etc., which can be represented as fixed-size matrices, executable files are better suited to be represented as a graph structure. Since the rise of graph neural networks, a large amount of research has focused on the application of graph neural networks in malware detection [14–23]: Some use GNNs framework for malicious code classification based on function call graph structure [14, 15, 17, 18], some do the similar work based on control flow graph [19], the features represents nodes in graph from either statistical method like PageRank [14], HIN [21] or semantic learning methods [15]. However, all of these work does not give the analyst a basis to help them speed up their analysis, Therefore, analyst still need to spend nearly the amount of time validating the model's predictions as from scratch.

2.3 Interpretation of Metric Learning

Deep neural networks lose the interpretability of the model due to its overly complex network structure. Metric-based learning methods map samples into the feature space for classification learning, which has stronger visibility and interpretation. Triple t [24, 25] is a typical loss function. It define the loss value of different sample distributions through Eq. (1).

$$L_{BA}(\theta; X) = \overbrace{\sum_{i=1}^{P}\sum_{a=1}^{K}}^{all\ anchors}\ \overbrace{\sum_{\substack{p=1\\p\neq a}}^{K}}^{all\ pos}\ \overbrace{\sum_{j=1}^{P}\sum_{\substack{n=1\\j\neq i}}^{K}}^{all\ negatives} \left[m + d_{j,a,n}^{i,a,p}\right]_{+}, \qquad (1)$$

$$d_{j,a,n}^{i,a,p} = D\Big(f_\theta\big(x_a^i\big), f_\theta\big(x_p^i\big)\Big) - D\Big(f_\theta\big(x_a^i\big), f_\theta\big(x_n^i\big)\Big).$$

Where letter a means anchor, letter p means positive with the same class as anchor, letter n means negative, which has different class from anchor, letter D means distance function.

Meanwhile, a lot of work tried combine the KNN with deep neural network [26–28], and it is proved that KNN is more sensitive to new sample than deep learning network. In this thesis, we aim to provide an intuitive and verifiable family classification judgment by comparing the similarity of feature representations between samples using metric learning.

3 Method

3.1 Framework Overview

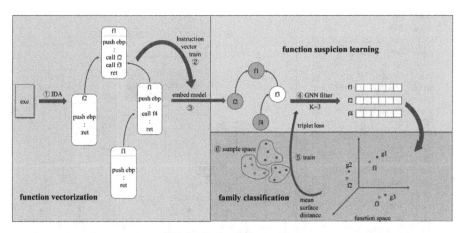

Fig. 1. Framework overview

As shown in Fig. 1, our proposed framework consists of three phases and six steps: the first phase is function vectorization, where the executable file is divided into blocks of instructions in functions after disassembly (serial number 1 in the figure). Asm2Vec [29] proposes a work to vectorize functions and proved that the semantic learning of assembly code can be used to determine the function of a function. However, Asm2Vec does not fully utilize the prior knowledge of the code, we observe that a large number of instruction operands actually characterize the same or close semantics, so we improve on Asm2Vec and significantly reduce the size of the embed table (serial number 2). The second phase is function suspicion learning, where we combine equation vectors with CG graphs to form a graph representation of the executable file (serial number 3), fuse the semantic information of different functions through graph neural network learning, and select the K most suspicious functions (serial number 4). The third stage is family classification, based on the filtered K most suspicious core functions, we learn their ensemble similarity (serial number 5) and determine their family information in the sample mapping space according to the KNN algorithm (serial number 6), which has the advantage of being sensitive to new data and robust to data drift.

3.2   Instruction Vectorization

At first we used IDA Pro to disassemble the binary file, extracting the list of functions in the binary file, the function call graph, and the assembly code inside each function. Each extracted assembly instruction is represented by a triplet-tuple: < opcode, operand 1 type, operand 2 type >. Each part of triplet is embedded into a d-dimensional vector, considering that some instructions have two operands and some have only one operand, we average the vector representation of operation as the operand embedding of the instruction, then concatenate it with opcode vector as the vector embedding of instruction.

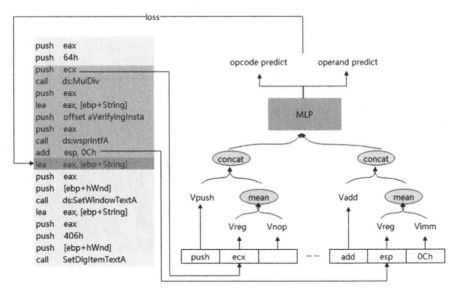

Fig. 2. Instruction vectorization structure, in this example we use first 8 instructions to predict the ninth instruction "lea eax, [ebp+String]"

To learn the semantic information of the assembly instructions, for each instruction we use the vectors of w instructions before it to predict its own type. We do not predict the intermediate op because the model could not learn the RET instruction in that case.

The specific network structure is shown in Fig. 2. Considering that although we unify a large number of operands of the same type but the remaining vocabulary is still large, statistics according to data set show that there are 524 possible types of opcode, we adopt the K-negative sample method.

3.3 Function Suspicion Learning

The vectorization at the instruction level is not sufficient, and in order to investigate a more comprehensive representation of functional semantics, we need to further investigate the vectorization of functions.

We use the average of all instruction vectors in the function as the function vector. After learning the vector representation of functions, the sample file can be represented as a graph representation structure with call graph as the topology and function semantic vectors as the node features, we aim to use graph neural network to combine the contextual relationship between functions to grasp the semantics of functions more accurately. In this way, we can automate the work of extracting the most interesting K-functions for each sample.

The network structure we use consists of three layers of GCN [32] accompanied by elu activation functions, with the number of channels in the GCN set to 32, after which we use a k-sort layer [33] to select K functions.

The vectors corresponding to the selected K functions will be extracted for family classification.

3.4 Family Classification

Finally, we use the selected K function vectors to complete the family classification of the sample. We cannot directly concatenate the representation vectors of these K functions and learn them later, because considering two samples A and B of the same family, the suspicious function x with the same semantics will appear in the K most salient features of both samples A and B. However, function x is ranked i in sample A but j in sample B. When $i! = j$, directly concatenate the vectors and learning them later will over emphasizes the order feature in the output vector set, which is likely to mislead our judgment, so we need a classification method that ignore the order of the output vectors in the output vector set. It is also inappropriate to directly average all the output vectors and then classify them, because when the feature points are uniformly distributed throughout the vector space, the representations of the two sets of functions may be completely different, yet the sum of their representations is similar. In fact, each function vector is a point in the D-dimensional feature space, and we can regard the sample similarity problem as a similarity measure between points sets consisting of K points in the sample space. Mean surface distance function is a common point set similarity measure function, and its calculation formula is shown in Eq. (2).

$$d_H(X, Y) = \frac{1}{||X|| + ||Y||} \left(\sum_{x \in X} min_{y \in Y} d(x, y) + \sum_{y \in Y} min_{x \in X} d(y, x) \right) \quad (2)$$

where X and Y are two different point sets, and d(.) is distance function between two points, in this work we choose Euclidean distance.

Now that we have defined the sample-to-sample distance function, we adopt triplet loss [25] (Eq. (1)) to optimize the model.

Triplet loss follows the basic idea that the same attracts and the different repels, which allows us to use the KNN algorithm for classification directly after the network learning is completed, and take advantage of the KNN algorithm's sensitivity to a small number of new samples. Enables the model to be robust to conceptual drift of malicious samples.

4   Experiments

4.1   Dataset

We use malware from the real world as the data set. The data set contains 17 families, including adware, backdoor, Trojan and virus. Each family has more than 1000 samples and total number reaches 19232 samples. In practice, we find that a large number of family sample show exactly the same appearance after IDA Pro script analysis. Their changes only come from the data area rather than the code area, which will be easily recognized by heuristic methods. For such samples, we filtered the samples representing the same characteristics. In the remaining samples, only 9 families still have more than 100 unique sample (see Table 1), it proves the widespread existence of code reuse in the real world. We selected them to form our training set and used the remaining samples to test the resistance of model to data drift.

Table 1. Sample remained distribution of each family.

Family	Number before filter	Number after filter
Adware.Win32.Mywebsearch.A	981	110
Backdoor.Win32.Bifrose.E	1054	187
Trojan.Win32.Autorun.1	1049	342
Trojan.Win32.Delf.B	901	169
Trojan.Win32.Kazy.9	1658	1247
Trojan.Win32.Shiz.1	1171	236
Virus.Win32.Chir.B	993	959
Virus.Win32.Otwycal.A	1310	1264
Virus.Win32.Resur.B	1100	312

The filtered data set is unbalanced, and it fits the actual situation. Notice that the reduction of Trojan and Virus is smaller. We think this is because the producers of Virus and Trojan pay more attention to hiding themselves, so they change the code more frequently.

When training the instruction vectorization model, these samples represent more than 100 million instructions.

4.2 Baseline

We implemented some other malware classification model for comparison, They include traditional machine learning methods, including classification according to the statistical characteristics of instructions. The specific models include KNN, SVM and RF; other model process binary files into images and learn further. They include CNN [31] and GLCM [30] processing.

4.3 Compare with Baseline

We randomly divided the data set into training set and verification set according to the ratio of 4:1. The results are shown in Table 2. From the experimental data, we know that the effect of visually processing malware and learning with CNN model is better than the model based on statistical data. And our model achieves the best effect on the test set. The GLCM+RF model achieves 100% accuracy in the training set, but only 65.6% in the test set, which indicates that there is a large over fitting problem in the model.

Table 2. Accuracy of models.

Model	Accuracy on train set	Accuracy on test set
Statistical+RF	84.6%	77.1%
Statistical+KNN	84.6%	75.6%
Statistical+SVM	74.5%	69.1%
GLCM+RF	**100%**	65.6%
GLCM+KNN	65.7%	53.0%
CNN	86%	80.7%
Our model	90.3%	**85.9%**

Table 3 and Table 4 show the classification ability of the model in each family. It can be seen that the accuracy of model in the training set has reached 90.3% and that in the test set has reached 85.9%. In the specific analysis, the model has the best detection effect on virus.Win32.Chir.B, and its recall rate has reached 97%, followed by Trojan.Win32.Shiz.1, its recall rate reached 95%, and the recall rate of a total of six families was more than 80%. The detection effect of Trojan.Win32.Delf.B is the worst, with only 68.5% recall rate. Which may be due to the Trojan horse software to hide itself.

Table 3. Confusion matrix on train set.

predict \ label	Trojan.Win32.Shiz.1	Backdoor.Win32.Bifrose.E	Trojan.Win32.Kazy.9	Virus.Win32.Resur.B	Trojan.Win32.Delf.B	Virus.Win32.Otwycal.A	Virus.Win32.Chir.B	Adware.Win32.Mywebsearch.A	Trojan.Win32.Autorun.1
Trojan.Win32.Shiz.1	192	4	7	0	1	1	0	2	3
Backdoor.Win32.Bifrose.E	1	120	20	3	13	8	2	0	12
Trojan.Win32.Kazy.9	0	6	924	11	6	18	17	4	26
Virus.Win32.Resur.B	3	2	3	211	7	21	1	3	11
Trojan.Win32.Delf.B	1	3	6	1	89	4	0	4	8
Virus.Win32.Otwycal.A	2	4	8	18	5	943	2	5	22
Virus.Win32.Chir.B	0	0	1	0	0	0	747	0	0
Adware.Win32.Mywebsearch.A	1	1	1	1	1	1	0	66	3
Trojan.Win32.Autorun.1	2	9	19	4	8	9	1	2	195

Table 4. Confusion matrix on test set.

predict \ label	Trojan.Win32.Shiz.1	Backdoor.Win32.Bifrose.E	Trojan.Win32.Kazy.9	Virus.Win32.Resur.B	Trojan.Win32.Delf.B	Virus.Win32.Otwycal.A	Virus.Win32.Chir.B	Adware.Win32.Mywebsearch.A	Trojan.Win32.Autorun.1
Trojan.Win32.Shiz.1	31	1	3	0	0	0	0	0	0
Backdoor.Win32.Bifrose.E	0	25	9	0	2	4	0	1	6
Trojan.Win32.Kazy.9	2	4	233	2	0	6	1	0	11
Virus.Win32.Resur.B	0	2	2	59	3	10	0	3	9
Trojan.Win32.Delf.B	1	0	1	0	26	6	0	1	2
Virus.Win32.Otwycal.A	0	1	3	1	1	226	1	2	5
Virus.Win32.Chir.B	0	0	1	0	0	1	187	0	0
Adware.Win32.Mywebsearch.A	0	1	0	1	0	4	0	15	1
Trojan.Win32.Autorun.1	0	4	6	0	7	2	0	2	28

4.4 Robustness to Data Drift

Data drift is a common problem in the field of machine learning. We investigated whether the proposed model is sensitive enough to new data and can identify it quickly and correctly in the original data set, the samples of four families did not enter the training set because the repeatability is too high. Their distribution after de duplication is shown in Table 5. We do not modify any parameters of the model and directly use it to predict the types of these families. Because we want the model to learn the ability to extract suspicious functions in a broad sense, rather than the ability to identify a specific family.

Table 5. Sample distribution for data drift test.

Family	Number before filter	Number after filter
Adware.Win32.Bundleinstaller.1	884	6
Adware.Win32.Fiseria.D	1027	12
Adware.Win32.Plugin.2	1133	6
Trojan.Win32.Downloader10.A	798	11

As shown in Table 6, the prediction accuracy of the new families reached 62.8%, which decreased by 26.9% compared with the test set. Experiments show that the model also has a certain classification ability for family samples outside the training set. Through in-depth analysis of the experimental data, we find that the model is more inclined to predict Trojan.Win32.Downloader10.A as Adware.Win32.Fiseria.D, because the Trojan horse software has better hiding function. Among the three kinds of adware family classification data, our family classification effect has reached 77.3%, which shows that the model can better classify the adware family.

Table 6. Confusion matrix in data drift experiment.

Predict \ label	Trojan.Win32. Downloader10 .A	Adware.Win32. Plugin.2	Adware.Win32. Fiseria.D	Adware.Win32. Bundleinstaller .1
Trojan.Win32.Downloader10.A	5	0	0	2
Adware.Win32.Plugin.2	0	4	1	2
Adware.Win32.Fiseria.D	6	1	11	0
Adware.Win32.Bundleinstaller.1	0	1	0	2

4.5 Validation of Help for Manual Analysis

In order to verify that the model can accelerate the verification of analysts, we manually analyzed some samples in the data set and analyzed the k-top function selected by the model. The following sample is classified as adware.Win32.Bundleinstaller.1, and the hash value is *00c354a953c554abe6ccd1787f1d475b8f3b1141*.

We set K to 4 and observe the sequence number of the selected function of the sample in the model. The result is number 50, 15, 31 and 84, and their corresponding function start addresses are 0x00402B3B, 0x00403D97, 0x00404EE8, 0x00406C40. The last one is automatically labeled as "GetFileVersionInfoA" and the first one is labeled as "DialogFunc" by IDA pro. Their functions are to obtain file version information and set up dialog boxes. Function 0x404EE8 is also a pop-up function with more comprehensive abilities. It undertakes the core functio.ns of adware such as creating threads, show window, responding to events and so on(see Fig. 3). Only four functions in the entire sample involve dialog. Combined with in-depth analysis and string content, we determine that this sample is an adware. It is a pity that the functions related to the registry are not output by the model.

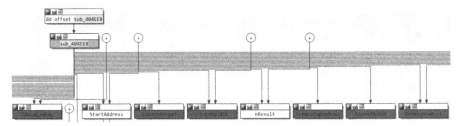

Fig. 3. Part of proximity browser for sub_0x404EE8, the function is related to key functions such as ShowWindow, CreateThread and GetWindowRect.

5   Conclusion

Malware detection has a long history of development as well as malware. With the continuous improvement of mathematical model and detection technology, malware can be more effectively characterized as a data structure in line with its own functions. In our work, we propose a pre-trained model that vectorises functions. We characterize malware as a graph model with function as node, and use graph neural network to learn and classify it, which is better than the model based on statistical data or computer vision. In addition, we find that the model is resistant to data drift, especially for adware. More importantly, we focus on the verifiability of the model and its impact on analysts in real-world scenarios.

According to the information we know, no one has done the verifiable output of graph neural network in the field of malware before our work.

6   Future Work

It is noted that the model performs significantly better on the training set than the test set, indicating that there is an overfitting problem and we will improve the model in the future to better fit the actual situation. The different pre-training models also introduce differences in the final classification results, and we will compare them further in future work.

Using the similarity of functions and function sets to classify samples is exciting, but it still requires researchers to spend a lot of time analyzing the specific effects of specific functions. We hope to establish a model that can correlate functions with their effects in future work and further release analysts.

Acknowledgments. The authors would like to thank the Editor-in-Chief, the Associate Editor, and the reviewers for their insightful comments and suggestions. We also thank Zhuopang Lin and Yue Ma for their help in the work. This work was supported by Youth Innovation Promotion Association, CAS (No.2020166), Key Laboratory of Network Assessment Technology, Chinese Academy of Sciences and Beijing Key Laboratory of Network Security and Protection Technology.

References

1. Ndibanje, B., Kim, K.H., Kang, Y.J., et al.: Cross-method-based analysis and classification of malicious behavior by API calls extraction. Appl. Sci. **9**(2), 239 (2019)
2. Shijo, P.V., Salim, A.: Integrated static and dynamic analysis for malware detection. Comput. Sci. **46**, 804–811 (2015)
3. Kim, H., Kim, J., Kim, Y., Kim, I., Kim, K.J., Kim, H.: Improvement of malware detection and classification using API call sequence alignment and visualization. Clust. Comput. **22**(1), 921–929 (2017). https://doi.org/10.1007/s10586-017-1110-2
4. Ki, Y., Kim, E., Kim, H.K., et al.: A novel approach to detect malware based on API call sequence analysis. Int. J. Distrib. Sens. Netw. **11**(6), 101 (2015)
5. Kang, J., Jang, S., Li, S., et al.: Long short-term memory-based Malware classification method for information security. Comput. Electr. Eng. **77**, 366–375 (2019)
6. Wang, P., Tang, Z., Wang, J.: A novel few-shot malware classification approach for unknown family recognition with multi-prototype modeling. Comput. Secur. **4**, 97 (2021)
7. Abou-Assaleh, T., Cercone, N., Keselj, V., Sweidan, R.: N-gram-based detection of new malicious code. In: Proceedings of the 28th Annual International Computer Software and Applications Conference, COMPSAC 2004, Hong Kong, China, 28–30 September 2004, vol. 2, pp. 41–42 (2004)
8. Santos, I., Laorden, C., Bringas, P.G.: Collective classification for unknown malware detection. In: Proceedings of the International Conference on Security and Cryptography, Seville, Spain, 18–21 July 2011, pp. 251–256 (2011)
9. Anderson, B., Storlie, C., Lane, T.: Improving malware classification: bridging the static/dynamic gap. In: Proceedings of the 5th ACM Workshop on Security and Artificial Intelligence, Raleigh, NC, USA, 19 October 2012, pp. 3–14 (2012)
10. Santos, I., Penya, Y.K., Devesa, J., Bringas, P.G.: N-grams-based File Signatures for Malware Detection. In: ICEIS(2), vol. 9, pp. 317–320 (2009)
11. Ye, Y., Chen, L., Wang, D., Li, T., Jiang, Q., Zhao, M.: SBMDS: an interpretable string based malware detection system using SVM ensemble with bagging. J. Comput. Virol. **5**, 283 (2009)
12. Islam, R., Tian, R., Batten, L., Versteeg, S.: Classification of malware based on string and function feature selection. In: Proceedings of the 2010 Second Cybercrime and Trustworthy Computing Workshop, Ballarat, Australia, 19–20 July 2010, pp. 9–17 (2010)
13. Liu, L., Wang, B.: Malware classification using gray-scale images and ensemble learning. In: Proceedings of the 2016 3rd International Conference on Systems and Informatics (ICSAI), Shanghai, China, 19–21 November 2016, pp. 1018–1022 (2016)
14. Lo, W.W., Layeghy, S., Sarhan, M., et al.: Graph neural network-based android malware classification with jumping knowledge (2022)
15. Wang, S., Zhao, Y., Liu, G., Su, B.: A hierarchical graph-based neural network for malware classification. In: Mantoro, T., Lee, M., Ayu, M.A., Wong, K.W., Hidayanto, A.N. (eds.) ICONIP 2021. LNCS, vol. 13111, pp. 621–633. Springer, Cham (2021). https://doi.org/10.1007/978-3-030-92273-3_51
16. Pei, X., Long, Y., Tian, S.: AMalNet: a deep learning framework based on graph convolutional networks for malware detection. Comput. Secur. **93**, 101792 (2020)

17. Feng, P., Ma, J., Li, T., et al.: Android malware detection based on call graph via graph neural network. In: 2020 International Conference on Networking and Network Applications (NaNA) (2020)

18. Xu, P., Khairi, A.E.: Android-COCO: Android malware detection with graph neural network for byte- and native-code. arXiv e-prints (2021)

19. Yan, J., Yan, G., Jin, D.: Classifying malware represented as control flow graphs using deep graph convolutional neural network. In: 2019 49th Annual IEEE/IFIP International Conference on Dependable Systems and Networks (DSN). IEEE (2019

20. Gao, H., Cheng, S., Zhang, W.: GDroid: Android malware detection and classification with graph convolutional network. Comput. Secur. **6**, 102264 (2021)

21. Hei, Y., Yang, R., Peng, H., et al.: HAWK: rapid android malware detection through heterogeneous graph attention networks. IEEE Trans. Neural Netw. Learn. Syst. **PP**(99), 1–15 (2021)

22. Li, S., Zhou, Q., Zhou, R., et al.: Intelligent malware detection based on graph convolutional network (2021)

23. Kargarnovin, O., Sadeghzadeh, A.M., Jalili, R.: Mal2GCN: a robust malware detection approach using deep graph convolutional networks with non-negative weights (2021)

24. Schroff, F., Kalenichenko, D., Philbin, J.: FaceNet: a unified embedding for face recognition and clustering. In: CVPR (2015)

25. Hermans, A., Beyer, L., Leibe, B.: In defense of the triplet loss for person re-identification (2017)

26. Mizrahi, I., Avidan, S.: kNet: a deep kNN network to handle label noise (2021)

27. Zhuang, J., Cai, J., Wang, R., et al.: Deep kNN for medical image classification (2020)

28. Papernot, N., Mcdaniel, P.: Deep k-nearest neighbors: towards confident, interpretable and robust deep learning (2018)

29. Ding, S.H.H., Fung, B.C.M., Charland, P.: Asm2Vec: boosting static representation robustness for binary clone search against code obfuscation and compiler optimization. IEEE Computer Society (2019)

30. Vv, A., Skm, A., Vbs, B.: Multiclass malware classification via first- and second-order texture statistics. Comput. Secur. **97**, 101895 (2020)

31. Krčál, M., Švec, O., Bálek, M., et al.: Deep convolutional malware classifiers can learn from raw executables and labels only (2018)

32. Kipf, T.N., Welling, M.: Semi-supervised classification with graph convolutional networks (2016)

33. Zhang, M., Cui, Z., Neumann, M., Chen, Y.: An end-to-end deep learning architecture for graph classification (2018)

Malware Detection Using Automated Generation of Yara Rules on Dynamic Features

Qin Si[1,2], Hui Xu[1(✉)], Ying Tong[3], Yu Zhou[3], Jian Liang[3], Lei Cui[1],
and Zhiyu Hao[1]

[1] Institute of Information Engineering, Chinese Academy of Sciences, Beijing, China
`{siqin,xuhui,cuilei,haozhiyu}@iie.ac.cn`
[2] School of Cyber Security, University of Chinese Academy of Sciences,
Beijing, China
[3] Jiangsu Provincial Public Security Department, Beijing, China

Abstract. With the explosive growth of malware and its variants, automated malware detection is a hot topic in security. In this paper, we propose a malware detection method based on automated Yara rule generation on dynamic behaviors, mainly aiming to improve malware detection in terms of automation and effectiveness. Firstly, we extract the API call sequences as features from dynamic behaviors obtained in the sandbox. Secondly, we focus on the impact of runtime parameters containing significant semantic information in API calls on maliciousness discrimination. Then, we leverage random forest and logistic regression algorithms in YaraML to calculate weights for features extracted from API calls and runtime parameters and output a set of Yara rules. Finally, we use these Yara rules to perform malware detection. We conduct a set of experiments on a dataset of malicious samples and benign samples. The experimental results show that our method is effective in terms of accuracy and precision upon malware detection.

Keywords: Malware · Yara rules · Dynamic feature · API sequences · Machine learning

1 Introduction

With the rapid development of the Internet of Everything and the mobile Internet, the number of malware and its variants has shown an explosive growth trend. According to the report [1], SonicWall detected that the total number of ransomware attacks worldwide in 2021 had exceeded 623 million, an increase of 105% compared to last year. At the same time, 442,151 new malware variants appeared, a year-on-year increase of 65%, which affected many industries such as finance, energy, medical care, and industry, posing a severe threat to the security of the entire cyberspace. Despite protective software such as anti-virus software and firewalls, it is still impossible to fully identify, capture, and prevent malware

© The Author(s), under exclusive license to Springer Nature Switzerland AG 2022
C. Su et al. (Eds.): SciSec 2022, LNCS 13580, pp. 315–330, 2022.
https://doi.org/10.1007/978-3-031-17551-0_21

and its variants. Therefore, how to automatically and efficiently identify, detect and defend against the massive new malware is still a challenging problem.

Traditional signature-based and heuristic-based malware detection techniques rely on manually formulated rules/patterns for malware detection [21], and thus cannot cope with the frequently appeared malware variants nowadays. With the rapid development of artificial intelligence, intelligent malware detection based on machine learning and deep learning has become the mainstream research direction to provide automated and effective malware detection. Intelligent malware detection can be divided into feature extraction, model training, and malware detection. Meanwhile, the features used for detection can be divided into static and dynamic features.

Static features, including strings, opcodes, and byte sequences, can be obtained by statically analyzing the contents of the portable executable(PE) file without actually executing the malware sample. Schultz et al. [18] first proposed to use the n-gram method on the Windows platform to extract the features of byte sequence and dynamic link library-related information, proving the effectiveness of static features in malware detection. However, static features suffer two challenges. On the one hand, static features are easily affected by obfuscation technology and encryption. On the other hand, static feature matching is limited to identifying the known malware, which may perform worse when facing the newly appeared malware, especially those who use the polymorphic transformation.

Dynamic features refer to the behavior features extracted from the actual execution of malware in a secure and protected virtual environment, making up for the deficiency of static features. Dynamic features include runtime information, network behavior, registry changes, system call sequence, memory usage, etc. The Windows API call sequence is considered one of the most representative features of all dynamic behaviors. It covers the operation of system objects such as files, networks, and processes and reflects programs' complete execution flow. Ye et al. [22] developed an intelligent malware detection system called IMDS, the first attempt to generate features using API calls. They adopted the association rules algorithm in data mining technology to find out rules that significantly influenced malware detection and used them to detect unknown malware. There are also studies [4,8,16,19,20] based on the system call sequence, using information gain, TF-IDF, and other methods to select the features with strong classification ability. Then, they use BP neural network, Bayesian network, Naive Bayes, KNN, SVM, decision tree, random forest, and deep neural networks to detect and classify malicious software.

However, since the obtained system calls are often numerous and complex, the researchers can rarely make full use of all relevant information. Most of the related work only retains features such as API name and frequency of API call sequences. However, the runtime parameters, which record useful semantic information, are always excluded, which hurts the performance upon malware detection. Therefore, it is critical to explore how to mine the features from both API calls and their runtime parameters for improving malware detection.

In this paper, we propose a malware detection method based on automatic Yara rule extraction of dynamic behaviors. It takes all the API call sequences involved during malware execution, and treats API calls and runtime parameters passed to API calls as dynamic features. Then, it uses the machine learning model to compute API sequences' maliciousness weight and automatically extracts Yara rules. With the rules, we further implement rule matching-based malware detection. The experimental results show that the proposed method can achieve 90.98% of recall, 89.06% of accuracy, and 89.27% of F1-score on a large dataset.

Contribution. To summarize, this paper makes the following contributions.

- First, we leverage the insight that parameters in API call sequence can assist malware detection and then propose a method to label the feature with weights, which explores the maliciousness discrimination upon machine learning (Sect. 3.1).
- Second, we employ logistic regression and random forest algorithms in YaraML to generate rules and implement a malware detection method using rule matching. We also optimize the generated Yara rules to improve the accuracy and precision of malware detection (Sect. 3.2).
- Third, we provide a fully-automated methodology that transforms dynamic behavior into weighted features, trains the model, generates the rule, and detects the malware (Sect. 3.3).
- Finally, we evaluate our method on a dataset including 20000 malware and benignware. The results demonstrate the effectiveness of our approach (Sect. 4).

2   Background

2.1   Dynamic Feature Extraction

Sandboxing is a security mechanism used to isolate running programs from the real environment, mainly aiming to reduce operating system crashes and the spread of malware. Since malware is destructive to a certain extent, the sandbox is often used to run malicious samples and obtain the sample's running behavior, used for the subsequent analysis. Among the typical sandbox, Cuckoo is an opensource malware analysis sandbox that supports automated analysis of executable files and collects comprehensive running information, which is then used to trace the behavior in an isolated environment.

Among the dynamic behaviors captured by the sandbox, the API call sequence is one of the most representative features. API (Application Programming Interface) is a set of pre-packaged function call interfaces consisting of the function name, return value, and passed parameters. API call sequences reflect the complete execution flow of the program, covering its operations on system objects such as files, networks, and processes. Moreover, the parameters passed in the API call sequence often contain deeper semantic information. In the Windows system, both benign software and malware interact with the kernel through the system calls called by APIs. For example, for the same behaviour of calling the *NtSetValueKey* function to modify the registry key value, when the parameter values are *AntiVirusDisableNotify*, *FirewallDisableNotify*, and *FirewallOverride*, they have significantly different effects on malware identification. Therefore, the operation object, threat level, and impact on malware identification of the same API call can be different due to different parameters passed.

Hence, when we extract the behavior features, we comprehensively consider the Windows API sequence and its parameters, which enrich the dynamic behavior information of malware. In addition, we propose to analyze the impact of parameters on program maliciousness discrimination by assigning weights to parameters to improve the detection accuracy further. Meanwhile, to solve the problem of the enormous amount of API calls, which is impossible to analyze only through manual experience, we apply the machine learning method to train all the API call sequences, covering all the parameter space as much as possible.

2.2 Yara Rules

Yara is an open-source, multi-platform tool aimed at (but not limited to) helping malware researchers identify and classify malware samples [3] and works with most hosts running Windows, Linux, or Mac operating systems. Using Yara, we can create rules that characterize malware families in strings, instruction sequences, regular expressions, and byte patterns and identify the malware by signature match. Meanwhile, Yara also supports scanning files or processes to identify whether they belong to rule-described malware.

Many intrusion detection systems (IDS), intrusion prevention systems (IPS), and anti-virus platforms use Yara rules to detect and block malware, including Symantec, FireEye, Kaspersky, VirusTotal, Antiy, and more. Yara's popularity stems from its simple and effective way of writing rules [10]. Each Yara rule is equipped with two fields: string and condition. The string field consists of a series of strings and a boolean expression. And in the condition field, the logic of rule matching is explained through regular expressions. We use YaraML to automate generating Yara rules for the API call sequence of malware under windows and use the generated Yara rules to detect and identify malware.

3   Implementation

3.1   Overview

We design and implement a novel malware detection method that performs automated Yara rule generation for dynamic behavior based on YaraML. YaraML [17] is a tool that automatically generates Yara rules from training data by translating logistic regression and random forest binary classifiers into the Yara language. We improve the feature extraction section and focus on the impact of parameters on API maliciousness. We borrow the idea of the statistic method in

TF-IDF and introduce the concept of weighted feature to find the most representative malicious API calls. Moreover, we design an optimized malware detection method based on the Yara rule matching, and the method performs well on the test dataset. The workflow of our method is shown in Fig. 1, which is divided into three phases: Data Preprocessing, Automated Rule generation, and Malware Detection.

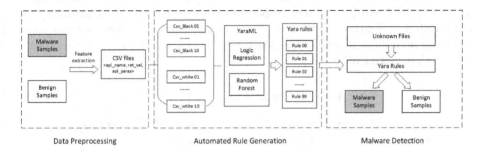

Fig. 1. The workflow of proposed malware detection methodology.

Data Preprocessing: First, we preprocess the original dataset, including malware and benignware samples. We extract all API call sequences and their parameters involved in the running time as dynamic features and save the features in CSV files. Each CSV file corresponds to a sample, and each line of API call in the CSV file represents a feature. The feature includes three fields: api_name, ret_value, and passed parameters used in the API call. Then, after labeling the black and white samples, the grouped feature CSV files are used as input and passed into the Automated Rule Generation module.

Automated Rule Generation: Second, We use two machine learning models of logistic regression and random forest in the automated Yara rule extraction tool (YaraML) to train the extracted dynamic features. We propose to analyze the impact of different parameters on the maliciousness of API calls. The weight value of each feature is calculated, and construct the condition expression of the Yara rule. Finally, this model automatically generates a rule file that conforms to the Yara rule form.

Malware Detection: Finally, we detect malware samples in the test set with the Yara rules obtained from different machine learning models. We continuously adjust the grouped method of the training set according to the feedback of the test results to optimize the Yara rule. The most effective Yara rule is finally determined and used for malware identification and detection.

3.2 Automated Yara Rule Generation for Dynamic Behavior Features

Feature Processing. We process the feature set passed in by the Data Preprocessing module into an eigenvector. We read all the API call sequences saved in the CSV sample file and take each row *[api_ name, ret_ value, argvs]* in the CSV file as a feature. Then we build a mapping relationship between the API and its frequency in the form of a dictionary, in which the key is the feature string, and the value is the frequency of the feature.

Specifically, firstly, construct a feature matrix. For example, the API call *[NtReadFile, 0, 1, C:\\ program\\ 1.exe]* and *[Fake_ SetFileHiddenOrReadOnly, 0, 2, C:\\ program\\ Function.dll, 000000a7]* appear in malicious and benign samples [64, 2] and [2, 0] times respectively. For clarity, the API features are abbreviated as Feature_1, Feature_2, ..., Feature_m. Therefore, we can construct an n*m-dimensional feature matrix composed of m features of n samples. We set that matrix to be X.

Table 1. The structure of matrix X.

	Feature_1	Feature_2	Feature_m	Lable(Malicious or not)
Sample_1	64	2	$\cdots$	Xnm	1
Sample_2	2	0	$\cdots$	Xnm	0
....	$\cdots$	$\cdots$	$\cdots$	$\cdots$	...
Sample_n	Xn1	Xn2	$\cdots$	Xnm	1

Secondly, label the feature. Set Y as the malicious label of the sample, where malware is 1 and non-malware is 0. Save *(X, Y)* as a *features_ and_ label.pkl* file and transform it into the training machine learning model.

The principle of Yara rule extraction with logistic regression and random forest models is described below.

Logistic Regression-Based Rule Generation. Logistic regression can be seen as a linear regression model normalized by the sigmoid function and is often used in binary classification problems. Its prediction principle is shown in formula 1 below. By estimating the probability, Logistic regression measures the correspondence between the input feature and the class label to be predicted.

$$P_{(y = 1|x; \theta)} = \frac{1}{(1 + e^{-\theta^T x})} \tag{1}$$

Note that formula 1 is derived by taking the output of the linear regression as the input of the Sigmoid function. The value of the Sigmoid function will infinitely approach 1 as the variable x continues to increase, while it will close to 0 as the variable x decreases. Meanwhile, it supports mapping any real number to the (0, 1) interval. Therefore, it can calculate the probability of correct prediction under the given conditions. Moreover, by solving the regression coefficients in the linear regression, a set of weight values θ can be obtained, representing each feature's contribution to the prediction process, which is convenient for evaluating the importance of different features. The steps of Logistic regression-based rule generation are as follows.

Calculate Feature Weights. For the Eigenvector obtained in the feature processing section, solve the best set of parameter vectors that make formula 1 with the largest probability, using maximum likelihood estimation. $\theta^T = [\theta_1, \theta_2, ..., \theta_n]$ is the weight corresponding to each feature (API call).

```
rule black01
{
    strings:
    $s0 = "NtCreateMutant,0,1,uxJLpe1m,,,," fullword  wide ascii // weight: 7.502
    $s1 = "NtWriteVirtualMemory,0,2,svchost.exe,864,,," fullword  wide ascii // weight: 6.342
    $s2 = "NtReadFile,0,1,C:\\temp\\DXSETUP.exe,,,," fullword  wide ascii // weight: 6.169

    $s205 = "LoadLibraryExW,0,1,C:\\WINDOWS\\system32\\riched20.dll,,,," fullword  wide ascii // weight: -0.9937
    $s206 = "LoadLibraryExW,0,1,C:\\WINDOWS\\WinSxS\\x86_Microsoft.VC80.CRT_1fc8b3b9a1e18e3b_8.0.50727.3053_x-ww_b80fa8ca
    \\msvcr80.dll ,,,," fullword  wide ascii // weight: -1.142
    $s207 = "LoadLibraryExW,0,1,C:\\WINDOWS\\system32\\winspool.drv,,,," fullword  wide ascii // weight: -1.159

    condition:
    ((#s0 * 7.502) + (#s1 * 6.342) + (#s2 * 6.169) + ..... + (#s205 * -0.994) + (#s206 * -1.142) + (#s207 * -1.159) + (-6.299)) > 0

}
```

Fig. 2. The generated Yara rule based on logistic regression model.

Construct Yara Rules. Firstly, fill the Yara rule's string field. List all string features with the form of *"$s0=[api_ name, ret_ value, argvs]"* and append the feature's weight at the end of each row.

Secondly, the condition field of the Yara rule is constructed by multiplying the feature and the weight value and accumulating all the results, plus an offset θ_0. Meanwhile, the judgment condition is set that when the result of the condition regular expression is greater than 0, the test sample is classified as malware.

Finally, with the generated Yara rule, we can develop malware detection. The generated Yara rule sample is shown in Fig. 2.

Random Forest-Based Rule Generation. Random Forest is an ensemble-based method that combines the results of multiple decision tree classifiers for a single output. Random Forest contributed an extra functionality to the bagging process by randomly drawing bootstrap samples from training data. Further, each selected sample grows as an unpruned tree, and a split decision at each node is based on the best-selected predictor from randomly chosen predictors. The label is assigned based on a majority voting by base classifiers in the testing phase.

For the original training set D(X, Y) with a total number of n samples, we build k decision trees and record all the malicious node. After we get the forest model, we construct Yara rules. First, fill the string field of the private rule of the Yara rule with the recorded malicious nodes in the k trees. Second, search the shortest paths from the root node of each tree to malicious nodes, and use the depth-first search method to construct the condition field of the private rule in the form of an AST tree. Finally, fill the condition field of the Yara rule with permutation and combination of multiple tree majority votes and get the last rule used for malware detection. The generated rule is shown as Fig. 3.

```
private rule tree0
{
    strings:
        $s0 = "LoadLibraryExW,0,1,C:\\WINDOWS\\system32\\lpk.dll,,,," fullword wide ascii
        $s1 = "NtReadVirtualMemory,0,2,RavMon.exe,1816,,," fullword wide ascii
        ......
    condition:
        ...
}
private rule tree1
{
    strings:
        $s0 = "LoadLibraryExW,0,1,C:\\WINDOWS\\system32\\lpk.dll,,,," fullword wide ascii
        $s1 = "NtReadVirtualMemory,0,2,RavMon.exe,1816,,," fullword wide ascii
        ......
    condition:
        ...
}
private rule tree2
{
    strings:
        $s0 = "LoadLibraryExW,0,1,C:\\WINDOWS\\system32\\version.dll,,,," fullword wide ascii
        $s1 = "NtReadFile,3c,1,C:\\WINDOWS\\WindowsShell.Manifest,,,," fullword wide ascii
        ......
    condition:
        ...
}
rule RF00
{
    condition:
        (tree0 and tree1)
        or (tree0 and tree2)
        or (tree1 and tree2)
}
```

Fig. 3. The generated Yara rule based on random forest model.

3.3 Malware Detection

Figure 4 shows that given a Yara rule, the Yara tool can identify and classify malicious samples through static rule matched.

```
rule black01
{
    strings:
    $s0 = "NtCreateMutant,0,1,uxJLpe1m,,,," fullword  wide ascii // weight: 7.502
    $s1 = "NtWriteVirtualMemory,0,2,svchost.exe,864,,," fullword  wide ascii // weight: 6.342
    $s2 = "NtReadFile,0,1,C:\\temp\\DXSETUP.exe,,,," fullword  wide ascii // weight: 6.169

    $s205 = "LoadLibraryExW,0,1,C:\\WINDOWS\\system32\\riched20.dll,,,," fullword  wide ascii // weight: -0.9937
    $s206 = "LoadLibraryExW,0,1,C:\\WINDOWS\\WinSxS\\x86_Microsoft.VC80.CRT_1fc8b3b9a1e18e3b_8.0.50727.3053_x-ww_b80fa8ca
    \\msvcr80.dll ,,,," fullword  wide ascii // weight: -1.142
    $s207 = "LoadLibraryExW,0,1,C:\\WINDOWS\\system32\\winspool.drv,,,," fullword  wide ascii // weight: -1.159

    condition:
    ((#s0 * 7.502) + (#s1 * 6.342) + (#s2 * 6.169) + ...... + (#s205 * -0.994) + (#s206 * -1.142) + (#s207 * -1.159) + (-6.299)) > 0

}
```

Fig. 4. Malware detection with the generated yara rule.

Specifically, the Yara tool scans the test sample and performs feature matching with the whole 208 API call features (i.e., $S0-S207$ listed in the string field). Then, according to the judgment in the condition field, all the matched features are weighted to calculate the maliciousness of the sample. If the weighted result is greater than 0, the test sample is malicious software; otherwise, it is benign software. The effectiveness of the Malware detection module is positively related to the efficiency and completeness of the rules and the volume of the test samples.

4   Evaluation

4.1   Experimental Setup

Our dataset consists of the dynamic running behavior of 40,000 WindowsPE files. These dynamic behaviors were obtained by running the samples in the cuckoo sandbox and further processing the generated dynamic behavior reports. We extracted the API traces contained in the dynamic behavior and divided this dataset equally into training and test sets. Both training and test sets contain 20,000 samples (10,000 malicious and 10,000 benign samples, respectively).

We used different machine learning models for automatic feature processing, training, and Yara rule generation on the training set. Eventually, we measured the performance from five metrics: Accuracy, FPR, Precision, Recall, and F1-score.

4.2   Malware Detection with the Generated Yara Rule

Section 3 described methods for automatically generating Yara rules. In order to explore the impact factors of malware detection results, we carried out experiments from the following aspects: dynamic feature extraction, training model, number of rules used for detection, rule categories, and training set volume. We divided the training set into subsets to generate multiple Yara rules and tested on the test set through rule stacking. Furthermore, one might argue that since our dataset does not consist of the dynamic behaviour according to a certain type of malware, it is not possible to generate Yara rules for a specific type of malware.

Feature Extraction. Firstly, group the training set. The malicious samples and benign samples in the training set were each divided into ten training subsets. Secondly, in order to evaluate the influence of the parameters passed by the API on the maliciousness of the program, we respectively trained the complete API sequence features, including API name and passed parameters, and the API features with no-parameters with logistic regression and random forest models. We passed 10 groups of malicious samples and benign samples with permutation and combination (i.e., in the form of *(blk0, wht0), (blk0, wht1)...(blk9, wht9)*) into two machine learning models and eventually got 100 generated Yara rules from the two models respectively. Thirdly, test the 200 generated rules on the test set. The experimental results are shown in Table 2. We analyzed the results from the following two aspects.

First, different features with the same training model. When using features including parameters, Yara rules generated by both models improved the accuracy of malware identification compared to features without parameters. The

Table 2. Performance of different features and training models.

Features	Training model	Rule_num	Acc[b]	FPR	R[b]	P[b]	F1-score
no-parameter API	LR[a]	100	0.76615	0.2004	0.7104	0.7995	0.7523
no-parameter API	RF[a]	100	0.83345	0.2408	0.9768	0.7590	0.8542
API with Paras	LR	100	0.8386	0.2084	0.9192	0.7915	0.8506
API with Paras	RF	100	0.86095	0.1836	0.9315	0.8163	0.8701

[a] LR (logistic regression), RF (random forest).
[b] Acc (accuracy), R (recall), P (precision).

accuracy of logistic regression and random forest improved by 9.5% and 3.3%, respectively, and the F1-score was improved by 13.1% and 1.9%, respectively. Meanwhile, with features including parameters, the recall of the logistic regression model was greatly improved by 29.4%, while the precision of random forest was increased by 7.5%, and FPR was reduced by 23.8%. It proves that the parameters passed by the API contain rich semantic information, which is of great significance to the maliciousness discrimination of the program.

Second, different training models with the same feature. Random forests performs better than logistic regression. When using features without parameters, random forests outperformed logistic regression models with 8.8% and 37.5% improvements in precision and recall, respectively. After training with the API parameters, the performance of logistic regression and random forest both improved. Specifically, compared with the logistic regression, the accuracy, recall and precision rate of the random forest model were improved by 2.7%, 1.3% and 3.1%, and FPR dropped by 11.9%. As can be seen, the rules generated by the random forest model are more efficient in malware detection than those generated by logistic regression, and the accuracy and F1-score have reached a relatively high level. To summarize, using the random forest model to train API traces with passed parameters, can we get the rules that perform better in malware detection.

Varying Number of Rules. In the previous section, we tested the performance of different features and different training models to generate Yara rules in malware detection. In this section, we measure the performance of malware detection with varying number of rules.

First, we used the 100 rules generated by the two models in the previous section on the test set and mapped the accuracy with the rule in a dictionary. The key was the rule name, and the value was the times of rule-matched.

Secondly, sort by value. The more times malicious samples were matched by the rule, the higher the rule was ranked. The rule ranked top was considered the best and most effective rule for malware detection. According to the sorted results, test on the test set with the top 100, 20, 15, 10, and 5 rules, respectively. The results of the rules generated by logistic regression and random forest are shown in Table 3 and Table 4, respectively.

Table 3. Performance of LR model with varying number of rules.

Rule_num	Acc	FPR	R	P	F1-score
100	0.8386	0.2084	0.9192	0.7915	0.8506
20	0.8450	0.1531	0.8435	0.8468	0.8451
15	0.84975	0.14351	0.8403	0.8564	0.8483
10	0.84355	0.12855	0.806	0.8714	0.8374
5	0.84395	0.1046	0.7789	0.8953	0.8331

Table 4. Performance of RF model with varying number of rules.

Rule_num	Acc	FPR	R	P	F1-score
100	0.86095	0.18836	0.9315	0.8163	0.8701
20	0.8880	0.1312	0.9161	0.8637	0.8891
15	0.8906	0.1238	0.9098	0.87615	0.8927
10	0.89015	0.1106	0.8912	0.8890	0.8901
5	0.8561	0.0980	0.7994	0.9016	0.8474

According to the experimental results in Table 3 and Table 4, we found that the detection effect of malicious samples was not completely positively correlated with the number of rules; that is, not the more number of rules leads to a better detection effect. By analyzing the metrics in the table, we found that as the number of rules increased, the accuracy first increased and then decreased, the recall gradually increased, and the precision gradually decreased. However, as we reduced the number of rules, which meant improving the quality of rules and selecting more effective rules with higher rankings, we found that the FPR did gradually decrease, and the drop of FPR was in line with our expectations.

As recall gradually increased and precision decreased, we used F1-score to evaluate recall and precision comprehensively. Considering the metrics of Accuracy and F1-score, we found that when the number of rules was 15, the accuracy and F1-score reached the peak simultaneously; that is, the effectiveness of malware detection was the best.

On the other hand, comparing Table 4 with Table 3, we found that, compared with the rules generated by the logistic regression model, the rules generated by the random forest model performed better in malicious sample detection. Taking Rule_num=15 as an example, compared with logistic regression, the Accuracy and F1-score of the random forest increased by 4.8% and 5.2%, and the FPR decreased by 13.7%. It can be concluded that when the rules generated by a single model are used for malware detection, the random forest model is recommended for training, and the number of rules is recommended to be 15, to get the best malware detection effect.

Rules Stacking. However, due to the complex judgment logic, although the rules generated by the random forest performed better on rule-based matching, it worked slow. Considering the efficiency and effectiveness, we tried to detect malware by stacking the rules of the two models. Take the random forest rule_num equal to 5 (the shortest time and better performance), and the logistic regression model rules_num are 5, 10, 15, and 20, respectively. The experimental results are shown in Table 5.

Table 5. Performance of stacking varying number of LR rules and 5 RF rules

LR Rule_num	Acc	FPR	R	P	F1-score
20	0.85975	0.16249	0.8927	0.8375	0.8642
15	0.86395	0.1550	0.8915	0.8449	0.8676
10	0.8607	0.14435	0.8678	0.85564	0.8617
5	0.86912	0.1308	0.8580	0.86912	0.8635

As shown from the table, compared to malware detection with the rules generated by a single model, it can further improve the detection effect using the stacking of different model rules. For example, the Accuracy and F1-score of 5 random forest rules stacked on n logistic regression rules improved by 1.5% and 1.9% compared to 5 random forest rules. Similarly, 15 logistic regression rules stacked with 5 random forest rules improved by 1.7% and 2.3% compared to 15 logistic regression rules alone.

Grouping Method of Training Set. In order to further improve the effect of malware detection, we changed the grouping method of the training set. As shown above, the first grouping method divided the malicious samples and benign samples in training set into ten subsets. Each subset consisted of 1000 malicious samples and 1000 benign samples. Our second grouping method is that only malicious samples were randomly divided into ten groups, and benign samples were not divided. Each training subset includes 1000 malicious samples and 10000 benign samples. By passing the training subsets into the two machine learning models, we eventually got 20 Yara rules. Followed the same experimental steps as the previous section, we carried out the test on the test set with single and stack model rules. The results are shown in Table 6.

Table 6. The effectiveness of rules training with second grouping method.

Rule_num	Training model	Acc	FPR	R	P	F1-score
10	LR	0.82245	0.02349	0.6609	0.9765	0.7882
10	RF	0.7455	0.01748	0.5	0.9825	0.6627
20	LR+RF	0.8292	0.0298	0.6792	0.97014	0.7990

As can be seen from Table 6, comparing the Yara rules generated by the second grouping method with rules in first grouping method, although the accuracy and f1-score of second grouping method were not as good as the results in group 1, the precision metrics of the second grouping method was much higher than that of the first grouping method with a significant improvement. The precision could be as high as 98.25% with the rules generated by the logistic regression model. Considering Accuracy and F1-score, we found the precision could also be as high as 97.01% with rules generated by the logistic regression model and random forest model.

5   Related Work

Considerable research has been conducted in malware detection and analysis. In principle, the dynamic behavior of whether a program carries out malicious operations is a representative feature to detect malware effectively. An approach followed by most researchers is to consider API calls. APIs are the only way for a program to interact with the underlying operating systems and its resources. Thus, most of the malicious operations carried out by a piece of malware involve one or more APIs. Therefore, by analyzing the sequence of API calls, the dynamic behavioral features of malware can be obtained, which can then be used for malware detection.

5.1   API Call Feature-Based Work

Rieck et al. [15] obtained the API of the program through the dynamic analysis method and constructed features by statistics the occurrence frequency of each API. Qiao et al. [13] constructed features based on the frequency of API being called. Eskandari et al. [7] believe that in addition to obtaining the API of the program, it is also necessary to preserve the calling sequence information of the API. They obtain the API sequence and extract API sequence features with the n-gram method, which makes up for the lack of API calling sequence research in some related works to a certain extent. Ahmed et al. [2] also extracted features at runtime through dynamic analysis. They used spatial features and sequential features. Spatial features are composed of API parameters and return values, and sequential features are composed of API call sequences. Park et al. [12] did not directly use the APIs as a feature but the obtained system call sequence as a feature by dynamically running the analyzed program in a sandbox. Zhang et al. [23] proposed API-Graph, which built API calling graphs to represent the internal relationships between various programming entities. Moreover, they fed the API graphs into Random Forest, Model Pool, SVM, and DNN to train malware detectors.

5.2   Yara Related Work

In recent years, the Yara rules technique has emerged as a widely accepted technique for malware analysis due to its flexible and customizable nature, allowing malware analysts to develop Yara rules according to their specific requirements in targeting specific types of threats [11]. Therefore, generating the most effective Yara rules is the biggest challenge in applying Yara rules for malware analysis. Yara rules can be generated either manually or automatically [5,14]. Generating Yara rules manually requires a highly-specialized skill-set in a specific security area, whereas generating Yara rules automatically with a tool is relatively easy. Three typical tools [6] yarGen, YaraGenerator, and Yabin are used to generate Yara rules automatically, and all of them are Python-based and open-source. Moreover, with the popularity of Yara, some excellent open-source projects maintain a repository to collect a complete set of Yara rules and keep it as up-to-date as possible. For example, the awesome-Yara Project [9] collected by InQuest is a collection of major manufacturers, such as FireEye, McAfee, spyre, and plenty of automated Yara rule generation tools and plugins are included, including ida_Yara, YaraGen-x64dbg-plugin, etc.

These studies inspire our proposed method. However, the main advantage of our work over these studies is that we pay attention to the parameter features' contribution to malware detection. Furthermore, we integrate and automate the feature extraction, training, automated Yara rules generation and malware detection, and eventually achieve better performance.

These studies inspire our proposed method. However, unlike employing the single feature of API, we weight API calls with the passed parameters and evaluate their sensitivities to malicious behavior. Then, we used a machine learning model to train the extracted dynamic features and automatically generate the Yara rule. The main advantage of our work over these studies is that we pay attention to the parameter features' contribution to malware detection and integrate and automate the feature extraction, training, automated Yara rules generation, and malware detection together, and finally achieve better performance.

6   Conclusion

In this paper, we propose a malware detection method using automatically generated Yara rules on dynamic behavioral features. First, we extract the dynamic behavior of the PE file under Windows and use its API calling sequence with the passed parameters as dynamic features to generate the embedding. After that, features are trained with two classic linear and nonlinear models in machine learning by YaraML. In addition, we focus on the impact of the parameters passed by the API call sequence on the maliciousness discrimination during the training process and introduce the concept of feature's weight into the Yara rule to weight each string (API call) used for static feature matched. Eventually, we use the automatically generated Yara rules to detect malware. Our method effectively improves the performance of malicious judgment for Windows PE files. Moreover, to a certain extent, it can effectively resist the obfuscation technologies such as packing, encryption, and polymorphism of malware. Furthermore, to improve the detection performance, we plan to use the DNN model to train the features in future work to mine deeper semantic information in dynamic features and get better performance.

Acknowledgements. This work is supported by the National Natural Science Foundation of China (Grant No. 62072453, 61972392), Youth Innovation Promotion Association of the Chinese Academy of Sciences (No. 2020164).

References

1. Sonicwall2022-cyber-threat-report.   https://www.sonicwall.com/2022-cyber-threat-report
2. Ahmed, F., Hameed, H., Shafiq, M.Z., Farooq, M.: Using spatio-temporal information in API calls with machine learning algorithms for malware detection. In: The 2nd ACM Workshop on Security and Artificial Intelligence, pp. 55–62 (2009)
3. Alvarez, V.M.: yara documentation4.2.0 (2022)
4. Ashraf, A., Aziz, A., Zahoora, U., Rajarajan, M., Khan, A.: Ransomware analysis using feature engineering and deep neural networks. arXiv preprint arXiv:1910.00286 (2019)
5. Brengel, M., Rossow, C.: {YARIX}: Scalable {YARA-based} malware intelligence. In: 30th USENIX Security Symposium, pp. 3541–3558 (2021)
6. Clark, C.: Yaragenerator. XenoSec (2013)
7. Eskandari, M., Khorshidpur, Z., Hashemi, S.: To incorporate sequential dynamic features in malware detection engines. In: 2012 European Intelligence and Security Informatics Conference, pp. 46–52. IEEE (2012)
8. Gupta, S., Kumar, P.: An immediate system call sequence based approach for detecting malicious program executions in cloud environment. Wireless Pers. Commun. **81**(1), 405–425 (2015)
9. InQuest: awesome-yara (2016). https://github.com/InQuest/awesome-yara
10. Jaramillo, L.E.S.: Detecting malware capabilities with Foss: lessons learned through a real-life incident. In: 2018 13th Iberian Conference on Information Systems and Technologies (CISTI), pp. 1–6. IEEE (2018)
11. Naik, N., Jenkins, P., Cooke, R., Gillett, J., Jin, Y.: Evaluating automatically generated yara rules and enhancing their effectiveness. In: 2020 IEEE Symposium Series on Computational Intelligence (SSCI), pp. 1146–1153. IEEE (2020)
12. Park, Y., Reeves, D., Mulukutla, V., Sundaravel, B.: Fast malware classification by automated behavioral graph matching. In: Proceedings of the Sixth Annual Workshop on Cyber Security and Information Intelligence Research, pp. 1–4 (2010)
13. Qiao, Y., Yang, Y., Ji, L., He, J.: Analyzing malware by abstracting the frequent itemsets in api call sequences. In: 2013 12th IEEE International Conference on Trust, Security and Privacy in Computing and Communications, pp. 265–270. IEEE (2013)
14. Raff, E., Zak, R., et al.: Automatic Yara rule generation using biclustering. In: The 13th ACM Workshop on Artificial Intelligence and Security, pp. 71–82 (2020)
15. Rieck, K., Holz, T., Willems, C., Düssel, P., Laskov, P.: Learning and classification of malware behavior. In: Zamboni, D. (ed.) DIMVA 2008. LNCS, vol. 5137, pp. 108–125. Springer, Heidelberg (2008). https://doi.org/10.1007/978-3-540-70542-0_6
16. Saxe, J., Mentis, D., Greamo, C.: Visualization of shared system call sequence relationships in large malware corpora. In: Proceedings of the Ninth International Symposium on Visualization for Cyber Security, pp. 33–40 (2012)
17. Saxe, J.: Yaraml (2020). https://github.com/sophos-ai/yaraml_rules/

18. Schultz, M.G., Eskin, E., Zadok, F., Stolfo, S.J.: Data mining methods for detection of new malicious executables. In: Proceedings 2001 IEEE Symposium on Security and Privacy. S&P 2001, pp. 38–49. IEEE (2000)
19. Tandon, G., Chan, P.K.: Learning useful system call attributes for anomaly detection. In: FLAIRS Conference, pp. 405–411 (2005)
20. Varghese, S.M., Jacob, K.P.: Anomaly detection using system call sequence sets. J. Softw. **2**(6), 14–21 (2007)
21. Ye, Y., Li, T., Adjeroh, D., Iyengar, S.S.: A survey on malware detection using data mining techniques. ACM Comput. Surv. (CSUR) **50**(3), 1–40 (2017)
22. Ye, Y., Wang, D., Li, T., Ye, D.: IMDS: intelligent malware detection system. In: Proceedings of the 13th ACM SIGKDD International Conference on Knowledge Discovery and Data Mining, pp. 1043–1047 (2007)
23. Zhang, X., et al.: Enhancing state-of-the-art classifiers with API semantics to detect evolved android malware. In: The 2020 ACM SIGSAC Conference on Computer and Communications Security, pp. 757–770 (2020)

Mobile System Security

Question Answering Models for Privacy Policies of Mobile Apps: Are We There Yet?

Khalid Alkhattabi[✉], Davita Bird, Kai Miller, and Chuan Yue[✉]

Colorado School of Mines, 1500 Illinois St, Golden, CO 80401, USA
{kalkhattabi,davitabird,kbhoshijo,chuanyue}@mines.edu

Abstract. Increasing interest in assisting users by accurately and automatically answering their questions has spawned numerous efforts on using Deep Learning (DL) to solve Question Answering (QA) problems. These efforts have resulted in different QA models capable of answering questions on various topics. Research shows that existing QA models perform well on generic questions (e.g., about sports, news, and common knowledge); however, the ability of QA models to answer basic but important questions about mobile apps' privacy policies is unknown. In this paper, we first derived a set of 43 basic questions concerning mobile apps' privacy policies based on global privacy laws. Then, we constructed two datasets of labeled (Passage, Question, Answer) 3-tuples. Finally, we conducted two main experiments to evaluate the ability and effectiveness of existing QA models in answering basic questions about mobile apps' privacy policies. Our experimental results show that (1) existing QA models perform poorly in answering basic questions about mobile apps' privacy policies, and (2) fine-tuning existing QA models using our QA datasets can help improve their performance. We hope our datasets and findings can help researchers build better QA models for more accurately answering questions about mobile apps' privacy policies.

Keywords: Privacy policy · Mobile app · Question Answering · NLP models

1 Introduction

A mobile app's privacy policy is a legal document describing how users' information is collected, used, stored, and shared by the mobile app. Ideally, users should read a mobile app's privacy policy and they may look for answers to their specific questions such as the types of the information that could be collected. However, such policies are often long and complex, making them difficult to read and understand [10,12]. Thus, it is beneficial to develop tools to help users by accurately and automatically answer their questions about mobile apps' privacy policies.

Recently, there are lots of research efforts on developing Question Answering (QA) models that can answer a variety of questions from users. These efforts

© The Author(s), under exclusive license to Springer Nature Switzerland AG 2022
C. Su et al. (Eds.): SciSec 2022, LNCS 13580, pp. 333–352, 2022.
https://doi.org/10.1007/978-3-031-17551-0_22

have taken Deep Learning (DL) as the primary approach. For example, the Bi-directional Attention Flow (BiDAF) model uses recurrent neural network (RNN) hierarchical layers of long short-term memory (LSTM) to tackle the QA problem [19]. The Bidirectional Encoder Representations from Transformers (BERT) model [11] and the Text-to-Text Transfer Transformer (T5) model [15] both use the transformer architecture [20], and they can be used to build QA models.

These QA models perform well on generic questions (e.g., about sports, news, and common knowledge). However, their ability to answer basic but important questions about mobile apps' privacy policies remains unknown. Basic questions are a set of questions that ask about the major aspects of a mobile app's privacy policy. For example: What information is collected from users? What is the effective date of the privacy policy? How can a user contact the app developer or provider with further questions? These are basic but important questions that any user may ask about a mobile app's privacy policy. Ideally, these questions should have the corresponding answers clearly written in each mobile app's privacy policy.

Prior studies have investigated QA models regarding privacy policies [9,18]. They built privacy policy datasets to train and test different QA models. Their datasets were created by reviewing privacy policies either from authors themselves [9] or from crowdworkers [18]. However, the datasets (especially the questions in them) created directly from privacy policies are often not comprehensive because many privacy policies are not well written in the first place; meanwhile, responses provided by crowdworkers often contain errors. Correspondingly, evaluating QA models based on these datasets will be insufficient.

In this paper, our primary goal is to evaluate the ability and effectiveness of existing QA models in answering basic questions about mobile apps' privacy policies. Specifically, we have the following three research questions:

- RQ1: What is a basic set of privacy policy questions about mobile apps?
- RQ2: How well can existing QA models answer this basic set of privacy policy questions about mobile apps, and which questions are difficult to answer?
- RQ3: How can the performance of existing QA models be improved to better answer the privacy policy questions about mobile apps?

Our RQ1 aims to derive a set of basic questions about mobile apps' privacy policies that are consistent with the principles and guidelines in global privacy laws. These questions will be designed to explore the major aspects of mobile apps' privacy policies. We derived 43 basic questions, which are considered in the scope of the mobile apps' privacy policies. Further, we checked these 43 basic questions by reviewing 20 mobile apps' privacy policies. We found answers to most of our questions in those privacy policies. We also found that one of the privacy policies contains the answers to all our 43 basic questions.

Our RQ2 is to assess the ability of the existing QA models in answering the basic questions about mobile apps' privacy policies. To do this, we first used the 43 basic questions and the 20 mobile apps' privacy policies to construct two datasets that will be used in our evaluation. Dataset1 contains 41,754 unique (Passage, Question, Answer) 3-tuples, including both questions that have an answer and questions to which an answer does not exist. Dataset2 is a subset of Dataset1, and it contains 2,225 unique (Passage, Question, Answer) 3-tuples in which each question has an answer in the corresponding passage. We then selected three state-of-the-art QA models BiDAF [19], BERT [11], and T5 [15] to evaluate their performance on our two datasets. For each of the three models, we used the average F1 as our primary metric for assessing the overall performance. We also pursued to understand which of those 43 basic questions were difficult for the existing QA models to answer.

Our RQ3 aims to improve QA models to better answer the basic questions about mobile apps' privacy policies. As a starting point, we combined our datasets with the existing datasets to improve the performance of QA models.

Our evaluation results show that the existing QA models perform poorly in answering basic questions about mobile apps' privacy policies. The overall performance for all three models (BiDAF, BERT, and T5) is 19.78%, 45.12%, and 47.01% on F1 scores, respectively, when they were trained on SquadV1, tested on Dataset2, and evaluated based on the top answer. In contrast, the overall performance of the three models increased to 33.20%, 61.90%, and 59.01% on F1 scores, respectively, when they were evaluated based on the top-3 answers. Furthermore, we found that questions about the policy update dates and effective dates are more straightforward to answer by the models than other questions. On the other hand, questions related to data collection purposes and third-parties are much more challenging to answer than other questions. Finally, we found that combining our datasets with existing datasets results in an improvement in the performance of the QA models.

The main contributions of this paper are as follows:

- We derived a set of 43 basic questions about mobile apps' privacy policies.
- We constructed two datasets (labeled by three of us) based on the 43 basic questions and 20 mobile apps' privacy policies; these datasets can be used by researchers to measure or evaluate the performance of QA models.
- We evaluated the effectiveness of three state-of-the-art QA models, and found that they perform poorly in answering the basic questions about mobile apps' privacy policies.
- We found that fine-tuning existing QA models using our datasets can help improve their performance.

2   Background and Related Work

2.1   Background

Question Answering (QA). QA is a Natural Language Processing (NLP) task for answering users' questions automatically on any given passage. Recently, DL techniques have become a widely used approach to tackle the problem. As a result, various state-of-the-art QA models have become available. Some representative models are Bi-directional Attention Flow (BiDAF), Bidirectional Encoder

Representations from Transformers (BERT), and Text-To-Text Transfer Transformer (T5).

BiDAF has a hierarchical architecture with seven layers to process the input data (passage and question) and generate the output (answer) [19]. These layers include: Character Embedding, Word Embedding, Highway Network, Contextual Embedding, Attention Flow, Modeling, and Output [19]. These layers use a variety of neural networks including a recurrent neural network (RNN) and bi-directional Long Short-Term Memory (LSTM) models. BiDAF uses an attention mechanism that helps find context-to-question and question-to-context attentions, thus identifying the most relevant words in a passage to a question and vice versa [19]. Among the three QA models, what makes BiDAF unique is the use of LSTM within the contextual embedding layer, which allows it to keep track of all useful information without forgetting or ignoring during learning [14].

The BERT model was released by Google in 2019 [11]. It is pretrained on two large datasets. The main objectives of BERT are to predict the masked tokens and to predict the next sentence. Meanwhile, it can reuse information to solve a new problem by using transfer learning or fine-tuning. The BERT model is built on an original transformer that has an encoder, used for reading inputs, and a decoder, used for making the prediction [20]. The BERT model uses an attention mechanism, termed self-attention, that takes every word in a sequence and generates an embedding for it based on its spatial relationships with other words in the same sequence [20].

T5 is a new model released in 2020, also by Google [15]. T5 outperforms most existing models on many NLP tasks [15]. It is pretrained on the Colossal Clean Crawled Corpus (C4). Similar to the BERT model, T5 can reuse information to solve many NLP tasks with transfer learning. T5 is a unified framework to convert any NLP task to a text-to-text problem to solve [15]. BERT and T5 differ from BiDAF in that they use transformers and are better suited for transfer learning techniques.

2.2   Related Work

Question Answering for Privacy Policies. Prior studies have investigated QA for privacy policies. Some studies have created new QA datasets to train and validate QA models [9,13,18]. For instance, Abhilasha et al. [18] built the PrivacyQA dataset for mobile apps' privacy policies with more than 3,600 pairs of questions and answers. The questions in the PrivacyQA dataset were generated by crowdworkers, each of whom provided five questions by reading mobile apps' descriptions and screenshots. However, constructing questions based on app descriptions can be inaccurate and incomplete.

In a similar vein, Wasi et al. [9] constructed PolicyQA, a large dataset for websites' privacy policies curated from an existing corpus of OPP-115 [21]. PolicyQA has 25,017 (Passage, Question, Answer) 3-tuples, 714 questions of which were written by domain experts by reviewing 115 websites' privacy policies. In another work, Hamza et al. [13] built a new QA dataset consisting of questions posted by Twitter users about privacy policies. However, questions asked by users on social networking sites, such as Twitter, may not cover all aspects of the policies or may be beyond the scope of privacy policies.

In a different vein, Benjamin et al. [10,12] analyzed the readability of privacy policies of websites, showing that privacy policies are still challenging to read. The authors' finding shows that, on average, a privacy statement's readability level is above the average of an American's reading level.

3   Methodology and Datasets

In this section, we first provide a brief overview of the methodology we follow to evaluate the existing QA models. Also, we elaborate on how we derive 43 basic questions about mobile apps' privacy policies from global privacy laws. We further describe how we construct two datasets based on the 43 basic questions and 20 mobile apps' privacy policies.

3.1   Overview of Our Methodology

Figure 1 shows an overview of our methodology for evaluating the existing QA models for mobile apps' privacy policies. First, we used global privacy laws as the source for deriving 43 basic questions about mobile apps' privacy policies. Next, we answered those 43 questions for each paragraph of a set of 20 mobile apps' privacy policies. With our answers, we constructed two datasets: Dataset1 and Dataset2. Both datasets consist of (Passage, Question, Answer) 3-tuples. Dataset1 contains questions that have an answer and questions to which an answer does not exist. Dataset2 only contains questions that have the answers in passages.

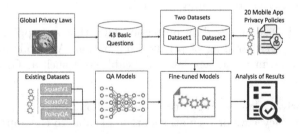

Fig. 1. Overview of our methodology.

After constructing the two datasets, we selected the existing datasets we would use to fine-tune QA models. Next, we selected the candidate QA models to use in our evaluation. After that, we fine-tuned these selected QA models by using the most common QA datasets available in the existing research. Finally, we tested the fine-tuned QA models on our two newly generated datasets and analyzed the results.

3.2   Using Global Privacy Laws to Derive 43 Basic Questions

To derive a set of basic questions concerning mobile apps' privacy policies, we turned to global privacy laws. We sourced seven national, state, and international privacy laws from the UK, Canada, South Africa, Australia, Brazil, California, and European Union [1–6,8]. These global privacy laws provide privacy policy principles and checklists that guide businesses for the development of privacy policies and the protection of individuals' data.

Ideally, the privacy policy of a mobile app should be comprehensive enough to address all principles and outlines expressed in these laws. For example, mobile apps' privacy policies should have the information about data collection, data use, users' rights, etc. Correspondingly, when users install or consider to install an app, they may ask basic questions about the major aspects of its privacy policy to decide if using the app would incur privacy risks. However, such a set of basic but important questions that can well capture the global privacy laws does not exist.

Therefore, we set out to first derive such a set of basic questions that can be representative and relevant to mobile apps' privacy policies. We surveyed the aforementioned seven global privacy laws and looked closely at each privacy principle expressed in the laws. We then derived the major questions from the text of each principle. Eventually, we formed a set of 43 basic questions about mobile apps' privacy policies as listed below. We describe them in groups, and the questions in the same group are closely related or similar but with different words that appear in practice.

Questions 1 and 2 ask about the business or app name and its services. The official name of the business or mobile app is an important part of a privacy policy.

- Q1: What is the name of the app?
- Q2: What services does the app provide?

Questions 3 and 4 ask about data protection laws that are applicable to complaints regarding the handling of private information. A mobile app's privacy policy should conform to privacy laws applicable to it such as GDPR and UK laws.

- Q3: What privacy laws or regulations do we follow?
- Q4: What privacy laws or regulations are applicable to the app?

Questions 5 through 12 ask about the data collection activities of first parties. They inquire about what data is collected, used, or disclosed and why.

- Q5: What information do we collect from you?
- Q6: What personal data or information do we collect from you?
- Q7: How do we collect information from you?
- Q8: How do we collect personal data or information from you?
- Q9: How do we use the collected information?
- Q10: How do we use the collected personal data or information?

- Q11: What is the purpose of collecting your information?
- Q12: What is the purpose of collecting your personal data or information?

Questions 13 through 21 ask about the activities of third parties regarding information collected, shared, sold to, or sold by. Question 17 asks for the names of third parties that receive the information or personal data.

- Q13: What information is collected by third parties?
- Q14: What personal data or information is collected by third parties?
- Q15: What information do we share with third parties?
- Q16: What personal data or information do we share with third parties?
- Q17: What are the names of third parties related to our app?
- Q18: What information do we sell to third parties?
- Q19: What personal data or information do we sell to third parties?
- Q20: What is the purpose of sharing information to third parties?
- Q21: What is the purpose of sharing personal information or data to third parties?

Questions 22 through 28 ask about the rights of users to control their own information and choices under the applicable privacy laws including the rights of users to opt-out of privacy settings.

- Q22: What are your rights?
- Q23: How can you submit a request or question regarding your rights?
- Q24: How can you withdraw or opt-out of your consent?
- Q25: How can you withdraw or opt-out of data collection?
- Q26: How can you opt-out of receiving targeted advertisements?
- Q27: How can you opt-out of using cookies?
- Q28: How long does it take for us to process withdrawing or opt-out requests?

Question 29 asks how users will be notified if privacy policies will be changed. How a company informs users of privacy policy changes is important. Companies may inform users via email, phone, or text message.

- Q29: How will we notify you if we make any changes to this privacy policy?

Question 30 and 31 ask about the original effective date and update date for privacy policies. Every privacy policy must contain an effective date about when the current privacy policy became effective and an update date about when the privacy policy was last updated.

- Q30: What is the effective date of this privacy policy?
- Q31: When was this privacy policy updated?

Question 32 asks about the measures businesses or apps take to protect users' data and privacy. Ideally, every mobile app's privacy policy should describe the criteria and procedures used for data protection such as encryption.

- Q32: What security measures do we use to protect your personal data or information?

Questions 33 and 34 ask about children's privacy under applicable privacy laws.

- Q33: What information do we collect from children?
- Q34: What personal data or information do we collect from children?

Questions 35 through 37 ask about the retention of data by a business under data privacy laws. A statement that describes how long the data will be stored and where it will be stored should ideally be included in every mobile app's privacy policy.

- Q35: What is the data retention policy?
- Q36: How long do we store the data or information we collected from you?
- Q37: Where do we store the collected data or information?

Questions 38 through 40 ask about the procedure for handling complaints and inquiries. They also ask who is responsible for a particular complaint or inquiry.

- Q38: What is the procedure to respond to your complaints or inquiries?
- Q39: Who will respond to your complaints or inquiries?
- Q40: How long does it take to respond to your complaints or inquiries?

Question 41 asks about international data transferring policy, which is especially applicable to businesses and apps whose operations run across borders.

- Q41: What is the international data transferring policy?

Questions 42 and 43 ask about the contact information of a business or app. A mobile app's privacy policy should provide the contact information (e.g., name, email address) that users may use to communicate with the app owner or other involved parties.

- Q42: How can you contact us if you have questions?
- Q43: Whom should you contact if you have questions?

Relevance and Comprehensiveness of Our Basic Questions. To validate the relevance of the 43 questions, we ran an experiment to measure if our questions covered the major aspects of mobile apps' privacy policies. We examined 20 privacy policies from 20 different mobile apps. We selected ten mobile apps from the top-100 free mobile apps in the Google Play store, and the other ten randomly from a list of over 3M mobile apps in the Google Play store. We then mapped all the questions and their answers from the mobile apps' privacy policies.

Table 1 shows the 20 apps and the number of questions (out of 43) that we have the answers in each mobile app's privacy policy. We found that, on average, 30.8 (71.6%) of our 43 basic questions had an answer in each top mobile app's privacy policy. Overall, this set of 43 basic questions about mobile apps' privacy policies is relevant and comprehensive. Therefore, we moved forward using these questions and their answers to construct two datasets for evaluating the ability of QA models. Note that top apps contain the answers to more questions than randomly chosen apps. For example, one top app even covers 100% of the 43 basic questions.

3.3 Constructing and Labeling Our Two Datasets

After finalizing the above set of 43 questions, we followed one common practice in NLP to divide each of the 20 privacy policies (of the 20 mobile apps listed in Table 1) into paragraphs (segments) each with a maximum of 512 tokens. Next, three of us independently went through the 20 privacy policies paragraph by paragraph to identify the answers to all the 43 questions. If a question has a concrete answer in a paragraph, we wrote down the answer; otherwise, we noted that the paragraph does not contain an answer to the question.

Next, we aggregated our team members' answers to all the questions. We wanted our final dataset to contain just one answer for each of the 43 questions for each paragraph, so this aggregation was necessary. We followed the following two rules in aggregating the three sets of answers:

Table 1. Mobile apps and questions covered

Mobile app	Random or Top app	Questions covered
actiongames.games.sfd	Random	19 (44.18%)
addnote.vnps.addnotes	Random	28 (65.11%)
addtomob.lndv6.kitabcha	Random	29 (67.44%)
ae.adnec.android	Random	19 (44.18%)
af.ahg.buberdriver	Random	30 (69.7%)
agengineering.cardio	Random	6 (13.95%)
ai.capitalise.mobile	Random	34 (79.06%)
ai.cloudmall.android	Random	23 (53.48%)
ai.z1	Random	27 (62.79%)
air.air.BeautifyKira	Random	27 (62.79%)
cn.danatech.xingseus	Top	29 (67.44%)
com.abi.draw.onepart.dop	Top	20 (46.51%)
com.amazon.avod.thirdpartyclient	Top	34 (79.06%)
com.anotherplaceproductions.fat2fit	Top	35 (81.39%)
com.bgg.jump	Top	43 (100%)
com.catwalk.fashion.star	Top	31 (72.09%)
com.cdgames.fidget3d	Top	14 (32.55%)
com.cleanteam.oneboost	Top	30 (69.7%)
com.contextlogic.wish	Top	37 (86.04%)
com.amazon.mShop.android.shopping	Top	35 (81.39)

- If two or three members of our team wrote down an answer to a question, we labeled the answer existing (E).
- If no member of our team wrote down an answer to a question, we labeled the answer not existing (N/E).

Following the aggregation rules above, we obtained a dataset containing 45,116 (Passage, Question, Answer) 3-tuples. Using majority voting, our three team members agreed on 94.4% (42,580) of the 45,116 3-tuples that had answers or were left blank (no answers exist). Out of those 42,580 3-tuples, 40,355 (94.7%) had no answer, leaving a set of 2,225 3-tuples with agreed answers clearly contained in the passages (each of which is a paragraph in a privacy policy). The remaining 5.6% of the 45,116 3-tuples, for which our team members could not agree on the existence or non-existence of an answer, were rejected and deleted from our dataset.

Our last step was to delete the redundant data in this large dataset, leaving our final dataset with 41,754 annotated 3-tuples - this is referred to as **Dataset1**. We refer to the subset of Dataset1, which contains 2,225 3-tuples all with answers in the corresponding passages, as **Dataset2**.

Next, we performed data preprocessing to transform the passages in the 3-tuples into a more digestible format, which is a common practice that can often help enhance the accuracy of NLP models. We removed HTML tags and extra whitespaces. We also replaced digits with a special token <digit>, email addresses with a special token <email>, phone numbers with a special token <phone>, URLs with a special token <url>, and punctuations with the whitespace, etc. Meanwhile, we converted all accented characters to ASCII characters and made all the text lowercase.

In the end, we finalized the construction of Dataset1 and Dataset2. Those 20 privacy policies contain 954 unique paragraphs with a total of 1,096,781 words (among which 2,734 are unique words). Most sentences have 3 to 50 words in length. The average sentence length is 34.88 words.

4   Experiments and Analyses

Using the two datasets constructed above, we conducted two main experiments to evaluate the effectiveness of existing QA models in answering the 43 basic questions about mobile apps' privacy policies. Experiment 1 assesses the ability of QA models from four perspectives: evaluating QA models based on the top answer, evaluating QA models based on the top-3 answers, evaluating QA models that are fine-tuned using our datasets, and identifying the easy and difficult questions for the existing QA models to answer. Experiment 2 aims to improve QA models to better answer the basic questions about mobile apps' privacy policies. In this section, we present the experimental setup, evaluation metrics, and the detailed evaluation results.

4.1   Experimental Setup

In this subsection, we describe how we set up the experimental environment, including the selection of existing datasets and QA models.

Selecting Existing Datasets for Fine-Tuning QA Models. Various QA datasets are available for fine-tuning or training a QA model. In this work, we selected the most common QA datasets available to us: SquadV1 [17], SquadV2 [16], and PolicyQA [9]. The first two datasets, SquadV1 and SquadV2, are the largest and most popular datasets for fine-tuning QA models. These two datasets are large and diverse, consisting of 100,000+ questions on a set of Wikipedia articles [16,17]. The third dataset is PolicyQA, which contains 25K data samples on a set of 115 websites' privacy policies. PolicyQA is a large and dedicated QA dataset for websites' privacy policies. We rejected some datasets, such as PrivacyQA [18] because it is a binary dataset with each question being labeled according to its relevance or not to the text. See Table 2 for more comparison between our Dataset1, PrivacyQA, and PolicyQA.

Table 2. Comparison of PolicyQA, PrivacyQA, and Our Dataset1

	PolicyQA	Our Dataset1	PrivacyQA
Dataset source	115 website privacy policies	20 mobile app privacy policies	35 mobile app privacy policies
Question source	Privacy policies	Privacy laws	App descriptions
Question creators	Authors	Authors	Crowdworkers
Number of questions	714	43	1,750
Answer creators	Authors	Authors	domain experts
Dataset size	25,017	41,754	3,500
Answered questions	25,017	2,225	3,500

Selecting QA Models. To select QA models for our evaluation, we reviewed the existing literature on QA and made a shortlist of models to evaluate. We rejected some models due to the lack of official source code or instructions to train and test them. After further research and investigation, we found that the most relevant QA models are built using two main techniques: Long Short Term Memory (LSTM) [14] and Transformer [20]. Finally, we chose three QA models BiDAF, BERT, and T5 (as reviewed in Sect. 2) that were built upon these two techniques as the basis for our study.

These three models are representative and they are also widely used as foundations for other QA models. We further fine-tuned each of these three models using each of our three selected existing datasets. We used transformers HaggeFace [4] and ByTorch [7] to fine-tune the QA models.

Fine-Tuning QA Models. When fine-tuning the three QA models, we used the same parameters as in the original source code to ensure the accuracy and fairness of an evaluation. In Table 3, we reported the parameters used in the original models and correspondingly in our experiments.

Table 3. Parameters used for our experiments

Parameters	BERT	T5	BiDAF
Train_batch_size	24	24	12–16
Learning_rate	3.00E-05	3.00E-05	0.5–0.0002
Num_train_epochs	5	5	5–12-15
Max_seq_length	384	384	400
Word embedding	Glove_300d	Glove_300d	Glove_100d-300d
Optimizer	Adam	Adam	Adam-AdaDelta

Table 4. Experimental replications

Models	Dataset	Originaly Reported		Replicated	
		F1%	EM%	F1%	EM%
BERT	SquadV1	88.5	80.8	87.48	79.56
	SquadV2	77.1	74.4	74.88	71.21
	PolicyQA	61.2	32.7	59.11	30.95
T5	SquadV1	92.08	85.44	92.08	85.44
	SquadV2	X	X	78.65	74.44
	PolicyQA	X	X	52.2	1.9
BiDAF	SquadV1	77.3	67.7	74.6	63.7
	SquadV2	*	*	*	*

We then moved on to test the accuracy of those models on the original test data. This is to verify that the models performed correctly as reported in the original studies [9,11,15,19]. Table 4 shows the top answer performance of our trained (replicated) models and that of the models reported in the original papers. The differences between the originally reported and our replicated performance results are quite small, indicating the correct fine-tuning and replications of those models in our experimental environment.

After fine-tuning and testing the three models on the original datasets (SquadV1, SquadV2, and PolicyQA), we tested them on our own datasets, Dataset1 and Dataset2, to evaluate their performance.

4.2   Identifying Metrics Used to Evaluate QA Models

The most popular metrics used to evaluate QA models are F1 and exact matches (EM) as we just saw in Table 4. We now provide more details about these two metrics. F1 is used to measure the precision and recall in a balanced manner, while EM is used to measure the exactness of a question-answer match. F1 can be computed by calculating how often a word represented in a model's predicted answer appears in the true answer. EM refers to whether the true answer is precisely the same as the model's prediction. Both metrics were used in the literature, but most studies mainly used F1 to measure the performance of a QA model. Thus, we decided to primarily use F1 in this study. We report EM results just as additional information.

In calculating F1, we followed the common practice to interpret the True Positive (TP), False Positive (FP), and False Negative (FN) as follows:

– TP indicates the number of shared (correlation) tokens between the actual answer and the predicted answer for a given question.
– FP represents the number of tokens in the predicted answer but not included in the actual answer for a given question.
– FN means the number of tokens in the actual answer but not in the predicted answer for a given question.

F1 is calculated by using the following formula:

$F1 = 2*(Precision * Recall)/(Precision + Recall)$, where $Precision = TP/(TP + FP)$ and $Recall = TP/(TP + FN)$.

We ran all of our experiments on our local server with 4 GPUs and with 32 GB RAM for each Tesla V100 GPU.

4.3 Experimental Design, Evaluation, and Analysis of Results

Experiment 1 for Answering RQ2: How Well Can Existing QA Models Answer Our Basic Set of 43 Privacy Policy Questions About Mobile Apps, and Which Questions Are Difficult to Answer? In this experiment, we aimed to evaluate the ability of QA models to answer basic questions about mobile apps' privacy policies. In particular, we measured the overall performance of QA models by using our Dataset1 and Dataset2.

We will analyze the overall performance of QA models from four perspectives: 1) evaluation based on the top answer, 2) evaluation based on the top-3 answers, 3) evaluating these models by fine-tuning them on our datasets, and 4) identifying the easy and difficult questions for QA models.

Sub-Experiment 1: Evaluating the Overall Performance Based on the Top Answer

Experimental Design: This sub-experiment sought to measure the ability of QA models to correctly identify answers to basic questions about mobile apps' privacy policies in terms of the top answer. We tested each QA model on our Dataset1 and Dataset2 and only considered the returned top answer for each question. Then, we calculated the average F1 score based on all the questions and answers.

Result: Figures 2 and 3 show the performance of QA models on our Dataset2 (2,225) and Dataset1 (41k), respectively. On Dataset2, the top answer results of this experiment show that when QA models were fine-tuned with SquadV1, the average F1 score was 45.12%, 47.01%, and 19.78% for BERT, T5, and BiDAF, respectively. This performance was significantly worse than expected, as even the highest 47.01% F1 score is far from being satisfying for users. This result leaves considerable room for future researchers to improve QA models.

Meanwhile, Fig. 2 shows that fine-tuning the models using PolicyQA resulted in worse performance than when using SquadV1 on our Dataset2. This result was surprising, since PolicyQA is a dataset dedicated to privacy policy tasks. It indicates that PolicyQA is not general enough for building accurate QA models for answering questions about privacy policies.

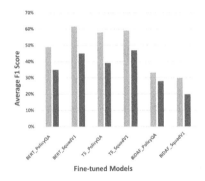

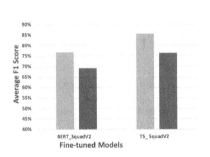

Fig. 2. Performance of BERT, T5, and BiDAF on Our Dataset2 under Two Cases: Top Answer and Top-3 Answers.

Fig. 3. Performance of BERT, T5, and BiDAF on Our Dataset1 under Two Cases: Top Answer and Top-3 Answers.

When we fine-tuned BERT and T5 using the SquadV2 dataset, they generated high average F1 scores on our Dataset1 at 69.31% and 76.77%, respectively, as shown in Fig. 3. The reason for the increased F1 scores is that within our 41K samples in Dataset1, 94.5% of the questions had no answers. SquadV2 enables a QA model to respond well to the questions that do not have the answers in the passages, whereas SquadV1 is not suited to those questions.

Overall, when assessing the average F1 scores of these various QA models, we can see that BERT and T5 consistently outperform BiDAF. BERT and T5 generally can be expected to perform similarly, likely because both rely on the Transformer architecture.

Sub-Experiment 2: Evaluating the Overall Performance Based on the Top-3 Answers

Experimental Design: This sub-experiment sought to measure the performance of the models by modifying them to provide the three most possible answers to any given question, rather than the single top answer. After getting the top-3 answers, we checked if any one of them matches the real answer. Providing top-3 answers can be helpful in practice by better including the real answers for users to further choose.

Result: When models were asked to produce the top-3 answers, they yielded a performance improvement of up to 18% on the F1 score over the previous sub-experiment (which focused on top answers), as shown in Figs. 2 and 3. For example, when BERT_SquadV1 was tasked with finding only top answers, its F1 score was 45.12%, but the same fine-tuned model yielded 61.59% on the F1 score when tasked with finding the top-3 answers.

Sub-Experiment 3: Fine-Tuning the Existing QA Models Using Our Datasets

Experimental Design: In this sub-experiment, we fine-tuned and evaluated the existing QA models using our QA datasets. To do this, we divided each dataset (Dataset1 and Dataset2) into two parts: one for training and the other for testing. The training part included data pertaining to 15 mobile apps' privacy policies. The data of the remaining five mobile apps' privacy policies was used for the testing. Thereby, our Dataset1 was divided into 35,451 3-tuples for training and 6,303 3-tuples for testing. Similarly, Dataset2 was divided into 1,818 3-tuples for training and 407 3-tuples for testing.

After this division, we fine-tuned the QA models by using the training partitions and then used the test partitions to evaluate the fine-tuned QA models. To compare our results, we used the aforementioned test partitions to evaluate QA models that were fine-tuned on SquadV1, SquadV2, and PolicyQA datasets. This design is important to make the comparison fair.

Result: Overall, we saw significant improvement on the performance of QA models when we fine-tuned them on datasets as shown in Table 5 (rows 7–8). On Dataset1, BERT and T5 achieved 94.07% and 94.02% on F1 scores, respectively. If we compare this performance with BERT and T5 fine-tuned on SquadV2 (row 5), we made improvements up to 22.60% and 12.90% on the F1 scores for BERT and T5, respectively. Moreover, we found BERT and T5 had 99.03% and 98.38% F1 scores, respectively, in predicting no answer to a question that has no answer. This is an important result because users may often first wonder if an answer to a specific question exists in a mobile app's privacy policy or not.

Table 5. Experimental results on the test partitions from Dataset1 and Dataset2

QA dataset	BERT				T5				BiDAF			
	Dataset1		Dataset2		Dataset1		Dataset2		Dataset1		Dataset2	
	F1%	ME%	F1%	ME%	F1%	ME%	F1%	ME%	F1%	ME%	F1%	ME%
SquadV1	7.32	5.50	44.92	16.74	3.39	1.50	45.51	16.25	*	*	16.91	1.23
SquadV2	71.47	70.39	26.12	9.35	81.12	80.00	29.40	12.06	*	*	*	*
PolicyQA	1.98	0.34	30.31	4.92	2.43	0.57	37.12	8.12	*	*	23.79	2.45
Dataset1	92.67	91.52	22.01	13.05	94.02	92.87	30.64	12.80	*	*	*	*
Dataset2	3.10	1.33	48.24	20.68	4.28	2.07	61.81	27.58	*	*	50.27	16.50
Dataset1 + SquadV2	94.18	93.14	32.31	16.25	94.11	89.79	26.11	11.82	*	*	*	*
Dataset2 + SquadV1	4.29	2.18	61.08	28.32	4.12	1.79	63.08	26.84	*	*	22.57	1.47
Dataset2 + PolicyQA	3.86	1.36	59.73	20.93	4.06	1.44	63.03	22.41	*	*	54.46	16.25

*: the given dataset is not supported by the original model.

On Dataset2, the T5 model achieved the best performance with 61.81% on the F1 score compared to 48.24% and 50.27% for BERT and BiDAF, respectively. We compared these results with those of the same QA models fine-tuned on

SquadV1 and PolicyQA, as shown in Table 5 (rows 4 and 6). BERT on Dataset2 made an improvement up to 17.93% on the score. T5 on Dataset2 improved up to 24.69% on the F1 score. Lastly, BiDAF on Dataset2 improved up to 33.36% on the F1 score. Despite the small size of our Dataset2, we made significant improvements on all QA models.

Sub-Experiment 4: Identifying Difficult Questions for QA Models

Experimental Design: Our goal in this sub-experiment was to understand which of the 43 basic questions were easy for the models to answer, and which questions posed challenges to the models. Similar to Sub-Experiment 1 in Sect. 4.3, we first fine-tuned the existing QA models on SquadV1, SquadV2, and PolicyQA. Then, we analyzed each model's performance on every question individually.

In the experimental design, we first divided our Dataset2 into 43 distinct groups based on the 43 basic questions. Each QA model was then used to answer the basic question within that group for different passages. Finally, we calculated the average F1 scores for QA models per each group (or basic question).

Result: Figure 4 shows the results of this experiment. There are great variations in how each QA model answered the individual questions in our Dataset2. As shown in Fig. 4, within our set of 43 basic questions, the more straightforward questions, which asked about elements like update dates and effective dates, were answered with the highest accuracy. In contrast, the difficult basic questions for QA models are those related to data collection purposes and related to third-parties (regarding their collection and use of data); those questions are harder to answer and also have high variations on the answer accuracy.

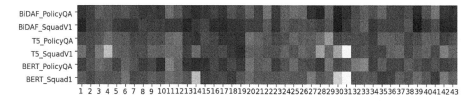

Fig. 4. Heatmap: the easy (light color) vs. difficult (dark color) questions for six QA models.

Experiment 2 for Answering RQ3: How Can the Performance of Existing QA Models Be Improved to Better Answer the Privacy Policy Questions About Mobile Apps?

Experimental Design: Our goal was to investigate how to improve QA models to better answer the basic questions about mobile apps' privacy policies. To this end, we combined our two datasets with existing datasets SquadV1, SquadV2, and PolicyQA. When combining datasets, we take into account the characteristical similarities between our datasets and the other datasets. For example, we combined our Dataset1 with SquadV2 because both datasets contain unanswerable questions. Similarly, we combined our Dataset2 with SquadV1 and PolicyQA because all of them only contain questions that have a corresponding answer within the passage.

We then moved towards fine-tuning the QA models by using the combined datasets. Next, we tested the fine-tuned models on the testing partitions that we constructed in the previous Sub-Experiment 3 in Sect. 4.3. Finally, we compared the results when using a combination of datasets against when using the datasets individually.

Result: The result is shown in Table 5 (rows 9-11). All QA models made obvious improvements when we combined our datasets with the existing datasets compared to when we used only one alone. For example, we saw obvious improvements when we added our Dataset2 to SquadV1 and fine-tuned the QA models. When we fine-tuned the T5 model with a combined dataset (Dataset2 and SquadV1), the F1 score jumped from 45.51% (when we used SquadV1 alone) to 63.08% (when fine-tuned with the combined datasets). These findings indicate that our datasets can be used to augment the existing datasets to improve the accuracy of the QA models in answering basic questions about mobile apps' privacy policies.

5   Discussion

Our experiments showed that existing QA models are far from being able to accurately answer basic questions about mobile apps' privacy policies. One of the reasons for this is the lack of large and high-quality QA datasets explicitly dedicated to mobile apps' privacy policies. We checked three large QA datasets (SquadV1, SquadV2, and PolicyQA), none of which was dedicated to mobile apps' privacy policies. None of them helped answer basic questions about mobile apps' privacy policies with good performance. Therefore, there is a need for a large and comprehensive QA dataset dedicated to developing accurate QA models concerning mobile apps' privacy policies.

We also found that when a QA model was fine-tuned on the PolicyQA dataset, the model performed much worse than when fine-tuned on SquadV1, despite the fact that PolicyQA is dedicated for websites' privacy policies while SquadV1 is for general topics. There are two possible reasons: 1) the size and diversity of the QA dataset used to fine-tune models matter (SquadV1 is much larger and more diverse than PolicyQA); 2) the PolicyQA dataset is not general enough for building accurate QA models for answering questions about privacy policies.

We also observed that the existing QA models perform better when considering the correct answer within the top-3 answers. There is a higher probability of getting the correct answer within the top-3 answers than just from the top answer. Therefore, it is useful to customize QA models to identify top-3 possible answers to better capture the correct answers to the basic questions about mobile apps' privacy policies.

Furthermore, we observed that BERT and T5 have the best performance on most of the test cases that we performed. In addition, T5 slightly outperforms BERT model for answering basic questions about mobile apps' privacy policies in most test cases. Therefore, it could be helpful to adopt T5 as a baseline for building QA models for mobile apps' privacy policies.

As a result of this study, we built three datasets: one consists of 43 basic questions concerning mobile apps' privacy policies, and the other two datasets, Dataset1 and Dataset2. Initially, the 43 basic questions are designed to evaluate QA models. However, in the future we can use these basic questions for other purposes, such as examining the completeness of a mobile app's privacy policy or using them as a guideline for writing more complete privacy policies for mobile apps. On the other hand, Dataset1 and Dataset2 are used to evaluate QA models, fine-tune QA models, and augment existing QA datasets to improve the ability of QA models on answering basic questions about mobile apps' privacy policies.

Limitations: One limitation of this work is that we derived the 43 basic questions concerning mobile apps' privacy policies only from seven privacy laws in different geographic regions. Although there are other privacy laws, such as those in China, Indonesia, and Malaysia, we only chose the most well-known privacy laws for their popularity, clarity of principles, and accessibility.

The second limitation of our work is regarding the methodology of deriving the set of 43 basic questions. We derived these basic questions based on our understanding and analysis of the text in privacy laws and principles. When we validated the relevance of the 43 basic questions on 20 mobile apps' privacy policies, we found these questions were relevant and comprehensive. Nevertheless, it can be beneficial if some domain experts (e.g., lawyers or law makers) would help us review those questions or derive more questions based on their deeper understanding of privacy laws and principles.

6   Conclusion

In this paper, we sought to evaluate the ability and effectiveness of existing QA models in answering basic questions about mobile apps' privacy policies. We derived a set of 43 basic questions concerning mobile apps' privacy policies from global privacy laws. We further constructed two QA datasets, Dataset1 and Dataset2. We evaluated three QA models (BiDAF, BERT, and T5) on existing and our QA datasets. Our findings show that existing QA models perform poorly in answering basic questions about mobile apps' privacy policies; however, the same models performed better when fine-tuned using our datasets. We hope these findings and our datasets can help researchers build better QA models to more accurately answer users' questions about mobile apps' privacy policies.

Acknowledgment. We thank reviewers for their comments. Khalid was supported by the Tabuk University. All authors were supported by the Colorado School of Mines.

References

1. Brazilian general data protection law (LGPD, English translation). https://iapp. org/resources/article/brazilian-data-protection-law-lgpd-english-translation/. Accessed 03 Mar 2022
2. California Consumer Privacy Act (CCPA) — State of California - Department of Justice - Office of the Attorney General. https://oag.ca.gov/privacy/ccpa. Accessed 03 Mar 2022
3. Gapp privacy: 10 generally accepted privacy principles. https://linfordco.com/ blog/the-10-generally-accepted-privacy-principles/. Accessed 03 Mar 2022
4. How to read a privacy policy — State of California - Department of Justice - Office of the Attorney General. https://oag.ca.gov/privacy/facts/online-privacy/ privacy-policy. Accessed 03 Mar 2022
5. Pipeda Fair Information Principles - Office of the Privacy Commissioner of Canada. https://www.priv.gc.ca/en/privacy-topics/privacy-laws-in-canada/the-personal-information-protection-and-electronic-documents-act-pipeda/. Accessed 03 Mar 2022
6. The principles — ICO. https://ico.org.uk/for-organisations/guide-to-data-protection/guide-to-the-general-data-protection-regulation-gdpr/principles/. Accessed 03 Mar 2022
7. Pytorch hub — PyTorch. https://pytorch.org/hub/. Accessed 03 Mar 2022
8. Read the Australian privacy principles - home. https://www.oaic.gov.au/privacy/ australian-privacy-principles/read-the-australian-privacy-principles. Accessed 03 Mar 2022
9. Ahmad, W., Chi, J., Tian, Y., Chang, K.W.: PolicyQA: a reading comprehension dataset for privacy policies. In: Findings of the Association for Computational Linguistics: EMNLP (2020)
10. Bowers, J., Sherman, I.N., Butler, K.R., Traynor, P.: Characterizing security and privacy practices in emerging digital credit applications. In: Proceedings of the Conference on Security and Privacy in Wireless and Mobile Networks (2019)
11. Devlin, J., Chang, M.W., Lee, K., Toutanova, K.: BERT: pre-training of deep bidirectional transformers for language understanding. In: Conference of the North American Chapter of the Association for Computational Linguistics: Human Language Technologies (2019)
12. Fabian, B., Ermakova, T., Lentz, T.: Large-scale readability analysis of privacy policies. In: Proceedings of the International Conference on Web Intelligence (2017)
13. Harkous, H., Fawaz, K., Lebret, R., Schaub, F., Shin, K.G., Aberer, K.: Polisis: automated analysis and presentation of privacy policies using deep learning. In: Proceedings of the USENIX Security Symposium (2018)
14. Huang, Z., Xu, W., Yu, K.: Bidirectional LSTM-CRF models for sequence tagging. CoRR abs/1508.01991 (2015)
15. Raffel, C., et al.: Exploring the limits of transfer learning with a unified text-to-text transformer. J. Mach. Learn. Res. (2020)
16. Rajpurkar, P., Jia, R., Liang, P.: Know what you don't know: unanswerable questions for squad. In: Annual Meeting of the Association for Computational Linguistics (2018)
17. Rajpurkar, P., Zhang, J., Lopyrev, K., Liang, P.: Squad: 100,000+ questions for machine comprehension of text. In: Conference on Empirical Methods in Natural Language Processing (EMNLP) (2016)

18. Ravichander, A., Black, A.W., Wilson, S., Norton, T., Sadeh, N.: Question answering for privacy policies: combining computational and legal perspectives. In: Conference on Empirical Methods in Natural Language Processing and the International Joint Conference on Natural Language Processing (2019)

19. Seo, M.J., Kembhavi, A., Farhadi, A., Hajishirzi, H.: Bidirectional attention flow for machine comprehension. In: Proceedings of the International Conference on Learning Representations, ICLR (2017)

20. Vaswani, A., et al.: Attention is all you need. In: Proceedings of the Advances in Neural Information Processing Systems (2017)

21. Wilson, S., et al.: The creation and analysis of a website privacy policy corpus. In: Annual Meeting of the Association for Computational Linguistics (2016)

Design of End-To-End Security for MQTT 5.0

Hung-Yu Chien[✉] [iD]

National Chi Nan University, PuLi, Taiwan, R.O.C.
hychien@ncnu.edu.tw

Abstract. Owing to its simplicity and easiness to use, Message Queue Telemetry Transport (MQTT) is very popular and there are many deployments globally. The experiences from the widely deployments also manifest its critical weaknesses: lack of enough security support and poor flexibility/scalability. In light of these experiences and reports, the newest MQTT standard called MQTT 5.0 amends several new functions and extensions. MQTT 5.0 has the great potentials to extend and increase new functions and features. One of the mostly-discussed limitations of the its precedent MQTT systems is its lack of end-to-end (publisher-to-subscriber) security support. In this paper, we design two end-to-end security schemes for MQTT 5.0. To the best of our knowledge, this is the first end-to-end security support designed for MQTT 5.0.

Keywords: Internet of Things (IoT) · MQTT · Authentication · Security · Encryption

1 Introduction

MQTT [1, 2] has gained its popularity and there are many deployments globally, because it is simple, efficient, and easy to use. It is one of the most popular IoT communication protocols. The applications of MQTT have covered several domains like smart office, smart agriculture, consumer IoT scenarios, Industrial IoT scenarios, and so on. These widely deployments also manifest the weaknesses of its precedent standards (MQTT 3.1 and its earlier versions). These weaknesses/ limitations include poor security support and poor scalability/flexibility [3].

MQTT is a message-oriented protocol and is based on the publish/subscribe interaction pattern. A MQTT system consists of a set of clients (publishers and subscribers) and a broker who acts as an intermediary among the clients. The message exchange among clients is based on the concept of "topic". The broker receives the messages from the publishers, and forward them to those subscribers who subscribe the topic.

Conventionally, MQTT itself does not support enough security like authentication and privacy. It supports simple authentication of identity and password. It assumes the deployments could enable SSL/TLS in the underlying layers to protect the privacy of the transmission. The TLS/SSL links are separately built for publisher-to-broker and broker-to-subscriber. Therefore, in such environments, the broker can peek at the contents and violates the privacy of the publisher-subscriber transmissions. It is also not convenient

C. Su et al. (Eds.): SciSec 2022, LNCS 13580, pp. 353–363, 2022.
https://doi.org/10.1007/978-3-031-17551-0_23

for MQTT systems to implement conventional request-response interactions which are popular in many conventional client-server architectures.

In light of the experiences and feedbacks from many deployments, the newest standard called MQTT 5.0 has been released in 2019. MQTT 5.0 has added several new features like the Enhanced Authentication [4], User Properties [5], and so on. Several experts and organizations like [4–6] start to share some tutorials of the new standard, and point out the great potentials of the new features.

This paper designs two End-to-End (E2E) security mechanisms using MQTT 5.0. Compared to its counterparts, the contributions of this work are listed as follows.

(1)   To the best knowledge, it is the first design of MQTT 5.0 E2E security.
(2)   It prevents a broker peeking at the content for an honest-but-curious broker model that a broker would honestly follow the protocols but might try to peek at the content.
(3)   Our design is much more flexible and practical because we do not need to assume the strict timeliness of the actions of publishers and subscribers.

The rest of this article is organized as follows. Section 2 introduces the related work. Section 3 first reviews some MQTT background and new features, and then introduces our designs. Section 4 analyzes the security and evaluates the performance. Section 5 states our conclusions and future works.

2   Related Work

Since MQTT standards and platforms have been released, there exist many deployments in various application domains. This paper focuses on the security; therefore, we will introduce those features and related publications that are security-related.

Some researchers designed customized key agreement schemes to enhance the security of MQTT systems; some of these MQTT-aware key agreement schemes are symmetric-key-based [7–11] while others like [12, 13] are asymmetric-key-based. Many of the previous MQTT-aware key agreement schemes do not consider the compatibility with the existent MQTT Application Interfaces (API). Chien et al. [10] proposed a two-phase authentication mechanism for MQTT 3.1-compatible. In [11], Chien et al. extended the work to support group communication.

There exist some works tackling the E2E security of MQTT. Mektoubi et al. [12] propose to assign a specific certificate for each topic, a publisher encrypts its messages using the public key of the topic certificate, and a legitimate subscriber who owns the corresponding private key can decrypt the messages. This approach can provide E2E security for MQTT systems; however, the public-key-based encryption and decryption is a huge overhead for the clients. Chien et al. [11] proposed to let the broker maintain a topic-centric group key for each topic and securely distributes the group keys to those legitimate clients; all the clients use the symmetric key to encrypt/decrypt the messages; this approach is efficient but the broker can peek at the message contents. Lee et al. [14] proposed the MQTLS scheme to allow a publisher to securely share its E2E keys via publisher's-subscriber's ephemeral Diffie-Hellman session keys; this approach effectively facilitates a publisher the job of E2E key distribution to its subscribers; however, the publishers and the subscribers perform the key distribution during their MQTT connection phases (which involve the MQTT CONNECT APIs). It requires all the sub-scribers issue their CONNECT request before the publisher issue its CONNECT request; this requirement is impractical. Furthermore, all these E2E security mechanisms target at the previous MQTT standards like MQTT 3.1; none of them are designed for MQTT 5.0. Ciou and Chien [15] recently designed and implemented a Challenge-Response authentication using MQTT 5.0 Enhanced Authentication framework, but they did not consider the E2E security.

3 Two End-To-End Security Designs for MQTT 5.0

3.1 Some MQTT 5.0 New Features

MQTT 5.0 provides several new features and framework that facilitates designers the design and implementations of MQTT-aware authentication, "User properties" for trans-mitting information between a publisher and its subscribers, "Response Topic" for imple-menting conventional request-response interaction, and so on. Here, we will focus on those features that are used in our design.

Enhanced Authentication. The MQTT 5.0 Enhanced Authentication Framework aims at facilitating designers the design and implementation of MQTT-aware authenticated key agreement schemes by providing new AUTH APIs and new fields including Authen-tication method (referred as auth_id in the rest of this paper) and Authentication data (referred as auth_data). The new AUTH API and CONNECT/CONNACK API with new fields can be used to initiate the corresponding authentication method and passing the corresponding authentication data in AUTH/CONNECT/CONNACK API. A simplified protocol stack with these APIs is shown in Fig. 1.

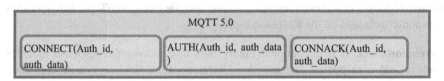

Fig. 1. MQTT 5.0 enhanced authentication protocol stack

One simple example is to let a client and a broker perform the TLS mutual authen-tication. The client specifies AUTH_id="TLS" and Auth_data="Client Hello, ..." in its CONNECT API. After retrieving the AUTH_id="TLS" from the CONNECT request, the broker initiates the corresponding TLS authentication method and responds with AUTH API with the specified AUTH_id="TLS" and AUTH_data="ServerHello", ...). The rest several interactions are TLS flows embedded in the AUTH APIs until the broker finally sends back CONNACK with the result of the authentication. Figure 2 depicts a simplified message flow of MQTT 5.0-aware TLS.

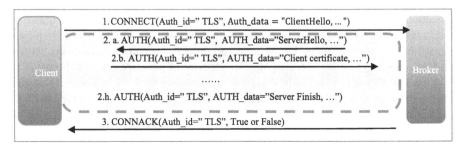

Fig. 2. A simplified flow of a TLS authentication within MQTT 5.0 context

User Properties. User properties are user-defined metadata shared among publishers, brokers, and subscribers. They are represented as UTF-8 key/value pair. One example of sharing clientId/topic/certificate via a PUBLISH API is specified as follows. PUBLISH(topic ='IoT/P1', retain=TRUE, UserProperties={"ClientId:P1", "Topic:IoT/P1", "Certificate: xxx", …}. In this example, the retain flag being set to TRUE; therefore, the broker will keep this message until the next PUBLISH message with "retain=TRUE" and will deliver this message to those clients who subscribe the same topic later. When the subscribers get the messages, they will get the metadata shared by the publisher P1. This new feature "User Properties" is very powerful and flexible, and it provides users the great potentials of designing new functions.

Request-Response interaction via Response Topic. It is not friendly to implement the conventional request-response interactions between a publisher and a subscriber in the precedent MQTT standards. MQTT 5.0's "ResponseTopic" property makes the design and implementation much easier. ResponseTopic is an optional UTF-8 string in a PUBLISH or a CONNECT packet. A client can specify its ResponseTopic in its packets; the receivers (a broker or a subscriber) retrieves the specified ResponseTopic and publishes its response messages on the ResponseTopic.

Correlation Data. It is an optional binary data that follows the response topic. A requestor and a responder can use this CorrelationData field to synchronize their request-response messages.

3.2 Two Ene2End Security Designs for MQTT 5.0

Here we design two E2E security designs, using MQTT 5.0, for two IoT application scenarios. The first scenario is for the cases where there are few publishers and many potential subscribers for each publisher; one example application is many subscribers subscribing valuable/sensitive data from the publishers; for such cases, the publishers chooses the E2E keys and securely distributes the keys to its subscribers.

The second scenario is for the cases where there are many publishers and only few subscribers; one application example is the Industrial IoT (IIoT) in which few serverswould collect data from many sensors; for such cases, the servers choose the E2E keys and securely distribute them to the sensors.

In the following two scenarios, we all assume that the clients and brokers perform TLS as their authentication method during the connection establishment. Any other suitable authentication methods could be used. Here we focus on the E2E security designs, using MQTT 5.0. Both schemes for the two scenarios consist of three phases: client connection phase, E2E security establishment phase, and E2E-MQTT-message publishing phase. Both the client connection phase and the E2E-MQTT-message phases are the same for the two schemes. Now we introduce the two schemes respectively as follows. Table 1 summarizes the notations.

Table 1. The notations.

P1.Cert, S1.Cert	The certificates of the publisher P1 and the subscriber S1 respectively P1.Cert specifies its public key as g^a; S1.Cert specifies its public key as g^b. Here we simplify notations without explicitly specifying the underlying fields, and any secure fields like Elliptic Curve Cryptographies could be used
$E2E_{key}$	The End-to-End session keys between a publisher and its subscribers or between several publishers and a subscriber
DH_{key}	The Diffie-Hellman key between a publisher and a subscriber. This key is used to securely deliver the E2E key. One example of $DH_{key} = g^{ab}$ which is based the public key and private key of their certificates
$Enc_{key}[], Dec_{key}[]$	Encryption/decryption using the key

[Scenario 1: Publisher choosing E2E keys]. Figure 3 depicts the flow of the scheme.

The Client Connection Phase (Phase 1). A client (either a publisher or a subscriber) initiates its connect request via its CONNECT packet in which the AUTH_id specifying the authentication method (in this example, we assume TLS) and the AUTH_data. When the broker receives the request, it retrieves the AUTH_id field and the AUTH_data, and responds the request by sending AUTH packet (the content would depend on the authentication method). After several runs of AUTH packets, the broker sends CONNACK to indicate the result of the authentication. If the result is successful, then the client and the broker share a client-broker session key. Because we focus on the E2E security, the tedious steps of the TLS flow would be skipped here.

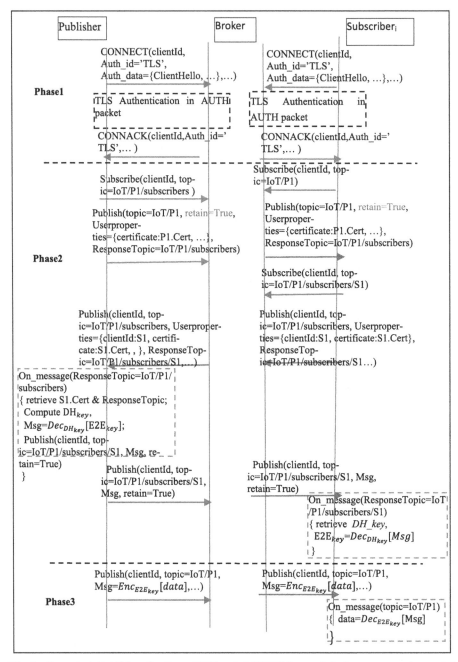

Fig. 3. Scenario 1: Publisher distributes E2E key in MQTT 5.0. →: original message; →: forwarded message;

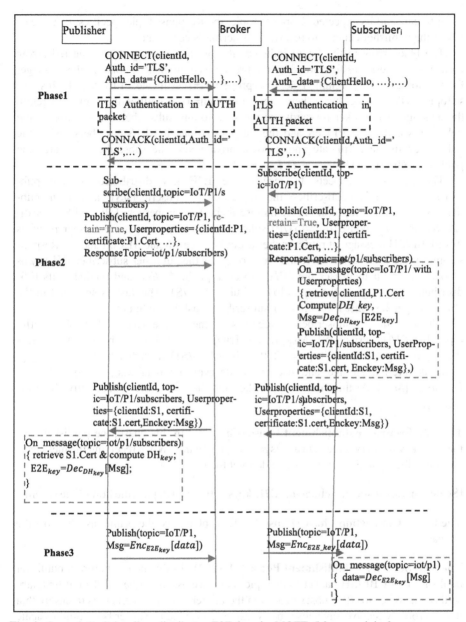

Fig. 4. Scenario2: Subscriber distributes E2E key in MQTT 5.0. →: original message; →: forwarded message;

The E2E Security Establishment Phase (Phase 2). In this phase, before a publisher publishes its PUBLISH packet to its topic (here, we assume it be IoT/P1), it first subscribes the topic=IoT/P1/subscribers from the broker; this arrangement is to ensure that it will properly receive any subscriber's response of which a subscriber would indicate its certificate and its expected ResponseTopic; the ResponseTopic specifies the topic of which the publisher expects to receive a subscriber's certificate.

The blue arrow in the figure indicates the original messages, and the red arrow indicates the messages forwarded by the broker. The publisher publishes the message: Publish(topic=IoT/P1, retain=True, Userproperties={certificate:P1.Cert, …}, ResponseTopic=IoT/P1/subscribers); here the field retain=True notifies the broker to retain the message. The broker forwards the message to any subscriber which retrieves the publisher's certificate P1.Cert and the ResponseTopic=IoT/P1/subscribers; using the public key in the certificate and its own private key, the subscriber computes the publisher-subscriber-DH-key as $DH_{key} = g^{ab}$.

The subscriber expects to receive the E2E key distributed by the publisher; therefore, it subscribes the topic=IoT/P1/subscribers/S1 and then publishes Publish(clientId, topic=IoT/P1/subscribers, Userproperties={clientId:S1, certificate:S1.cert}, ResponseTo-ic=IoT/P1/subscribers/S1…); when the publisher receives this PUBLISH message, it retrieves the subscriber's certificate S1.Cert and the Responsetopic=IoT/P1/subscribers/S1, and then computes the publisher-subscriber-DH-key as $DH_{key} = g^{ab}$; it then uses the DH_{key} to encrypt the $E2E_{key}$ and publishes its E2E distribution message in the topic=IoT/P1/subscribers/S1. This task is specified in the On_message(ResponseTopic=IoT/P1/subscribers) task in the figure.

When the subscriber receives the message Publish(clientId, topic=IoT/P1/subscribers/S1, Msg, retain=True) forwarded by the broker, it performs the On_message(ResponseTopic=IoT/P1/subscribers/S1) in which it retrieves the DH_{key} from its internal storage and uses it to decrypt the data Msg to get $E2E_{key}= Dec_{DH\_key}[Msg]$. At this end, the publisher and the subscriber successfully share the $E2E_{key}$.

The E2E Security Establishment Phase (Phase 3). In this phase, the publisher uses the E2E_key to encrypt the data as Msg=$Enc_{E2E_{key}}[data]$. When receiving the messages, the subscribers use the key $E2E_{key}$ to decrypt the messages.

[Scenario 2: Subscriber choosing E2E keys]. Figure 4 depicts the flow of the scheme.

The Client Connection Phase (Phase 1). This phase is the same as that of the Scenario 1.

The E2E Security Establishment Phase (Phase 2). In this phase, before a publisher publishes its PUBLISH packet to its topic (here, we assume it be IoT/P1), it first subscribes the topic=IoT/P1/subscribers from the broker; this arrangement is to ensure that it will properly receive any subscriber's response of which a subscriber would indicate its certificate and its expected ResponseTopic; the ResponseTopic specifies the topic of which the subscriber expects to sends its certificate and its encrypted E2E key.

The publisher publishes the message: Publish(topic=IoT/P1, retain=True, Userproperties={certificate:P1.Cert, …}, ResponseTopic=IoT/P1/subscribers). The broker forwards the message to any subscriber which retrieves the publisher's certificate P1.Cert and the ResponseTopic=IoT/P1/subscribers.

When a subscriber receives the above PUBLISH message, it retrieves the publisher's certificate P1.Cert and the ResponseTopic=IoT/P1/subscribers, and then computes the publisher-subscriber-DH-key as $DH_{key} = g^{ab}$; it then uses DH_{key} to encrypt the $E2E_{key}$ and publishes its E2E distribution message in the topic=IoT/P1/subscribers. This task is specified in the On_message(topic=IoT/P1/ with Userproperties) task in the figure. When the publisher receives the forwarded message Publish(clientId, topic=IoT/P1/ subscribers, Userproperties={clientId:S1, certificate:S1.cert, Enckey:Msg}), it retrieves the certificate S1.cert, computes the $DH_{key} = g^{ab}$, and uses DH_{key} to decrypt the data to get the $E2E_{key}$. At this end, the publisher and the subscriber successfully share the $E2E_{key}$.

The E2E Security Establishment Phase (Phase 3). This phase is the same that of the Scenario 1.

4 Security Analysis and Performance Evaluation

4.1 Security Analysis

Due to page limitation, this conference version does not include the analysis.

4.2 Performance Evaluation

Because the first phase is a TLS client-broker channel establishment phase and the third phase is just a normal MQTT publish-forward process, the evaluation will focus on the second phase- the E2E security establishment phase.

The second phase of the first scheme takes seven message packets, and these messages requires 5 message runs (some messages do not have dependency and they can be sent simultaneously and be arranged in a single run). The second phase of the second scheme takes 6 message packets in 3 message runs. As we know that MQTT message transmission is very simple and efficient, the second phases of the two schemes could be efficiently executed. Regarding the message length, only a certificate demands larger overhead (say 2K to 4 K bytes); luckily, there are some researches on small-size IoT certificates. Table 2 summarizes the performance of the proposed schemes.

Table 2. Summary of the performance of the proposed schemes

Scheme	E2E security	E2E key distributor	Number of messages in the 2nd phase	Number of runs in the 2nd phase
Scheme 1	Yes	Publisher	7	5
Scheme 2	Yes	subscriber	6	3

5 Conclusions and Future Works

In this paper, we have pointed out the lack of the end-to-end security support in most MQTT deployments. With the MQTT 5.0 new features, we have designed two end-to-end security mechanisms. The analysis shows that the proposed schemes could efficiently achieve the goals. To the best of our knowledge, they are the first end-to-end security designs for MQTT 5.0. We have implemented the protypes of the authentication in the enhanced authentication, and will implement the end-to-end security mechanisms. As MQTT 5.0 new features are simple but very flexible, we believe there exist greats potentials to design the end-to-end security for MQTT, and hope this pioneering works could give a reference work for other researchers to design their mechanisms.

References

1. ISO/IEC 20922:2016, Information technology -- Message Queuing Telemetry Transport (MQTT) v3.1.1. https://www.iso.org/standard/69466.html. Accessed 25 Mar 2022
2. OASIS, MQTT Version 5.0, 07 March 2019. https://docs.oasis-open.org/mqtt/mqtt/v5.0/mqtt-v5.0.html. Accessed 01 Apr 2022
3. Andy, S., Rahardjo, B., Hanindhito, B.: Attack scenarios and security analysis of MQTT communication protocol in IoT system. In: Proceedings of EECSI 2017, Yogyakarta, Indonesia, 19–21 September 2017, pp. 19–21 (2017)
4. HiveMQ Homepage, Enhanced Authentication. https://www.hivemq.com/blog/mqtt5-essentials-part11-enhanced-authentication/. Accessed 02 Apr 2022
5. HiveMQ Homepage, User Properties - MQTT 5 Essentials Part 6. https://www.hivemq.com/blog/mqtt5-essentials-part6-user-properties/. Accessed 24 Mar 2022
6. Steve Internet Guide, Understanding and Using MQTT v5 Request Response. http://www.steves-internet-guide.com/mqttv5-request-response/. Accessed 14 Mar 2022
7. Rizzardi, A., Sicari, S., Miorandi, D., Coen-Porisini, A.: AUPS: an open source authenticated publish/subscribe system for the Internet of Things. Inf. Syst. **62**, 29–41 (2016)
8. Neisse, R., Steri, G., Baldini, G.: Enforcement of security policy rules for the internet of things. In: 2014 IEEE 10th International Conference on Wireless and Mobile Computing, Networking and Communications (WiMob), Larnaca, pp. 165–172 (2014)
9. Shin, S. H., Kobara, K.: Efficient Augmented Password-Only Authentication and Key Exchange for IKEv2. IETF RFC 6628, Experimental, June 2012. https://tools.ietf.org/rfc/rfc6628.txt. Accessed 05 Feb 2022
10. Chien, H.Y., et al.: A MQTT-API-compatible IoT security-enhanced platform. Int. J. Sens. Netw. **32**(1), 54–68 (2020)
11. Chien, H.-Y., Lin, P.C., Chiang, M.L.: Efficient MQTT platform facilitating secure group communication. J. Internet Technol. **21**(7), 1929–1940 (2020)
12. Mektoubi, A., Lalaoui, H., Belhadaoui, H., Rifi, M., Zakari, A.: New approach for securing communication over MQTT protocol A comparison between RSA and Elliptic Curve. In: 2016 Third International Conference on Systems of Collaboration (SysCo), Casablanca, pp. 1–6 (2016)
13. Singh, M., Rajan, M.A., Shivraj, V.L., Balamuralidhar, P.: Secure MQTT for internet of things (IoT). In 2015 Fifth International Conference on Communication Systems and Network Technologies, IEEE, India, pp. 746–751, 4–6 April 2015
14. Lee, H., Lim, J., Kwon T.: MQTLS: toward secure MQTT communication with an untrusted broker. In: 2019 International Conference on Information and Communication Technology Convergence (ICTC), pp. 53–58 (2019)

15. Ciou, P.-P., Chien, H.-Y.C.: An implementation of challenge-response authentication for MQTT 5.0 IoT system. In: The 2021 International Conference on Emerging Industry and Health Promotion (EIHP 2021), Puli, 3–4 July 2021

DroidFP: A Zero-Permission Detection Framework for Android Devices Based on Gated Recurrent Unit

Xinyu Liu[1,2], Wu Zhao[3], Langping Chen[1,2(✉)], and Qixu Liu[1,2]

[1] Institute of Information Engineering, Chinese Academy of Science, Beijing, China
{liuxinyu,liuqixu}@iie.ac.cn
[2] School of Cyber Security, University of Chinese Academy of Science, Beijing, China
chenlangping18@mails.ucas.ac.cn
[3] Beijing Hua Shun Xin An Technology Co. Ltd., Beijing, China
lvxiaoyu@baimaohui.net

Abstract. The Android market is booming, and the unique identification of user devices by APPs helps track attackers. Although Google has designed unique identifiers such as IMEI, users' permission is required to obtain such identifiers. There are currently some methods to forge such identifiers through the Android emulator. To resist identifier forgery attacks and accurately identify Android devices, in this paper, we propose a zero-permission detection framework for an Android device called DroidFP, which does not require any permissions to generate an Android fingerprint. DroidFP consists of emulator detection and Android device identification, which uses GRU to associate the fingerprint changes for the same device. We collected actual device data and emulators data using data enhancement to expand the dataset to 16200. Experiment results show that emulator detection is essential, and DroidFP has high robustness and accuracy in device identification.

Keywords: Android emulator detection · Device identification · Gated Recurrent Unit

1 Introduction

The ACFE survey in 2020 shows that in the field of security, fraud will cause trillions of dollars in losses globally every year, and the concealment of user identities on virtual networks is the basis for fraudsters, which makes identification technology an essential part of the security field [2]. When a user accesses a system through a mobile device, the system can authenticate the user's identity so that an attacker trying to impersonate the device will be detected [6].

Traditional methods use unique device identifiers to identify devices, such as International Mobile Equipment Identity (IMEI) and International Mobile Subscriber Identity (IMSI). However, these identifiers can be forged through the Android emulator, and obtaining these permissions requires user authorization. Therefore, to track attackers

C. Su et al. (Eds.): SciSec 2022, LNCS 13580, pp. 364–374, 2022.
https://doi.org/10.1007/978-3-031-17551-0_24

more accurately, we need to get identifiers that more uniquely represent the user's identity in a zero-permission way. Some advertising operators use geographic coordinates and IP addresses to identify Android and iOS devices [1]. However, these two attributes are variable and are not suitable as a substitute for device identifiers. Device identifiers need to be sufficiently stable and unique.

This paper first judges whether the currently used device is an Android emulator or an actual Android phone to solve the above problems. Second, considering the stability and low collision of device fingerprints, we choose as many identifiers as possible to mark Android devices and generate fingerprints by combining them. We use the random forest to build an emulator detection model and Gated Recurrent Unit (GRU) to construct a device identification model. Both perform well and can quickly recognize devices without user authorization. The main contributions of our paper are as follows:

1. We have proposed an Android device identification framework DroidFP which consists of data collection, emulator detection, and device identification. More than 100 identifiers from basic, CPU and thermal feature sets are utilized to build DroidFP. Moreover, all identifiers can be obtained without user authorization.
2. With the understanding and permission of some volunteers, we collected their device fingerprints to form a fingerprint dataset. Besides, the device fingerprint generated by the Android emulator was artificially added to the dataset and marked.
3. We are the first to add emulator detection to the Android device identification method. This module dramatically improves the efficiency of DroidFP and reduces database storage overhead.

2 Related Work

First presented at HitCon 2013, the purpose of the Anti-emulator is to detect emulated Android environments using various methods [2]. Thanasis et al. proposed using heuristics to detect Android emulators, where static heuristics detected the emulated environment by checking the presence and content of a unique device identifier. Dynamic heuristics tried registering a sensor listener and determining whether it is an emulated environment by the value and time interval of two calls to the sensor [3]. EasyProtector is a third-party open-source library that detects all aspects of Android systems, using baseband information, sensor, and installer detection to identify emulators [4]. It can see most open-source emulators in the market but not the niche ones. Most emulators currently can bypass this framework's detection.

At present, a lot of techniques for device identification have been proposed in academia and industry to assist in user authentication and intrusion tracing. Since explicit identifiers such as IMEI can be easily forged, more and more researchers are currently using other identification technologies. Dey S et al. researched Android's three-axis accelerator [5]. They believed that due to process issues in the sensor manufacturing process, even the same sensor, its sensor chip will respond differently to the same motion stimulus. However, this method requires the device to turn on the vibration mode, and it takes about 30 s to obtain and analyze the data. Wenjia Wu et al. proposed a method to uniquely identify users by collecting the identifiers of user devices [6]. They focused on the uniqueness of the user and did not propose an excellent way to identify the emulator and the actual user device. Many researchers have conducted dynamic analyses of specific types of devices (emulators or actual devices) [7, 8]. Although these methods are helpful, they are not fast enough and require more professional knowledge. All of these dynamic approaches can be evaded by malware that uses anti-emulation. Wenjia Wu et al. proposed a method to uniquely identify users by collecting the identifiers of user devices [6]. Their focus is on the uniqueness of the user, and they do not propose a good way to identify the emulator and the real user device.

3   The DroidFP Framework

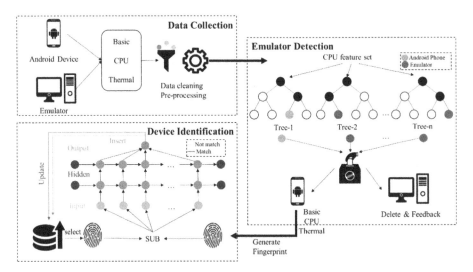

Fig. 1.   Overview of DroidFP.

3.1   DroidFP Overview

Shown in Fig. 1, DroidFP is composed of data collection, emulator detection, and device identification. In Feature collection, DroidFP collects features from every Android device. These three feature sets have been experimentally validated to significantly impact device identification in Sect. 4.3, while battery information performing not good. Due to the variety of data categories of features, data cleaning and pre-processing are indispensable. All features pre-processing will be converted to the numeric type in pre-processing.

The following module is emulator detection, an essential step to distinguish whether the user is using an actual Android device or a computer-based emulator. We construct the emulator detection module with the random forest algorithm, using the CPU information as the model features. The emulator detection module is a binary classification model whose result is either an actual Android device or an emulator.

The last module is device identification which compares the device fingerprint with every Android fingerprint in the database using the GRU algorithm. This module sends the device fingerprint and an Android fingerprint to the GRU model trained from our training dataset. And this model is also a binary classification model whose result is whether the two fingerprints come from the same device. Each of the results corresponds to a different treatment, as described in Sect. 3.4.

3.2   Feature Set and Pre-processing

This section mainly introduces the various features of the Android device we used to generate the integrated fingerprint and the pre-processing methods to transform various types of data into a uniform format.

Feature Set. We divide these features into four categories according to the classification to which they belong: basic, CP, battery, and thermal information. We mainly obtain the features of the Android device by directly getting the features or methods of the corresponding class, receiving the return value by executing the corresponding system command, and reading the related file information. Google provides some APIs to help developers obtain device information [9]. This paper uses only APIs that do not need permissions for data collection.

Basic Information. The basic information refers to some basic configuration of the device, such as the model, version, and manufacturer. Many of the features we collected are related to user settings. Because everyone has different habits, even if two users use the same model of devices, they will set various options, which leads to the device being recognized.

CPU Information. Although it is possible to perform complex calculation functions by calling the CPU of the target device, the difference in calculation capabilities between the emulator and the actual phone can be easily judged from the results, but this requires a long calculation time (10 s or more) and will generally use the device to the user cause serious impact. Therefore, we only obtain the CPU information of the device by reading the file and executing system commands.

Battery Information. Battery information can also be used for device fingerprinting. It can be got directly from *BatteryManager*, and the current battery status can be got by registering *BroadcastReceiver*. But this feature set performs not well in experiments.

Thermal Information. To provide effective thermal relief when the phone overheats, Android introduces the thermal system for abstracting the interfaces to the thermal subsystem hardware devices. The hardware interfaces include temperature sensors and thermistors on the device surface, battery, GPU, CPU, and USB ports. This paper collects all the heat information, and the corresponding data is collected only once to ensure the identification rate. To foster further research, the feature sets are public[1].

---

[1] Our feature set is publicly available at https://github.com/ImCaviar/DroidFP.

Pre-processing. The dataset we collected from users' Android devices contains various data types, such as integer, float, string, and Boolean. However, when the values are sent to the emulator detection or device identification module, they must be processed into a uniform data format. The most challenging part of this process lies in converting string data to numeric data. Nevertheless, academia has no uniform methods for converting data of string type to a numeric type. Therefore, we propose the following pre-processing methods representing strings numerically while retaining the maximum amount of information.

Enumeration. Generate a list for each attribute separately, determine whether the current attribute value appears in the list, add it to the list if it has not appeared before, and finally return the index of the attribute value in the list. This method works for a limited number of attribute values, such as *DeviceName*, and *Manufacturer*.

Values Extraction. For data in numerical form, the value is extracted directly, and the blank data is recorded as -1. For the sub-attributes contained in the attribute value, the segmentation is first performed based on the names of the sub-attributes, and then the data portion of the sub-attribute values is extracted. For example, some sub-attributes can be extracted from *MemoryInfo*, such as *MemTotal*, *MemFree*, *MemAvailable*, and *Active*. These sub-attributes can be distinguished by line feeds, and each sub-attribute name is followed by a colon and a string of numbers, such as "*MemTotal: 3816244 kB*". Therefore, we extract the number behind the colon as *3816244*.

Boolean. Boolean data consists of TRUE or FALSE. TRUE corresponds to the number 1; FALSE corresponds to the number 0.

String Splitting. Some attributes consist of meaningful strings that are joined by some punctuation and have weak interrelationships. Such as *NotificationSound*, which uses a file path to represent the system's default notification ringtone. For such attribute values, we split the string by punctuation and spaces, add the ASCII codes of the split strings, and then weight the sum.

In addition, a large amount of temperature information of the devices is collected in the thermal feature set. We extract the sub-attributes of five dimensions. Considering that the data recorded in the dataset is the result of multiplying the actual degree Celsius by 1000, we define the temperature between 20,000 and 75,000 as a typical value. The sub-attributes of the five dimensions are the number of valid temperature values, the maximum value, the minimum value, the mean value, and the variance of the valid temperature values.

3.3 Emulator Detection

For some applications that identify the IMEI value as the unique identifier of the Android device, the Android emulator can change the IMEI value at will, which profoundly affects the safe operation of the application. It can tamper with some Android fingerprint features and interfere with recognizing Android device fingerprints.

Emulator detection is a critical aspect of DroidFP, effectively reducing the time overhead and data storage overhead of invalid device fingerprinting as DroidFP does not perform the device identification or store the device fingerprint forged by the Android emulator in the database. Additionally, we will feedback to APP developers.

DroidFP constructs the module of emulator detection using random forest, an integrated machine learning method with a decision tree as the basic unit. Random forest is a flexible and practical algorithm with excellent accuracy among all current algorithms, capable of handling input samples with high-dimensional features and evaluating the importance of each feature on the classification problem.

The pre-processed CPU features are input to the random forest module, and the model uses binary classification with a classification result of 0 or 1. When the classification result is 0, it means that a device is a real machine, and when the classification result is 1, it means that the device is an Android emulator. When the device is detected as an actual phone, all the feature values collected from this device form the Android fingerprint and are delivered to the next module. When a device is detected as an emulator, all features collected from that device are discarded. DroidFP no longer performs the detection of the device identification module and makes feedback in the APP as described above.

3.4 Device Identification

Device identification is the core module of DroidFP. Fingerprints of Android devices from non-emulator devices are fed to this module for further device identification. The device identification module aims to identify each Android device by a set of device features collected to form an Android device fingerprint. Considering the possibility that Android device fingerprints change over time, we use a GRU-based approach to construct a dynamic Android device identification model.

Since software updates and system upgrades of devices may lead to changes in Android device fingerprints, it is not practical to identify them using an exact match approach. The dynamic recognition method allows the device fingerprint to change to a certain extent, meaning that even if the device changes by a small amount, DroidFP can still match it to the correct device and accurately identify it.

The full name of the GRU algorithm is Gate Recurrent Unit, which simplifies the Long Short-Term Memory network. Consider that there is a specific internal relationship between features. For example, the device manufacturer has a particular connection with the device's name, and a part of the platform information with the browser name, browser version number, etc., will be included in the user agent. The input vector, which consists of feature values, covers this relationship. We choose GRU to replace the internal relationship with a time series. The GRU model is an improvement of the original Recurrent Neural Network (RNN) to solve the problem faced by RNN, i.e., it is difficult for RNN to model long-range dependencies due to the gradient disappearance or gradient explosion problem that exists with backpropagation.

The device identification module takes the basic, CPU, and thermal information of the Android device as features for input. Considering that the multi-classification model treats each device as a class, it has little effect when the number of samples is small. Still, when the number of samples increases in the order of magnitude, the recognition accuracy of the multi-classification model gradually decreases. As a result, DroidFP uses a binary classification method to match the device fingerprint with each fingerprint in the database.

The device fingerprint is input to the device identification module in pairs with each fingerprint in the database. First, the SUB operation is performed, i.e., the feature values of one fingerprint are subtracted from the feature values of the other fingerprint, and the absolute values are taken. After that, each feature value forms an input vector and is fed into the GRU. After the computation of the neural network, the GRU outputs 0 or 1, where 0 indicates that the pair of fingerprints come from different devices and 1 indicates that the pair of fingerprints are from the same device.

Suppose the pair of fingerprints are from different devices. In that case, the search continues for other fingerprints from the database to match the device fingerprint until the last fingerprint in the database is searched. If no match is made, the fingerprint to be matched is inserted into the database. If there is a difference between the two fingerprints when the pair is successfully matched, the old fingerprint in the database is updated with the device fingerprint. Otherwise, it is not updated.

4   Experiment and Result

4.1   Dataset

Through the above introduction, we have compiled relevant APP to collect the corresponding data, obtained the connected device information by letting people download it, and passed it back to our database. We continued to collect data for one month. During the data collection, we clarify to the user which data types are collected in the experiment and where they would be used. After data preprocessing, data cleaning, and data enhancement, we finally got about 16000 data, of which about 16% were emulator data, and the rest were the actual phone data.

4.2   Android Emulator Detection

Identifying Android emulators is essentially a binary classification question, whether a device is an actual device or an Android emulator. We use the random forest algorithm for emulator detection. We utilize accuracy, recall, precision, and f1-score to validate the Android emulator detection model.

Android Emulator Detection Result. The pre-processed CPU features are used to detect whether the device is an Android emulator or not. The above four metrics are used to measure the random forest model. Table 1 shows that random forest performs well in emulator detection. This is because random forest uses a multiple decision tree voting mechanism, and the mode of the category output determines its judgment result by the decision tree.

Table 1. Random forest experiment results.

Indicator	Accuracy	Recall	Precision	F1-score
value	99.68%	99.06%	98.87%	98.93%

Using CPU information alone can do an excellent job of distinguishing between actual Android devices and Android emulators. In terms of the randomness of random forests, for each tree, random forests randomly and with replacement take samples from the training set as the training set of the tree and randomly select some features from all the features as the feature subset. Each time the tree is split, the optimal feature is selected from the feature subset, which makes the random forest not easy to fall into the dilemma of overfitting. In addition, it can also automatically extract more critical features and detect the mutual influence between features. It can also obtain good results for the default value problem.

4.3 Android Device Identification

We have done some experiments to evaluate the performance of the Android device identification model. Similarly, we utilize accuracy, recall, precision, and f1-score to validate this model.

Performance of Different Feature Sets. Considering that the effect of different feature sets on device identification may not be the same, we examined the performance of each feature set separately. We randomly selected 12000 pieces of data as the training set and 4000 pieces of data as the test set. The effect of the feature set consisting of the basic, battery, CPU, and thermal information on the GRU model is shown in Fig. 2. The training set in GRU is split into 7:3 for model training, the batch size is set to 50, and the value of epoch is increased from 50 to 300. We put two hidden layers in the GRU model, where the first layer consists of 256 nodes and the second layer consists of 32 nodes.

From Fig. 2, we can see that when the training epochs of the GRU reach 200 rounds, the model can already achieve good results on basic, CPU, and thermal feature sets. Therefore, we set the epoch value to 200 in the subsequent experiments. GRU performs well when running on basic, CPU, and thermal feature sets. When running on basic feature sets, GRU can achieve 96.78% accuracy and 94.08% f1-score (epoch = 250). And GRU performs better on both CPU and thermal feature sets, which means basic, CPU and thermal information significantly contribute to device identification. Conversely, the battery feature set performs worse than these three, which means battery information does not apply to building device fingerprints to identify Android devices. As a result, we use only the basic, CPU and thermal information to construct the device fingerprint without using the battery information.

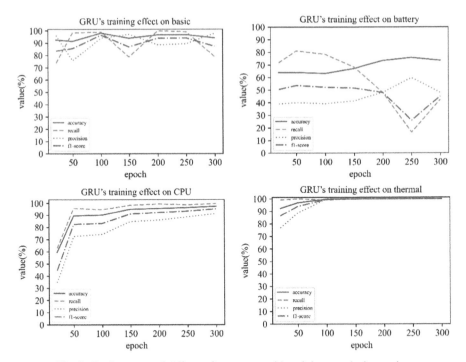

Fig. 2. Performance of different feature sets with training epochs increasing.

Compared with Multi-classification. The device identification we proposed is a binary classification model because we conjecture that the binary classification model performs better than the multiclassification model on the device fingerprint dataset with a large amount of data. To verify our conjecture, in this part, we compare the binary classification model and the multi-classification model in terms of test results. The result is shown in Fig. 3.

From the result of the figure, we can see that binary classification performs better on all feature sets. The recall of multi-classification is much lower than binary classification on the basic feature set, while their precision is not much different. This shows that the multi-classification method has a low false alarm rate but a high miss rate, which means that small changes in Android fingerprints are prone to misclassification by the multi-classification model, which can identify the fingerprints from an old device as a new device fingerprint. The binary classification model outperforms the multiclassification model in terms of performance and robustness.

Efficiency. We test the efficiency of the emulator detection module and device identification module separately. It takes an average of 2 ms for emulator detection to process 2000 pieces of data. For device identification, it takes an average of 96 ms to compare 2000 pairs of device fingerprints.

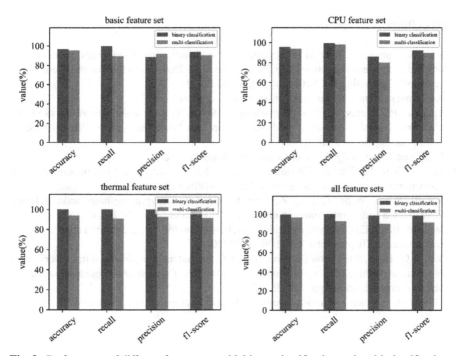

Fig. 3. Performance of different feature sets with binary classification and multi-classification.

5 Conclusion

In this paper, we introduce how to obtain the features of Android devices to generate fingerprints and get them from an Android device that does not require the user to grant any permissions to the APP. We propose an Android device identification framework called DroidFP using the random forest algorithm to build an emulator detection module and the GRU algorithm to construct a device identification module. The experimental results show that the Android emulator can be distinguished well by the CPU feature set. In addition, we use the basic, CPU, and thermal information to construct the device fingerprint, which is used to identify the user's device. In addition, GRU performs well in device identification when it is a binary classification model. In the future, we hope to apply our Android device fingerprints to the actual environment and collect more anonymous information to improve our system.

Acknowledgements. We thank the reviewers for their valuable comments and suggestions. This work is supported by the Youth Innovation Promotion Association CAS (No.2019163), the Strategic Priority Research Program of Chinese Academy of Sciences (No. XDC02040100), the Key Laboratory of Network Assessment Technology at Chinese Academy of Sciences and Beijing Key Laboratory of Network security and Protection Technology.

References

1. Sung, K., Huang, J., Corner, M.D., Levine, B.N.: Re-identification of mobile devices using real-time bidding advertising networks. In: Proceedings of the 26th Annual International Conference on Mobile Computing and Networking, pp. 1–13 (2020)
2. Anti-emulator. https://github.com/strazzere/anti-emulator
3. Thanasis, P., Giannis, V., Elias, A., Michalis, P., Sotiris, I.: Rage against the virtual machine: hindering dynamic analysis of Android malware. In: Proceedings of the 7th EUROSEC, Amsterdam, pp.5:1–5:6 (2014)
4. EasyProtector. https://github.com/lamster2018/EasyProtector
5. Dey, S., Roy, N., Xu, W., Choudhury, R.R., Nelakuditi, S.: AccelPrint: imperfections of accelerometers make smartphones trackable. In: NDSS. Citeseer (2014)
6. Wu, W., Wu, J., Wang, Y., Ling, Z., Yang, M.: Efficient fingerprinting-based android device identification with zero-permission identifiers. IEEE Access **4**, 8073–8083 (2016)
7. Irolla, P., Filiol, E.: Glassbox: dynamic analysis platform for malware android applications on real devices. arXiv preprint arXiv:1609.04718 (2016)
8. Wu, W.C., Hung, S.H.: DroidDolphin: a dynamic android malware detection framework using big data and machine learning. In: Proceedings of the 2014 Conference on Research in Adaptive and Convergent Systems, pp. 247–252 (2014)
9. Google play services — google developers. https://developers.google.com/android

System and Web Security

An Intrusion Detection System Based on Deep Belief Networks

Othmane Belarbi[1], Aftab Khan[1]([✉]), Pietro Carnelli[1],
and Theodoros Spyridopoulos[2]

[1] Bristol Research and Innovation Laboratory, Toshiba Europe Ltd., Bristol, UK
{othmane.belarbi,aftab.khan,pietro.carnelli}@toshiba-bril.com
[2] School of Computer Science and Informatics, Cardiff University, Cardiff, UK
spyridopoulost@cardiff.ac.uk

Abstract. The rapid growth of connected devices has led to the proliferation of novel cyber-security threats known as zero-day attacks. Traditional behaviour-based Intrusion Detection Systems (IDSs) rely on Deep Neural Networks (DNNs) to detect these attacks. The quality of the dataset used to train the DNNs plays a critical role in the detection performance, with underrepresented samples causing poor performances. In this paper, we develop and evaluate the performance of Deep Belief Networks (DBNs) on detecting cyber-attacks within a network of connected devices. The CICIDS2017 dataset was used to train and evaluate the performance of our proposed DBN approach. Several class balancing techniques were applied and evaluated. Lastly, we compare our approach against a conventional Multi-Layer Perceptron (MLP) model and the existing state-of-the-art. Our proposed DBN approach shows competitive and promising results, with significant performance improvement on the detection of attacks underrepresented in the training dataset.

Keywords: Network Intrusion Detection System · Deep learning ·
Deep Belief Networks · Class balancing

1 Introduction

Traditional Intrusion Detection Systems (IDSs) are signature-based, relying on existing signatures of known attacks. They are designed to detect single attacks or families of attacks based on their particular characteristics. However, the vast amount of data that needs to be daily processed to develop new signatures renders their timely generation a challenging task. Furthermore, the generation of signatures for complex attacks that have evolved from previously known threats is not straightforward and requires additional effort [32].

Behaviour analysis techniques have also been explored by researchers to detect intrusions [32]. Most of these systems use machine learning techniques to model system behaviour and detect malicious activity. Compared to signature-based IDSs, machine learning techniques can detect large families of attack

C. Su et al. (Eds.): SciSec 2022, LNCS 13580, pp. 377–392, 2022.
https://doi.org/10.1007/978-3-031-17551-0_25

variants regardless of their complexity. Typical machine learning techniques for classification are used to train models of malicious behaviour based on existing labelled datasets of system activity [1,18]. Classification can be binary (i.e. normal or malicious) or multi-class. In multi-class classification, the model can also detect the type of attack based on the classes/labels in the training set.

The quality of the dataset plays a critical role in the detection performance of the trained IDS model. When a type of attack is underrepresented in the dataset, typical in IDS datasets, the resulting model performs poorly on the detection of attack variants that belong to the infrequent attack type. Several attempts have been proposed to mitigate the issues caused by imbalanced IDS datasets, focusing mainly on the data sampling and class balancing techniques [25].

In this paper, we propose a multi-class classification Network Intrusion Detection System (NIDS) based on Deep Belief Networks (DBNs)[1]. DBN is a generative graphical model formed by stacking multiple Restricted Boltzmann Machines (RBMs). It can identify and learn high-dimensional representations. A DBN is first pre-trained in an unsupervised way by using a greedy layer-by-layer learning algorithm and then fine-tuned using the back-propagation technique in a supervised manner. As shown in our experimental results, this two-stage training process improves the detection performance against infrequent attack samples whilst retaining a high performance against the rest of the attacks.

This paper's contributions can be summarised as follows:

1. We demonstrate that our DBN-based NIDS outperforms MLP-based NIDSs, especially when there is a small number of attack samples in the dataset.
2. We conducted a series of class balancing experiments on the highly imbalanced CICIDS2017 dataset [26], which includes benign network traffic and twelve attacks. Our experimental results demonstrate that our class balancing approach improves the detection performance in terms of F1-score.
3. The classification results of our NIDS, after applying our class balancing approach, are compared against the state-of-the-art. Our proposed method demonstrates significant improvement in F1-score from 0.873 to 0.94.

The rest of the paper is organised as follows. In Sect. 2, we present recent related work on IDSs and DBNs. Section 3 describes the proposed methodology for the DBN-based NIDS. In Sect. 4, we analyse the pre-processing approach we followed on the CICIDS2017 dataset and the model architecture we used, and report the performance results of the study comparing them against the state-of-the-art. Finally, we conclude the paper and present pathways for future work in Sect. 5.

2   Related Work

In general, all ML-based IDSs comprise multiple components including data collection, pre-processing, feature extraction/selection and decision engine [5].

---

[1] https://github.com/othmbela/dbn-based-nids.

NIDS rely on capturing and analysing inbound and outbound network traffic in the under analysis system. In most cases, they are separate devices attached to the network gateway. Depending on the application and the related privacy policy, they may collect and analyse only the headers of the network traffic packets or require access to the packet payload as well [19]. Our work focuses on the pre-processing, the feature extraction/selection and the decision engine for the implementation of NIDS. Our NIDS model relies on the CICIDS2017 dataset [26], which was generated by analysing full-packet network traffic. However, the extracted data and our generated features do not rely on the payload of the network packets nor on the source/destination IP address and port number. Therefore, our model preserves user privacy to an extent. Nevertheless, user privacy largely depends on the way data are captured on the network, which is outside the scope of our research.

Various machine learning methodologies have been researched for the development of NIDS [4,13,17]. Among these, Support Vector Machines (SVMs) have been one of the most commonly used [7,11,12]. Researchers in [7] combined SVMs with ensemble learning to increase the generalisation ability of the model and improve its performance on the unknown data samples. However, both the Fuzzy-C Means (FCM) clustering method and the k-fold cross validation method used to train and test the final SVM can be problematic when applied to network traffic time series datasets. A similar issue is evident in other current SVM-based NIDS works [11]. Additionally, research conducted in [3] demonstrated that SVMs can take a significantly longer time to classify unseen data.

Recent work has demonstrated that deep learning techniques are quite efficient in identifying cyber-attacks on networks [27]. In [31], the authors proposed a deep learning approach for intrusion detection using Recurrent Neural Networks (RNNs). The proposed RNN-IDS effectively recognised the type of intrusion with a higher accuracy and detection rate than traditional ML-based IDS in both binary and multi-class classification. However, it performed poorly against the minority classes in multi-class classification, a common issue in cyber-security datasets. In a similar work [21], it was demonstrated that an ensemble of RNNs can perform binary classification with 94% accuracy within the first 5 s of execution. However, no discussion was provided by the authors around the performance of the approach against the minority classes of imbalanced datasets.

In [22], the authors implemented and tested four classifiers for Distributed Denial Of Service (DDoS) attack detection using deep learning models such as MLP, 1D-Convolutional Neural Network (CNN), LSTM and 1D-CNN+LSTM. The models were built based on the CICIDS2017 dataset [26]. The dataset was balanced by using the duplicating method. The experimental results demonstrated that the CNN+LSTM performed better than the rest of the deep learning models achieving an accuracy of 97.16%.

The researchers in [8] presented a deep learning detection system for DDoS attacks, called LUCID. LUCID is a CNN-based IDS for binary classification of DDoS attacks. The proposed approach can be used in online resource-constrained environments thanks to its ability to ensure low processing overhead and attack

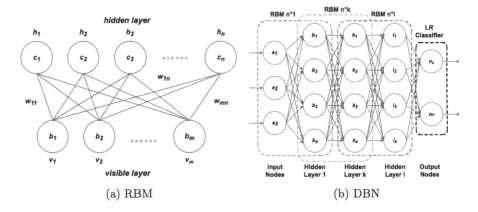

(a) RBM   (b) DBN

Fig. 1. Algorithm structure

detection time. The evaluation results showed that the CNN-based IDS recognises DDoS attack on the CICIDS2017 dataset with an accuracy of 99.7%.

The authors in [9] focused on real time detection of malicious traffic in large-scale high-throughput networks. The proposed approach, named Whisper, leverages frequency domain analysis to extract and analyse sequential information of the network traffic. Whisper can effectively detect 42 sophisticated attacks from the WIDE MAWI dataset in high throughput with at least 90% detection accuracy. Even though our work does not focus on large-scale networks, combining it with frequency domain analysis is an interesting concept we would like to explore in future work.

Researchers in [29] used an RBM to extract fundamental features from the traffic data and then train an SVM classifier. This approach was able to shorten the training time whilst preserving performance of the classifier. In a similar work [20], a NIDS based on deep learning was built using the KDD CUP'99 dataset. The authors used an RBM to extract higher-level features from the input data followed by a back-propagation neural network to classify intrusions. The suggested model showed significant improvement in accuracy over traditional ML-based NIDS. Finally, a system that classifies network intrusions using DBNs (a stack of RBMs) was implemented in [2]. In that work, the DBN-IDS achieved an accuracy of around 97.5% using 40% of the dataset in the training process. However, the evaluation metrics were only limited to accuracy, with no discussion around recall and precision. The proven ability of RBMs to improve the performance of existing classifiers, along with the lack of an in-depth analysis of DBNs as NIDS and the limited work on tackling imbalanced cyber-security datasets, inspired the research presented in this paper.

2.1   Restricted Boltzmann Machines

RBMs are Energy-Based Models (EBMs) that have been largely used for several tasks such as feature extraction, feature reduction and collaborative filtering

[15,23]. RBMs are two-layer undirected models where the layers are the visible layer and the hidden layer as illustrated in Fig. 1a.

An RBM captures the dependency between the visible and hidden units, v and h, by associating an energy to each configuration of the variables. The energy function takes low values when the two variables are compatible and higher values when h is less compatible with v.

The energy function of a joint configuration (v, h) has an energy given by [16]:

$$E(v,h) = -\sum_{i \in visible} b_i v_i - \sum_{j \in hidden} c_j h_j - \sum_{i,j} v_i h_j w_{ij} \tag{1}$$

where:

- v_i, h_j are the binary states of visible unit i and hidden unit j.
- b_i, c_j are the biases of visible unit i and hidden unit j.
- w_{ij} is the weight between the visible unit i and hidden unit j.

The joint probability distribution of a pair of a visible vector v and a hidden vector h is defined via the energy function as:

$$p(v,h) = \frac{1}{Z} e^{-E(v,h)} \tag{2}$$

where Z, the partition function, is defined as the summation over all possible pairs of visible and hidden vectors:

$$Z = \sum_{v,h} e^{-E(v,h)} \tag{3}$$

The probability of the visible vector v is given by marginalising out the hidden vector h:

$$p(v) = \frac{1}{Z} \sum_{h} e^{-E(v,h)} \tag{4}$$

During the training phase, RBMs adjust their weights based on the Contrastive Divergence (CD) algorithm in which the second expectation term of the gradient descent, Eq. 5, is approximated after running k steps of the Gibbs sampler.

$$\Delta w_{ij} = \epsilon \left(<v_i h_j>_{data} - <v_i h_j>_{recon} \right) \tag{5}$$

where:

- ϵ is the learning rate.
- $<v_i h_j>_{data}$ is the product of v_i, h_j before reconstruction
- $<v_i h_j>_{recon}$ is the expected value of v_i, h_j after k-step reconstruction

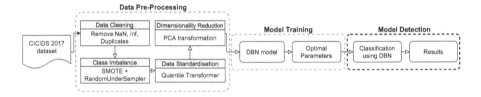

Fig. 2. High-level architecture of our DBN-based NIDS

2.2 Deep Belief Network

A DBN is a deep architecture of multiple stacks of RBMs sequentially connected as shown in Fig. 1b. Each RBM model performs a non-linear transformation on its input vectors and produces outputs vectors that will serve as input for the next RBM model in the sequence. Except for the first and final layers of the DBN, every layer serves as a hidden layer to the nodes that come before and as a visible/input layer to the nodes that comes after. DBNs can be used in both unsupervised learning for generating images and in supervised learning for classification [24]. DBNs are pre-trained layer by layer and fine-tuned using the back-propagation technique.

3 Methodology

In this paper, we aim to evaluate DBNs for network intrusion detection and address the issue of high-class imbalance in network traffic datasets. Figure 2 illustrates the high level architecture of our approach. In the next sections we present and analyse the key processes in our architecture.

3.1 Training Data Pre-Processing

We split the dataset into training, validation, and testing sets. The training set is used to train the model; the model learns the mapping function from this data. The validation set is used to perform the initial testing and tuning of the model, while the testing set is used to evaluate the model's performance. In datasets with high-class imbalance (as is generally observed in IDS datasets), a stratified split of the data is very important allowing a fairer assessment of the model's performance [14]. Stratified data splitting preserves the proportion of samples for each target class essentially ensuring that enough samples of the minority class are included in the training set.

Class Imbalance: As highlighted above, IDS datasets generally suffer from higher class imbalance compared to datasets from other domains. For example, datasets such as NSL-KDD and CICIDS2017 have 95% and 90% benign samples respectively, with the rest containing different types of attacks. This can fundamentally be attributed to the nature of these attacks, even in real-world deployments where the majority of the network traffic is expected to be benign in nature. High-class imbalance in datasets introduces bias in favour of the majority class (benign), which makes the classification of the minority classes very challenging. There are multiple methods introduced in the literature that can handle such class imbalance. We evaluate the following methods in this paper:

Under-Sampling and Over-Sampling: Under-sampling methods re-sample the *majority* class by removing some of the instances. Typically, a random undersampler is employed in which the majority class samples are removed at random. Over-sampling methods on the other hand re-sample the *minority* classes by duplicating or creating new artificial instances with algorithms such as the SMOTE [6].

Class Weight Strategy: Models could consider the underrepresented classes without re-sampling the training set by adding weights to the loss function of the algorithm [28]. The class weight strategy penalises the wrong classification of the minority classes more than the misclassification of the majority class. Hence, each class will have equal importance on gradient updates, on average, regardless of the number of samples.

Sample Weight Strategy: Another method consists of associating a weight to each training sample where the weight is computed as described above. In this strategy, the dataset is re-balanced by ensuring that each batch of data is proportionally distributed.

Data Standardisation: IDS datasets are sometimes high dimensional in nature (e.g. CICIDS2017 dataset has 78 features). In the case of such higher-dimensional datasets without any form of normalization, machine learning models in general do not optimise very well or take much longer to train. Standardising the input variables to overcome this issue can become skewed or biased, due to the large number of outliers in the highly imbalanced security datasets. Dropping outliers may help, however, it is not recommended since there is a risk of losing essential information required for correctly classifying attacks. There are different methods to overcome this problem by using statistics that are robust to outliers. Unlike other scalers, robust scaler and quantile transformation methods are not influenced by the impact of marginal outliers (because they are based on percentiles and quantiles respectively). In robust scaling, the median of a given feature is subtracted from values and divided by the interquartile range. The resulting range is larger than the other scalers. The quantile transformation is another standardization method that is robust to outliers. This method estimates the cumulative distribution function of the input variables and transforms the values to a uniform distribution $[0, 1]$. Then, the obtained values are mapped to the desired distribution using the associated quantile function.

Dimensionality Reduction: One of the most important steps in typical machine learning toolchains is dimensionality reduction. This can be achieved through feature selection or other methods such as Principal Components Analysis (PCA). PCA is a data analysis technique that transforms the possible correlated features set to uncorrelated features set. It can be used to reduce the dimensionality feature space by ignoring the components containing the least variance of the original feature space.

Table 1. Class distribution of CICIDS2017 dataset.

Category	Labels	# samples
Benign	Benign	1,807,787
DoS/DDoS	Heartbleed, DDoS DoS Hulk, DoS GoldenEye DoS Slowloris, DoS Slowhttptest	320,269
PortScan	PortScan	57,305
Brute Force	FTP-Patator, SSH-Patator	8,551
Web Attack	Web Attack – Brute Force Web Attack – XSS Web Attack – SQL Injection	2,118
Botnet	Bot	1,943

3.2 Model Training

The DBN model requires two steps in the training process: unsupervised pre-training and supervised fine-tuning. In the first phase, each RBM is trained to reconstruct its input by adjusting its weights and feeding the input layer of the next RBM. This process is repeated until each RBM layer is pre-trained (greedy learning). In supervised fine-tuning, all the weights are optimised by using the stochastic gradient descent and back-propagation. Details of the specific architectures, hyperparameters, and performance metrics are provided in Sect. 4. Finally, in the case of intrusion datasets that mainly suffer from high-class imbalance, the accuracy metric cannot be relied upon [10]. Therefore, we chose the F1-score, precision, and recall as our metrics to evaluate the models.

4   Experiments

All the experiments were conducted using a 64-bit Intel(R) Core(TM) i7-7500U CPU with 16 GB RAM in Windows 10 environment. The models have been implemented in Python v3.8.2 using the PyTorch v1.9.0 library.

4.1   Dataset

In order to test the proposed DBN-based NIDS, we used the CICIDS2017 dataset created by the Canadian Institute for Cyber-security (CIC) which satisfies the eleven criteria described in [26]. The dataset includes samples of benign activity and common attacks over a period of five days. A B-Profile system described in [26] was used to generate realistic benign traffic. The benign traffic corresponds to the human interaction of 25 users based on standard network protocols such as HTTP(S), FTP, SSH, IMAP and POP3. Several attacks were then initiated. Each record in the dataset has 78 network features extracted with a network traffic analyser, CICFlowMeter [26].

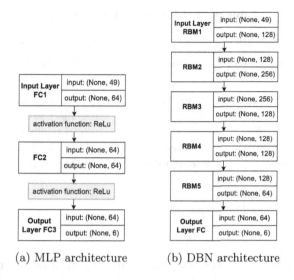

(a) MLP architecture   (b) DBN architecture

Fig. 3. Model architecture

We removed ten features that had no variance and seventeen highly correlated features from the dataset since they were bringing redundant information to the model. A detailed description of our pre-processing can be found on the github repository(See footnote 1). The dataset was then split into training, validation, and testing sets in the proportions of 60%, 20%, and 20% respectively. The CICIDS2017 dataset contains many outliers. Therefore, we used the quantile transformation to deal with outliers and transform our features to a uniform distribution [0, 1].

Table 1 shows how we created new attack classes by merging minority classes that had similar characteristics and behaviour. After merging the classes, we explored different class balancing techniques to further reduce the class imbalance rate and improve the prevalence ratio of the dataset. The "Infiltration" class was removed because of its small portion of the overall dataset.

We then performed a PCA transformation on the CICIDS2017 dataset to reduce the dimensional feature space and simplify the learning process. As stated in the previous section, it is important to preserve as much information as possible. After a series of experiments we concluded that 99% of the explained variance can be retained for only 25 principal components. The feature space has been almost halved without losing any significant information.

4.2 MLP and DBN Architecture

In this study, we have implemented and tuned two different deep learning classifiers, MLP and DBN. Figure 3a shows the architecture of the implemented MLP. It consists of multiple fully connected layers. 49 nodes were used in the input layer to represent the number of input features. After fine-tuning, two hidden

Table 2. Model design and parameters.

(a) DBN				(b) MLP	
Parameter	Pre-training	Fine-tuning		Parameter	
Epochs	10	30		Epochs	10
Learning rate	0.1	0.001		Learning rate	0.02
Batch size	64	128		Batch size	64
Momentum	0.9	-		Momentum	0.9
Optimiser	SGD	Adam		Weight decay	-
Loss function	-	cross-entropy		Optimiser	SGD
Gibbs step	1 step	-		Loss function	cross-entropy
Weight init.	Xavier initialiser	-			
Bias init.	Zeros (0)	-			

layers with 64 nodes each were set and the ReLU activation function was used in the hidden layers. Six nodes were used in the output layer, each node representing one class. Finally, the Soft-Max function was used in the output layer to perform a multi-class classification.

Figure 3b shows the architecture of the implemented DBN. After fine-tuning, five RBMs are stacked with (49, 128), (128, 256), (256, 128), (128, 128), and (128, 64) visible/hidden nodes set per RBM respectively. The output from the last RBM is connected to a fully connected layer with 6 nodes for multi-class classification using the Softmax function. The training parameters of the DBN and MLP are shown in Table 2.

4.3   Results

We compare the performance of the different class balancing techniques using the evaluation metrics defined in Sect. 3.2.

Figure 4 shows the F1-score, precision, and recall that the DBN-based NIDS achieved for various class balancing techniques. The model has a high precision and recall, thus a high F1-score, for the "Benign", "Brute Force", "DoS/DDoS", and "PortScan" classes. However, for the "Web Attack" and "Botnet" classes, either high recall and low precision, or vice versa is observed. It may not always be possible to have high values for both precision and recall. Hence, a trade-off between the precision and the recall is required. In the context of cyber-security, it is important to be able to detect all the malicious activities on the network (high recall). However, it is less severe if few false alarms are raised (low precision). Figure 4 shows that the combination of SMOTE and random under-sampler achieved the best results. The recall value of every class is at least equal to 99%, which means that most of the attacks are successfully detected. Moreover, this method has the best precision for the Botnet class in comparison to the other class balancing techniques.

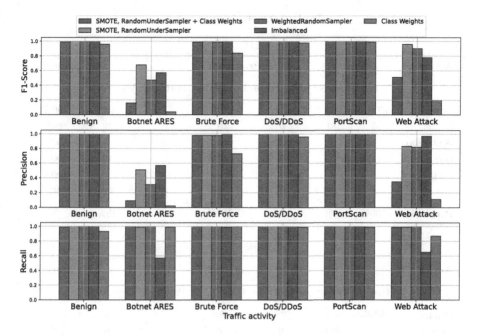

Fig. 4. F1-Score, Precision and Recall achieved by the proposed DBN-based multi-class classification for the different balancing techniques

Table 3 shows the confusion matrix of the DBN and MLP on the testing set. The number of misclassifications and correct classification are summarised with count values for each label. We can see that both models can correctly classify most of the network traffic samples. However, significant differences can be seen between these two models in terms of precision. The MLP classifies precisely only 49% of the "Web Attack"; 407 benign traffic packets were misclassified as "Web Attack". On the other hand, the DBN model classifies "Web Attacks" with a precision of 83%. This suggests that the DBN model has developed a more meaningful pattern for these attacks, potentially due to its two-stage training.

We also compare our DBN and MLP models against the state-of-the-art intrusion detection approaches that use the CICIDS2017 dataset. All studied approaches trained their models using supervised learning methods. However, some of the studies perform binary rather than multi-class classification. We compare our approach against six methods. DeepGFL [30] is a framework that can extract deep features from attributed network flow graphs. LSTM and 1D-CNN [22] are deep learning models that perform binary classification. 1D-CNN+LSTM [22] is a combination of the two latter models for binary classification. LUCID [8] uses CNNs to detect DDoS attacks. Table 4 summarises the performance results of the aforementioned models and compares them against our models.

The DeepGFL [30] framework used for the classification of twelve classes produced worse results than our proposed approach in terms of recall and F1-

Table 3. Confusion matrices.

(a) MLP

Actual	Predicted						Recall
	Benign	Botnet	Brute Force	DoS/DDoS	PortScan	Web Attack	
Benign	360810	500	29	101	7	407	100%
Botnet	6	381	0	0	0	0	98%
Brute Force	4	0	1689	0	0	0	100%
DoS/DDoS	113	0	0	63717	0	17	100%
PortScan	3	4	1	23	11366	4	100%
Web Attack	2	0	0	2	0	408	99%
Precision	100%	43%	98%	100%	100%	49%	

(b) DBN

Actual	Predicted						Recall
	Benign	Botnet	Brute Force	DoS/DDoS	PortScan	Web Attack	
Benign	361350	358	28	52	6	60	100%
Botnet	3	384	0	0	0	0	99%
Brute Force	3	0	1691	0	0	0	100%
DoS/DDoS	119	0	0	63707	0	21	100%
PortScan	6	4	0	17	11371	3	100%
Web Attack	5	0	0	1	0	406	99%
Precision	100%	51%	98%	100%	100%	83%	

score. The DeepGFL approach classified correctly only 44.8% of the malicious activities. The differences in the results could be explained either by the nature of the model itself or the different pre-processing technique used.

Furthermore, our DBN approach achieved higher classification results than the MLP, 1D-CNN and LSTM in [22]. Although these classifiers were designed for the detection of DDoS attacks, our approach performed better while classifying six different types of attacks. For instance, the MLP proposed by [22] and our MLP achieve the same F1-score but differences can be seen in terms of precision and recall. Although our MLP presents a slightly smaller precision there has been a major improvement in the recall. As mentioned in Sect. 4.3, we prefer higher recall over precision since it is fundamental to be able to detect all malicious activities on computer networks even if it comes at the expense of a few false positives. Finally, LUCID [8] and 1D-CNN+LSTM [22] performed slightly better than our DBN approach. However, these two models were only used for binary classification whereas our DBN approach achieved a high recall while performing a multi-class classification.

Table 4. Performance comparison against existing methods using the CICIDS2017 dataset, the target number of classes is shown in the last column.

Study	Method	F1-score	Recall	Precision	#Classes
Our Study	DBN	0.940	0.997	0.887	6
Our Study	MLP	0.873	0.995	0.817	6
[30]	DeepGFL	0.531	0.448	0.948	12
[22]	MLP	0.872	0.862	0.884	2
[22]	LSTM	0.895	0.898	0.984	2
[22]	1D-CNN	0.939	0.901	0.981	2
[22]	1D-CNN+LSTM	0.982	0.991	0.974	2
[8]	LUCID	0.996	0.999	0.993	2

5 Conclusion and Future Work

In this paper, we researched the use of DBNs for Network Intrusion Detection. We developed two NIDS based on DBNs and MLPs. We conducted multiple experiments using the CICIDS2017 dataset with various class-balancing techniques. The proposed MLP-based and DBN-based NIDS achieved an F1-score of 87.3% and 94% respectively using a combination of SMOTE and random under-sampler. Our experimental results demonstrate that DBNs surpass traditional MLPs on the classification of network intrusions, especially when the attacks have a small number of samples. Moreover, we compared our proposed DBN-based NIDS against the state-of-the-art ML-based IDS methods. Our NIDS outperforms all other multi-class classification approaches and shows competitive results against binary classification methods with a major improvement in terms of recall.

Currently, our method requires a centralised network sampler in order to monitor network traffic for our DBN-based NIDS. However, in certain applications this may not be possible due to increased data volumes, relevant privacy issues or complex network configurations. As such, a distributed approach might be necessary. We are currently working towards this direction exploring the various capabilities of DBNs when deployed in a distributed manner.

References

1. Al-Qatf, M., Lasheng, Y., Al-Habib, M., Al-Sabahi, K.: Deep learning approach combining sparse autoencoder with SVM for network intrusion detection. IEEE Access **6**, 52843–52856 (2018). https://doi.org/10.1109/ACCESS.2018.2869577
2. Alom, M.Z., Bontupalli, V., Taha, T.M.: Intrusion detection using deep belief networks. In: National Aerospace and Electronics Conference (NAECON), pp. 339–344 (2015). https://doi.org/10.1109/NAECON.2015.7443094

3. Anthi, E., Williams, L., Słowińska, M., Theodorakopoulos, G., Burnap, P.: A supervised intrusion detection system for smart home iot devices. IEEE Internet Things J. **6**(5), 9042–9053 (2019). https://doi.org/10.1109/JIOT.2019.2926365

4. Ashfaq, R.A.R., Wang, X.Z., Huang, J.Z., Abbas, H., He, Y.L.: Fuzziness based semi-supervised learning approach for intrusion detection system. Inf. Sci. **378**, 484–497 (2017). https://doi.org/10.1016/j.ins.2016.04.019

5. Bridges, R.A., Glass-Vanderlan, T.R., Iannacone, M.D., Vincent, M.S., Chen, Q.G.: A survey of intrusion detection systems leveraging host data. ACM Comput. Surv. **52**(6) (2019). https://doi.org/10.1145/3344382

6. Chawla, N.V., Bowyer, K.W., Hall, L.O., Kegelmeyer, W.P.: Smote: synthetic minority over-sampling technique. J. Artif. Intell. Res. **16**, 321–357 (2002). https://doi.org/10.1613/jair.953

7. Chitrakar, R., Huang, C.: Selection of candidate support vectors in incremental SVM for network intrusion detection. Comput. Secur. **45**, 231–241 (2014). https://doi.org/10.1016/j.cose.2014.06.006

8. Doriguzzi-Corin, R., Millar, S., Scott-Hayward, S., Martínez-del Rincón, J., Siracusa, D.: Lucid: a practical, lightweight deep learning solution for DDOS attack detection. IEEE Trans. Netw. Serv. Manage. **17**(2), 876–889 (2020). https://doi.org/10.1109/TNSM.2020.2971776

9. Fu, C., Li, Q., Shen, M., Xu, K.: Realtime robust malicious traffic detection via frequency domain analysis. In: Proceedings of the 2021 ACM SIGSAC Conference on Computer and Communications Security, November 2021. https://doi.org/10.1145/3460120.3484585

10. Galar, M., Fernandez, A., Barrenechea, E., Bustince, H., Herrera, F.: A review on ensembles for the class imbalance problem: bagging, boosting, and hybrid-based approaches. IEEE Trans. Syst. Man Cybernet. Part C (Appl. Rev.) **42**(4), 463–484 (2012). https://doi.org/10.1109/TSMCC.2011.2161285

11. Gu, J., Lu, S.: An effective intrusion detection approach using SVM with Naïve Bayes feature embedding. Comput. Secur. **103**, 102158 (2021). https://doi.org/10.1016/j.cose.2020.102158

12. Gu, J., Wang, L., Wang, H., Wang, S.: A novel approach to intrusion detection using SVM ensemble with feature augmentation. Comput. Secur. **86**, 53–62 (2019). https://doi.org/10.1016/j.cose.2019.05.022

13. Guo, C., Ping, Y., Liu, N., Luo, S.S.: A two-level hybrid approach for intrusion detection. Neurocomputing **214**, 391–400 (2016). https://doi.org/10.1016/j.neucom.2016.06.021

14. Hammerla, N.Y., Plötz, T.: Let's (not) stick together: pairwise similarity biases cross-validation in activity recognition. In: ACM International Joint Conference on Pervasive and Ubiquitous Computing, New York, NY, USA, pp. 1041–1051. Association for Computing Machinery (2015). https://doi.org/10.1145/2750858.2807551

15. Hinton, G.E., Salakhutdinov, R.R.: Reducing the dimensionality of data with neural networks. Science **313**(5786), 504–507 (2006). https://doi.org/10.1126/science.1127647

16. Hinton, G.E.: Training products of experts by minimizing contrastive divergence. Neural Comput. **14**(8), 1771–1800 (2002). https://doi.org/10.1162/089976602760128018

17. Kim, G., Lee, S., Kim, S.: A novel hybrid intrusion detection method integrating anomaly detection with misuse detection. Expert Syst. Appl. **41**(4, Part 2), 1690–1700 (2014). https://doi.org/10.1016/j.eswa.2013.08.066

18. Kunang, Y.N., Nurmaini, S., Stiawan, D., Suprapto, B.Y.: Attack classification of an intrusion detection system using deep learning and hyperparameter optimization. J. Inf. Secur. Appl. **58**, 102804 (2021). https://doi.org/10.1016/j.jisa.2021.102804

19. Matyás, V., Kur, J.: Conflicts between intrusion detection and privacy mechanisms for wireless sensor networks. IEEE Secur. Priv. **11**(5), 73–76 (2013). https://doi.org/10.1109/MSP.2013.111

20. Peng, W., Kong, X., Peng, G., Li, X., Wang, Z.: Network intrusion detection based on deep learning. In: 2019 International Conference on Communications, Information System and Computer Engineering (CISCE), pp. 431–435 (2019). https://doi.org/10.1109/CISCE.2019.00102

21. Rhode, M., Burnap, P., Jones, K.: Early-stage malware prediction using recurrent neural networks. Comput. Secur. **77**, 578–594 (2018). https://doi.org/10.1016/j.cose.2018.05.010

22. Roopak, M., Yun Tian, G., Chambers, J.: Deep learning models for cyber security in iot networks. In: 2019 IEEE 9th Annual Computing and Communication Workshop and Conference (CCWC), pp. 0452–0457 (2019). https://doi.org/10.1109/CCWC.2019.8666588

23. Salakhutdinov, R., Mnih, A., Hinton, G.: Restricted Boltzmann machines for collaborative filtering. In: Proceedings of the 24th International Conference on Machine Learning, pp. 791–798. ICML 2007 (2007). https://doi.org/10.1145/1273496.1273596

24. Salama, M.A., Hassanien, A.E., Fahmy, A.A.: Deep belief network for clustering and classification of a continuous data. In: The 10th IEEE International Symposium on Signal Processing and Information Technology, pp. 473–477 (2010). https://doi.org/10.1109/ISSPIT.2010.5711759

25. Sapre, S., Islam, K., Ahmadi, P.: A comprehensive data sampling analysis applied to the classification of rare iot network intrusion types. In: 2021 IEEE 18th Annual Consumer Communications Networking Conference (CCNC). pp. 1–2 (2021). https://doi.org/10.1109/CCNC49032.2021.9369617

26. Sharafaldin, I., Lashkari, A.H., Ghorbani, A.A.: Toward generating a new intrusion detection dataset and intrusion traffic characterization. In: Proceedings of the 4th International Conference on Information Systems Security and Privacy. SCITEPRESS - Science and Technology Publications (2018). https://doi.org/10.5220/0006639801080116

27. Singla, A., Bertino, E., Verma, D.: Preparing network intrusion detection deep learning models with minimal data using adversarial domain adaptation. In: Asia Conference on Computer and Communications Security (2020). https://doi.org/10.1145/3320269.3384718

28. Wang, S., Liu, W., Wu, J., Cao, L., Meng, Q., Kennedy, P.J.: Training deep neural networks on imbalanced data sets. In: 2016 International Joint Conference on Neural Networks (IJCNN), pp. 4368–4374 (2016). https://doi.org/10.1109/IJCNN.2016.7727770

29. Yang, J., Deng, J., Li, S., Hao, Y.: Improved traffic detection with support vector machine based on restricted Boltzmann machine. Soft. Comput. **21**(11), 3101–3112 (2015). https://doi.org/10.1007/s00500-015-1994-9

30. Yao, Y., Su, L., Lu, Z.: Deepgfl: deep feature learning via graph for attack detection on flow-based network traffic. In: MILCOM 2018–2018 IEEE Military Communications Conference (MILCOM), pp. 579–584 (2018). https://doi.org/10.1109/MILCOM.2018.8599821

31. Yin, C., Zhu, Y., Fei, J., He, X.: A deep learning approach for intrusion detection using recurrent neural networks. IEEE Access **5**, 21954–21961 (2017). https://doi.org/10.1109/ACCESS.2017.2762418

32. Zhong, W., Yu, N., Ai, C.: Applying big data based deep learning system to intrusion detection. Big Data Mining and Analytics 3(3), 181–195 (2020). https://doi.org/10.26599/BDMA.2020.9020003

HINCDG: Multi-Meta-Path Graph Auto-Encoders for Mining of Weak Association Malicious Domains

Jiawei Sun[1,2], Guangjun Wu[2(✉)], Junnan Yin[1,2(✉)], Qiang Qian[1,2], Junjiao Liu[1,2], Jun Li[1,2], and Yong Wang[1,2]

[1] School of Cyber Security, University of Chinese Academy of Sciences, Beijing, China
{sunjiawei,yinjunnan,qiangqian,liujunjiao,lijun,wangyong}@iie.ac.cn
[2] Institute of Information Engineering, CAS, Beijing, China
wuguangjun@iie.ac.cn

Abstract. Due to the lack of interaction with other domain names or entities and the scarcity of access records, it is extremely challenging to detect malicious domain names in the early stages of the life cycle. The detection methods based on association relationships have high robustness and are difficult to escape. However, these related methods require a time window to accumulate relations. For the sparse of newly emerged DNS, it's difficult to detect malicious domain names in its early life cycle. We regard the lack of initial association relationship of domain name nodes as a missing data problem. A variety of heterogeneous association relationships are extracted from the dynamic evolution graph of HINS containing structural neighbourhood information and temporal features, and then we randomly dropped out some meta-path domain name associations, construct missing initial associations, increase the ability to reason about missing associations, and improve the detection ability of newly emerging malicious domains with weak associations. The HINCDG has been evaluated in the ISP DNS traffic (one billion queries per hour), the experimental results (97% F1-Measure) illustrate the efficiency and accuracy.

Keywords: Temporal graph network · Malicious domain mining · Malware activities · Heterogeneous information networks

1 Introduction

Due to the flexibility and accessibility of domain names, DNS brings us convenience also potential security risks.Cyber criminals almost use malicious domain names in various malicious activities.With the development of detection technology and its counter detection technology, existing malicious domain detection work shifts from traditional manual features (structural features, language features, time features, etc.) to more robust correlation detection methods. The detection method based on behavioral features or association relationships has

© The Author(s), under exclusive license to Springer Nature Switzerland AG 2022
C. Su et al. (Eds.): SciSec 2022, LNCS 13580, pp. 393–406, 2022.
https://doi.org/10.1007/978-3-031-17551-0_26

higher robustness. The latest techniques use graph neural networks and heterogeneous information networks (HIN) to detect malicious domain names and achieve good results, with the advantages of working with non-Euclidean data, GNN can aggregate information of both graph structure and static features to generate the underlying representation of nodes for classification tasks, and HIN could get more rich association relationships. However, these methods require a time window to accumulate a sufficient number of domain requests or resolution relationships before they can infer and classify, which causes a lag in detection.

Many malicious activities appear very briefly, and malicious domain names have a short life cycle. In 2019, IoT botnets are generally active for a short period and control a small scale, a single IP address active within three days or less accounting for more than 60% (cncert,2020 [1]). Many malware propagations use 0 day vulnerability, which has a wide propagation in the pre-patching of vulnerabilities, so it is crucial to detect the malware in the early stage of malware.

Due to the long time window of detection, existing malicious detection uses correlation cannot detect quickly, which can be weeks to several days. For example, MANADHATA.2014 [14]. has a time window of 1 week, which may cause missing the best period for malicious domain blocking. Therefore, it is difficult for these methods to detect fastly. Moreover, newly emerged malicious domains stemming from a short registration time so as to have little relationship with other entities and lacks valuable information.

To overcome the aforementioned limitations of existing methods, we present a novel domain name detection approach called HINCDG, which can detect malicious domain in the early stage of malware's propagation. The dynamic evolution graph method of HINCDG detects that propagation and evolution characteristics of malicious domain names.

To deal with lacks of valuable information, we extend the dynamic evolution graph in heterogeneous information networks to use more information to enhance the detection of these weakly associated domains. On the basis of this, to improve the detection ability of newly emerged malicious domain names with weak association relations, we consider the missing initial association of domain nodes as a missing data problem, we randomly drop out some meta-paths of domain association relations during the training process, construct missing initial association relations, and increase the inference ability for missing associations. We focus on missing association relations that are similar to a cold start in a recommender system, which we call the cold start of malicious domain nodes.

Since we construct an evolution graph for each domain name node from the initial state to detect malicious domain names, the cold start of malicious domain name nodes is crucial meaningful. Under missing initial states, the use of multiple association relations and the reasoning are effective.

In order to verify the feasibility of our approach HINCDG, we implement a prototype system as a case study and evaluate its effectiveness by experiencing large-scale DNS tracing of incoming ISPs.

Experiments show that our approach can achieve significant scalability and accuracy on large-scale data from ISPs. Compared with existing state-of-the-art detection systems, our approach can quikly discover newly generated malicious domains with fewer as-associations. Overall, the main contributions of our work are summarized as follows:

Dynamic evolution graphs of malicious domain graphs are used to capture the evolutionary features of malicious domains in both structural and temporal dimensions.

Consider missing initial association relations of domain nodes as a missing data problem. For multiple association relations in HIN, we increase the inference capability of missing association relations and improve the inference prediction of malicious domain names with weak association relations.

2   Related Work

Malicious domain detection has always been a hot issue in botnet detection. Compared with others, DNS traffic is much less than others, and it worked before the attack. Moreover, the openness and transparency of DNS and the penetration characteristics of firewalls make DNS the first choice of attackers. In the past few years, a lot of research has been proposed on botnets detection. These researches are mainly divided into two categories, domain-based detection and behaviour-based detection. The domain-based detections usually use feature engineering and machine learning methods to detect malicious domain names. EXPOSURE [16] proposed by Bilge et al. reduces the training dataset and time constraints and can detect unknown types of malicious domains. It designs four sets of features and uses the J48 decision tree algorithm to achieve good detection results. These methods use a lot of rich data and many artificially designed features to achieve high accuracy, but the acquisition of rich data is sensitive and time-consuming, and the adversary can easily adjust the features to avoid detection.

Behaviour-based methods usually use periodic behaviour characteristics of domain names, group behaviour characteristics, and co-occurrence of domain names to detect malicious domain names. Manadhata et al. [14] constructed a bipartite graph of host domain names accessed by domain names through server logs and used the Belief Propagation algorithm on the graph to predict the probability that the domain name is malicious.The FProbe proposed by Sun et al. [4] uses the similarity of the number of queries to cluster domain names and then uses the correlation characteristics of the domain groups to classify the domain groups using supervised learning.

3   Background and Motivation

3.1   Background

Heterogeneous Information Network. Heterogeneous Information Network (HIN). An HIN is defined as a graph $G = (V, E, A, R, \phi, \varpi)$, where V and E are the sets of nodes and edges, respectively. Each node v and edge e are associated with their type mapping functions $\phi : V \rightarrow A$ and $\varpi : E \rightarrow R$, where A and R denote the sets of node and edge types such that $|A| + |R| > 2$.

Network Schema. Network Schema. The Network Schema is denoted as S = (A, R). It is a meta template for an HIN G = (V,E) with the object type mapping $\phi : V \rightarrow A$ and the edge type mapping $\varpi : E \rightarrow R$.

Meta-path. Meta-path [23]. Given an HIN $G = (V, E, A, R, \phi, \varpi)$, a meta-path ρ is denoted in the form of $A_1 \rightarrow R_1 \rightarrow A_2 \rightarrow R_2 \rightarrow ...R_l \rightarrow A_{l+1}$, which describes a composite relation between v_1 and v_l.

3.2   Motivation

Attackers use a variety of techniques to evade detection, such as Sub-Grouping, Fake-Query and One-Time domain, Fast-Flux, Domain-Flux, Double-Flux and other technologies. Change the association relationship, resulting in the inability to use association detection methods for fast and accurate detection. For example, DGA is often used to block C&C channels by providing a number of alternative domains. In addition, sophisticated attackers also try to evade detection systems by modifying temporal and spatial features, for example, they obfuscate domain name request intervals, synchronization temporal features, and resource sharing features. Attackers use various evasion methods to hide these associations, especially in each time window, the malicious domain names contained in these time windows will be in different periods of their respective life cycles, since we cannot include the entire life of malicious domain names in each time window. Therefore, the malicious domain names in each time window are always in different initial states. We model the lack of data in these initial states and the lack of association caused by evasion techniques as the lack of a certain type of data in multiple associations problem, and designed HINCDG according to the following various associations.

(1) Clients infected by the same attacker tend to query the same (or partially overlapping) set of malicious domain names. Meanwhile, benign clients have no reason to query these domains, as most of them exist to support malicious services.
(2) Attackers. Due to economic constraints, it is hard for attackers to own many network resources. Therefore, they have to reuse network resources. For example, when analyzing DNS response traffic, we can find a few DGA generated domains are all resolved to a certain IP address.
(3) The co-occurrence relationship of domain name access. In human behavior, it is difficult to generate some specified query patterns similar to the program. These fixed query patterns are the co-occurrence associations between domain names.

In the early stage of malicious domain name activity, domain name activity records were sparse, to incorporate richer information, HINCDG models various entities and relationships in DNS as HINs(Heterogeneous Information Network). Since Graph Convolutional Network (GCN) has achieved great success on non-Euclidean data such as graph data, we simultaneously handle domain features and the various associations among domains with Heterogeneous GCN. At the same time, due to the short life cycle of malicious domain name activity, HINCDG models the sparse problem of domain name activity records in it's early stage or the hidden behavior of domain name malicious activity as a certain type of data missing problem in various associations in order to quickly detect it at an early stage; and consider to the dynamic nature of DNS and the time-varying properties of domain name propagation, GCN is used to handle both domain features and associations between domains. However, existing methods focus on rich informative features to detect malicious domains and are not suitable for real-world data with sparse records. Therefore, we propose a heterogeneous GCN model named HINCDG that can capture the propagation evolution features to generalize the propagation evolution features under covert behavior and the complex graph structure in HIN.

4 The Overview of HINCDG

In this part, we propose a novel malicious domain name detection method, which is called the dynamic evolution heterogeneous graph detection method of malicious domain names. We state the problem as a time snapshot node classification problem with a weak association or lack of association. The architecture of the graph neural network represented by our dynamic graph is shown in Fig. 1. First, we extracted meaningful multi meta-paths on HINS to extract subgraphs, which effectively enhanced the relationship between domain names and domain names. To extract the subgraphs of each meta-path, we use independent graph neural network coding for learning, learn semantic embedding based on meta-paths, and then aggregate the semantic embeddings of multiple meta-paths into a complete representation. In the process of training and learning this complete representation, we randomly delete some meta-path representations and then use the decoder to reconstruct this complete multi-path representation to complete the inference of missing related information. This allows us to have the feature detection capabilities of heterogeneous information network features and increase the corresponding reasoning and judgment capabilities and be able to detect the evasion behaviour with a carefully designed meta-path. We input the full representation in each time window to the temporal sequence module. The module uses multiple historical time window steps to capture the evolution characteristics of the domain names' propagation in the graph structure over time, to learn the evolution characteristics of each malicious domain name in the early stage of propagation Fig. 1.

4.1 Preprocessing

Preprocessing. Over the passive DNS traffic collected by local recursive resolvers, preprocessing module filters out the traffic to reduce computing resources and normalize the traffic further. Firstly, we filter out the popular domains in the DNS traffic requested by multi clients. The more clients that the

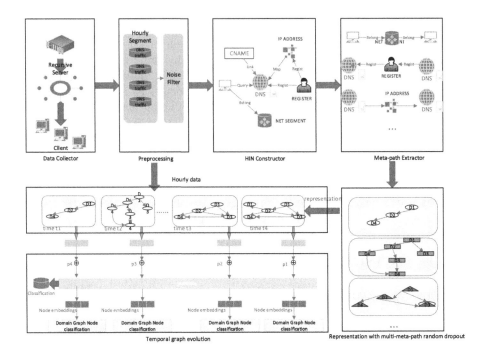

Fig. 1. Architecture.

domain is requested by, the less possible it is to be suspicious. By this means, lots of public services domains, cloud servers, and popular CDN could be filtered out.

Furthermore, we also use Alexa Top 1 million domains as the whitelist to reduce the amount of passive DNS data. For the remaining data, we use the character feature to filter out the disposable domains generated by popular software or local hardware, such as BitTorrent domains ending with "tracker", router domains ending with "in.arpa", McAfee disposable domains ending with "mcafee". Secondly, NXdomains can be generated by DGA malware as well as benign hosts. Therefore we remove the noise irrelevant to suspicious NXdomains, such as misused DNS, misconfigured DNS.

Construction of Dynamic Graph. The malicious domain name dynamic graph is defined as a series of static graph snapshots, $G = G^1, ..., G^T$, where T is the number of steps in the time window, each malicious domain name static graph snapshot $G^T = (V, E^T)$ is the set of domain name nodes at time step t, the edge E is the set of relations between domain names(link with the HIN relationship). The purpose of the dynamic graph representation of malicious domain names is to learn the potential representation of each domain name node at time step t = 1,2,..., T so that the potential representation of the node retains the relationship between the domain name node and other domain names'local graph association relationship expression. Meanwhile, it also retains the evolution features of domain name nodes over time.

HIN Constructor. Based on the collected data, inspired by [24], HINCDG naturally models the DNS scene as a HIN consisting of six types of nodes, namely clients (C), domains (D), IP addresses (I), accounts (A), CNAME records (R), and network segments (S). We represent their relations as follows. For more details, telephone and Email from WHOIS dataset represent the registrant accounts.

R1: domains and IP matrix M where element M(i,j) = 1 if domain i is mapped to IP j; otherwise, M(i,j) = 0.

R2: clients and domains matrix Q where element Q(i,j) = 1 if client i query domain j; otherwise, Q(i,j) = 0.

R3: domain and the CNAME record matrix U where each element $U_{i,}) \in 0, 1$ denotes whether domain i shows in CNAME record j or not.

R4: domains and registrant account matrix Od where element Od(i,j) = 1 if domain i is registered by account j; otherwise, Od(i,j) = 0.

R5: IP addresses and registrant accounts matrix where element Op(i,j) = 1 if IP address i is registered by account j, otherwise, Op(i,j) = 0.

R6: client-belong-segment matrix B where element $B_{i,j} \in 0, 1$ denotes whether client i belongs to network segment j.

Among them, P1 describes that the cname domain of a benign domain is unlikely to be malicious. P2 represents the clients' query behaviours :The malicious domain set queried by infected clients of the same attackers tend to be the same (or partially overlapped), while regular clients have no reasons to reach out for them. P3 reveals the resource aggregation of attackers, domains resolved to the same IP address in a period tend to belong to the same class. P4 is chosen for the same reason. A domain becomes more suspicious if it is under an account that has registered other malicious domains. P5 implies that adjacent clients are vulnerable to the same attacks. P6 represents the association that two domains are resolved to IP addresses that the same account or organization owns (Fig. 2).

4.2 Training the Representation with Random Dropout on Meta-path

Multi-meta-path Graph Encoders. We leverage graph attention network (GAT) as the aggregation mechanism to aggregate the neighbour's representation with different importance to form a node embedding. Here we let node i as the centre node and N_i as its neighbours set to simply illustrate how the GAT work. Due to the heterogeneity of nodes, different types of nodes have different feature spaces [22]. So we first project them to the same node space and then calculate the attention score.

$$\alpha_{ij} = \frac{exp(LeakyReLU(a^T[Wh_i||Wh_j]))}{\sum_{k \in N_i} exp(LeakyReLU(a^T[Wh_i||Wh_k]))}, \forall j \in N_i$$

where $W \in R^{F' \times F}$ and $a \in R^{2F' \times l}$ denote linear transformation. T represents transposition. N_i denotes the neighbors set of node i. We apply LeakyReLU

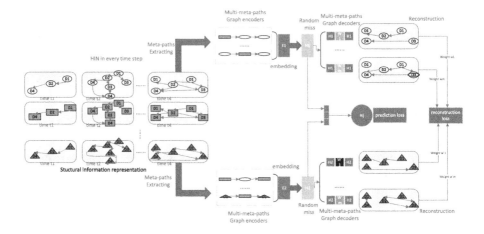

Fig. 2. missing data problem training.

with negative input slope $\alpha = 0.2$ as activation function. Then we aggregate information from N_i, $h'_i = \sigma(\sum_{j \in N_i} \alpha_{ij} h_j + h_i)$, where $\sigma(\cdot)$ denotes the activation function. There are multiple meta-paths for the target node.

Random Dropout on Meta-path. Inspired by denoising auto-encoders that train a model to reconstruct the input from its corrupted version and the cold-start [23] in the recommendation. We regard the lack of initial data as a missing data problem.

After obtaining each meta-paths embeddings, we then fuse them to get a complimentary representation.

$$h_e = \frac{1}{M} \sum_{m=1}^{M} MLP(h_e^m)$$

where m denotes the m meta-path and M is the number of meta-paths. During training, we aim to generalize the model to adjust to the cold start scenario which goal is to produce accurate representations when parts of the input are missing. Specifically, we randomly drop out some meta-paths based. Then the complementary representations are modified as:

$$h_e = \frac{1}{M} \sum_{m=1}^{M} MLP(h_e^m) * S(m)$$

where $S(m) \in 0, 1$ indicates that whether m-th meta-paths is dropped out or not. First, this training with dropout encourages the model to pay more attention to capturing the informative features from helpful auxiliary views. In case of missing the data, it is also capable of producing meaningful representations with more robustness. In this way, the multi-meta-paths graph encoders can generalize to the cold start scenario naturally. On the other hand, dropout can be used to regularise the model to avoid over-fitting.

Multi-Meta-Path Graph Decoding. In order to better model the representation similarity of domains and clients, motivated by [18], we transform the
original auxiliary relationships to domain-domain relationships. Concretely, we
utilize the second-order proximity [19] to capture the similarity between two
domain names, for the reason that second-order proximity can describe the similarity of graph structure to the other node.

For each type meta-path, it requires reconstructing the multi meta-paths
graph data $A^{(1)}, ..., A^{(M)}$ from the fusion representation H. H is an embedding
matrix where each row represents the node embedding.

Each meta-paths has its corresponding decoders $\{P(\hat{A}^{(m)}|H, W_m)\}_{m=1}^{M}$,
which aims to predict whether there is a link between two nodes in view m, W_m
is the weights for meta-path m, and D is the embedding dimension. Specifically,
we reconstruct a multi-meta-paths graph based on the fusion representation:

$$\sum_{m=1}^{M} p(\hat{A}^{(m)}|H, W_m) = \sum_{m=1}^{M} sigmoid(H \cdot W_m \cdot H^T)$$

Finally, through the encoder and decoder, we can learn and infer a more
robust embedded representation of malicious domain name encoding Then
extract the malicious domain name embedding representation in each time window, and then combine this structural neighbourhood representation with the
time evolution sequence to capture the time evolution features of malicious
domain name propagation with multiple heterogeneous relationships.

4.3   Capture the Propagation Features

In this section we use the representation learned in these graph time window as
input, and use LSTM with attention to keep the history information of each node.

Structural Information Representation. As illustrated in Fig. 1, we capture
the local structure feature around a node at each time step. We denote the node
representations as $h_v^1, h_v^2, ..., h_v^T, h_v^t \in R^F$, which feed as input to the temporal
block.

In our graph encoders, there are independent encoder networks instantiated
as meta path-guided heterogeneous GAT. Then, we aggregate all the meta-paths
embeddings with the dropout operation to get more robust complementary representations as input to the Temporal graph evolution.

Temporal Graph Evolution. First, we capture the ordering information in
the temporal attention module by using position embeddings [21], $p^1, ..., p^T, p^t \in R^F$, which embed the absolute temporal position of each snapshot. The position
embeddings are then combined with the output of the structural attention block to
obtain a sequence of input representations: $h_v^1 + p^1, h_v^2 + p^2, ..., h_v^T + p^T$ for node v
across multiple time steps. This block also follows a similar structure with multiple
stacked temporal self-attention layers. The final layer outputs pass into a position-
wise feed-forward layer to give the final node representations $e_v^1, e_v^2, ..., e_v^T$.

Graph Context Prediction. To enable the learned representations to capture structural evolution, our objective function preserves the local structure around a node across multiple time steps. We use the dynamic representation of a node v at time step t, e_v^t to preserve local proximity around v at t.

$$L = \sum_{t=1}^{T} \sum_{v \in V} (\sum_{u \in N^t} -log(\sigma(< e_u^t, e_v^t >)) - w_n \cdot \sum_{u' \in P_n^t(v)} log(1 - \sigma(< e_u'^t, e_v^t >)))$$

where σ is the sigmoid function, denotes the inner product operation, P_n^t is a negative sampling distribution for snapshot G,w_n, the negative sampling ratio, is a tunable hyper-parameter to balance the positive and negative samples.

5 Experiment

5.1 ISP Data and Ground Truth

We collected DNS traces in ISP recursive servers during the two days from December 7th to December 8th, 2019. There is 1.5t data per day with an amount of 0.8 billion data per hour, which contains various types of DNS records. Due to the limitation of storage space and computing resources, we sample the scale of 1/10 every hour, 4 times in total.

We collected 21558 different second-level domains from multiple authoritative blocklists, including malware domain.com, Zeus tracker, malwaredomainlist.com, malc0de.com [15], Ban Benecke Consulting. We also use all DGA data from DGArchive [7] until December 31, 2018, a total of 87 DGA families or variants, 88614672 different domain samples.

5.2 Performance Evaluation

We provide the results of multiple limited time window sizes on real-world data and evaluation. Four indicators are used to evaluate the performance of our model and compare it with the baseline.(Accuracy, Precision, Recall,TP,FP,FN,TN)

To evaluate the performance of the proposed method. We compare with the public advanced baseline model(FANCI and Node2vec).

FANCI uses 21 domain name features, including structural features, language features and statistical features. It uses machine learning SVM and random forest to detect malicious domains. But FANCI only uses lightweight language features, ignoring the neighbourhood structure relationship and time-series relationship between domain names.

Node2vec maps nodes to feature vectors in low-dimensional space, preserves neighbourhood features, learns the node embedding representation of the network structure, and then uses the random forest to classify domain names. Its

Table 1. Comparison of detection performance over HINCDG, FANCI and Node2vec with 5-fold

Application	Metrics	1	2	3	4	5	Average
HINCDG	TPR	0.966	0.962	0.968	0.967	0.966	0.9670
HINCDG	FPR	0.020	0.019	0.022	0.020	0.021	0.0204
HINCDG	ACC	0.971	0.963	0.967	0.970	0.968	0.9693
FANCI	TPR	0.907	0.901	0.922	0.900	0.922	0.9104
FANCI	FPR	0.026	0.020	0.027	0.022	0.020	0.0276
FANCI	ACC	0.940	0.935	0.938	0.937	0.948	0.9396
Node2vec	TPR	0.904	0.898	0.912	0.926	0.926	0.9132
Node2vec	FPR	0.028	0.029	0.026	0.024	0.029	0.0272
Node2vec	ACC	0.932	0.929	0.947	0.928	0.937	0.9346

function is to learn the relationship between neighbouring nodes through unsupervised learning. For the embedding of new nodes, it needs to relearn the global relationship.

This paper uses a standard 5-Fold cross-validation method to evaluate the experiment effect. This experiment was all run on two Intel(R) Xeon(R) CPU E5-2609 V4 CPUs and four NVIDIA Corporation GK210GL Tesla K80.

Table 1 lists the detection effects of the HINCDG model compared to the FANCI and Node2vec algorithms on the training set data through 5-Fold cross-validation. Node2vec can achieve TPR, 91.3% accuracy and 93.4% accuracy rate on average, FANCI can reach a TPR of 91%, and an accuracy rate of 93.9%. Therefore, under the classification and detection algorithm of the HINCDG model, HINCDG can effectively detect malicious domain names (Table 2).

Table 2. Performance over HINCDG, FANCI and Node2vec

Methods	Accuarcy	Precision	Recall	F1-Measure
HINCDG	0.9670	0.9733	0.9724	0.9728
FANCI	0.9396	0.9178	0.9257	0.9217
Node2vec	0.9146	0.9120	0.9064	0.9091

5.3   Effectiveness of Malicious Domain Graph with Cold-Start

To validate the effectiveness of HINCDG, we compare it with three systems to check the effectiveness of HINCDG with Cold-Start, HINCDG with no Cold-Start, Temporal Dynamic Evolution Graphs(ITG) and Graph detecting method of GraphSAGE.

Table 3 show the performance of each method. Temporal Dynamic Evolution Graphs performs better than GraphSAGE because it not only uses the local associated structure information but also uses the time evolution characteristics of node edges as global information features. The characteristics of the specific shape of the subgraph in the time snapshot can distinguish the propagation evolution of the malicious domain name node by the subgraph. HIN Temporal Dynamic Evolution Graphs outperforms both of them, as it can jointly handle the node features together with the complex structural information in HIN. Our proposed algorithm SHetGCN achieves the best performance; neither methods model HINs under traditional supervised learning settings, ignoring the gaps between training and inference procedures. The decoder's reconstruction in domain names' relationship makes the features of the similar domain in the meta-paths closer together.

Table 3. Performance over HINCDG, HINCDG without Cold-Start, ITG and Graph-SAGE

Methods	Accuarcy	Precision	Recall	F1-Measure
HINCDG	0.9670	0.9733	0.9724	0.9728
No Cold-Start	0.9589	0.9531	0.9454	0.9492
ITG	0.9346	0.9120	0.9066	0.9092
GraphSAGE	0.8802	0.8471	0.8390	0.8430

5.4   Detection in the Early Stage

An essential function of HINCDG is to detect malicious domain names in the early stage of the malware life cycle. Therefore, detecting newly generated (zero-day) and rarely used malicious domains is an important indicator of the system. We applied the model directly to the real situation, and we found 8,778 potentially suspicious malicious domains.

We use two methods to verify these detected potentially malicious domains. One is to use the publicly available excellent systems, FANCI and LSTM. These two systems respectively use machine learning and deep learning techniques to distinguish between benign domains and malicious domains. The detection results of the two systems for potentially suspicious domains are shown in the Table 4. Secondly, we use VirusTotal's public blacklist for detection, while VirusTools uses authoritative malicious blacklists of multiple companies. For the newly-emerged domain names in the early stage of the spread of malware, because of their few associations, it is difficult to be confirmed. Therefore, we consider domain names that appear at least once as malicious domain names. As a result, the 309 new malicious domains we discovered were exposed in the form of domains or IPs. We observed that there are 468 domain names without qualitative judgment. Through analysis, a total of 8,310 malicious domains were found, and we have 93.5% confidence that our system is capable of responding to new threats.

For unassociated or weakly associated domains, our method is equivalent to detecting the propagation and evolution of the domain name in the early stage of the domain name's life cycle, so it has a certain detection effect for this type of unassociated or weakly associated domains.

Table 4. ProLongation result

Application	Prolongation	TPs	FNs	Percent
LSTM	8220	7028	1192	0.855
FANCI	8220	7315	905	0.89

6 Conclusion

This paper proposes HINCDG, a novel temporal evolution dynamic graph neural network for detecting malicious domain names. As far as we know, this is the first time that a temporal HIN cold-start graph neural network applied for malicious domain detection. HINCDG integrates node neighbourhood structure information and temporal evolution information at the same time and considers the content characteristics of domain name nodes. ISP network experiments show that HINCDG can meet the requirements of the technical specifications and can detect the propagation and evolution of malicious domain names faster than other malicious domain detection technologies. One potential limitation is that HINCDG cannot distinguish the specific service categories used by malicious domains, such as phishing, spam, C2, etc. In the future, we plan to use more knowledge bases or basic facts to classify specific types of domain name abuse to obtain the distribution of different malicious categories.

Acknowledgments. We are grateful to the anonymous reviewers for their work and insightful feedback. This work was supported by the National Key Research and Development Program of China under Grant 2021YFB3101503.

References

1. Rahbarinia, B., Perdisci, R., Antonakakis, M.: Segugio: efficient behavior-based tracking of malware-control domains in large ISP networks. In: 2015 45th Annual IEEE/IFIP International Conference on Dependable Systems and Networks, pp. 403–414. IEEE (2015)
2. DNS-BH (2019). http://www.malwaredomains.com/
3. Khalil, I., Yu, T., Guan, B.: Discovering malicious domains through passive DNS data graph analysis. In: Proceedings of the 11th ACM on Asia Conference on Computer and Communications Security, pp. 663–674 (2016)
4. Sun, J., Zhou, Y., Wang, S., et al.: FProbe: detecting stealthy DGA-based botnets by group activities analysis. In: 2020 IEEE 39th International Performance Computing and Communications Conference (IPCCC), pp. 1–8. IEEE (2020)
5. Schuppen, S., Teubert, D., Herrmann, P., Meyer, U.: FANCI: feature-based automated NXDomain classification and intelligence. In: 27th USENIX Security Symposium (USENIX Security 2018), pp. 1165–1181 (2018)

6. Antonakakis, M., et al.: From throw-away traffic to bots: detecting the rise of DGA-based malware. In: USENIX security symposium, vol. 12 (2012)

7. Plohmann, D., Yakdan, K., Klatt, M., Bader, J., Gerhards-Padilla, E.: A comprehensive measurement study of domain generating malware. In: USENIX Security Symposium, pp. 263–278 (2016)

8. Wang, T.-S., Lin, H.-T., Cheng, W.-T., Chen, C.-Y.: DBod: clustering and detecting DGA-based botnets using DNS traffic analysis. Comput. Secur. **64**, 1–15 (2017)

9. Sankar, A., Wu, Y., Gou, L., et al.: Dysat: deep neural representation learning on dynamic graphs via self-attention networks. In: Proceedings of the 13th International Conference on Web Search and Data Mining, pp. 519–527 (2020)

10. Zeustracker (2019). https://zeustracker.abuse.ch/blocklist.php

11. Lee, J., Lee, H.: GMAD: graph-based malware activity detection by DNS traffic analysis. Comput. Commun. **49**, 33–47 (2019). Malware Domain List (2019). http://www.malwaredomainlist.com/

12. Gao, H., Yegneswaran, V., Jiang, J., et al.: Reexamining DNS from a global recursive resolver perspective. IEEE/ACM Trans. Netw. **24**(1), 43–57 (2014)

13. Porras, P., Saidi, H., Yegneswaran, V.: An analysis of conficker's logic and rendezvous points. Computer Science Laboratory, SRI International, Technical Report, 36 (2009)

14. Manadhata, P.K., Yadav, S., Rao, P., Horne, W.: Detecting malicious domains via graph inference. In: Kutyłowski, M., Vaidya, J. (eds.) ESORICS 2014. LNCS, vol. 8712, pp. 1–18. Springer, Cham (2014). https://doi.org/10.1007/978-3-319-11203-9_1

15. Malc0de.com (2019). https://malc0de.com/bl/ZONES

16. Bilge, L., Kirda, E., Kruegel, C., et al.: EXPOSURE: finding malicious domains using passive DNS analysis. In: NDSS, pp. 1–17 (2011)

17. Yadav, S., Reddy, A.K.K., Reddy, A.L.N., et al.: Detecting algorithmically generated malicious domain names. In: Proceedings of the 10th ACM SIGCOMM Conference on Internet Measurement, pp. 48–61 (2010)

18. Zhao, J., et al.: Intentgc: a scalable graph convolution framework fusing heterogeneous information for recommendation. In: Proceedings of the 25th ACM SIGKDD International Conference on Knowledge Discovery and Data Mining, pp. 2347–2357 (2019)

19. Goyal, P., Ferrara, E.: Graph embedding techniques, applications, and performance: a survey. Knowl.-Based Syst. **151**(2018), 78–94 (2018)

20. Kendall, A., Gal, Y., Cipolla, R.: Multi-task learning using uncertainty to weigh losses for scene geometry and semantics. In: Proceedings of the IEEE Conference on Computer Vision and Pattern Recognition, pp. 7482–7491 (2018)

21. Fan, S., et al.: Metapath-guided heterogeneous graph neural network for intent recommendation. In: Proceedings of the 25th ACM SIGKDD International Conference on Knowledge Discovery and Data Mining, pp. 2478–2486 (2019)

22. Wang, X., et al.: Heterogeneous graph attention network. In: The World Wide Web Conference, pp. 2022–2032 (2019)

23. Zheng, J., Ma, Q., Gu, H., et al.: Multi-view denoising graph auto-encoders on heterogeneous information networks for cold-start recommendation. In: 27th KDD, pp. 2338–2348 (2021)

24. Sun, X., Tong, M., Yang, J., et al.: HinDom: a robust malicious domain detection system based on heterogeneous information network with transductive classification. In: 22nd International Symposium on Research in Attacks, Intrusions and Defenses (RAID 2019), pp. 399–412 (2021)

AttVAE: A Novel Anomaly Detection Framework for Multivariate Time Series

Yi Liu[1,2] , Yanni Han[1(✉)] , and Wei An[1]

[1] Institute of Information Engineering, Chinese Academy of Sciences, Beijing, China
hanyanni@iie.ac.cn
[2] School of Cyber Security, University of Chinese Academy of Sciences,
Beijing, China

Abstract. Anomaly detection plays a significant role in building a secure and reliable system. Multivariate time series contain important system information, such as system load and time delay. Temporal-dependent methods like RNNs are usually used for anomaly detection on time series. However, inner correlations of time series have shown great potentials in anomaly detection than temporal-dependent methods. In this paper, we propose a novel anomaly detection framework, namely AttVAE, which utilizes attention mechanisms on multivariate time series. This attention mechanism exploits the inner correlations of different time-series dimensions to discover the robust latent variables. Extensive experiments are conducted on two real-world datasets, and results show that AttVAE achieves the best F1-score at 0.79 and 0.97 compared with existing traditional and sophisticated methods. In addition, the missing and false alarm rate by AttVAE is reduced by 20% on average compared with the state-of-the-art models.

Keywords: Multivariate anomaly detection · Attention mechanism · Variational auto-encoder

1 Introduction

Anomaly detection is an important task to protect systems from those intended or unintended malicious attacks, such as network intrusion, information fraud, industrial sabotage, system abnormalities, etc. However, with the rapid development of computer science, the monitored data metrics have become increasingly complex, which makes anomalies diverse and imperceptible [1]. In addition, unknown errors caused by non-artificial reason in system can destroy the secure and reliable operating environment. The accuracy and efficiency of anomaly detection has become a major challenge for the further development of the information society.

Currently, the monitoring of multivariate time series is an essential part of large scale systems. Multivariate time series record the operating status of the system in

This work is supported by the Cooperation project between Chongqing Municipal undergraduate universities and institutes affiliated to CAS (HZ2021015).

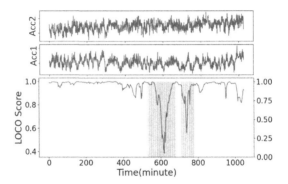

Fig. 1. Local Correlation scores (LOCO) of two accelerometer metrics (Acc1 & Acc2) from SKAB datasets and red bars indicate the anomaly intervals. (Color figure online)

real time to assist administrators diagnose system errors and failures. Traditionally, temporal dependent methods dominated the time series anomaly detection field, such as Long Short Term Memory Recurrent Neural Networks (LSTM-RNN) [2–5], Gate Recurrent Unit (GRU) [6]. However, spatial dependent approaches [7–9] gained attention in recent years due to their capability of scaling up to increasingly dynamic complex multivariate datasets. Unlike univariate time series, multivariate time series have rich information among indicators. Therefore, detecting anomalies from a multivariate level has more practical significance for building reliable and secure systems. The inner correlations among metrics can also extract anomalies distinctively. *Liang et al.* work [10] has proved that anomalies behave conspicuously in correlation scores among multivariate metrics. Local correlation score [11] compares the local auto-covariance matrices of series to generate a time evolved similarity score. Figure 1 shows the local correlation scores calculated from SKAB datasets, which the metrics in terms of two accelerometer values (Acc1 & Acc2) show a distinctive correlation under normal conditions(closed to 1.0). In this figure, when an anomaly event occurs, the curve fluctuates greatly with rapid descending of local correlation scores. Thus, capturing the inner correlation patterns of multivariate time series plays an important role in anomaly detection.

In this paper, we propose a novel reconstruction method, namely AttVAE (Attention based Variational AutoEncoder). The motivation of this method is to extract the inner correlation with the self-attention module and thereby construct robust latent variables via variational autoencoder. Unlike existing temporal dependent methods, our attention-based model is effective because the hidden features can be extracted from sets of time series and subsequently use a deep network to ingests attention features to estimate the reconstruction probability of a time interval in time. The inner correlation attention features of observed time series sequences are extracted by self-attention module and converted to robust latent representations. At each time period, one target time series sequence is used to query its reconstruction probability from the generated latent representations. Based on the reconstruction probability, anomaly intervals are determined using the generated distribution of target sequences as the anomaly scores.

To make our reconstruction model more effective, the loss function of Evidence Lower Bound(ELBO) [12] of VAE is utilized to maximize the likelihood of the input, while maintaining the normal distribution of latent variables. Then, to determine point outliers, dislocation summation is developed to calculate the average anomaly probability for each timescale. Finally, the reconstruction probability of the time series is obtained, and the abnormal state is marked with the determined threshold. The lower reconstruction probability the more likely the state is abnormal. Our main contributions in this paper are listed as follows:

- We propose an attention-based variational autoencoder (AttVAE) framework with self-attention module and VAE, which can infer the robust latent variables and generate the reconstructed distribution to address the multivariate anomaly detection.
- To overcome the inadequacy that time-dependent methods on aperiodic series, a self-attention mechanism is exploited for extracting hidden correlations of observed multivariate time series and querying correlations of target series.
- Extensive experiments are carried out for evaluating the performance of our proposed AttVAE framework, and these results reveal that it can achieve superior anomaly detection compared with five baselines methods with two real-world datasets.

The remainder of this paper is organized as follows. Section 2 reviews the related work. In Sect. 3, the proposed AttVAE anomaly detection framework is explained in detail. Section 4 presents experimental results. Finally Sect. 5 concludes the paper.

2   Related Work

Anomaly detection in time series is an active topic that has plenty of solutions. In this section, a literature review of some traditional anomaly detection methods and state-of-art deep neural network solutions are introduced, which can be categorized into two types.

2.1   Traditional Methods

One traditional type is distance models. Based on constant or piecewise constant models, [13,14] are used to obtain median value, median deviation, or expected values from the past sequence to obtain a criterion for time series. These statistic values are used to compare the Euclidian or other distances with future data to detect anomalies. Similarly, [15] constructs a k-Nearest Neighbor (kNN) algorithm to compute anomaly scores from the k nearest neighbors' average distance of the dataset. Exponentially Weighted Moving Average (EWMA) [16] applied a smoothing window sliding on time series. The weight influence on each value decreases exponentially with time. The closer the time is to the current moment, the greater the weighted influence of the data. The autoregression-based methods, Autoregressive Integrated Moving Average (ARIMA) [17] and Autoregressive Moving Average (ARMA) [18] collect temporal dependencies in the sliding windows, then predict data to discover anomaly detection. Other classic methods include support vector machine (SVM) [19], correlations methods [20], extreme value theory [21], etc. Although these methods have proven their effectiveness in various applications, it is invalidate to multivariate time series, because they cannot correctly capture the correlation among complex metrics. Generally, these models are sensitive to noises and usually lead to false-positive results.

2.2   Deep Learning Methods

Besides traditional algorithms, deep learning based algorithms also developed rapidly and have outstanding performance. AutoEncoder (AE) is a popular network for dimension-reduced processing and has many applications in anomaly detection problems [3,6,7,10]. Recurrent Neural Networks (RNN) specialize in model time dependency, which behaves actively in multivariate anomaly detection problems. [4] extracts time dependencies of time series by LSTM (a variant of RNN) networks on the encoder-decoder structure. [3] simply combines LSTM and VAE (variational autoencoder) to introduce stochastic variables to improve the robustness of the model. [6] novelty glues GRU(another variant of RNN) and VAE together to construct stochastic connections in hidden layers getting well performance on spacecraft and server machine datasets. SDFVAE [10] considered static and dynamic features of multivariate metrics simultaneously with using BiLSTM (Bi-directional LSTM). Convolutional Neural Networks (CNN) was also applied to present as learning-based anomaly detection algorithms [8,22]. In addition, Graph Deviation Network [9] utilize graph neural networks (GNN) on anomaly detection. Recently, attention based methods have shown great power in sequential data processing to discover reliable long-range temporal dependencies [23,24], especially for anomaly detection [25]. However, existing previous methods focused on temporal dependence of time series sequences, while they ignore the benefit of correlations. To combat these disadvantages, this paper is characterized by a new attention based criterion. Inspired from the previous usage of deep networks, our deep model features in designing self-attention models for learning more metrics internal correlations.

3   AttVAE Framework

AttVAE consists of two components. Self-attention modules and VAE modules alternate in the Encoder-Decoder structure. The overall framework has shown in Fig. 2. This Encoder-Decoder structure facilitates the learning of robust latent variables from attention patterns.

Suppose a system of M metrics is monitored and observations are recorded at equal intervals over time. The observed multivariate time series $\mathcal{X}$ is denoted by a set of time points $\mathcal{X} = \{x_1, x_2, x_3 \ldots x_N | x_t \in \mathbb{R}^M\}$, where N is the total length of time-series and M indicates that $\mathcal{X}$ is an M-dimensional time series dataset. x_t represents the observation of time t. The anomaly detection problem of multivariate time series is to determine whether x_t is anomalous or not

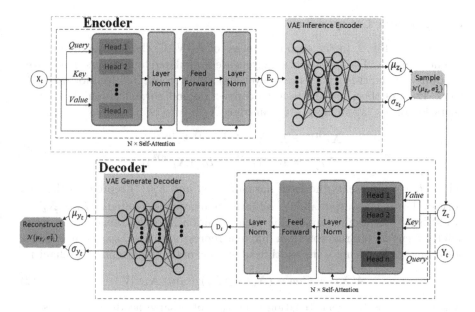

Fig. 2. The overall framework of AttVAE.

without labels. At time t, time series $\mathcal{X}$ is divided into target and observation sequences by windows of equal length. The observation sequence is denoted as $\boldsymbol{X}_t = \{x_{t-L}, \ldots, x_{t-2}, x_{t-1}, x_t\}$ and $\boldsymbol{X}_t \in \mathbb{R}^{M \times L}$, where $L(L \leq N)$ is the window length of the observation input. The target sequence is denoted as $\boldsymbol{Y}_t = \{x_{t-K}, \ldots, x_{t-2}, x_{t-1}, x_t\}$ and $\boldsymbol{Y}_t \in \mathbb{R}^{M \times K}$, where $\boldsymbol{Y}_t \subset \boldsymbol{X}_t$. The target sequence is a sub-sequence of the observation sequence.

The observation sequence $\boldsymbol{X}_t$ is the input of the encoder of AttVAE. The self-attention encoder extracts the attention features $\boldsymbol{E}_t$ from the sequence. Then, variables have been converted to latent distributions $\mathcal{N}\left(\boldsymbol{\mu}_{Z_t}, \boldsymbol{\sigma}_{Z_t}^2\right)$ by the VAE inference encoder. Latent variables $\boldsymbol{Z}_t$ are sampled from the distribution by *reparameterization* trick [12]. There are two sequences input to the decoder. Target sequence $\boldsymbol{Y}_t$ is transmitted as *Query* matrix and latent variables $\boldsymbol{Z}_t$ are *Key* and *Value* matrices. D_t is the attention feature extracted from the self-attention decoder. The VAE generate decoder reconstructs the target sequence distribution $\mathcal{N}\left(\boldsymbol{\mu}_{Y_t}, \boldsymbol{\sigma}_{Y_t}^2\right)$. Finally, the anomaly score $\boldsymbol{S}_t$ is generated by computing the reconstruction probability of $\boldsymbol{Y}_t$. Anomaly time points usually derive lower reconstruction probability score. Thus, thresholds are applied to distinguish anomaly intervals.

AttVAE emphasizes that the idea of multivariate time series anomaly detection is to learn internal correlations and use random latent variables. Self-attention mechanism in AttVAE is used to discover more information relationships on metrics and VAE enhances the robustness of latent variables through random sampling. The overall Encoder-Decoder structure is conductive to unsupervised learning, since most anomaly detection datasets lack labels.

3.1   Encoder Component

As shown in Fig. 2, in the encoder process of AttVAE, the first module is self-attention layers. The self-attention layers are formulated by N layers. Each layer contains one multi-head attention layer and a fully connected feed-forward network. Each of them has the residual connection and normalization. The representation of n_{th} layers input are defined as $\boldsymbol{X_t}^{(n)}$:

$$
\begin{aligned}
\boldsymbol{X_t}^{(n)*} &= L_n(\boldsymbol{X_t}^{(n-1)} + A(\boldsymbol{X_t}^{(n-1)})) \\
\boldsymbol{X_t}^{(n)} &= L_n(\boldsymbol{X_t}^{(n)*} + L_{ff}(\boldsymbol{X_t}^{(n)*}))
\end{aligned}
\tag{1}
$$

where $L_n(*)$ represents the layer normalization and $L_{ff}(*)$ represents the feed forward layer. The output after N self-attention layers is denoted as $\boldsymbol{E_t} = \boldsymbol{X_t}^{(N)}$. Multi-head attention is applied on each attention layer, allowing the model to jointly focus on information from different representation subspaces at different locations. $A(\boldsymbol{X_t})$ denotes the multi-head method of the self-attention mechanism:

$$
A(\boldsymbol{X_t}) = Con[a_1(\boldsymbol{X_t}), a_2(\boldsymbol{X_t}), ..., a_h(\boldsymbol{X_t})]W^h
\tag{2}
$$

where $Con[*]$ is the concatenation operation of h same heads, and W^h is the weight parameters of multi-heads. For attention computing, an inner attention process is formulated for the observation sequence $\boldsymbol{X_t} = \{x_{t-L}, ..., x_{t-1}, x_t\}$ to extract attention features. Typically, the definition of self-attention $a_h(*)$ is scaled dot production [26], and the input Q_t, K_t, V_t are initialized by the observation sequence:

$$
\begin{aligned}
a_h(\boldsymbol{X_t}) &= f_d\left(h_s\left(\frac{Q_t K_t^T}{\sqrt{d_k}}\right)V_t + \boldsymbol{X_t}\right) \\
Q_t &= W^Q \boldsymbol{X_t} \\
K_t &= W^K \boldsymbol{X_t} \\
V_t &= W^V \boldsymbol{X_t}
\end{aligned}
\tag{3}
$$

where, $W^Q \in \mathbb{R}^{d_q*M}, W^K \in \mathbb{R}^{d_k*M}, W^V \in \mathbb{R}^{d_v*M}$ are training parameters, M is the dimension of the observation sequence, and d_q, d_k, d_v are dimensions of Q_t, K_t and V_t. The $f_d(*)$ means that the dropout function randomly sets the attention value to 0 with a certain probability to avoid overfitting. $h_s(*)$ is the *softmax* function.

After extracting attention features from multi-head self-attention encoder layers, the latent variables $\boldsymbol{Z_t}$ is generated from the dense layer of VAE. There are two sets of dense layers. One is for generating the mean value $\boldsymbol{\mu}_{Z_t}$ and the other is for the standard deviation $\boldsymbol{\sigma}_{Z_t}$:

$$
\begin{aligned}
\boldsymbol{\mu}_{Z_t} &= \mathrm{w}^{\mu_z} h_r\left(\boldsymbol{E_t}\right) + \mathrm{b}^{\mu_z} \\
\boldsymbol{\sigma}_{Z_t} &= h_{sp}\left(\mathrm{w}^{\sigma_z} h_r\left(\boldsymbol{E_t}\right) + \mathrm{b}^{\sigma_z}\right) + \epsilon^{\sigma_z}
\end{aligned}
\tag{4}
$$

where $h_r(*)$ denotes the *Relu* activation function and $h_{sp}(*)$ denotes the *softplus* activation function. $\boldsymbol{\mu}_{Z_t}$ and $\boldsymbol{\sigma}_{Z_t}$ are derived from the full connection layer with different activation functions. The small value ϵ^{σ_z} is a very important bias to prevent the numerical overflow of the loss value. In Eq. (4), b, w are training parameters of their corresponding layers. Finally, using the *reparameterization* trick [12], our latent variable Z_t is sampled from the Gaussian distribution $\mathcal{N}\left(\mu_{Z_t}, \sigma_{Z_t}{}^2\right)$:

$$Z_t = \mu_{Z_t} + \delta_t \sigma_{Z_t} \tag{5}$$

where $\delta_t \sim \mathcal{N}(0,1)$. The *reparameterization* trick guarantees the backpropagation through a random node. Specifically, the latent dimension of Z_t is equal to the dimension of the target sequence Y_t, because in the decoder stage, Y_t will query its pattern on the *Key* and *Value* matrices of Z_t.

3.2   Decoder Component

As shown in Fig. 2, the decoder is composed of a self-attention module and a VAE generate decoder. The self-attention module in the decoder is also formulated by N self-attention layers with the multi-head trick, feed forward layers and normalization layers. The output after N self-attention layers is denoted as $D_t = Z_t{}^{(N)}$. However, attention computing is differently defined as:

$$
\begin{aligned}
a_h(Z_t) &= f_d\left(h_s\left(\frac{Q_t K_t^T}{\sqrt{d_k}}\right) V_t + Z_t\right) \\
Q_t &= W^Q Y_t \\
K_t &= W^K Z_t \\
V_t &= W^V Z_t
\end{aligned} \tag{6}
$$

where W is training parameters in the decoder attention layers. Y_t is input as the target *Query* sequence to query the inner attention features with regard to latent representation Z_t. Then D_t is further processed by dense layers of VAE generating network to generate the reconstructed distribution with mean value and standard deviation pairs $< \mu_{Y_t}, \sigma_{Y_t} >$:

$$
\begin{aligned}
\mu_{Y_t} &= w^{\mu_y} h_r\left(D_t\right) + b^{\mu_y} \\
\sigma_{Y_t} &= h_{sp}\left(w^{\sigma_y} h_r\left(D_t\right) + b^{\sigma_y}\right) + \epsilon^{\sigma_y}
\end{aligned} \tag{7}
$$

Also, $h_r(*)$ is the activation function *Relu* and b, w are training parameters in dense layers. The distribution of reconstructed data $Y_t' \sim \mathcal{N}\left(\mu_{Y_t}, \sigma_{Y_t}^2\right)$ is the Gaussian distribution, which generates from latent variable Z_t and the query target sequence Y_t. Finally, anomaly intervals can be detected based on the reconstruction probability of Y_t on the Gaussian distribution: $\mathcal{N}\left(\mu_{Y_t}, \sigma_{Y_t}^2\right)$.

3.3   Loss Function

The loss function (Eq. 8) is defined based on two main sections. For the input observation sequence $\{x_{t-L}, ..., x_{t-1}, x_t\}$, the model encoder generates their latent representation pairs $\{ < \mu_{z_{t-K}}, \sigma_{z_{t-K}} >, ..., < \mu_{z_{t-1}}, \sigma_{z_{t-1}} >, < \mu_{z_t}, \sigma_{z_t} > \}$. L and K denote the observation sequence length and the target sequence length separately. The overall process of the encoder inference network can be written as inferring $q_\theta(z_t|x_t)$. The prior $p_\theta(z_t)$ for z_t usually follows the Gaussian distribution. So in the optimization, the first section is to minimize the value of KL divergence between $q_\theta(z_t|x_t)$ and $p_\theta(z_t)$. The second section is the reconstruction error. For the target sequence $\{y_{t-K}, ..., y_{t-1}, y_t\}$, the decoder generating network reconstructs its normal distribution pairs $\{< \mu_{y_{t-K}}, \sigma_{y_{t-K}} >, ..., < \mu_{y_{t-1}}, \sigma_{y_{t-1}} >, < \mu_{y_t}, \sigma_{y_t} >\}$. The reconstruction error is the reconstructed probability $p_\phi(y_t|z_t)$. Eventually, similar to VAE models, AttVAE model can be optimized by ELBO function [12]. Hence, for the L-length observation sequence X_t and K-length target sequence Y_t, the loss function can be formulated as:

$$loss(\theta, \phi) = \frac{1}{K} \sum_{i=t-K}^{t} \sum_{j=1}^{M} \left(\log(p_\theta(z_i^j)) - \log(q_\theta(z_i^j \mid x_i^j)) \right.$$
$$\left. + \log(p_\phi(y_i^j \mid z_i^j)) \right) \tag{8}$$

3.4   Anomaly Criterion

Anomaly intervals are defined based on reconstruction probabilities. The reconstruction Gaussian distribution pairs are $\{< \mu_{y_{t-K}}, \sigma_{y_{t-K}} >, ..., < \mu_{y_{t-1}}, \sigma_{y_{t-1}} >, < \mu_{y_t}, \sigma_{y_t} >\}$. Then the anomaly intervals module samples reconstructed y_i' for times, and compute the mean reconstruction error as anomaly scores S_t in the time interval $\{t - K : t\}$:

$$S_t = P(Y_t \mid Z_t)$$
$$= \sum_{i=t-L}^{t} \sum_{j=1}^{M} \frac{1}{\sqrt{2\pi}\sigma_{y_i}^j} \exp\left(-\frac{(y_i^j - \mu_{y_i}^j)^2}{2\sigma_{y_i}^{j\,2}} \right) \tag{9}$$

S_t is the anomaly scores of K-length anomaly intervals. Identifying point outliers makes it convenient to compare anomaly detection performance between algorithms. Simply, the point anomaly score s_t is defined as the average value on every equal-length slipping window:

$$s_t = \frac{1}{K} \sum_{i=t}^{t+K} S_i \tag{10}$$

As for anomaly detection, a determined threshold is applied to annotate normal and abnormal states through anomaly scores. Formally, when the time point has a higher anomaly score (higher reconstruction probability), it means that this time point is more likely to be treated as normal states. The lower the score (lower reconstruction probability), the more likely the time point is to be considered as abnormal states.

4 Evaluation

In this section, AttVAE is extensively evaluated on two datasets with five baselines methods for practical applications.

Datasets: Two benchmark datasets SKAB [27] and SWaT [28] are used to evaluate the performance of AttVAE and other baseline methods. (1) Skoltech Anomaly Benchmark (SKAB)[1] was designed for the evaluation of multivariate anomaly detection algorithms. The version we used is v0.9 and this dataset is still updating. This dataset was collected from water circulation systems. It contains 8 dimensions of time series from different modules including water pumps, electric motors, pressure and flow meters, thermocouples, etc. In particular, this dataset contains more than 30 individual test data files in *.csv* format. However, the amount of data per file is only around 1000 lines. Thus all testsets are aggregated to give an average evaluation result. (2) Secure Water Treatment (SWaT)[2] was provided by *iTrust*, Centre for Research in Cyber Security, Singapore University of Technology and Design. The version we used is SWaTA1&A2_Dec2015. The system continued to run for 11 days, under 7 days normal operation and 4 days attacked scenarios. Sensors and actuators collected 51 time series and all data are labeled according to normal or abnormal behaviors. The research team designed several attack scenarios to attack the system and labeled the datasets.

Evaluation Metrics: For the evaluation, F1-scores, FAR (false alarm rate), and MAR (Missing alarm rate) are selected as our criteria. Since AttVAE does not define a certain method in the anomaly criterion module to specify the threshold, this paper traverses all thresholds and selects the best F1-score as the final result, denoted as F1-best. F1-best measures the accuracy of the anomaly detection problem and takes into account both the precision and recall of the classification model. FAR means that the anomaly does not occur, but the detection algorithm gives a fault alarm. While MAR means that the anomaly occurs and should be alarmed, the detection algorithm ignores it:

$$\mathrm{FAR} = \frac{FP}{FP + TN}$$
$$\mathrm{MAR} = \frac{FN}{FN + TP} \qquad (11)$$

where TP is True Positive, FP is False Positive. Likewise, FN is False Negative and TN is True Negative. By definition, the sum of FAR and Recall is exactly 1. These indicators provide reliable and comprehensive evaluations of the performance of algorithms on the dataset and provide correct guidance for engineering tasks.

---

[1] https://github.com/waico/SKAB.

[2] https://itrust.sutd.edu.sg/itrust-labs_datasets/dataset_info/.

Implementation Details: AttVAE model uses the *pytorch* framework. The length of the observation sequence was set to 128 and the target sequence length was set to 115 according to Sect. 4.1 below. Three sublayers ($N = 3$) were placed on self-attention modules and the number of multi-heads was 4. The dense layer of VAE had three layers with 128 hidden cells. The batch size and epochs was set to 50 and 20 respectively. During training, *Adam* optimizer was used and the learning rate was set to 10^{-4}. The computing device used in the experiment is NVIDIA GeForce GTX TITAN X, and 4 cores Intel(R) Xeon(R) Silver 4210R CPU @ 2.40 GHz.

Baseline Methods: We extensively compare our model AttVAE with five baseline models under different categories, including the autoregressive model ARIMA [17], CNN based unsupervised model MSCRED [22], density estimation model DAGMM [7], temporal recurrent reconstruction model Omnianomaly [6], TCN based model DDxNet [29]. ARIMA is designed as a prediction-based method and the depth is shallow. It is an algorithm focused on univariate time-series, so we applied it to every dimension for M-dimensional times. DAGMM is a deep stochastic Autoencoder for multi-variate data. The observation sequence of DAGMM is only a one-time-point, which narrows its visual Field. MSCRED is designed to handle noisy data by introducing signature matrices. It combines convolutional LSTM and attention mechanisms to capture spatial information and temporal dependence hidden in multivariate time series. Omnianomaly builds a stochastic model capturing the temporal dependence of observation sequence by GRU units. However, in Omnianomaly, the internal correlation process is simple, with only dense layers for cross-dimensional information exchange. DDxNet is a TCN based densely connected network with dilated causal convolutions to learns the spatial features of time series.

4.1   Performance Comparison

Table 1 shows the F1-score, FAR, and MAR of AttVAE, ARIMA, MSCRED, DAGMM, Omnianomaly and DDxNet on two real-world datasets. The best evaluation metrics are emphasized in bold-face and the second best results are indicated by underline. AttVAE outperforms all baseline methods in two datasets.

Table 1. Evaluation results for algorithms on datasets

	SKAB			SWaT		
Algorithms	F1-best	FAR(%)	MAR(%)	F1-best	FAR(%)	MAR(%)
ARIMA [17]	0.52	65.01	<u>12.01</u>	–	–	–
MSCRED [22]	0.64	39.93	13.56	0.94	56.35	7.16
DAGMM [7]	0.32	79.46	20.54	0.93	84.42	<u>6.51</u>
Omnianomaly [6]	0.55	64.04	27.30	<u>0.96</u>	<u>11.95</u>	9.97
DDxNet [29]	<u>0.76</u>	**32.75**	14.6	0.93	28.59	9.43
AttVAE(proposed)	0.79	<u>37.62</u>	**3.29**	**0.97**	**3.97**	**4.81**

For F1-best scores, AttVAE gets the best with 0.79 (SKAB) and 0.97 (SWaT). The F1 score of SWaT is generally higher than that of SKAB, because TP accounts for a larger proportion on the SWaT dataset. Next, we analyze the performance of every baseline method.

The above results validate that AttVAE has an outstanding performance on multivariate real-world time series. Compared with autoregression-based methods such as ARIMA, AttVAE is a deep encoder-decoder based model, which mines the deep pattern of observation sequences. ARIMA even fails to learn complex time series patterns in SWaT and performs poorly on SKAB because of its shallow network. Unlike DAGMM, AttVAE introduces long inputs with L-length observations. With richer historical information, the reconstruction of the target sequence is close to the normal pattern. Moreover, stochastic variables brought by VAE enhance the robust property of AttVAE. This is why MSCRED has higher MAR without stochastic variables. Time series in SKAB datasets show fewer periodic characters. Consequently, RNN based model, like Omnianomaly failed to use its GRU encoder to capture temporal dependence features. As for DDxNet, the reconstruction structure and stochastic latent variables are important in multivariate time series analysis, which is the shortcoming of DDxNet. In Table 1, AttVAE has got a better evaluation performance on SWaT (50 dimensions) than on SKAB (8 dimensions), because SWaT has richer features. It demonstrates that capturing the internal correlation of metrics is beneficial for anomaly detection.

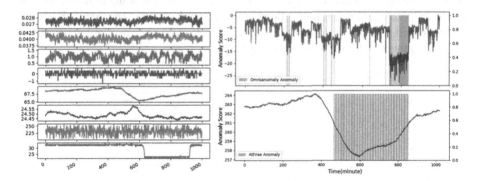

Fig. 3. Anomaly scores on No. 15 testsets of SKAB dataset. The left figure is the multivariate time series of the test sets. The vertical axis of right figures are the reconstruction anomaly score s_t of Omnianomaly and AttVAE. The horizon axis represents time (Unit minute). Red bars on the two figures are anomaly intervals detected by Omnianomaly(0.42) and AttVAE(0.97) with determined thresholds. (Color figure online)

4.2 AttAVE Anomaly Score Performance

The reconstruction probabilities of target sequences, plotted with blue lines, are shown on the right side of Fig. 3. The multivariate time series of No. 15 testsets of SKAB are shown on the left side of Fig. 3. The right figures show the anomaly scores s_t calculated by Omnianomaly (F1: 0.42) and AttVAE (F1: 0.97). The red vertical bars indicate anomaly intervals detected by models. The reconstruction probability anomaly scores of AttVAE successfully separate the normal pattern and abnormal outliers. While the score of Omnianomaly fluctuates significantly and anomalies could not be well detected. The reason is that Omnianomaly is highly dependent on periodic of the time series with GRU nets. However, in No.15 testsets, most of multivariate time series exhibited fixed trends or irregularities. The anomaly score of AttVAE is relatively stable with less fluctuation.

4.3 Effects of Sequence Length

Sequentiality is a major feature of time series, but the length of the input sequence is not as long as possible. In this section, the influence of target sequence length K is evaluated at intervals of 5. The result is graphed in Fig. 4. For the observation sequence, the length is fixed to $L = 128$, while the target sequence length K ranges from 1 to 125. From $K = 1$ to $K = 15$, the F1 score is equal to 0, and the MAR and FAR rates remain unchanged, which means that the model does not converge in such settings. From $K = 20$ to $K = 70$, three evaluation metrics fluctuate violently, which means that the model state is unstable and can only converge occasionally. From $K = 75$ to $K = 125$, the AttVAE model is stable and reaches the optimal state at $K = 115$. Therefore, the length of the target sequence is finally chosen to be 115.

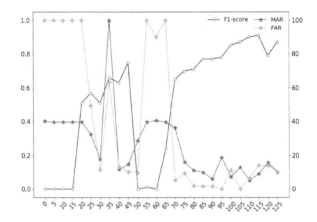

Fig. 4. F1-score, MAR, FAR variation in SKAB datasets via target length K ranges from 1 to 125.

5   Conclusion

Multivariate anomaly detection is of great significance for building secure and reliable system operating environment. In this paper, we have proposed a novel anomaly detection method, namely AttVAE, which utilizes attention mechanisms on multivariate time series. It have effectively captured the inner correlations of metrics on the observation sequence, and successfully built the reconstruction distribution of target sequences for anomaly detection. Further, extensive experiments have been conducted on two real-world datasets and have proven that our AttVAE significantly outperforms the other five baseline algorithms.

References

1. Chandola, V., Banerjee, A., Kumar, V.: Anomaly detection: a survey. ACM computing surveys (CSUR) **41**(3), 1–58 (2009)
2. Hundman, K., Constantinou, V., Laporte, C., Colwell, I., Soderstrom, T.: Detecting spacecraft anomalies using LSTMs and nonparametric dynamic thresholding. In: Proceedings of the 24th ACM SIGKDD International Conference on Knowledge Discovery & Data Mining, pp. 387–395 (2018)
3. Park, D., Hoshi, Y., Kemp, C.C.: A multimodal anomaly detector for robot-assisted feeding using an LSTM-based variational autoencoder. IEEE Robot. Autom. Lett. **3**(3), 1544–1551 (2018)
4. Malhotra, P., Ramakrishnan, A., Anand, G., Vig, L., Agarwal, P., Shroff, G.: LSTM-based encoder-decoder for multi-sensor anomaly detection. arXiv preprint arXiv:1607.00148 (2016)
5. Nguyen, N., Quanz, B.: Temporal latent auto-encoder: a method for probabilistic multivariate time series forecasting. In: Proceedings of the AAAI Conference on Artificial Intelligence, vol. 35, pp. 9117–9125 (2021)
6. Su, Y., Zhao, Y., Niu, C., Liu, R., Sun, W., Pei, D.: Robust anomaly detection for multivariate time series through stochastic recurrent neural network. In: Proceedings of the 25th ACM SIGKDD International Conference on Knowledge Discovery & Data Mining, pp. 2828–2837 (2019)
7. Zong, B., et al.: Deep autoencoding gaussian mixture model for unsupervised anomaly detection. In: International Conference on Learning Representations (2018)
8. Munir, M., Siddiqui, S.A., Dengel, A., Ahmed, S.: DeepAnT: a deep learning approach for unsupervised anomaly detection in time series. IEEE Access **7**, 1991–2005 (2018)
9. Deng, A., Hooi, B.: Graph neural network-based anomaly detection in multivariate time series. In: Proceedings of the AAAI Conference on Artificial Intelligence, vol. 35, pp. 4027–4035 (2021)
10. Dai, L., et al.: SDFVAE: static and dynamic factorized VAE for anomaly detection of multivariate CDN KPIS. In: Proceedings of the Web Conference 2021, pp. 3076–3086 (2021)
11. Papadimitriou, S., Sun, J., Philip, S.Y.: Local correlation tracking in time series. In: Sixth International Conference on Data Mining (ICDM 2006), pp. 456–465. IEEE (2006)

12. Kingma, D.P., Welling, M.: Auto-encoding variational Bayes. arXiv preprint arXiv:1312.6114 (2013)
13. Basu, S., Meckesheimer, M.: Automatic outlier detection for time series: an application to sensor data. Knowl. Inf. Syst. **11**(2), 137–154 (2007)
14. Mehrang, S., Helander, E., Pavel, M., Chieh, A., Korhonen, I.: Outlier detection in weight time series of connected scales. In: 2015 IEEE International Conference on Bioinformatics and Biomedicine (BIBM), pp. 1489–1496. IEEE (2015)
15. Hautamaki, V., Karkkainen, I., Franti, P.: Outlier detection using k-nearest neighbour graph. In: Proceedings of the 17th International Conference on Pattern Recognition, 2004. ICPR 2004, vol. 3, pp. 430–433. IEEE (2004)
16. Carter, K.M., Streilein, W.W.: Probabilistic reasoning for streaming anomaly detection. In: 2012 IEEE Statistical Signal Processing Workshop (SSP), pp. 377–380. IEEE (2012)
17. Zhang, Y., Hamm, N.A., Meratnia, N., Stein, A., Van De Voort, M., Havinga, P.J.: Statistics-based outlier detection for wireless sensor networks. Int. J. Geogr. Inf. Sci. **26**(8), 1373–1392 (2012)
18. Brockwell, P.J., Davis, R.A.: Time Series: Theory and Methods. Springer Science & Business Media (2009)
19. Manevitz, L.M., Yousef, M.: One-class SVMs for document classification. J. Mach. Learn. Res. **2**(Dec), 139–154 (2001)
20. Kriegel, H.P., Kröger, P., Schubert, E., Zimek, A.: Outlier detection in arbitrarily oriented subspaces. In: 2012 IEEE 12th International Conference on Data Mining, pp. 379–388. IEEE (2012)
21. Siffer, A., Fouque, P.A., Termier, A., Largouet, C.: Anomaly detection in streams with extreme value theory. In: Proceedings of the 23rd ACM SIGKDD International Conference on Knowledge Discovery and Data Mining, pp. 1067–1075 (2017)
22. Zhang, C., et al.: A deep neural network for unsupervised anomaly detection and diagnosis in multivariate time series data. In: Proceedings of the AAAI Conference on Artificial Intelligence, vol. 33, pp. 1409–1416 (2019)
23. Kitaev, N., Kaiser, Ł., Levskaya, A.: Reformer: the efficient transformer. arXiv preprint arXiv:2001.04451 (2020)
24. Wu, H., Xu, J., Wang, J., Long, M.: Autoformer: decomposition transformers with auto-correlation for long-term series forecasting. Adv. Neural Inf. Process. Syst. **34**, 22419–22430 (2021)
25. Chen, Z., Chen, D., Zhang, X., Yuan, Z., Cheng, X.: Learning graph structures with transformer for multivariate time series anomaly detection in IoT. IEEE Internet Things J. (2021)
26. Vaswani, A., Shazeer, N., Parmar, N., Uszkoreit, J., Jones, L., Gomez, A.N., Kaiser, Ł., Polosukhin, I.: Attention is all you need. Advances in neural information processing systems 30 (2017)
27. Katser, I.D., Kozitsin, V.O.: Skoltech anomaly benchmark (SKAB). http://www.kaggle.com/dsv/1693952 (2020). https://doi.org/10.34740/KAGGLE/DSV/1693952
28. Goh, J., Adepu, S., Junejo, K.N., Mathur, A.: A dataset to support research in the design of secure water treatment systems. In: International Conference on Critical Information Infrastructures Security, pp. 88–99. Springer (2016). https://doi.org/10.1007/978-3-319-71368-7_8
29. Thiagarajan, J.J., Rajan, D., Katoch, S., Spanias, A.: DDxNet: a deep learning model for automatic interpretation of electronic health records, electrocardiograms and electroencephalograms. Sci. Rep. **10**(1), 1–11 (2020)

BASNEA: Threat Hunting for Ethereum Smart Contract Based on Backtrackless Aligned-Spatial Network Entity Alignment

Xiangyu Du[1,2], Zhengwei Jiang[1,2], Jun Jiang[1,2], Kai Zhang[1], Zijing Fan[1,2(✉)],
Fangming Dong[2], Ning Li[1], and Baoxu Liu[1,2]

[1] Institute of Information Engineering, Chinese Academy of Sciences, Beijing, China
fangzijing@iie.ac.cn
[2] School of Cyber Security, University of Chinese Academy of Sciences,
Beijing, China

Abstract. Ethereum, a blockchain-based platform with a large number of decentralized applications, has been facing vast attacks and suffered significant financial losses. Threat hunting on Ethereum fails to detect attacks in time, resulting in abundant attacks being discovered only after vendors or developers take property inventory count. We propose BASNEA, a backtrackless aligned-spatial network entity alignment algorithm, to identify attacks, suspicious, and benign behaviors by comparing the attack provenance graphs constructed by the Ethereum threat intelligence with transaction provenance graphs generated from the Ethereum sync node. We also use attack investigation to the analysis of suspicious behaviors, and feedback is given to the analysis model to identify more potential threats. The experiments show that based on the collected 1,220 attack events, BASNEA can show more accurate and robust results in Ethereum smart contract threat hunting, which identifies 14 vulnerability types, and 8,814 attack events, including 1,122 known attack behaviors, and 7692 suspected attack behaviors. After the attack investigation, we discovered the hidden information behind the attack, which can help us better identify unknown threats.

Keywords: Ethereum · Smart contract · Threat hunting · Network entity alignment

1 Introduction

Blockchain technology has been widely used in online trading platforms, digital storage, and public services which facilitates people's work, life, and economy.

Supported by Youth Innovation Promotion Association, CAS (No. 2020166), this work is also supported by the Program of Key Laboratory of Network Assessment Technology, the Chinese Academy of Sciences, Program of Beijing Key Laboratory of Network Security and Protection Technology.

Ethereum, as the second generation of blockchain platform, has become the largest smart contract platform and the second-largest trading platform.

However, the economic property of blockchain has attracted a lot of hacker attacks. For example, the Parity event froze hundreds of millions of dollars, the FOMO event lost tens of millions of dollars and the famous APT organization Lazarus stole over 8,100 dollars from Bangladesh Central Bank.

Many security companies, researchers, and developers publish a lot of Ethereum threat intelligence to describe attack events and vulnerabilities. Security analysts read and understand attack patterns to discover attacks in Ethereum, which difficult to identify threats quickly and accurately. We seek to detect attack which has not been reported and find more threats through learning attack pattern automatically in open source threat intelligence.

There are difficulties in the detection of smart contracts. Firstly, the attacker does not follow the pattern and also the debugging process is never necessarily on the chain nor logged. Seconding, attackers debug attack code continuously for a long time and the time span is too large. Finally, the operation of various events has been mixed and many people attempt to attack without further action after the attack.

To address these challenges, we extract attack features from open source threat intelligence and performed multi-source verification in the Ethereum database. Then we constructed them into transaction origin graph and attack behavior graph which represents behavior features better. To speed up the attack investigation process, to achieve rapid threat hunting.

The contributions of this paper are as follows:

- Entity alignment is applied to the threat hunting for the first time. We find potential attacks from the prospect of threat actors, attack tools, and targets.
- Aiming at the threat hunting and discovery task of Ethereum, a new back-trackless aligned-spatial network entity alignment(BASNEA) algorithm is proposed to identify attackers, attack tools and victims. Meanwhile, we judge known types of attack behaviors, suspicious behaviors and normal behaviors by using the transaction timing graph editing distance(GED) method according to the actual transaction process.
- We accelerate the investigation process of attack, realize the rapid threat hunting, and reveal the behavior pattern behind the operation of attackers by distinguishing suspicious behaviors according to the attack methods by using the clustering method.

2 Background

2.1 Ethereum

Ethereum is a community-run technology that supports the cryptocurrency Ethereum and thousands of decentralized applications [1]. Ethereum is made up of blocks and each of which packages transactions that take place over a period of time. **Transaction** is initiated by one account against another. Transactions are hashed in 32-bit hexadecimal format. The main fields of an Ethereum transaction are shown in Table 1. Transactions are divided into external transactions and internal transactions. **External transactions** are often called transactions, which are initiated directly by the sender and can be seen intuitively. **Internal transactions** are usually called traces, which are the inter-account operations called by the smart contract or other smart contracts in transactions. Accounts are classified into two types, **EOAs**(external Owned Accounts) and **smart contracts**, which are uniquely identified by a 20-byte public key. EOAs are human-controlled addresses, while smart contracts are created by other accounts (BOTH EOAs and other smart contracts) in the form of code running in EVM(Ethereum Virtual machine) that automatically performs predefined functions.

Table 1. Parsed ethereum transaction data

Fields	Meaning	Sample
Hash	The hash is a unique 66-character identifier that is generated whenever a transaction is executed	0xfa5e20de...
Status	The status of the transaction	Success
Block	Number of the block in which the transaction is recorded	14797857
Time	The time when the transaction is last seen in the network pool	1653572752
From	The sending party of the transaction	0xe7e6c8....
To	The receiving party of the transaction	0x1c76e0....
Value	The value being transacted in Ether and fiat value	0xaa2cc....
Gas	The amount paid to miners	0x3454b
MethodID	The function signature	0xab834bab
Data	Content submitted in a transaction	0xab834b...

2.2 Threat Hunting

Threat hunting is the process of actively and repeatedly searching the network and sake for detecting and isolating advanced threats that evade existing security solutions. Threat hunting is a semi-automated way to detect suspicious behavior patterns in data, summarize patterns or TTPs (Tactics, Techniques and Procedures), and build automated analysis capabilities.

Unlike threat intelligence, threat hunting is not just about using external information, such as IoC (Indicators of Compromise), snort, or other detection rules, which perform well in detecting known attacks and become ineffective once the attacker fine-tunes them. Attack behavior also includes many attack features. The IoB (indicator of behavior) based on attack patterns can better discover potential attacks that cannot be found by detection rules.

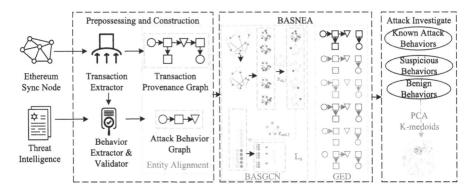

Fig. 1. Overview of Backtrackless Aligned-Spatial Network Entity Alignment (BAS-NEA)

2.3   Graph Convolutional Neural Networks

Graph convolutional neural network (GCN) is a natural extension of convolutional neural network in the field of graph. It is applicable to nodes and graphs of any topology structure since it can learn node feature information and structure information end-to-end at the same time. In the task of node classification and edge prediction, the results of open dataset are much better than other methods. GCN can process non-euclidean data like Ethereum transactions, molecular structures and other spatial structures that do not have rules. These atlas structures are different for each node connection. Each node in the atlas contains features information and structural information. In this kind of graph data, we should consider the feature information and structure information of nodes at the same time rather than rely on manual rules to extract since it would lose a lot of implicit and complex patterns.

A GCN model consists of multiple stacked GCN layers. The input to the l-th layer of the GCN model is a vertex feature matrix, $H^{(l)} \in \mathbb{R}^{n \times d^{(l)}}$. Let $G = (V, E), |V| = n$, A is a $n \times n$ connectivity matrix that represents the structure information of the graph; $\hat{A} = A + I$; $\hat{D}$ is the diagonal node degree matrix of $\hat{A}$. The input to the l-th layer of the GCN model is a vertex feature matrix, where n is the number of vertices and $d^{(l)}$ is the number of features in the l-th layer. The output of the l-th layer is a new feature matrix $H^{(l+1)}$ by the following convolutional computation [15]:

$$H^{(l+1)} = \sigma(\hat{D}^{-\frac{1}{2}} \hat{A} \hat{D}^{-\frac{1}{2}} H^{(l)} W^{(l)}) \tag{1}$$

where $W^{(l)} \in \mathbb{R}^{d^{(l)} \times d^{(l+1)}}$ is the weight matrix of the l-th layer in the GCN, $d^{(l+1)}$ is the dimensionality of new vertex features. The activation function σ is chosen as $ReLU(\cdot) = max(0, \cdot)$.

3   The Proposed Framework

3.1   System Model

The main goal of this framework is to conduct threat hunting in Ethereum to discover potential attacks. As shown in the Fig. 1, the input of this framework consists of two parts, one is transaction data from Ethereum synchronization nodes, and the other is threat intelligence recording Ethereum attack events. We preprocessed and constructed the data, including constructing the Ethereum data as a transaction Provenance graph, as well as extracting key information from threat intelligence and constructing an attack behavior graph. The key to threat hunting in this paper is the BASNEA method in the middle of the figure, which uses the BASGCN and GED algorithms to align entities. It calculates the similarity between the threat subject, which is in the transaction origin graph and the attack behavior graph, and the attacked target to discover potential attack behaviors. The last is the attack investigation. Based on the results obtained by the BASNEA method and threat intelligence information, the results are classified into known attacks, suspected attacks and normal behaviors through principal component analysis and the K-Medoids clustering algorithm. Combined with expert analysis, we can judge whether the suspected attack is an attack variant.

3.2   Prepossessing

As shown in the left figure of Fig. 1, we first preprocess the data through three extractors.

Ethereum Transaction Extractor. We query the transaction and internal transaction information of Ethereum through the API interface, which is parsed into fields according to yellow paper [16] such as from and to, as shown in Table 1.

Attack Behavior Extractor and Validator. We collect threat intelligence information from CVEs, Dapp vendors' announcements, security companys' blogs, and researcher blogs. Then we generate threat indicators by using regularities to filter attack transaction hashes, malicious smart contract addresses, attacked application addresses, attacking and attacked functions. However, the quality of multi-source threat intelligence is difficult with no guarantees, and the results we extract may be inaccurate because we verify threat indicators. We have searched the threat indicator in the Ethereum data to determine whether the retrieved transactions match the description.

3.3   Construction

We construct a transaction provenance graph from transaction behaviors of the Ethereum Sync Database and an attack behavior graph from the extracted attack behavior of threat intelligence.

Transaction Provenance Graph. For each transaction, we construct a transaction origin graph $G = (V, E)$, where G is a directed hypergraph with attributes. We define $V = (v_1, v_2, ...v_i, ..., v_n)$ as the node set of the graph, that is, all accounts in the transaction, which includes EOA and smart contracts, v_i is a node in the graph, that is, the node in transaction. We define $v_i = (d_{i1}, d_{i2}, ..., d_{ij}, ..., d_{im})$, where d_{ij} is the attribute of node v_i, such as account type, first active transaction time, last transaction time, smart contract function list and smart contract fuzzy hash, etc. We define $E = (e_1, e_2, ..., e_p, ..., e_k)$ as the edge set of the graph, that is, the relationship between transactions and their internal transactions, such as ether transfer, smart contract invocation, suicide and other behavior definitions. e_p is an edge of the graph, that is, a behavior in the transaction. We define $e_k = (f_1, f_2, ..., f_q, ...f_l)$, where f_q is the attribute of the edge e_k, such as the amount of ether, the amount of tokens, the generation of Coin type, calling function, calling parameters and calling sequence, etc.

Attack Behavior Graph. Compared to the complete transaction graph, the attack graph appears sparse. Since the attack graph comes from the threat intelligence we collected, which was a high-level summary of the attack behavior. It may not include the detailed information of the attack, but only the conclusive or evidentiary information of the attack and the constructed graph may be incomplete. The attack graph has the same structure as the transaction graph. However, there will be many missing nodes and relationships because of the incomplete intelligence. Simultaneously, the *calling function* may appear in the form of a name instead of an *id*, and the *calling order* is a relative order, that is, only the order of the edges is indicated.

3.4 BASNEA

In this paper, the BASNEA model is proposed, which can significantly reduce the tottering problem of spatial GCN entity alignment and solve the bottleneck of analysis performance of massive high-speed transactions to make new transactions timely and effectively processed. This method takes the information of transaction heterogeneous attribute graph into account and can also represent the transaction graph features to the end-to-end learning framework of threat hunting task.

Given a sample graph G(V,E) with its aligned vertex grid structure $\overline{X} \in \mathbb{R}^{M \times c}$ and the associated backtrackless aligned grid vertex adjacency matrix $\overline{A}^D \in \mathbb{R}^{M \times M}$ the proposed backtrackless spatial graph convolution operation takes the following forms [2]:

$$Z_{in}^h = Relu(\overline{D}_{in}^{-1} \overline{A}_{in} \sum_{j=1}^{c} (\overline{X} \odot W^h)_{[:,j]})$$ (2)

and

$$Z_{out}^h = Relu(\overline{D}_{out}^{-1}\overline{A}_{out} \sum_{j=1}^{c} (\overline{X} \odot W^h)_{[:,j]}) \tag{3}$$

where $\odot$ represents the element-wise Hadamard product, in-adjacency matrix $\overline{A}_{in} = (\overline{A}^D)^T$, out-adjacency matrix $\overline{A}_{out} = \overline{A}^D$, $\overline{D}_{in}$ is the in-degree matrix of $\overline{A}_{in}$, and $\overline{D}_{out}$ is the out-degree matrix of $\overline{A}_{out}$. More specifically, Eq. 2 corresponds to the in-spatial graph convolution operation. Equation 3 corresponds to the out-spatial graph convolution operation. The in-spatial and out-spatial convolution operations share the same trainable parameter matrix $W^h \in \mathbb{R}^{M \times c}$ for both their h-th convolution filters with the filter size $M \times 1$ and the channel number c. Relu is the rectified linear units function (i.e., a nonlinear activation function), and $Z_{in}^h \in \mathbb{R}^{M \times 1}$ and $Z_{out}^h \in \mathbb{R}^{M \times 1}$ are the output activation matrices for the in-spatial and out-spatial convolution operations.

In addition to node information, network structure information is also important for entity alignment tasks. Therefore, Z is divided into structure vector z_s and attribute vector z_a [15]. Z_s^0 is initialized with random input and updated with training, while Z_a^0 is initialized with entity vector and will not be updated in subsequent training. Therefore, the structure vector and attribute vector of output activation matrices for the in-spatial and out-spatial convolution operations in this paper are as follows:

$$[Z_s^{l+1}; Z_a^{l+1}] = ReLU(\overline{D}^{-1}\overline{AD}^{-1}[Z_s^l W_s^l; Z_a^l W_a^l]) \tag{4}$$

After several rounds of updates, for comparison of graph G_1 and G_2, nodes are v_{1i} and v_{2j}, edges are e_{1i} and e_{2j}, functions are called m_{1i} and m_{2j}, parameters are transferred d_{1i} and d_{2j}, and Ethereum is transferred v_{1i} and v_{2j}. We use graph editing distance to measure similarity between entities.

$$D(v_{1i}, v_{2j}) = \beta \frac{f(z_s(v_{1i}), z_s(v_{2j}))}{d_s} = (1-\beta) \frac{f(z_a(v_{1i}), z_a(v_{2j}))}{d_a} \tag{5}$$

where $f(x, y)$ represents the graph editing distance between x and y as Eq. 6, $z_s(\cdot)$ and $z_a(\cdot)$ denote the structure embedding and attribute embedding of an entity respectively. d_s and d_a are dimensionalities of structure embeddings and attribute embeddings. β is a hyper-parameter that balances the importance of two kinds of embeddings.

$$f(g_1, g_2) = \sum_{\substack{e_{1i} \in e_{1function}, \\ e_{2i} \in e_{2function}}} (\{ \begin{matrix} 3, if\ count(e_{1i}) = 1 \\ 1, other \end{matrix} + \{ \begin{matrix} 10, if\ e_{1i} \in Privile \\ 0, other \end{matrix})$$

$$+ \sum_{\substack{e_{1i} \in e_{1parameter}, \\ e_{2i} \in e_{2parameter}}} \{ \begin{matrix} 0, if\ e_{1i} = e_{2i} \\ 0, else\ if\ type(e_{1i}) = type(e_{2i}) = address \\ |e_{1i} - e_{2i}|/(e_{1i} + e_{2i}), else\ if\ type(e_{1i}) = type(e_{2i}) = number \\ 1, other \end{matrix}$$

$$+ \sum_{\substack{e_{1i} \in e_{1money}, \\ e_{2i} \in e_{2money}}} \{ \begin{matrix} \frac{|e_{1i}-e_{2i}|}{\max(e_{1i}, e_{2i})}, if\ e_{1i} + e_{2i} > 0 \\ 0, other \end{matrix} + \sum_{\substack{e_{1i} \in e_{1order}, \\ e_{2i} \in e_{2order}}} \frac{|e_{1i} - e_{2i}|}{\max(e_{1i}, e_{2i})} \quad (6)$$

$$+ \sum_{\substack{v_{1i} \in v_{1address}, \\ v_{2i} \in v_{2address}}} (\{ \begin{matrix} 0, if\ type(v_{1i}) = type(v_{2i}) \\ 10, other \end{matrix} + \{ \begin{matrix} 0, if\ dapp(v_{1i}) = dapp(v_{2i}) \\ 10, other \end{matrix})$$

$$+ \sum_{\substack{v_{1i} \in v_{1function}, \\ v_{2i} \in v_{2function}}} 5 * Jaccard(v_{1i}, v_{2i})) + \sum_{\substack{v_{1i} \in v_{1opcode}, \\ v_{2i} \in v_{2opcode}}} 5 * simhash(v_{1i}, v_{2i})$$

$$+ \frac{|t_1 - t_2|}{30} + \{ \begin{matrix} 0, if\ v_{1sender} = v_{2sender} \\ 10, other \end{matrix} + \{ \begin{matrix} 0, if\ e_{1sender} = e_{2sender} \\ 10, other \end{matrix}$$

where all variables' description in Table 2.

Based on the types of vulnerability exploitation we have collected, we set the cost of nodes and edges in graph editing distance for these attack methods and define the cost function:

$$D(g_1, g_2) = \alpha \min_{(o_1, \dots, o_k) \in o(g_1, g_2)} \sum_{i=1}^{k} c(o_i) + \beta \triangle t + \gamma r \quad (7)$$

Meanwhile, ordinary adjacency matrix A cannot handle relations, considering that two entities that are connected to aligned entities by different relations are likely to be unequal [15]. We use the following method to calculate A of KG and make it represent the extent to which alignment information is propagated from the i-th entity to the j-th entity.

$$fun(r) = \frac{\#Head\_Entities\_of\_r}{\#Triples\_of\_r} \quad (8)$$

$$ifun(r) = \frac{\#Tail\_Entities\_of\_r}{\#Triples\_of\_r} \quad (9)$$

Table 2. Variable Name List of Eq. 6

Variable name	Description
g_1	transaction provenance graph
g_2	attack behavior graph
$e_{1function}, e_{2function}$	function of edges of g_1 and g_2
$count(e_{1i})$	the number of called functions e_{1i} in g_1
$Privile$	a privileged functions set
$e_{1parameter}, e_{2parameter}$	the called function's parameter list of the e_1 and e_2
$type(e_{1i}), type(e_{2i})$	data type of the parameter in e_1 and e_2's called function
e_{1money}, e_{2money}	the amount of money traded on the edges in g_1
e_{1order}, e_{2order}	the order of the edges in the graph
$v_{1address}$	the address of the account corresponding to the node
$type(v_{1i}), type(v_{2i})$	the type of account corresponding to the node, which is divided into eoa and smart contract
$dapp(v_{1i}), dapp(v_{2i})$	the dapp name corresponding to the node
$v_{1function}, v_{1function}$	function list of the smart contract corresponding to node
$Jaccard(v_{1i}, v_{2i})$	the jaccard distance of a function set of nodes v_{1i}, v_{2i}
$v_{1opcode}, v_{2opcode}$	the preprocessed operation code of the node v_{1i}, v_{2i}
$simhash(v_{1i}, v_{2i})$	the fuzzy hash of node v_{1i}, v_{2i} bytecode
$v_{1sender}, v_{2sender}$	the sender's account type of g_1 and g_2
$e_{1sender}, e_{2sender}$	the called function of the initial edge of g_1 and g_2
t_1, t_2	the transaction timestamp of g_1, g_2

For each element a_{ij} in A:

$$a_{ij} = \sum_{<e_i, r, e_j> \in G} ifun(r) + \sum_{<e_j, r, e_r> \in G} fun(r) \tag{10}$$

$\#Head\_Entities\_of\_r$ indicates the number of header entities in relationship r, and $\#Tail\_Entities\_of\_r$ indicates the number of tail entities in relationship r. $\#Triples\_of\_r$ represents the number of triples of the relation r. a_{ij} represents the effect of the i-th entity on the j-th entity. We adopts margin-based ranking loss as loss function:

$$L_s = \sum_{(e,v) \in S} \sum_{(e',v') \in S'_{e,v}} ReLU[f(z_s(e), z_s(v)) + \gamma_s - f(f(z_s(e'), z_s(v')))] \tag{11}$$

We minimize the cost loss function:

$$\mathcal{L} = D + L_s \tag{12}$$

3.5 Attack Investigate

The BASNEA method finds the attack objects and attackers described in the threat intelligence. We divide the results into unreported known attack behaviors, suspicious attack behaviors and normal behaviors according to the similarity with known attack events. For suspicious attack behaviors, we extract attack pattern features such as attack function, attack step size, authority change, capital flow, attack time, attack code and attacked target, etc.

We use principal component analysis to reduce the dimensionality of the above features, and k-Medoids to cluster suspicious behaviors into different attack methods. Finally, we sent it to auditors for further analysis to reduce the manual screening time and accelerate the attack discovery process.

The singular value decomposition method is used to reduce the dimension of principal component analysis. Assume data sample $X_{p \times n}$, which can be decomposed into:

$$X = U_{p \times n} \Sigma_{n \times n} V_{n \times n}^T \tag{13}$$

where V is orthogonal matrix, Σ is diagonal matrix.

4 Evaluation

4.1 Datasets

Ethereum Transaction. There are four ways to obtain Ethereum data: browser (etherscan), online query interface (etherscan, infura), submitting code to run (google big query) and querying Ethereum nodes. In order to quickly analyze the data on a large scale, we choose openethereum, and use packaging patterns for data synchronization.

Dapp List. We collected dapp lists and crawled their current and historical versions from data sources such as dappradar [4], dappreview [11], stateofthedapps [5], ethereumscan [6], and others. Some functionally complex dapps are made up of multiple smart contracts to facilitate the replacement of certain functions, or to modularize certain functions. There are many smart contracts for such dapps, which cause certain confusion in the analysis. In addition, these dapp lists are not necessarily complete since collected by operators or volunteers. We identify more untagged dapps through analyzing the code similarity of other smart contracts created by the dapp creator's account, 6,276 in total.

Threat Intelligence. We collect threat intelligence information from blockchain security companies, dapp vendors, CVE, and researchers' blogs. Then we filter out transaction hashes, account addresses, and function hashes through regular expressions, and obtain function names through a 4byte database. As shown in Table 3, We obtain 815 attacker eoas, 173 malicious smart contract addresses and 298 attacked dapp from 1220 incident reports.

Table 3. Threat intelligence statistic

Source	Incidents	Eoas	SM	Dapps
CVEs	535	631	142	352
PeckShield	117	86	20	72
Slowmist	132	115	31	68
Lianantech	102	67	16	45
Dapp vendors	46	6	0	38
Medium	182	76	33	153
Anquanke	54	42	8	39
Freebuf	52	38	11	43
Summary	1220	815	173	298

Table 4. Precision, Recall and F1-score for six methods

Method	Precision	Recall	F1-score
RNN	0.84	0.9	0.87
RecGNNs	0.89	0.91	0.9
GAE	0.87	0.89	0.88
GCN	0.87	0.82	0.84
BASGCN	0.9	0.91	0.9
BASNEA	**0.92**	**0.94**	**0.93**

4.2 Experimental Setup

We use python to implement all functions. Transaction Extractor uses the ipc interface of openethereum to obtain Ethereum transaction data. The data field is the type of parameters analyzed through the eth_abi library, and the field representing the number of tokens is selected through the 4 byte dictionary library to determine whether it is a sensitive function. Smart contract byte-code is parsed into opcodes by the pyevmasm library. Behavior Extractor & Validator is collected through the scrapy framework, and the XPath method is parsed into the required threat intelligence. Transaction Provenance Graph and Attack Behavior Graph are built through the Networkx library using MultiDi-Graph (directed hypergraph). The backtrackless convolution part of the BAS-NEA model is implemented by the tensorflow library, and the GED is implemented by the optimize_graph_edit_distance method of Networks. Attack Investigator is implemented through the K-medoids method of the Scikit-learn library after principal component analysis.

4.3 Evaluation Metrics

In order to verify the experimental effect, We split each incident in the threat intelligence data 7:3 randomly based on training data and test data. We carry out five verifications, and take the average of the five results. We regard the same data as threat intelligence in the results as unreported known attack behaviors, data with a similarity greater than 0.9 with threat intelligence as suspicious attack behaviors, and the rest as normal behaviors. After inspection by 3 experts, and suspicious attack behavior was confirmed.

We use the precision rate, recall rate, and F1-score to evaluate the model effect. In order to compare the effects, we use RNN, RecGNNs, GAE, GCN, BASGCN and our proposed BASNEA model for analysis. We run the experiments after running 20 times and take the average results in Table 4.

The first column shows the methods of comparing experiments and the last three columns are the evaluation index, which are accuracy rate precision, recall rate and F1-score respectively. In Table 4, the algorithm comparison experiment results show that BASNEA returns the best results among the six methods. Therefore, BASNEA can show more accurate and robust results in Ethereum smart contract threat hunting.

4.4 Attack Analysis

In order to gain insight into attacks, we analyze suspicious behaviors based on selected four types of experimental results, including overflow, privilege, code error, and replay.

Attack Time Distribution. According to our statistics on attack events, as shown in the Fig. 2a, we can find that the attack is explosive, focusing on the application online, the first appearance of vulnerability exploitation, and the appearance of analysis reports. We conducted statistics according to 1 day, 3 days, 7 days and 30 days. As shown in the Table 2b, we found that 5% of the attacks were concentrated in 3 days after the application went online, 30% of the attacks were concentrated in 1 day after the exploit occurred, and 30% of the attacks concentrate on 7 days after the analysis report appears.

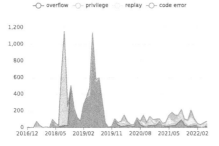

item	1d	3d	7d	30d
Time of dapp creation	53	441	528	2204
Time to first exploit	617	2027	2732	4143
Time of report release	264	1498	2468	4671

(a) time distribution of attack incidents   (b) time difference of attack incidents

Fig. 2. Time analysis of attack events

Attacker. We analyze the attackers and their target, as shown in the Fig. 3a, from which we find the preference information of the attacker for Dapp. It can be seen from the figure that there were many attacks on June 18 and July 19. During that time, gambling and token applications prospered, but security protection was not done well, and there were many privileges and overflow attacks.

We analyzed the vulnerability types attacked by DAPP, as shown in the Fig. 3b. Attackers can be roughly divided into two categories. 80% of attackers attack against a single vulnerability type, and 12% of them attack the same vulnerability more than 10 times. Only 3% of them cash out through exchanges. 8% of attackers will attack more than three types of vulnerability, which is a large number of attacks with high frequency, and 5% of the attackers will cash through exchanges.

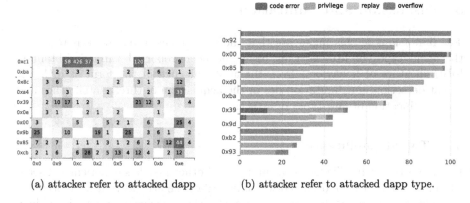

(a) attacker refer to attacked dapp

(b) attacker refer to attacked dapp type.

Fig. 3. Attacker refer to attacked dapp type

Attacker Group. We analyzed the relationship between the attacker and the target, as shown in the Fig. 4b. It is found that the targets of the attackers are consistent. In the figure, the yellow attacker attacks the Beauty Coin as well as the SmartMesh, Old Token and UGChain, while the green attacker attacks the SpankChain, PrivateBank and Morph applications. We counted the attack time, and 80% of the attacks took place within three days.

We sorted out common relationships between attacker accounts: (1) Direct transfer: attacker A transfers money to attacker B; (2) Indirect transfer: Attacker A invokes smart contract, and smart contract transfers to attacker B; (3) Call. Attacker A invokes the attack code created by attacker B, or attacker A and attacker B invoke the same attack code. We analyze the attacker based on these relationships, as shown in the Fig. 4a.

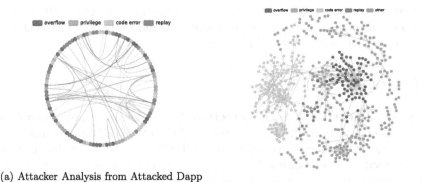

(a) Attacker Analysis from Attacked Dapp Perspective

(b) Attacker Analysis from Attacker Perspective.

Fig. 4. Attacker group (Color figure online)

5   Discussion and Limitation

The limitations of this paper are that the main focus of our work is to detect the same types of attacks that have not been reported through obtaining IoB(Indicators of behaviors) from threat intelligence in the form of IoC. For threat detection, our limitation lies in the acquisition of threat intelligence and the identification of new types of attacks.

5.1   Threat Intelligence

Ethereum threat intelligence is a summary of other people's experience of security incidents that have occurred which describes the attacks that have occurred and contain many attack features. Its effective sharing can positively help enhance the overall security capability of the industry. As the input data of the method in this paper, threat intelligence is used to identify attacks consistent with the attack behavior described by threat intelligence. However, the richness of threat intelligence also limits the number of unreported attack events that can be found in this paper. Attacks, however, varied but has similarity. In this paper, some achievements have been made in extending the existing attack events, and 95% of the attack events have been extended. For attack patterns not mentioned in threat intelligence, the research based on code analysis and attacker relationship analysis can better discover new attacks. We can continue to identify new attack events based on the results of these studies.

5.2   New Type of Attack Incidents

In this paper, the attack behavior pattern is extracted from the existing attack events to detect the same type of attack that has not been reported before, but it is difficult to accurately identify the attack type that has not occurred before. In the future, we seek to consider multi-view learning methods to identify events of unknown attack types from the perspectives of money flow, smart contract byte-code and account relationship behavior, etc.

6   Related Work

Entity Alignment for Attack Detection. Entity Alignment, also known as Entity Matching, refers to finding the same Entity in the real world among entities in the heterogeneous database. Ligatti [12] collects the IOC of threat intelligence as seeds, selects multiple features to match malicious applications developed by malicious attackers in the android application markets, and uses the pruning method to reduce the impact of path explosion. Milajerdi [10] collects threat intelligence data, manually extracts information to construct graph structure, and searches incomplete subgraphs by entity alignment to discover attack behavior. Gao [7] collects threat intelligence and automatically extracts information to discover attack activities through building relationships into TBQL language. Hadar [8] identifies vulnerabilities and potential exploits in enterprise environments according to threat intelligence by using the entity alignment method.

Theat Hunting by Behavior. In recent years, more and more studies have shown the effectiveness of identifying threats from behavioral perspectives. Wang [14] tracks money flow behavior, compares it with the behavior extracted in the code, and identifies anomalies through inconsistent behavior. Torres [13] matches attack patterns with known behaviors at run-time for discovering the fraud. Liu [9] detect threats through results of fuzzing smart contracts to detect the reentrant vulnerabilities. Chen [3] extracts a large number of behavioral features and identifies phishing activities in Ethereum through gradient regression. Zhou [17] collects threat intelligence information and builds result trees and behavior graphs in Ethereum to detect attacks by comparing similarities.

7 Conclusion

For threat hunting on Ethereum, we propose BASNEA to extract attack patterns from threat intelligence and find known attack and their variants, speeding up the investigation process. First of all, we maintain an Ethereum node that synchronizes the transaction data in real-time, then import them into the transaction behavior database to generate the transaction provenance graph. Meanwhile, we collect 1,220 Ethereum threat intelligence, extract attack features and generate attack behavior graphs. Afterward, we apply the BASNEA model to compare the attack provenance graphs with transaction provenance graphs for identifying threats. The comparison experiment results show that BASNEA performs more accurate and robust results in Ethereum threat hunting. After verification, we identify 8814 attack behaviors of 14 vulnerability types with the accuracy of 92% through 1220 attack events. Finally, we analyze the results from the perspectives of time distribution, attack behavior, and various relationships, and discover the hidden information in the attack to help confirm the attack. Our work makes sense for the Ethereum threat hunting, which can accelerate attack detection and improve the accuracy of discovery to avoid further losses as quickly as possible.

References

1. Ethereum community. https://ethereum.org/. Accessed 3 May 2022
2. Bail, L., Cui, L., Jiao, Y., Rossi, L., Hancock, E.R.: Learning backtrackless aligned-spatial graph convolutional networks for graph classification. IEEE Transactions on Pattern Analysis and Machine Intelligence PP(99), 1–1
3. Chen, W., Guo, X., Chen, Z., Zheng, Z., Lu, Y.: Phishing scam detection on ethereum: towards financial security for blockchain ecosystem. In: IJCAI, pp. 4506–4512. ijcai.org (2020)
4. dappradar: Dappradar - the world's dapp store — blockchain dapps ranked. https://dappradar.com/. Accessed 3 May 2022

5. of the Dapps, S.: A next-generation smart contract and decentralized application platform. https://www.stateofthedapps.com/. Accessed 3 May 2022

6. etherscan: The ethereum blockchain explorer. https://cn.etherscan.com/. Accessed 3 May 2022

7. Gao, P., et al.: Enabling efficient cyber threat hunting with cyber threat intelligence. In: ICDE, pp. 193–204. IEEE (2021)

8. Hadar, E., Hassanzadeh, A.: Big data analytics on cyber attack graphs for prioritizing agile security requirements. In: RE, pp. 330–339. IEEE (2019)

9. Liu, C., Liu, H., Cao, Z., Chen, Z., Chen, B., Roscoe, B.: Reguard: finding reentrancy bugs in smart contracts. In: ICSE (Companion Volume), pp. 65–68. ACM (2018)

10. Milajerdi, S.M., Eshete, B., Gjomemo, R., Venkatakrishnan, V.N.: POIROT: aligning attack behavior with kernel audit records for cyber threat hunting. In: Cavallaro, L., Kinder, J., Wang, X., Katz, J. (eds.) Proceedings of the 2019 ACM SIGSAC Conference on Computer and Communications Security, CCS 2019, London, UK, 11–15 November, 2019, pp. 1813–1830. ACM (2019). https://doi.org/10.1145/3319535.3363217, https://doi.org/10.1145/3319535.3363217

11. Review, D.: A next-generation smart contract and decentralized application platform. https://dapp.review/. Accessed 3 May 2022

12. Sebastián, S., Caballero, J.: Towards attribution in mobile markets: Identifying developer account polymorphism. In: Ligatti, J., Ou, X., Katz, J., Vigna, G. (eds.) CCS 2020: 2020 ACM SIGSAC Conference on Computer and Communications Security, Virtual Event, USA, 9–13 November, 2020, pp. 771–785. ACM (2020). https://doi.org/10.1145/3372297.3417281, https://doi.org/10.1145/3372297.3417281

13. Torres, C.F., Baden, M., Norvill, R., Jonker, H.: Ægis: smart shielding of smart contracts. In: CCS, pp. 2589–2591. ACM (2019)

14. Wang, H., Li, Y., Lin, S., Ma, L., Liu, Y.: Vultron: catching vulnerable smart contracts once and for all. In: ICSE (NIER), pp. 1–4. IEEE/ACM (2019)

15. Wang, Z., Lv, Q., Lan, X., Zhang, Y.: Cross-lingual knowledge graph alignment via graph convolutional networks. In: Proceedings of the 2018 Conference on Empirical Methods in Natural Language Processing (2018)

16. WOOD, D.G.: Ethereum: A secure decentralised generalised transaction ledger. https://ethereum.github.io/yellowpaper/paper.pdf. Accessed 3 May 2022

17. Zhou, S., Yang, Z., Xiang, J., Cao, Y., Yang, M., Zhang, Y.: An ever-evolving game: evaluation of real-world attacks and defenses in ethereum ecosystem. In: USENIX Security Symposium, pp. 2793–2810. USENIX Association (2020)

Multi-region SRAM-Based TCAM for Longest Prefix

Qian Zou[1,2], Ning Zhang[1,2(✉)], Feng Guo[1,2], Qingshan Kong[1], and Zhiqiang Lv[1,2]

[1] Institute of Information Engineering, Chinese Academy of Sciences, Beijing, China
{zouqian,zhangning,guofeng,kongqingshan,lvzhiqiang}@iie.ac.cn
[2] School of Cyber Security, University of Chinese Academy of Sciences, Beijing, China

Abstract. Ternary content-addressable memory (TCAM) plays an important role in network. TCAM is used as high-speed search engine to achieve packet classification. Software-defined network (SDN) data plane is a typical application field where achieves network communication and security protection. Field-programmable gate array (FPGA) offers a programmable hardware platform to emulate TCAM based on static random-access memory (SRAM). However, block RAM resource on FPGA is finite and SRAM-based TCAM structure consumes a large number of block RAMs. Existing methods aim memory utilization to do lots of research. However, memory resources remain to be tight with increasing demand of network packet complexity. Aiming to memory utilization, this paper presents a multi-region SRAM-based TCAM structure. Our method divides entry into address field and data field. The first data pre-processing determines suitable parameter closely related to memory utilization and classification principle in two types of field. The second mapping mechanism is mapping data field to SRAM memory cell combined with longest prefix feature for IP address. The proposed design efficiently reduces consumed numbers of block RAMs on FPGA. Our proposed design is implemented on a Xilinx Virtex FPGA device. Compared to existing SRAM-based TCAMs, our method reduces 33.5938% memory space for a rule set with size of 2048 × 64. With increasing scale of rule sets, proposed design has better and more stable memory utilization.

Keywords: Block RAM (BRAM) · SRAM-based TCAM · Field programmable gate array (FPGA) · Memory utilization · Longest prefix

1 Introduction

Ternary content-addressable memory (TCAM) is a high-speed search device. It compares search content with all the words stored in TCAM in parallel. Due to hardware parallelism, TCAM can search a word in one clock. Every bit in TCAM has three states: 0, 1 and X (don't care) state.

TCAM is widely used in networking communication and security, pattern recognition, artificial intelligence, database management and compression, big-data processing, translation look-aside buffers (TLBs) in microprocessors and

© The Author(s), under exclusive license to Springer Nature Switzerland AG 2022
C. Su et al. (Eds.): SciSec 2022, LNCS 13580, pp. 437–452, 2022.
https://doi.org/10.1007/978-3-031-17551-0_29

graph equality search [1–4]. When using TCAM for data query and match, data is processed efficiently. TCAM has high throughput and can process more data at the same time compared to other ways. With rapid development of the network, a large number of packets need to be identified and processed in a special time. And network communication also results in network security issues. Software-defined network (SDN) [5,6] is a hot research in recent years. SDN divides network device into control and data plane communicated by OpenFlow [7] protocol. OpenFlow switch [8] is used by data forwarding in data plane. Packet classification [9,10] is an imperative technique in OpenFlow switch. It needs to store many rules and when inputting a packet, packet compares with stored rules and switch device performs corresponding action such as forwarding or dropping for packets according to match result. The rules build up access control and security filtering. Network device achieves normal network communication and security protection by matching rules. IP address is an important field in OpenFlow rules. It has longest prefix feature [11]. TCAM can directly implement an entry with mask due to three state in TCAM. Due to high-speed processing, TCAM is popular in network security protection and communication.

Traditional TCAM is based on application specific integrated circuits (ASIC). The ASIC TCAM can achieve quick search, however ASIC TCAM occupies a large circuit area and has high power consumption. ASIC is for specific requirement and can not be reconfigured repeatedly with less flexibility. The features make ASIC unable to meet requirement of plenty of packets processing flexibly in modern network. Field-programmable gate array (FPGA) is a hardware platform that can be programmable and processes data in parallel. Hardware is reconfigured based on FPGA. However, there is no available TCAM device unit on FPGA. TCAM can not be used directly. Researchers make TCAM emulation with existing resources of FPGA [12,13]. TCAM emulation contains several procedure: storage, match and priority arbitration. The part consuming the most resources is storage. At present, FPGA can offer flip-flops (FFs), lookup tables (LUTs) and block RAMs (BRAMs) resources to achieve storage function. For TCAM based on FF and LUT, more entries can result in more FFs and LUTs used, however, it increases complexity of place and route. For SRAM-based TCAM emulation, SRAM blocks are arranged in arrays regularly. With increasing of stored entries, more SRAM blocks need to be used. For one entry, if width of entry increase linearly, number of SRAM blocks used will increase exponentially. However, FPGA resources are limited. Therefore, efficient storage in TCAM emulation design is necessary.

Narrow memory resources in SRAM-based TCAM design limit scale of application. To find appropriate and efficient memory structure is an urgent demand. Our proposed TCAM structure aims to achieve memory resource saving.

The contributions of this work are as follows:

- A multi-region SRAM-based TCAM structure for longest prefix is proposed.
- The proposed design achieves approximately 33.5938% memory area reduction per bit.

– For rule sets of large scale, the proposed design has better memory performance compared to smaller scales.

The rest of this paper is organized as follows. Section 2 surveys the related work. The proposed multi-region SRAM-based TCAM structure for longest prefix is described in detail in Sect. 3. Implementation and results of proposed design are given in Sect. 4. Section 5 presents the performance evaluation of proposed design. Section 6 concludes the paper.

2 Related Work

The TCAM emulation design on FPGA mainly includes three types: FF-based, LUTRAM-based and SRAM-based TCAM.

The FF-based TCAM design utilizes FFs on FPGA as memory unit [14–17]. FF-based TCAM structure is mainly based on G-AETCAM [14]. It contains two FFs in one TCAM cell to describe stored bit and mask bit. RPE-TCAM [16] divides multiple banks and controls part of unused banks off at one time to reduce power consumption based on G-AETCAM [14]. At the same time, instead of comparator in FF-based unit, multiplexer (MUX) is used to save some hardware overhead. The design in [17] aims match lines to change hardware structure. It splits match lines into multiple segments controlled by several clocks. When the front match lines segments not match, the rest segments can not be performed to reduce power consumption. Two FFs describe one TCAM bit, and interconnection in FFs is huge and complex with stored data scale increasing. Using logic to implement TCAM has a narrow limitation of storage capacity. For large size of rule sets, methods based on logic are hard to store.

The LUTRAM-based TCAM design mainly uses LUT resources on FPGA [18–21]. Frac TCAM [18] proposed a fracturable pipelined structure to store more TCAM bits. It efficiently reduces LUT resources. However, it increases extra logic resources and FFs. Dure-TCAM [19] reduces update latency. It supports word searching during updating. The searching operation is not overlapped. Searching operation results in large power consumption due to whole hardware activity. D-TCAM [20] efficiently utilizes FFs in slices to build two-level pipelines structure. It improves data throughout. However, it essentially not reduces memory areas. The large LUTRAM can result in routing congestion. LUT-FF pairs are easily appeared in some TCAM structures, however actually only LUTs are used and this results in waste of FF resources.

The SRAM-based TCAM design is based on block RAMs on FPGA. Many research works are proposed [22–29]. HP-TCAM [22] arranges SRAM blocks to store data presence and entry address information. E-TCAM [23] and Z-TCAM [24] optimize HP-TCAM structure. E-TCAM [23] reduces indicator bits and Z-TCAM [24] deletes data information that not exits in entries to compress memory space. UE-TCAM [25] achieves a systematic framework. The words are mapped to SRAM address and indexes are mapped to SRAM unit contents. However, width of words is limited by depth of SRAM block address and large entries can result in many SRAM blocks used. The design in [26] divides SRAM addresses into several parts with internal clocks controlling to improve memory utilization. RS-TCAM [27] aims match lines redundancy to reduce SRAM blocks usage in SRAM array width. However, the decreasing is limited. The scheme in [28] achieves fast update and search. It reduces update latency. EE-TCAM [29] splits multiple sub-tables with valid splitting and removes memory space with empty information to reduce memory occupied areas.

Our proposed design is based on UE-TCAM [25] and method in [26]. It divides words into two fields to store in a multi-region TCAM structure to compress memory space and achieve efficient memory utilization.

3   Proposed Method

3.1   Basic Idea

The proposed multi-region SRAM-based TCAM divides TCAM bits in every entry into two parts, where one part is mapped to address of SRAM memory, and the other part along with index is mapped to columns of SRAM memory together.

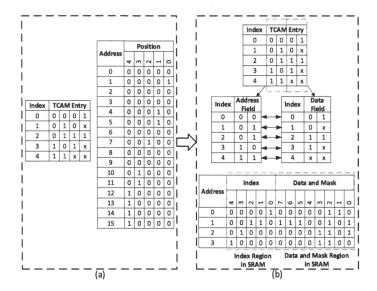

Fig. 1. (a) An example of mapping with traditional TCAM method. (b) An example of mapping with proposed multi-region TCAM method.

Framework Design. The proposed framework is shown in Fig. 1. Figure 1(a) shows an example of UE-TCAM [25] implementation for a 5 × 4 TCAM entry table. TCAM bits are mapped to address of SRAM block. The indexes are mapped to different columns of SRAM block. Storing a 5 × 4 entry table uses a

16 × 5 SRAM block. Figure 1(b) shows proposed multi-region TCAM implementation. Entry table is divided into two sub-tables. The left sub-table is named as address field and mapped to SRAM address. The right sub-table is named as data field. It converts to data and mask, then mapped to column of data and mask region in SRAM block. Index is mapped to column of index region. For 5 × 4 TCAM entry table, it consumes 4 × 13 SRAM block. As a whole, 4 × 13 SRAM block with proposed method is smaller than 16 × 5 SRAM block with traditional method in area. The proposed multi-region TCAM reduces memory consumption storing same entry table.

Field Conversion. The value of address field is directly converted to SRAM address. Index converts SRAM column. Figure 2(a) shows a field conversion example. For example, address field 0001 is mapped to SRAM address 1. Index 1 is mapped to middle column in index region of SRAM. Proposed method aims to entry of IP address, which has longest prefix feature. In middle process, data field x-bit is converted to data 1-bit and mask 0-bit. In data and mask region, data bits and number of mask 1-bit are stored. As shown in Fig. 2(a), when index is 1, data field 101x converts data 1011 and mask 1110 in middle process. In SRAM block, it converts data 1011 and mask number 011 that means there are three 1-bits in mask 1110 to store in the data and mask region.

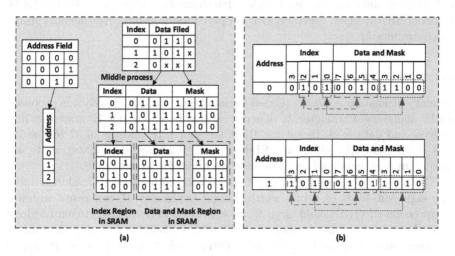

(a)   (b)

Fig. 2. (a) An example of conversion of address field, index and data field in SRAM block. (b) An example of connection between index and data field in SRAM block.

Connection Between Index and Data Field. When address field in many entries is same, address row of SRAM needs to store multiple indexes and data fields. The principle to store is that higher 1-bit in index region corresponds to higher data field in data and mask region. The connection between index and data field is built by order of position. As shown in Fig. 2(b), the left table shows higher index 1-bit corresponds to higher bits 0010 in data and mask region, and lower index 1-bit corresponds to lower bits 1100. Similarly, the right table put index and data field with the same way. It is noted that index corresponding to data and mask region is different between the two tables. 1-bit in index region corresponds to data and mask region, and 0-bit corresponds nothing.

Analysis of Consumed SRAM Memory. For a TCAM entry table with size of $T_N \times T_W$, we divide half entry bits of $\frac{T_W}{2}$ width into address field, and the rest into data field. Address field determines depth $2^{\frac{T_W}{2}}$ of SRAM block. The data field converts data and mask region. One data field with size of $\frac{T_W}{2}$ width is mapped to data region of $\frac{T_W}{2}$ width and mask region of $\log_2(\frac{T_W}{2}) + 1$. For one entry, data and mask region is $\frac{T_W}{2} + \log_2(\frac{T_W}{2}) + 1$ bit width. In proposed method, same address field results in an width increase in data and mask region. The maximum in entry numbers of same address field in entry table is defined as M, then width of data and mask region is $(\frac{T_W}{2} + \log_2(\frac{T_W}{2}) + 1) \times M$. The index region and data and mask region determine $T_N + (\frac{T_W}{2} + \log_2(\frac{T_W}{2}) + 1) \times M$ width of SRAM block together. Our proposed method improves memory usage by controlling M.

3.2   Data Pre-processing

Memory utilization is closely related to parameter M. Our approach is proposed for IP addresses. Parameter M depends on that how to divide IP addresses into address and data field. In entries, there are source IP address of 32 bits width and destination IP address of 32 bits width. IP addresses of 32-bit width are divided into address field and the rests are divided into data field.

Due to dotted decimal feature of IP address, 64-bit width IP address splits into eight sub-fields of 8 bits width. Larger parameter M can result in lower compression effect. To avoid large M, we select exact IP sub-fields to map address field. N_E is defined as number of exact address field entries. N_E determines compression scale. $TCAM_s$ is defined as entries including exact source IP address and $TCAM_d$ is defined as entries including exact destination IP address. Our proposed method is filtering out $TCAM_s$ of N_{Es} entries and $TCAM_d$ of N_{Ed} entries respectively. In $TCAM_s$, source IP address is split by four sub-fields of 8 bits width. We need to count appearance frequency of every value in every sub-field and get maximum frequency M_s. By the same way as $TCAM_s$, we get maximum frequency M_d in $TCAM_d$. When $\frac{M_s}{N_{Es}}$ is smaller than $\frac{M_d}{N_{Ed}}$, source IP address is set as address field and destination IP address as data field, and parameter M is M_s. Otherwise, result is opposite.

Figure 3 shows a simple example of data pre-processing. N_{Es} is 3 and N_{Ed} is 3. M_s is 2 in $TCAM_s$ and M_d is 3 in $TCAM_d$. $\frac{M_s}{N_{Es}}$ is smaller than $\frac{M_d}{N_{Ed}}$, then parameter M is M_s and address field is source IP and data field is destination IP.

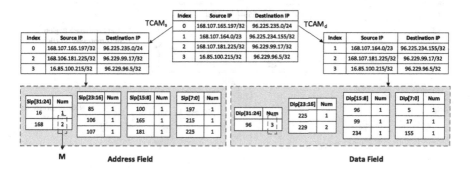

Fig. 3. An example of parameter $M = 2$, address field is source IP and data field is destination IP.

In proposed method, smaller parameter M and larger N_E can achieve more efficient memory utilization. Data pre-processing for rule sets aims to get the most appropriate parameter M to achieve maximum compression effect.

3.3 Multi-region SRAM Array

An entry table with size of $T_N \times T_W$ is divided into two portions including compression portion and non-compression portion. The size of configured SRAM block unit is defined as $S_D \times S_W$. Compression portion corresponds to index region with $R_I \times C_I$ SRAM blocks and data and mask region with $R_D \times C_D$ SRAM blocks for N_E exact address fields. The non-compression portion corresponds to index region with $R_N \times C_N$ SRAM blocks for $T_N - N_E$ non-exact address fields.

The multi-region SRAM array is shown in Fig. 4. For depth S_D of SRAM block in all portions, a SRAM block is divided into P SRAM sub-blocks of 8 bits width. A sub-block is an address loop to describe width of entry table. P equals $S_D/2^8$. In index region of compression portion, width S_W corresponds to indexes. In data and mask region of compression portion, width S_W corresponds to $S_W/12$ data fields. The basic unit of one data field includes data of 8 bits width and mask of 4 bits width. In non-compression portion, indexes are stored similar with index region in compression portion. For fields, there are no address and data fields. Whole entry fields are mapped to SRAM address. The difference is that non-compression portion needs to express width T_W using SRAM blocks, however compression portion only needs to express $T_W/2$ width and the other $T_W/2$ width is converted to data field to store with index together.

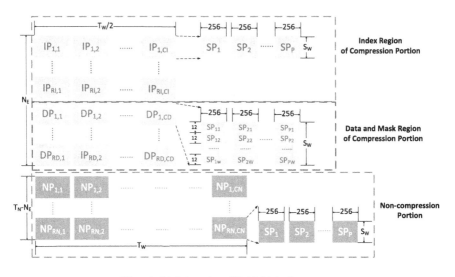

Fig. 4. Multi-region SRAM block array.

3.4   Multi-region Mapping

The principle of writing a new word is that higher 1-bit in index lines corresponds to higher data of 12 bits width in data lines. Figure 5 only shows way of inserting a new word with 4 bits data instead of actual 12 bits. As the bottom table shown in Fig. 5, when inserting a new word of index 1, the 1st column in index region is written 1-bit. The position of index 1 is between index 3 and index 0. In data and mask region, columns ranging from 3 to 0 remain original and describe data of index 0. However, columns ranging from 7 to 4 in top table move to columns ranging from 11 to 8 and describe data of index 3. New data of index 1 is inserted in columns ranging from 7 to 4. It achieves that higher index corresponds to higher data and mask.

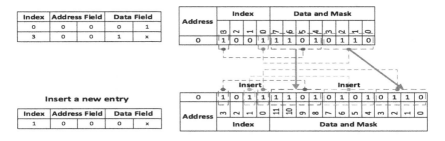

Fig. 5. An example of writing a new word in SRAM.

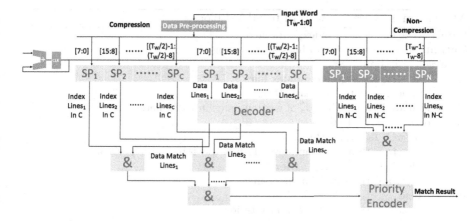

Fig. 6. Flow path of mapping and matching.

When storing a word in compression portion, address field of $\frac{T_W}{2}$ width transforms into multiple SRAM addresses of 8 bits width. In a SRAM block, we roll around 8 bits width address by controlling internal clock counter. Figure 6 shows flow path of mapping and matching. Index converts to index lines. Index positions of SRAM are valid, and the other positions remain original value. The data field of 8 bits width converts 8 bits data and 4 bits mask. If data field is longer than 8 bits, it is divided into many sub data fields of 8 bits width.

Algorithm 1 shows how to write a new word in compression region. When SRAM address rolls down value of address field, SRAM write enable turns on. New written 12 bits data lines need to be inserted. We calculate location loc_{index} of written index in 1-bits of index lines to insert correctly.

3.5   Searching

When inputting a word to search, index lines and data lines in compression portion and index lines in non-compression portion can be gotten from SRAM blocks according to address field of input word. As shown in Fig. 6, for data and mask, data lines are decoded by data match lines of data field in parallel by decoder. We merge data match lines with index lines in index region of compression portion to get match lines in compression portion. We execute "bit-and" operation on match lines in compression portion and index lines in non-compression portion. Results in compression and non-compression portion are sent to priority encoder to get the final match result.

One SRAM block generates P lines with internal clock. Address field of input word in one SRAM block is divided into P sub address fields named $raddr_i$. The data field of input word in one SRAM block is divided into P sub data fields named $rdata_i$.

In compression portion, for one $raddr_i$, we get index lines and data lines. We compare the data lines including data and mask with input data field $rdata_i$ and

Algorithm 1. write a new word to SRAM blocks

Input: write enable w_{en}, index, data field
Output: index lines and data lines after writing
 1: **if** $w_{en} = 1$ **then**
 2:     1-bit $\rightarrow$ index position of index lines
 3:     data field $\rightarrow$ data and mask DM_w
 4:     calculate location loc_{index} of written index in index lines
 5:     **for** $m = M - 1$ to 0 **do**
 6:         **if** $(m > loc_{index})$ **then**
 7:             data with m position moves 12 bits width to higher position
 8:         **else if** $(m < loc_{index})$ **then**
 9:             data with m position no change
10:         **else**
11:             new $DM_w \rightarrow$ data with m position
12:         **end if**
13:     **end for**
14: **end if**

---

get data match lines where describe data field match result. Index lines and data match lines are merged to get match lines. Due to rolling of i, we get P match lines in turn and execute "bit-and" operation to get match lines for one SRAM block. For multiple SRAM blocks, we can get multiple match lines in parallel and execute "bit-and" operation to get final match lines ml_c in compression portion.

In non-compression portion, there is only index region. Input word only converts address fields. For one $raddr_i$, one SRAM block outputs P index lines and "bit-and" operation merges P index lines. The index lines of multiple SRAM blocks are executed "bit-and" again to get final match lines ml_{nc} in non-compression portion.

Priority encoder selects out final match result between final match lines in compression and non-compression portion.

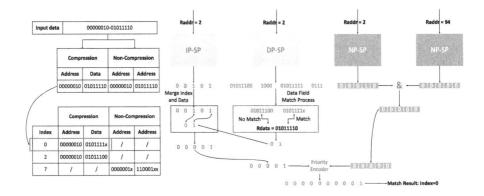

Fig. 7. An example of searching a word.

Figure 7 shows an example of searching an input word. In Fig. 7, input data field $rdata_i$ is 01011110. By reading DP-SP block, SRAM outputs two data lines of 12 bits width. Data lines convert data of 8 bits width that every bit has three states. The one 01011100 not match with $rdata_i$ 01011110. The another 0101111x matches with $rdata_i$. Data match lines are 01, which means that the 1st data lines not match and the 0st data lines match. The data match lines 01 execute "bit-and" operation with position of 1-bit in index lines 00101 to get match line 00001. For NP-SP, input word is divided into two address fields to search two NP-SPs. Index lines merge to 00000 by "bit-and". Match lines 00001 in compression portion and 00000 in non-compression portion merge and priority encoder outputs match result that index is 0.

4   Implementation and Results

The proposed design is implemented on a Xilinx FPGA device (XCVU190). This FPGA device supports a large number of 3780 Block RAMs. Our proposed design is implemented and verified based on Xilinx Vivado 2018.3 design tool and Modelsim simulation tool. Classbench tool [30] is used to generate Access Control List (ACL) and Firewall (FW) rule sets with different scales.

The proposed method aims to IP address with longest prefix. Experiments test source and destination IP address of 64 bits width in ACL and FW rule sets with different scales ranging from 512 to 10K. For rule sets of IP address, the scale of rule set is equivalent to size of TCAM entry. The width of TCAM entry is 64 bits and depth is ranging from 512 to 10K.

Figure 8 and Fig. 9 shows Block RAM usage numbers in five types of ACL and FW rule sets respectively. Figure 10 and Fig. 11 shows block RAM consumption comparison based on different methods in ACL and FW rule sets of different scales. The proposed method consumes smaller block RAMs. Table 1 shows Block RAM resource consumption and performance comparison based on different method. In table 1, results in proposed case I-III are for ACL rule sets in different scales. The result shows memory consumption with our proposed design decreases obviously compared to other previous methods. Figure 12 and Fig. 13 compares Block RAM consumption per bit in different scales of ACL and FW rule sets. With the scale of rule sets increasing, memory consumption per bit decreases. Results indicate that the proposed method has better memory utilization in larger scales of rule sets.

5   Performance Evaluation

Memory resource usage is an important metric in TCAM emulation designs due to expensive cost. Table 1 shows memory resource usage comparison in different methods. BRAM in Table 1 means Block RAM usage numbers of 18Kb BR_{18Kb} and 36Kb BR_{36Kb} together on FPGA. Memory Usage describes total area of Block RAM occupied. Memory Usage is defined as formula (1) shown below:

$$Memory\ Usage = BR_{18Kb} \times 18 + BR_{36Kb} \times 36 \qquad (1)$$

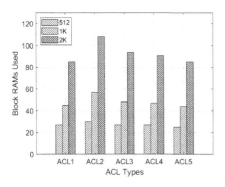

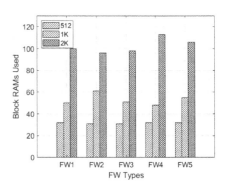

Fig. 8. Block RAMs usage numbers in ACL rule sets of different types.

Fig. 9. Block RAMs usage numbers in FW rule sets of different types.

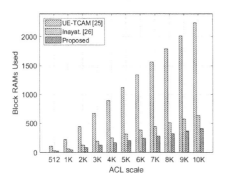

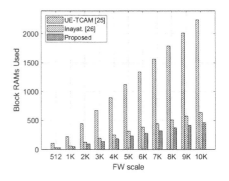

Fig. 10. Block RAMs usage numbers in ACL rule sets of different scales.

Fig. 11. Block RAMs usage numbers in FW rule sets of different scales.

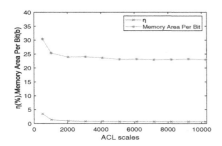

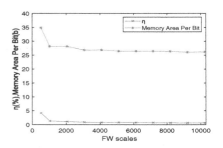

Fig. 12. Memory area per bit and η in ACL rule sets of different scales.

Fig. 13. Memory area per bit and η in FW rule sets of different scales.

Table 1. Performance comparison of the proposed method with previous methods.

Architecture	TCAM size($\mathbf{T_N} \times \mathbf{T_W}$)	BRAM (18 Kb, 36 Kb)	Memory Usage (Kb)	Memory Area Per Bit(b)
HP-TCAM- [22]	512 × 36	16,48	2016	112
E-TCAM- [23]	512 × 36	16,32	1440	80
Z-TCAM- [24]	512 × 36	16,32	1440	80
UE-TCAM- [25]	512 × 36	0,32	1152	64
Inayat- [26]	512 × 32	0,16	576	36
EE-TCAM- [29]	512 × 36	0,32	1152	64
Azhar- [28]	512 × 36	64,0	1152	64
Proposed CASE-I	512 × 64	0,27	972	30.375
Proposed CASE-II	1024 × 64	0,45	1620	25.3125
Proposed CASE-III	2048 × 64	0,85	3060	23.90625

In proposed method, required numbers of Block RAMs are defined as BR_e for N_E TCAM entries and BR_{n-e} for $T_N - N_E$ TCAM entries. Total numbers of Block RAMs are defined as BR_{pro} thus

$$BR_e = \frac{N_E + 12 * M}{S_W} \times \frac{\frac{T_W}{2}}{\frac{S_D}{2^8} \times 8} \tag{2}$$

$$BR_{n-e} = \frac{T_N - N_E}{S_W} \times \frac{T_W}{\frac{S_D}{2^8} \times 8} \tag{3}$$

$$BR_{pro} = BR_e + BR_{n-e} \tag{4}$$

Memory area per bit is defined as a performance metric to describe memory consumption for a TCAM bit in entry. It is shown in formula (5) below:

$$Memory\ area\ per\ bit = \frac{Memory\ Usage \times 1024}{T_N \times T_W} \tag{5}$$

Smaller memory area per bit consumes less memory and has better memory utilization. Table 1 shows our proposed method achieves 33.5938% and 62.6465% reduction of Block RAMs in memory area per bit with ACL-2K rule sets compared to Inayat. [26] and UE-TCAM [25] respectively. As it shown, our proposed method has smaller memory area per bit compared to other methods and achieve memory compression.

The proposed method has two related parameters M and N_E in memory compression performance. Parameter M determines consumed Block RAMs width in compression portion. The proposed method occupies less Block RAMs with smaller M. This paper analyzes rule set features by data pre-processing to get smaller M. Parameter N_E determines the entry number in compression portion. Parameter N_E depends on rule sets features. The proposed method tends to hand out more entries in compression portion to achieve better memory utilization. Larger N_E helps to increase compression degree of memory space. For parameters M and N_E, we use $\frac{M}{N_E}$ to describe instead of two parameters. Smaller M and larger N_E can result in smaller $\frac{M}{N_E}$. η is defined as formula (6) below:

$$\eta = \frac{M}{N_E} \tag{6}$$

Smaller η achieves better memory utilization. Figure 12 and Fig. 13 shows that tendency of η and memory area per bit with scale increasing. With scales of rule sets increasing, η and memory area per bit become smaller and more stable. Results show that our proposed method has a more significant effect in memory utilization with larger scale of rule sets. Obviously, our proposed method achieves better memory utilization and has better memory compression performance in larger rule sets due to smaller η.

The proposed design is used in hardware switch of SDN data plane to accommodate more security rules. The results of occupied memory area per bit show that our proposed design achieves 33.5938% and 62.6465% increment in numbers of storing security rules given the same size of memory space compared to Inayat. [26] and UE-TCAM [25] respectively. Storing more security rules means that classification rules of network packets are more precise and processing complex network packets is more flexible. The hardware safety protection platform with proposed design becomes safer and more reliable in achieving network packets access control and security filter.

6   Conclusion

SRAM-based TCAM high-speed searching engine on FPGA hardware platform plays an important role in network communication and security protection. Existing SRAM-based TCAM designs suffer from large memory area. We presents a multi-region SRAM-based TCAM structure for IP address. It divides into multiple regions including index region and data and mask region and changes mapping way in part of field to avoid sustained increasing depth of SRAM block array. We utilize IP address feature of longest prefix to further reduce consumed memory cell. The experiment results shows our proposed design reduces 33.5938% and 62.6465% memory consumption in rule sets of 2K compared to Inayat. [26] and UE-TCAM [25] respectively. Obviously, the proposed method has a significant improvement in memory utilization. For rule sets of larger scales, our proposed method has better memory utilization compared to smaller rule sets.

Our proposed design can accommodate more security rules due to memory utilization improvement. The hardware security protection platform based on proposed design achieves safer and more reliable protection mechanism in access control and security filter for diverse network packets.

Acknowledgement. This work is supported by Project of Chinese Academy of Sciences (Grant No. KGFZD-145-21-03).

References

1. Huang, J.Y., Wang, P.C.: TCAM-Based IP Address Lookup Using Longest Suffix Split. IEEE/ACM Trans. Networking **PP**(2), 1–14 (2018)
2. Omer, M., Zahid, U., Hassan, M., et al.: Fast Pattern Recognition through an LBP driven CAM on FPGA. IEEE Access, 1 (2018)
3. Guerra-Hernandez, E.I., Espinal, A., Batres-Mendoza, P., et al.: A FPGA-based neuromorphic locomotion system for multi-legged robots. IEEE Access, pp. 8301–8312 (2017)
4. Karam, R., Puri, R., Ghosh, S., et al.: Emerging trends in design and applications of memory-based computing and content-addressable memories. Proc. IEEE **103**(8), 1311–1330 (2015)
5. Hu, F., Hao, Q., Bao, K.: A survey on software-defined network and OpenFlow: from concept to implementation. Commun. Surv. Tutorials IEEE **16**(4), 2181–2206 (2014)
6. Kreutz, D., Ramos, F., Verissimo, P.E., et al.: Software-defined networking: a comprehensive survey. Proceedings of the IEEE 103(1) (2014)
7. Mckeown, N., Anderson, T., Balakrishnan, H., et al.: OpenFlow: Enabling innovation in campus networks. ACM SIGCOMM Comput. Commun. Rev. **38**(2), 69–74 (2008)
8. Sindhura, B., Shobha, K.R.: Implementation and testing of openflow switch using FPGA. In: International Conference on Computing. IEEE Computer Society (2017)
9. Norige, E., Liu, A.X., Torng, E.: A ternary unification framework for optimizing TCAM-based packet classification systems. IEEE/ACM Trans. Networking, 1–14 (2018)
10. Chen, T.S., Lee, D.Y., Liu, T.T., et al.: Dynamic Reconfigurable Ternary Content Addressable Memory for OpenFlow-Compliant Low-Power Packet Processing[J]. Circuits and Systems I: Regular Papers, IEEE Transactions on **63**(10), 1661–1672 (2016)
11. Ghosh, S., Baliyan, M.: A hash based architecture of longest prefix matching for fast IP processing. In: TENCON 2016–2016 IEEE Region 10 Conference. IEEE (2016)
12. Ullah, Z., Jaiswal, M.K., Chan, Y.C., et al.: FPGA Implementation of SRAM-based ternary content addressable memory. In: Parallel & Distributed Processing Symposium Workshops & Phd Forum. IEEE (2012)
13. Jiang, W.: Scalable ternary content addressable memory implementation using FPGAs. In: 2013 ACM/IEEE Symposium on Architectures for Networking and Communications Systems (ANCS). ACM (2013)
14. Irfan, M., Ullah, Z.: G-AETCAM: gate-based area efficient ternary content-addressable memory on FPGA. IEEE Access PP(99), 1 (2017)
15. Ullah, Z.: LH-CAM: logic-based higher performance binary CAM architecture on FPGA. IEEE Embedded Syst. Lett., 1 (2017)
16. Irfan, M., Ullah, Z., Chowdhury, M.H., et al.: RPE-TCAM: reconfigurable power-efficient ternary content-addressable memory on FPGAs. IEEE Trans. Very Large Scale Integr. (VLSI) Syst. PP(99), 1–5 (2020)
17. Fouzder, T., Hafeez, A., Rehman, N.U., et al.: Power efficient FPGA-based TCAM architecture by using segmented matchline strategy. In: 2019 International Conference on Advances in the Emerging Computing Technologies (AECT) (2020)

18. Zahir, A., Khattak, S.K., Ullah, A., et al.: FracTCAM: Fracturable LUTRAM-Based TCAM Emulation on Xilinx FPGAs. IEEE Trans. Very Large Scale Integr. (VLSI) Syst. (2020)
19. Ullah, I., Ullah, Z., Afzaal, U., et al.: DURE: An energy- and resource-efficient TCAM architecture for FPGAs with dynamic updates. IEEE Trans. Very Large Scale Integr. (VLSI) Syst. PP(99), 1–10 (2019)
20. Irfan, M., Ullah, Z., Cheung, R.: D-TCAM: a high-performance distributed RAM based TCAM architecture on FPGAs. IEEE Access (2019)
21. Zhuo, Q., Margala, M.: Low power RAM-based hierarchical CAM on FPGA. In: International Conference on Reconfigurable Computing & Fpgas. IEEE (2015)
22. Ullah, Z., Ilgon, K., Baeg, S.: Hybrid partitioned SRAM-based ternary content addressable memory. IEEE Trans. Circuits Syst. I: Regular Papers 59(12), 2969–2979 (2012)
23. Ullah, Z., Jaiswal, M.K., Cheung, R.C.: E-TCAM: an efficient SRAM-based architecture for TCAM. Birkhauser Boston Inc. (2014)
24. Ullah, Z., Jaiswal, M.K., Cheung, R.C.C.: Z-TCAM: an SRAM-based architecture for TCAM. IEEE Trans. Very Large Scale Integr. Syst. 23(2), 402–406 (2015)
25. Ullah, Z., Jaiswal, M.K., Cheung, R., et al.: UE-TCAM: an ultra efficient SRAM-based TCAM. Tencon IEEE Region 10 Conference. IEEE (2015)
26. Ullah, I., Ullaha, Z., Lee, J.A.: Efficient TCAM design based on multipumping-enabled multiported SRAM on FPGA. IEEE Access, 1 (2018)
27. Zhang, J., Yang, R., Cao, X., et al.: A resource-saving TCAM structure based on SRAM. In: 2019 IEEE 5th International Conference on Computer and Communications (ICCC). IEEE (2019)
28. Qazi, A., Ullah, Z, Hafeez, A.: Fast mapping and updating algorithms for a binary CAM on FPGA (2021)
29. Ullah, Inayat, Zahid, et al. EE-TCAM: an energy-efficient SRAM-based TCAM on FPGA. Electronics (2018)
30. Turner, D.: ClassBench: a packet classification benchmark. IEEE/ACM Trans. Networking 15(3), 499–511 (2007)

Security in Financial Industry

.

A Solution for the Offline Double-Spending Issue of Digital Currencies

Zhexuan Hong and Jiageng Chen[✉]

Central China Normal University, No. 152, Luoyu Road, Hongshan District, Wuhan,
Hubei, China
zh119@uowmail.edu.au, Jiageng.chen@ccnu.edu.cn

Abstract. Digital currencies are legally valid legal tender issued by the country's central bank, equivalent to the paper currencies currently on the market, with value characteristics and legal solvency, manufactured and managed by the central bank. User privacy and the security against the double spending issues are among the most important factors of the electronic currency. Features such as the anonymity, one time and the unforgeability are of great importance to the digital currency in order to replace the existing paper money in the market. In this paper, we effectively achieve the one-time feature of the digital currencies based on the one-time signature power delegation technique, so as to successfully avoid the "double spending" issue when users are offline.

Keywords: Digital currencies · Group signature · Double spend · One time

1 Introduction

In this study, we will use the transaction process of digital RMB proposed by the People's Bank of China as an example to analyze the specific processes and problems of digital currency consumption, and then further propose several effective solutions to deal with the related security issues.

1.1 Background

Since People's Bank of China formally started the development of Digital Currency Electronic Payment (DCEP) in 2017, the digital currency has gradually entered people's daily life with the primary purpose of replacing the existing currency in circulation and improving the international competitiveness of Chinese RMB [14,15]. With the main purpose of protecting the public property, research institutions have designed a DCEP scheme that basically meets the needs of the public and is safe and secure. However, there are still some security risks without being mentioned in detail. In the patent for the offline payment using digital currency chip card applied by the Institute of Printing Science and Technology of the People's Bank of China in 2016 [15], the problem of double-spend may

C. Su et al. (Eds.): SciSec 2022, LNCS 13580, pp. 455–471, 2022.
https://doi.org/10.1007/978-3-031-17551-0_30

exist when both sides of the transaction are offline, which is a significant factor endangering the security of public property.

People's Bank of China released a white paper on the progress of research and development of China's digital RMB on July 16, 2021, and the description of security in the digital RMB design features in Chap. 3 also mentions the use of technologies such as digital certificate systems, digital signatures, and secure encryption to achieve non-repeatable spending. Nevertheless, there is no detailed explanation of the double-spending problem in specific double-offline payment scenarios [16].

1.2   Related Work

Double-spending problem of the electronic money is one of the important issues studied previously. Since the introduction of Bitcoin, society has been devoting more and more attention to digital currency. Central Bank Digital Currency (CBDC), which is a strong guarantee of national credit authority, has also been proposed, such as RScoin in the UK and Ubin in Singapore [17]. Bitcoin, a decentralized peer-to-peer electronic cash system, relies on timestamps and unspent transaction outputs (UTXO) to solve the double-spending problem. And many existing third-party software, such as China's Alipay and WeChat, prevent double spending by modifying balances in real time. Of course, all of the above solutions are based on the condition that both parties to the transaction are online. When offline electronic cash was first proposed, the double-spending problem could only be detected but not effectively blocked [2]. In this paper, the DCEP model based on one-time signature power delegation technology and one-time procedures can stop double-spending when both parties of the transaction are not online, but it requires the support of a security chip from the user's mobile device.

In this research, the one-time signature delegation technique used to solve the double-spending problem in the case of double offline transactions is similar to the previous t-times credential, where the primary function of the t-times credential is to prevent users from presenting the same credential more than t times. For some unscrupulous users, i.e., those who show the same credential more than the threshold value t, the system administrator can perform revocation of the anonymous credential [13]. For example, the administrator can use the accumulator, which enables revocation for individual users and guarantees the anonymity of the revoked and legitimate users [9]. Although this approach has been used in many scenarios, it is still insufficient to stop the above problem, since we need immediate revocation of displayed credentials. In summary, to achieve the feature of "one-time", the user needs the support of other hardware holding key secret values when he needs to spend e-cash, and the user cannot make any independent consumption [4,8], i.e., some of the parameters computation process during the transaction requires the participation of mobile security hardware, and such security hardware should have the ability to refuse to participate in the same e-cash transaction parameters for a second computation.

Group signature has been used in many areas such as electronic transactions, electronic voting, etc. [6] because of its anonymity and traceability. Group signatures and their derivative versions of anonymous proxy signatures are essentially a delegation of signature power. However, in the case of the above DCEP patent where both parties to the transaction are offline, the basic group signature is not sufficient to solve the problem of double spending in that case because it does not have a one-time delegation of signature right. Therefore, a scheme with a one-time delegation of signature right can be used to effectively solve the double-spending problem in DCEP [1,3].

1.3 Organization

This paper is organized as follows: Sect. 2 introduces the preparatory knowledge of this paper, and Sect. 3 gives the specific construction of the DCEP scheme and its problems. In Sect. 4, we provide an effective solution to the possible double-spending problem in the case of dual offline users. In Sect. 5, we give the security proof and efficiency analysis of the scheme in this paper followed by the summary of the paper.

2 Basic Knowledge

The proposed method is mainly based on group signatures and anonymous credentials, and the related concepts and basics are introduced below.

2.1 Bilinear Groups

The bilinear group in this paper consists of three cyclic groups, $\mathbb{G}_1$, $\mathbb{G}_2$, $\mathbb{G}_T$, and their ranks are all prime p. The size of p is related to the security level. For example, you can choose $p = 256$. The generators of the groups $\mathbb{G}_1$, $\mathbb{G}_2$ are g and $\widetilde{g}$, respectively, denoted as $\mathbb{G}_1 = \langle g \rangle$, $\mathbb{G}_2 = \langle \widetilde{g} \rangle$. There exists a bilinear pairing $e : \mathbb{G}_1 \times \mathbb{G}_2 \to \mathbb{G}_T$, and has the following properties:

(1) Bilinear: $\forall g \in \mathbb{G}_1$, $\widetilde{g} \in \mathbb{G}_2$, and α, $\beta \in \mathbb{Z}_p$, $e(g^\alpha, \widetilde{g}^\beta) = e(g, \widetilde{g})^{\alpha\beta}$.

(2) Non-degeneracy: $\forall$ $g \neq 1_{\mathbb{G}_1}$ and $\widetilde{g} \neq 1_{\mathbb{G}_2}$, then $e(g, \widetilde{g}) \neq 1_{\mathbb{G}_T}$.

(3) Pairing e can be computed efficiently.

2.2 Okamoto-Schnorr Signature

The Okamoto-Schnorr signature scheme is based on the Okamoto-Schnorr knowledge proof scheme, which is converted into a valid signature scheme by applying the Fiat-Shamir transformation [10]. The initialization defines the same parameters p, H as in the original Schnorr scheme [7]. The specific process is shown below.

1. $KeyGen(1^\chi) \rightarrow (sk,\ pk)$: we choose the generating element $g_1,\ g_2, ...,\ g_n \in \mathbb{G}_1$. Set the signature key to $x_1,\ x_2, ...,\ x_n \in \mathbb{Z}_p^n$, and the public key is $pk = (g_1,\ g_2,\ ...,\ g_n,\ x,\ p), x = g_1^{x_1} \cdot g_2^{x_2} \cdot ... \cdot g_n^{x_n}$.
2. $Sign(sk,\ m) \rightarrow (c,\ v_1,\ v_2, ...,\ v_n)$: pick n random numbers $r_1,\ r_2,\ ...,\ r_n \in \mathbb{Z}_p$, compute $T = g_1^{r_1} \cdot g_2^{r_2} \cdot ... \cdot g_n^{r_n}$, $c = H(T \parallel m)$, $v_i = r_i - c \cdot x_i (i = 1,\ 2, ...,\ n)$.
3. $Verify(m,\ pk,\ (c,\ v_1,\ v_2)$: check if the Eq. 1 holds to determine if the signature is valid.

$$H(m \parallel g_1^{v_1} \cdot g_2^{v_2} \cdot ... \cdot g_n^{v_n} \cdot x^c) \overset{?}{=} c \tag{1}$$

If the above equation holds, output 1, otherwise output 0.

4. $SigIssue(U(pk,\ m),\ S(x_1,\ x_2, ...,\ x_n))$:
   (a) S selects n random numbers $r_1,\ r_2, ...,\ r_n$, send $R \leftarrow g_1^{r_1} g_2^{r_2} ... g_n^{r_n}$ to the user.
   (b) The user randomly selects $a_1,\ a_2, ...,\ a_n,\ b \in \mathbb{Z}_p$, compute $c' \leftarrow H(R \cdot g_1^{a_1} g_2^{a_2} ... g_n^{a_n} \cdot x^b)$, send $c \leftarrow c' - b \bmod p$ to S.
   (c) The signer sends $v_i = r_i - c \cdot x_i \bmod p\ (i = 1,\ 2, ...,\ n)$ to the user.
   (d) If $R = g_1^{v_1} g_2^{v_2} ... g_n^{v_n} \cdot x^c$, the user computes $v_i' = v_i + a_i \bmod p\ (i = 1,\ 2, ...,\ n)$, calculating the signature of the original message $\sigma = (c',\ v_1',\ v_2', ...,\ v_n')$, otherwise the calculation is terminated.

2.3   Pok of the Pedersen Commitment

The Pedersen commitment is a statistically hidden, computationally bound additive homomorphic commitment scheme [11], and here we give a proof of knowledge about the value of the Pedersen commitment. The specific protocol is shown below:

Set-up phase: the prover has the commitment value $C = \prod_{i=1}^{n} g_i^{x_i}$.

Execution Phase:

1. The prover chooses the random value r_i used to hide the commitment value x_i and sends $C' \leftarrow \prod_{i=1}^{n} g_i^r$ to the verifier.
2. The verifier sends the random value $c \in \mathbb{Z}_p$ to the prover.
3. The prover computes and sends $z_i \leftarrow r_i + c \cdot x_i \bmod p$.
4. If the Eq. 2 holds, the verifier accepts the fact that the prover knows the relevant commitment value.

$$C' \cdot C^c = \prod_{i=1}^{n} g_i^{z_i} \tag{2}$$

2.4   Addable Secret Sharing

In this study, the secret sharing technique is used to split the target secret value into multiple subparts (the sum of the subparts is equal to the target secret value), and then the subparts are distributed to multiple protocol participants

[12]. At the end of the protocol, the user constructs the target secret value by obtaining the relevant sub-parts from the participants that have the sub-parts of the secret value. Here we assume that the number of secret values is 2. Moreover, the original scheme uses MAC to verify that the subparts of the secret values sent by the actual participants are correct. We assume that the two secret values are a, b, the MAC key is L, the MAC tag is La, Lb, the messages are m, m' and the protocol participants are P, P'.

- Input: $a = a_1 + a_2 \bmod p$, $b = b_1 + b_2 \bmod p$, $L = L_1 + L_2 \bmod p$, $L \times a_1 = m^{a_1} + m'^{a_2} \bmod p$, $L \times b_1 = m^{b_1} + m'^{b_2} \bmod p$.
- Output: participant 1 and participant 2 reconstruct the secret value $s = c \times a + c' \times b \bmod p$ if MAC passes the test(c, c' are the system parameters known to participants). The verification process is specified as follows:

1. The participants P_1, P_2 publish the secret sub-part $S_1 = c \times a_1 + c' \times b_1$ and $S_2 = c \times a_2 + c' \times b_2$ respectively, which they own. Here the coefficients c and c' are known for P_1, P_2.

2. The participants P_1, P_2 compute the reconstructed secret value $S = S_1 + S_2 \bmod p$.

3. The participants P_1, P_2 compute the verification values $V_1 = L_1 \times S - (c \times m^a + c' \times m^b)$, $V_2 = L_2 \times S - (c \times m'^a + c' \times m'^b)$ respectively.

4. The participants P_1, P_2 compute $V_1 + V_2 \overset{?}{=} 0$, and if the above equation holds, the participant accepts S as the correct reconstructed secret value.

Since the security chip inside the mobile phone will be used as the secret value holder in this study, the verification part of the original scheme [12] can be omitted, which greatly improves the efficiency of the implementation.

3 The Digital Currency System and Related Issues

In this section, we will first briefly introduce the general procedure of digital currency. Here we use DCEP as a special case for analysis to help readers understand the general mechanism of digital currency consumption. Then the related security problems are summarized by various models.

3.1 The Overall Framework and Transaction Process of DCEP

The general framework of DCEP is shown in Fig. 1, the whole process can be divided into issuance, DCEP chip card manufacturing, chip card application and DCEP redemption. The above four processes correspond to steps 1, 2, 3 and 4 in the Fig. 1.

3.2   Trading and Offline Double-Spend Model

DCEP transactions can be divided into online payment transactions, face-to-face online (or single offline) transactions and face-to-face double offline transactions. This research focuses on the "double spend" problem in the face-to-face double offline transactions. Dual offline payment is a significant advantage of DCEP over WeChat Pay and Alipay Pay. Specifically, both parties can transact offline through a wireless connection, such as NFC and Bluetooth, which enables offline transactions to be carried out in the same way as paper money. The general flow is shown in Fig. 2.

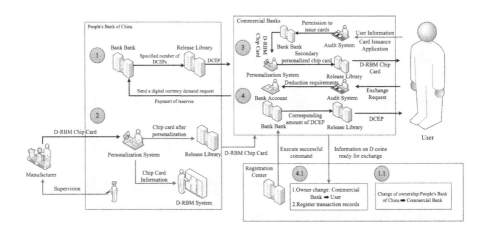

Fig. 1. DCEP master framework.

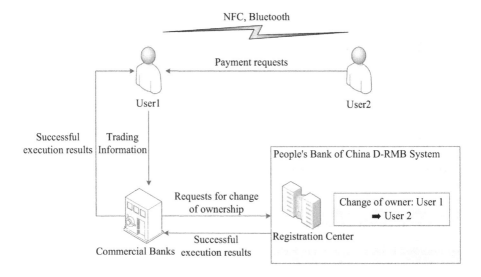

Fig. 2. Dual offline payment process.

DCEP's dual offline payment method is not a typical electronic payment method, but it can lead to double spending problems. The main reason is that the payer's wallet does not delete the DCEP that have been spent once until it receives the notification of a successful change of DCEP ownership, giving some malicious users the opportunity to spend the same DCEP for second time illegally. The approximate steps of the double spend model in the above double offline case is shown in Fig. 3.

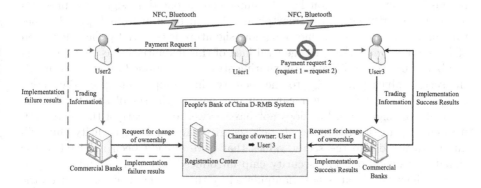

Fig. 3. Double spend process

The existing digital RMB patents only mentioned the use of post-facto recourse to reduce this situation [15], which is clearly not enough. This study will then address this issue using a one-time signature right delegation technique.

4   Digital RMB One-Time Spending Scheme

In this section we will specify the digital currency one-time spending scheme, respectively the specific implementation of the one-time signature rights delegation and the one-time anonymous credential presentation. For the purposes of this research, a one-time signature authorization is mean that the commercial bank embeds a one-time signature program into the user's digital wallet and that the signing program can only be used only once for the same DCEP. However, this does not mean that the DCEP minting rights are transferred, as only a DCEP certified by the central bank can be used, and the embedding of the signature by the commercial bank is only one part of the process of bringing the currency to market and making it available for use. For convenience, we will call such programs S_{otp}. Running S_{otp} requires the mobile device of the DCEP owner to interact with its internal security hardware, but does not require the involvement of a commercial bank. And the security hardware is security chip in our phone. Such a security chip can act as security hardware that stores critical information and can delete such data at a given moment. Let us assume that the message entered by the user, i.e. the D-coin, is represented as d_i (i = 1, 5, 10,

20, 50, 100). And suppose that the one-time signed execution of some program F is $[F]_{S_{otp}}$. For example, the one-time implementation of the Okamoto-Schnorr signature can be written in the form of the Eq. 3:

$$[OS.\ sign(sk,\ m)]_{S_{otp}} = \langle g_1,\ g_2, ...,\ g_n,\ x,\ p,\ \{[r_i - c \times x_i\ mod\ p]\}_{i=1}^{n}\rangle \quad (3)$$

4.1   Instantiation of One-Time Signature Delegation

In this section we focus on how to implement a one-time signature program using the security chip in a smartphone. As can be seen from Eq. 3, the one-time procedure for the Okamoto-Schnorr signature is essentially the calculation of $\{r_i - c \times x_i\ mod\ p\}$, so the general idea of this instantiation is that commercial banks use the additive secret sharing strategy mentioned above to transmit the secret values $\{r_i,\ x_i\}_{i=1}^{n}$ to the security chip component inside the phone and to the user, i.e. the user can only use part of the set of secret values to calculate the signature, but does not have access to the part of the secret values temporarily stored in the phone's security chip, and the security chip will automatically delete the secret values that have already been involved in the signature calculation. The security chip introduced here can be understood as security hardware that is not manipulated by the user, i.e. it does not keep the secret values that have been used for the signature operation, allowing a malicious user to take advantage of it, thus ensuring a good performance. In the following, we assume for convenience that the total number of secret values is 2, i.e. that there are secret values $\{r_1,\ x_1\}$, $\{r_2,\ x_2\}$. They are held by the user and the internal security chip, respectively. When the user sends a request, the security chip sends the key information $\{r_2,\ x_2\}$ it holds to the user and deletes it. The approach of separating and then merging effectively enables the one-time use of critical information $\{r,\ x\}$.

First, we define an idealized function $F_{S_{otp}}$ corresponding to our protocol, where the user is allowed to perform only one computation of $r_i - c \times x_i\ mod\ p$. Sid represents the session number of the user and the security chip, and Qid represents the query number. Sim represents the simulator. S_i represents the security component $(1 \leq j \leq n)$ with number j inside the phone's security chip.

1. Request to generate S_{otp}: idealize function $F_{S_{otp}}$ input $(S_{otp}Req,\ bank,\ sid)$ sent by user, record $(S_{otp}Req,\ bank,\ user,\ sid)$, transmit $(S_{otp}Req,\ bank,\ user,\ sid)$ to Sim. After Sim returns a confirmation transmit $(S_{otp}Req,\ user,\ sid)$ to the bank.
2. Generate S_{otp}: idealize the function $F_{S_{otp}}$ by entering $(S_{otp}Gen,\ user,\ sid,\ g,\ g',\ x_1,\ x_2,\ p)$ sent by the commercial bank. Transmit the following messages in order to user $user$, simulator Sim and security chip S. For the user, transmit $(S_{otp}Gen,\ bank,\ user,\ sid)$ to Sim. After receiving a confirmation reply from Sim, transmit $(S_{otp},\ bank,\ sid)$ to the user. For the security chip, transmit $(S_{otp}Gen,\ bank,\ S_i,\ sid)$ to Sim. After receiving a confirmation reply from Sim, transmit $(S_{otp}share,\ sid,\ bank)$ to the security chip inside the phone.

3. Run S_{otp}: idealise function $F_{S_{otp}}$ Enter $(S_{otp}, user, x_1, x_2, r_1, r_2, p)$ sent by user, transmit $(S_{otp}Run, \{qid\}_{i=1}^n, user, sid)$ to S. transmit $(S_{otp}Run, bank, \{v\}_{i=1}^2, sid, \{qid\}_{j=1}^n)$ to the user after receiving S's confirmed reply.

Next, we elaborate on the S_{otp} generation protocol in the idealized function $F_{S_{otp}}$. Suppose that the commercial bank has a signing secret key $sk = (x_1, x_2)$ and a public key $pk = (g, g', x = g^{x_1}g'^{x_2}, p)$. And we assume that at the beginning of the protocol, the commercial bank has stored its public key and the public key of the mobile security chip in an idealized public key authority CA.

1. The user's mobile device receives the command $(S_{otp}Req, bank, sid)$ to generate S_{otp} and transmit it to the commercial bank.
2. The   commercial bank receives the user message and outputs $(S_{otp}Req, user, sid)$. The commercial bank inputs $(S_{otp}Gen, user, g, g', p, x_1, x_2, sid)$, selects random values $r_1, r_2 \in \mathbb{Z}_p$, and calculates $R = g^{r_1}g^{r_2}$. At this point the commercial bank will decompose the secret value $\{r_i, x_i\}_{i=1}^2$ randomly into $r_i = r_i' + r_i'' \bmod p$ and $x_i = x_i' + x_i'' \bmod p$.
3. In order to efficiently share the secret value r_i', x_i' to the security chip component S_j inside the phone, the commercial bank decomposes the secret value r_i', x_i' into n subparts and distributes them to n security chip components, i.e. $\left\{r_{i,\,j}', x_{i,\,j}'\right\}_{i=1,\,2}^{1\leq j\leq n}$, j represents the serial number of the chip set, as shown in the Eq. 4:

$$r_i' = \sum_{j=1}^n r_{i,\,j}' \bmod p, \quad x_i' = \sum_{j=1}^n x_{i,\,j}' \bmod p \tag{4}$$

4. The commercial bank obtains the public key $\{pk_{S_j}\}_{j=1}^n$ of n secure chip components from CA, then transmit $(Enc(pk_{S_j}, \left\{r_{i,\,j}', x_{i,\,j}'\right\}_{i=1}^2), sid)$ is sent to the security chip.
5. The commercial bank transmits $(Enc(pk_{user}, S), sid)$ to the user, S_{otp} S in the form is shown below:

$$S = \left\langle \left\{r_i'', x_i''\right\}_{i=1}^2, g, g', g^{x_1}g'^{x_2}, g^{r_1}g'^{r_2}, p, sid \right\rangle \tag{5}$$

6. The security chip component S_j will temporarily store $\left\langle \left\{r_{i,\,j}', x_{i,\,j}'\right\}, sid \right\rangle$, sid once it receives $(Enc(pk_{S_j}, \left\{r_{i,\,j}', x_{i,\,j}'\right\}), sid)$.
7. User receives $(Enc(pk_{user}, S), sid)$ from a commercial bank, stores S, and outputs $(S_{otp}, bank, sid)$.

Finally, we will describe the S_{otp} running protocol in detail. In this protocol, the user needs to work with the security chip component S_j inside the phone in order to effectively run S_{otp} and obtain a legitimate signature. Suppose the user has

S_{otp} S from a commercial bank and enters $c' \leftarrow c - \beta$, $c \leftarrow H(d||R \cdot g^{a_1} g'^{a_2} y^b)$, a_1, a_2, $b \in \mathbb{Z}_p$ are randomly selected, and d is a series of D-coins that need to be signed by the user, i.e. the D-coins that the user will use for the transaction. The protocol flow is shown below:

1. The user receives $(S_{otp}Run, \{qid_j\}_{j=1}^n, c', sid)$ and immediately transmit $(qid_j, Enc(pk_{S_j}, pk_{user}, c'), sid)$ to the security chip inside the phone to obtain j secret values share.
2. The secure chip inside the phone receives and decrypts the message from the user using the private key to get $(Enc(pk_{S_j}, pk_{user}, c'), qid_j, sid)$. The security chip computes its own stored secret value $v'_{i,j}(i = 1, 2)$ in the form shown below:

$$v'_{i,j} \leftarrow r'_{i,j} - c' \cdot x'_{i,j} \bmod p \tag{6}$$

After transmitting, the internal secret share and other information about the transaction is deleted immediately, i.e. $\left\langle \{r'_{i,j}, x'_{i,j}\}_{i=1}^2, sid \right\rangle$, which effectively prevents the user from wanting to make a second transaction for the same D-coin within the same transaction. for the same transaction. The security chip then transmits the calculated result to the user as $(Enc(pk_{user}, \{v'_{i,j}\}_{i=1}^2), qid_j, sid)$.
3. The user receives and decrypts the message sent by the security chip to get $\{v'_{i,j}\}_{i=1}^2$. At this point, the user can then compute the Eq. 7 to get the final signature component v'_1, v'_2.

$$v'_i = r_i - c' x_i = (\sum_{j=1}^n v'_{i,j}) + (r''_i - c' x''_i) \bmod p \tag{7}$$

Finally, the user outputs $(S_{otp}run, \{v'_i\}_{i=1}^2, sid, qid)$. At this point, we have finished describing the general mechanism for instantiating S_{otp} run, and we will now propose a new anonymous credentialing scheme based on the one described above.

4.2   Application of One-Time Anonymous Credential

Next we will combine the above scheme with anonymous credentials, so that commercial banks do not need to embed their master signature key directly into S_{otp}. The main idea of one-time anonymous credentials is that an anonymous credential held by a user for a series of D-coins can only be verified once by the verifier. In a sense, the credential holder would be prevented from displaying multiple holdings of the credential, rather than transmitting duplicate payment verification to check for double-spending, as in the digital RMB patent, which connects to a commercial bank and then performs duplicate payment detection [2]. Here we use the multi-message signature scheme in short random signatures proposed by David as the basic scheme for anonymous credentials [5], thus enabling the ability to consume multiple DCEP of different denominations at once.

Here we use the following scheme combining short random signatures and S_{otp}: The commercial bank issues a series of D-coins with random values $a_{1, S_{otp}}$, $a_{2, S_{otp}} \in \mathbb{Z}_p$ embedded in the D-coins. And transmit a S_{otp} containing critical information $a_{1, S_{otp}}$, $a_{2, S_{otp}}$ to the user. If the user wants to spend the D-coin, he needs to use the S_{otp} sent by the bank to perform a proof of knowledge about $a_{1, S_{otp}}$, $a_{2, S_{otp}}$, which effectively implements a one-time credential using the one-time of S_{otp}. We then describe the specific scheme for one-time credentials in detail. We assume that the user in the following scenario spends $d_1, d_5, d_{10}, d_{20}, d_{50}, d_{100}$ on six D-coins of different denominations at the same time.

1. $DCEP.\ Setup(\chi)$: generate public parameter $params = (\mathbb{G}_1, \mathbb{G}_2, \mathbb{G}_T, p, e)$.
2. $DCEP.\ KeyGen(params,\ n)$:select the generators $g_1 \in \mathbb{G}_1$, $g_2 \in \mathbb{G}_2$, and the random values $(r_1, r_5, r_{10}, r_{20}, r_{50}, r_{100}, a_{1, S_{otp}}, a_{2, S_{otp}}, d_t, x) \in \mathbb{Z}^{10}$. Compute the following two equations.

$$(D_1,\ ...,\ D_{100},\ D_{1, S_{otp}},\ D_{2, S_{otp}},\ X,\ D_t) \leftarrow (g_1^{r_1}, ..., g_1^{r_{100}},\ g_1^{a_{1,\ S_{otp}}}, \\ g_1^{a_{2,\ S_{otp}}},\ g_1^x,\ g_1^{d_t}) \tag{8}$$

$$(D_1',\ ...,\ D_{100}',\ D_{1, S_{otp}}',\ D_{2, S_{otp}}',\ X',\ D_t') \leftarrow (g_2^{r_1}, ..., g_2^{r_{100}},\ g_2^{a_{1,\ S_{otp}}}, \\ g_2^{a_{2,\ S_{otp}}},\ g_2^x,\ g_2^{d_t}) \tag{9}$$

The $(D_i,\ D_i')$ in the above two equations is linked to the D-coin d_i ($i = 1, 5, 10, 20, 50, 100$). The bank's public key $pk_{bank} = (g_1, D_i, D_{1, S_{otp}}, D_{2, S_{otp}}, D_t, g_2, D_i', D_{1, S_{otp}}', D_{2, S_{otp}}', D_t')$, the bank's private key is $sk_{bank} = X$.
3. $DCEP.\ Auth(bank(sk_{bank}),\ user(d_1, d_5, d_{10}, d_{20}, d_{50}, d_{100})))$ is the interaction protocol between the bank and the user, as shown in the following steps.
   (1) If the user needs anonymous credentials for the D-coins in this transaction, i.e. $d_1, d_5, d_{10}, d_{20}, d_{50}, d_{100}$ as described above, the user calculates the commitment value $c \leftarrow D_1^{d_1} D_5^{d_5} D_{10}^{d_{10}} D_{20}^{d_{20}} D_{50}^{d_{50}} D_{100}^{d_{100}} \cdot D_t^\alpha \cdot g_1^{SN_u}$, $\alpha,\ SN_u \in \mathbb{Z}_p$ is chosen randomly. Transmit the commitment value c to the commercial bank.
   (2) The user side generates a proof of knowledge about the above commitment c and transmits it to the commercial bank. The proof of knowledge takes the following concrete form as shown below.

$$PK((d_1,\ d_5,\ d_{10},\ d_{20},\ d_{50},\ d_{100},\ \alpha,\ SN_u) : c = D_1^{d_1} D_5^{d_5} D_{10}^{d_{10}} D_{20}^{d_{20}} D_{50}^{d_{50}} D_{100}^{d_{100}} \cdot g_1^\alpha \cdot D_t^{SN_u}) \tag{10}$$

   (3) If the knowledge about the commitment value c proves that PK is valid, the commercial bank selects random values $a_{1, S_{otp}}$, $a_{2, S_{otp}}$,

$r_{1, S_{otp}}$, $r_{2, S_{otp}}$, SN_b, a and transmits the signatures θ and S_{otp} S to the user. The exact form is shown below.

$$\theta = (\theta_1, \theta_2) = (g_1^a, (g_1^x \cdot D_{1, S_{otp}}^{a_1, S_{otp}} \cdot D_{2, S_{otp}}^{a_2, S_{otp}} \cdot D_t^{SN_b} \cdot c)^a) \tag{11}$$

$$S_{otp} S = \langle SN_b, p, D'_{1, S_{otp}}, D'_{2, S_{otp}}, D_{1, S_{otp}}^{\prime a_1, S_{otp}}, D_{2, S_{otp}}^{\prime a_2, S_{otp}},$$
$$D_{1, S_{otp}}^{\prime r_1, S_{otp}}, D_{2, S_{otp}}^{\prime r_2, S_{otp}}, \{r_{i, S_{otp}} - c \cdot a_{i, S_{otp}} \bmod p\}_{i=1}^2 \rangle \tag{12}$$

(4) The user has obtained $(d_1, d_5, d_{10}, d_{20}, d_{50}, d_{100}, a_{1, S_{otp}}, a_{2, S_{otp}}, SN)$, $SN = SN_b + SN_u$. Compute the signature of this transaction as:

$$\sigma = (\sigma_1, \sigma_2) = (\theta_1, \theta_2/\theta_1^r) = (g_1^a, (g_1^x \cdot D_{1, S_{otp}}^{a_1, S_{otp}} \cdot D_{2, S_{otp}}^{a_2, S_{otp}} \cdot D_t^{SN} \cdot$$
$$D_1^{d_1} D_5^{d_5} D_{10}^{d_{10}} D_{20}^{d_{20}} D_{50}^{d_{50}} D_{100}^{d_{100}})) \tag{13}$$

So the credential Cre for this transaction can be expressed as $(\sigma, (d_1, d_5, d_{10}, d_{20}, d_{50}, d_{100}, a_{1, S_{otp}}, a_{2, S_{otp}}, SN), S)$. $SN = SN_b + SN_u$ The verification equation for this signature is shown in Eq. 14:

$$e(\sigma_1, g_2^x \cdot D_{1, S_{otp}}^{\prime a_1, S_{otp}} \cdot D_{2, S_{otp}}^{\prime a_2, S_{otp}} \cdot D_t^{\prime SN} \cdot D_1^{d_1} D_5^{d_5} D_{10}^{d_{10}} D_{20}^{d_{20}} D_{50}^{d_{50}} D_{100}^{d_{100}}) \overset{?}{=} e(\sigma_2, g_2) \tag{14}$$

4. *DCEP. Spend(merchant(pk_{bank}, σ, SN), user(Cre, d_i))* is the interaction protocol between the user and the recipient (merchant), $i = 1, 5, 10, 20, 50, 100$. The user needs to provide a proof of knowledge about the signature of the D-coin of the transaction. Here it is easy to obtain the proof of knowledge of the transaction information directly through the above signature verification 16, referring to the Eq. 15 for the specific transformation form.

$$e(\sigma_1, D_t')^{SN} \cdot e(\sigma_1, D_1^{\prime d_1} \cdot D_5^{\prime d_5} \cdot D_{10}^{\prime d_{10}} \cdot D_{20}^{\prime d_{20}} \cdot D_{50}^{\prime d_{50}} \cdot D_{100}^{\prime d_{100}}) \cdot$$
$$\prod_{i=1}^2 e(\sigma_1, D_{i, S_{otp}}')^{a_i, S_{otp}} \overset{?}{=} e(\sigma_2, g_2)/e(\sigma_1, g_2^x) \tag{15}$$

The proof of knowledge about $d_1, d_5, d_{10}, d_{20}, d_{50}, d_{100}, a_{1, S_{otp}}, a_{2, S_{otp}}, SN$ can be obtained from the verification Eq. 15, $(i = 1, 5, 10, 20, 50, 100)$, where the user side needs to run S_{otp} S and announce the sequence number SN to obtain a proof of knowledge sent to the recipient with the following information in the form shown in Eq. 16:

$$\langle PK(\{d_i\}_{(i=1, 5, 10, 20, 50, 100)}, \{a_{i, S_{otp}}\}_{i=1, 2}, SN) : \prod_{i=1}^2 e(\sigma_1, D_{i, S_{otp}}')^{a_i, S_{otp}}$$
$$\cdot e(\sigma_1, D_t')^{d_i} \cdot e(\sigma_1, D_t')^{SN} \cdot e(\sigma_1, g_2^x) = e(\sigma_2, g_2) \rangle \tag{16}$$

The merchant verifies the fact that the payer is the owner of the above-mentioned series of D-coins and the legitimacy of the D-coins through the user's proof of knowledge regarding the signature of the transaction information, and completes the transaction. As to how the merchant gets that portion of the digital currency, the merchant can provide the bank with information about the transaction after it happened. If the information or credentials provided are valid, then the bank will change the ownership of the digital currency spent by the initiator of the transaction, and the receiver's account will later get the corresponding share of digital currency.

5   Security and Efficiency Analysis

In this section we present a detailed security proof for the digital currency consumption schemes proposed in this study. For the digital currency one-time spending scheme, we mainly verify its one time, user privacy, and unforgeability. And we also give the comparison between our scheme with some popular digital currencies consumption scheme.

5.1   One Time

The one-time that we want to achieve in this study means that the user cannot sign and publish the relevant credentials for a transaction involving D-coins more than once, i.e. the user is not allowed to spend the same D-coin a second time.

In the payment phase of the second scenario, the user will pay by presenting anonymous credentials, as the user has no knowledge of the $a_{1, S_{otp}}$, $a_{2, S_{otp}}$ embedded inside the D-coin by the commercial bank, and so can only use the S_{otp} S sent by the commercial bank for proof, which is an effective way to achieve one-time.

5.2   Invisibility

The invisibility that we want to achieve in this study means that the commercial bank is invisible to the D-coins involved in the user's transaction, which effectively protects the user's privacy and does not prevent the bank from issuing valid credentials for the series of D-coins.

Under the Pedersen commitment scheme, the D-coins used in transactions submitted by users to the bank are theoretically invisible to commercial banks during the credential issuance phase of the anonymous credential scheme i.e. d_1, d_5, d_{10}, d_{20}, d_{50}, d_{100}.

5.3   Digital RMB Unforgeability

The non-forgeability of digital RMB in this study means that a malicious user cannot forge a legitimate signature on a D-coin using a transaction signature generated by a commercial bank based on the user's legitimate commitment to the transaction information, thus allowing the malicious user to forge the D-coin and conduct the transaction.

Definition 1 (EUF-CMA). *If a signature scheme is an $EUF - CMA$, then for any polynomial-time attacker A, the probability of A winning the following attack game is negligible.*

1. setup phase: challenger C runs setup and key generation algorithm to obtain pk, sk and transmits public key pk to attacker A.
2. interrogation phase: attacker A transmits up to q signed interrogation messages m_1, m_2, ..., m_q. Challenger replies to each query with a signature σ_i, $i = 1, 2, ..., q$.
3. Forgery phase: The attacker A finally transmits a forged signature (m', σ') to the challenger, and passes the verification, where $\forall i \in [1, q]$, $m' \neq m_i$, the attacker wins the game.

Lemma 1. *Short randomized signature schemes are next to unforgeable under selective plaintext attacks.*

Definition 2 (non-existential forgery of blind signatures). *If the blind signature of the authorization phase of $DCEP$ in the anonymous credentialing scheme in this study is non-forgeable, then for any polynomial-time attacker A, the probability of A winning the following attack game is negligible.*

1. *setup phase: the challenger runs the one-time anonymous credential setup and key generation program to get the system parameters params, and (pk_I, sk_I) and transmits the credential publisher's public key and public parameters to the attacker.*
2. *Credential issuance phase: The attacker with pk_I runs the credential issuance program of the one-time anonymous credential protocol with the challenger. The number of successful executions of this program is counted here as n.*
3. *Credential presentation phase: The attacker A executes the credential presentation procedure with the verifier. The number of successful executions of this procedure is n'.*

If the final $n' > n$, the attacker wins the game.

Theorem 1. *A short random signature scheme based on the security of S_{otp} with a random prediction machine model, where the signature in the credential issuance phase of a one-time anonymous credential scheme is unforgeable.*

Proof. We introduce the simulator Sim to play the attacker of the non-existent forgery in the short random signature scheme and to play the challenger of the non-existent forgery game in this scheme. The basic idea is that if there is an attacker who can break this scheme, then the simulator Sim can use this advantage to win the $EUF - CMA$ game against the external challenger C_e in the basic scheme. We define two attack games $game_0$, $game_1$, representing the unforgeability game under the selective message attack in the original scheme and the unforgeability game in this study's scheme, respectively.

1. The external challenger C_e in $game_0$ transmits pk_I to the simulator Sim, which in turn transmits pk_I to the attacker A in $game_1$.

2. Attacker A computes and transmits commitment

$$C = g_1^r \cdot D_1^{d_1} D_5^{d_5} D_{10}^{d_{10}} D_{20}^{d_{20}} D_{50}^{d_{50}} D_{100}^{d_{100}}$$

Give the simulator Sim. Sim extracts d_i and r using the internal knowledge extractor $E(i = 1, 5, 10, 20, 50, 100)$.

3. Sim randomly selects $a_{1, S_{otp}}$, $a_{2, S_{otp}}$ and transmits $(a_{1, S_{otp}}, a_{2, S_{otp}}, d_i)$ to challenger C_e.

4. Challenger C_e generates a signature σ_1 on $(a_{1, S_{otp}}, a_{2, S_{otp}}, d_i)$ and transmits it to Sim.

5. Sim generates the signature σ_2 of the commitment C. Then transmit σ_2 and S_{otp} S containing $a_{1, S_{otp}}$, $a_{2, S_{otp}}$ to the attacker A, i.e. (σ_2, S).

6. At this point the attacker A gets the signature containing the D-coin information and a series of messages to obtain the anonymous credentials Cre from the σ_2, S sent to him. Here we assume that A succeeds in obtaining and issuing the credentials n, n' respectively. If $n' > n$, then Sim can know that at least one of the $CreShow$ executions is a forgery.

7. Sim randomly selects Cre_i with subscript i $(1 \leq i \leq n)$ for the credential posting phase and extracts $(d_i', \left\{ a_{i, S_{otp}}' \right\}_{i=1}^2)$ using extractor E.

8. Sim signs the above extracted message $(d_i', \left\{ a_{i, S_{otp}}' \right\}_{i=1}^2)$ and transmits it to C_e.

Since the Okamoto-Schnorr signature has witness indistinguishability, the probability that the message $(d_i', \left\{ a_{i, S_{otp}}' \right\}_{i=1}^2)$ has not been signed by Sim for interrogation in $game_0$ is non-negligible, i.e. Sim can use this message signature pair to break the basic scheme of $EUF - CMA$. This conflicts with our Lemma 1, so the possibility that there exists an attacker A who can break the unforgeability of the one-time anonymous credential scheme is negligible.

5.4   Efficiency Analysis

In this subsection, we compare the payment environments that can be supported by the three digital currency payment schemes in turn, as well as the anti double spending in the online case, the anti double spending in the single offline case, and the anti double spending in the double offline case.

As can be seen from the Table 1, the model proposed in this study can effectively prevent the double consumption problem by using digital signatures and anonymous credentials at once when all users are offline, which is a major advantage of the model over existing studies and payment methods.

Table 1. Comparison between electronic money spending schemes

Scheme	Wechat, Alipay	PST of PBOC	Our scheme
Payment environment	*online, single offline*	*online, single offline, dual offline*	*online, single offline, dual offline*
Anti online double spend	*Yes*	*Yes*	*Yes*
Anti single and offline double-spending	*Yes*	*Yes*	*Yes*
Anti single and offline double-spending	*No*	*No*	*Yes*
Anti-Double Spending Strategy	*None*	*Post-incident accountability*	*Disposable Digital Currency*

6   Conclusion

This study applies the one-time signature delegation authority technique to the Chinese digital RMB double offline payment, which effectively solves the double spend problem that can exist in the digital RMB patent when both users are offline for the transaction, and effectively replaces the solution of transmitting duplicate payment detection for post-event recovery mentioned in the previous offline payment patent.

Acknowledgement. My advisor, Mr. Chen, has been extremely helpful and supportive throughout the research and dissertation process. I would like to express my great gratitude to Mr. Chen.

References

1. Chaum, D., van Heyst, E.: Group Signatures. In: Davies, D.W. (ed.) EUROCRYPT 1991. LNCS, vol. 547, pp. 257–265. Springer, Heidelberg (1991). https://doi.org/10.1007/3-540-46416-6_22
2. Chaum, D., Fiat, A., Naor, M.: Untraceable electronic cash. In: Goldwasser, S. (ed.) CRYPTO 1988. LNCS, vol. 403, pp. 319–327. Springer, New York (1990). https://doi.org/10.1007/0-387-34799-2_25
3. Bellare, M., Shi, H., Zhang, C.: Foundations of group signatures: the case of dynamic groups. In: Menezes, A. (ed.) CT-RSA 2005. LNCS, vol. 3376, pp. 136–153. Springer, Heidelberg (2005). https://doi.org/10.1007/978-3-540-30574-3_11
4. Nishide, T.: One-time delegation of unlinkable signing rights and its application. In: Nguyen, K., Wu, W., Lam, K.Y., Wang, H. (eds.) ProvSec 2020. LNCS, vol. 12505, pp. 103–123. Springer, Cham (2020). https://doi.org/10.1007/978-3-030-62576-4_6
5. Pointcheval, D., Sanders, O.: Short randomizable signatures. In: Sako, K. (ed.) CT-RSA 2016. LNCS, vol. 9610, pp. 111–126. Springer, Cham (2016). https://doi.org/10.1007/978-3-319-29485-8_7
6. Camenisch, J., Stadler, M.: Efficient group signature schemes for large groups. In: Kaliski, B.S. (ed.) CRYPTO 1997. LNCS, vol. 1294, pp. 410–424. Springer, Heidelberg (1997). https://doi.org/10.1007/BFb0052252

7. Okamoto, T.: Provably secure and practical identification schemes and corresponding signature schemes. In: Brickell, E.F. (ed.) CRYPTO 1992. LNCS, vol. 740, pp. 31–53. Springer, Heidelberg (1993). https://doi.org/10.1007/3-540-48071-4_3

8. Goldwasser, S., Kalai, Y.T., Rothblum, G.N.: One-time programs. In: Wagner, D. (ed.) CRYPTO 2008. LNCS, vol. 5157, pp. 39–56. Springer, Heidelberg (2008). https://doi.org/10.1007/978-3-540-85174-5_3

9. Acar, T., Nguyen, L.: Revocation for delegatable anonymous credentials. In: Catalano, D., Fazio, N., Gennaro, R., Nicolosi, A. (eds.) PKC 2011. LNCS, vol. 6571, pp. 423–440. Springer, Heidelberg (2011). https://doi.org/10.1007/978-3-642-19379-8_26

10. Fiat, A., Shamir, A.: How to prove yourself: practical solutions to identification and signature problems. In: Odlyzko, A.M. (ed.) CRYPTO 1986. LNCS, vol. 263, pp. 186–194. Springer, Heidelberg (1987). https://doi.org/10.1007/3-540-47721-7_12

11. Pedersen, T.P.: Non-interactive and information-theoretic secure verifiable secret sharing. In: Feigenbaum, J. (ed.) CRYPTO 1991. LNCS, vol. 576, pp. 129–140. Springer, Heidelberg (1992). https://doi.org/10.1007/3-540-46766-1_9

12. Shamir, A.: How to share a secret. Commun. ACM **22**(11), 612–613 (1979). https://doi.org/10.1007/978-3-642-15328-0_17

13. Teranishi, I., Furukawa, J., Sako, K.: k-times anonymous authentication (extended abstract). In: Lee, P.J. (ed.) ASIACRYPT 2004. LNCS, vol. 3329, pp. 308–322. Springer, Heidelberg (2004). https://doi.org/10.1007/978-3-540-30539-2_22

14. Fanusie, Y., Jin, E.: China's Digital Currency (2021)

15. Qian, Y., et al.: Method and system for offline payment using digital currency chip card [P], Beijing: CN107230079B 2020-10-09 (in Chinese)

16. People's Bank of China. White paper on the progress of research and development of China's digital RMB [R/OL] (2021-7-16) [2021-7-25] (in Chinese). http://www.pbc.gov.cn/goutongjiaoliu/113456/113469/4293590/index.html

17. Anna: Digital dollar:purpose of issuance, basic architecture, application scenarios and challenges to China's central bank digital currency DC/EP. New Finance. 11(2020), 21–26 (in Chinese). DOI:CNKI:SUN:XJRO.0.2020-11-004

A Hierarchical Macroeconomic Copula Model for Cyber Damages Based on Current Cyber Insurance Prices

Daniel Kasper[(✉)] and Jens Grossklags

Technical University of Munich, 85748 Garching, Germany
dkasper@cyber-economics.com, jens.grossklags@in.tum.de

Abstract. The cyber insurance market has expanded dramatically over the last decade; however, the underlying risk is still poorly understood by both cyber insurers and academic researchers. Although the quantification of cyber damage is a mainstay in the literature and of ongoing interest for researchers, several research questions requiring at least a somewhat accurate stochastic model for industry or countrywide cyber damages, are mostly disregarded by the academic community or only discussed in qualitative terms. Thus, this paper proposes a macroeconomic framework for generating plausible damage estimates based on current cyber insurance rate schedules, along with a nested hierarchical copula model for implementing the correlation between cyber damages. The resulting sample datasets will be made available to researchers to help spur an additional quantitative push in the literature.

Keywords: Cyber insurance · Cyber risk quantification · Cyber risk modeling

1 Introduction

The proverbial holy grail of cyber risk modeling is the "true" cyber loss distribution for any given firm or entity and the aggregation of these distributions to industry sector levels, countrywide damages or the global economy. The short history of the risk itself, the incompleteness and unstructured nature of available claims data, and the dynamically changing threat landscape lead to diminished value of the already little data that is available. Thus, compared with other insurance lines of business, this currently remains a distant goal. Although the global premium volume for cyber insurance is growing quickly, the confidence of industry stakeholders in the current quantitative modeling capabilities (especially when it comes to higher reinsurance risk transfers that are overly sensitive toward the tail correlation of the underlying policies) is still limited (see, for example, a current report from Marsh [7]).

This presents a high barrier of entry for academic research into cyber risk, as robust estimates for cyber risk damages are required to analyze and model a plethora of essential scenarios, such as the evaluation and comparison of public policy instruments to foster market development. Although several attempts have been made in the literature to quantify cyber risks (see, e.g., [1,3]), usually fitting statistical distributions to existing cyber damages or insurance claims data, they are partly dependent on outdated data or limited in their applicability and thus offer diminished predictive value.

A promising alternative approach to classical actuarial techniques was described in Woods et al. [10], where the authors used an evolutionary algorithm (EA) to derive cyber loss distributions from 23 rate schedules of United States cyber insurers. In theory, this approach reverses the standard order of procedure of insurers, that base their loss distribution assumptions on damage estimates or historic claims data culminating in the final rate schedule. The method, therefore, provides a good estimate of the current expectations and sentiments toward cyber risk by leading insurers, akin to how options, futures, and other derivatives allow to gauge the expectations of the financial markets. However, although this approach can provide appropriate damage distributions for individual risk owners, it only offers implicit information on the correlation of damages between multiple risks.

To fill this gap in the literature and provide researchers and industry practitioners with datasets as a basis for further modeling and analysis, we propose a macroeconomic framework, loosely inspired by Dreyer et al. [2], consisting of individual loss distributions for firms in 11 industry sectors, which are derived from a current rate schedule of one of the largest cyber insurers in the United States. We develop a nested Archimedean copula with three hierarchy levels that are provided for five sample parameter constellations, ranging from moderate to high correlation. The resulting dataset that consists of roughly 100GB of data in .csv format will be made available to researchers and other interested parties at www.cyber-economics.com/GermanDamageDataset.

2   Model Choices

In the following, we explain the method used to infer loss distributions from insurance prices (Sect. 2.1), introduce the rate schedule used to calculate said loss distributions (Sect. 2.2) and discuss nested Archimedean copulas (Sect. 2.3). We further describe the real German economy and the model economy based on it (Sect. 2.4). Finally, we discuss the inherent limitations of the utilized approach (Sect. 2.5).

2.1   Inferring Loss Distributions from Insurance Prices

For many established property and casualty insurance types with a rich history of data, the standard actuarial approach is to fit several commonly used statistical distributions via a severity-frequency framework to existing data. However, even in well-established lines of business, final insurance prices may represent not only the fair price according to the statistical methods used, but also insurer sentiments toward future loss events, additional loading factors (i.e., safety margins) to account for potential accumulation risks, or purely commercial factors, like maximizing profit when the demand for a particular product or coverage is inelastic. With cyber insurance's volatile and rapidly evolving underlying risk, it is especially valuable to not only look into the history, but also consider the sentiment and beliefs of current market participants toward the future, similar to how central banks provide forward guidance to investors regarding interest rate decisions.

Woods et al. [10] introduced a procedure to infer loss distributions from insurance prices. We refer to their paper for a detailed technical description of the algorithm and additional reasoning for the soundness of the method. We use the method as described with the following key changes:

1. We explicitly incorporate α, a parameter mentioned by the authors, but not directly implemented in the optimization procedure. The parameter captures the probability of no loss, thus turning the fitted distribution into a mixed continuous distribution. Instead of stretching or compressing pure distributions ex-post, this allows the optimization to directly find the best-fitting mixed distribution.
2. Instead of the EA particle swarm optimization (PSO), we employ another EA, namely differential evolution (DE). This approach outperforms and provides more robust results than PSO on most real-valued numerical optimization problems (see [11]), as it directly works with the differences in real-valued vectors.
3. The log-normal and polynomial distributions were almost identical in their explanatory value for a given rate schedule, with an overlap of 98%. Therefore, we omit the polynomial distribution from the fittings and continue with the five resulting distributions.

2.2 Travelers Insurance 2020 Rate Schedule

In contrast to Woods et al. [10], we only model the implied loss distributions for a single rate schedule from Travelers Insurance, which was published on the Californian SERFF Filling System on March 2, 2020. The pricing logic of the rate schedule is based on a multiplicative pricing approach, where the central coverage is differentiated between business interruption (BI) and non-business interruption (nBI). The core nBI coverage includes 15 first- and third-party modules with associated factor ranges, such as security and privacy costs (0.6–1.0), privacy breach notification (0.05–0.45), and media liability (0.15–0.55). The base premium rate is calculated based on turnover for nonfinancial companies, while for financial corporations it is based on assets under management (AUM). The pricing logic encompasses 27 private, public and non-profit company lines of business (e.g., agriculture, healthcare, retail) and 23 types of financial institutions (e.g., bank, broker, hedge fund); each has an associated factor range that indicates a premium reduction/increase for the respective company types (e.g., healthcare 1.1–1.5, broker 1.0–1.4). The premiums and deductibles for BI and nBI coverage are calculated separately, with no stated upper limit, even though the actual policies are still subject to underwriting approval and are likely only of theoretical importance. There are several additional factors listed in the schedule, for example, discounts for good cyber security hygiene and modifiers for policies that consist of BI and nBI coverage.

The policy triples required for the optimization, consisting of a (base) price, coverage limit, and deductible, are based on the nBI damages with a multiplier of 1.0. The 744 triples used for the optimization consist of 124 different coverage limits, ranging from \$25,000 to \$2 billion. For each coverage limit, there are six relative deductible levels, ranging from 10% to 100% of the coverage sum.

2.3   Nested Archimedean Copulas

According to Sklar's theorem, any cumulative multivariate distribution F of the variable Y can be expressed by mapping the univariate marginal distributions F_i with a suitable copula C. Formally (see e.g. [8]):

$$
\begin{aligned}
&Let\ Y = [Y_1, \cdots, Y_n]' \sim F,\ with\ Y_i \sim F_i \\
&then\ \exists\ C\ : [0,1]^n \to [0,1] \\
&s.t.\ F(y)\ = C(F_1(y_1), \cdots, F_n(y_n)) \forall\ y\ \in \mathbb{R}^n
\end{aligned}
\tag{1}
$$

Archimedean copulas are a special class of copulas that are computationally easy to sample and can capture different tail dependencies. However, their exchangeability, that is, symmetry of the positive and negative tails, is a shortcoming that is especially noticeable in higher dimensional modeling. The class of nested Archimedean copulas enables the implementation of hierarchical dependence structures, each with its own correlation factors, to allow for asymmetric tails while retaining the computational advantages (see [5]).

The implemented model consists of three hierarchical levels and can be seen in Fig. 2 in the Appendix, where the structure is schematically shown for three sectors. The global correlation parameter guides the correlation of all industry sectors below it, whereas a specific industry correlation parameter determines the intra sector correlation between the four different enterprise sizes within each industry sector (three for financial). For simplicity, the correlation parameters used in this paper are assumed to be equal at all hierarchy levels and are analyzed for five levels (0.05, 0.10, 0.15, 0.25, and 0.50).

2.4   German Economy and Model Economy

The model economy consists of 11 industry sectors and is derived from recent data on the German economy. As the rate schedule of Travelers is based on the turnover for most industries and AUM of financial institutions, the turnover must be mapped to the GDP/value added contribution of the respective enterprise. The data for the turnover of the respective industries and GDP are based on current estimates of the Federal Statistical Office of Germany (Statistisches Bundesamt). However, the breakdown of enterprise sizes is based on a 2014 estimate. In addition, the 2014 estimate only provides the share of large firms in turnover. To calculate the micro, small, and medium enterprise share, we break down the small and medium-sized enterprises according to a ratio based on the overall turnover share of the respective companies in overall GDP.

According to data from the Federal Statistical Office of Germany [9], large corporations contributed approximately about 70% of the total annual turnover in 2018, whereas their share of total firm numbers was only 1%–2% in many industry sectors (Table 1).

Table 1. Turnover share of different enterprise sizes of the German economy in 2014

Enterprise type	Number of employees	Turnover limit	Turnover share in 2018
Micro	<10	<€2 Mil	6,6%
Smallest	10–49	€10 Mil	11,3%
Medium	50–249	€50 Mil	12,2%
Large	>249	>€50 Mil	69,9%

Table 6 in the Appendix shows the share of firms and turnover for 10 of the 11 sectors, except for the financial corporations that use other metrics. After several necessary adjustments, such as the distribution of the value-added of companies classified as "other" to the other sectors, these numbers serve as the foundation for the model economy. Based on the German economy's GDP contribution and sector makeup, the model economy consists of 693,751 firms across the eleven sectors (Table 2).

Table 2. Number of firms in the German model economy

Sector	Micro	Small	Medium	Large
Financial	-	500	60	1
Business and professional services	103,478	20,696	27,594	166
Manufacturing	60,385	12,077	16,103	636
Construction	72,115	14,423	19,231	44
Telecom, technology and electronics	17,403	3,481	4,641	106
Transportation and storage	23,423	4,685	6,246	105
Utilities	3,464	693	924	115
Wholesale and retail	59,732	11,946	15,928	262
Accommodation and food services	12,214	2,443	3,257	7
Real estate	118,199	23,640	31,520	120
Mining	589	118	157	3

The nonfinancial companies are assumed to have a turnover of 0.5, 5, 100, and 1,000 Mil Euro at the micro, small, medium, and large level, respectively. For financial corporations, the AUM is assumed to be 1, 60, and 500 Bn Euro. Financial corporations were simplified to include only three firm sizes, as a "micro-bank" with AUM of around $50 or $100 Mil is more of an exception than the norm.

2.5   Interpreting, Transferring, and Adjusting Derived Cyber Loss Distributions

Cyber insurance coverage continues to differ between carriers, many offering dozens of optional coverage elements and/or endorsements; thus, a key underlying question is what the term "cyber damages" encompasses from the perspective of an insurance rate schedule. The cyber distribution of a Californian small enterprise is different from an identical company in Bavaria in terms of size and other business metrics. For one, the regulatory requirements, potential fines, and possible litigation costs vary by jurisdiction. Meanwhile, language or software stacks used should influence the specific risks of concrete attack types (e.g., phishing). Therefore, the results of the derived prices of the Californian rate schedule are only partially portable and applicable to other countries, and because it was published in 2020, it is valid only for a limited time.

However, although this limited transferability affects precision and validity of the derived distributions, the main goal of our work is to generate various, plausible estimates for a wide parameter space to provide future researchers with a quantitatively sound foundation on which to build upon. To counteract these shortcomings and increase the validity and transferability of the derived results, we norm the expected value of damages to a certain percentage of the overall GDP; in this exemplary implementation 0.5% of the German GDP. While this calibration certainly loses information about the absolute levels of damages, which are embedded within the rate schedule, the most important attributes of the resulting datasets are not primarily precision but robustness and plausibility.

3   Results

This section presents the results of the marginals distribution fittings and gives an overview of the modeled cyber loss damages.

3.1   Loss Distribution Fitting

DE was used to fit the marginal distributions for each corporate type, following the method outlined in Woods et al. [10], while considering the changes outlined in Sect. 2.1. The optimization was carried out using the deoptim R package, with 1,000 optimization epochs (called itermax in the package) and a starting population (NP) of 300. The employed optimization strategy is the default strategy DE / local-to-best / 1 / bin (strategy 2). Moreover, the initial population was constrained in its initialization to limit the search space to probable parameter constellations. For the log-normal distribution, for example, the starting population was initialized with $\mu, \sigma \in (0, 30)$.

Table 3. Mean absolute deviation for different turnover sizes of nonfinancial companies.

Turnover	0.5 Mil	5 Mil	100 Mil	1,000 Mil
Log-Normal	**0.098**	0.154	**0.064**	**0.093**
Pareto	0.123	0.297	0.217	0.255
Burr	0.110	**0.118**	0.165	0.311
Gamma	0.453	0.507	0.478	0.523
Weibull	0.161	0.180	0.089	0.147

Table 4. Mean absolute deviation for different turnover sizes of financial companies.

AUM	1 Bn	60 Bn	500 Bn
Log-Normal	0.174	**0.096**	**0.160**
Pareto	0.222	0.202	0.235
Burr	**0.158**	0.399	0.480
Gamma	0.506	0.478	0.523
Weibull	0.194	0.145	0.198

Overall, the best-fitting distribution for the four nonfinancial (Table 3) and three financial (Table 4) enterprise sizes is the log-normal distribution, which provided for five out of the seven total parameter constellations the best fit. Although the Burr distribution offered the best fit for the remaining two, we will use the log-normal distribution for all firms to keep the marginals consistent. As noted by [10], the fittings should be at least partially understood as corresponding to the insurer's sentiments, that have been likely calibrated on its own claims data, but also forward looking factors. Overall, the fittings for the nonfinancial sectors are better than for the financial ones. Compared to the fittings of [10], which had an absolute deviation of 15% to 20% for most rate schedules, the fitted loss distributions, particularly for the nonfinancial corporations, have a better overall fit, giving us confidence that the method adjustments in the algorithm outlined in Sect. 2.1 have improved the fitting quality.

Table 5. Best fitting parameters of log-normal distribution for different enterprise sizes

Type	Nonfinancial				Financial		
Size	Micro	Small	Medium	Large	Small	Medium	Large
μ	3.68	2.15	8.5	9.44	3.22	10.2	12.1
σ	3.24	4.59	3.64	3.71	4.34	3.43	3.52
α	0.88	0.93	0.95	0.9	0.00	0.00	0.00

The best fitting marginal parameters for the log-normal distribution are shown in Table 5, where the parameter α is the probability of no loss, which turns the resulting distribution into a mixed distribution.

3.2   Archimedean Copula Implementation and Resulting Datasets

This section presents a brief overview of the German model economy's resulting overall cyber loss distribution. A more detailed description of the resulting datasets will be provided in a follow-up paper using the generated data as basis to estimate the impact of several public policy instruments. Joining the marginal distributions with the nested Archimedean copula, we determine that the simulated cyber damages of the model economy are increasingly kurtotic in an increase in the correlation parameters. As mentioned, the damages are normed to cause an expected annual damage of 0.5% of the German GDP (without taxes and subsidies); about 15 billion Euro. For the graphical representation (see Fig. 1), the aggregated 500 runs per parameter constellation were drawn from the 10,000 available data rows per firm and correlation.

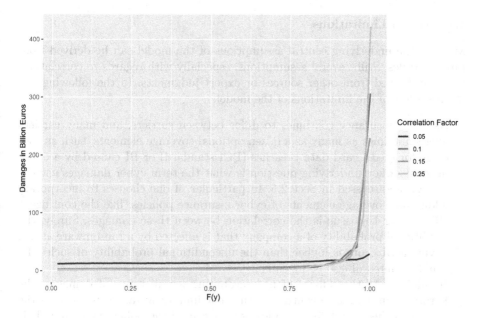

Fig. 1. Cyber damage distributions of the model economy for different correlation factors, normed to 0.5% of German GDP

The resulting graph showcases the inherent volatility and kurtosis of the final distributions, as the 0.10 correlation curve surpasses the 0.15 curve at the maximum loss due to the limited sample size. The absolute value of damage can be imposed by stretching or contracting the distribution according to one's need; thus, the only fixed elements that shift the probability mass are the correlation parameters. The worst case loses of the aggregated sample datasets are varying drastically. For a correlation of 0.05 the 1-in-50 worst case is just 30 billion Euro, about twice the annually expected damages. The 1-in-50 losses for a correlation of $0.1, 0.15, 0.25$ are 307, 229, and 421 billion Euro, respectively. As the tail-behavior is of particular interest, the datasets offer a wide range of scenarios concerning worst case losses.

4   Discussion

In the following, we outline the current limitations of the underlying model, how they can be overcome, how to empirically verify or calibrate the parameters, and how the generated data can be used in future research.

4.1   Model Limitations

Many of the underlying central assumptions of the model can be derived from rate schedules. Still, several assumptions, especially with regards to correlation, must be derived from other sources or expert judgments. In the following, we discuss a few of the limitations of the model.

1. As cyber insurance continues to differ between carriers, and many carriers offer sometimes as many as a dozen optional coverage elements, such as coverage for credit card data breaches (PCI standard) or BI caused by a cyber incident, a key underlying question is what the term cyber damages encompasses, as discussed in Sect. 2.5. In particular, if one chooses to incorporate additional coverage elements of cyber insurance policies, like the contingent BI, another key issue is the correlation between these damages. Surely, the conditional probability of a company that is affected by a ransomware attack having a BI claim is higher than the unconditional probability of such a BI claim ex-ante, all else being equal.
2. In addition to these flaws of not accounting for all types of damages, the nature of an insurance contract with a maximum coverage sum, renders the insurer in theory indifferent to losses that exceed the policy maximum. This indifference is an additional constraint when deriving the cyber economic damages from insurance prices, as they are likely to exceed the policy limit in the case of medium and large enterprises. Although the fitted distributions used to model cyber damages to insurance prices allow inference of the losses exceeding the available policy limit, the approach introduces new challenges with regard to the tail-behavior of damages. Some of the fitted distributions have extremely heavy tails, which have a significant impact on the expected

value of damages, as well as the maximum possible loss. These tails, however, are of relatively low concern for an insurer who, at most, might cover $20 million of a potential hundred-million-dollar loss for a large corporation. Particularly, in future model applications, a necessary condition for commonly used microeconomic utility families of functions, such as the CRRA (constant relative risk aversion) class, is that a loss cannot exceed the initial wealth of the respective entities. Thus, it might become necessary to cut of the damages of a specific cyber attack at a high percentage of the available net worth, for example, 90% of net worth or AUM.

3. Although nested Archimedean copulas allow for the modeling of asymmetric correlation parameters, the stable condition for a nested Archimedean copula, which requires the correlation of lower hierarchies to be larger or equal to higher ones, rules out plausible parameter constellations. This is especially true for parameter constellations that feature a low correlation between firms in the same industry and/or similar size but a high global correlation between all cyber damages.

5   Application, Calibration, and Outlook

This paper is an attempt to provide reasonable estimates of country wide cyber damages (including the important correlation between damages) that can be used for the following research questions:

1. As mentioned, the datasets can be used to analyze the effect of several possible public welfare and market development instruments, like an insurer-of-last-resort solution, or reduction of cyber insurance premiums. This analysis usually involves the explicit modeling of the utility of enterprises, insurers, and potential other stakeholders of the insurance value chain, like reinsurers or the capital market.

2. As demonstrated in [4], the examination of potential cumulative aggregation scenarios can be used to infer whether the cyber insurance market would be able to compensate for a massive tail-event in terms of incident response capacity and financial value-at-risk.

3. Akin to [6], the underlying data can be used to price and simulate possible payouts of cyber-bonds or other higher risk transfers.

We hope that the datasets will allow researchers to investigate the aforementioned and other research questions and inspire them and industry practitioners to produce new datasets going in the future. As copulas allow the independent modeling of the multivariate dependency from the single risks, it will in the future be easy to exchange either for better or more up to date estimates. For example, a new rate schedule could be easily fitted for its best fitting loss distribution and replace the estimates of the Travelers 2020 rate schedule. It is also possible to substitute a different copula family or hierarchy specification for the nested Archimedean copula used here. Another option to calibrate the model is to empirically verify the copula structure, i.e., to fit several copula types to a set of empirical multivariate data. In particular, for nested Archimedean copulas, with their hierarchical structure, it would be interesting to understand which structure/specification provides the best explanatory value (e.g., does a structure where enterprises are first grouped by size and then by sector offer a better fit than the current model).

Acknowledgment. We thank the anonymous reviewers for their feedback.

6   Appendix

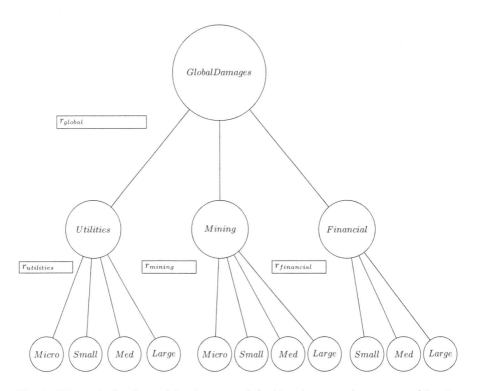

Fig. 2. Schematic for the multivariate nested Archimedean copula structure (showing 3 of 11 sectors)

Table 6. Parameters for model economy

Industry	Value added 2020 (Bn Eur)	Year of data	# Firms	Share firms SM	Share firms L	Share turnover SM	Share turnover L	Travelers nBi factor	Value added to turnover ratio SM	Value added to turnover ratio L	nBi factors avg.
Financial	116.91	2020	-	-	-	-	-	0.65–1.05	-	-	- 0.85
Business and professional services	337.63	2020	372,561	99.80%	0.20%	63.90%	36.10%	0.70–1.10	60.53%	41.20%	0.9
Manufacturing	593.85	2020	207,847	97.40%	2.60%	21.20%	78.80%	0.50–0.90	35.91%	22.14%	0.7
Construction	182.47	2020	243,112	99.90%	0.10%	82.40%	17.60%	0.50–0.90	39.65%	28.60%	0.7
Telecom, technology and electronics	114.46	2018	92,869	99.30%	0.70%	31.70%	68.30%	1.00–1.40	52.09%	42.23%	1.2
Transportation and storage	125.86	2020	89,704	98.90%	1.10%	38.80%	61.20%	0.70–1.10	41.32%	31.51%	0.9
Utilities	91.603	2019	6675	89.39%	10.61%	7.88%	92.12%	1.00–1.40	37.73%	9.66%	1.2
Wholesale and retail	317.69	2020	581,762	99.20%	0.80%	39.20%	60.80%	0.55–0.95	19.53%	10.60%	0.75
Accommodation and food services	30.387	2020	222,203	99.80%	0.20%	83.80%	16.20%	1.00–1.40	46.81%	45.73%	1.2
Real estate	334.374	2020	196,831	99.90%	0.10%	73.70%	26.30%	0.80–1.20	68.05%	48.48%	1
Mining	3.44	2019	1,767	98%	2%	35.70%	64.30%	0.70–1.10	37.95%	45.33%	0.9

References

1. Böhme, R., Schwartz, G.: Modeling cyber-insurance: towards a unifying framework. In: Workshop on the Economics of Information Security, June 2010. http://citeseerx.ist.psu.edu/viewdoc/summary?doi=10.1.1.165.4129
2. Dreyer, P., et al.: Estimating the global cost of cyber risk: methodology and examples (2018). https://www.rand.org/pubs/research_reports/RR2299.html
3. Eling, M., Wirfs, J.: Cyber risk: too big to insure? risk transfer options for a mercurial risk class (2016). https://www.ivw.unisg.ch/~/media/internet/content/dateien/instituteundcenters/ivw/studien/cyberrisk2016.pdf
4. Hillairet, C., Lopez, O.: Propagation of cyber incidents in an insurance portfolio: counting processes combined with compartmental epidemiological models. Scand. Actu. J. **2021**(8), 671–694 (2021). https://doi.org/10.1080/03461238.2021.1872694
5. Hofert, M., Mächler, M.: Nested archimedean copulas meet R: the nacopula package. J. Stat. Softw. **39**(9), 1–20 (2011). https://doi.org/10.18637/jss.v039.i09
6. Kasper, D.: Analyzing the feasibility of cyber bonds by stochastically solving a copula-based model with differential evolution (2019). http://rgdoi.net/10.13140/RG.2.2.30180.40325
7. Marsh. Cyber insurance market overview: Fourth quarter 2021 (2022-02). https://www.marsh.com/us/services/cyber-risk/insights/cyber-insurance-market-overview-q4-2021.html
8. Patton, A.J.: A review of copula models for economic time series. J. Multivariate Anal. **110**, 4–18 (2012). https://doi.org/10.1016/j.jmva.2012.02.021
9. Söllner, R.: The economic importance of small and medium-sized enterprises in Germany. Wirtschaft und Statistik **1**, 40–51 (2014). https://www.destatis.de/EN/Methods/WISTAScientificJournal/Downloads/the-economic-importance-soellner-12014.pdf?__blob=publicationFile. English Version
10. Woods, D.W., Moore, T., Simpson, A.C.: The county fair cyber loss distribution: drawing inferences from insurance prices. Digital Threats Res. Pract. **2**(2), 1–21 (2021). https://doi.org/10.1145/3434403
11. Zhang, J., Sanderson, A.C.: JADE: adaptive differential evolution with optional external archive. IEEE Trans. Evol. Comput. **13**(5), 945–958 (2009). https://doi.org/10.1109/TEVC.2009.2014613

Social Engineering and Personalized Security

Cyber Social Engineering Kill Chain

Rosana Montañez Rodriguez[1] and Shouhuai Xu[2(✉)]

[1] Department of Computer Science, University of Texas at San Antonio,
San Antonio, TX 78249, USA
`rosana.montanezrodriguez@my.utsa.edu`
[2] Department of Computer Science, University of Colorado Colorado Springs,
Colorado Springs, CO 80918, USA
`sxu@uccs.edu`

Abstract. Cyber attacks are often initiated with a social engineering attack to penetrate a network, which we call Cyber Social Engineering (CSE) attacks. Despite many studies, our understanding of CSE attacks is inadequate in explaining why these attacks are prevalent and why humans are still the weakest link in cybersecurity. This paper aims to deepen our understanding of CSE attacks and help design effective defenses against them. Specifically, we propose a framework, dubbed *CSE Kill Chain*, for systematically modeling and characterizing CSE attacks. To demonstrate the usefulness of the framework, we perform a case study in which we apply it to analyze a real-world CSE attack.

Keywords: Cybersecurity · Cyber attacks · Cyber social engineering kill chain · Human factors · Social engineering · Cybersecurity modeling · Science of cyber security

1 Introduction

Cyber Social Engineering (CSE) attacks are cyber attacks that use humans as an attack vector. They have become prevalent as humans are often the weakest link in cybersecurity. For example, Verizon Annual Data Breach Investigation Report [6] shows that 85% of the data breach incidents occurring in the year 2020 involved a human component. Although CSE attacks are prevalent, our understanding of them remains to be improved as the prevalence of attacks suggests the lack of effective defenses.

The lack of effective defenses can be attributed to the fact that most existing defenses against CSE attacks, or CSE defenses for short, focus on detecting and filtering social engineering messages [30]. However, this approach fails to address the source of the problem: poor security decision-making resulting from errors in human judgment. As a consequence, the inadequate understanding of what makes humans vulnerable to CSE attacks results in limited approaches to mitigating this inherent vulnerability. This problem motivates the present study, which aims to propose a systematic framework for characterizing CSE attacks in

C. Su et al. (Eds.): SciSec 2022, LNCS 13580, pp. 487–504, 2022.
https://doi.org/10.1007/978-3-031-17551-0_32

a fashion similar to how we characterize technological cyber attacks. In addition to possibly leveraging the resulting framework to guide the design of effective defenses, it can also facilitate the incorporation of CSE attacks into existing technological cyber attacks frameworks.

Our Contributions. In this paper, we make three contributions. First, we establish a direct relationship between psychological constructs and CSE attacks. By doing so, we provide a "bridge" to facilitate cross-pollination between the fields of psychology, human factors, and cybersecurity. This bridge enables researchers across multiple disciplines to explore new approaches to defending against CSE attacks by leveraging the knowledge from the relevant fields.

Second, the preceding bridge guides us to propose a framework, dubbed *CSE Kill Chain*, for modeling CSE attacks. This means that the framework accommodates human psychology by relating cognitive and social psychological constructs to CSE attacks. This also means that as the term suggests, the framework is partly inspired by the Lockheed-Martin Cyber Kill Chain [21], which focuses on technological cyber attacks, not CSE attacks. Rather than offering adaptions to the Lockheed-Martin Cyber Kill Chain, the framework further incorporates elements of the MITRE ATT&CK framework [51], especially the concepts of attack *tactics* and *techniques*. Therefore, the present study can achieve the best of both worlds (i.e., these two frameworks) when coping with CSE attacks. This alignment with well-accepted frameworks is important for practitioners and researchers to adopt the CSE Kill Chain framework. All these together make the framework a foundation for studying CSE attacks in a systematic fashion.

Third, in principle, the framework can have many applications, such as modeling real-world CSE attacks and leveraging these models to prevent and/or detect ongoing CSE attacks, which requires the availability of datasets. To demonstrate the usefulness of our framework, we present a case study to provide an in-depth analysis of a real-world, new CSE attack. The case study leads to valuable insights, including: (i) the framework can guide the identification of the connection between a cyber attack and a previously known scam in the physical world; (ii) the framework can extend the knowledge of CSE attacks exploiting social media; and (iii) the framework can demonstrate how human psychological constructs can be weaponized.

Related Work. The prior studies that are closely related to the present one are the attempts at understanding CSE attacks. These attempts typically adapt social engineering attacks in the physical world to cyberspace. As a consequence, they fail to capture the attacker-user-defender interactions that are unique to CSE attacks and absent in the physical world (e.g., the success of a CSE attack may require the cooperation of a victim user, while evading the defenses that are employed). Moreover, they fail to establish connections between human psychological vulnerabilities and CSE attacks, fail to integrate CSE attacks with cyber attacks frameworks, and fail to provide insights into developing defenses against CSE attacks. Four representative prior attempts are briefly reviewed below.

The earliest study is the Social Engineering Cycle (SEC) [33] based on the experience of the authors on social engineering attacks in the physical world. It divides a social engineering attack into four phases: research, developing rapport and trust, exploiting trust, and utilizing information. However, SEC is a high-level description of social engineering attacks and does not present any tactical or operational guidance that can be actioned for cyber defense. Our framework fills this void by mapping social engineering attack processes to existing cyber attack processes, specifically the MITRE ATT&CK framework [51].

The Social Engineering Attack Framework [36] refines the aforementioned SEC and divides social engineering attacks into six phases: attack formulation (newly added), information gathering (replacing "research" in SEC), preparation (newly added), developing relationship (replacing "developing rapport and trust" in SEC), exploiting relationship (replacing "exploiting trust" in SEC), and debrief (replacing "utilizing information" in SEC). However, this framework does not explore the psychological constructs that make social engineering attacks successful.

The Attack Cycle (AC) [48] follows an approach which is similar to the aforementioned SEC. It divides a social engineering attack into four phases: information gathering, establishing relations and rapport, exploitation, and execution. Although AC is more detailed than SEC, it neither describes any attack-victim interactions nor relates psychological principles to social engineering attacks.

The Cycle of Deception framework [38], which is based on criminal manipulations (i.e., grooming), divides social engineering attacks into five phases: goal and plan, map and bond, execution, recruiting and cloaking, and evolving/regressing. However, it does not describe how to apply each phase in practice. For example, it is unclear how to execute the recruiting and cloaking phase, which requires a continuous relationship with the victim, but this relationship is not always present in social engineering attacks.

Putting the present study into a broader context, it is important to realize that understanding, characterizing, and incorporating CSE attacks is integral to the emerging Science of Cyber Security since CSE attacks are integral to most, if not all, cyber attacks. For example, the Cybersecurity Dynamics framework aims to explicitly model human factors from a holistic perspective [63–65,70]. Moreover, the specific family of Cybersecurity Dynamics models known as preventive and reactive defense dynamics models [17,27–29,61,62,67–69,71] have explicitly modelled *pull-based* cyber attacks, which include CSE attacks (e.g., phishing and drive-by download).

Paper Outline. The remainder of this paper is organized as follows. Section 2 presents the CSE Kill Chain framework. Section 3 describes a case study on applying the CSE Kill Chain framework to analyze a real-world CSE attack. Section 4 discusses the limitations of the present study. Section 5 concludes the paper with open problems for future research.

2   The Cyber Social Engineering (CSE) Kill Chain

The premise of the CSE Kill Chain framework is human psychology. From a psychological perspective, a successful CSE attack is when the attacker's external sensory input, combined with the victim's internal cognitive processes, leads the victim to behave in the way desired by the attacker (e.g., clicking a link in a malicious email). In what follows, we start with a discussion on the cognitive and psychological foundation of the CSE Kill Chain framework, including the following psychological constructs: information processing, trust, framing, persuasion, deception, risk acceptance, and attention. These constructs collectively lead to the desired behavior.

2.1   Cognitive and Psychological Foundation of CSE Kill Chain

The success of a CSE attack depends on the attacker's ability to influence a victim individual's response. This is because, in order for an attacker to accomplish this goal, the attacker must influence the victim's internal cognitive processes by manipulating the elements in the attack (e.g., tailored message in spearphishing). The cognitive processes pertinent to CSE attacks are the ones that are involved in human information processing, which is naturally affected by psychological constructs such as trust, attention, and risk. Table 1 summarizes the relationships between the constructs that are discussed in the present subsection and the techniques that are described later in Sect. 2.2. The relationships are elaborated below.

Table 1. Mapping between psychological constructs and CSE attack techniques

Psychological Constructs	CSE Kill Chain Technique	
Trust	Trusted Relationship (CSE-1201)	Affection Trust (CSE-T1204)
Framing	Personalization (CSE-T1110)	Contextualization (CSE-T1101)
Persuasion	Persuasion (CSE-T1108)	Foot-in-the-Door (FITD) (CSE-T1205)
Deception	Impersonation (CSE-T1102)	Visual Deception (CSE-T1103)
	Website or App. Spoofing (CSE-T1104)	URL Spoofing (CSE-T1105)
	Rev. Social Engineering (CSE-T1202)	Pretexting (CSE-T1203)
	Scamming Techniques (CSE-T1207)	
Risk Acceptance	Incentives & Motivators (CSE-T1109)	Quid-Pro-Quo (CSE-T1206)
Attention	Urgency Cues (CSE-T1106)	Attention Grabber (CSE-T1107)

Human information processing combines internal cognitive processes with external stimuli and information. The output of this process is reflected by an individual's response to the external input. Some researchers believe that there is a dual-processing system involving intuitive (heuristic) and analytic thinking [23]. Intuitive thinking is automatic and fast as it is based on general rules and recognizable patterns; analytical thinking is often slow because it is effortful and involves deliberations and deep analyses [23]. Several models attempt to explain the interactions between these two systems [7,41,42]. We leverage the three-stage dual-processing model described in [41] as it provides the insights relevant to the present study, supported by observations of several social engineering experiments. Specifically, this model states that conflict monitoring mediates the switching from intuitive to analytic processing, where a conflict is a deviation from the expected rules or known patterns. Once the analytical processing is engaged, there are two possible outcomes: the individual can generate a different response to resolve the conflict (i.e., decouple) or justify (i.e., rationalize) the initial response to resolve the conflict. Consequently, a failed social engineering attack is when message inconsistencies are detected, triggering suspicion [14, 53,58]. A successful social engineering attack is when conflict is not detected, or when conflict is detected, the individual still rationalizes their decision to comply. The later case helps explain why individuals can knowingly fall victims to phishing scams [26]. Using the preceding model as a point of departure, we can dissect the elements of a successful social engineering attack into two scenarios, which will guide us in designing the CSE Kill Chain framework.

In the first scenario (i.e., conflict not detected), the attacker avoids raising conflict by projecting trust, which is the belief that the other party is acting in good faith. Trust counters suspicion in both the real world [11,24] and social engineering [35]. For example, a social engineering message that projects trust is indistinguishable from a benign message and thus encourages the recipient to comply. The psychological constructs relevant to our research that encourage compliance are framing, persuasion and deception. The effect of framing and persuasion on compliance has been the subject of extensive research in consumer psychology, and marketing [10,23,42]. The effect of deception on compliance has been studied in research on the psychology of consumer scams [25,26,50]. Our previous studies [30,34,35] show that these psychological constructs are relevant to cyber social engineering attacks. At a high level, framing is a technique that can be used to increase the appeal of a social engineering message by manipulating its interpretation to evoke a particular emotion [23]; framing can be used in social engineering through personalization and contextualization. Persuasion is the use of arguments to encourage a specific behavior [10]; the use of persuasion techniques (e.g., foot-in-the-door) in CSE attacks is discussed in [35]. Deception is the use of arguments to encourage a false belief [5]. Deception techniques are widely used in CSE attacks, and may involve using visual elements associated with a brand, mirroring the "look-and-feel" of legitimate websites or applications, mimicking legitimate website addresses, or encouraging communication with the attacker [34].

In the second scenario (i.e., rationalization), we observe that social engineering attack can succeed because the individual justifies their initial response and accepts the risk of the action. Risk acceptance is a process through which an individual tolerates the prospect of a potential loss. Rationalization may lead an individual to believe that the perceived reward of complying with the request outweighs the perceived potential loss [19,26,30]. Rewards commonly used in CSE attacks are monetary rewards in return of a favor, free goods, or the opportunity to perform a good deed.

An attacker can manipulate attention in both scenarios to make the message noticeable. Attention is a key component of human information processing as it moderates the prioritizing of information [57]. Attention is directed to the most salient information. To increase CSE message saliency, an attacker can use emotional triggers like urgency cues or graphical and auditory elements to redirect attention, such as attention grabber.

2.2 Framework Overview

Figure 1 presents a high level view of the framework, which is based on the CSE attacks lifecycle of four phases: pre-stage; resource development; execution; and exploitation. The lifecycle is inspired by the Lockheed Martin Cyber Kill Chain [21], where each phase builds on the success of the previous one. Inspired by the MITRE ATT&CK framework [51], each phase is decomposed into *tactics* and *techniques*, where a *tactic* defines the short-term objective of an attack and a *technique* is the activities that support a tactic. Table 2 decomposes each phase into tactics and techniques. The phases and their associated tactics and techniques are elaborated below.

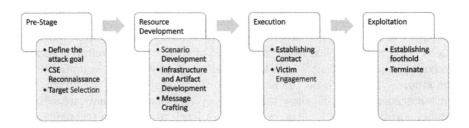

Fig. 1. The four phases and their associated tactics of the CSE Kill Chain framework.

2.3 The Pre-Stage Phase

In this phase, the attacker identifies opportunities to increase their success. This phase consist of three tactics: *Define the Attack Goal, CSE Reconnaissance,* and *Target Selection.*

Table 2. CSE kill chain matrix (inspired by the MITRE ATT&CK matrix). Note that ATT&CK techniques (e.g., T1957) may be leveraged to instantiate some CSE techniques (e.g., CSE-T1003) as discussed in the text.

PHASE	Pre-Stage	Resource Development				Execution			Exploitation	
TACTIC	Define the goal (CSE-TA01)	CSE Reconnaissance (CSE-TA02)	Target Selection (CSE-TA03)	Scenario Development (CSE-TA04)	Infrastructure and Artifact Development (CSE-TA05)	Message Crafting (CSE-TA06)	Initial Contact (CSE-TA07)	Victim Engagement (CSE-TA08)	Establish Foothold (CSE-TA09)	Terminate (CSE-TA10)
TECHNIQUES	Steal Proprietary Information	Passive Surveillance (CSE-T1001)	Analyze Vulnerabilities (CSE-T1004)	Contextualize. (CSE-T1101)	Compromise Infrastructure (T1584)	Urgency Cues (CSE-T1106)	Replication through Removable Media (T1091)	Pretexting (CSE-T1203)	Command and Scripting Interpreter (T1059)	Funds Transfer (CSE-T1301)
	Financial Fraud	Dumpster Diving (CSE-T1002)	Identify Available Resources (CSE-T1005)	Impersonation (CSE-T1102)	Develop Capabilities (T1587)	Attention Grabber (CSE-T1107)	Phishing (T1566)	Affection Trust (CSE-T1204)	Exploitation for Client Execution (T1203)	Information Transfer (CSE-1302)
	Steal Personal Information	Open Source Recon. (CSE-T1003)	Identify Env. Limitations (CSE-T1006)		Obtain Capabilities (T1588)	Persuasion (CSE-T1108)	Drive-By Compromise (T1198)	FITD (CSE-T1205)	Native API (T1106)	
	Acquire Information		Determine Impact (CSE-T1007)		Stage Capabilities (T1608)	Incentives & Motivators (CSE-T1109)	Trusted Relationships (CSE-T1201)	Quid-Pro-Quo (CSE-T1206)	Scheduled Task/Job (T1053)	
	Gain Access to a Network		Select Attack Conduit (CSE-T1008)		Visual Deception (CSE-T1103)	Personalization (CSE-T1110)	Rev. Social Engineering (CSE-T1202)	Scamming Techniques (CSE-T1207)	Software Deployment Tools (T1072)	
			Determine Exploitability (Exposure) (CSE-T1009)		Website or Application Spoofing (CSE-T1104)				System Services (T1569)	
					URL Spoofing (CSE-T1105)				User execution (T1204)	

FITD = Foot-in-the-Door

The "Define the Attack Goal" Tactic (denoted by CSE-TA01). This tactic identifies the desired outcome of a CSE attack to maximize success. Possible CSE attack goals include: *steal proprietary information, financial fraud, steal personal information, acquire information,* and *gain access to a network,* which are self-explaining. Understanding attackers' goals can help design effective defense to prevent, detect, and attribute CSE attacks.

The "CSE Reconnaissance" Tactic (denoted by CSE-TA02). This tactics gathers information to identify vulnerabilities and opportunities to conceal a CSE attack by mimicking legitimate activities, interactions, expected behaviors and norms in the environment and/or exploiting the widely accepted biases and beliefs that are unique to the environment. This tactic can be supported by the following CSE techniques: (i) *Passive Surveillance* (denoted by CSE-T1001), which is the close monitoring of a targeted location to identify activity patterns, entry and exit points, and to assess security [16]; (ii) *Dumpster Diving* (denoted by CSE-T1002), which is the act of searching through the trash for useful information, such as corporate phone books, corporate letterheads, calendar of events, or system manuals [47]; and (iii) *Open-Source Reconnaissance* (denoted by CSE-T1003), which is the process of gathering information available online and in social media [39], and can be instantiated as the following MITRE ATT&CK techniques [51]: *"gather victim identity information"* (denoted by T1589 in [51]), *"gather victim organization information"* (denoted by T1591 in [51]), *"search closed sources"* (denoted by T1597 in [51]), *"search open technical database"* (denoted by T1593 in [51]), *"search open websites/domain"* (denoted by T1596 in [51]), and *"search victim-owned websites"* (denoted by T1594 in [51]).

The "Target Selection" Tactic (denoted by CSE-TA03). This tactic selects a target based on its exploitability and how much the exploitation contributes to achieving the attacker's goal. Factors that affect exploitability are environmental limitations, attacker's available resources, weakness exposure [4], and attack conduit. This tactic can be supported by the following CSE techniques: (i) *Analyze Vulnerabilities* (denoted by CSE-T1004); (ii) *Identify Available Resources* (denoted by CSE-T1005); (iii) *Identify Environmental Limitations* (denoted by CSE-T1006); (iv) *Determine Impact* (denoted by CSE-T1007); (v) *Select Attack Conduit* (denoted by CSE-T1008); and (vi) *Determine Exploitability* (denoted by CSE-T1009).

2.4   The Resource Development Phase

In this phase, the attacker crafts the resources that are necessary to launch a CSE attack. This phase has three tactics: *Scenario Development, Infrastructure and Artifact Development,* and *Message Crafting.*

The "Scenario Development" Tactic (denoted by CSE-TA04). This tactic develops a scenario to provide a credible reason for contacting the victim. A scenario consists of two parts: backstory and persona. A backstory sets the stage for the attacker to approach the victim. A persona is a fake identity that aligns with the backstory and adds credibility. A persona can also increase the victim's cooperation. This tactic is supported by the following techniques: *contextualization* (denoted by CSE-T1101), which incorporation of details in the backstory to project the appearance of belonging to a group [35]; and *impersonation* (denoted by CSE-T1102), which creates a persona to increase cooperation by leveraging societal norms and expectations [2,15,16,46].

The "Infrastructure and Artifacts Development" Tactic (denoted by CSE-TA05). This tactic creates the artifacts and infrastructure that make a scenario believable [56]. Artifacts serve as evidence of the credibility of a CSE message and increase a victim's trust perception of the CSE message. For artifact hosting, an attacker can build the infrastructure or use a compromised third-party infrastructure. This tactic is supported by the following CSE techniques: (i) *Compromise Infrastructure* (T1584, inherited from the ATT&CK framework [51]), which entails the process of gaining control of a third-party infrastructure to reuse it in a cyber attack; (ii) *Develop Capabilities* (T1587, inherited from ATT&CK [51]), which involves the building of capabilities by the attacker; (iii) *Obtain Capabilities* (T1588, inherited from ATT&CK [51]), which involves the purchase or stealing of capabilities by the attacker; (iv) *stage capabilities* (T1608, inherited from ATT&CK [51]), which involves the action of preposition capabilities for an attack; (v) *Visual Deception* (denoted by CSE-T1103), which is the manipulation of known artifacts to project credibility, such as high-quality artifacts (e.g., logos, images, videos, or name spoofing [12]) and proper grammar, implicit third-party endorsement (SSL padlocks, use of HTTPS, antifraud statements, corporate protection), and content presentation [52]; (vi) *Website or Application Spoofing* (denoted by CSE-T1104), which is the mimicking of a legitimate website or application; and (vii) *URL Spoofing* (denoted by CSE-T1105), which is the replacement of visually similar characters in a legitimate URL to create a malicious URL (e.g., replacing "w" with "vv" in a URL [12]).

The "Message Crafting" Tactic (denoted by CSE-TA06). This tactic creates a CSE message to persuade a victim, by lowering the victim's risk perception, to perform the action that is desired by the CSE attacker [26]. This tactic is supported by the following techniques, which may be used individually or in combination. (i) *Urgency Cues* (denoted by CSE-T1106), which encourages an automatic response from a victim based a perceived sense of urgency [54]; (ii) *Attention Grabbers* [37] (denoted by CSE-T1107), which is the use of visual and auditory elements to force an individual to switch their attention to a message [30]; (iii) *Persuasion* [10] (denoted by CSE-T1108), which involves the use of persuasion principles in the message to encourage a behavior like clicking a link or providing personal information [35]; (iv) *Incentives and Motivators* (denoted by

CSE-T1109) [46], which are the rewards that encourage a desired victim behavior [15,49]; and (v) *Personalization* (denoted by CSE-T1110), which involves implying a connection with the victim, by expressing personal knowledge of a victim, such as addressing a victim by name, using appropriate pronouns, and aligning a message with the recipient characteristics (e.g., interests, biases and beliefs, and personal information) [20,35,55].

2.5   The Execution Phase

This phase convinces a victim to comply with the attacker's request and has two tactics: *Initial Contact* and *Victim Engagement*.

The "Initial Contact" Tactic (denoted by CSE-TA07). This tactic initiates a contact with a victim. This tactic is supported by the following techniques: (i) *Replication through Removable Media* (T1091, inherited from ATT&CK [51]), which is the use of removable media to copy malware into a system; (ii) *Phishing* (T1566, inherited from ATT&CK [51]), which involves the use of emails to deliver malicious content to gain access to a system; (iii) *Drive-By Compromise* (T1198, inherited from ATT&CK [51]), which is about gaining access to a system by alluring a victim to visit a compromised website; (iv) *Trusted Relationship* (denoted by CSE-T1201), which is adapted from the ATT&CK Trusted Relationship technique (T-1199 [51]) to social engineering attacks and involves leveraging relations or connections to other agents, or exploiting third parties (e.g., social media sites, dating sites, etc.) to increase perceived credibility [1]; and (v) *Reverse Social Engineering* (denoted by CSE T-1202), which triggers the victim to initiate a communication with the attacker.

The "Victim Engagement" Tactic (denoted by CSE-TA08). This tactic establishes continuous communications with the victim to increase compliance. This tactic is often employed when an attack involves a high-risk request (e.g., money wire transfer). This tactic is supported by the following techniques: (i) *Pretexting* (denoted by CSE-T1203), which is the use of pretenses to entice a victim into willingly disclosing information [18]; (ii) *Affection Trust* (denoted by CSE-T1204), which involves establishing an emotional connection through continuous communications to increase a victim's risk tolerance and compliance [31]; (iii) *Foot-in-the-Door* (denoted by CSE-T1205), which manipulates a victim to comply with a large request by making several smaller requests over time [13]; (iv) *Quid-Pro-Quo* (denoted by CSE-T1206), which promotes a victim's compliance by promising a future reward for the victim's help [19]; and (v) *Scamming* [49] (denoted by CSE-T1207), which is the use of deceptive elements to encourage a false belief [5].

2.6   The Exploitation Phase

This phase makes an attack that achieves its goal. It has two tactics: *Establishing a Foothold* and *Terminate*.

The "Establish Foothold" Tactic (denoted by CSE-TA09). This tactic leverages a victim's compliance with the attack's request to penetrate into a network. For example, clicking on a link could trigger the installation of a malicious software, which enables the attacker to gain access to a network or launch a ransomware attack [3]. This tactic can be supported by the following ATT&CK techniques: (i) *Command and Scripting Interpreter* (T1059, inherited from ATT&CK [51]), which is the use of commands, scripts or binaries to compromise a system; (ii) *Exploitation for Client Execution* (T1203, inherited from ATT&CK [51]), which is the exploitation of a vulnerability in the software installed in a system; (iii) *Native API* (T1106, inherited from ATT&CK [51]), which is the use of native Operating System programming interfaces to compromise a systems; (iv) *Scheduled Task/Job* (T1053, inherited from ATT&CK [51]), which is the use of the task scheduling functionality to compromise a system; (v) *Software Deployment Tools* (T1072, inherited from ATT&CK [51]), which is the use of a third-party enterprise applications to conduct lateral movement in a network; (vi) *System Services* (T1569, inherited from ATT&CK [51]), which is the abuse of system services to execute commands and programs; and (vii) *User Execution* (T1204, inherited from ATT&CK [51]), which is execution of an action by a victim to help the attacker gain access into a system.

The "Terminate" Tactic (denoted by CSE-TA10). Once the victim performs the desired action, the attack terminates. This tactic can be supported by the following techniques: (i) *Financial Transfer* (denoted by CSE-T1301), which may be conducted by an employee to transfer funds to a foreign bank account [22] or by an individual to transfer money to a romantic [45] or venture partner [19]; and (ii) *Information Transfer* (denoted by CSE-T1302), which involves the movement of information to an asset that is under the attacker's control.

3   Case Study

This section presents a case study to demonstrate how the CSE Kill Chain can be applied to analyze a real-world CSE attack described in [1]. This attack is a cyberspace variant of the recruiting scam in the physical world described in [50]. The attack involves the four phases of the CSE Kill Chain. The attack uses a social media platform to exploit the victims. To demonstrate the usefulness of the framework, we leverage the findings of the case study to generate an attack pattern that describes the implementation of each technique (Table 3). These two products synthesize details of a CSE attack to assist characterization.

3.1   The Pre-stage Phase of the Attack

The CSE attack in this case study mirrors the Recruitment Scam described in [50], meaning that the attacker just has to recreate the scam elements in the digital space. At this phase, the CSE attacker uses three tactics. (i) Corresponding to the "Define the Attack Goal" tactic (CSE-TA01), the attack attempts

Table 3. Illustration of generating attack patterns from the case study [1], where attack patterns can help identify distinct elements in an attack to define a signature for the attacker.

Tactic	Technique	Implementation
SE Recon. (CSE-TA02)	Open Source Recon.	Online research on potential targets and methods of exploitation
Target Selection (CSE-TA03)	Analyze Vul.	Features that allow a attacker to operate undetected
	Identify Available Resources	Platform recruiting tools, job seeker analysis tools, and job adverting tools
	Identify Env. Limitations	Violations of use of the platform services
	Determine Impact	Attract job seeker with financial means
Scenario Develop. (CSE-TA04)	Contextualiz.	Construction Company hiring project managers
	Impersonation	Hiring Manager Persona
Inf. & Artifact Development (CSE-TA05)	Visual Deception	High quality images and brand logos
	Website/App. Spoofing	Carbon copy website from legitimate construction company
Message Crafting (CSE-TA06)	Persuasion	o Authority: Hiring manager demands in-person interview o Social Compliance: Interview would determine if candidate is a good fit for their culture
	Incentives & Motivators	High paying salary
Initial Contact (CSE-TA07)	Rev. SE	Job seekers contact the attacker
	Trusted Relationships	Using LinkedIn, a site the job seekers trust, for job posting
Victim Engagement (CSE-TA08)	Pretexting	Invitation for an in-person interview used for request personal information and money
	FITD	Gradual increase of request: o 1st request: resume o 2nd request: personal information o 3rd request: money
	Scamming Tech.	Distraction: job seeker fails to notice inconsistent, e.g., paying for travel cost for an interview
Terminate (CSE-TA10)	Funds Transfer	Job seeker transfer money to attacker's bank account
	Information Transfer	Job seeker send copy of passport and identification

to steal a victim's personal information and money (i.e., financial fraud). (ii) As part of the "CSE Reconnaissance" tactic (CSE-TA02), the attacker identifies the social media platforms that would better support its goal by using technique CSE-T1003 (Open Source Reconnaissance) and, more specifically, the ATT&CK technique T1596 (Search Open Website/Domains). Since the attack is a digital version of the Recruitment Scam, the attacker would gather information on available employment sites, the users, the cost of corporate membership, and membership benefits. (iii) The "Target Selection" tactic (CSE-TA003) focuses on selecting an employment platform to wage the attack. The employment platform would (indirectly) recommend potential victims. This can be achieved by using the technique CSE-T1004 (Analyze Vulnerabilities), whereby the attacker identifies platform features that can benefit the attacker in evading detection. Furthermore, by using the technique CSE T-1005 (Identify Available Resources), the attacker evaluates the platform features to recommend victims and increase the visibility of the (fake) job posting. By using the technique CSE T-1006 (Identify Environmental Limitations), the attacker evaluates the employment platforms based on the conditions that violate the user agreement. As described in CSE-T1007 (Determine Impact), the attacker must attract individuals with financial means. The attacker may focus on white-collar professionals, especially project managers.

3.2   The Resource Development Phase of the Attack

From the previous phase, the attacker selects LinkedIn to connect with job seekers. At this phase, the CSE attacker uses three tactics. (i) As part of the "Scenario Development" tactic (CSE-TA04), the attacker uses the technique CSE-T1101 (Contextualization) to create a fictional company and job postings for project managers. The attacker also uses technique CSE-T1102 (Impersonation) to assume the persona of a Hiring Manager. (ii) In support of the "Infrastructure and Artifact Development" tactic (CSE-TA05), the attacker uses technique CSE-T1104 (Website or Application Spoofing) to create a copy of a legitimate company website and modify it to align with the scenario in question. The attacker also uses technique CSE-T1103 (Visual Deception) by displaying legitimate logos and professional graphics on the website to increase its credibility. Using technique T1608 (Stage Capability), the attacker activates the website in a web hosting platform. (iii) Corresponding to the "Message Crafting" tactic (CSE-TA06), the attacker uses techniques CSE-T1109 (Incentives) to offer a high salary range of $105K-$160K. By using CSE-T1108 (Persuasion Techniques) which exploits the principle of authority [10] or social compliance [49], the attacker demands an in-person interview for a candidate to demonstrate that the candidate is a proper fit to the chief project manager of a company. Summarizing the preceding discussion, we draw:

Insight 1. *Understanding how human perception is formed is key to detecting CSE attacks.*

3.3   The Execution Phase of the Attack

At this phase, a CSE attacker uses two tactics. (i) Corresponding to the "Initial Contact" tactic (CSE-TA07), the attacker uses technique CSE-T1202 (Reverse Social Engineering) by posting the job announcement on LinkedIn, which automatically advertises the position to suitable candidates. A victim contacts the attacker by applying for the job and providing their curriculum and personal information. Using LinkedIn also leverages technique CSE-T1201 (Trusted Rela-tionship). (ii) Corresponding to tactic CSE-TA08 (Victim Engagement), the attacker uses CSE technique CSE-T1203 (Pretexting) to request the victim's personal information (VISA/travel information, passport, identification, etc.) with the pretext of arranging for an in-person job interview. Using technique CSE-T1205 (FITD), the attacker obtains a victim's compliance by gradually increasing the size of the request (i.e., the attacker initially requests a victim's resume, then personal information, and finally, a money transfer). Using tech-nique CSE-T1207 (Scamming Technique), the attacker uses the prospect of a well-paying job as a distraction to prevent a victim from noticing the inconsisten-cies in their interaction. Examples of inconsistency include: providing personal information without an interview or job offer and covering travel costs upfront for a job interview. Summarizing the preceding discussion, we draw:

Insight 2. *Social media enables a CSE attacker to increase the credibility and trustworthiness of CSE attacks.*

3.4   The Exploitation Phase of the Attack

At this phase, and as described in the "Terminate" tactic (CSE-TA10), the attacker uses techniques CSE-T1302 (Information Transfer) and CSE-T1301 (Funds Transfer) to receive a victim's personal information and money trans-fer into a designated bank account. Once the funds are received, the attacker terminates communications with the victim.

4   Limitations

The present study has several limitations, which need to be overcome by future studies. First, because it focuses on attacks, the CSE Kill Chain does not accom-modate the victim attributes that contribute to the success of CSE attacks. For example, it does not capture victims' temporal psychological attributes (e.g., stress and workload), which can contribute to social engineering victimization by reducing victims' attention and vigilance. Second, the CSE Kill Chain does not account for the environment where the attacker-victim interaction occurs (e.g., workplace, home office), which can affect a victim's risk acceptance. For example, a user may be more willing to click on a link in a CSE message when receiving a message on a network which employs multiple defense layers. Third, more case studies are needed to evaluate the effectiveness of the CSE Kill Chain.

5   Conclusion

We have presented the CSE Kill Chain framework, which describes CSE attacks in four phases: pre-stage, resource development, execution, and exploitation. We established connections between the CSE Kill Chain and the MITRE ATT&CK framework, which does not consider CSE attacks. Therefore, it is hopeful that the

CSE Kill Chain can be adopted to accompany the MITRE ATT&CK framework to accommodate CSE attacks.

We hope this work will inspire many more studies on defending against CSE attacks. There are several outstanding open problems for future research. In addition to addressing the limitations of the present study as described above, we mention the following: How can we apply the CSE Kill Chain to make existing warning models (e.g., the Communication-Human Information Processing model [57]) more effective in communicating security threats to users? How can we apply the CSE Kill Chain to identify an attacker's psychological signature so as to enhance attack attributions? How can we leverage the CSE Kill Chain to characterize the relationship between suspicion and cognitive engagement so as to defend from CSE attacks? How can we transform the CSE Kill Chain framework into mathematical models for quantitative analysis purposes? This would require to defining pertinent cybersecurity metrics [8,9,32,40,66] and conducting quantitative studies to characterize CSE attacks [43,44,59,60].

Acknowledgement. We thank the anonymous reviewers for their comments that helped us in improving the paper. Approved for Public Release; Distribution Unlimited. Public Release Case Number 21–1635.The first author is also affiliated with The MITRE Corporation, which is provided for identification purposes only and is not intended to convey or imply MITRE's concurrence with, or support for, the positions, opinions, or viewpoints expressed by the authors.©2022 The MITRE Corporation. ALL RIGHTS RESERVED. This work was supported in part by ARO Grant #W911NF-17-1-0566, NSF Grants #2122631 and #2115134, and Colorado State Bill 18–086.

References

1. Allodi, L., Chotza, T., Panina, E., Zannone, N.: The need for new antiphishing measures against spear-phishing attacks. IEEE Secur. Priv. **18**(2), 23–34 (2019)
2. Anderson, R.: Security Engineering: a Guide to Building Dependable Distributed Systems. John Wiley & Sons (2020)
3. Applegate, S.D.: Social engineering: hacking the wetware! Inf. Secur. J. a Glob. Perspect. **18**(1), 40–46 (2009)
4. Barrett, N.: Penetration testing and social engineering-hacking the weakest link. Inf. Secur. Tech. Rep. **4**(8), 56–64 (2003)
5. Buller, D.B., Burgoon, J.K.: Interpersonal deception theory. Commun. Theory **6**(3), 203–242 (1996)
6. Center, V.T.R.A.: 2021 data breach investigation report. Tech. rep, Verizon Threat Research Advisory Center (2021)
7. Chen, S., Chaiken, S.: The heuristic-systematic model in its broader context. In: Dual-process theories in social psychology, pp. 73–96. The Guilford Press (1999)
8. Cho, J., Hurley, P., Xu, S.: Metrics and measurement of trustworthy systems. In: Proceedings IEEE MILCOM (2016)
9. Cho, J., Xu, S., Hurley, P., Mackay, M., Benjamin, T., Beaumont, M.: STRAM: measuring the trustworthiness of computer-based systems. ACM Comput. Surv. **51**(6), 1–47 (2019)

10. Cialdini, R.B., Cialdini, R.B.: Influence: the psychology of persuasion, vol. 55. Collins New York (2007)
11. Deutsch, M.: Trust and suspicion. J. Conflict Resolut. **2**(4), 265–279 (1958)
12. Dhamija, R., Tygar, J.D., Hearst, M.: Why phishing works. In: Proceedings of the SIGCHI conference on Human Factors in computing systems, pp. 581–590 (2006)
13. Freedman, J.L., Fraser, S.C.: Compliance without pressure: the foot-in-the-door technique. J. Pers. Soc. Psychol. **4**(2), 195 (1966)
14. Gavett, B.E., Zhao, R., John, S.E., Bussell, C.A., Roberts, J.R., Yue, C.: Phishing suspiciousness in older and younger adults: the role of executive functioning. PLoS ONE **12**(2), e0171620 (2017)
15. Gragg, D.: A multi-level defense against social engineering. SANS Reading Room **13**, 1–21 (2003)
16. Greenlees, C.: An intruder's tale - [it security]. Engineering & Technology, pp. 55–57 (2009)
17. Han, Y., Lu, W., Xu, S.: Preventive and reactive cyber defense dynamics with ergodic time-dependent parameters is globally attractive. IEEE TNSE **8**(3), 2517–2532 (2021)
18. Hechler Baer, M.: Corporate policing and corporate governance: what can we learn from Hewlett-Packard's pretexting scandal. Univ. Cincinnati Law Rev. **77**, 523 (2008)
19. Herley, C.: Why do Nigerian scammers say they are from Nigeria? In: WEIS (2012)
20. Hirsh, J.B., Kang, S.K., Bodenhausen, G.V.: Personalized persuasion: tailoring persuasive appeals to recipients' personality traits. Psychol. Sci. **23**(6), 578–581 (2012)
21. Hutchins, E.M., Cloppert, M.J., Amin, R.M., et al.: Intelligence-driven computer network defense informed by analysis of adversary campaigns and intrusion kill chains. Leading Issues Inf. Warfare Secur. Res. **1**(1), 80 (2011)
22. Junger, M., Wang, V., Schlömer, M.: Fraud against businesses both online and offline: crime scripts, business characteristics, efforts, and benefits. Crime Sci. **9**(1), 1–15 (2020). https://doi.org/10.1186/s40163-020-00119-4
23. Kahneman, D.: Thinking, fast and slow. Macmillan (2011)
24. Kirmani, A., Zhu, R.: Vigilant against manipulation: the effect of regulatory focus on the use of persuasion knowledge. J. Mark. Res. **44**(4), 688–701 (2007)
25. Langenderfer, J., Shimp, T.A.: Consumer vulnerability to scams, swindles, and fraud: a new theory of visceral influences on persuasion. Psychol. Marketin. **18**(7), 763–783 (2001)
26. Lea, S.E., Fischer, P., Evans, K.M.: The Psychology of Scams: Provoking and Committing Errors of Judgement. Tech. rep, Office of Fair Trading (2009)
27. Li, X., Parker, P., Xu, S.: Towards quantifying the (in) security of networked systems. In: 21st IEEE International Conference on Advanced Information Networking and Applications (AINA2007), pp. 420–427 (2007)
28. Li, X., Parker, P., Xu, S.: A stochastic model for quantitative security analyses of networked systems. IEEE TDSC **8**(1), 28–43 (2011)
29. Lin, Z., Lu, W., Xu, S.: Unified preventive and reactive cyber defense dynamics is still globally convergent. IEEE/ACM ToN **27**(3), 1098–1111 (2019)
30. Longtchi, T., Rodriguez, R.M., Al-Shawaf, L., Atyabi, A., Xu, S.: Internet-based social engineering attacks, defenses and psychology: a survey. arXiv preprint arXiv:2203.08302 (2022)
31. McAllister, D.J.: Affect-and cognition-based trust as foundations for interpersonal cooperation in organizations. Acad. Manag. J. **38**(1), 24–59 (1995)

32. Mireles, J., Ficke, E., Cho, J., Hurley, P., Xu, S.: Metrics towards measuring cyber agility. IEEE T-IFS **14**(12), 3217–3232 (2019)
33. Mitnick, K.D., Simon, W.L.: The art of deception: controlling the human element of security. John Wiley & Sons (2003)
34. Montañez, R., Atyabi, A., Xu, S.: Social engineering attacks and defenses in the physical world vs. cyberspace: a contrast study. In: Cybersecurity and Cognitive Science, pp. 3–41. Elsevier (2022)
35. Montañez, R., Golob, E., Xu, S.: Human cognition through the lens of social engineering cyberattacks. Front. Psychol. **11**, 1755 (2020)
36. Mouton, F., Malan, M.M., Leenen, L., Venter, H.S.: Social engineering attack framework. In: 2014 Information Security for South Africa, pp. 1–9. IEEE (2014)
37. Nelms, T., Perdisci, R., Antonakakis, M., Ahamad, M.: Towards measuring and mitigating social engineering software download attacks. In: 25th {USENIX} Security Symposium ({USENIX} Security 16), pp. 773–789 (2016)
38. Nohlberg, M., Kowalski, S.: The cycle of deception - a model of social engineering attacks, defenses and victims. In: HAISA (2008)
39. Pastor-Galindo, J., Nespoli, P., Gómez Mármol, F., Martínez Pérez, G.: The not yet exploited goldmine of OSINT: opportunities, open challenges and future trends. IEEE Access **8**, 10282–10304 (2020). https://doi.org/10.1109/ACCESS.2020.2965257
40. Pendleton, M., Garcia-Lebron, R., Cho, J., Xu, S.: A survey on systems security metrics. ACM Comput. Surv. **49**(4), 1–35 (2016)
41. Pennycook, G., Fugelsang, J.A., Koehler, D.J.: What makes us think? a three-stage dual-process model of analytic engagement. Cogn. Psychol. **80**, 34–72 (2015)
42. Petty, R.E., Cacioppo, J.T.: The elaboration likelihood model of persuasion. In: Communication and Persuasion: Central and Peripheral Routes to Attitude Change, pp. 1–24. Springer, New York (1986). https://doi.org/10.1007/978-1-4612-4964-1_1
43. Pritom, M., Schweitzer, K., Bateman, R., Xu, M., Xu, S.: Characterizing the landscape of COVID-19 themed cyberattacks and defenses. In: IEEE ISI'2020 (2020)
44. Pritom, M., Schweitzer, K., Bateman, R., Xu, M., Xu, S.: Data-driven characterization and detection of COVID-19 themed malicious websites. In: IEEE ISI'2020 (2020)
45. Rege, A.: What's love got to do with it? exploring online dating scams and identity fraud. Int. J. Cyber Criminol. **3**(2) (2009)
46. Riegelsberger, J., Sasse, M.A., McCarthy, J.D.: The researcher's dilemma: evaluating trust in computer-mediated communication. Int. J. Hum.-Comput. Stud. **58**(6) (2003)
47. Robinson, S.W.: Corporate espionage 101. https://www.giac.org/paper/gsec/1587/corporate-espionage-101/102941 (2003). Accessed 19 Jun 2021
48. Social Engineer, L.: The attack cycle. https://www.social-engineer.org/framework/attack-vectors/attack-cycle/. Accessed 22 June 2021
49. Stajano, F., Wilson, P.: Understanding Scam Victims: Seven Principles For Systems Security. University of Cambridge, Computer Laboratory, Tech. rep. (2009)
50. Stajano, F., Wilson, P.: Understanding scam victims: seven principles for systems security. Commun. ACM **54**(3), 70–75 (2011)
51. Strom, B.E., Applebaum, A., Miller, D.P., Nickels, K.C., Pennington, A.G., Thomas, C.B.: Mitre att&ck design and philosophy. Tech. rep., MITRE (2020). Accessed 25 June 2021
52. Van Der Heijden, A., Allodi, L.: Cognitive triaging of phishing attacks. In: 28th {USENIX} Security Symposium ({USENIX} Security 19), pp. 1309–1326 (2019)

53. Vishwanath, A., Harrison, B., Ng, Y.J.: Suspicion, cognition, and automaticity model of phishing susceptibility. Commun. Res. **45**(8), 1146–1166 (2018)
54. Vishwanath, A., Herath, T., Chen, R., Wang, J., Rao, H.R.: Why do people get phished? testing individual differences in phishing vulnerability within an integrated, information processing model. Decis. Support Syst. **51**(3), 576–586 (2011)
55. Wang, J., Chen, R., Herath, T., Rao, H.R.: An exploration of the design features of phishing attacks. Inf. Assur. Secur. Priv. Serv. **4**(29), 178–199 (2009)
56. Wathen, C.N., Burkell, J.: Believe it or not: factors influencing credibility on the web. J. Am. Soc. Inform. Sci. Technol. **53**(2), 134–144 (2002)
57. Wogalter, M.S.: Communication-human information processing (c-hip) model. In: Forensic Human Factors and Ergonomics, pp. 33–49. CRC Press (2018)
58. Wright, R.T., Marett, K.: The influence of experiential and dispositional factors in phishing: An empirical investigation of the deceived. J. Manag. Inf. Syst. **27**(1) (2010)
59. Xu, L., Zhan, Z., Xu, S., Ye, K.: An evasion and counter-evasion study in malicious websites detection. In: IEEE CNS, pp. 265–273 (2014)
60. Xu, L., Zhan, Z., Xu, S., Ye, K.: Cross-layer detection of malicious websites. In: Third ACM Conference on Data and Application Security and Privacy (CODASPY'13), pp. 141–152 (2013)
61. Xu, M., Da, G., Xu, S.: Cyber epidemic models with dependences. Internet Math. **11**(1), 62–92 (2015)
62. Xu, M., Xu, S.: An extended stochastic model for quantitative security analysis of networked systems. Internet Math. **8**(3), 288–320 (2012)
63. Xu, S.: Emergent behavior in cybersecurity. In: HotSoS 2014: Proceedings of the 2014 Symposium and Bootcamp on the Science of Security, pp. 1–2 (2014)
64. Xu, S.: Cybersecurity dynamics: a foundation for the science of cybersecurity. In: In: Wang, C., Lu, Z. (eds.) Proactive and Dynamic Network Defense. AIS, vol 74. Springer, Cham (2019). https://doi.org/10.1007/978-3-030-10597-6_1
65. Xu, S.: The cybersecurity dynamics way of thinking and landscape (invited paper). In: ACM Workshop on Moving Target Defense (2020)
66. Xu, S.: SARR: a cybersecurity metrics and quantification framework (keynote). In: Proceedings of the 2021 International Conference on Science of Cyber Security (2021)
67. Xu, S., Lu, W., Xu, L.: Push- and pull-based epidemic spreading in networks: thresholds and deeper insights. ACM Trans. Auton. Adapt. Syst. **7**(3), 1–26 (2012)
68. Xu, S., Lu, W., Xu, L., Zhan, Z.: Adaptive epidemic dynamics in networks: thresholds and control. ACM Trans. Auton. Adapt. Syst. **8**(4), 1–19 (2014)
69. Xu, S., Lu, W., Zhan, Z.: A stochastic model of multivirus dynamics. IEEE Trans. Dependable Secure Comput. **9**(1), 30–45 (2012)
70. Xu, S.: Cybersecurity dynamics. In: Proc. HotSoS'14, pp. 1–2 (2014)
71. Zheng, R., Lu, W., Xu, S.: Preventive and reactive cyber defense dynamics is globally stable. IEEE TNSE **5**(2), 156–170 (2018)

Towards Practical Personalized Security Nudge Schemes: Investigating the Moderation Effects of Behavioral Features on Nudge Effects

Leilei Qu[ID], Ruojin Xiao, and Wenchang Shi[✉]

Renmin University of China, Beijing, People's Republic of China
{llqu,ruojinx,wenchang}@ruc.edu.cn

Abstract. The concept of "personalized security nudges" promises to solve the contradictions between people's heterogeneity and one-size-fits-all security nudges, whereas the psychological traits needed for personalization are not easy to obtain. To address the problem, we propose to leverage users' behaviors logged by information systems, from which multiple behavioral features are extracted. A between-subjects lab experiment was conducted, during which participants' behavioral features and responses to three famous security nudges (the so-called nudge effects) were logged. To test the feasibility of our proposal, we analyzed the relationships between the behavioral features with the nudge effects and discovered the significant moderation effects expected for all the three security nudges involved. The results indicate the feasibility of personalizing security nudges according to user behaviors, liberating the personalized security nudge schemes from the dependence on psychological scales.

Keywords: Nudge · Personalization · Behavioral features

1 Introduction

As cybersecurity becomes increasingly important [43], individuals are constantly faced with tangled cybersecurity decision-making scenarios, such as the choices of passwords and public free WiFi [50]. However, partially due to the incomplete and asymmetric information, most individuals are unable to make an informed choice, which leads to the prevalent "insecure" behaviors among the whole user base [3].

Thus, it is widely recognized that the designers and developers of information systems should provide users with more cues to aid their decision-making process when confronting cybersecurity problems [2,3]. Typical examples include a password meter that tells users how weak their passwords are [42] and the *Telepathwords* proposed by Komanduri et al. [22] that shows how predictable a

© The Author(s), under exclusive license to Springer Nature Switzerland AG 2022
C. Su et al. (Eds.): SciSec 2022, LNCS 13580, pp. 505–521, 2022.
https://doi.org/10.1007/978-3-031-17551-0_33

password is, the former of which is one of the most common password nudges in our daily life.

Nudge, a notion proposed by Thaler and Sunstein [41], implies altering individuals' behavioral intentions by libertarian paternalism. In other words, typical nudge schemes do not force people to choose a specific option or another; instead, they focus on the design of policies and systems to make some specific options more "attractive", effectively guiding people towards them [40]. Recently, due to the numerous effective nudges designed and implemented in the domain of HCI, i.e., the so-called "digital nudge" [8], an increasing number of cybersecurity researchers have turned to nudges to improve users' security awareness and the adoption rates of security policies [10,12,27]. Typical examples include a time delay [45], the information of the potential audiences of a social media post [45], the phraseology of how the consequences of risky behaviors are described [4,29], and the number of times users' location information has been shared [5]. All the clues can nudge users towards more secure and privacy-preserve decisions. Thus, the application of nudge to cybersecurity is promising since slight changes in the choice architecture can lead to noticeable behavioral changes.

However, people are different, and everyone makes decisions differently. A risk-aversion and cautious person may find bungee scary, but it can be a pleasure for a risk-seeking person. Thus, a nudge effective for a group of people may not show the same impact on another group [11]. The number of shared locations can be a useful decision-making clue for people who are rational and sensitive to numbers. However, the people who do not care about this kind of information are not rare. Assuming users' heterogeneity and their responses to nudges, we are supposed to design various nudges targeted at different groups of people instead of the current one-size-fits-all approach with the "average users" in mind [11,24, 26,36].

The General Decision-Making Styles (GDMS) model divides individuals' manners of decision-making into five types: Rational, Avoidant, Dependent, Intuitive, and Spontaneous, each type with its unique characteristics [37]. The significant moderation effects of individuals' GDMS on nudge effects discovered by Peer et al. [26] indicate that individuals' responses to various cybersecurity nudges are dependent on their decision-making styles. Take the password meter as an example. According to Peer et al. [26], the password meter merely benefits people who always turn to others for advice when making decisions (typical "dependent" decision-makers); others, by contrast, will not respond positively.

To address the challenges posed by human heterogeneity, several researchers have been devoted to the paradigm of "personalized security nudges" [11,17,24, 26,36], and most of them focus on the GDMS mentioned above. For example, Malkin et al. [24] customized browser warnings according to the different mindsets of people with different GDMS. As a result, they found that the Statistics nudge characteristic of detailed data could effectively nudge rational decision-makers towards more "secure" choices. Besides, based on the moderation effects of the GDMS on nudge effects, Peer et al. [26] designed a personalization scheme by using Monte-Carlo simulation, selecting the "best" nudge type for each decision-making style. The scheme was considered a success since it significantly improved users' average password strength in a field experiment.

Despite the progress made, the GDMS-based approach has an obvious flaw, over-reliance on psychological scales. Specifically, in a typical experimental setting, it is common to ask the participants to fill out the psychological scales to measure their GDMS. It is unusual, however, that any psychological scales show up when users are busy with their daily affairs for a typical information system.

To solve the problem, we propose to leverage users' system-use behaviors, which are actually the actions performed by users on information systems. Compared to the previously used GDMS, the system-use behaviors and the corresponding log files are more available for system designers and administrators. Furthermore, with the objective data collected by systems, we can avoid, wherever possible, the potential biases caused by the self-reported GDMS, typical subjective data [34].

The abundant research on utilizing user behaviors to build user profiles and recommend personalized content and advertisements [23, 39] illustrate the potential of our proposal. However, hardly any compelling evidence can demonstrate the feasibility of applying the approach to the domain of security nudge. Thus, to explore the feasibility, we analyze the data collected from a between-subjects lab experiment ($N = 312$) to investigate the relationships between the effectiveness of various password nudges and users' behaviors recorded by system logs. Specifically, we extract behavioral features from the log files and investigate the moderation effects of the behavioral features on nudge effects, i.e., how the behavioral features affect the effectiveness of the nudges on password strength. The results show that the proposed behavioral features, as more practical alternatives than the GDMS, moderate the effectiveness of security nudges on password strength. We contribute to the community by indicating the feasibility of establishing a behavior-based personalization scheme for security nudges.

2   Related Work

Our research is built on previous work on personalization, especially personalized security nudge schemes.

2.1   Personalization

One of the earliest fields where personalization has been widely applied is online recommendation systems. Behavioral targeting is a technique that delivers advertisements to targeted users based on the prediction of their preferences, which are built upon their browsing behaviors [47]. It is used to increase the CTR (Click-Through Rates) of the advertisements. Social media platforms also adopt personalization in their online recommendations [38]. They infer users' cognitive states based on their profile, interests, history, and current actions, which are further used to match the most relevant content and recommend it to them.

Due to the increasing attention to user experiences, personalization has been widely used in many sub-areas of HCI, one of which is gamification. The concept "gamification" refers to applying game design elements to non-game contexts in order to attract users and maintain their attention [18]. To maximize the impact of gamification, several researchers are now advocating the use of personalization in gamification. For example, Jia et al. [18] investigated how people with different personality traits perceived the influence of different motivational affordances in a 248-participant online survey. They advocated personality-targeted gamification and provided valuable guidelines. Despite the same focus on gamification, Orji et al. [25] tried another direction to explore the correlations between users' personality traits and their perceived persuasiveness of various persuasive strategies. Their findings and design suggestions for personality-driven persuasive gamification have further stressed the importance of personalization.

Apart from recommendation systems and gamification, personalization has appeared in other areas, including a cognition-centered personalization framework for cultural-heritage content [31] and personalized tools for privacy configuration [44,48]. The tool *VeilMe* proposed by Wang et al. [44] is an interactive visualization tool that helps users decide whether and how to share the data about their personality traits derived from social media data, precisely the privacy configuration. Notably, it initializes and personalizes new users' privacy configuration leveraging their personality traits.

2.2 Personalized Security Nudge Scheme

Table 1. A summary of the related work on personalized security nudge

Author	Scheme
Malkin et al. [24]	Customize security warnings based on the mindsets of people with various GDMS characteristics
Qu et al. [30]	Customize security warnings based on the mindsets of people with various CFC characteristics
Peer et al. [26]	Allocate various existing security nudges to individuals who are most likely to benefit (with corresponding GDMS characteristics)
Schöning et al. [36]	Allocate various privacy notices to individuals who are most likely to benefit (with corresponding cognitive styles)

The field of cybersecurity has begun to adopt personalization in recent years [11], especially personalized security nudges. We present a summary of the existing schemes of personalized security nudges in Table 1.

By designing six customized HTTPS warnings according to the various mindsets of people with different GDMS characteristics, Malkin et al. [24] discovered that only a data-centric nudge worked as expected. Specifically, its effects on altering security behaviors were positively correlated with the possibility of being a rational decision-maker. From a similar perspective, Qu et al. [30] designed two security nudges targeted at the mindsets of people with different CFC (Consideration for Future Consequences) [19] and tested their effects on changing security attitudes via an online survey. They found significant correlations between individuals' CFC and the effectiveness of one of the two nudges, but their results were limited to changes in security attitudes instead of essential behavioral changes [30]. Peer et al. [26] analyzed the correlations between the impact of several popular password nudges and users' GDMS by conducting two large-scale online experiments. They achieved many significant results and proved that allocating security nudges in a personalized manner based on users' differences in decision-making styles could motivate them to choose stronger passwords [26]. Apart from security warnings, personalization also happens in privacy notices. When users receive a privacy notice that matches their cognitive style, they tend to have lower privacy concerns and risk perceptions [36].

The research mentioned above illustrates that the success of personalized security nudges can not be divorced from the acquisition of users' psychological traits, such as the GDMS, CFC, and cognitive styles mentioned above. However, deploying the schemes in real systems is challenging, if not impossible, since psychological scales are not natural for typical information systems. Thus, motivated by the abundant research on recommendation systems, we attempt to leverage the user behaviors logged and explore the feasibility of building a behavior-based personalization security nudge scheme.

3   Feature Selection and Research Goal

Researchers have proposed several effective personalization schemes based on the significant correlations between users' GDMS and their responses to various security nudges. For example, rational decision-makers like to evaluate alternatives logically [37], so detailed data generally appeals to them. Motivated by this, Malkin et al. [24] designed a data-centric nudge to emphasize the security benefits of security measures. The results indicated that the effectiveness of the nudge was significantly correlated with an individual's possibility of being a rational decision-maker. Besides, by implementing various famous security nudges and measuring the responses of users with different GDMS, Peer et al. [26] found that the effects of the password meter (tells users how strong their passwords are), the Crack-Time nudge (informs users how long it would take to crack their passwords), and the CHBS (Correct Horse Battery Staple) nudge (shows users how to create strong passwords) were all moderated by their GDMS traits. Thus, due to the correlations (moderation effects) between GDMS and nudge effects, the feasibility of building a GDMS-based personalization scheme has been validated.

By contrast, due to the lack of relevant evidence, a clear idea of the relationship between behavioral features and nudge effects is absent, unable to illustrate whether it is feasible to build a personalized nudge scheme based on the behavioral features. To address the problem, we propose to leverage the user behaviors related to personality traits. According to Gratian et al. [16], individuals' differences in personality traits, risk-taking preferences, and decision-making styles were all significantly correlated with their security intentions, including the responses to cybersecurity warnings and notices. However, compared to the rich research on predicting personality traits from behavioral features [7,14,15,39], hardly any studies have touched on the correlations between behavioral features and the other two psychological traits, the risk-taking preferences and the decision-making styles. Thus, based on the correlations between personality traits and security intentions, if the behavioral features we choose are related to personality traits, it is reasonable to hypothesize the correlations (e.g., moderation effects) between the behavioral features and the cybersecurity-related intentions.

Therefore, to select the promising features to establish a behavior-based personalization scheme, we focus on the user behaviors proven to be associated with personality traits previously. Notably, the chosen features must be applicable to the majority of information systems so that the results can be extended to other contexts. Finally, a total of three types of behavioral features are incorporated:

1. **Password Features.** Much work has proved that individuals' password choices reflect their personality traits [1,17,20,32]. Motivated by this, we chose to leverage the characteristics of passwords to represent user behaviors. Differing from the previous work [17] focusing on "local" features (i.e., whether the password contained several "weak" structures such as keyboard patterns and repetitive digits), our study concentrated on "global" ones. Specifically, we treated a password as a whole and calculated its guessing times (P_{guess}), strength score ($P_{strength}$), length (P_{length}), number of character types incorporated (P_{type}), and similarity to usernames ($P_{similarity}$). The former two were measured by zxcvbn [46], a famous password strength estimator.

2. **Mouse Features.** In cybersecurity, it is widely acknowledged that mouse movement data is helpful for biometric authentication [33]. Namely, we can uniquely identify a user by monitoring his/her mouse use habits. Besides, previous studies on mouse use suggested that motion patterns in computer mouse operations could be utilized to predict personality traits accurately [21, 49]. Based on the findings, we tracked participants' mouse behaviors and calculated the average arc length (M_{arc}), average linear velocity (M_{v_lin}), average radians (M_{radian}), and average angular velocity (M_{v_ang}).

3. **Account Features.** Daily observations and pre-study interviews offered additional insights. We learned that some people always let the passwords shown clearly visible during password entry, and some succeeded in entering the correct email verification code by trying multiple times. We assumed that the two phenomena also reflected users' internal personality traits. Thus, we used $A_{visible}$ to represent whether a participant let his/her password shown visible and A_{evc} to record the times that he/she tried to input the correct email verification code.

Finally, the goal of the research is to explore the feasibility of establishing a behavior-based personalization scheme by studying the moderation effects of the eleven features above on the effectiveness of security nudges.

4 Methodology

To investigate the correlations between the proposed behavioral features and nudge effects, we analyzed the user data collected from a between-subjects lab experiment conducted in China. The experiment was approved by the IRB (Institutional Review Board) of the organization.

4.1 Testbed

The lab experiment was conducted in a role-play scenario so that users' natural responses to security nudges could be monitored and collected.

Partially due to the long history and the widespread deployment of password-based systems, the password is one of the most frequently researched areas in cybersecurity for nudge-related studies [17, 26]. Thus, based on the rich literature in this area, we chose it as the testbed of our behavior-based personalization scheme. That is, in this paper, we focus on the effectiveness of password nudges and will investigate their correlations with the proposed behavioral features.

Role-Play Scenario. As Fig. 1 suggests, each participant in the experiment was asked to imagine registering a critical financial account, for which we developed a simulation system that was similar to typical financial websites in China. They were supposed to input usernames, passwords, email verification codes, and CAPTCHAs during the process.

Experimental Condition. The simulation system would ask the participants to reset their passwords no matter what they had set for the first time through a security warning (see Fig. 2). Therefore, each participant would have two passwords: the password created before the security warning (noted as PW_{old}) and the password created afterward (noted as PW_{new}). Importantly, to aid the decision-making process during password resetting, the system would provide the participants with various security nudges. The nudges provided were actually the different conditions of the between-subjects lab experiment with a random policy. Namely, the experimental condition was the nudge type, and the system would randomly allocate a nudge type for each participant. In other words, the system would divide the participants into four groups (experimental conditions), three nudge groups (see Fig. 3) and a control group. According to Fig. 3, the participants assigned to the nudge groups would see the corresponding security nudge during the resetting process. By contrast, there was nothing except for the regular registration page as Fig. 1 in the control group. Thus, by comparing the

(a) Chinese Version   (b) English Version (translated)

Fig. 1. Screenshot of the registration page

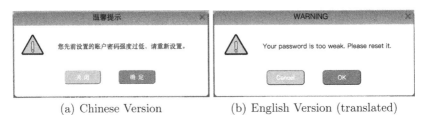

(a) Chinese Version   (b) English Version (translated)

Fig. 2. Screenshot of the security warning

two passwords (PW_{old} and PW_{new}) in strength across all the experimental conditions, we could measure the effectiveness of the nudges involved on improving password strength.

The password nudges implemented in the nudge groups mentioned above were designed based on previously published ones that had been proven effective:

- **Recommendation.** Generating and recommending a stronger alternative by modifying several characters of the previous password [42] (see Figs. 3(a) and 3(b)). The number of guesses needed to crack the alternative password must be at least 15 times as many as the one of the original user password.
- **Social-Positive.** Comparing a user's password to the whole user base and telling him/her how "strong" it is via real-time feedback "Your password is stronger than *percentage* of the users." (see Figs. 3(c) and 3(d)), a specific form of social proof in cybersecurity [10]. The social-proof nudge is widely acknowledged as one of the most effective nudges by researchers from various domains [10,40].
- **Social-Negative.** A variant of the *Social-Positive* nudge. We designed it by reframing the "positive" social proof as a "negative" comparison result, from

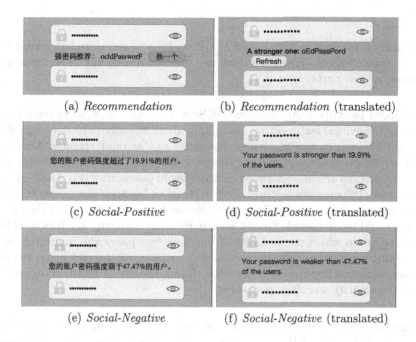

(a) *Recommendation*

(b) *Recommendation* (translated)

(c) *Social-Positive*

(d) *Social-Positive* (translated)

(e) *Social-Negative*

(f) *Social-Negative* (translated)

Fig. 3. Screenshots of the security nudges involved

"Your password is stronger than *percentage* of the users." to "Your password is weaker than *percentage* of the users." (see Figs. 3(e) and 3(f)). Numerous studies on framing effects in cybersecurity have shown that a simple change to the description of the decision-making problem will significantly affect the outcomes [2,6,13,29,35].

4.2 Recruitment, Compensation, and Demographics

A total of 312 participants were recruited for the lab experiment from Credemo [9], a Chinese crowdsourcing platform commonly used to recruit participants for large-scale online surveys and experiments. To avoid potential biases, we did not inform the participants of our real purposes during the recruitment process, but everyone was debriefed individually when the experiment was over. The compensation for their valuable time and feedback was RMB ¥5.

Among the 312 participants: (1) there were 146 males and 165 females; (2) all were adults and about 78.8% were aged between 18 and 29; (3) over ninety percent had at least experienced undergraduate education; (4) half were students, and most of the remaining were clerical support persons.

4.3   Data

As mentioned above, the prime goal of the study is to correlate behavioral features to nudge effects. Thus, the data we collected during the experiment was composed of two parts.

Behavioral Features. As mentioned in Sect. 3, in this paper, when referring to the term "behavioral features", we are talking about the user behaviors regarding password choices, mouse movement patterns, and account settings, based on which an eleven-dimension feature vector was established. First, we recorded each participant's original password choice (the old password PW_{old}) and utilized it to extract the password features needed. Next, an instance of a mouse-tracking program ran in the background to record mouse data precisely so that the mouse features could be extracted. Finally, each participant's account settings would be logged, based on which the visibility of the plain-text passwords and error times of inputting verification codes were observed. Notably, all the user behaviors and the corresponding features were obtained during the initial registration process before the security warnings popped up.

Nudge Effects. Due to the study design, each participant in our study had two passwords, PW_{old} and PW_{new}, and they were created before and after the security warnings, respectively. Notably, for the participants allocated to the nudge groups, the resetting process was accompanied by the corresponding security nudges. Thus, by comparing the two passwords in strength, we could evaluate the effectiveness of the three nudges implemented. Specifically, we chose the password strength estimator *zxcvbn* [46] mentioned above to calculate the minimum orders of magnitudes of the guesses required to crack the two passwords, noted as $Guess_{old}$ and $Guess_{new}$. Next, the difference between the two variables was calculated as follows so that a quantitative measurement of nudge effects was achieved.

$$Effect = Guess_{new} - Guess_{old}$$

5   Results

Previous research on the GDMS-based personalization scheme was mostly based on the moderation effects of the GDMS on nudge effects. Namely, the impact of various security nudges depended on users' GDMS, so we could predict whether a nudge would take effect if the corresponding user's GDMS was known. Following the idea, to investigate the feasibility of the behavior-based proposal, we analyzed the data collected from the lab experiment, focusing on the moderation effects of the behavioral features on the nudge effects (i.e., the variable $Effect$ indicating the improvement in password guessability).

More specifically, to test the moderation effects, we compared each nudge group to the control group and analyzed each component of the eleven-dimension behavioral feature by nudge interaction using the Johnson-Neyman technique [28] with a 95% confidence interval.

With the Johnson-Neyman technique, we could identify the range of the behavioral features where the nudges significantly affected users' decision-making during password creation, the so-called "regions of significance". Furthermore, since the technique uses bootstrapping methods, the "significance" is determined mainly by the confidence interval instead of the usual p-value. Specifically, if the confidence interval does not include zero, the moderation effect is significant.

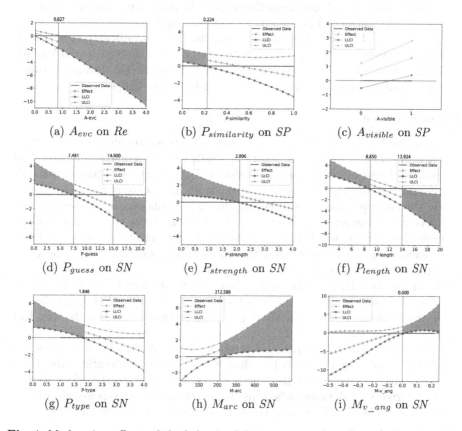

(a) A_{evc} on Re (b) $P_{similarity}$ on SP (c) $A_{visible}$ on SP

(d) P_{guess} on SN (e) $P_{strength}$ on SN (f) P_{length} on SN

(g) P_{type} on SN (h) M_{arc} on SN (i) M_{v_ang} on SN

Fig. 4. Moderation effects of the behavioral features on nudge effects (subscripts: Re for *Recommendation*, SP for *Social-Positive*, SN for *Social-Negative*)

Figure 4 shows the significant moderation effects discovered. In Fig. 4, (1) the coral and red lines indicate the limits of the confidence intervals; (2) the cyan lines indicate the effect sizes; (3) the brown-colored areas show the regions of the behavioral features where the moderation effects are statistically significant. More details are provided in the following.

Recommendation.

- According to Fig. 4(a), the moderation effects are significant and negative when the value of A_{evc} is greater than .827. We inferred that the *Recom-*

mendation nudge would discourage the individuals who were apt to make mistakes when inputting the email verification code.

Social-Positive.

- According to Fig. 4(b), the moderation effects are significant and positive when the value of $P_{similarity}$ is less than .224. We inferred that the *Social-Positive* nudge would encourage the people who did not use similar structures in their usernames and passwords to improve password strength.
- According to Fig. 4(c), the moderation effects are significant and positive when the value of $A_{visible}$ is 1 (Note: $A_{visible}$ is a discrete variable). We inferred that people who let the passwords shown visible during password entry would respond positively to the *Social-Positive* nudge.

Social-Negative.

- According to Fig. 4(d), (1) the moderation effects are significant and positive when the value of P_{guess} is less than 7.481; (2) the moderation effects are significant and negative when the value of P_{guess} is greater than 14.900. We inferred that the *Social-Negative* nudge significantly encouraged users to create a stronger password when their original passwords were highly predictable. By contrast, the nudge showed adverse effects on people who already had an unpredictable password. It is in accord with our intuition because it looks ridiculous when a warning says, "Your password is weaker than 1% of users. Please choose a stronger one.".
- According to Fig. 4(e), the moderation effects are significant and positive when the value of $P_{strength}$ is less than 2.086. We inferred that the *Social-Negative* nudge significantly affect password setting only when the user had a weak password.
- According to Fig. 4(f), (1) the moderation effects are significant and positive when the value of P_{length} is less than 8.850; (2) the moderation effects are significant and negative when the value of P_{length} is greater than 13.924. We inferred that the users who loved to create long passwords were less likely affected by the *Social-Negative* nudge than those whose password strings were short.
- According to Fig. 4(g), the moderation effects are significant and positive when the value of P_{type} is less than 1.846. We inferred that people who used merely one character type (e.g., only digits or only lowercase letters) to generate a password would benefit from the *Social-Negative* nudge.
- According to Fig. 4(h), the moderation effects are significant and positive when the value of M_{arc} is greater than 212.588. We inferred that an individual with numerous mouse trails of great distances would be possibly encouraged by the *Social-Negative* nudge to choose a strong password.
- According to Fig. 4(i), the moderation effects are significant and positive when the value of M_{v_ang} is positive. We inferred that people who moved the mouse clockwise were more likely to be motivated by the *Social-Negative* nudge than those who moved in an anticlockwise direction.

These findings indicate that users' system-use behaviors significantly affect the effectiveness of security nudges. That is, people who behave differently when using systems indeed respond differently to security nudges.

6   Limitation and Future Work

There are several limitations in this paper. On the one hand, the experiment was conducted in a role-play scenario, so the results might not apply to real password-setting contexts. Nonetheless, the primary goal of the study is to investigate the feasibility of utilizing behavioral features when personalizing security nudges, which has been achieved with the role-play scenario. To enhance the ecological validity of the study, we plan to take a deeper look at the moderation effects by studying users' responses to various nudges when making security decisions in the "real" world. On the other hand, despite the significant moderation effects discovered, it is still unknown whether the behavior-based personalization scheme can really improve the effectiveness of security nudges and how much the improvement can be. Thus, in the future, we plan to design a behavior-based personalization scheme surrounding the behavioral features proposed in the paper and test its effects on nudging security decision-making.

7   Conclusion

The primary motivation of the study was to make personalized security nudges closer to real life. It is widely acknowledged that personalization can mitigate the risks of sacrificing the welfare of some sub-populations while improving the persuasiveness and effectiveness of security nudges [11,17,24,26]. Targeted at the heterogeneity among populations, personalized security nudges are an improvement in benefiting the public in security decision-making over current one-size-fits-all approaches. Despite the significant improvements achieved [24,26], there is still a gap in the real implementation of personalized security nudges since the psychological characteristics necessary for personalization are not easy to obtain. Asking each user to fill out lengthy questionnaires is not realistic in actual systems, so more practical solutions are needed. Thus, following the idea of leveraging user behaviors in personalizing online content and advertisements, we explore the feasibility of establishing a behavior-based approach by investigating the moderation effects of behavioral features.

We analyzed the user data collected via a between-subjects lab experiment (N = 312) and discovered the significant moderators for all the security nudges incorporated. For example, the *Recommendation* nudge will likely motivate a user who often makes mistakes when inputting the email verification code to choose a stronger password, whereas others might not be affected. In summary, the key contribution of the work is that we prove that the behavioral features have similar moderation effects on security nudges to the GDMS so that they can be practical alternatives for future personalization schemes of security nudges. We advocate that system designers, especially those who work on security nudges, pay more attention to user behaviors and make full use of them to allocate the nudge to people who are most likely to respond positively.

Acknowledgements. This work was supported by the National Natural Science Foundation of China under Grant No. 61472429 and Grant No. 61772538; the National Key R&D Program of China under Grant No. 2017YFB1400702 and Grant No. 2020YFB1005600.

References

1. Abdrabou, Y., Abdelrahman, Y., Khamis, M., Alt, F.: Think harder! Investigating the effect of password strength on cognitive load during password creation. In: Extended Abstracts of the 2021 CHI Conference on Human Factors in Computing Systems. Association for Computing Machinery, New York (2021). https://doi.org/10.1145/3411763.3451636
2. Acquisti, A., et al.: Nudges for privacy and security: understanding and assisting users' choices online. ACM Comput. Surv.(CSUR) **50**(3), 44 (2017). https://doi.org/10.1145/3054926
3. Acquisti, A., Brandimarte, L., Loewenstein, G.: Privacy and human behavior in the age of information. Science **347**(6221), 509–514 (2015)
4. Adjerid, I., Acquisti, A., Brandimarte, L., Loewenstein, G.: Sleights of privacy: framing, disclosures, and the limits of transparency. In: Proceedings of the ninth symposium on usable privacy and security. SOUPS 2013, p. 9. ACM, New York (2013). https://doi.org/10.1145/2501604.2501613
5. Almuhimedi, H., et al.: Your location has been shared 5,398 times!: A field study on mobile app privacy nudging. In: Proceedings of the 2015 CHI Conference on Human Factors in Computing Systems. CHI 2015, pp. 787–796. ACM, New York (2015). https://doi.org/10.1145/2702123.2702210
6. Bahirat, P., Willemsen, M., He, Y., Sun, Q., Knijnenburg, B.: Overlooking context: how do defaults and framing reduce deliberation in smart home privacy decision-making? In: Proceedings of the 2021 CHI Conference on Human Factors in Computing Systems. Association for Computing Machinery, New York (2021). https://doi.org/10.1145/3411764.3445672
7. Berkovsky, S., Taib, R., Koprinska, I., Wang, E., Zeng, Y., Li, J., Kleitman, S.: Detecting personality traits using eye-tracking data. In: Proceedings of the 2019 CHI Conference on Human Factors in Computing Systems. CHI 2019, pp. 1–12. Association for Computing Machinery, New York (2019). https://doi.org/10.1145/3290605.3300451
8. Caraban, A., Karapanos, E., Gonçalves, D., Campos, P.: 23 ways to nudge: a review of technology-mediated nudging in human-computer interaction. In: Proceedings of the 2019 CHI Conference on Human Factors in Computing Systems. CHI 2019, p. Paper No. 503. ACM, New York (2019). https://doi.org/10.1145/3290605.3300733
9. Credemo: Credemop (2021). https://www.credamo.com
10. Das, S., Kramer, A.D., Dabbish, L.A., Hong, J.I.: Increasing security sensitivity with social proof: a large-scale experimental confirmation. In: Proceedings of the 2014 ACM SIGSAC Conference on Computer and Communications Security, pp. 739–749. ACM, New York (2014)

11. Egelman, S., Peer, E.: The myth of the average user: improving privacy and security systems through individualization. In: Proceedings of the 2015 New Security Paradigms Workshop. NSPW 2015, pp. 16–28. ACM, New York (2015). https://doi.org/10.1145/2841113.2841115

12. Felt, A.P., et al.: Improving SSL warnings: comprehension and adherence. In: Proceedings of the 2015 CHI Conference on Human Factors in Computing Systems. CHI 2015, pp. 2893–2902. ACM, New York (2015). https://doi.org/10.1145/2702123.2702442

13. Gluck, J., et al.: How short is too short? Implications of length and framing on the effectiveness of privacy notices. In: Twelfth Symposium on Usable Privacy and Security ({SOUPS} 2016), pp. 321–340. USENIX Association, Washington, D.C. (2016)

14. Golbeck, J., Robles, C., Edmondson, M., Turner, K.: Predicting personality from twitter. In: 2011 IEEE Third International Conference on Privacy, Security, Risk and Trust and 2011 IEEE Third International Conference on Social Computing, pp. 149–156. IEEE (2011)

15. Golbeck, J., Robles, C., Turner, K.: Predicting personality with social media. In: CHI 2011 Extended Abstracts on Human Factors in Computing Systems, pp. 253–262 (2011)

16. Gratian, M., Bandi, S., Cukier, M., Dykstra, J., Ginther, A.: Correlating human traits and cyber security behavior intentions. Comput. Secur. **73**, 345–358 (2018)

17. Guo, Y., Zhang, Z., Guo, Y., Guo, X.: Nudging personalized password policies by understanding users' personality. Comput. Secur. **94**(3), 101801 (2020)

18. Jia, Y., Xu, B., Karanam, Y., Voida, S.: Personality-targeted gamification: a survey study on personality traits and motivational affordances. In: Proceedings of the 2016 CHI Conference on Human Factors in Computing Systems. CHI 2016, pp. 2001–2013. Association for Computing Machinery, New York (2016). https://doi.org/10.1145/2858036.2858515

19. Joireman, J., Shaffer, M.J., Balliet, D., Strathman, A.: Promotion orientation explains why future-oriented people exercise and eat healthy: evidence from the two-factor consideration of future consequences-14 scale. Pers. Soc. Psychol. Bull. **38**(10), 1272–1287 (2012)

20. Katsini, C., Fidas, C., Raptis, G.E., Belk, M., Samaras, G., Avouris, N.: Influences of human cognition and visual behavior on password strength during picture password composition. In: Proceedings of the 2018 CHI Conference on Human Factors in Computing Systems. CHI 2018, p. 87. ACM, New York (2018). https://doi.org/10.1145/3173574.3173661

21. Khan, I.A., Brinkman, W., Fine, N., Hierons, R.M.: Measuring personality from keyboard and mouse use. In: Abascal, J., Fajardo, I., Oakley, I. (eds.) ECCE 2008 - The Ergonomics of Cool Interaction, European Conference on Cognitive Ergonomics 2008, Funchal, Madeira, Portugal, 16–19 September 2008, p. 38. ACM (2008). https://doi.org/10.1145/1473018.1473066

22. Komanduri, S., Shay, R., Cranor, L.F., Herley, C., Schechter, S.: Telepathwords: preventing weak passwords by reading users' minds. In: 23rd {USENIX} Security Symposium ({USENIX} Security 14), pp. 591–606. USENIX Association, Washington, D.C. (2014)

23. Li, L., Chu, W., Langford, J., Schapire, R.E.: A contextual-bandit approach to personalized news article recommendation. In: Proceedings of the 19th International Conference on World Wide Web. WWW 2010, pp. 661–670. Association for Computing Machinery, New York (2010). https://doi.org/10.1145/1772690.1772758

24. Malkin, N., Mathur, A., Harbach, M., Egelman, S.: Personalized security messaging: nudges for compliance with browser warnings. In: 2nd European Workshop on Usable Security. EuroUSEC 2017, pp. 1–12. Internet Society, Reston (2017). https://doi.org/10.14722/eurousec.2017.23008

25. Orji, R., Nacke, L.E., Di Marco, C.: Towards personality-driven persuasive health games and gamified systems. In: Proceedings of the 2017 CHI Conference on Human Factors in Computing Systems CHI 2017, pp. 1015–1027, Association for Computing Machinery, New York (2017). https://doi.org/10.1145/3025453.3025577

26. Peer, E., Egelman, S., Harbach, M., Malkin, N., Mathur, A., Frik, A.: Nudge me right: Personalizing online security nudges to people's decision-making styles. Comput. Hum. Behav. **109**(12), 106347 (2020)

27. Petelka, J., Zou, Y., Schaub, F.: Put your warning where your link is: improving and evaluating email phishing warnings. In: Proceedings of the 2019 CHI Conference on Human Factors in Computing Systems. CHI 2019, p. 518. ACM, New York (2019). https://doi.org/10.1145/3290605.3300748

28. Preacher, K.J., Curran, P.J., Bauer, D.J.: Computational tools for probing interactions in multiple linear regression, multilevel modeling, and latent curve analysis. J. Educ. Behav. Stat. **31**(4), 437–448 (2006)

29. Qu, L., Wang, C., Xiao, R., Shi, W., Liang, B.: Towards better security decisions: applying prospect theory to cybersecurity. In: Extended Abstracts of the 2019 CHI Conference on Human Factors in Computing Systems. CHI EA 2019, p. Paper No. LBW2613. ACM, New York (2019). https://doi.org/10.1145/3290607.3312782

30. Qu, L., Xiao, R., Wang, C., Shi, W.: Design and evaluation of CFC-targeted security nudges. In: Extended Abstracts of the 2021 CHI Conference on Human Factors in Computing Systems. Association for Computing Machinery, New York (2021). https://doi.org/10.1145/3411763.3451624

31. Raptis, G.E., Fidas, C.A., Katsini, C., Avouris, N.M.: Towards a cognition-centered personalization framework for cultural-heritage content. In: Extended Abstracts of the 2018 CHI Conference on Human Factors in Computing Systems. CHI EA 2018, pp. 1–6. Association for Computing Machinery, New York (2018). https://doi.org/10.1145/3170427.3190613

32. Raptis, G.E., Katsini, C., Cen, A.J.l., Arachchilage, N.A.G., Nacke, L.E.: Better, funner, stronger: a gameful approach to nudge people into making less predictable graphical password choices. In: Proceedings of the 2021 CHI Conference on Human Factors in Computing Systems. Association for Computing Machinery, New York (2021). https://doi.org/10.1145/3411764.3445658

33. Rose, J., Liu, Y., Awad, A.: Biometric authentication using mouse and eye movement data. In: 2017 IEEE Security and Privacy Workshops, SP Workshops 2017, San Jose, CA, USA, 25 May 2017, pp. 47–55. IEEE Computer Society (2017). https://doi.org/10.1109/SPW.2017.18

34. Rosenman, R., Tennekoon, V., Hill, L.G.: Measuring bias in self-reported data. Int. J. Behav. Healthc. Res. **2**(4), 320–332 (2011)

35. Samat, S., Acquisti, A.: Format vs. content: the impact of risk and presentation on disclosure decisions. In: Thirteenth Symposium on Usable Privacy and Security ({SOUPS} 2017), pp. 377–384. USENIX Association, Washington, D.C. (2017)

36. Schöning, C., Matt, C., Hess, T.: Personalised nudging for more data disclosure? On the adaption of data usage policies format to cognitive styles. In: Proceedings of the 52nd Hawaii International Conference on System Sciences. HICSS 2019, pp. 4395–4404. University of Hawaii at Manoa, Honolulu (2019). https://doi.org/10.24251/HICSS.2019.532

37. Scott, S.G., Bruce, R.A.: Decision-making style: the development and assessment of a new measure. Educ. Psychol. Meas. **55**(5), 818–831 (1995)
38. Shi, Y., Ye, D., Goder, A., Narayanan, S.: A large scale machine learning system for recommending heterogeneous content in social networks. In: Proceedings of the 34th International ACM SIGIR Conference on Research and Development in Information Retrieval. SIGIR 2011, pp. 1337–1338. Association for Computing Machinery, New York (2011). https://doi.org/10.1145/2009916.2010189
39. Stachl, C., et al.: Predicting personality from patterns of behavior collected with smartphones. Proc. Natl. Acad. Sci. **117**(30), 17680–17687 (2020)
40. Sunstein, C.R.: Nudging: a very short guide. J. Consum. Policy **37**(4), 583–588 (2014)
41. Thaler, R.H., Sunstein, C.R.: Nudge: Improving Decisions About Health, Wealth, and Happiness. Penguin, New York (2009)
42. Ur, B., et al.: Design and evaluation of a data-driven password meter. In: Proceedings of the 2017 CHI Conference on Human Factors in Computing Systems. CHI 2017, pp. 3775–3786. ACM, New York (2017). https://doi.org/10.1145/3025453.3026050
43. Wang, W., Srivastava, G., Lin, J.C.W., Yang, Y., Alazab, M., Gadekallu, T.R.: Data freshness optimization under CAA in the UAV-aided MECN: a potential game perspective. IEEE Trans. Intell. Transp. Syst. 1–10 (2022). https://doi.org/10.1109/TITS.2022.3167485
44. Wang, Y., Gou, L., Xu, A., Zhou, M.X., Yang, H., Badenes, H.: Veilme: an interactive visualization tool for privacy configuration of using personality traits. In: Proceedings of the 33rd Annual ACM Conference on Human Factors in Computing Systems. CHI 2015, pp. 817–826. Association for Computing Machinery, New York (2015). https://doi.org/10.1145/2702123.2702293
45. Wang, Y., Leon, P.G., Acquisti, A., Cranor, L.F., Forget, A., Sadeh, N.: A field trial of privacy nudges for Facebook. In: Proceedings of the 2014 CHI Conference on Human Factors in Computing Systems. CHI 2014, pp. 2367–2376. ACM, New York (2014). https://doi.org/10.1145/2556288.2557413
46. Wheeler, D.L.: ZXCVBN: low-budget password strength estimation. In: 25th {USENIX} Security Symposium ({USENIX} Security 16), pp. 157–173. USENIX Association, Washington, D.C. (2016)
47. Yan, J., Liu, N., Wang, G., Zhang, W., Jiang, Y., Chen, Z.: How much can behavioral targeting help online advertising? In: Proceedings of the 18th International Conference on World Wide Web. WWW 2009, pp. 261–270. Association for Computing Machinery, New York (2009). https://doi.org/10.1145/1526709.1526745
48. Zhang, B., Sundar, S.S.: Proactive vs. reactive personalization: can customization of privacy enhance user experience? Int. J. Hum.-Comput. Stud. **128**, 86–99 (2019)
49. Zhao, Y., Miao, D., Cai, Z.: Reading personality preferences from motion patterns in computer mouse operations. IEEE Trans. Affect. Comput. 1 (2020). https://doi.org/10.1109/TAFFC.2020.3023296
50. Zimmermann, V., Renaud, K.: The nudge puzzle: matching nudge interventions to cybersecurity decisions. ACM Trans. Comput. Hum. Interact. **28**(1), 7:1–7:45 (2021). https://doi.org/10.1145/3429888

Spear Phishing Email Detection with Multiple Reputation Features and Sample Enhancement

Zhiting Ling[1,2(✉)], Huamin Feng[3(✉)], Xiong Ding[4], Xuren Wang[5(✉)],
Chang Gao[5], and Peian Yang[1(✉)]

[1] Institute of Information Engineering, Chinese Academy of Sciences, Beijing, China
{lingzhiting,yangpeian}@iie.ac.cn
[2] University of Chinese Academy of Sciences, Beijing, China
[3] Beijing Electronic Science and Technology Institute, Beijing, China
fenghm@besti.edu.cn
[4] Hangzhou Dbappsecurity Co., Ltd., Beijing, China
peter.ding@dbappsecurity.com.cn
[5] Information Engineering College Capital Normal University, Beijing, China
wangxuren@cnu.edu.cn

Abstract. Spear phishing is a complex targeted attack which has rapidly increased in recent years. The traditional email features based on the sender's behavior portrait cannot accurately characterize the spear phishing email, and the detection is often hampered when the data set is small. In order to tackle these problems, in this paper, we present a new approach for detecting spear phishing attacks in the full help of the local and external reputation features. Our method extracts 8 local and 6 external reputation features derived from an analysis of spear phishing emails, combined with 4 forwarding features and 20 general features for more accurate detection. Synthetic Minority Oversampling Technique (SMOTE) algorithm and an improved KM-SMOTE are applied on enhancing samples. We evaluate features on a multi-source data set of over 41 thousand emails and achieve the recall of 86.89%, the accuracy of 88.33% in identifying spear phishing emails. With SMOTE, we improve the recall and precision to 91.80% and 93.55%, and the false positive rate is reduced by at least 22%. With KM-SMOTE, we achieve better maximum recall of 95.08%, precision of 93.55% and F1-score of 94.31%.

Keywords: Spear phishing email · Threat intelligence · Reputation features · KM-SMOTE

1 Introduction

Phishing is the most common type of cyber crime in 2020 [1], which increased from 114,702 in 2019 to 241,324 in 2020. Reported in [2], 65% of active hacker

Supported by Youth Innovation Promotion Association, CAS (No. 2020166), Key Laboratory of Network Assessment Technology, Chinese Academy of Sciences and Beijing Key Laboratory of Network Security and Protection Technology.

groups rely on spear phishing to implement infection. According to Verizon [3], 96% of targeted attacks use email as a carrier. Phishing is the most common cause of data breaches in 2019, with 22% of 2019 data breaches involving phishing. Phishing is also the leading issue in complaints to the FBI's Internet Crime Complaint Centre (IC3) in 2020. Phishing incidents more than doubled compared to the previous year, and cost victims over \$54 million in direct losses. At present, the existing detection researches use signal detection theory (SDT) to investigate students' ability to distinguish between phishing emails and real emails [4]. Some work performs user interaction detection for phishing emails in the general sense [5]. Spear phishing emails may contain disguised executable files. P.Unchit et al. [6] use time-based behavior modeling on email sending behavior to prevent advanced email attacks that cannot be detected by traditional protection systems, which is an important step in detecting advanced spear attacks. David T et al. [7] develop the SPEar phishing Attack Detection system (SPEAD) to analyze all incoming emails on a network for the presence of spear phishing attacks. Reference [8–10] extracts 20 features from the subject and body of spear phishing emails, including 6 subject features, 12 body features, and 2 attachment features. But in [8], the data set is not public and it's hard to do comparison in the same data set as [8]. In [11], they extract entity's reputation features, which relied on this entity appearing times in the scene, to measure its credibility. In [12], they detect spear phishing emails with features like domain reputation, sender reputation, recipient reputation, suspicious words, etc.

Spear phishing email is targeted and looks much more realistic, thus harder to detect. The traditional single features based on the sender's behavior portrait cannot characterize the spear phishing email accurately. Additionally, compared with general emails, spear phishing email is rare. With such a small number of known spear phishing instances, standard machine learning approaches seem unlikely to succeed: the training set is too small and the class imbalance too extreme.

To overcome these challenges, we introduce two key contributions. First, we present an analysis of differences from multiple perspectives that we argue are essential differences between spear phishing emails and other emails. With threat intelligence data, we derive a set of typical features and forwarding relationships of emails. Second, in order to solve the problem of sparse spear phishing emails, we introduce the Synthetic Minority Oversampling Technique (SMOTE) and a developed one KM-SMOTE to alleviate the problem of sample imbalance. Combining these two ideas together , we do some experiments to evaluate features and compare results. Experiments have proved that the introduction of reputation features and sample enhancement will effectively improve various performance indicators of spear phishing email detection.

2   Related Work

2.1   Spear Phishing Email

Spear phishing email contains counterfeit messages that appear to be legitimate. Its target is not ordinary individual, but specific company, organization or important personnel. Its purpose is to acquire key information or highly sensitive information, such as financial data, personnel credentials, intellectual property rights, and customer privacy information. There are four common deceiving ways of spear phishing emails:

Sender address spoofing. The sender's email address is real, but the sender's name is counterfeit. For example, change the sender's name "Alice good" to "Alice". The attacker deceives the recipient with the real address of the sender. In this case, the recipient sees the real email address and trusts this email is from sender.

Sender name spoofing. The sender's name is real, but the sender's email address is counterfeit. For example, change the real email address "Alice@companyX.com" to "Alice@evil.com". The attacker deceives the recipient with the sender's real name. Many emails hide the sender's email address by default and only show the sender's name. In this case, the recipient sees the sender's name is familiar and trusts this email is authentic.

Third-party service impersonation. The attacker usually impersonates third-party service provider or technical support, such as account support, credit card service, etc. If recipient has already applied relevant service, when he receives this email, it is easy to trust its content and perform operations.

Real user hijack. The attacker controls the real user's email account. Thus, the sender's name and email address are the same as the real user's. The attacker sends emails by this controlled account. When the recipient see this counterfeit email from a legitimate user, he is very likely to perform dangerous operations.

Spear Phishing Email Attack Methods. In a spear phishing attack, the adversary sends a targeted email designed to trick the recipient into performing a dangerous action. Once the attacker has gained the recipient's trust, he then needs to exploit this trust by inducing the recipient to do what he what. There are two spear phishing email attack methods:

Malicious attachment attack. The attacker often uses malicious attachments, and the attached files usually have 0-day vulnerabilities. If the recipient opens the attachment and executes it, malicious code will be executed.

Credential theft attack. Attack methods based on phishing URLs are also called certificate-based spear phishing emails. The attacker embeds a phishing URL in the email body, script, or attachment, and the URL contains malware or leads to a phishing web page made by the attacker in advance. It is difficult for recipients to identify counterfeit websites, and they are easily tricked into revealing their credentials.

Moreover, there are often some urgent words in spear phishing emails, such as: "Are you busy now?" "Do you have time to do something very urgent? "

"There is an item requiring urgent payment." In case of emergency, the recipient is easy to be deceived, and remits the money to the account controlled by the attacker, causing financial loss.

Spear Phishing Emails Features Analysis. Figure 1 shows a phishing email, which includes basic elements such as sender, recipient, subject, body (including URL address), and sending time. Therefore, the features of phishing email detection are mainly divided into the following aspects: subject-based features, body-based features, URL-based features, script-based features, and sender-based features. These features are usually statistical features or binary features. For example, URL-based features are extracted from the body of the email, including the IP address of the URL, the number of the URL, the number of domain names which are corresponding to all URLs, and whether the URL is embedded in the picture, whether the URL contains the "@" character, whether there is a word such as "click" or "login" in front of the URL, and whether URL contains information such as port.

For email analysis, the word2vec is usually used to convert the body of the email into a word vector, and the TF-IDF is usually used to obtain the weight of the word, then the machine learning or deep learning is used for detection. For example, using the bidirectional long and short-term memory network Bi-LSTM for training and learning.

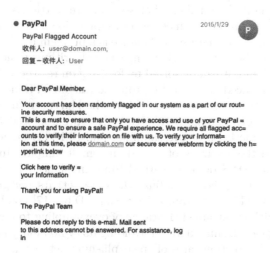

Fig. 1. A phishing email example.

2.2   Threat Intelligence Data Source

We learned external reputation of spear phishing emails from cyber threat intelligence data. There are three main threat intelligence data sources we used: The

China National Cyberspace Threat Intelligence Collaboration (CNTIC), operated from 2020, is a platform providing threat intelligence services. It contains tens of billions of cyber threat reputation information. As to phishing emails, five types of data are provided, including IP, sender's mailbox, URL, domain, and malicious email. And the reputation intelligence is given in the form of threat level as malicious, non-malicious, and undetermined malicious. It also provides multiple mailing tags for phishing emails, spam emails and pornographic emails.

Virus Total, established in 2004, is a free suspicious file analysis service website. It can help to query the reputation information of email attachments, URLs, email addresses and so on. Virus Total uses dozens of anti-virus engines to scan files or web pages and show them in list. The ratio of malicious amount and anti-virus engine amount is the result of analyzing the sample's reputation to be reported.

Phish Tank, established in 2006, is a free community site where anyone can submit, verify, track and share phishing data. Phish Tank adopts manual evaluation criteria, users vote for confirmation and then publicize. It downloads the verified phishing link to the local server for subsequent queries. When users query, three results will be returned as phishing emails, non-phishing emails or no results.

2.3   SMOTE and KM-SMOTE Data Enhancement

The condition of multiple imbalanced classes is more restrictive when the aim of the final system is to obtain the most accurate precision for each of the concepts of the problem [13]. Thus, data set imbalance is a problem need to be solved. On the one hand, it can be solved by changing some algorithms to adapt to the data set. On the other hand, it can be solved by focusing on restructuring the data set to make it more balanced. Chawla [14] proposed the SMOTE method to enhance sample data by synthesizing new data. This method has been successfully applied in many aspects. For example, ZHANG M [15] preprocessed the unbalanced data set with the methods of oversampling and SMOTE enhancing the data set, and improved the accuracy of identifying small samples. In [16], a system detecting malicious DNS domain learned from unbalanced DNS data set, and used under-sampling method to adjust the data set. Its recognition rate was over 95%. KM-SMOTE was proposed by Xiong Ding [17] combining K-means and SMOTE, which constrained the range of oversampling to a cluster obtained by K-means on spear phishing data set avoiding fuzzy boundary problems. Ding's work showed good detection rates of spear phishing detection.

3   Spear Phishing Email Feature Extraction Model

The difference between the spear phishing email, the ordinary phishing email and the legitimate email is analyzed in this paper. We present the spear phishing email feature extraction model to depict spear phishing email more comprehensively and accurately, which is shown in Fig. 2.

There are three types of features: (i) 20 general features of emails obtained from the mail subject, body, attachment, sender and recipient's metadata, (ii) 4 forwarding features, combining with the existing email data, describe the forwarding relationship of the recipient, and (iii) 14 reputation features of emails obtained from threat intelligence and third-party open-source data statistics query platform.

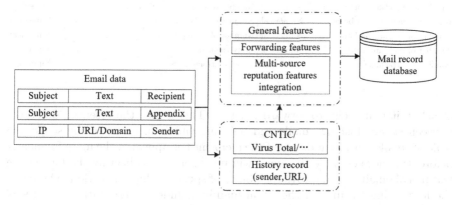

Fig. 2. Multi-dimensional mail feature extraction.

3.1 General Email Feature Extraction

Based on the work of reference [8], the general email features are obtained, which are suitable for the spear phishing email detection, from the metadata of the email subject, body, attachments, sender and recipient. The general email features include statistical features like "the number of subject words", "the number of URLs", "richness", and also include Boolean binary features like "whether the body contains attachments". "Richness" is the ratio of the number of words to the number of characters. The richness of the topic and body are calculated, and its calculation formula is shown in formula (1). Displayed equations are centered and set on a separate line.

$$Richness = \frac{\#of\,words}{\#of\,characters} \tag{1}$$

General email features are analyzed and sorted out as shown in Table 1. Among them, the "function words" in features refer to the words commonly used in phishing emails, such as bank, account, password, recent, risk... and other relatively sensitive information.

3.2 Email Forwarding Feature Extraction

The spear phishing email is highly targeted and closely related to the recipient or the recipient's organization. When the recipient receives the email sent by the

Table 1. General email features

Feature	Type	Feature	Type
Subject is "reply"	Boolean	Subject contains function words such as "bank"	Boolean
Subject contains "verification"	Boolean	Number of topic words	Numerical
Number of subject words	Numerical	Theme richness	Numerical
Body contains "verification"	Boolean	Body contains pause words	Boolean
Body contains "attachment"	Boolean	Body contains the phone number	Boolean
Number of function words in body	Numerical	Number of single words in body	Numerical
Number of new lines in body	Numerical	Number of URLs in body	Numerical
Number of domains in body	Numerical	Number of words in body	Numerical
Number of separate words	Numerical	Body richness	Numerical
Number of attachments	Numerical	Type of attachments	Numerical

attacker, it is unlikely to forward it again. This is also the essential difference between spear phishing emails and phishing emails in terms of the scope and scale of emails sent. In addition, if the recipient has appeared the more frequently before, the more credible the email will be. Therefore, collecting the forwarding features of emails can improve the ability of spear phishing detection. Therefore, the forwarding features of the email mainly include the reputation features of the recipient and the forwarding situation of this email.

Recipient Reputation Feature Extraction. The feature of recipient reputation was first proposed by Grant Ho et al. [18]. They calculate the Jaccard similarity between the current recipient and the previous recipient set, the formula as shown in formula (2). The maximum similarity is took as the recipient's reputation feature. If the current recipient has appeared multiple times in the previous recipient set, indicating that there is a certain relationship between current and previous recipients, thus, the mail is less likely suspicious. Displayed equations are centered and set on a separate line.

$$J(A, B) = \frac{|A \cap B|}{|A \cup B|} = \frac{|A \cap B|}{|A| + |B| - |A \cap B|} \tag{2}$$

Email Forwarding Situation Feature Extraction. In order to obtain the current forwarding feature data of an email, we are facing the permission problem caused by privacy and security. Therefore, we cannot directly control the email account of each user. We obtain the email forwarding relationship chain based on each user's sending and receiving emails to solve this problem. The email forwarding features mining process is shown in Fig. 3. As shown in formula (3), this paper concatenates the subject name and body of the email, uses the hash algorithm SimHash to calculate the fingerprint of the email, and gets the result as Email Entity. Displayed equations are centered and set on a separate line.

$$EmailEntity = SimHash(SubjectName + Body) \tag{3}$$

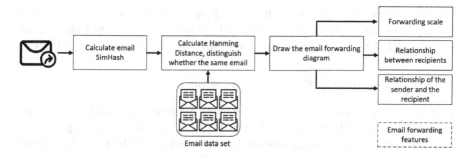

Fig. 3. Email forwarding features mining process.

Then the Chinese words are segmented with Jieba, and get a 64-bit binary number, as shown below:

"1001000000101100101101001101101110100011101111001000011100001100"

When the unique identification of an email is obtained with SimHash, this paper uses Hamming distance to calculate the similarity of emails to determine whether two mails are the same. Hamming distance, also known as text distance, is used to calculate the similarity degree of text. With SimHash, it can quickly and efficiently distinguish whether the text is the same or not. As shown in formula (4), based on empirical values, if $Distance_{AB} < 5$, it is deemed that email A and email B are the same, otherwise, the two emails are considered different. Displayed equations are centered and set on a separate line.

$$Distance_{AB} = Hamming\_Distance(EmailEntity(A), EmailEntity(B)) \quad (4)$$

The same email is searched and identified by traversing the entire email data set. The search of all the same email can be completed for each traversal, then the forwarding relationship chain of each same email is obtained. We store the result in the way of map database storage, and extract the forwarding features including forwarding scale, the relationship between recipients, and the relationship of the sender and the recipient. The email forwarding features are shown in Table 2, including the recipient reputation feature and the forwarding situation feature.

Table 2. Email forwarding features

Feature	Feature description	Type
Recipient reputation	The frequency of recipient appearance previously	Numerical
Forwarding scale	Total number of email forwarding	Numerical
Relationship between recipients	Whether recipients are in the same organization	Boolean
Relationship of the sender and the recipient	Whether the sender and the recipient are from the same organization	Boolean

4   Reputation Feature Extraction of Spear Phishing Email

The spear phishing email commonly uses spear phishing links and high-risk attachments as attack methods. The reputation features of emails are obtained by the current rapidly developing threat intelligence and third-party open-source data statistics query platform. Our research focus on the spear phishing emails based on URL links, and obtain the reputation features related to email links.

4.1   Local Reputation Feature Extraction

Grant Ho [18] first proposed the local reputation features of emails, which were only used to extract the reputation features of links in emails. This paper makes extension to it and adds features related to the sender and the sender's address. Table 3 lists 8 local reputation features extracted.

The attacker embeds a phishing link in the email, and sends this spear phishing email to the recipient, then he requires the recipient to click on the link and enter relevant information or download relevant software and execute it. No matter if the recipient clicks on the link, the relevant assumptions are as follows: (i) the more frequently the email's sender appears, the more credible the email is; (ii) the more frequently the email sender's address appears, the more credible the email is; (iii) the more frequently the email's embedded link appears, the more credible the email is.

In Table 3, the Fully Qualified Domain Name (FQDN) is selected instead of URL or domain name because the granularity of FQDN is relatively moderate. If the URL is too fine-grained, the URL received each time may not be found in the history record. And if the domain name is too coarse-grained, when the attacker deploys the phishing URL on the second-level domain of this domain name, this possibility may be missed.

Table 3. Email local reputation features

Feature	Type
Number of FQDN occurrence	Numerical
The time interval between the last occurrence of FQDN	Numerical
Number of the sender's name occurrence	Numerical
The time interval between the last occurrence of the sender's name	Numerical
Number of the sender's address occurrences	Numerical
The time interval between the last occurrence of the sender's address	Numerical
Number of the sender's name and address occurrences	Numerical
The time interval between the last occurrence of the sender's name and address	Numerical

4.2   External Reputation Feature Extraction

Attacker's External Reputation Feature Extraction. Before sending spear phishing emails, the attacker has obtained the relevant information of the recipient in the preliminary detection process, including the possible access to the website of the company or organization. Meanwhile, the attacker makes a corresponding phishing website following his own goals. Apart from the slight difference between the URL and the real URL, the page elements are almost the same as the real page elements, which is too difficult for the recipient to distinguish. For example, the real ICBC website is "http://www.icbc.com.cn/icbc/", and the website created by the attacker may be "http://www.lcbc.com.cn/icbc/". The attacker replaces the letter "i" with the letter "l". If you do not check it carefully, it is difficult for the recipient to find that the URL embedded in the email is a highly counterfeit page. After creating the website and composing the email, the attacker sends the email to the recipient, and then waits for the recipient to click on and fill sensitive information.

The attacker needs to register a domain name, supporting the website's resolution and operation, from a domain name registration agency to create a highly counterfeit phishing website. It's doesn't need a long time for the attacker to register the domain name, to create a phishing website, and to send the email to the recipient. After completing the production of phishing website, the attacker is most probably to send the phishing email to the recipient within a very short time, instead of waiting for a long time. What's more, the website created by the attacker will not have many visitors.

Based on the two assumptions above, the global ranking website Alexa and the domain name information query website WHOIS are introduced to obtain email links and domain name reputation information. Alexa is used to query the ranking of email links. The higher the global ranking of a website (the closer the ranking is to the first), the higher the popularity of the website and the lower the possibility that the website is a phishing link and the email is a spear phishing email. For the links that cannot be queried, a default ranking value is gave to them, and the default ranking is 1000000. The link with default ranking value will be thought as suspected phishing link.

WHOIS is a transmission protocol used to query information such as IP and owner of a domain name. It can query whether a domain name has been registered and show the complete registration information. WHOIS can be used to query the domain name and obtain its registration information. The closer the website's registration date, the more suspicious the website is. Conversely, the farther the website's registration date and the closer the website's update date, the more legitimate the website is. If the global ranking of a website is higher and the registration date is farther, the less suspicious it is, and vice versa.

External Reputation Feature Extraction Based on Threat Intelligence. As shown in Table 4, threat intelligence platform CNTIC and specialized third-party intelligence platform VirusTotal, PhishTank, URLscan are used to obtain external reputation features of emails. The phishing link or IP address used in spear phishing emails is specific, and no one has received the email before the recipient receives the email, in this way there is no result in the threat intelligence source. The result of a query from an external threat intelligence source may be one of several situations: For legitimate email, the result of the threat intelligence query is empty or benign; For phishing email or spam, the result of the threat intelligence query is empty, or it is a phishing email or spam; For spear phishing email, the result of the threat intelligence query is empty or marked as suspicious.

Table 4. Email external reputation features

Features	Data sources	Type
Global ranking of domain names	Alexa	Numerical
Domain name registration date	WHOIS	Numerical
URL reputation value	CNTIC/VirusTotal/PhishTank/URLscan	Numerical
Domain name reputation value	CNTIC/VirusTotal	Numerical
Sender's IP reputation value	CNTIC/VirusTotal	Numerical
Sending address reputation value	CNTIC/VirusTotal	Numerical

Finally, when the reputation features of IP, links, etc. are obtained from multiple sources, the lowest reputation value is took uniformly, that is, using the most suspicious result as the reputation feature for subsequent training.

5   Experiments

5.1   Experimental Data Collection

Authorized by relevant state departments, we collected 202 spear phishing emails from January to May 2019, randomly selected 13916 non-spear phishing emails (including legitimate emails, phishing emails, etc.) in the second week of April 2019, and 25920 legitimate emails from the Enron data set. We collected 1113 phishing emails from the 2018 International Workshop on Security and Privacy Analytics (IWSPA) competition data specifically targeting phishing emails. These emails are put all together to constitute the experimental data.

5.2   Experimental Indicators

In order to evaluate the detection effect, the following test indicators are used. True Positive (TP) means the number of samples whose real category is malicious and the model classification result is also malicious. False Positive (FP) means the number of samples whose real category is benign but the model classification result is malicious. False Negative (FN) means the number of samples whose real category is malicious but the model classification result is benign. And True Negative (TN) means the number of samples whose real category is benign and the model classification result is benign.

This paper uses Recall to describe the detection ability, uses Precision to describe the detection accuracy, uses F1 to do a comprehensive assessment, uses

False Positive Rate (FPR) to measure the utility of the model. The formulas are shown as (5),(6),(7) and (8).

$$Recall = \frac{TP}{TP + FN} \tag{5}$$

$$Precision = \frac{TP}{TP + FP} \tag{6}$$

$$F1 = 2 * \frac{Precision * Recall}{Precision + Recall} \tag{7}$$

$$FPR = \frac{FP}{FP + TN} \tag{8}$$

5.3 Experiments Based on General Email Features

The general email features were used to do some experiments, and 20 dimensions email vector features were generated in this paper. 4 common machine learning models were applied: Random Forest, Decision Tree, Logistic Regression and Support Vector Machine to detect the spear phishing email data set. The experiments served not only as the basic experiments of this article, but also as the comparative experiments for follow-up work.

In Table 5, Recall, Precision, F1 and FPR judgement indicators are used to describe the detection results of the 4 machine learning models. As shown in the table, the best and most stable experimental result was the Random Forest, the Recall rate was 82.93%, the Precision rate and F1 score were more than 82%, and FPR was as low as 0.24%. From the overall results, the analysis results of Decision Tree, Logistic Regression and Support Vector Machine were likely to be the same. The Recall rate and Precision rate were basically close to 80%, and the FPR is less than 0.5%. As a whole, for the detection of spear phishing emails, the index of the Recall rate was far from the practical requirements, an average of 18% of the FN meant there was a considerable part of the spear phishing emails had been missed.

Table 5. Detection results based on general email features

Model	Recall	Pre	F1	FPR
Random	83.61%	82.26%	82.93%	0.24%
Decision Tree	81.97%	79.37%	80.65%	0.31%
Logistic Regression	80.32%	83.05%	81.67%	0.24%
Support Vector Machine	83.61%	80.95%	82.26%	0.29%

5.4 Experiments Based on External Features

In order to evaluate the detection effect with forwarding features, especially external reputation features, we did some experiments and compared the detection results of the work with only conventional statistical features in [18] and the work with the addition of reputation features or forwarding features. As shown in Table 6, the addition of reputation features did not improve the Recall rate, which was still 83.61%, the Precision rate and F1 score increased by 8% and 5% respectively, and the FPR effectively decreased by two times. With the addition of forwarding features, the Recall rate, Precision rate and F1 score all increased by about 5%, and the FPR decreased by one-fourth.

Table 6. Experimental comparison on different feature sets

Feature set	Recall	Pre	F1	FPR
Prateek Dewan [18]	83.61%	82.26%	82.93%	0.24%
Basic features + reputation features	83.61%	91.07%	87.18%	0.12%
Basic features + forwarding features	86.89%	88.33%	87.60%	0.18%

Algorithm 1: SMOTE data enhancement.

Input: Spear phishing email sample:$\{x_1, x_2, ..., x_m\}$; enhanced ratio.
Output: New sample:$\{y_1, y_2, ..., y_n\}$.

1 For each sample x_k in the minority class, calculate the k nearest neighbors of x_k ;

2 According to the enhancement ratio, randomly select a neighbor sample node from the k neighbors of x_k, denoted as $\{y_1, y_2, ..., y_n\}$;

3 For each $y_j \in \{y_1, y_2, ..., y_n\}$ construct n new samples based on
$x_k : x_{new}^j = x_k + random \times (y_j - x_k), 1 \leq j \leq n.$

4 Repeat the above steps until all the samples in the minority class are traversed.

5.5 Experiments Based on SMOTE and KM-SMOTE Sample Enhancement

The proportion of spear phishing email samples in the experimental data set was less than 0.5%. In order to alleviate the extreme imbalance of the data set, the SMOTE in Algorithm 1 was used to increase the number of spear phishing email samples in experimental data set. KM-SMOTE first used K-means to obtain 5 clusters. If there existed noise data in a cluster, e.g., a sample or samples from majority class, noise samples were deleted from the cluster and recalculated cluster center again. Then SMOTE was used to enhance the sample r from minority class within the range of the cluster that r belonged to. In this way, the problems were efficiently solved like imbalanced data sets learning, indistinct border and so on.

This paper used Random Forest as a verification method, and gradually adjusted the value of the sample enhancement ratio. We repeated trials, when the enhancement radio increased from 1.0 to 1.8, the detection effect was getting better and better, but when the radio continued to increase, the detection effect was getting worse. So, 1.8 is chose as the enhancement ratio and the experimental comparison results are shown in Table 7. As shown in table, when all the features are used for SMOTE sample enhancement, each detection index improves greatly. The Recall rate and Precision rate increase by at least 5% and 2%, the F1 score increases by at least 2.4%, and the FPR decreases by one-fifth. This suggested that SMOTE can effectively improve the detection accuracy of spear phishing emails while reducing the false alarm rate.

We did a comparative experiment, when the enhancement ratio reached to 1.8 and continued increasing, the detection results based on SMOTE dropped while the detection results based on KM-SMOTE were still stable. It indicates that the excessive enhancement of samples affects SMOTE experimental effect. The comparative experiment result is showed in Fig. 3. Experiment combined all the features and applied KM-SMOTE with the enhancement ratio of 1.8 to examine detecting performance using random forest. We achieved a maximum Recall rate of 95.08%, Precision rate of 93.55% and F1 score of 94.31%, which improved respectively by 2%, 3%,3% over SMOTE. It can also clearly get the conclusion that the improved KM-SMOTE algorithm has better enhancement performance.

Table 7. Experimental comparison on samples after SMOTE enhancement

Detection model	Recall	Pre	F1	FPR
Prateek Dewan [18]	83.61%	82.26%	82.93%	0.24%
Basic features + reputation features	83.61%	91.07%	87.18%	0.12%
Basic features + forwarding features	86.89%	88.33%	87.60%	0.18%
All features, SMOTE sample enhancement	91.81%	90.33%	91.05%	0.14%

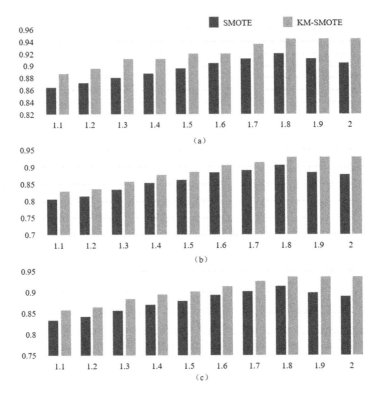

Fig. 4. The Precision(a), Recall(b) and F1-score(c) of SMOTE and KM-SMOTE algorithms with different enhancement ratios detected by random forest.

6   Conclusion and Future Work

In this paper, 8 local reputation features related to the senders and links, 6 external reputation features using threat intelligence platform information, 4 forwarding features based on the forwarding relationship chain and 20 general features derived from an analysis of spear phishing emails are introduced to improve the ability of identifying spear phishing emails. In order to alleviate the extreme imbalance samples, SMOTE and KM-SMOTE are applied to enhance the spear phishing email samples. Our approach is evaluated on contrast experiments which showed our approach significantly improved the Recall rate, the Precision rate and F1 score, and the false alarm rate has been greatly reduced. In general, the introduction of reputation features and the addition of forwarding features can better detect spear phishing emails.

There are some limitations of our approach, if there are no threat intelligence information about the phishing link or IP address in spear phishing emails, the external reputation features can't be extracted. Our next step is to conduct the research on improving classification algorithms, sample enhancement algorithms, and automatic feature extraction to further improve the effect of spear phishing email detection.

References

1. Internet Crime Report. https://www.ic3.gov/Media/PDF/AnnualReport/2020_IC3Report.pdf (2020)
2. Internet Security Threat Report. https://docs.broadcom.com/doc/istr-24-2019-en (2019)
3. Data Breach Investigations Report. https://www.verizon.com/business/en-gb/resources/reports/2020-data-breach-investigations-report.pdf (2020)
4. Unchit, P., Das, S., Kim, A., Camp, L.J.: Quantifying susceptibility to spear phishing in a high school environment using signal detection theory. In: Clarke, N., Furnell, S. (eds.) HAISA 2020. IAICT, vol. 593, pp. 109–120. Springer, Cham (2020). https://doi.org/10.1007/978-3-030-57404-8_9
5. Hongfu, H.U., Peng, G.: Mechanism of phishing email detection based on user interaction and its realization. Comput. Eng. Appl. (2017)
6. Stringhini, G., Thonnard, O.: That ain't you: blocking spearphishing through behavioral modelling. In: Almgren, M., Gulisano, V., Maggi, F. (eds.) DIMVA 2015. LNCS, vol. 9148, pp. 78–97. Springer, Cham (2015). https://doi.org/10.1007/978-3-319-20550-2_5
7. Spear phishing attack detection. https://apps.dtic.mil/sti/pdfs/ADA540272.pdf (2011)
8. Dewan, P., Kashyap, A., Kumaraguru, P.: Analyzing social and stylometric features to identify spear phishing emails. In: 2014 APWG symposium on electronic crime research (ecrime), pp. 1–13. IEEE (2014)
9. Amiri, I.S., Akanbi, O.A., Fazeldehkordi, E.: A machine-learning approach to phishing detection and defense. Syngress (2014)
10. Adewumi, O.A., Akinyelu, A.A.: A hybrid firefly and support vector machine classifier for phishing email detection. Kybernetes (2016)
11. L.W.G: Research on harpoon attack model and detection in advanced persistent threats, Ph.D. dissertation, University of Electronic Science and Technology of China (2020)
12. Chi, Y.P., Ling, Z.T., Ping, X.U., Yang, J.X.: Method of spearphishing attack detection. In: Computer Engineering and Design (2018)
13. Fernández, A., LóPez, V., Galar, M., Del Jesus, M.J., Herrera, F.: Analysing the classification of imbalanced data-sets with multiple classes: binarization techniques and ad-hoc approaches. Knowl.-Based Syst. **42**, 97–110 (2013)
14. Chawla, N.V., Bowyer, K.W., Hall, L.O., Kegelmeyer, W.P.: Smote: synthetic minority over-sampling technique. J. Artif. Intell. Res. **16**, 321–357 (2002)
15. Z.M.: Identification of encrypted traffic as small sample of class-imbalance, Ph. D. dissertation, Harbin Institute of Technology (2013)
16. Liu, Z., Zeng, Y., Zhang, P., Xue, J., Zhang, J., Liu, J.: An imbalanced malicious domains detection method based on passive DNS traffic analysis. Secur. Commun. Netw. **2018**(4), 1–7 (2018)

17. Ding, X., Liu, B., Jiang, Z., Wang, Q., Xin, L.: Spear phishing emails detection based on machine learning. In: 2021 IEEE 24th International Conference on Computer Supported Cooperative Work in Design (CSCWD), pp. 354–359. IEEE (2021)
18. Ho, G., et al.: Detecting and characterizing lateral phishing at scale. In: 28th USENIX Security Symposium (USENIX Security 19), pp. 1273–1290 (2019)

Privacy and Anonymity

TraceDroid: A Robust Network Traffic Analysis Framework for Privacy Leakage in Android Apps

Huajun Cui[1,2], Guozhu Meng[1,2], Yan Zhang[1,2(✉)], Weiping Wang[1,2],
Dali Zhu[1,2], Ting Su[3], Xiaodong Zhang[1,2], and Yuejun Li[1,2]

[1] Institute of Information Engineering, Chinese Academy of Sciences, Beijing, China
`zhangyan80@iie.ac.cn`
[2] School of Cyber Security, University of Chinese Academy of Sciences, Beijing, China
[3] Software Engineering Institute, East China Normal University, Shanghai, China

Abstract. Network traffic analysis is an appealing approach for the security auditing of mobile apps. Prior research employs various techniques (e.g., Man-in-the-Middle, TCPDUMP) to capture network traffic from apps and further recognize security/privacy risks inside. However, these techniques suffer from limitations such as traffic mixing, proxy evasion, and SSL pinning. Possible solutions are to modify and customize the Android system. However, existing studies are mainly based on Android OS 6/7. Contemporary apps generally cannot work properly on these archaic Android OS, which has become a stumbling block for further traffic analysis research. To address the above problems, we propose a new network traffic analysis framework-TraceDroid. We first leverage the dynamic hooking technique to hook the critical functions for sending network requests, and then save the request data along with code execution traces. Besides, TraceDroid proposes an unsupervised way to identify third-party libraries (TPLs) inside apps for facilitating the liability analysis between apps and TPLs. Utilizing TraceDroid, we conduct a large-scale experiment on 9,771 real-world apps to make an empirical study of the status quo of privacy leakage. Our findings show that TPLs account for 44.45% of privacy leakage in contemporary apps, and files transmitted from user devices contain much more detailed privacy data than network requests. We bring to light the over-data harvest and cross-library data harvest issues in apps. Furthermore, we unveil the relationship between TPLs and their visiting domains that previous research has never discussed.

Keywords: Network traffic · Privacy · Android · Third-party library

1 Introduction

As the most widely used mobile platform, the Android operating system brings great convenience to our society but also introduces lots of security problems like

C. Su et al. (Eds.): SciSec 2022, LNCS 13580, pp. 541–556, 2022.
https://doi.org/10.1007/978-3-031-17551-0_35

privacy leakage [12,38], advertisement fraud [8,9,16], and malware [13,34], etc. Network traffic analysis has been demonstrated as one of the most prominent methods to mitigate security concerns by plenty of researches. Generally, existing traffic analysis studies [6,17,23–25,32,40] usually employ TCPDUMP or Man-in-The-Middle (MITM) technique to capture network traffic. However, TCPDUMP cannot handle the traffic encryption problem, thus MITM tools have become the most used method to capture and inspect encrypted traffic. The MITM technique runs on a proxy mechanism, which means users need to install the custom certificate of MITM tools, trust the certificate, and configure a proxy (MITM server) on their devices. By doing so, all traffic of the device should go through the proxy server before reaching the target servers. With custom certificates, the proxy server can decrypt the network traffic by acting as a middleman in the communication path. However, this mechanism fails to handle the traffic mixing problem–background traffic (Android OS traffic, background service traffic), app traffic, and TPL traffic are mixed together, which prevents the fine-grained traffic analysis. In addition, some other limitations caused by MITM tools have not been well addressed (Sect. 2.1).

To mitigate the traffic mixing problem, prior studies [19,30,37] use a whitelist of "User-Agent" or "Host" in the HTTP request header to identify ad-library traffic. However, this method requires practitioners to maintain a list containing known domains and TPLs, and the list needs to be updated frequently. Obviously, as new TPLs keep emerging, this approach may result in low accuracy and the out-of-date lists cannot satisfy contemporary apps [39].

To distinguish the network traffic, an alternative mechanism is to modify and customize the Android operating system. However, this way is heavy-weight that necessitates a recompilation of the Android system every time for a code update. What's more, current studies in this area are mainly on Android 6/7 [6,23,24], such archaic Android system versions are not appropriate to run contemporary apps. In addition, on newer Android systems, new problems will appear (Sect. 3.2), which are not addressed by existing works.

To this end, we propose a new framework, TraceDroid, for network traffic analysis. The proposed TraceDroid can simultaneously address the above problems without any modification of the Android system. Specifically, we leverage the dynamic hooking technique to add additional code in the functions which are responsible for performing HTTP(S) requests, and then save the unencrypted data and the corresponding code execution traces. To present a fine-grained liability study of privacy leakage between host apps and TPLs, we propose an unsupervised method to identify TPLs by correlating the requests and code execution traces, and use this method to distinguish the traffic between host apps and TPLs. With the help of TraceDroid and TPL identification, we conduct a large-scale experiment on 9771 real-world apps and make a comprehensive analysis on the collected data to identify the status quo of privacy leakage in modern apps. Our new findings are as follows: 1) 44.45% of privacy leakage requests are initiated by TPLs, which indicates that TPLs have become a non-negligible channel for privacy leakage. 2) Device ID (e.g., IMEI, IMSI, SN) is the most appealing privacy data. 3) Over-data harvest of privacy information widely exists in contemporary apps and TPLs. The user's private data is sent to multiple back-end servers without noticing them. 4) Files transmitted from the user device tend to contain much more detailed privacy information than that in HTTP(S) requests,which has long been ignored by the research communities. 5) The relationship between TPLs and their visiting domains is a many-to-many correlation, and the domains can be classified into self-owned, authorization, and host app domains (Sect. 4.5).

Contributions. Our key contributions are summarized as follows:

- *We propose a new framework for Android network traffic analysis.* To our knowledge, TraceDroid is the first work that can solve traffic mixing, proxy evasion, traffic encryption, and SSL pinning simultaneously without any OS modification. Besides, TraceDroid can address the new challenges of running contemporary apps on modern Android systems (Sect. 3). Furthermore, TraceDroid is light-weight, making it easy to expand or modify. To foster further research, we released TraceDroid to the research community at https:// github.com/TraceDroid/TraceDroid-SciSec2022.
- *We design a new method to identify TPLs in apps.* An unsupervised method is proposed to identify TPLs by correlating HTTP(S) requests and the code execution traces. Compared to prior works, our method does not require any prior knowledge of TPLs or whitelists. We identified more than 300 TPLs in our app corpus and released the TPLs and their visiting domains on our Github repository.
- *A large-scale analysis of privacy leakage in contemporary apps is conducted.* We perform an empirical study on 9,771 apps, to analyze the transmission manners of leaked privacy data and the liable parties (Sect. 4.2 and 4.3), the over-data harvest and cross-library data harvest (Sect. 4.4), and the relationship between TPLs and their visiting domains (Sect. 4.5).

2   Background

2.1   MITM-based Traffic Capturing

As mentioned in Sect. 1, various MITM tools [7,10,18,20] use the proxy server and the custom certificate to capture and inspect HTTP(S) traffic. Unfortunately, we found some limitations of this method by investigating our app corpus and concluded them as follows:

Traffic Mixing. Mobile systems and apps are running a number of daemon processes, such as Google Framework Service and Push Service. Their traffic is mixed with the app traffic as background noise and is captured by the MITM server. As a result, it is non-trivial to distinguish the network traffic from the background traffic, app traffic, and TPL traffic.

Anti-debugging. Apps can detect whether a proxy is configured and refuse to communicate or change network behaviors. It is largely attributed to preventing apps from being debugged. For instance, the app *"com.outfit7.mytalkingtom.qihoo"* will not show any ads if a proxy is present.

Proxy Evasion. Apps are allowed to establish a direct connection to the target server even when a proxy server is configured on Android. For instance, the public method *"openConnection(Proxy proxy)"* in *java.net.URLConnection* can use a parameter *"Proxy.NO_PROXY"* to ignore the proxy server and create a direct socket connection that bypasses the proxy server.

SSL Pinning. It is the ability to trust specific certificates preinstalled in an app. With SSL pinning, an app can validate the server's certificate to ensure the uniqueness and security of communication between the app and the server. As a result, the custom certificate generated by the MITM tools will not work.

2.2   Hook-Based Traffic Capturing

Hooking (or Instrumentation) refers to injecting additional code into a program to collect runtime information. Once a code is injected into the target process, it has full access to the process memory and can modify its components. Developers can use this ability to alter the target process memory components, allowing them to replace or modify the API functions.

To capture network traffic, we can hook the corresponding APIs and inject additional codes into them to get the request data. Android app developers usually use various networking libraries [1,3,11,21,22,26,27,31] to perform network requests. Take Okhttp [21] as an example, it is a widely used networking library in Android development. The developer usually creates a *"httpClient"* object, builds a *"request"*, and uses its method *"request.set()"* to set the key-value parameters like "content-type:application/json" in the request header. The function *"perform(request)"* is finally called for sending out this HTTP request. In this case, we can hook the function *"perform(request)"* and save its parameter *"request"* to get the request data. We will show how to get the unencrypted request data in Sect. 3.1.

Compared with MITM tools, hook-based traffic capturing has the following advantages: 1) Hooking is only for the particular APIs in a certain target app (specific app process ID in the Android operating system), so the captured traffic does not contain traffic other than the app. 2) Hooking does not change the logic integrity of the original program, and it is transparent to apps, so it is not affected by anti-debugging and proxy evasion. Moreover, it does not need a custom certificate, so the pinning cannot stop us from getting request data.

3   Approach

As shown in Fig. 1, TraceDroid proceeds in four phases–*network hooking*, to instrument Android devices for traffic capturing; *traffic triggering*, to make apps produce more network traffic and parse the traffic to restore network requests, files, and call stacks; *TPL identification*, to identify TPLs in apps based on the captured requests and call stacks, which can benefit our liability analysis in Sect. 4.2; and *privacy leakage analysis*, to conduct a large-scale study on our apps corpus to identify the status quo of privacy leakage in modern apps.

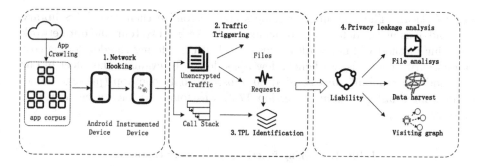

Fig. 1. System overview of TraceDroid

3.1 Network Hooking

As mentioned in Sect. 2.2, we use the hook-based traffic capturing method to overcome the limitations of MITM tools. Our idea is to hook all functions responsible for performing HTTP(S) requests. Nevertheless, there exist dozens of networking libraries [1,3,11,21,22,26,27,31]. It will be labor-intensive and time-consuming to hook all these libraries because this needs to do case by case study and instrument dozens of APIs. To this end, we turn to the underlying APIs that are depended by the networking libraries.

We manually analyzed the networking libraries and found that they rely on the OpenSSL library to perform SSL connections. OpenSSL (or named BoringSSL after Android 6) is the default SSL/TLS library in the Android system [5]. It contains two parts–libssl and libcrypto. Among them, libssl is the implementation of the SSL protocol, and the Android system uses its built-in functions (i.e., "*SSL_Read*" and "*SSL_Write*") to handle HTTPS requests. "*SSL_Read*" is used to read data from an established SSL session and put it into a buffer. "*SSL_Write*", on the contrary, writes data to the buffer and sends it to the remote server. Note that the functions in libcrypto will be invoked to decrypt and encrypt the data before "*SSL_Read*" or after "*SSL_Write*" is invoked, so the data read and written here is plain text (unencrypted data).

To illustrate how our network hooking method works, we take "*SSL_Write*" as an example. Its function prototype is "*int SSL_Write(SSL *ssl, const void *buf, int num)*", the API parameter "*ssl*" is the specified SSL connection, "*buf*" is the buffer that this function writes data into, "*num*" is the data (measured in number of bytes) will be written into "*buf*". As mentioned above, the libcrypto will be automatically invoked to encrypt the data after this function, and finally, the data is sent to the remote server. So we hook the function "*SSL_Write*", inject additional code into it, and save "*num*" bytes data from the "*buf*"–so we get the unencrypted request data (that is, we get the data before it is encrypted).

Similarly, we hook two APIs –"java.net.SocketOutputStream.socketWrite0" and "java.net.SocketInputStream.socketRead0" as they are the default HTTP APIs in the Android system. Table 1 shows the hooking functions in TraceDroid.

Evaluation. Theoretically, developers can customize their own TLS library instead of using the default one provided by the Android system, and our network hooking method will not work in this case. But considering the developing cost and security concerns, we believe few apps do so. To evaluate the effect of our method, we randomly investigated 80 apps, and only one app (package name: "*com.ss.android.ugc.aweme*", version 17.3) was found to have a custom TLS library.

Table 1. Hooking functions for network capturing

Traffic hooking	HTTPS	libssl SSL_Write
		libssl SSL_Read
	HTTP	java.net.SocketOutputStream.socketWrite0
		java.net.SocketInputStream.socketRead0
Call stack hooking	HTTPS	ConscryptFileDescriptorSocket$SSLOutputStream
		ConscryptFileDescriptorSocket$SSLInputStream
	HTTP	java.net.SocketOutputStream.socketWrite0
		java.net.SocketInputStream.socketRead0

3.2 Traffic Triggering

Obstacles Before App Execution. To capture app traffic, we install and execute apps to produce network traffic. However, with the evolution of the Android system, we found new obstacles before we can run apps in modern Android systems. First, apps may ask for permissions before users enter the app. Google introduced a runtime permission authorization mechanism [2] after Android 6.0 (API 23), and dangerous permissions like "android.permission.CALL_PHONE" have to be granted during runtime. As shown in Fig. 2 a), a dialog asking for permissions likely appears and blocks app execution unless the permission request is confirmed by the user. Second, many apps present various pop-up prompts or splash screens when launched. As shown in Fig. 2 b), a prompt dialog may present a user agreement or privacy policy that defines the responsibilities of each party, and the prompt dialog also needs confirmation from the user. As shown in Fig. 2 c), a splash screen is usually an introduction for apps while it is loading, and users have to swipe left/right on these screens to complete the procedure.

To mitigate these obstacles, we design and implement an automatic tool *obsCleaner* to satisfy them. The idea is to recognize the obstacle-related Android widgets on a screen and make certain UI operations to accomplish them. Specifically, for permission requests and pop-up prompts, we randomly tested 200 apps and distilled a keywords list related to these obstacles(e.g., "ok", "agree", "continue", and "start"). According to the keywords list, we locate the coordinate of the obstacles on the screen and imitate human operations to generate related events to satisfy them. We consider this work a one-time effort because these words are not updated frequently, and the list can be extended easily. For splash screens, we swipe the screen for a certain times K, and we set K to 5 because all the 200 apps can be satisfied by 5 times in our manual test. We have released *obsCleaner* on our Github repository to foster future research.

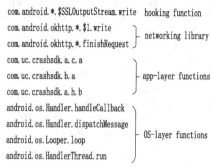

Fig. 2. Obstacles before app execution   **Fig. 3.** An example of call stacks

Triggering More Traffic. An important task in network traffic analysis is to generate as much traffic as possible. Previous works usually use the Android UI fuzzing tool Monkey to trigger traffic from apps. However, Monkey's random events are not efficient in triggering traffic. In this paper, we use the tool in our previous work–*AutoClick* [4], to do this. *AutoClick* is a lightweight and efficient tool to trigger network traffic. It is based on the *"click first"* principle, which automatically clicks all *"clickable"* layout elements on an Android activity. Our previous work demonstrated that it outperforms about 85% in generating distinct traffic during a limited time than Monkey.

3.3   TPL Identification

TPL identification refers to detecting the presence of TPLs in apps, and it is an important task to facilitate fine-grained traffic analysis. We manually employed existing TPL identification tools [14,15,28,35] to 20 randomly selected apps to see their accuracy. Unfortunately, the result shows that although they have a good performance on known TPLs (TPLs that they have trained), they lead to very low accuracy for the newly-emerged TPLs like *"com.bytedance.*"*, and this conclusion is in line with the prior study [39]. Nevertheless, the newly-emerged TPLs usually produce large traffic as a majority of apps integrate them, making them an indispensable part of our research.

The lucky thing is that previous work [29] shows that network traffic generated from the same TPL has similar network behaviors across different apps. That is to say, their HTTP(S) requests are similar in structure.

Algorithm 1: TPL identification

Input: $G : request \rightarrow call\_stack$: a visited graph mapping HTTP(S) requests
        to the corresponding call stacks
Output: $libs$: TPLs in apps

1   $libs \leftarrow \emptyset$;
2   Identify *domains* visited by all requests in G;
3   **for** *domain* $\in$ *domains* **do**
4   Obtain *reqs* that visit *domain*, and *reqs* $\in$ $G\langle request\rangle$;
5      $clusters \leftarrow performClustering(reqs)$;
6   **for** *cluster* $\in$ *clusters* **do**
7   **for** *req* $\in$ *cluster* **do**
8              $cstack \leftarrow G(req)$;
9              $cstack' \leftarrow filter(cstack)$ by removing hooking and networking
            libraries;
10   **for** *call* $\in$ *cstack'* **do**
11                 $lib \leftarrow truncate(call)$;
12                 $libs.append(lib)$;
13             $libs.deduplicate()$ by removing redundant libs;

14 **return** libs;

Hence, we propose an unsupervised manner of associating network requests
with call stacks to identify TPLs. Algorithm 1 shows our TPL identification process. First, we obtain the domains visited by more than M apps,
and M is empirically set to 10 (line 2). For each domain, we extract signatures from all the corresponding requests as *reqs* (line 4), and a *req* is
$\langle protocol, method, URL, host, path, key\_list\rangle$. A clustering analysis is performed
where the requests with the same signature are grouped together (line 5). Then,
we get the corresponding call stacks for each request to obtain the candidate TPL
(line 6). A call stack is a list of functions with a bottom-to-up code execution
trace shown in Fig. 3. We filter the stack by deleting our hooking functions in
Sect. 3.1 and networking libraries such as Okhttp3 (line 9) mentioned in Sect. 3.1
to get the candidate TPL. Next, we truncate the top three package names of the
candidate TPL and remove redundant ones to get final TPLs (line10-13).

Here we take a call stack as an example in Fig. 3. For ease of presentation, we have omitted irrelevant parts. The code execution trace contains four parts: OS-layer functions, app-layer functions, networking libraries,
and hooking functions. TraceDroid first deletes the hooking functions, networking library–"*com.android.okhttp.**", and the OS-layer functions (e.g.,
"*android.os.**"). In this way, we get the remaining package names with the
prefix of "*com.uc.crashsdk.**". We truncate the top three package names and do
de-duplication of these package names to obtain the TPL –"*com.uc.crashsdk*".

Parameter Setting. We conducted a statistic showing how many apps visit
each domain. It exhibits a long-tailed distribution with 95.8% of domains visited

by less than 10 apps, so we set M to 10 to obtain the candidate domains for further analysis. We have manually checked 53 TPLs identified by our method, and all of them are real TPLs (results are also released on our Github repository).

4 Evaluation and Measurement

Implementation and Experiment Setup. We implement TraceDroid with about 6K lines of Python and JavaScript code based on UIAutomator2 and Frida. For obstacle elimination, we use UIAutomator2 API "*XPath()*" to locate the coordinates of obstacles according to the keywords list; for network hooking, we use the Frida API "Interceptor.attach()" to hook the functions. For each app, TraceDroid installs it, triggers it for 10 min, and collects network traffic during runtime. After the test time, TraceDroid terminates the app and uninstalls it. TraceDroid sends the collected data to our server, and the device is ready for the next test app. Our experiment was conducted with two Pixel3 phones with Android 9 for about 33 days.

4.1 Dataset Construction

We crawled 9,771 apps from multiple app stores, among which 5,503 apps are from alternative app stores like Xiaomi [36] and 4,268 apps from Google Play. For each app store, we download the TOP list apps of each category. As shown in Table 2, TraceDroid collected 16.9 GB .pcap files and 6.2 GB call stack files. By parsing these files, we get 301,381 HTTP(S) requests and their corresponding call stacks. We restored 55,843 downloaded files and 2,914 uploaded files from the captured traffic.

Table 2. Manifest of experimental data and result

Data	Count	Description
Android apps	9,771	5,503 from alternative markets and 4,268 from Google
.pcap files	16.9 GB	The volume of captured traffic
Call stack	6.2 GB	The volume of function call stacks
Requests	301,381	HTTPS: 174,486 (57.9%) HTTP: 126,895 (42.1%)
Files	58,757	55,843 downloaded files, 2914 uploaded files

4.2 Liability Analysis

To conduct a liability analysis of privacy leakage between host apps and TPLs, we follow the privacy definition of the previous work [25] to categorize privacy data into three types: 1) device information (e.g., IMEI, Serial Number); 2) Location information (e.g., base station, GPS); 3) Network information (e.g., WiFi state, IP address). We collect the above information of our two Pixel3 phones for further analysis.

In our experiment, TraceDroid identifies 357 TPLs using the method proposed in Sect. 3.3. Based on the result, we conducted a fine-grained liability analysis of privacy leakage, that is, to show whether privacy data is leaked by TPLs or host apps. We denote the requests which transmit privacy data as *privacy requests*, and TraceDroid uses 5-tuple–$\langle appPackageName, source\ IP, sourcePort, destIP, destPort \rangle$ to correlate HTTP(S) requests with call stacks. TraceDroid searches the call stacks of *privacy requests*, if a TPL package name exists in the call stack, we consider the TPL initiates the privacy request; otherwise, it is initiated by the host app. We find that TPLs initiate 44.45% of privacy requests. More detail, about 39% of device information, 45.8% of location information, and 42.6% of network information leakage are transmitted by TPLs. Our result demonstrates that TPLs have become a non-negligible channel for privacy leakage and more regulation should be given to TPLs.

4.3   Privacy Leakage Through Files

Prior works mainly focus on network request analysis. However, files are also an essential part of network traffic, and surprisingly, no work analyzes the content in files, which makes it long been ignored by the research community. In this section, we make the first attempt to examine the contents of files. Benefiting from our packet-level hooking ability, TraceDroid restored 2,914 uploaded files (involving 329 apps). Using our liability analysis, we find that 1,793 files were transmitted by host apps, and 1,121 files were transmitted by TPLs (involving 84 TPLs).

First, we manually analyze files sent by TPLs and find that all these files are not human readable, and most of them do not have a suffix indicating the file type. For further investigation, we inspect these files with a binary viewer to analyze the encoding or encryption method and find that: 1) Files sent by different TPLs have similarities in the file name. For example, 810 file names end with "*stm_d*" or "*stm_p*", and 154 file names end with "*.*.pvuv.log*". 2) The first ten bytes in "*stm_d*" and "*stm_p*" files are the same.

Second, TraceDroid inspects all files generated by host apps and tries to decompress them if necessary. However, due to the various encoding formats, it is difficult to deal with them automatically, so we perform a semi-automatic analysis on these files. We first manually analyze some files to see whether they are human-readable and automatically analyze similar files (either with the same file names or sent by the same host app). Surprisingly, we find that these files tend to contain much more detailed privacy information than requests. For example, a file contains network status (mobile operator APN name, it indicates the operator name or WiFi name), app name, app version, distribution channel, client time stamp, device model, OS version, Android ID, and the rest of this file contains user operations like "user clicks the button in the Main activity at 11:00am". More details are shown in Table 3.

Table 3. Information transmitted through files

Process info	Memory info	CPU info
process id, thread id	RAM total,free,available	abi,processor,manufacturer, utility
Device info	**Battery info**	**Disk Info**
model, brand	voltage, health, temperature	disk total, available, block size
Root status	**Kernel info**	**Network info**
isRoot, su permission	Linux kernel info, Dalvik version	WiFi, mobile operator, SIM card
Installed app list	**Location info**	**Device IDs**
apps installed in the device	gps, city	IMEI,IMSI,SN,UUID,UDID
User action info	**Permission info**	**Phone number**
pvuv info	permissions app applied	user phone number

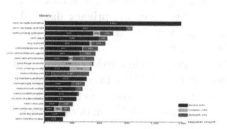

Fig. 4. Privacy leakage from TPLs

Fig. 5. TPL numbers per app

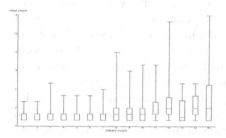

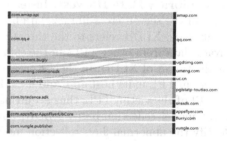

Fig. 6. TPL number&privacy domain

Fig. 7. TPL visiting Graph

To sum up, in this section, we present a fine-grained privacy leakage analysis on files transmitted from user devices. Our findings are as follows: 1) Files transmitted by TPLs have good encoding/encryption, which could prevent the file content from being extracted. However, some TPLs may use the same encoding/encryption method, if someone reverses one TPL, he may have the ability to decode other TPL's files. 2) Files transmitted by host apps do a poor job of protection, and they contain much more detailed privacy data than HTTP(S) requests, which has long been ignored by the research community.

4.4   Privacy Data Harvest

Over-Data Harvest. Figure 4 shows the privacy data transmitted by TOP 20 TPLs. It shows that 4 TPLs only transfer one type of privacy data, 6 TPLs transfer two types of privacy data, and 10 TPLs transfer three types of privacy data. Our further analysis shows that 33% of apps simultaneously transmit privacy data with TPLs, which means both the host apps and TPLs collect privacy data to deliver their service. However, users cannot control when and how often these data be collected and how they will be used.

Another question we intend to answer is, how many TPLs are integrated into an app, and does over-data harvest exists among TPLs? Fig. 5 shows that 78.5% of apps integrate less than 5 TPLs, 18.5% integrate 6 to 10 TPLs, and only about 3% of apps integrate more than 10 TPLs. Figure 6 shows the relationship between the TPL number and the domain number receiving privacy data. We can see that the more TPLs in an app, the more domains receive privacy data, indicating that over-data harvest does exist among TPLs.

Our findings demonstrate that over-data harvest widely exists among host apps and TPLs. Considering the broad integration of TPLs in apps, we point out that app developers should pay more attention to the collection behavior of TPLs, because if the TPLs collect privacy information in violation of regulations, it will have a destructive impact on the reputation of apps.

Cross-Library Data Harvest. Instead of collecting privacy data from the user device or the server, cross-library data harvest (XLDH) is a new attack model in recent years. XLDH refers to the threat model in that a malicious TPL collects privacy data from other TPLs in the same host app. Wang et al. [33] first point out the threat of XLDH. In their study, a malicious TPL checks the presence of the victim TPL in its host app, and uses the Java reflection mechanism to invoke the API of the victim TPL, thus acquiring the privacy data from it. We call this threat model reflection-based XLDH, and Wang et al. proposed a method to identify the abnormal Java reflection mechanism in order to detect this threat.

In our experiment, we bring to light a new XLDH model - instrumentation-based XLDH. In this model, a TPL uses instrumentation techniques to harvest data from other TPLs in the same host app. Specifically, we conducted an analysis based on the idea of "call stack chain inconsistency", that is to say, we check how a TPL is invoked across different apps to see whether there is any inconsistency among them. We select the 20 most commonly used TPLs in our dataset, extract their call stacks, compare their call stack chain across different apps, and search for the "call stack chain inconsistency". For example, we analyze all call stacks of a TPL "*com.uc.crashsdk*" and find that a TPL named "*com.networkbench.agent*" is invoked by it in the host app "*com.wondertek.paper*". However, "*com.uc.crashsdk*" does not invoke "*com.networkbench.agent*" in other apps. To figure out why this phenomenon occurs, we manually read the developer guide for these two TPLs. We found they belong to different vendors, and "*com.uc.crashsdk*" should not invoke "*com.networkbench.agent*" according to their developer guide, which means that such a phenomenon is suspicious. To find out the truth, we then decompile the app, manually analyze the source code, call stack, and network requests, finding that *"com.networkbench.agent"* instruments *"com.uc.crashsdk"* to harvests privacy data from it, and finally transmits privacy data to the domain *"network-bench.com"*, which is in line with the requests we observed in our dataset. Based on the "call stack chain inconsistency" idea, we found 2 apps that have the behavior of instrumentation-based XLDH in our app corpus, and both of them have tens of thousands of downloads from the app store. What's worse, instrumentation-based XLDH can evade the detection method proposed by Wang et al. [33] as it does not rely on the Java reflection mechanism. We believe this is a new XLDH model, and large-scale, automatic approaches should be studied in future research to deal with this threat.

To sum up, in this section, we present an empirical analysis of data harvest in modern apps. Our findings are as follows: 1) Privacy over harvest exists between host apps and TPLs. Developers should pay more attention to the behavior of TPLs, as they may damage the app's reputation if they violate the regulatory regulations. 2) Cross-library data harvest is a new and covert way to collect privacy data, and new methods should be proposed to detect this threat automatically.

4.5 Relationship Between TPLs and Domains

In this section, we aim to give a clear relationship between TPLs and their visiting domains. Libspector [40] concluded that there is no strict 1-to-1 correlation between TPLs and domains, but what exactly is the correlation remains unclear.

We collected the visiting domains of the 53 manually checked TPLs. Figure 7 is the visiting graph of some example TPLs: the left is TPL names, the right is their visiting domains, and the flow between left and right represents the traffic volume. The graph shows that TPL usually visits more than one domain, and a domain may be visited by more than one TPL, which is in line with the conclusion of Libspector [40]. Nevertheless, why does this phenomenon occur? What is the relationship between them? To figure things out, we read the TPL development documents and searched domains in the app source code to study their connections. We found that, for a particular TPL, the visiting domains can be categorized into three types: 1) self-owned domain: owned by the TPL provider, and the domain will be visited by the TPL across different apps; 2) authorization domain: domains providing an authorization mechanism for those who want to use its service. This is useful when some TPLs need to cooperate with each or provide a public service. The authorization mechanism can be a "key" that anyone who wants to use the service must register or apply for a "key" to access the API provided by the domain; 3) host app domain: owned by the host app provider. Apps use this domain to deliver their service.

Here we take an app named *"com.antutu.ABenchMark"* as an example. It integrates a library named *"com.umeng.commonsdk"*. For this library, *"umeng.com"* is a self-owned domain, and *"qq.com"* is an authorization domain. Note that there is a request initialized by *"com.umeng.commonsdk"* that visits a domain named "*autovote.antutu.net*". Figure 7 does not show the domain because the traffic volume between them is too small. But indeed, "*autovote.antutu.net*" is the host app domain for "*com.umeng.commonsdk*". The reason for "*umeng*" visiting "*antutu.net*" is that the TPL has a call-back API for the caller to deliver their service, and when developers invoke it, they can use the call-back API to visit their domains.

To sum up, in this section, we make an effort toward a clear correlation between TPLs and domains. Based on a large number of data analyses, we conclude that there is a many-to-many relationship between TPLs and domain. Further, we categorize the domains into three types and illustrate the reasons behind the visiting phenomenon between TPLs and domains.

5   Conclusion

This paper proposed a new framework TraceDroid for network traffic capturing and analysis. Compared with existing works, TraceDroid is more robust and efficient as it addresses the limitations of traffic mixing, proxy evasion, and SSL pinning. With the help of TraceDroid, we proposed an unsupervised way to identify Third-party libraries (TPLs), and then conducted a large-scale and comprehensive analysis of privacy leakage on 9,771 real-world apps. We present new findings on the privacy leakage caused by TPLs and files, and we also evaluated the phenomenon of over-data harvest between TPLs and host apps. Besides, we bring to light a new and covert data harvest way that should be studied further–instrumentation-based cross-library data harvest. Finally, we make the first attempt to give a clear relationship between TPLs and their visiting domains. To foster future research, we released all of the source code and experiment results on our Github repository.

Acknowledgment. This work is supported by the National Key Research and Development Program of China (No.2019YFB1005205).

References

1. https://developer.android.com/reference/java/net/HttpURLConnection (2021)
2. https://developer.android.google.cn/about/versions/marshmallow/android-6.0-changes?skip_cache=false (2021)
3. Async-http (2021). https://github.com/android-async-http/android-async-http
4. AutoClick (2021). https://github.com/BlcDle/AutoClick
5. BroingSSL (2021). https://boringssl.googlesource.com/boringssl/
6. Caputo, D., Pagano, F., Bottino, G., Verderame, L., Merlo, A.: You can't always get what you want: towards user-controlled privacy on android. arXiv preprint arXiv:2106.02483 (2021)
7. Charles (2021). https://www.charlesproxy.com/
8. Dong, F., et al.: Frauddroid: automated ad fraud detection for android apps. In: Proceedings of the 2018 26th ACM Joint Meeting on European Software Engineering Conference and Symposium on the Foundations of Software Engineering, pp. 257–268 (2018)

9. Dong, F., Wang, H., Li, L., Guo, Y., Xu, G., Zhang, S.: How do mobile apps violate the behavioral policy of advertisement libraries? In: Proceedings of the 19th International Workshop on Mobile Computing Systems & Applications, pp. 75–80 (2018)

10. Fiddler (2021). https://www.telerik.com/fiddler

11. HttpClient (2021). https://hc.apache.org/httpcomponents-client-5.1.x/

12. Li, L., et al.: ICCTA: detecting inter-component privacy leaks in android apps. In: 2015 IEEE/ACM 37th IEEE International Conference on Software Engineering, vol. 1, pp. 280–291. IEEE (2015)

13. Li, L., Li, D., Bissyandé, T.F., Klein, J., Le Traon, Y., Lo, D., Cavallaro, L.: Understanding android app piggybacking: a systematic study of malicious code grafting. IEEE Trans. Inf. Forensics Secur. **12**(6), 1269–1284 (2017)

14. Li, M., et al.: Libd: scalable and precise third-party library detection in android markets. In: 2017 IEEE/ACM 39th International Conference on Software Engineering (ICSE), pp. 335–346. IEEE (2017)

15. LibRadar (2021). https://github.com/pkumza/LibRadar

16. Liu, T., Wang, H., Li, L., Bai, G., Guo, Y., Xu, G.: Dapanda: detecting aggressive push notifications in android apps. In: 2019 34th IEEE/ACM International Conference on Automated Software Engineering (ASE), pp. 66–78. IEEE (2019)

17. Liu, T., et al.: Maddroid: characterizing and detecting devious ad contents for android apps. In: Proceedings of The Web Conference 2020, pp. 1715–1726 (2020)

18. Lumen (2021). https://www.haystack.mobi/

19. Ma, Z., Wang, H., Guo, Y., Chen, X.: Libradar: fast and accurate detection of third-party libraries in android apps. In: Proceedings of the 38th International Conference on Software Engineering Companion, pp. 653–656 (2016)

20. Meddle (2021). https://meddle.mobi/

21. Okhttp: https://square.github.io/okhttp/ (May 2021)

22. OpenFeign (2021). https://github.com/OpenFeign/feign

23. Razaghpanah, A., et al.: Haystack: In situ mobile traffic analysis in user space, pp. 1–13. arXiv preprint arXiv:1510.01419 (2015)

24. Reardon, J., Feal, Á., Wijesekera, P., On, A.E.B., Vallina-Rodriguez, N., Egelman, S.: 50 ways to leak your data: an exploration of apps' circumvention of the android permissions system. In: 28th USENIX security symposium (USENIX security 2019), pp. 603–620 (2019)

25. Ren, J., Rao, A., Lindorfer, M., Legout, A., Choffnes, D.: Recon: revealing and controlling pii leaks in mobile network traffic. In: Proceedings of the 14th Annual International Conference on Mobile Systems, Applications, and Services, pp. 361–374 (2016)

26. RestTemplate (2021). https://docs.spring.io/spring-framework/docs/current/javadoc-api/org/springframework/web/client/RestTemplate.html

27. Retrofit (2021). https://square.github.io/retrofit/

28. Soh, C., Tan, H.B.K., Arnatovich, Y.L., Narayanan, A., Wang, L.: Libsift: automated detection of third-party libraries in android applications. In: 2016 23rd Asia-Pacific Software Engineering Conference (APSEC), pp. 41–48. IEEE (2016)

29. Taylor, V.F., Spolaor, R., Conti, M., Martinovic, I.: Robust smartphone app identification via encrypted network traffic analysis. IEEE Trans. Inf. Forensics Secur. **13**(1), 63–78 (2017)

30. Tongaonkar, A., Dai, S., Nucci, A., Song, D.: Understanding mobile app usage patterns using in-app advertisements. In: Roughan, M., Chang, R. (eds.) PAM 2013. LNCS, vol. 7799, pp. 63–72. Springer, Heidelberg (2013). https://doi.org/10.1007/978-3-642-36516-4_7

31. Volley (2021). https://developer.android.com/training/volley/index.html/
32. Wang, H., et al.: Beyond google play: a large-scale comparative study of Chinese android app markets. In: Proceedings of the Internet Measurement Conference 2018, pp. 293–307 (2018)
33. Wang, J., et al.: Understanding malicious cross-library data harvesting on android. In: 30th USENIX Security Symposium (USENIX Security 2021), pp. 4133–4150 (2021)
34. Wang, W., et al.: Constructing features for detecting android malicious applications: issues, taxonomy and directions. IEEE Access **7**, 67602–67631 (2019)
35. Wang, Y., Wu, H., Zhang, H., Rountev, A.: Orlis: obfuscation-resilient library detection for android. In: 2018 IEEE/ACM 5th International Conference on Mobile Software Engineering and Systems (MOBILESoft), pp. 13–23. IEEE (2018)
36. XiaoMi: Xiaomi app store (2021). https://app.mi.com/
37. Xu, Q., Erman, J., Gerber, A., Mao, Z., Pang, J., Venkataraman, S.: Identifying diverse usage behaviors of smartphone apps. In: Proceedings of the 2011 ACM SIGCOMM Conference on Internet Measurement Conference, pp. 329–344 (2011)
38. Yang, Z., Yang, M., Zhang, Y., Gu, G., Ning, P., Wang, X.S.: Appintent: analyzing sensitive data transmission in android for privacy leakage detection. In: Proceedings of the 2013 ACM SIGSAC Conference on Computer & Communications Security, pp. 1043–1054 (2013)
39. Zhan, X., et al.: Automated third-party library detection for android applications: are we there yet? In: 2020 35th IEEE/ACM International Conference on Automated Software Engineering (ASE), pp. 919–930. IEEE (2020)
40. Zungur, O., Stringhini, G., Egele, M.: Libspector: context-aware large-scale network traffic analysis of android applications. In: 2020 50th Annual IEEE/IFIP International Conference on Dependable Systems and Networks (DSN), pp. 318–330. IEEE (2020)

A k-Anonymity-Based Robust Watermarking Scheme for Relational Database

Jing Yu[1,2], Shuguang Yuan[1,2], Yulin Yuan[1,2], Yafan Li[1,2], and Chi Chen[1,2(✉)]

[1] State Key Laboratory of Information Security,
Institute of Information Engineering, Chinese Academy of Science,
Beijing 100093, China
{yujing,yuanshuguang,yuanyulin,liyafan,chenchi}@iie.ac.cn
[2] School of Cyber Security, University of Chinese Academy of Sciences,
Beijing 101400, China

Abstract. In the era of big data, secure and controlled data publishing becomes increasingly vital. When data holders publish dataset to data demanders, data holders often (1) protect the copyright of the published dataset and (2) anonymize user's data by k-anonymity for privacy purpose. Hence, there is a realistic demand of watermarked k-anonymity dataset for ownership. However, there are two important challenges to be addressed: the lack of primary key and the narrow bandwidth channel for watermarked k-anonymity dataset. In this paper, we try to address above challenges by proposing a k-anonymity-based robust watermarking scheme in anonymized dataset by an "one-time" way to achieve both protection of privacy and copyright. This scheme is primary key independent and meets the requirement of keeping the same form with k-anonymity. Experimental studies prove the robustness of watermarking scheme against subset deletion and subset addition attacks.

Keywords: Database watermarking · Ownership · k-anonymity

1 Introduction

In the era of big data, with the development of technologies such as data mining and information sharing, data often need to be published to other organizations for use, analysis and research. Consider a scenario that merchants (called "data holders") publish dataset to buyers (called "data demanders"). Some dishonest data demanders (called "traitors") may collect, share or sell published dataset for profits without permission from the data holders. The data holders may use a watermarking scheme to embed a specific mark into their dataset for asserting ownership. In relational database, many robust watermarking schemes [5,6,19,20,23,26] for ownership have been proposed.

For privacy purpose, privacy preserving data publishing schemes including k-anonymity [16,22] have developed. Data holders could anonymize user's data

C. Su et al. (Eds.): SciSec 2022, LNCS 13580, pp. 557–573, 2022.
https://doi.org/10.1007/978-3-031-17551-0_36

before publishing dataset. Hence, there is a realistic demand of copyright identification of leaked anonymized data in that contained sensitive information such as medical health data. To the best of our knowledge, some works [13,17,18] aim to fingerprint anonymized dataset. By applying different anonymization patterns, they achieved traitor-tracing. And the [8] implements sanitization and fingerprinting by adding and removing tuples from the anonymized dataset. These works achieved the goal of traitor-tracing. But the goal of identification of dataset copyright can't reach due to the lack of identifiable watermarks. However, we hope to protect privacy while asserting data ownership through k-anonymity and watermarking techniques.

However, there are two important challenges of watermarking in k-anonymity dataset need be addressed. The first challenge is that the lack of primary key. In k-anonymity scenario, the primary key is defined as explicit identifiers which must be deleted. For most watermarking schemes [1,2,5,10,26], the primary key is used to locate watermarks. Hence, types of classical watermarking schemes can't adapt k-anonymity dataset. The second challenge is that narrow bandwidth channel. The structure of k-anonymity is classified into four types: explicit identifiers (EIs), quasi-identifiers (QIs), sensitive attributes (SAs) and non-sensitive attributes (NSAs). The EIs will be deleted. And any modifications in QIs and SAs are intolerant for privacy objective of k-anonymity. NSAs are often considered as data that are not important. The fact is that NSAs are more likely to be destroyed with a higher priority. Hence, the places and bandwidth of watermark are limited in k-anonymity dataset.

1.1   Contribution and Paper Organization

To address above challenges, we analyze the existing three types of watermarking strategies in k-anonymity in detail in Sect. 2: Watermark then Anonymize (WA), Anonymize then Watermark (AW) and Integrated Strategy, and propose a k-anonymity-based watermarking scheme for relational database. The main contributions of our work include:

1. We discuss and analyze the operable watermarking possibilities in anonymization scenario, and try to find available bandwidth in QIs for watermarking.
2. We propose a novel watermarking algorithm by an "one-time" way to achieve both protection of privacy and copyright. It's primary key independent and meets the requirement keeping the same form with k-anonymity.
3. Experimental studies prove the robustness of the watermarking algorithm against subset deletion and subset addition attacks.

Organization: Sect. 2 introduces background and motivation. Section 3 presents the proposed watermark scheme. In Sect. 4, data-driven experiments are demonstrated. Section 5 demonstrates related works. Section 6 concludes this paper.

2 Background and Motivation

In this section, we first introduce the background knowledge related to anonymization, then describe our motivation for studying k-anonymity-based watermarking scheme.

2.1 Background

Researchers have proposed many studies targeting anonymized data. Most of the current consider that the data to be anonymized in the form of explicit identifiers (EIs), quasi-identifiers (QIs), sensitive attributes (SAs) and non-sensitive attributes (NSAs), where EIs are attributes that explicitly identify tuple owners (e.g. name and ID), QIs are attributes that could be linked to external tables to identify the tuple owner (e.g. age and zipcode), SAs include sensitive information about individuals such as illness, salary, etc., and NSAs contain all attributes except for the previous three types. In fact, NSAs are often considered as data that are not important for research. Most works assume that the four sets of attributes are disjoint. To protect individuals privacy, EIs will be removed before the data is published. Thus the data holders publish an anonymized dataset, including QIs′, SAs and NSAs, among which QIs′ are the results of QIs being anonymized.

The k-anonymity model is one of the most widely anonymization methods. K-anonymity was first proposed by *Sweeney* and *Samarati* [16,22]. The k-anonymity model requires that any tuple in an anonymized dataset is indistinguishable from other k-1 tuples in QIs′. The set of tuples in the anonymized dataset containing the same QI values are defined as equivalence classes (ECs). That is, the size of all ECs in the anonymized dataset after k-anonymity is not smaller than k.

Table 1. Example dataset

| (a) An original table | | | | | | (b) 3-anonymity table | | | | |
| EI | QIs | | SAs | | NSA | QIs′ | | SAs | | NSA |
Name	Age	Zipcode	Disease	Salary	Score	Age	Zipcode	Disease	Salary	Score
Alex	24	53712	Heart disease	5000	98	[24,32]	[53712–53713]	Heart disease	5000	98
Beth	25	53711	Heart disease	6000	87	[25,30]	53711	Heart disease	6000	87
Carl	30	53711	Flu	10000	80	[25,30]	53711	Flu	10000	80
Ellen	30	53711	Cancer	5000	92	[25,30]	53711	Cancer	5000	92
Glen	32	53712	Heart disease	4000	79	[24,32]	[53712–53713]	Heart disease	4000	79
Helen	32	53713	Cancer	8000	96	[24,32]	[53712–53713]	Cancer	8000	96

For example, Table 1 (a) is an original dataset, where Name is an EI, $<Age,$ $Zipcode>$ are considered as QIs, Disease, Salary are considered as SAs, and Score is a NSA. Table 1 (b) shows the anonymized result obtained from Table 1 (a) after 3-anonymity. Tuples 2, 3 and 4 in Table 1 (b) form an equivalence class with respect to quasi-identifiers $<Age, Zipcode>$. Even if the data demanders know Beth's QI values, it is difficult to tell which of the three tuples he is.

The implementation of k-anonymity is divided into two methods depending on how the data is transformed: global recoding and local recoding. Global recording means that the same QIs values must be mapped to the same values or ranges in all tuples. Typical global recording algorithms include Incognito [14], Binary search [16] and Datafly [21]. Local recoding allows the same QIs values to be mapped to different values or ranges. Top-Down Specialization [7], Mondrian [15] and Bottom-Up Generalization [24] are typical local recoding algorithms.

2.2 Motivation

To protect privacy while achieving copyright protection, there are three solutions for data holders to use. We analyze the three solutions and thus illustrate the motivation of our research.

(1) Watermark then Anonymize (WA).

The meaning of WA is to embed watermark in the original dataset first and then anonymize the watermarked dataset. As we mentioned above, the original dataset usually consists of EIs, QIs, SAs and NSAs. However, since EIs can often correspond to unique individuals, they are usually removed when published. Therefore, in the following discussion, we only discuss scenarios where QIs, SAs and NASs are processed separately. In addition, due to the difficulty of embedding watermarks in categorical attributes, the attributes we discuss in the following are all numerical attributes.

- **Watermark on QIs.** First consider embedding watermark in QIs. We assume that the data holder embeds watermark in numerical QIs and then anonymizes the dataset. However, since the values of QIs are likely to change after k-anonymity, which may cause the watermark information to be rewritten, resulting in the watermark information not being detected properly.
- **Watermark on SAs.** We assume that the data holder embeds watermark in numerical SAs. Although SAs do not change after k-anonymity, and the anonymization process does not affect the watermark embedded in SAs. However, as important parameters for data usage and analysis, the accuracy of SAs after embedding watermarks can be affected.
- **Watermark on NSAs.** We consider the case of embedding watermark in numerical NSAs. Although watermark embedded in NSAs are similarly unaffected by the subsequent anonymization process, there are still some problems. Firstly, compared to other attributes, the number of NSAs is usually relatively small. This results in less space for watermarking information to be embedded. More importantly, since NSAs are often considered unimportant for research, they may be restricted from publishing, which results in the absence of watermark information in the published dataset.

(2) Anonymize then Watermark (AW).

AW means to anonymize the original dataset first and then embed watermark in the anonymized dataset. Since k-anonymity is only processed for QIs, we focus on the case of embedding watermark in QIs' in this section. And the cases of embedding watermark in SAs and NSAs are the same as the case in WA.

- **Watermark on QIs'.** We assume that the data holder performs *k*-anonymity on the original dataset first and then embeds watermark in QIs'. We know that for *k*-anonymity achieved by generalization or clustering methods, the value of QIs' in the anonymized dataset is presented as a range, such as [24,32] in Table 1 (b). Therefore, watermark information cannot be embedded in QIs' presented in the form of a range. Moreover, for *k*-anonymity achieved by microaggregation methods, although the values of QIs after anonymization are accurate values, the watermarks are still not suitable to be embedded in QIs'. This is because *k*-anonymity requires that the QI values in each equivalence class are the same, and the data holder must still ensure that the QI values in the equivalence classes are the same after embedding watermark. This will result in a significant reduction in the number of watermarks that can be embedded in anonymized dataset.

(3) Integrated Strategy.

Integrated strategy means that data holders combine the privacy protection and copyright protection into one integrated mechanism during dataset publishing. Only a few works belong to this type. The works [13,17,18] propose a fingerprinting method based on *k*-anonymity. The method distributes datasets with different generalization patterns to multiple data demanders, thus enabling tracing back to the traitors who caused the privacy disclosure. However, the method does not assert data ownership. In addition, the authors did not experimentally validate the method. The method proposed in [8] implements sanitization and fingerprinting by adding and removing tuples from the dataset. The method protects the privacy of individuals, while allowing traitors to be tracked in the event of illegal redistribution. However, the method also cannot assert data ownership. In addition, there is no experimental validation of the method in the article. The methods above combine privacy protection and fingerprinting, and are able to protect data privacy while tracing traitors. However, none of these methods can assert the ownership of the data.

3   Proposed Watermark Scheme

In this section, we introduce the *k*-anonymity-based watermarking scheme, including bandwidth channel, watermark architecture and algorithms.

3.1   Bandwidth Channel

According to above discussion, EIs, SAs attributes are excluded from watermarking. NSA attributes may be destroyed with a higher priority. Hence, we explore suitable places and bandwidth on QI attributes. This section we will discuss the bandwidth channel for watermarking in QIs attributes. Most watermark methods work under a general assumption that the original dataset can tolerate a certain degree of quality degradation. The tolerance is closely related to the bandwidth for watermark. The anonymized dataset consists of many ECs, each of which is guaranteed to contain at least k tuples. And the optimal upper reference bound of an EC is $2k - 1$, which has been strictly proved in reference [15]. Hence, there is a natural interval $[k, 2k - 1]$ for the number of tuples contained in each EC. Thus we advocate that the each EC in an anonymized dataset can actually tolerance degree change of tuple number in the interval $[k, 2k - 1]$, thereby providing the desired bandwidth channel for watermarking.

Example. Figure 1 showns a bandwidth channel for watermarking in a 3-anonymity table. We take the attribute $<Age>$ as QI to 3-anonymize and use a histogram to represent the 3-anonymity table. The abscissa represents the generalization interval of attribute $<Age>$, and the ordinate represents the tuple number in an EC, denoted by $|EC_i|$. Thus the bandwidth channel for watermarking in the 3-anonymity table is the interval of $[3, 5]$.

Based on the bandwidth channel which is unique to anonymized dataset, we propose a new watermarking architecture, under which we can generate ECs in which the number of tuples are controlled. The controllable tuple numbers in these special ECs can be as watermarks.

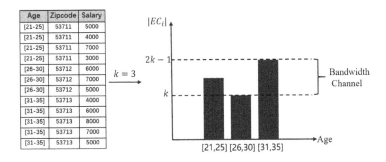

Fig. 1. The bandwidth channel for watermarking

3.2   Watermark Architecture and Algorithm

This section we will discuss the proposed watermark architecture of relational data that meet the dual requirements of privacy and copyright. The main architecture is presented in Fig. 2. The architecture includes the following three major phases: 1. Watermark Embedding, 2. k-anonymity and 3. Watermark Detection. Phase 1 and phase 2 belong to the data publishing stage, which must satisfy the k-anonymity specification in order to preserve the same data format. For ease of reference, we list notations that will be used in this paper in Table 2.

k-Anonymity Specification. The k-anonymity specification is used to regulate the watermark embedding function and the anonymity process, as in Fig. 2. It

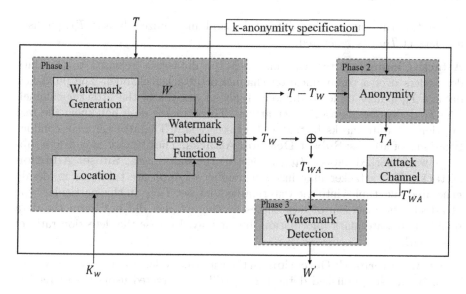

Fig. 2. Main architecture of the proposed watermarking scheme

requires that when executing the above two processes, the same set of QIs must be processed, while satisfying the anonymization parameter k.

Table 2. Notations

Notation	Description	Notation	Description
T	Original dataset	T_W	Watermarked dataset
T_A	Anonymized Dataset	T_{WA}, t_{WA}	Published Dataset and a tuple in T_{WA}
T'_{WA}	Published dataset that have been attacked	k	The system parameter for k-anonymity
W, W_g	Watermarks and the watermark in g-th EC	K_w	Watermark secret key
γ	A density control parameter	$\varDelta$	A redundant space for watermark
$QI_1, ..., QI_p$	QI attributes	s	A minimal step
t, N	A tuple and total number of tuples in T	n	Total number of watermarks
η	The proportion of successful watermark detection	τ	The watermark detection threshold

Phase1: Watermark Embedding. The main focus of watermark embedding phase is to embed watermark in such a way that it does not affect the privacy objective of k-anonymity. The original dataset T is transformed into watermarked dataset T_W. The original dataset T, watermark W, secret key K_w and k-anonymity specification are inputs. Watermark W and secret key K_w are only known to the data holders. And no one can detect the embedded watermark W without the secret key K_w.

Phase2: k-anonymity. In this phase, the main work is to anonymize the unmarked dataset $T - T_W$ to satisfy the k-anonymity specification. Thus, the published dataset can preserve the same data format with T_W and protect individual privacy. The output of this phase is the anonymized dataset T_A. By aggregating the watermarked dataset T_W and anonymized dataset T_A, publishing dataset T_{WA} is generated.

Attack Channel. After watermarking, the dataset is released to the data demanders over a communication channel or attacker channel. The published dataset T_{WA} may undergo different types of attacks in the attacker channel. The T'_{WA} denotes dataset under attack. The attacker dose not know the real positions of watermarks in that lack of secret key. The attacker may conduct two forms of attacks: **Subset Deletion Attacks.** The attacker may delete subset of watermarked dataset T_{WA} to destroy the watermarks. **Subset Addition Attacks.** The attacker may insert a number of duplicate tuples or randomly generated fake tuples into the watermarked dataset T_{WA}. In this particular type of attack, the insertion of new tuples by the attacker did not harm the data quality and watermark information, but it may decrease the detection ratio of watermark.

Phase3: Watermark Detection. In the watermark detection phase, the watermark W' in the published dataset T_{WA} will be extracted using the secret key K_w.

3.2.1   Watermark Embedding Phase. In the watermark embedding phase, three important tasks are accomplished: watermark generation, watermark location and watermark embedding.

(1) Watermark Generation. The watermark generation is based on the bandwidth channel, which is the interval $[k, 2k-1]$ in ECs.

Definition 1. Watermark Based on Bandwidth. The watermark W is composed of several variable intervals W_g, which controls the tuple numbers of the marked ECs.

$$W = (W_1, W_2, ... W_g, ..., W_n), 0 \leq |W_g| \leq k-1, 1 \leq g \leq n \qquad (1)$$

$$W_g = [a, b], 0 \leq a < b \leq k-1, |b-a| = \Delta \qquad (2)$$

where n represents the number of watermarks, g represents the g-th marked EC. Based on the bandwidth channel, the $|EC_g| = k + W_g$ and $k \leq |EC_g| \leq 2k-1$. Thus $0 \leq |W_g| \leq k-1$. The a and b are the positive integer, and $|b-a|$ relative to k-1 is a relatively smaller positive integer Δ, which provides a redundant space for watermark.

(2) Watermark Location. The potential ECs are selected to embed the watermark W. For the anonymized dataset, each QI attribute of a tuple t in an EC has an interval $[QI^{min}, QI^{max}]$. Thus, locating $t.QI^{min}$ is the key to form a special ECs. We use an one-way hash function (e.g.SHA1 or MD5) H to locate $t.QI^{min}$. The location function is as follow:

$$H(K_w|t.QI) = H(K_w|t.QI_1|...|t.QI_p) \qquad (3)$$

where K_w represents a secret key known only to the data holders, | represents concatenation. The $t.QI$ is the concatenation of the value for each QI attribute in tuple t. Then let H randomizes the values of K_w and the $t.QI$:

$$H(K_w|t.QI) \bmod \gamma = 0 \qquad (4)$$

When return value of formula (4) is 0, the tuples having value $t.QI_1, ..., t.QI_p$ will be selected, which can be as the start point of interval. Then the end point needs to be determined, making the number of tuples in the interval [start point, end point] equal to $|W_g|$. The γ is a control parameter that determines the density of watermarks. Note that, for ease of understanding and illustration, we represent tuples as points in space.

(3) Watermark Embedding. When the start point $t.QI^{min}$ is determined, we need to determine the end point to form EC that meet k-anonymity and watermark W requirement. However, there are many tuple sets satisfy watermarking requirement. Then the problem is how to choose the best one from the tuple sets which has minimal information loss. The normalized certainty penalty (NCP) [25] measure the information loss of each QI attribute in ECs. After the start point is located, we rank priority to candidate QIs with NCP for finding an end point as $t.QI^{max}$ that satisfy watermark W. From start point to end point of interval, tuples are selected to be grouped, which satisfies watermark W and has minimal information loss. Next, we generalize the selected tuple sets to form marked ECs. Finally, we take out the marked ECs to form an anonymized dataset with watermark sequence W.

$$T_W = EC_{W_1} \cup EC_{W_2} \cup ... \cup EC_{W_n} \qquad (5)$$

Example. Figure 3 shonws the procedure of watermark embedding, which contains three basic steps: Select the start points, Select tuple set and Generalization. Consider that dataset T has QIs $(QI_1, ..., QI_p)$, and assume that there is a order for each QI dimension. The tuples of T on $QI_1, ..., QI_p$ can then be represented as points in p-dimensional space. The Fig. 3 (a) shows a two-dimensional representation of a dataset, which Age and Weight are QI attributes. Each white dot represent a tuple. The overlapping points represent that these tuples have the same age-weight values.

Step 1: Select the Start Point. First, we should search the start point according to formula (3), (4). Take Fig. 3 (b) as a example, K_w is the watermark key. When $Age = a_2$, $Weight = w_2$, the value of formula (4) is 0. These two tuples are selected and one of them is used for subsequent calculations. This point is marked as black.

Step 2: Select Tuple Set. Next, we select the tuple set that satisfy k-anonymity and watermarking requirements. As shown in Fig. 3 (c), the anonymity parameter $k = 3$, the watermark $W_g = [a,b] (a = 0, b = 1)$. We choose $W_g = 1$, and two tuples has been selected in the step1. There are two alternative ways to select tuple set as shown by the dotted line in the figure. In order to select the better tuple set

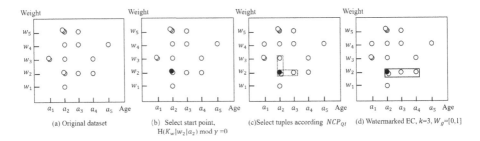

Fig. 3. Spatial representation of Age-Weight and selections based on k and W

which has less information loss, we calculate $NCP_{QI_{age}}$ and $NCP_{QI_{weight}}$ on these selected tuples in generalized data format. After calculation, the $NCP_{QI_{age}}$ is minimum. Thus, we select tuples according the Age attribute, and the result is shown in Fig. 3 (d). Note that, this step may repeat many times until the tuple number in the EC is greater than or equal to $k + W_g$.

Step 3: Generalization. Finally, we generalize these tuple to form marked ECs. As shown in Fig. 3 (d), we select the tuples including (a_2, w_2), (a_2, w_2), (a_3, w_2), (a_4, w_2). After generalization, the four tuples will be replaced by range $([a_2, a_4], w_2)$. These four tuples generate an marked EC.

3.2.2 k-anonymity Phase.
In the anonymity phase, the most important work is to anonymize the unmarked dataset $T - T_W$ to satisfy the k-anonymity specification. The k-anonymity algorithms using local recoding (LR) can be used to process unmarked dataset in our scheme. The generalization intervals generated by GR do not overlap, while the generalization intervals generated by the LR might potentially overlap. In other words, the LR allows the same QI values to be generalized into different intervals. If the GR is used in the anonymity phase, strict non-overlapping generalization intervals will be generated. It is easier for an attacker to identify the marked ECs. The LR will produce overlapping generalization intervals, thus, the attacker can not easily identify the marked ECs. Therefore, only the LR is suitable for our scheme. In anonymity phase, the processing of the unmarked dataset is as follows:

$$T_A = k - anonymity_{LR}(T - T_W) \tag{6}$$

where T_A is the anonymized dataset of $T - T_W$, the $k - anonymity_{LR}$ is the k-anonymity algorithms using local recoding. After phase 1 and phase 2, the published dataset T_{WA} is made (including marked EC_{W_g} and unmarked ECs), which adequately protects both individual privacy and data copyright (Fig. 4).

The basic algorithm is given in Algorithm 1, which describes the watermark embedding phase and the k-anonymity phase. Lines 2–8 determine all the starting points that will be marked when embedding the watermarks. Lines 10–25 implement the embedding of the watermarks. First, add one of the selected starting points to the *group* (lines 11–13). If the size of *group* is within the range

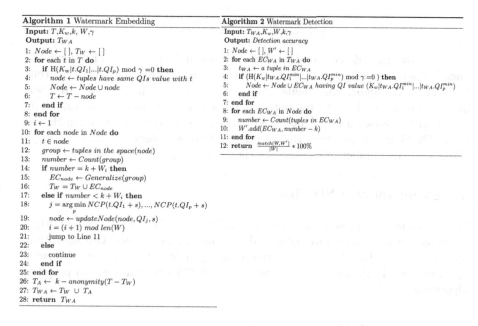

Fig. 4. Watermark embedding and detection algorithm

$k + W_i$, the *group* is generalized and added to T_W (lines 14–16). If the size of *group* is less than the minimum of this range, we uses NCP to expand the number of selected tuples on QI attributes (lines 17–21). Otherwise, these points are not processed (lines 22–24). Finally, *k-anonymity* on T-T_W does remaining work. The upper bound on the time complexity of the watermark embedding algorithm is $O(N * 2k)$.

3.2.3 Watermark Detection Phase.

In the watermark detection process, the first step is to locate the start points in the marked ECs using the secret parameters K_w and γ according to formula (3), (4). The next step is to calculate the tuple numbers in the marked ECs where the start points are located. The tuple numbers in each marked ECs minus the parameter k is the detected watermark W'. The last step is to compare W and W'. In our scheme, we can judge whether the watermark detection is successful according to formula (7), (8). First, we judge whether the watermark detection is successful in a marked EC according to formula (7). If the $W_g' \in [a, b]$, the watermark detection is successful. Then, we calculate the proportion η of ECs with successful watermark detection in the all marked ECs according to formula (8). We set the detection threshold τ, if $\eta \geq \tau$, the watermark detection for the T'_{WA} is successful.

$$f(EC_{W_{g'}}) = \begin{cases} 1, a \leq W_g' \leq b, 0 \leq g \leq n; \\ 0, otherwise. \end{cases} \tag{7}$$

$$\eta = \frac{\sum_{g=0}^{n} f(EC_{W_{g}'})}{n} * 100\% \tag{8}$$

The watermark detection algorithm is shown in Algorithm 2. The purpose of lines 2–7 is to find all equivalent classes EC_{WA} that contain watermark information. Then, the algorithm calculates the size of these EC_{WA} and records them in W' (lines 8–11). Finally, the detected W' is compared to W. The watermark detection is successful if the match proportion η is more than detection threshold τ. The time complexity of the watermark detection algorithm is $O(|EC_{WA}|)$. $|EC_{WA}|$ is the number of equivalence classes in T_{WA}.

4   Experimental Studies

In this section, we present the experimental studies of our practical algorithms in terms of watermarking robustness, data utility and efficiency. Our algorithms are k-anonymity-based robust watermarking algorithms, thus we named them k-RWA in short. In the later experiments, we use k-RWA to represent our proposed algorithms.

4.1   Experimental Setup

Our experimental setup includes the Dataset, Experimental Environment and Experimental Parameters.

Dataset. We evaluated our proposed scheme in the publicly available dataset INFORMS[1]. The dataset includes 102578 records and 18 attributes. And 9 numerical attributes in the INFORMS dataset were used in our experiment as QIs.

Experimental Environment. The experiments were conducted on a machine equipped with a 3.0 GHz Intel(R) Core(TM) i5 processor with 16 GB RAM. The operating system on the machine was Microsoft Windows 10. The programming language we used is Python in version 3.7.3.

Experimental Parameters. In our experiments, we choose the local recording algorithms Mondrian [15] and Top-Down Specialization [7] as k-anonymity algorithms in k-RWA. We use $k = 20$, QI $= 3$, $|W_g| = [0,10]$, $\gamma = 25$. Our experiments were repeated 10 times and the average of the results was calculated as the final result for each trial.

4.2   Robustness

In this section, we did experiments on the robustness of k-RWA with two types of attacks, "Subset Deletion" and "Subset Addition".

Subset Deletion. We randomly delete subset of tuples from published dataset T_{WA} with the ratio from 10% to 90%. The detection threshold is $\tau = 50\%$ with

---

[1] https://sites.google.com/site/informsdataminingcontest/.

red dotted line. In Fig. 5(a), experiments show the result of k-RWA (Mondrian) and k-RWA (Top-down), and even when the ratio of deleted tuples reach 90%, the watermark detection is successful.

Subset Addition. We add new tuples in the published dataset T_{WA} with the ratio from 20% to 200%. The source of new tuples for addition is from original dataset. The detection threshold is $\tau = 50\%$ too. Figure 5 (b) shows the experiment results of k-RWA (Mondrian) and k-RWA (Top-down) by adding tuples with the different ratios, and even when the ratio of addition tuples reach 200%, the watermark detection is successful.

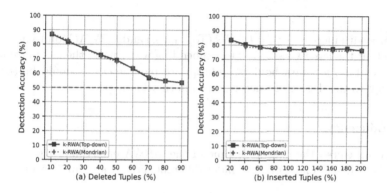

Fig. 5. The resilience to attack for k-RWA

Through the experiments above, k-RWA has good robustness against subset deletion and subset addition attacks.

4.3 Utility Evaluation

In this section, we report the experimental results of the k-RWA in terms of data utility. If the original dataset is processed only by Mondrian or Top-down, it will bring information loss to the original dataset, we called it I_k. If the original dataset is processed by k-RWA(Mondrian) or k-RWA(Top-down), it will also bring information loss to the original dataset, we called it I_{k-RWA}. In this experiments, we compare I_{k-RWA} with I_k using the GCP metric [9]. First, we compare I_{k-RWA} with I_k with different k and QI. We vary k from 20 to 100, and vary QI from 2 to 9. The results as shown in Fig. 6 (a) and (b) indicate that the information loss of k-RWA is higher than Mondrian or Top-down in most cases. This is due to the fact that the equivalence class chosen by k-RWA in order to embed the watermark may not be optimal for anonymization. The trade-off between privacy objective and watermarking objective, the latter must be achieved with high priority, which may causes extra information loss.

Then we analyze the impact of parameter γ on data utility. We vary γ from 25 to 200. The result as shown in Fig. 6 (c) demonstrates that GCP decreases

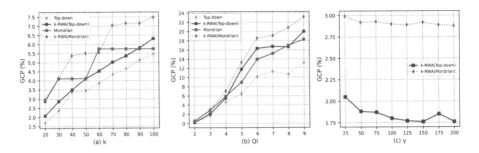

Fig. 6. Comparison of algorithms for the GCP with different value of k, QI and γ

gradually with increased γ for k-RWA(Top-down) and k-RWA(Mondrian), which proved that the less ECs selected for embedding watermark, the less information loss. Therefore, for data holders, appropriate parameters γ should be selected according to the degree of tolerance for information loss.

4.4   Efficiency

We also measured the execution time of the k-RWA embedding algorithm and the k-RWA detection algorithm under different dataset size and γ value.

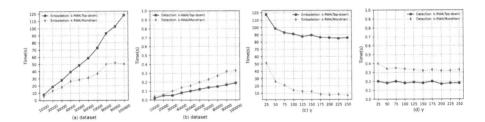

Fig. 7. Computation time for k-RWA

In Fig. 7 (a) and (b), we vary the dataset from 10000 tuples to 100000 tuples. The results show that the execution time of embedding and detection algorithms increases along with the size of embedded dataset. In Fig. 7 (c) and (d), we vary parameter γ from 25 to 250. The results show that the execution time of embedding and detection algorithms decreases along with the value increases of γ. Besides, the detection execution time shown in Fig. 7 (b) and (d) is much lower than the embedding execution time. The reason is that the information loss of each selected QI needs to be calculated when embedding watermarks, which has time consumption.

5 Related Work

Copyright protection is one of the most important issues in relational database for data holders. In [12], the database watermarking techniques are classified into three categories: Bit-Resetting Techniques (BRT), Data Statistics-Modifying Techniques (DSMT) and Constrained Data Content-Modifying Techniques (CDCMT). For BRT, selected bits are reset by a systematic process. Agrawal *et al.* [1,2] published the first relational databases watermarking scheme, which utilizes bits as watermarks. Following their research, a lot of watermarking models are proposed, such as [5,10,23,26]. For DSMT, data statistics such as mean, variance or distribution are used as watermarks. In [20], Sion *et al.* proposed a method that encoding of the watermark bit relies on altering the size of the "positive violators" set. Shehab *et al.* [19] formulated the database watermarking schemes as a constrained optimization problem. CDCMT schemes are based on modifying the contents of the data. For example, the schemes based on the ordering of the tuples (such as [4]) and insertion of extra spaces in attribute values (such as [3]). Such that watermarked data still remains useful. The zero-watermarking schemes [11] is also under this category. Our k-anonymity-based watermarking scheme belongs to the CDCMT.

6 Conclusion

In the current situation, data holders should not only protect data copyright, but also protect the privacy of users. To achieve dual protection goals, we proposed a database watermarking scheme based on k-anonymity. In our scheme, we propose an efficient watermark embedding algorithm and a watermark detection algorithm. Experimental results show that robustness, utility and efficiency of our scheme are good.

Acknowledgment. This work was supported by National Science and Technology Major Project of China under the Grant No. 2016ZX05047003.

References

1. Agrawal, R., Haas, P.J., Kiernan, J.: Watermarking relational data: framework, algorithms and analysis. VLDB J. **12**(2), 157–169 (2003)
2. Agrawal, R., Kiernan, J.: Watermarking relational databases. In: VLDB 2002: Proceedings of the 28th International Conference on Very Large Databases, pp. 155–166. Elsevier (2002)
3. Al-Haj, A., Odeh, A.: Robust and blind watermarking of relational database systems (2008)
4. Bhattacharya, S., Cortesi, A.: A distortion free watermark framework for relational databases. In: ICSOFT (2), pp. 229–234. Citeseer (2009)
5. Cui, X., Qin, X., Sheng, G.: A weighted algorithm for watermarking relational databases. Wuhan Univ. J. Nat. Sci. **12**(1), 79–82 (2007)

6. Franco-Contreras, J., Coatrieux, G.: Robust watermarking of relational databases with ontology-guided distortion control. IEEE Trans. Inf. Forensics Secur. **10**(9), 1939–1952 (2015)
7. Fung, B.C., Wang, K., Yu, P.S.: Top-down specialization for information and privacy preservation. In: 21st International Conference on Data Engineering (ICDE 2005), pp. 205–216. IEEE (2005)
8. Gambs, S., Lolive, J., Robert, J.M.: Entwining sanitization and personalization on databases. In: Proceedings of the 2018 on Asia Conference on Computer and Communications Security, pp. 207–219 (2018)
9. Ghinita, G., Karras, P., Kalnis, P., Mamoulis, N.: Fast data anonymization with low information loss. In: Proceedings of the 33rd International Conference on Very Large Data Bases, pp. 758–769 (2007)
10. Guo, F., Wang, J., Li, D.: Fingerprinting relational databases. In: Proceedings of the 2006 ACM Symposium on Applied Computing, pp. 487–492 (2006)
11. Hamadou, A., Sun, X., Gao, L., Shah, S.A.: A fragile zero-watermarking technique for authentication of relational databases. Int. J. Digit. Content Technol. Appl. **5**(5) (2011)
12. Kamran, M., Farooq, M.: A comprehensive survey of watermarking relational databases research. arXiv preprint arXiv:1801.08271 (2018)
13. Kieseberg, P., Schrittwieser, S., Mulazzani, M., Echizen, I., Weippl, E.: An algorithm for collusion-resistant anonymization and fingerprinting of sensitive microdata. Electron. Mark. **24**(2), 113–124 (2014). https://doi.org/10.1007/s12525-014-0154-x
14. LeFevre, K., DeWitt, D.J., Ramakrishnan, R.: Incognito: efficient full-domain k-anonymity. In: Proceedings of the 2005 ACM SIGMOD International Conference on Management of Data, pp. 49–60 (2005)
15. LeFevre, K., DeWitt, D.J., Ramakrishnan, R.: Mondrian multidimensional k-anonymity. In: 22nd International Conference on Data Engineering (ICDE 2006), pp. 25–25. IEEE (2006)
16. Samarati, P.: Protecting respondents identities in microdata release. IEEE Trans. Knowl. Data Eng. **13**(6), 1010–1027 (2001)
17. Schrittwieser, S., Kieseberg, P., Echizen, I., Wohlgemuth, S., Sonehara, N.: Using generalization patterns for fingerprinting sets of partially anonymized microdata in the course of disasters. In: 2011 Sixth International Conference on Availability, Reliability and Security, pp. 645–649. IEEE (2011)
18. Schrittwieser, S., Kieseberg, P., Echizen, I., Wohlgemuth, S., Sonehara, N., Weippl, E.: An algorithm for k-anonymity-based fingerprinting. In: Shi, Y.Q., Kim, H.-J., Perez-Gonzalez, F. (eds.) IWDW 2011. LNCS, vol. 7128, pp. 439–452. Springer, Heidelberg (2012). https://doi.org/10.1007/978-3-642-32205-1_35
19. Shehab, M., Bertino, E., Ghafoor, A.: Watermarking relational databases using optimization-based techniques. IEEE Trans. Knowl. Data Eng. **20**(1), 116–129 (2007)
20. Sion, R., Atallah, M., Prabhakar, S.: Rights protection for relational data. IEEE Trans. Knowl. Data Eng. **16**(12), 1509–1525 (2004)
21. Sweeney, L.: Guaranteeing anonymity when sharing medical data, the datafly system. In: Proceedings of the AMIA Annual Fall Symposium, p. 51. American Medical Informatics Association (1997)
22. Sweeney, L.: Achieving k-anonymity privacy protection using generalization and suppression. Int. J. Uncertain. Fuzziness Knowl.-Based Syst. **10**(05), 571–588 (2002)

23. Wang, H., Cui, X., Cao, Z.: A speech based algorithm for watermarking relational databases. In: 2008 International Symposiums on Information Processing, pp. 603–606. IEEE (2008)
24. Wang, K., Yu, P.S., Chakraborty, S.: Bottom-up generalization: a data mining solution to privacy protection. In: Fourth IEEE International Conference on Data Mining (ICDM 2004), pp. 249–256. IEEE (2004)
25. Xu, J., Wang, W., Pei, J., Wang, X., Shi, B., Fu, A.W.C.: Utility-based anonymization using local recoding. In: Proceedings of the 12th ACM SIGKDD International Conference on Knowledge Discovery and Data Mining, pp. 785–790 (2006)
26. Zhou, X., Huang, M., Peng, Z.: An additive-attack-proof watermarking mechanism for databases' copyrights protection using image. In: Proceedings of the 2007 ACM Symposium on Applied Computing, pp. 254–258 (2007)

Author Index

Alkhattabi, Khalid   333
An, Wei   407

Barba, Kevin   3
Belarbi, Othmane   377
Bird, Davita   333

Carnelli, Pietro   377
Castillo, Jorge   3
Chen, Chi   557
Chen, Jiageng   455
Chen, Langping   364
Chen, Qian   3
Chen, Tao   155
Chen, Xiao   302
Chien, Hung-Yu   353
Chiu, Wei-Yang   51
Cui, Huajun   541
Cui, Lei   315

Ding, Jiong   87
Ding, Xiong   522
Ding, Yu   287
Dong, Fangming   421
Du, Xiangyu   421

Fan, Zijing   421
Feng, Huamin   522
Feng, Yanchang   137
Fischmeister, Sebastian   260
Fu, Peipei   201

Gao, Chang   522
Ghodosi, Hossein   105
Gleerup, Thomas   245
Gou, Gaopeng   201
Grossklags, Jens   472
Guo, Feng   437
Guo, MengHan   287

Hamidi, Amirreza   105
Han, Yanni   407
Hao, Zhiyu   315
Hong, Zhexuan   455

Hsu, Po-Chu   121
Huang, Huawei   36

Jensen, Wictor Lang   51
Jessing, Sille   51
Jia, Kun   170
Jia, SiYu   287
Jiang, Jun   421
Jiang, Xiaohong   276
Jiang, Zhengwei   302, 421
Jing, Rongqi   302

Kang, Yanze   21
Kasper, Daniel   472
Khan, Aftab   377
Kong, Qingshan   437

Lachmayer, Roland   233
Lee, Taylor   260
Li, BinBin   287
Li, Chen   137
Li, Jun   393
Li, Ning   421
Li, Shuhao   217
Li, Wenjuan   245
Li, Yafan   557
Li, Yuejun   541
Li, Zhen   201
Liang, Jian   315
Ling, Chen   302
Ling, Zhiting   522
Liu, Baoxu   421
Liu, Feng   170
Liu, Jiazhi   170
Liu, Junjiao   393
Liu, Qixu   364
Liu, Xinyu   364
Liu, Yi   407
Liu, Yining   21
Lv, Zhiqiang   437

Meng, Guozhu   541
Meng, Weizhi   21, 51
Miller, Kai   333

Miyaji, Atsuko   121
Montanēz Rodriguez, Rosana   487
Mu, Yongheng   87

Noun, Hassan   233

Peng, Chengwei   186
Peng, Chunying   68

Qi, ZiSen   287
Qian, Qiang   393
Qiang, Qian   287
Qin, Wenjie   186
Qin, Yingchao   201
Qu, Leilei   505

Rajesh, G.   233
Rehm, Florian   233

Shen, Yulong   276
Shi, Wenchang   505
Shrestha, Sulav Lal   260
Si, Qin   315
Spyridopoulos, Theodoros   377
Su, Ting   541
Sun, Jiawei   393
Sun, Peishuai   217

Tan, Jiao   245
Tian, Changbo   186
Tong, Ying   315
Tu, Bibo   137

Wang, Bingxu   201
Wang, HaiPing   287
Wang, Qiuyun   302
Wang, Shuwei   302
Wang, Weiping   541
Wang, Wen   170

Wang, Xuren   522
Wang, Yong   393
Wang, Yu   245
Wen, Kun   155
Wu, Guangjun   393

Xiao, Ruojin   505
Xie, Jiang   217
Xing, Jian   287
Xiong, Gang   201
Xu, Haixia   68, 87
Xu, Hui   315
Xu, Shouhuai   487

Yan, Chuyi   87
Yang, Ling   36
Yang, Peian   522
Yin, Junnan   393
Yin, Tao   186
Yu, Jing   557
Yu, Xiaobo   21
Yuan, Shuguang   557
Yuan, Yulin   557
Yue, Chuan   333

Zeller, Guillaume   233
Zhang, Kai   421
Zhang, Ning   437
Zhang, Pinchang   276
Zhang, Xiaodong   541
Zhang, XiaoYu   287
Zhang, Yan   541
Zhao, Guangze   186
Zhao, Guozhu   276
Zhao, Wu   364
Zhou, Yu   315
Zhu, Dali   541
Zou, Qian   437